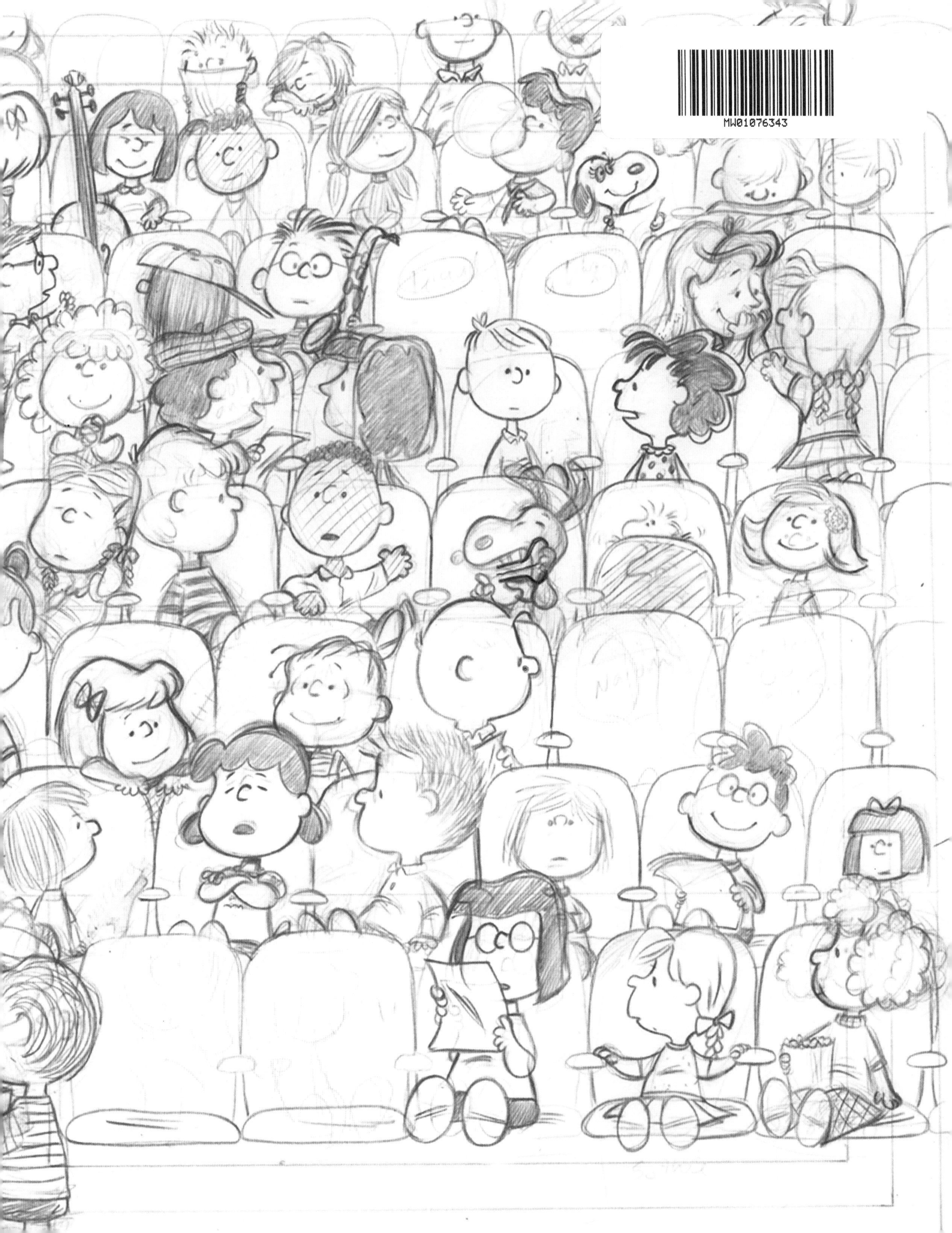

# THE COMPLETE
# PEANUTS
## FAMILY ALBUM

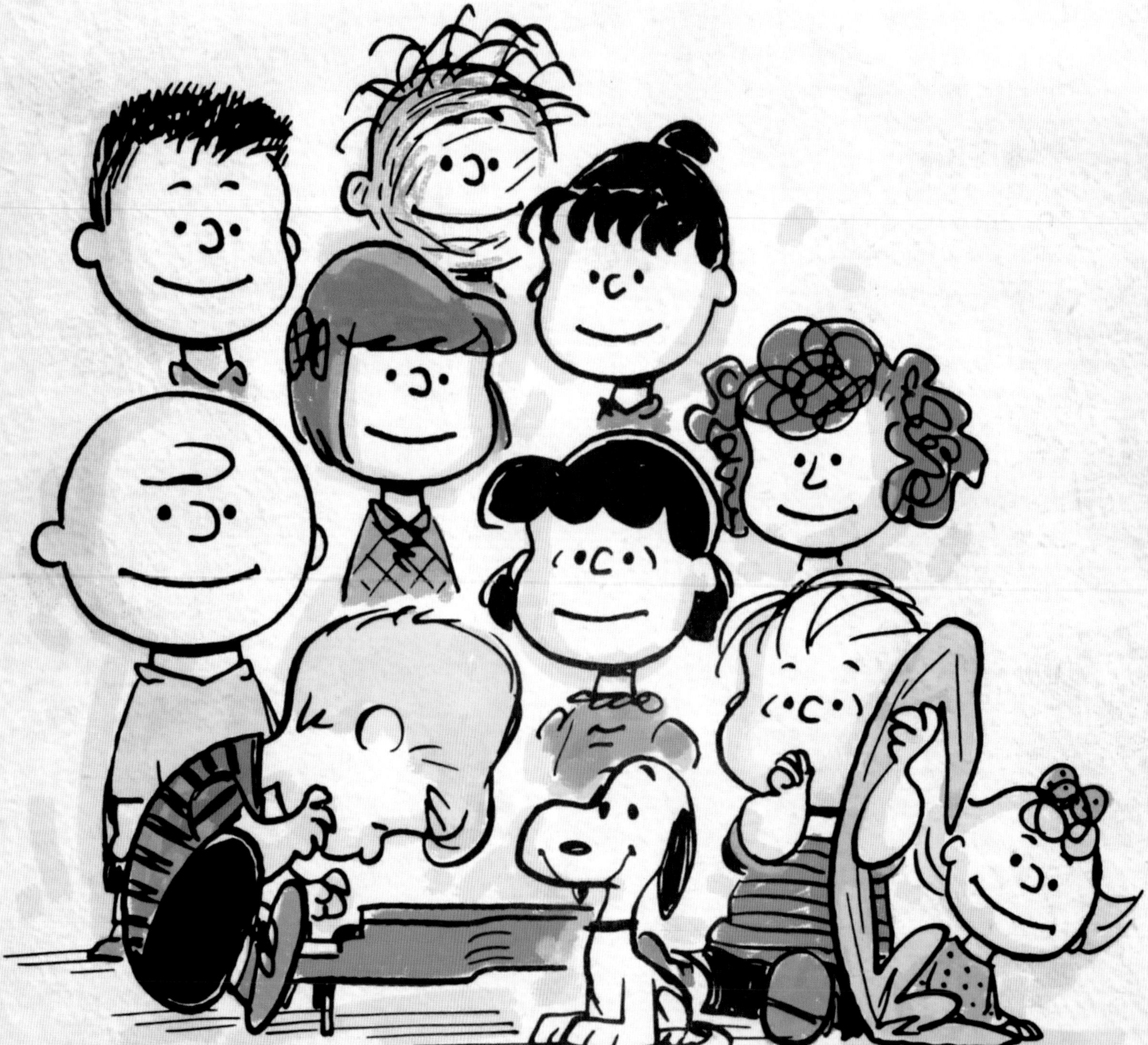
SCHULZ

# THE COMPLETE
# PEANUTS
# FAMILY ALBUM

## The Ultimate Guide to Charles M. Schulz's Classic Characters

**Andrew Farago**

Foreword by
**Berkeley Breathed**

Preface by
**Bob Peterson**

weldon**owen**

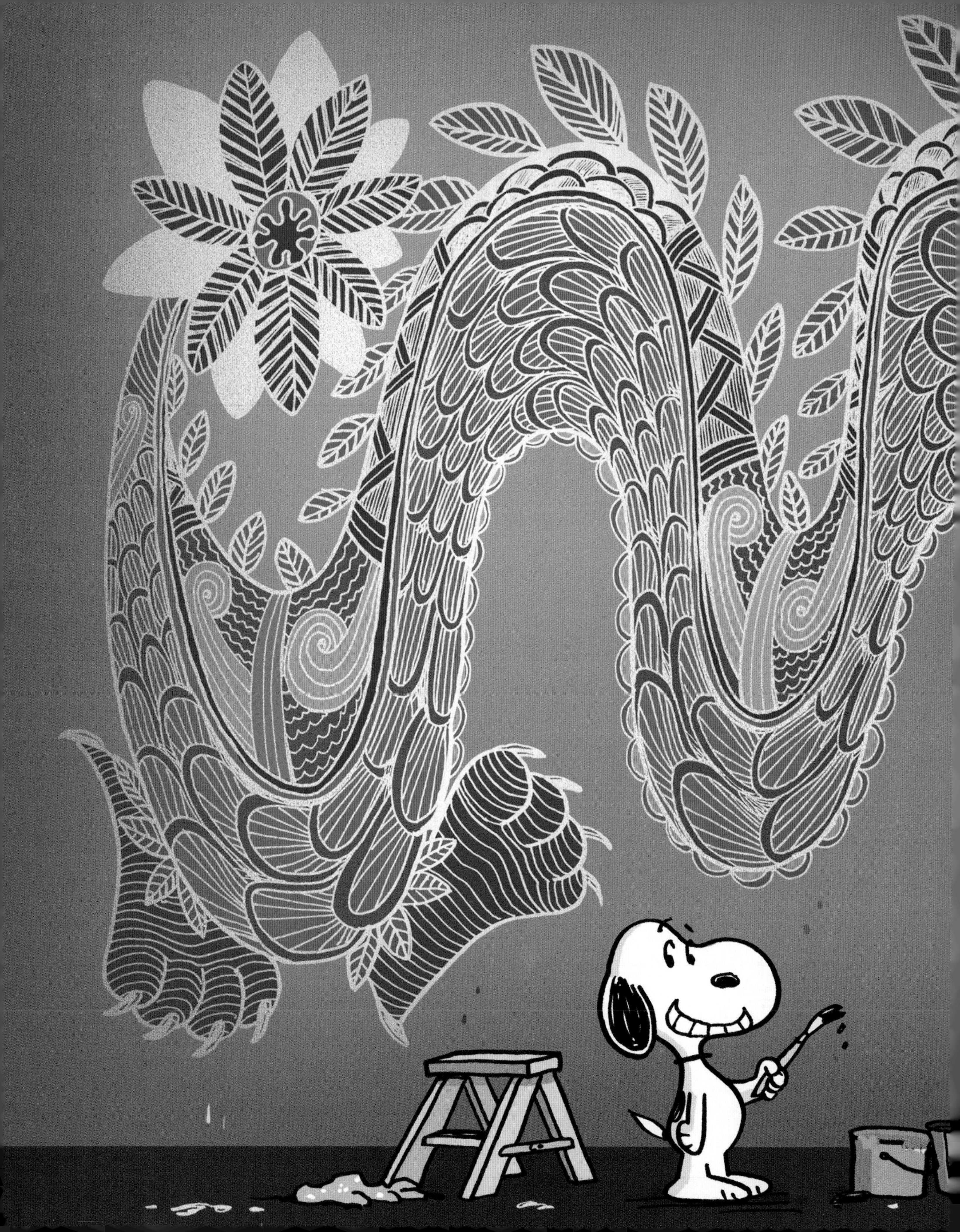

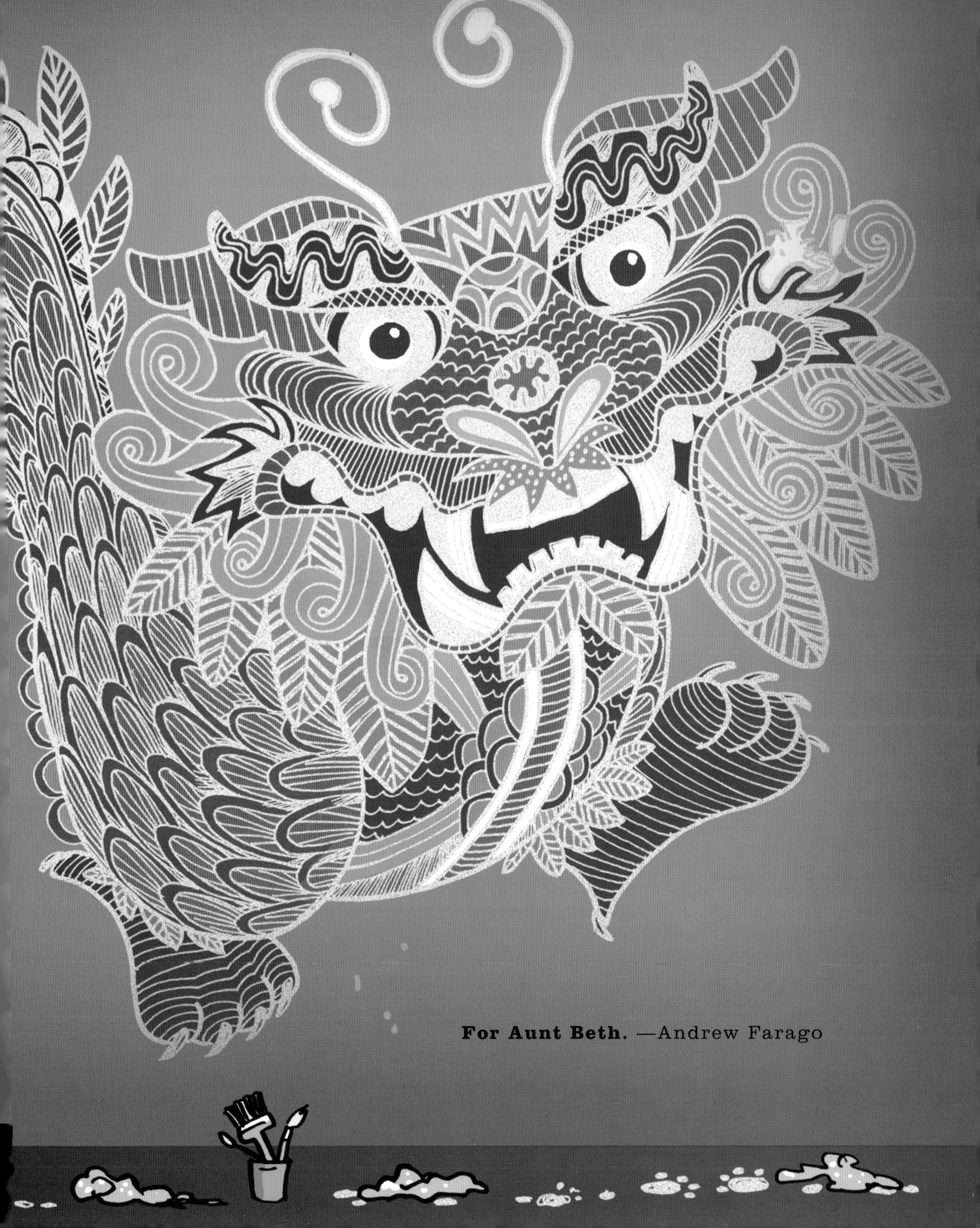

**For Aunt Beth.** —Andrew Farago

# CONTENTS

FOREWORD 8

PREFACE 11

INTRODUCTION 13

**Charlie Brown** 27

  The Eternal Optimist 30

  The Baseball Manager 34

  The Boy and His Dog 36

  The Lovable Loser 38

*You're a Good Man,*
*Charlie Brown* 40

*Valentine's Day* 42

Patty 45

Shermy 46

Violet 51

Charlotte Braun 55

Charlie Brown's
Pen(cil)-Pal 56

The Little Red-Haired Girl 57

Emily 58

*The Neighborhood Wall* 60

The Kite-Eating Tree 63

The Pitcher's Mound 64

Charlie Brown's Glove 64

Joe Shlabotnik 65

The Goose Eggs 66

Royanne Hobbs 67

*Summer Days* 68

Mr. Sack 70

Roy 72

Peggy Jean 73

Cormac 74

Ethan 75

**Schroeder** 77

*Schroeder's Piano* 80

**Lucy Van Pelt** 83

  The Fussbudget 86

  The Queen Bee 88

*Lucy's Psychiatric Booth* 90

**Linus Van Pelt** 93

*Linus's Security Blanket* 96

  The Philosopher 98

*The Great Pumpkin* 100

5, 3 & 4 104

Lydia 108

Truffles 109

Tapioca Pudding 110

Miss Othmar 111

*Halloween* 112

**Pig-Pen** 114

**Sally Brown** 121

  The Little Sister 124

The School 128

Eudora 129

Larry 130

Harold Angel 131

*Christmas Day* 132

Frieda & Faron 137

**Peppermint Patty** 141

  The All-Star Athlete 142

  The Hapless Student 144

José Peterson 148

Clara, Shirley,
& Sophie 149

Thibault 150

The Caddymaster 152

PAGE 1: *Spot art from strip – CSCA* | PAGE 2: *Original drawing by Charles M. Schulz* | PAGE 3: *Spot art from strip – Charles M. Schulz* | PAGES 4–5: Peanuts, *Issue #15, Boom! Studios cover, 2014 – CSCA* | ABOVE: *Character lineup model sheet – CSCA* | OPPOSITE: *Style Guide art – CSCA*

| | | | | | | |
|---|---|---|---|---|---|---|
| Maynard | 153 | The World Famous Author | 194 | World War II (The Cat Next Door) | 224 |
| *The Sporting Life* | 154 | The World Famous Attorney | 195 | Woodstock's Grandfather | 225 |
| Molly Volley | 159 | **The Masked Marvel** | 197 | **Marcie** | **227** |
| "Crybaby" Boobie | 160 | The Spy | 198 | Floyd | 232 |
| "Badcall" Benny | 161 | Lila | 200 | Joe Richkid | 233 |
| **Snoopy** | **163** | **Miss Helen Sweetstory** | 201 | **Franklin** | **235** |
| Master of Disguise | 166 | Poochie | 202 | **Rerun Van Pelt** | **241** |
| *Snoopy's Doghouse* | 174 | Loretta | 203 | The Artist | 242 |
| World War I Flying Ace | 176 | Spike | 204 | Joe Agate | 246 |
| The Red Baron | 178 | Joe Cactus | 205 | Supporting Cast | 247 |
| *Veteran's Day* | 179 | Naomi | 206 | Charlie Brown's Tentmate | 248 |
| *D-Day* | 181 | Daisy Hill Puppy Farm | 207 | Charlie Brown's Long-Lost Friend | 249 |
| Joe Cool | 182 | Olaf & Andy | 208 | Rerun's Classmate | 250 |
| "World-Famous" Snoopy | 186 | Belle | 209 | | |
| The World Famous Astronaut | 187 | Marbles | 210 | CHARLES M. SCHULZ | 252 |
| The World Famous Surgeon | 192 | Snoopy's Father & Mother | 211 | ACKNOWLEDGMENTS | 253 |
| The World Famous Sergeant-Major of the Foreign Legion | 193 | **Woodstock** | **213** | CREDITS | 255 |
| | | The Best Friend | 216 | COLOPHON | 256 |
| | | The Beagle Scouts | 222 | | |

# FOREWORD BY BERKELEY BREATHED

"Character counts" said my mother all too often, usually as a rebuke.

As always, I underestimated her shrewdness in literary matters, although she didn't know at the time she was being brilliant in areas apart from my attraction to dirty jokes at age twelve.

Character is the *only* thing in the business at hand—the one celebrated in this volume. It's the business I made my own not much after the above detour in preadolescent entertainment choices, and Charles Schulz's characters played a role, not surprisingly. To be in cartooning is to really be in "charactooning"—my term (I have no idea where "car" came from). The comic strips—or movies, or TV shows, or plays, or novels—that slip from memory do so for one simple reason that you may test at will: The personalities that inhabited these ephemeral vehicles were forgettable.

Character doesn't just *count* in comic strips; character is *everything*. Making even just a few of them distinct, fun, separate, and memorable when you only have four tiny frames each day is a herculean feat. Making dozens and dozens of them so is something else. Sparky Schulz did that.

Consider just one from *Peanuts*: my favorite, Lucy. From the position of a male writer who does this for a living, I can tell you that it's hard to create a female character without stumbling back on cliché. Lucy was wildly, wickedly free from the usual feminine banalities that girl characters attract like dumb lumbering bears to honey. She was the primary female character in *Peanuts* and by far the most complex in the whole gang. When Sparky invented the very simple allegory of the held (and inevitably withdrawn) football from the ever-hopeful Charlie Brown, he brought comic strips—and their real place in literature—into a larger world where complex character, as it should, rules. They gave Bob Dylan a Nobel Prize but neglected Charles Schulz. That's almost a punchline.

*Peanuts* wasn't a collection of gags (like most comic strips). It was an assemblage of personalities poured happily from the mind of one that very skillfully hid his creative, jubilant schizophrenia behind a genial smile and a straightforward heart. In 1986, I lay in a hospital bed with a broken spine after cracking up a small plane . . . and I opened a package that included a very rare *Peanuts* original strip, signed: *To Berkeley with friendship & every best wish—Sparky.*

"With friendship." I'd never met him. Character counts, indeed. In Sparky's case, his characters—in all their flaws and passions and idiosyncrasies—gave a collective voice to his own character of deep and undisguised humanity. Explore them here in *The Complete Peanuts Family Album* and marvel, like me, that they all came from *one* creative id. I wish I'd known him better when I had the chance. This volume may be the next best thing.

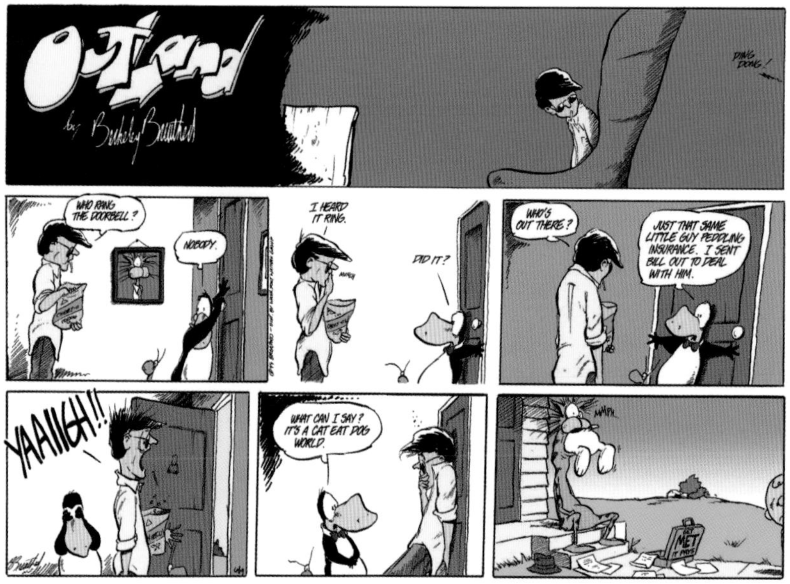
Outland
by Berkeley Breathed
DING DONG!
WHO RANG THE DOORBELL?
NOBODY.
I HEARD IT RING.
DID IT?
WHO'S OUT THERE?
JUST THAT SAME LITTLE GUY PEDDLING INSURANCE. I SENT BILL OUT TO DEAL WITH HIM.
YAAIIGH!!
WHAT CAN I SAY? IT'S A CAT EAT DOG WORLD.
MMPH.
MET

ABOVE: Outland *strip by Berkeley Breathed* | OPPOSITE: *Design by Cameron + Co*

I DON'T DO FLOWERS.. I DO
MORE ACTION! MORE COLOR!
UNDERGROUND COMICS
VL.3 — NO.8
.45 ¢
YES, MA'AM.. THESE WILL BE CONSECUTIVELY NUMBERED LIMITED EDITION PRINTS..
EACH PRINT WILL BE SIGNED AND ACCOMPANIED BY A CERTIFICATE OF AUTHENTICATION..

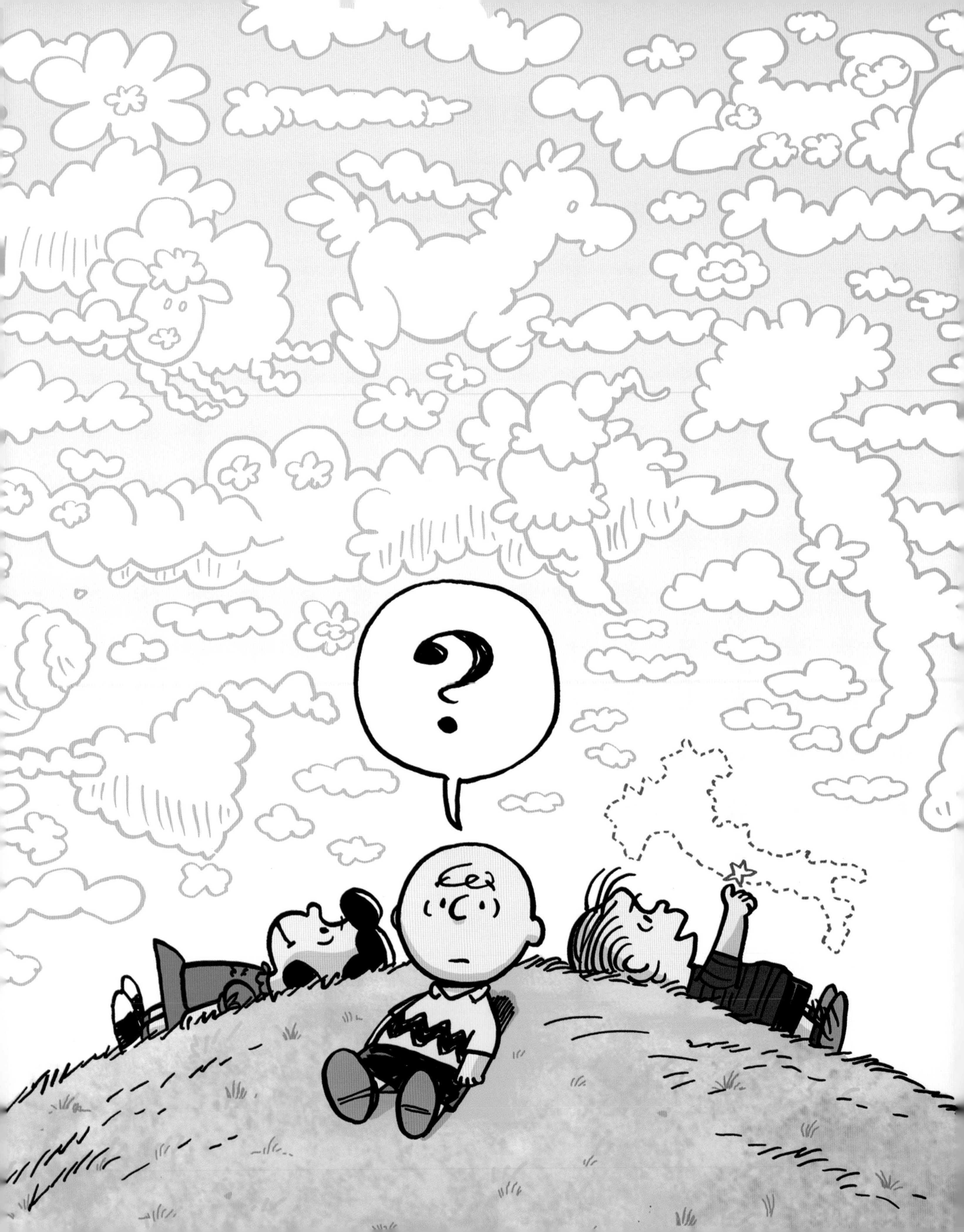
?

# PREFACE BY BOB PETERSON

I went as Charlie Brown for Halloween this past year. At age fifty-six, I got a few sideways glances. My beard and glasses with my Charlie Brown bald wig made me look more like Sigmund Freud Charlie. But I didn't care. The whole universe of *Peanuts* characters that Schulz created is sacred to me. I remember being in my pajamas as a four-year-old watching the Christmas special when it first ran on TV. I read every *Peanuts* book I could. I identified with Charlie Brown's insecurities. I was amazed at the secret, adventurous world of Snoopy. I was inspired by the spirituality of Linus and that he could endure the fussbudgetry of Lucy! I coughed on the sidewalk and then stomped on the germs. Schulz's work is in my artistic DNA now. He has many lessons for us.

*Peanuts* is such an interesting mix of emotional angst and surrealism. Somehow the two go together. Who among us hasn't felt that the world becomes surreal during times of angst? I've taken that Schulzian idea into my cartooning and animation career, which includes twenty-three years as a story artist and screenwriter at Pixar.

In graduate school at Purdue University, I drew a daily four-panel strip called *Loco Motives* for the *Purdue Exponent Newspaper*. There, I was exploring the angst of university life but overlaid with a surreal set of characters including a herbivorous plains-dwelling antelope who just happened to live with two dudes on campus. Blitzen, as I called him, could talk, and his antlers (much like Snoopy's) could reshape and reflect his emotions. There was no reason for putting this character in, but I was inspired by how Snoopy's surreal world of flying aces and bowling alleys in his dog house paired nicely with a normal round-headed boy who found the world mean and indecipherable.

This duality also inspired me on movies like *Up*, which is a mix of the grief of Carl Fredriksen and the surrealism of talking dogs ("Squirrel!"). The two balance and clarify each other. It seemed like the lower we took Carl in grief, the more outlandish we could go with Dug and the rest of the dog pack. Carl's grief stood out in stark contrast. His character was clear.

Which is another Schulz lesson: clarity and contrast of character—we all know what Lucy or Schroeder or Sally would say or do in any situation. It's what we in storytelling grapple with, and I am daily inspired by Schulz' mastery of it. In *Monsters, Inc.*, we spent a lot of time at the beginning just trying to define how Mike Wazowski would contrast Sulley. As an exercise, we put them in a situation of two roommates picking out a tie for Sully to go out for the evening. Mike fell into the role of the quick-tempered smart aleck; Sulley was more clear-headed and controlled. Each of the *Peanuts* characters had this—a clear personality type. But it is when Schulz puts them in contrast with other "side" characters that we get to see their depth. Linus's religious zealotry is put to the test in the Great Pumpkin patch by Sally. The little red-haired girl, whom we never see (a little red herring), brings out the romantic side in Charlie Brown. Without her, we only see the insecure Charlie. And on and on . . . Schulz created a world of characters in which contrast of the side characters clarified the main characters.

I am thankful every day that Schulz created this world and left a legacy of lessons for storytellers, and now I'm pondering next year's costume.

*Most of us familiar with Charles M. Schulz's artwork recognize it from the 17,897* Peanuts *comic strips he wrote and drew over his fifty-year career. And much of that artwork has been used and modified in a variety of media for almost as long, filtered through animation, commercial design, print, and character licensing across the world. The artwork presented in* The Complete Peanuts Family Album *comes from an array of sources and a diverse group of artists, including designers from Peanuts Worldwide (PW) and Charles M. Schulz Creative Associates (CSCA); some items come from the archives of the Charles M. Schulz Museum (CMSM) and some pieces have been specifically created for this book. Regardless of the source, all of the artwork presented here is lovingly inspired by Charles M. Schulz's original work.*

OPPOSITE: *Style Guide art – CSCA*

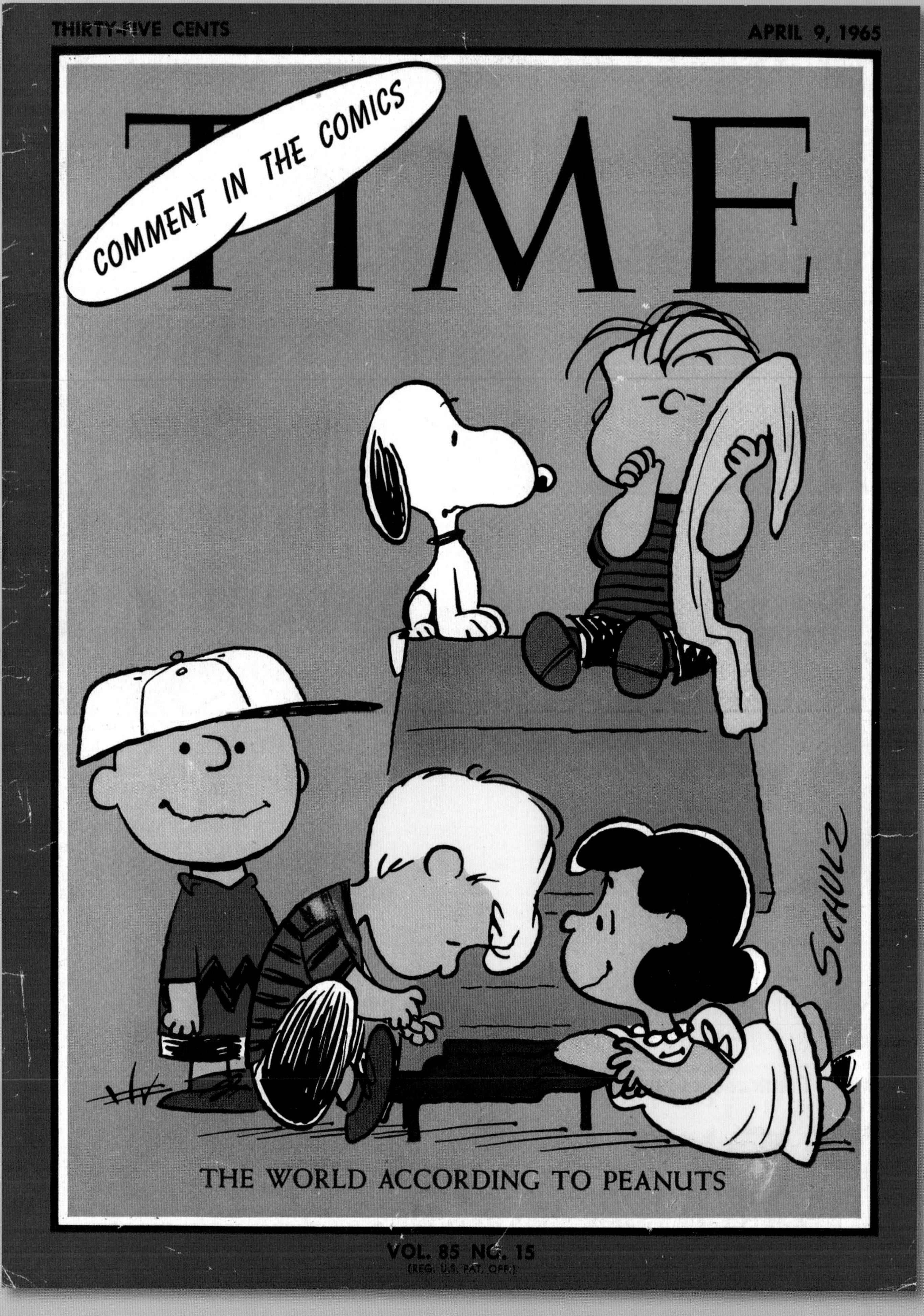
THIRTY-FIVE CENTS
APRIL 9, 1965
TIME
COMMENT IN THE COMICS
SCHULZ
THE WORLD ACCORDING TO PEANUTS
VOL. 85 NO. 15
(REG. U.S. PAT. OFF.)

# INTRODUCTION

Who's your favorite *Peanuts* character?

Or, to put it another way, what's wrong with you?

Maybe you have autophobia, the fear of loneliness. In that case, you probably relate to Charlie Brown and his endless list of anxieties, his wishy-washy nature, and his complete inability to fly a kite. (Science has not yet named the fear of Kite-Eating Trees, sadly.)

Do you have sedatephobia, the fear of silence? You'd probably get along well with Lucy, Miss Fussbudget of the Year since 1952, who has literally cursed the darkness rather than light a single candle.

It's possible you've got ailurophasia, the fear of cats, in which case you'd get along just fine with Snoopy and Woodstock—just don't tell Frieda.

And if you suffer from arithmophobia, the fear of numbers, you'd best avoid 555 95472 and his sisters, 3 and 4, altogether.

Whatever your affliction, rest assured that there's at least one *Peanuts* character who can sympathize with you over jelly-bread sandwiches and a frosty mug of root beer.

But what about problems more complex than the fear of cats, numbers, or numbers of cats? If that's the case, you may identify with some of these *Peanuts* characters that have never actually appeared in the strip (although none of them seem to actually have scopophobia, the fear of being seen).

Do you have a fear of sports? Perhaps you and Charlie Brown's unfortunate baseball idol Joe Shlabotnik suffer from athlimataphobia.

What about the fear of eggs? We'll never know why Linus was supposed to bring discarded eggshells to Miss Othmar's classroom, but that sounds like a classic case of ovaphobia, doesn't it?

And what if the Little Red Haired Girl wasn't avoiding Charlie Brown at all, but was simply frozen by chorophobia, the fear of dancing? Or even more tragic, philophobia, the fear of love itself? A single therapy session at Lucy's psychiatric booth could have completely changed her perspective on life.

There are a number of memorable unseen locales in *Peanuts*, too, including the interior of Snoopy's doghouse. A combination of the fear of houses, domatophobia, and the fear of dogs, cynophobia, may keep you from learning just how Snoopy has managed to fit a recreation room, a den, a cedar closet, a guest room, a whirlpool bath, and an Andrew Wyeth painting inside a standard-issue doghouse.

When *Peanuts* debuted in seven newspapers on October 2, 1950, its world was a little simpler. Charles Schulz's initial cast of characters consisted of Charlie Brown, his dog, Snoopy, and his friends Patty and Shermy. Their personalities weren't clearly defined in the strip's early days, but as new characters like Violet, Schroeder, Lucy, Linus, Pig-Pen, and Sally were introduced, everyone's role came into focus. By the end of the strip's first decade, *Peanuts* truly came into its own as the home of some of the most beloved characters in comic strip history.

The additions of Peppermint Patty, Marcie, and Franklin in the second half of the 1960s expanded the *Peanuts* universe across town to the neighboring school district. The extended cast provided Charles Schulz with even greater storytelling possibilities, and more opportunities for self-expression, as he noted in a 1984 interview. "I think anybody who is writing finds he puts a little bit of himself in all of the characters, at least in this kind of a strip. It's the only way that you can survive when you have to do something every day. You have to put yourself, all of your thoughts, all of your observations and everything you know into the strip."

While *Peanuts* seemingly introduced one iconic character after another, dozens of kids appeared for little more than a walk-on role in the strip. José Peterson, Thibault, and Cormac all came and went with only a

OPPOSITE: TIME® *magazine cover, April 9, 1965 – CMSM*

handful of appearances to their names. Molly Volley, "Crybaby" Boobie, and "Badcall" Benny never became global sports icons, and it's impossible to find any good Harold Angel merchandise at Christmastime. Loretta can be seen in only two panels in the strip's fifty-year history; Lila's only in one. Such is the life of a *Peanuts* supporting character.

But with more than sixty characters in the strip, ranging from the true cultural icon Snoopy to the would-be licensing superstar Tapioca Pudding, why settle for just one favorite character? Maybe you're one of the *Peanuts* fans who struggles daily with the condition that some scholars might call panpeanutophilia, better known as "love of all things *Peanuts*." (Not many scholars, mind you. But some.)

Sure, we all love Charlie Brown, but that doesn't mean we should forget Charlotte Braun. Live like Joe Cool, play like Joe Richkid. Or Joe Motorcross. Or Joe Grunge. Or Joe Shlabotnik.

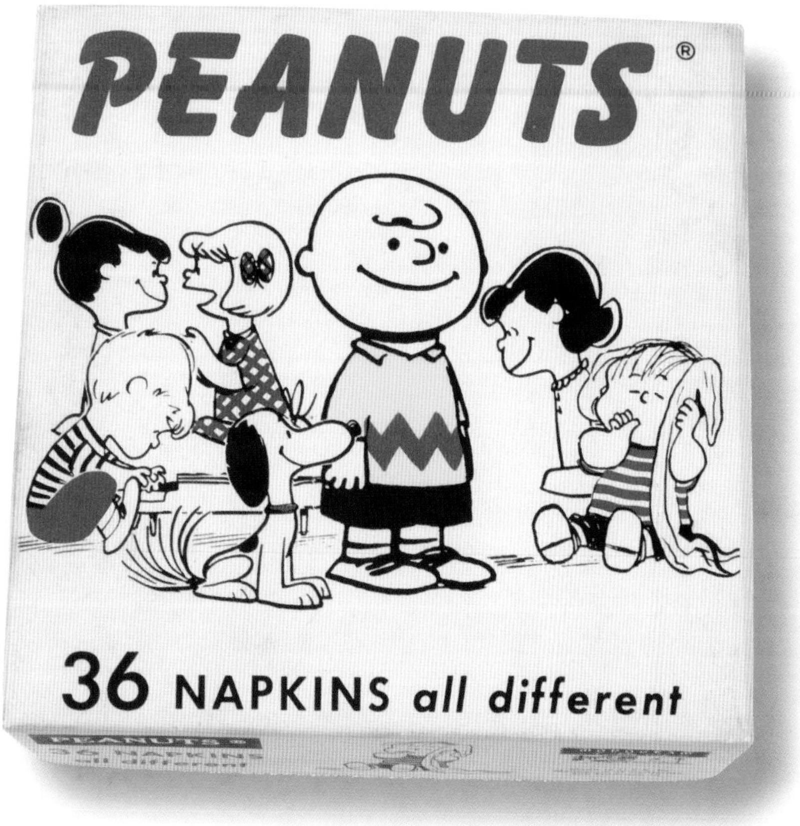
PEANUTS®
36 NAPKINS all different

You can play marbles with Joe Agate, or you can play by the gate with Snoopy's brother, Marbles. You can have truffles with Tapioca Pudding, or tapioca pudding with Truffles. For every Patty, there's a Peppermint Patty, and for every Shermy, there's a Shirley—and a Clara and a Sophie, to boot! It's enough to send you straight to Lucy's Psychiatric Booth for treatment.

**"I just draw what I think is funny, and I hope other people think it is funny, too."**

**– Charles M. Schulz**

But fortunately, to quote Lucy herself, "as they say on TV, 'the mere fact that you realize you need help indicates that you are not too far gone.'"

Read on and you'll learn the Van Pelt family tree from Rerun to Linus's blanket-hating grandmother, the names of Snoopy's brothers and sister from the Daisy Hill Puppy Farm, and the secret identities of The Masked Marvel and the mysterious Mr. Sack—and you'll have one less thing to worry about as you lie awake in bed at night.

And if that doesn't work, you can always join the French Foreign Legion.

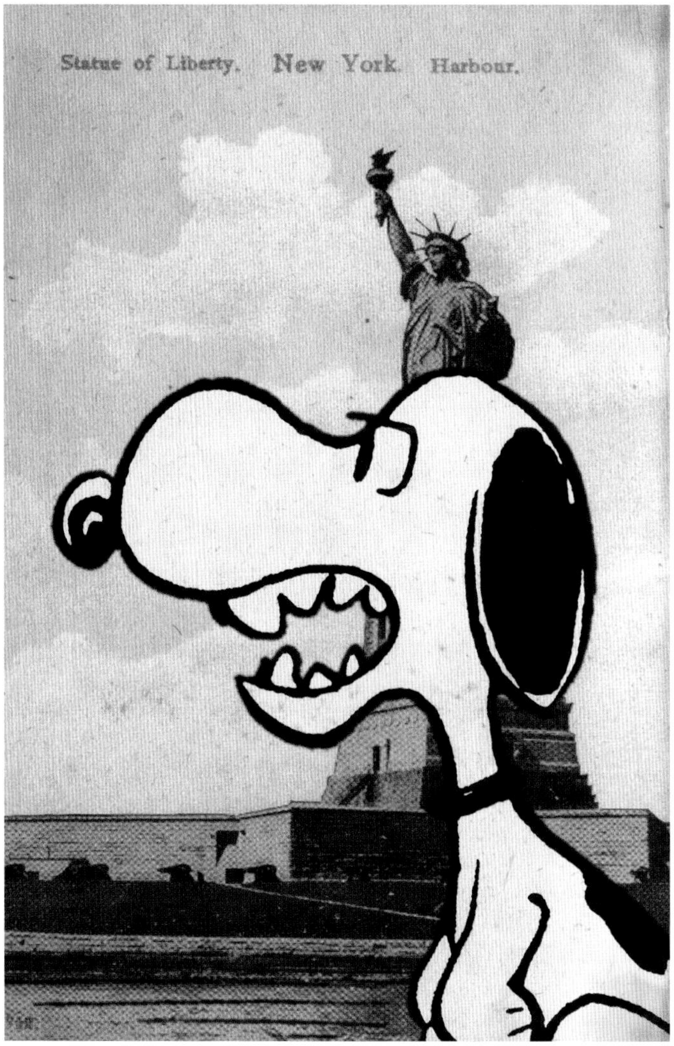
Statue of Liberty. New York. Harbour.

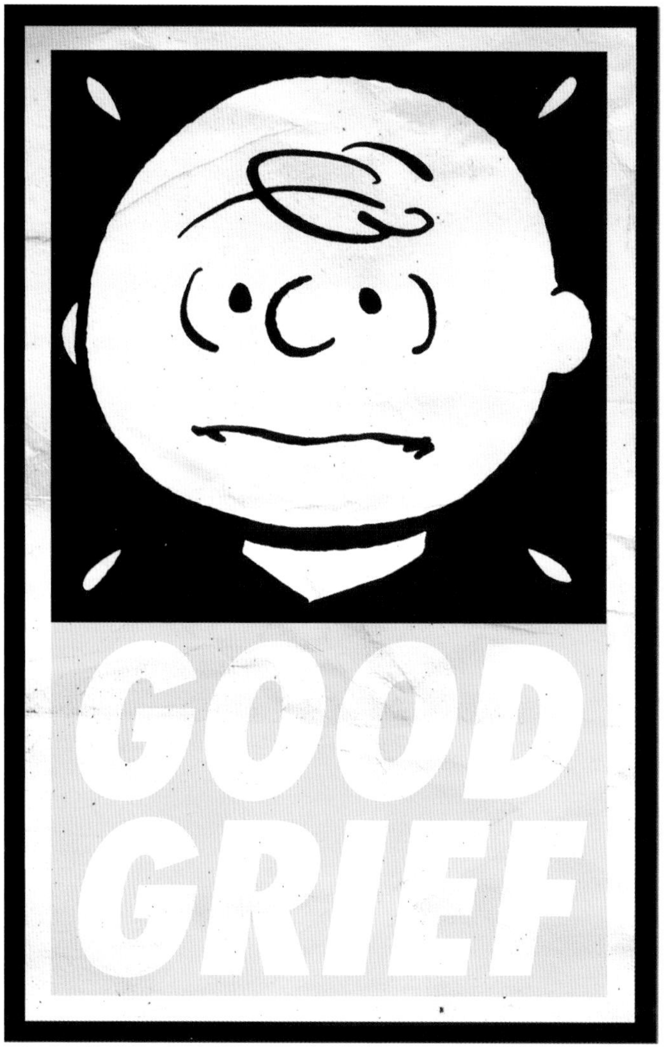
GOOD
GRIEF

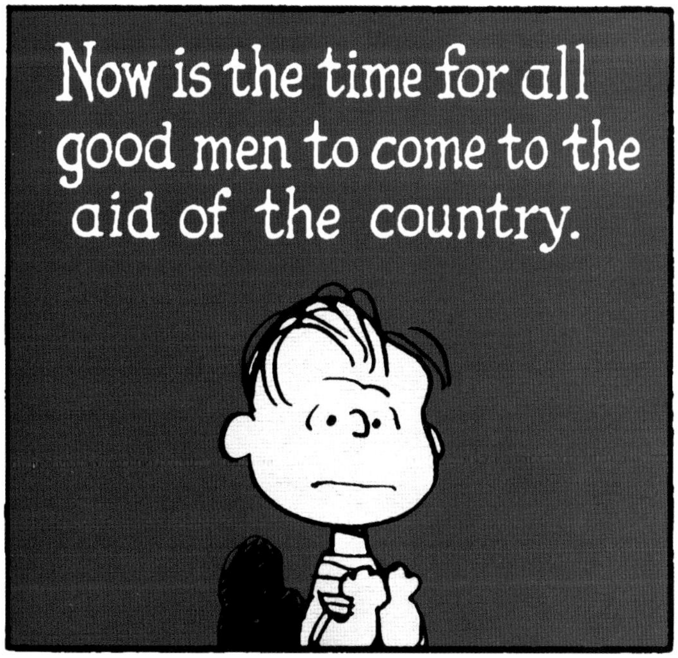
Now is the time for all good men to come to the aid of the country.

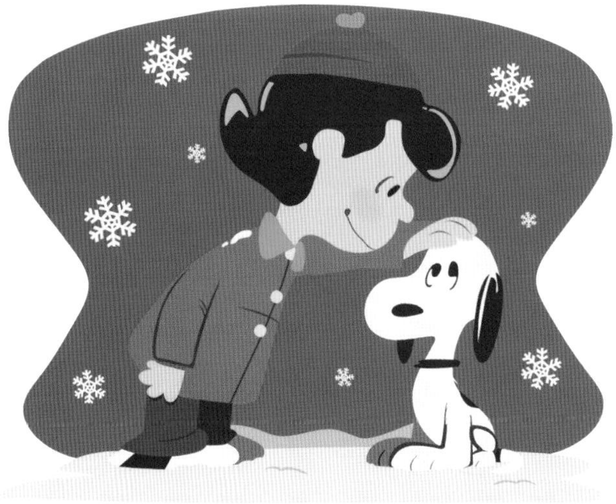

OPPOSITE: Peanuts *paper cocktail napkin box, created by Hallmark Cards, Inc., manufactured by Monogram, San Francisco, c. 1960 – CMSM* | ABOVE: *Style Guide art – CSCA*

# THE BOYS

From baseball to Beethoven, and from the Six Bunny-Wunnies to War and Peace, the boys in the neighborhood have a wide variety of interests and aspirations. Their personalities run the range from the wishy-washy Charlie Brown to the un-washy Pig-Pen, whose confidence in himself is unwavering.

1/Rerun 2/Franklin 3/Ethan 4/Snoopy 5/Larry 6/Cormac 7/Marbles 8/Spike 9/Maynard 10/Shermy 11/Austin 12/Leland 13/Linus 14/Charlie Brown 15/Milo 16/5 17/Joe Richkid 18/Thibault 19/Olaf 20/Faron 21/"Badcall" Benny 22/Floyd 23/Schroeder 24/Pig-Pen 25/Andy 26/Harold Angel 27/José Peterson 28/The Beagle Scouts (Conrad, Oliver, Bill, Fred) 29/Woodstock

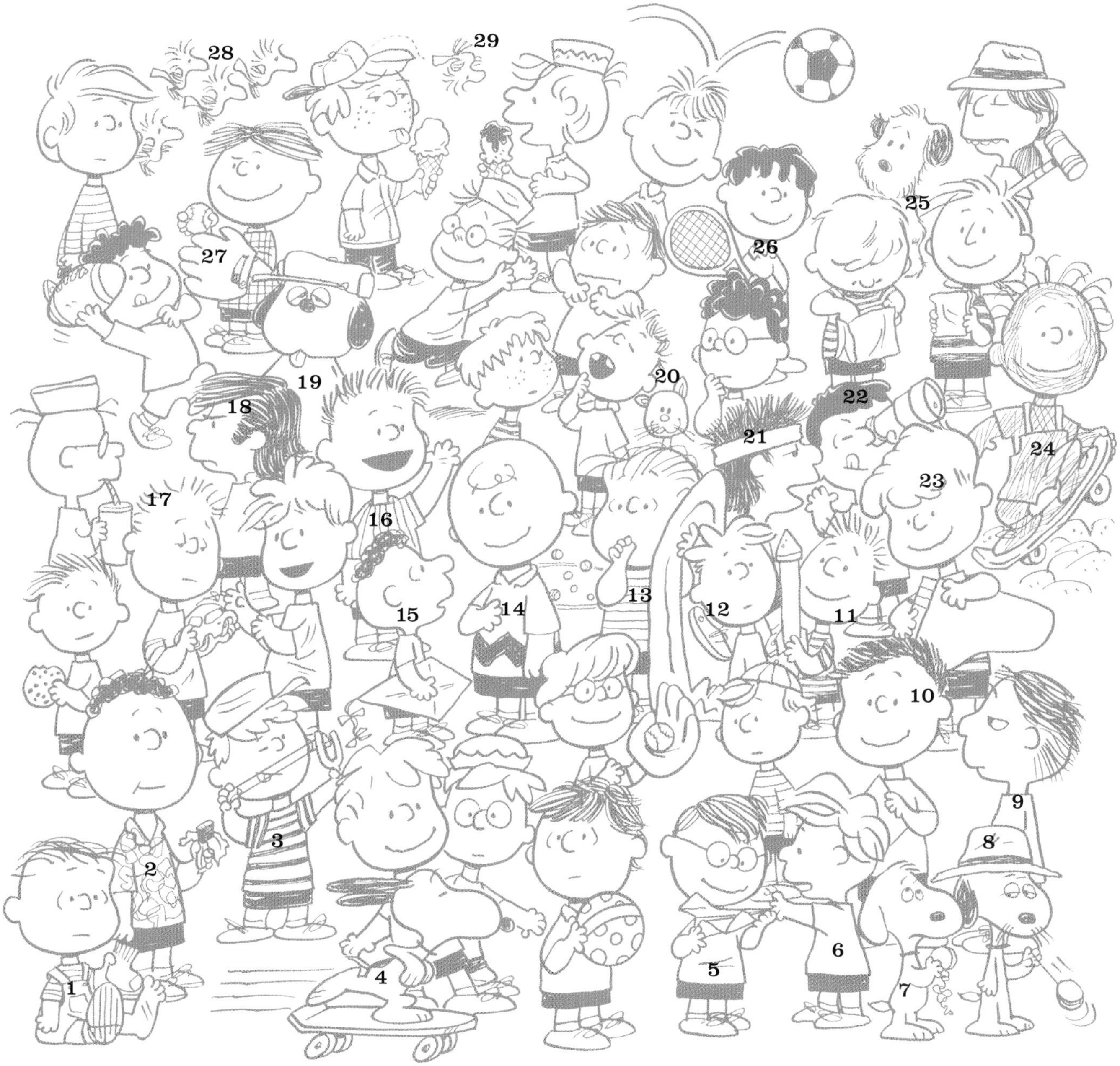
1
2
3
4
5
6
7
8
9
10
11
12
13
14
15
16
17
18
19
20
21
22
23
24
25
26
27
28
29

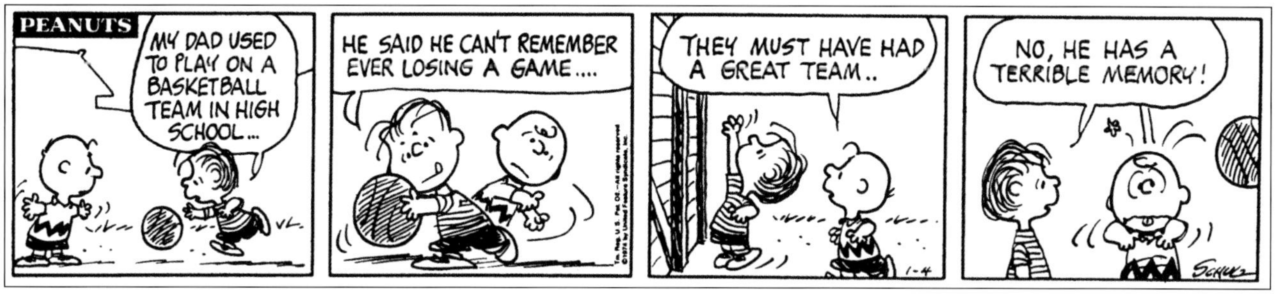
PEANUTS
MY DAD USED TO PLAY ON A BASKETBALL TEAM IN HIGH SCHOOL...
HE SAID HE CAN'T REMEMBER EVER LOSING A GAME....
THEY MUST HAVE HAD A GREAT TEAM..
NO, HE HAS A TERRIBLE MEMORY!

# THE GIRLS

**P**atty was the first girl in Charlie Brown's life, but she soon had a lot of company, as Violet, Lucy, and Frieda moved to the neighborhood. Between Lucy's status as the future Queen of the World, Peppermint Patty's athletic dominance, and Marcie's academic excellence, the girls in the neighborhood are second to the boys only when it comes to neuroses.

**1**/*Sophie* **2**/*Ruby* **3**/*Clara* **4**/*"Crybaby" Boobie* **5**/*Lydia* **6**/*Emily* **7**/*Peggy Jean* **8**/*3* **9**/*4* **10**/*Royanne Hobbs* **11**/*Marcie* **12**/*Peppermint Patty* **13**/*Lucy* **14**/*Violet* **15**/*Patty* **16**/*Sally* **17**/*Belle* **18**/*Truffles* **19**/*Naomi* **20**/*Frieda* **21**/*Eudora* **22**/*Tapioca Pudding* **23**/*Lila* **24**/*Molly Volley*

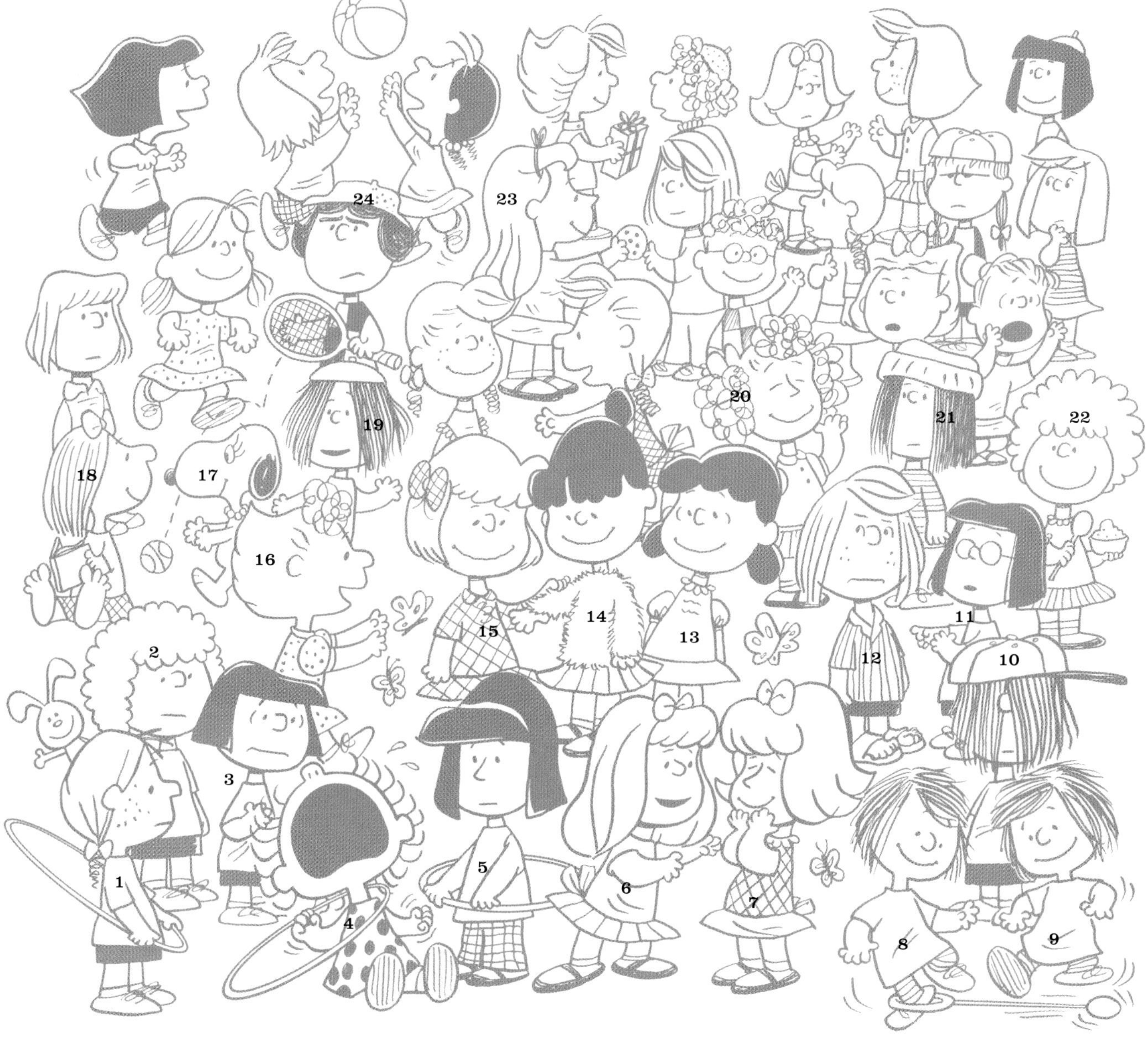
1
2
3
4
5
6
7
8
9
10
11
12
13
14
15
16
17
18
19
20
21
22
23
24

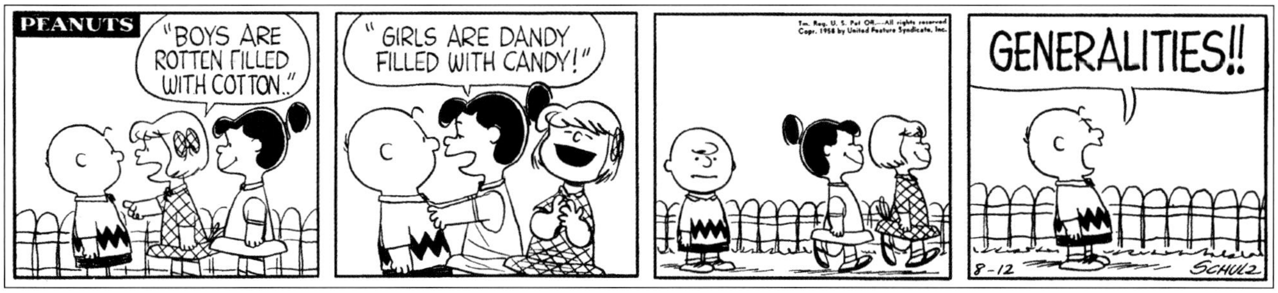
PEANUTS
"BOYS ARE ROTTEN FILLED WITH COTTON.."
"GIRLS ARE DANDY FILLED WITH CANDY!"
Tm. Reg. U. S. Pat Off.—All rights reserved Copr. 1958 by United Feature Syndicate, Inc.
GENERALITIES!!
8-12
SCHULZ

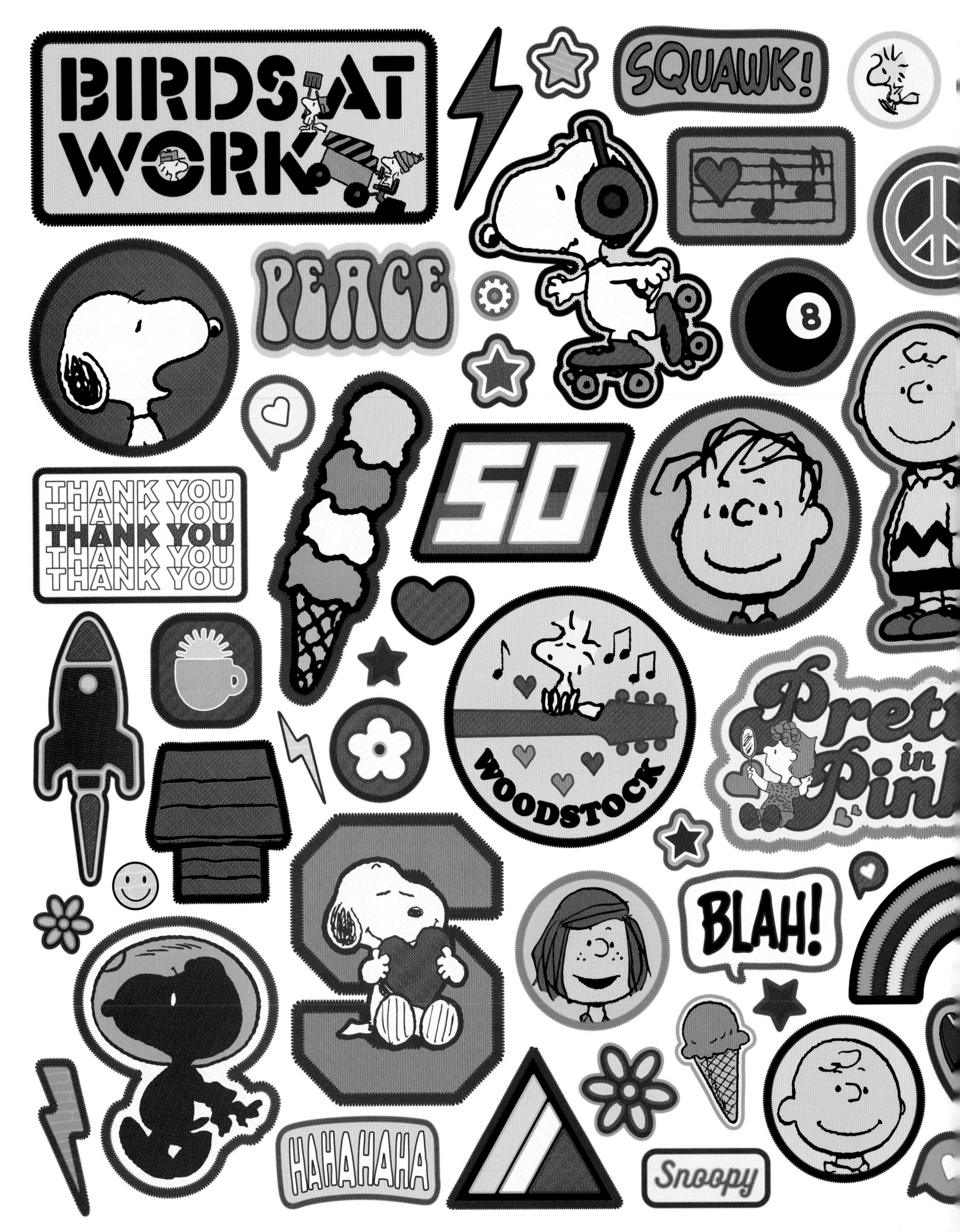
BIRDS AT WORK
SQUAWK!
PEACE
8
50
THANK YOU
THANK YOU
THANK YOU
THANK YOU
THANK YOU
WOODSTOCK
BLAH!
HAHAHAHA
Snoopy

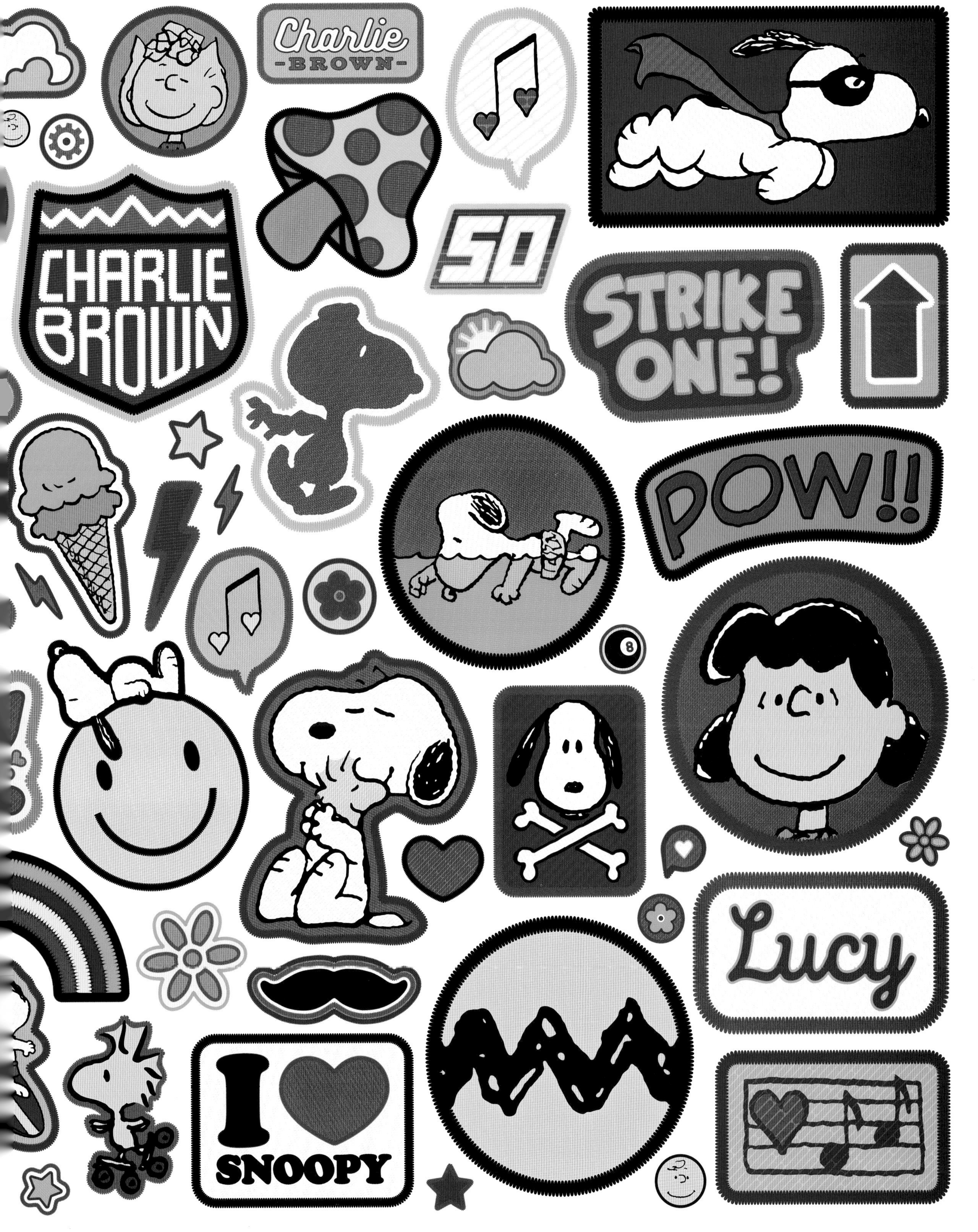
Charlie
-BROWN-
50
CHARLIE
BROWN
STRIKE
ONE!
POW!!
8
Lucy
I
SNOOPY

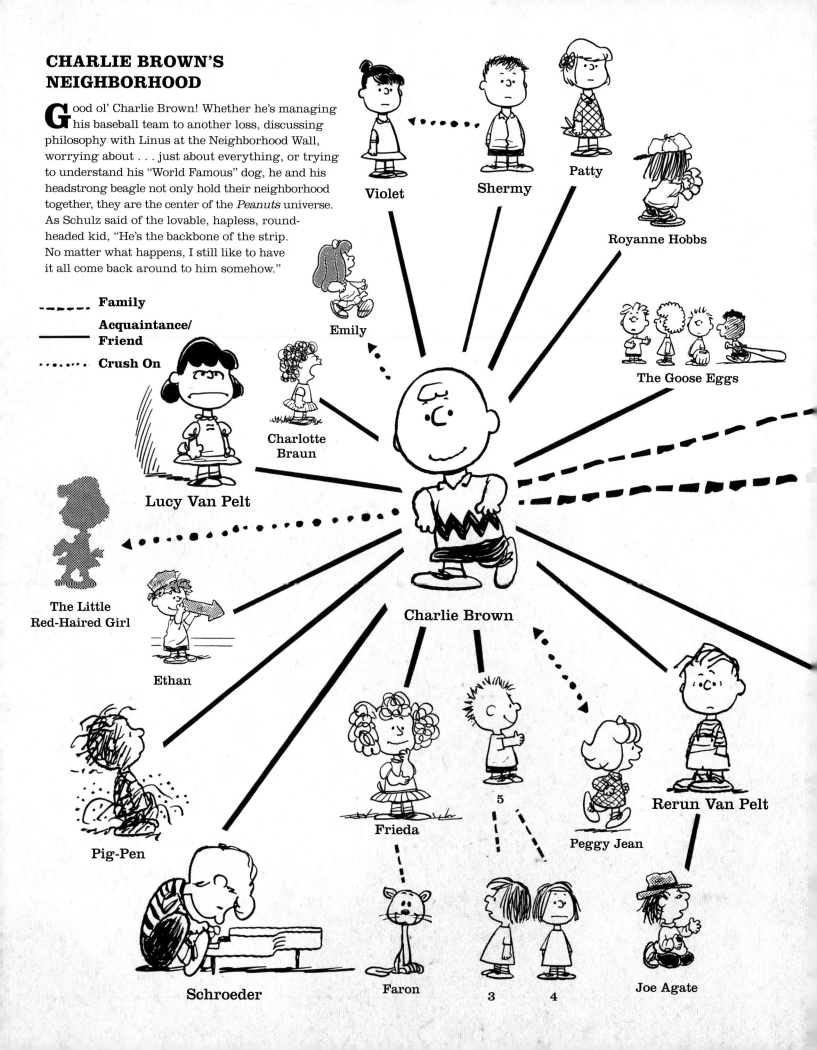

# CHARLIE BROWN'S NEIGHBORHOOD

**G**ood ol' Charlie Brown! Whether he's managing his baseball team to another loss, discussing philosophy with Linus at the Neighborhood Wall, worrying about . . . just about everything, or trying to understand his "World Famous" dog, he and his headstrong beagle not only hold their neighborhood together, they are the center of the *Peanuts* universe. As Schulz said of the lovable, hapless, round-headed kid, "He's the backbone of the strip. No matter what happens, I still like to have it all come back around to him somehow."

- - - - - **Family**
———— **Acquaintance/ Friend**
· · · · · · **Crush On**

Violet

Shermy

Patty

Royanne Hobbs

Emily

The Goose Eggs

Charlotte Braun

Lucy Van Pelt

Charlie Brown

The Little Red-Haired Girl

Ethan

Pig-Pen

Schroeder

Frieda

5

Faron

3

4

Peggy Jean

Rerun Van Pelt

Joe Agate

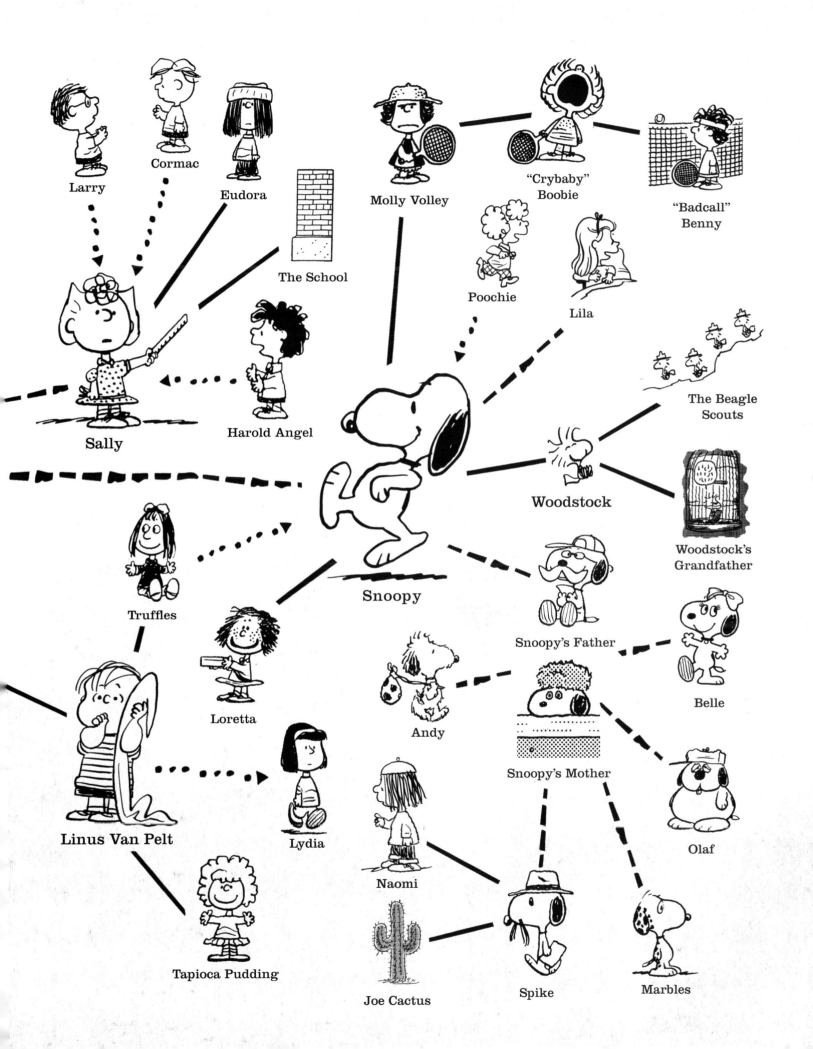

Larry

Cormac

Eudora

The School

Molly Volley

"Crybaby" Boobie

"Badcall" Benny

Poochie

Lila

The Beagle Scouts

Sally

Harold Angel

Snoopy

Woodstock

Woodstock's Grandfather

Truffles

Loretta

Andy

Snoopy's Father

Belle

Lydia

Naomi

Snoopy's Mother

Olaf

Linus Van Pelt

Tapioca Pudding

Joe Cactus

Spike

Marbles

## PEPPERMINT PATTY'S NEIGHBORHOOD

On the other side of town, Peppermint Patty manages a team that's practically the exact opposite of Charlie Brown's hapless squad, and her all-stars have a perfect undefeated record against his team. Although they're rivals on the field, Charlie Brown counts Peppermint Patty, Marcie, and Franklin among his closest friends.

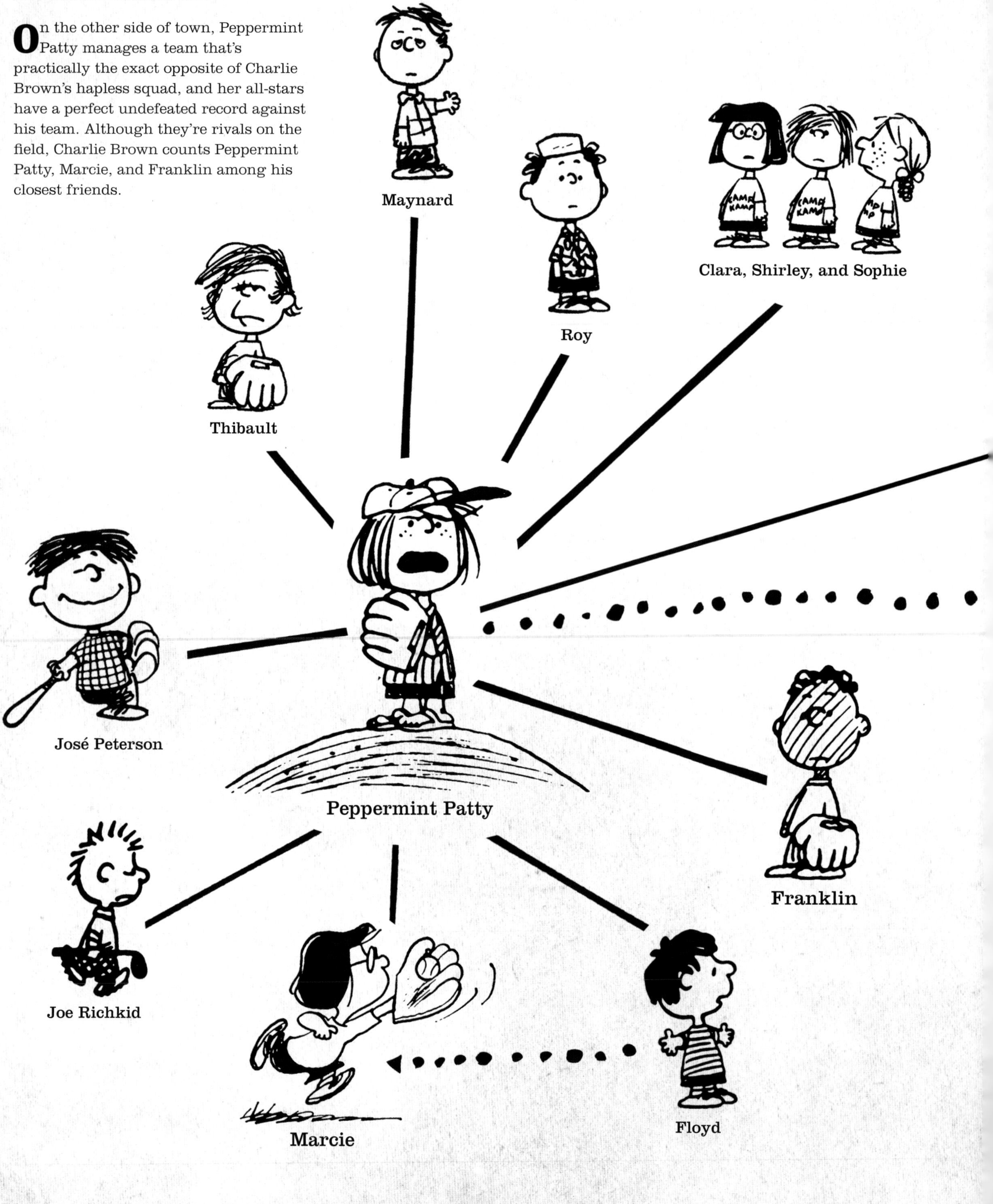
Maynard
Roy
Clara, Shirley, and Sophie
Thibault
José Peterson
Peppermint Patty
Franklin
Joe Richkid
Marcie
Floyd

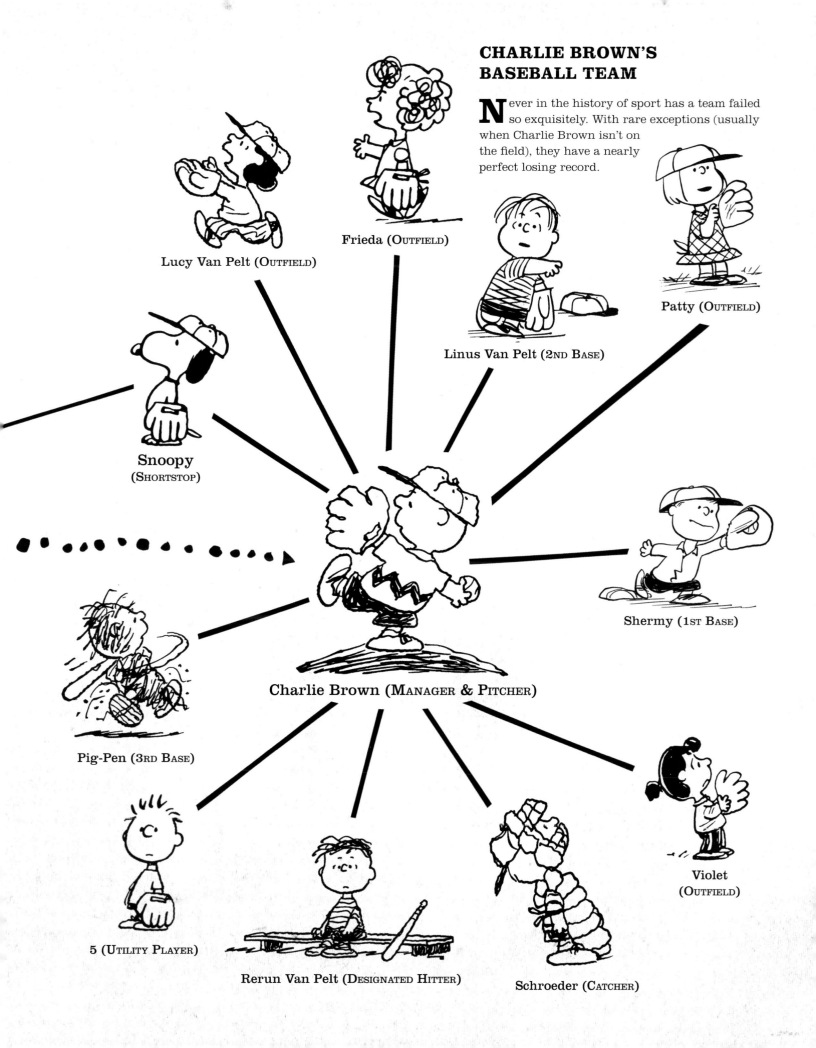

## CHARLIE BROWN'S BASEBALL TEAM

**N**ever in the history of sport has a team failed so exquisitely. With rare exceptions (usually when Charlie Brown isn't on the field), they have a nearly perfect losing record.

Lucy Van Pelt (OUTFIELD)

Frieda (OUTFIELD)

Linus Van Pelt (2ND BASE)

Patty (OUTFIELD)

Snoopy (SHORTSTOP)

Shermy (1ST BASE)

Pig-Pen (3RD BASE)

Charlie Brown (MANAGER & PITCHER)

Violet (OUTFIELD)

5 (UTILITY PLAYER)

Rerun Van Pelt (DESIGNATED HITTER)

Schroeder (CATCHER)

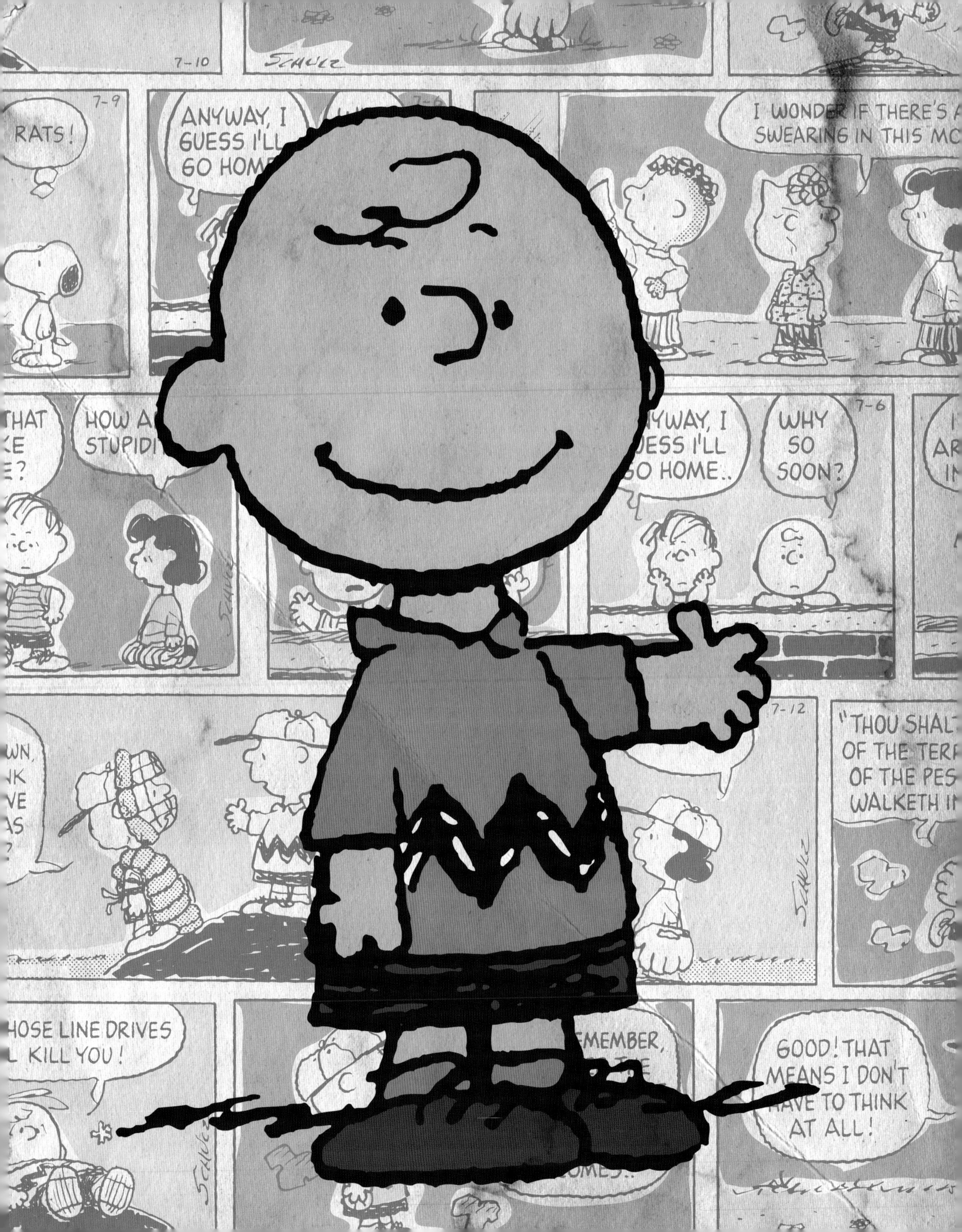
RATS!
WHY SO SOON?
GOOD! THAT MEANS I DON'T HAVE TO THINK AT ALL!

# CHARLIE BROWN

FIRST APPEARANCE
10/02/1950

Good ol' Charlie Brown, unlucky at love, unlucky at school, unlucky at sports. You name it—he finds some new and unusual ways to fail at it. But no matter what life throws at the wishy-washy, round-headed kid, he always tries his best and never gives up.

Charlie Brown eats, sleeps, and breathes baseball, but his love for the game never leads to success on the field. Each spring, he manages the world's worst team through yet another losing season. His performance as the team's pitcher results in some of the most spectacular highlights ever witnessed on the baseball diamond—for the other team. His cap, shirt, shoes, and socks are knocked off by line drives, and he even spends an inning upside down after a really solid hit. And with the exception of two home runs in his entire Little League career, he never comes through with a clutch performance when a close game is on the line.

His athletic difficulties aren't confined to a single season, as he's equally hapless at all sports. Every year, Lucy convinces him to attempt a placekick while she holds a football for him, and every year, she pulls it away and he lands flat on his back. Even the gentle pastime of kite flying has proven dangerous for him: He either ends up hopelessly tangled up in miles of string or stands by helplessly as the Kite-Eating Tree devours his latest flyer.

Charlie Brown is a thoroughly average student, although he could probably be an "A" student if not for his insecurities and performance anxiety. Fear of failure, fear of success, and, as Lucy once successfully points out, "fear of everything" always seems to hold him back. His unrequited crush on his classmate known only as the Little Red-Haired Girl goes unfulfilled in part because he can never bring himself to approach her. As he once observes, "They say opposites attract. . . . She's really something and I'm really nothing. . . . How opposite can you get?"

Despite his anxieties, or possibly because of them, his friends appreciate his company and know that they can always count on good ol' Charlie Brown, whether he wins or not. As Linus says, "Of all the Charlie Browns in the world, you're the Charlie Browniest!"

Charles Schulz and his lead character shared many similarities, and Schulz projected many of his own insecurities onto Charlie Brown. These universal feelings of anxiety and melancholy have been embraced by generations of readers worldwide. "Charlie Brown is the ultimate loser; that is both his magic and his destiny. If he weren't a loser, he'd have no incentive to keep on trying. The secret is not necessarily to win over adversity, but never to stop trying. That's the key, perhaps, to the human condition. Charlie Brown is the world's champion tryer. I think that's important."

Charlie Brown rarely caught a break under the pen of Charles Schulz, and that's a big part of his universal appeal. "I know one thing, humor doesn't come from a happy situation. Happy is not funny. Funny is when something happens to someone else and you identify with it and laugh at the luckless one at the same time. Disasters afflict Charlie Brown that come to all of us sometime; but to Charlie, everything bad happens all the time. He never gets anything right. But a nice kid. I like Charlie Brown."

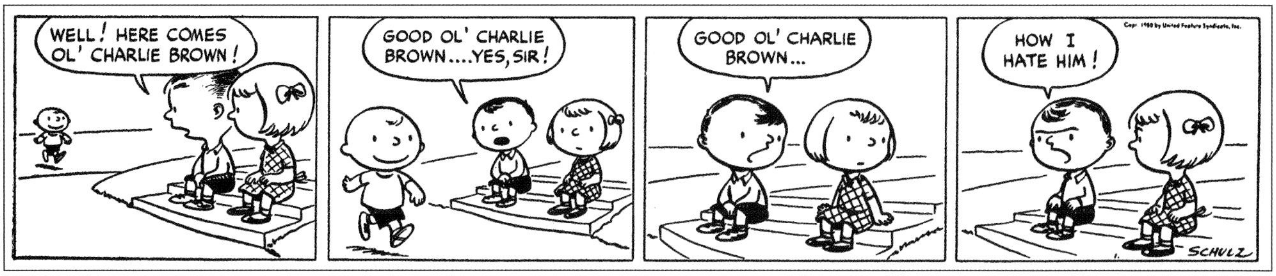
WELL! HERE COMES OL' CHARLIE BROWN!
GOOD OL' CHARLIE BROWN....YES, SIR!
GOOD OL' CHARLIE BROWN...
HOW I HATE HIM!
SCHULZ

OPPOSITE: *Spot art from strip – Charles M. Schulz*

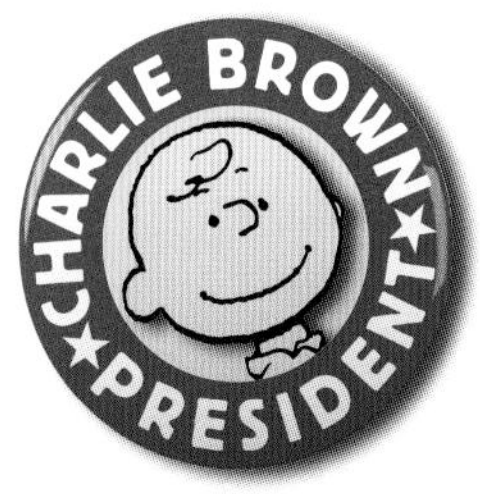
CHARLIE BROWN
PRESIDENT

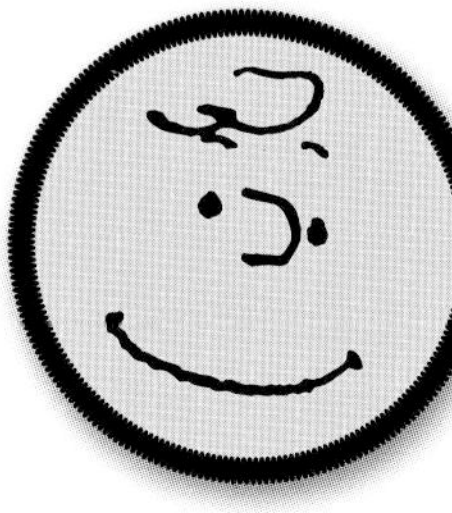

“I only dread one day at a time.”
—Charlie Brown

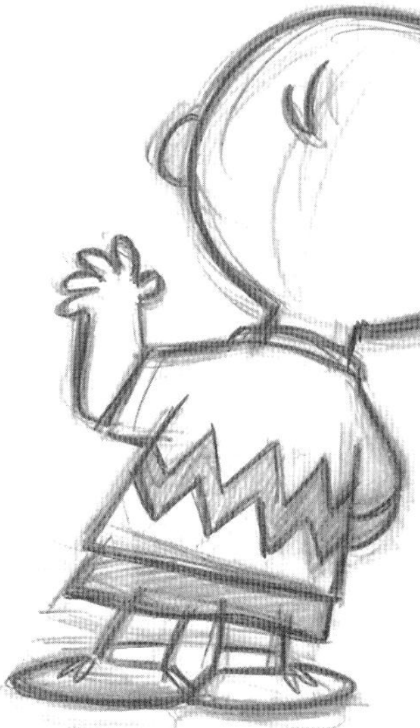

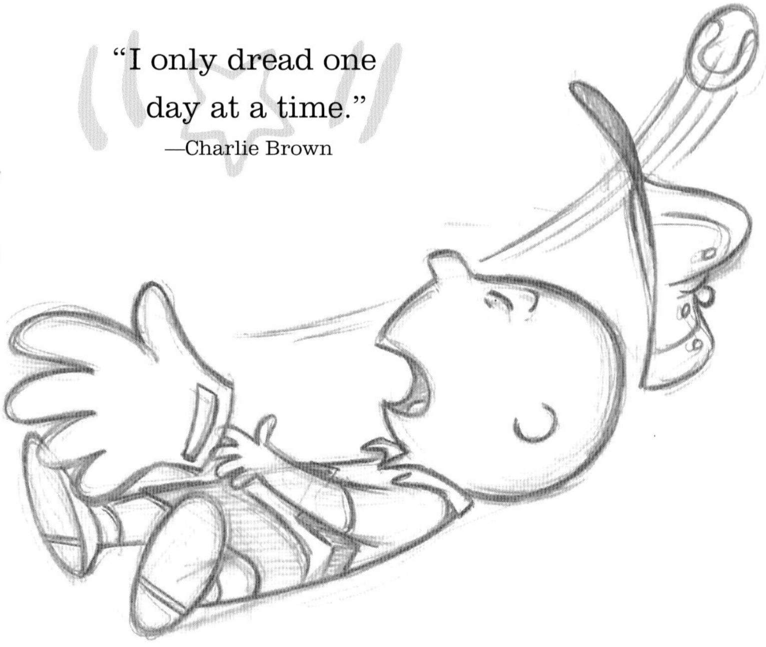

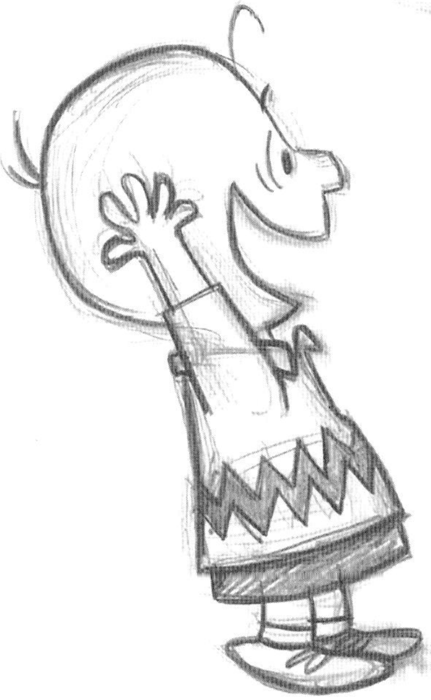

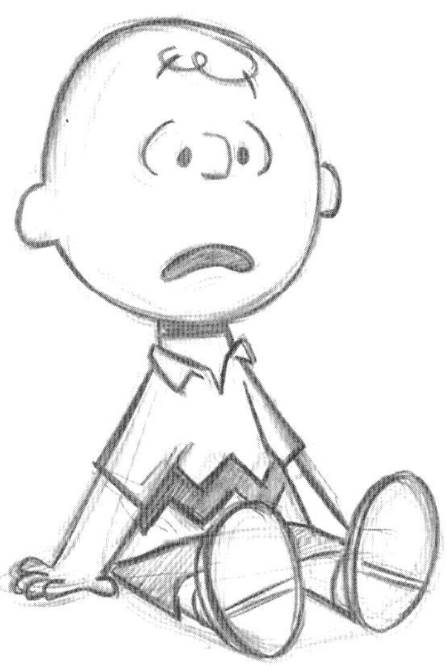

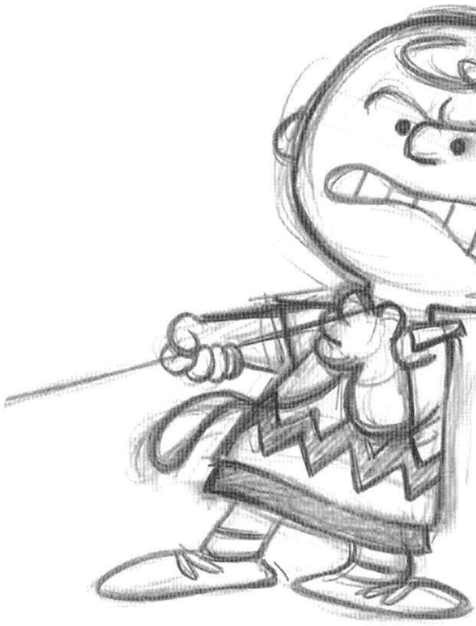

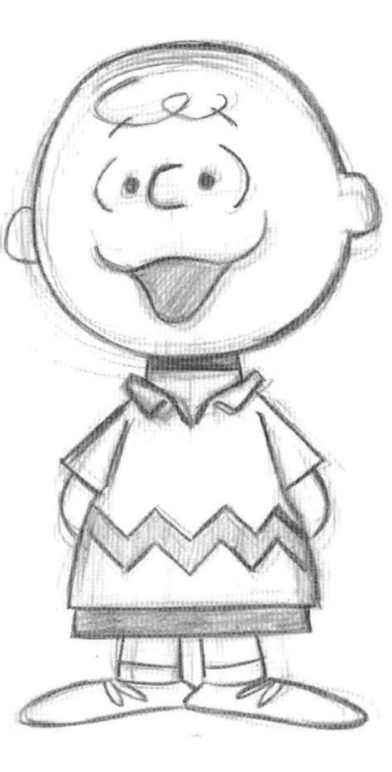

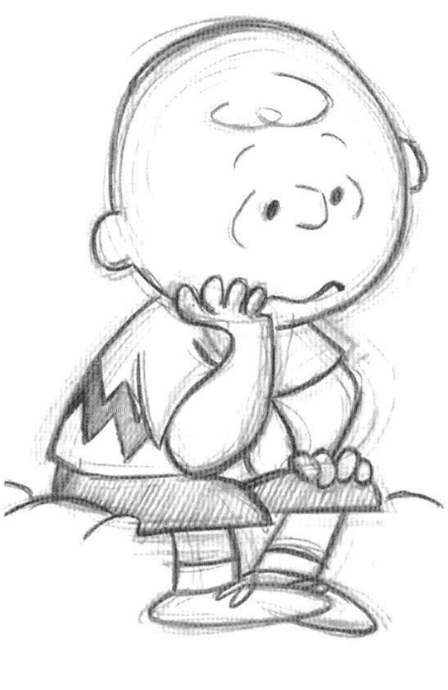

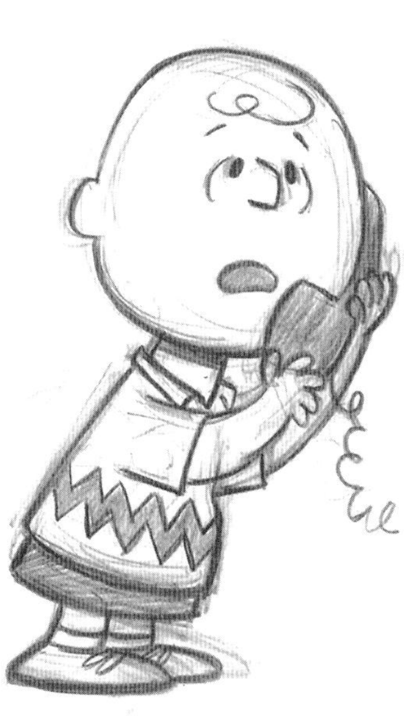

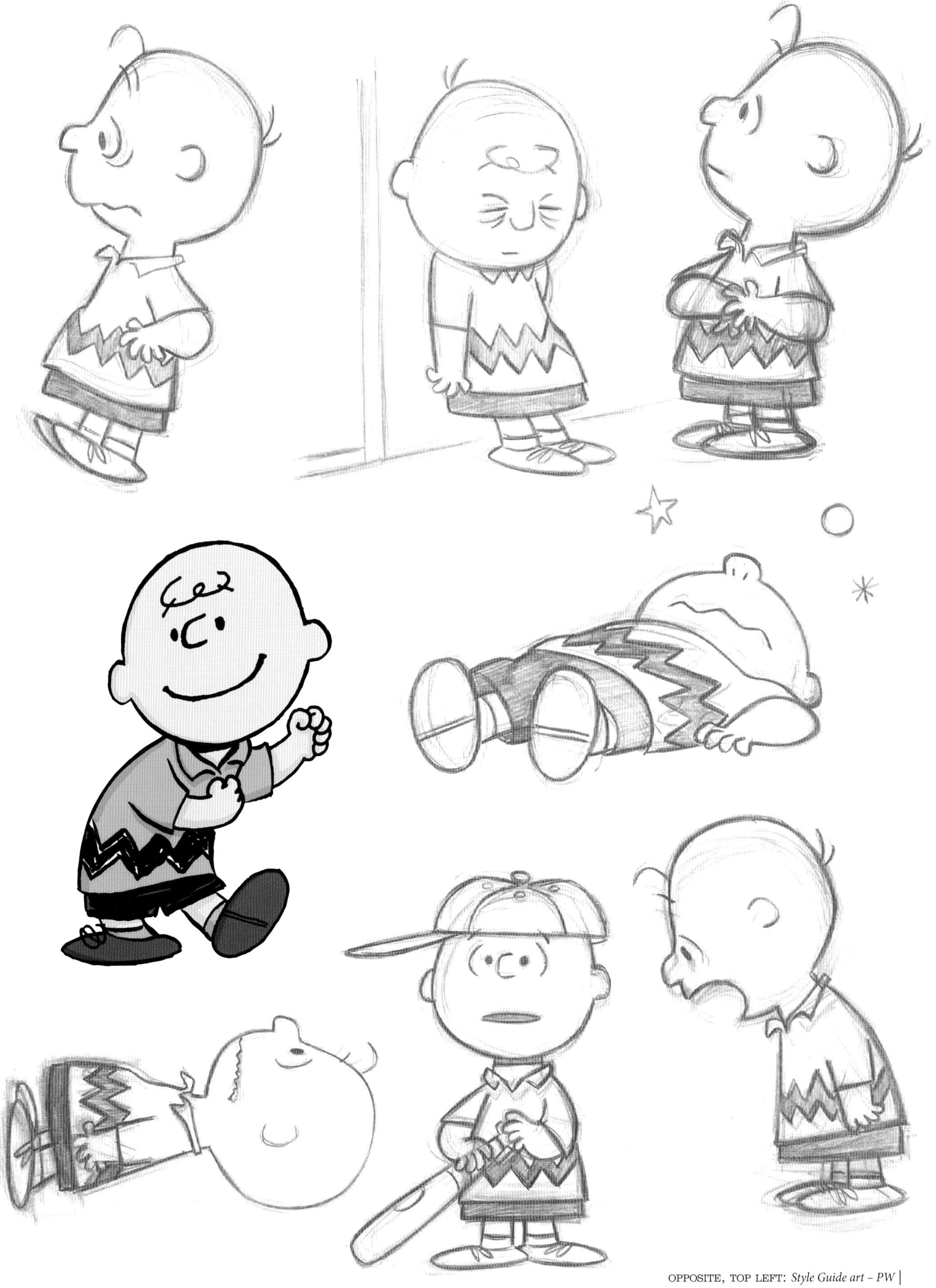

OPPOSITE, TOP LEFT: *Style Guide art – PW* | OPPOSITE AND ABOVE: *Charlie Brown model sheet – CSCA* | ABOVE CENTER: *Style Guide art – CSCA*

# THE ETERNAL OPTIMIST

It's a fall tradition. The football season doesn't really begin until Lucy convinces Charlie Brown—again—that she's going to hold a football in place so that he can kick it. Each time, he is justifiably skeptical, but she somehow convinces him that this is the year that she'll finally let him kick the football. And each and every year, she pulls the ball away at the last second, and Charlie Brown flies into the air and lands flat on his back. And every year, Lucy explains to Charlie Brown that his trust in her was misplaced, but both of them know that the cycle will repeat itself the following year.

This tradition was actually started by Violet, who first pulled the football away from Charlie Brown before Lucy moved into the neighborhood. Lucy soon took over the annual ritual, pulling the football on Charlie Brown's second attempt.

"PEANUTS"
HE'LL KICK MY HAND! I JUST KNOW HE WILL!
I CAN'T GO THROUGH WITH IT!
?
YOU DIDN'T KICK THE BALL, CHARLIE BROWN... WHY DIDN'T YOU KICK IT?
Copr. 1951 by United Feature Syndicate, Inc.
SCHULZ

PLEASE?

?
!
THUMP

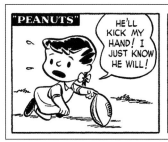

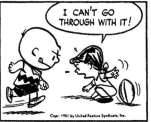

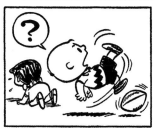

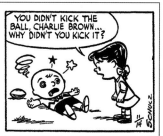

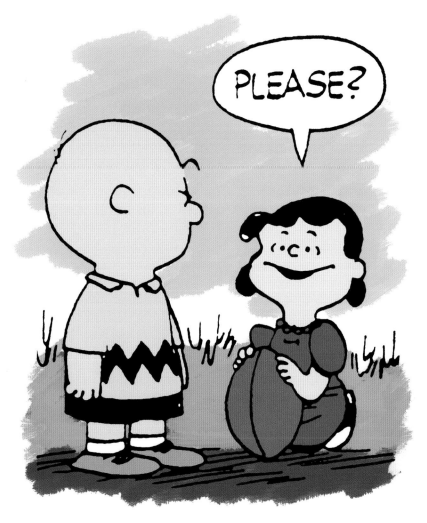

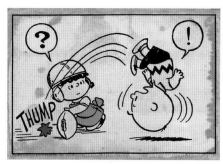

"This year has to be the year I kick that ol' ball."
—Charlie Brown

SHE DID IT AGAIN!

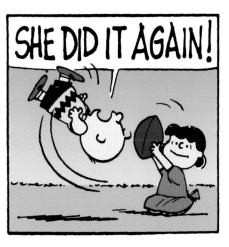

ABOVE: *Style Guide art – CSCA* | RIGHT: *Spot art from strip – Charles M. Schulz* | ABOVE RIGHT: *Art by Charles M. Schulz – CSCA* | OPPOSITE: *Style Guide art – CSCA* | OVERLEAF, LEFT: *Style guide art – PW* | RIGHT: *Comic-Con postcard, 2010 – CSCA*

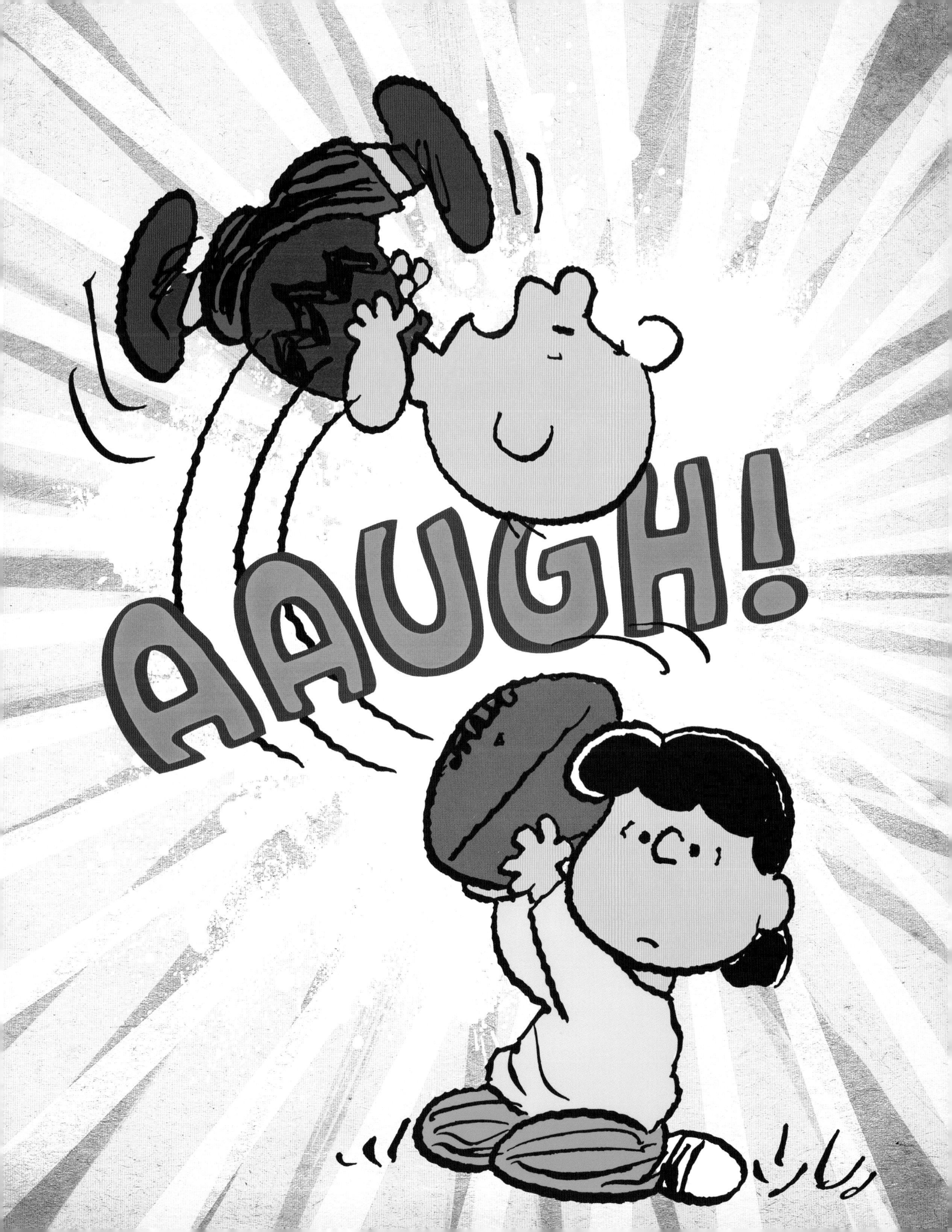
AAUGH!

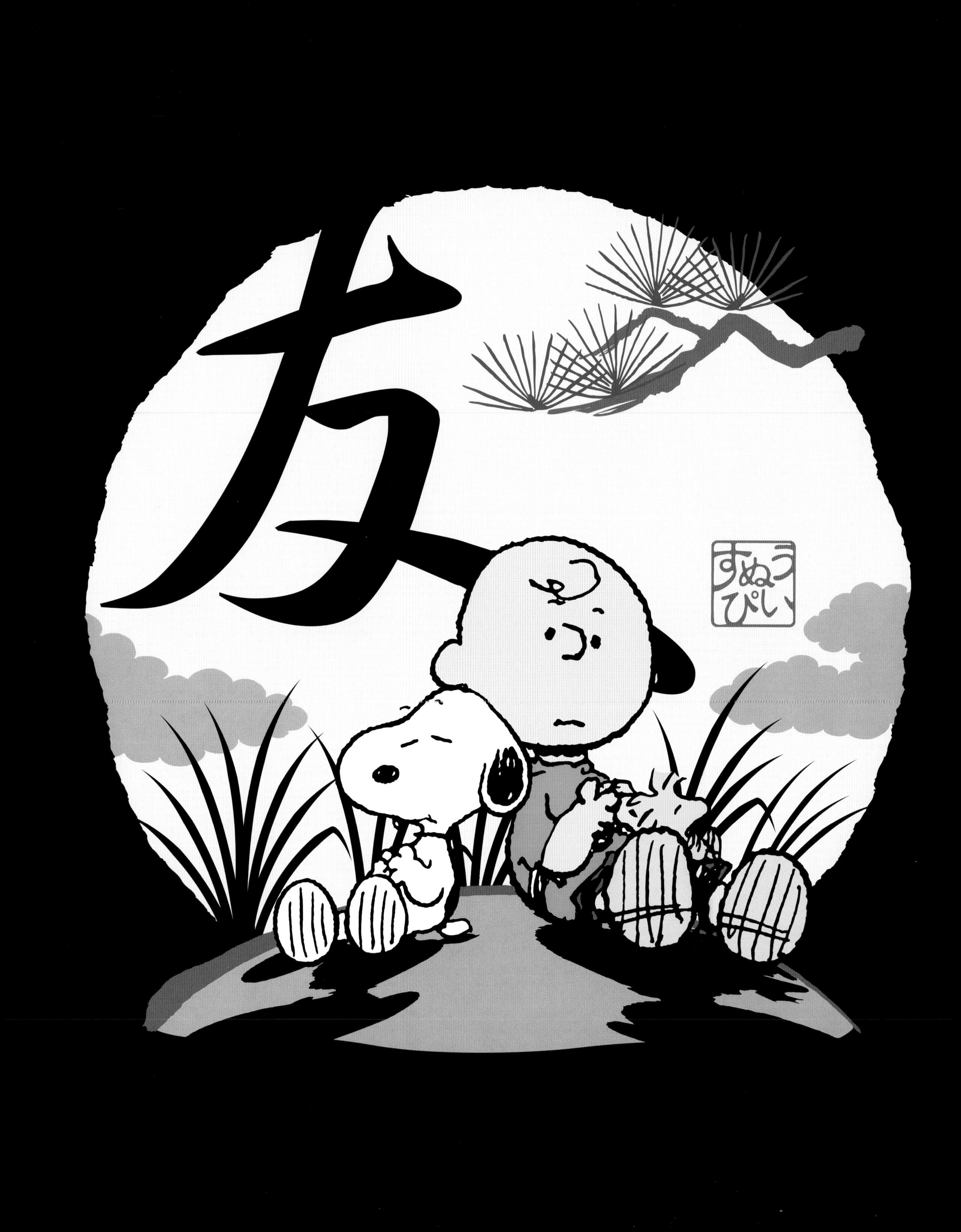
友
すぬうぴい

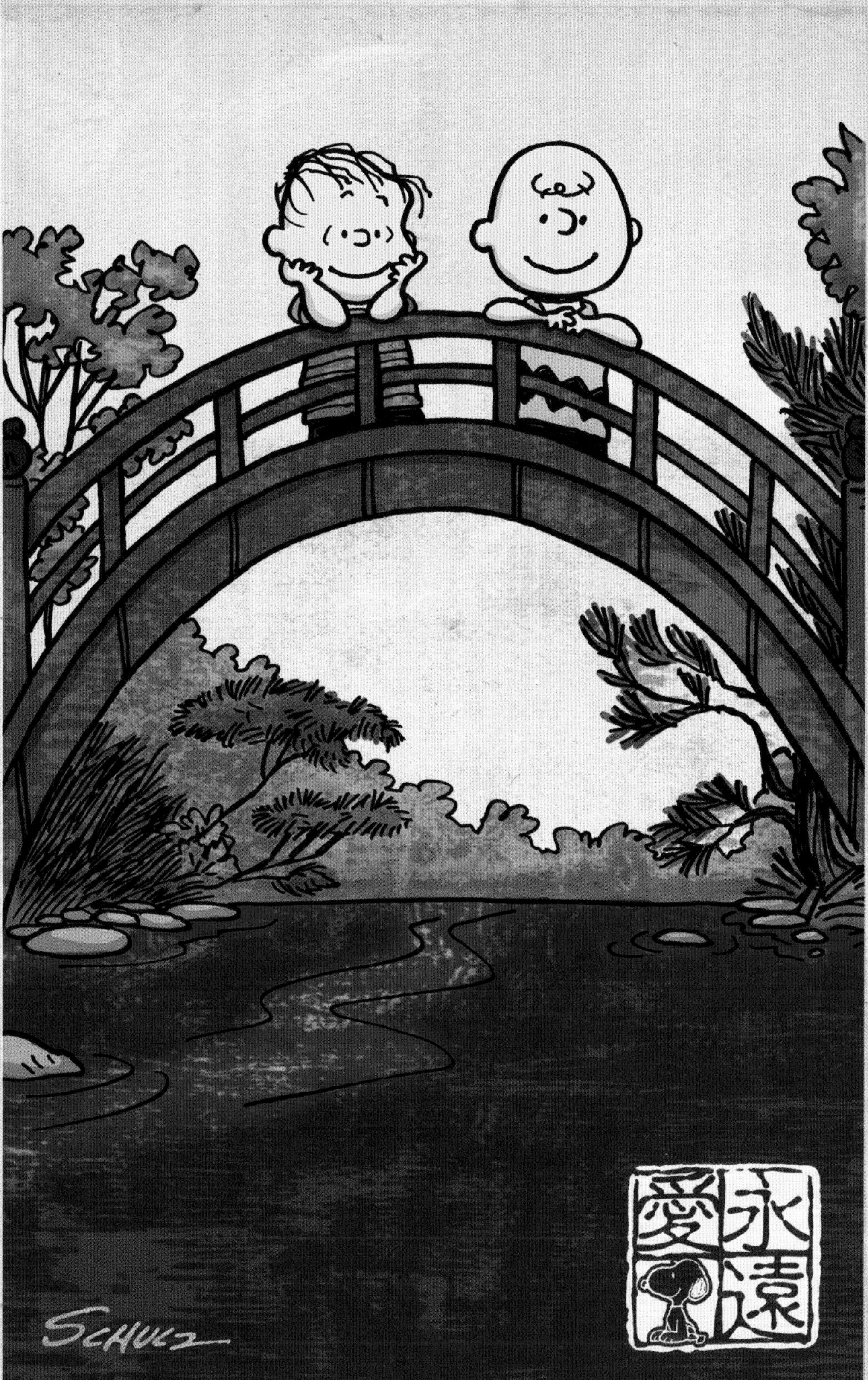
SCHULZ
永遠
愛

# THE BASEBALL MANAGER

Baseball is Charlie Brown's favorite sport. As his team's manager and pitcher, he spends each off-season analyzing statistics, carefully planning his team lineup, and studying his opponents. When spring comes around, he sets out determined to run a winning team. His teammates, however, have a much more lackadaisical approach. Each season, they manage to set new records in futility. Despite their losing record, Charlie Brown's love of baseball and his friends fill him with a renewed sense of optimism every season.

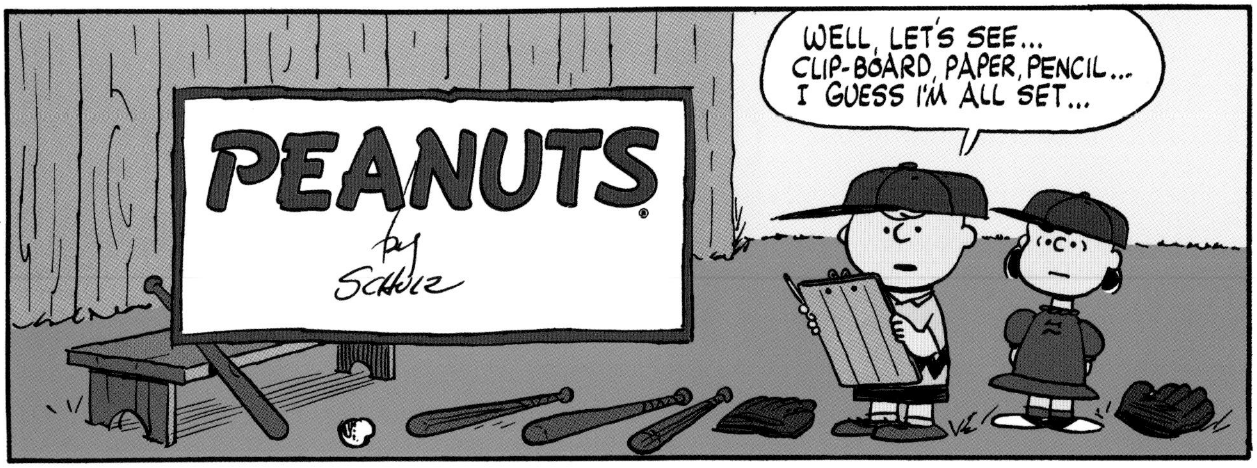
PEANUTS
by Schulz
WELL, LET'S SEE... CLIP-BOARD, PAPER, PENCIL... I GUESS I'M ALL SET...

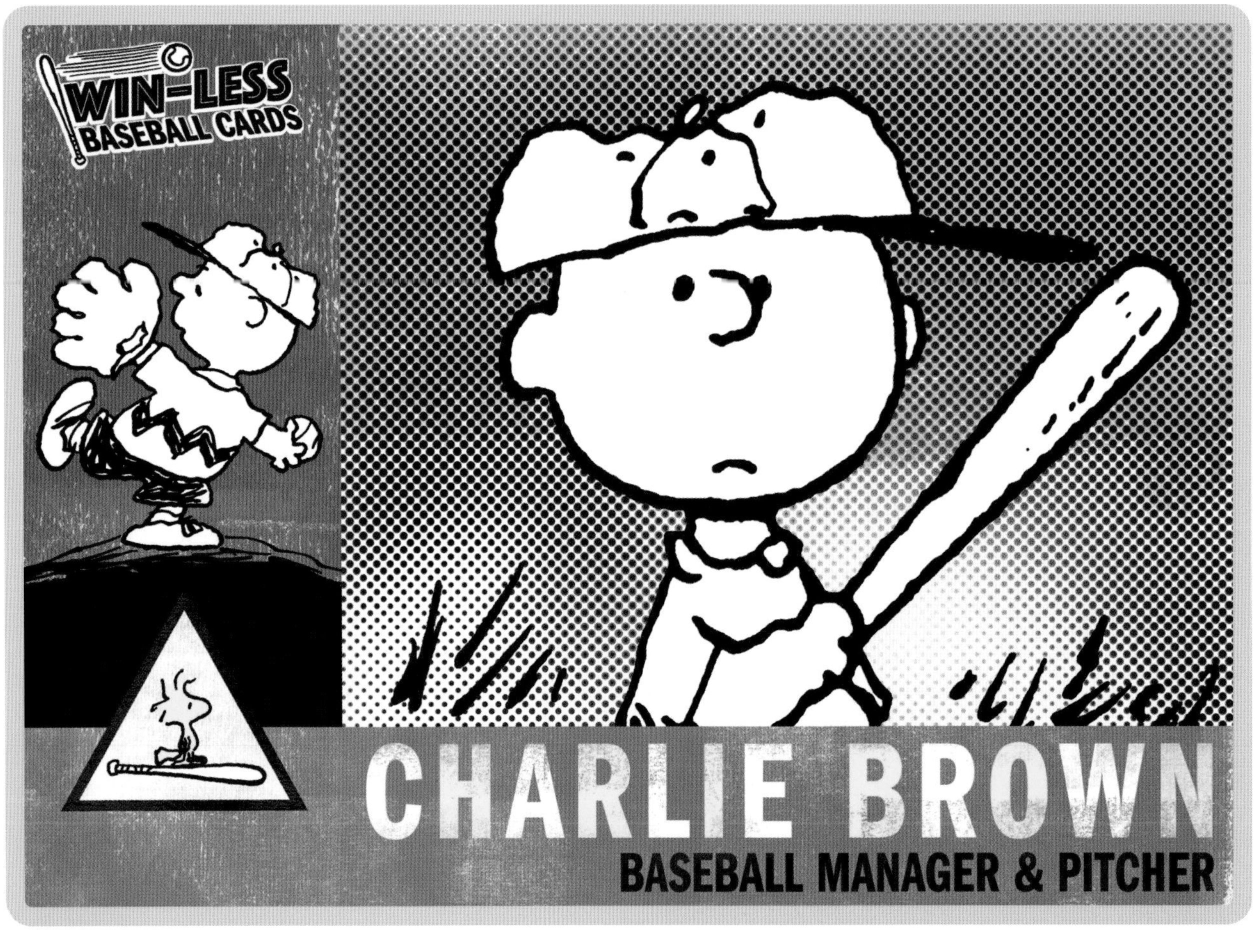
WIN-LESS BASEBALL CARDS
CHARLIE BROWN
BASEBALL MANAGER & PITCHER

"Just what I've always been afraid of . . . my team has built up an immunity to losing."

—Charlie Brown

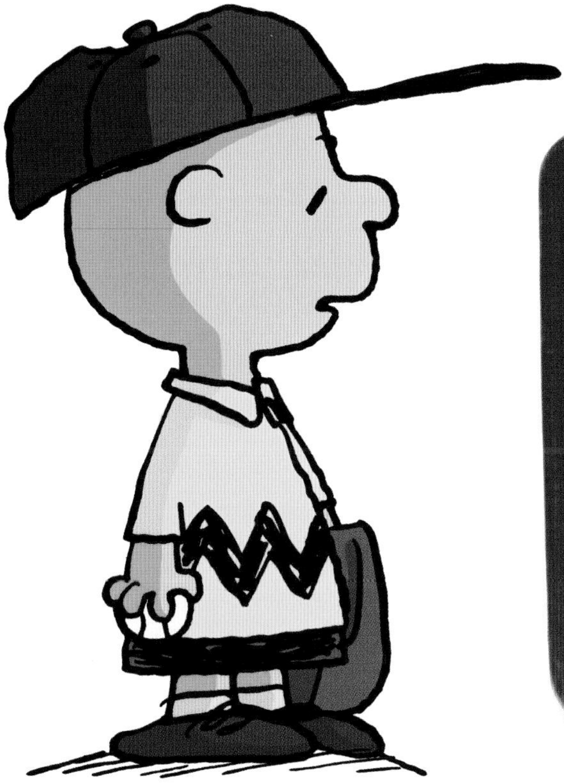

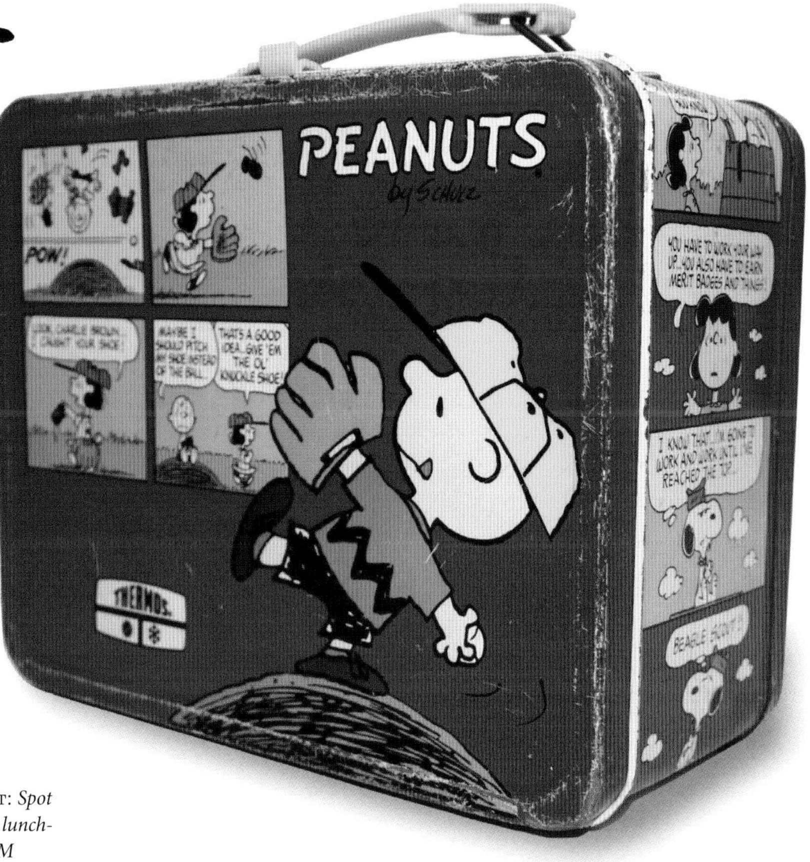

PEANUTS
by Schulz
POW!
MAYBE I SHOULD PITCH MY SHOE INSTEAD OF THE BALL...
THAT'S A GOOD IDEA...GIVE 'EM THE OL' KNUCKLE SHOE!
THERMOS
YOU HAVE TO WORK YOUR WAY UP...YOU ALSO HAVE TO EARN MERIT BADGES AND THINGS!
I KNOW THAT...I'M GOING TO WORK AND WORK UNTIL I'VE REACHED THE TOP!
BEAGLE SCOUT!!

OPPOSITE, BOTTOM: *Design by Cameron + Co* | ABOVE LEFT: *Spot art from strip – Charles M. Schulz* | ABOVE RIGHT: Peanuts *lunchbox, manufactured by King Seeley Thermos, c. 1975 – CMSM*

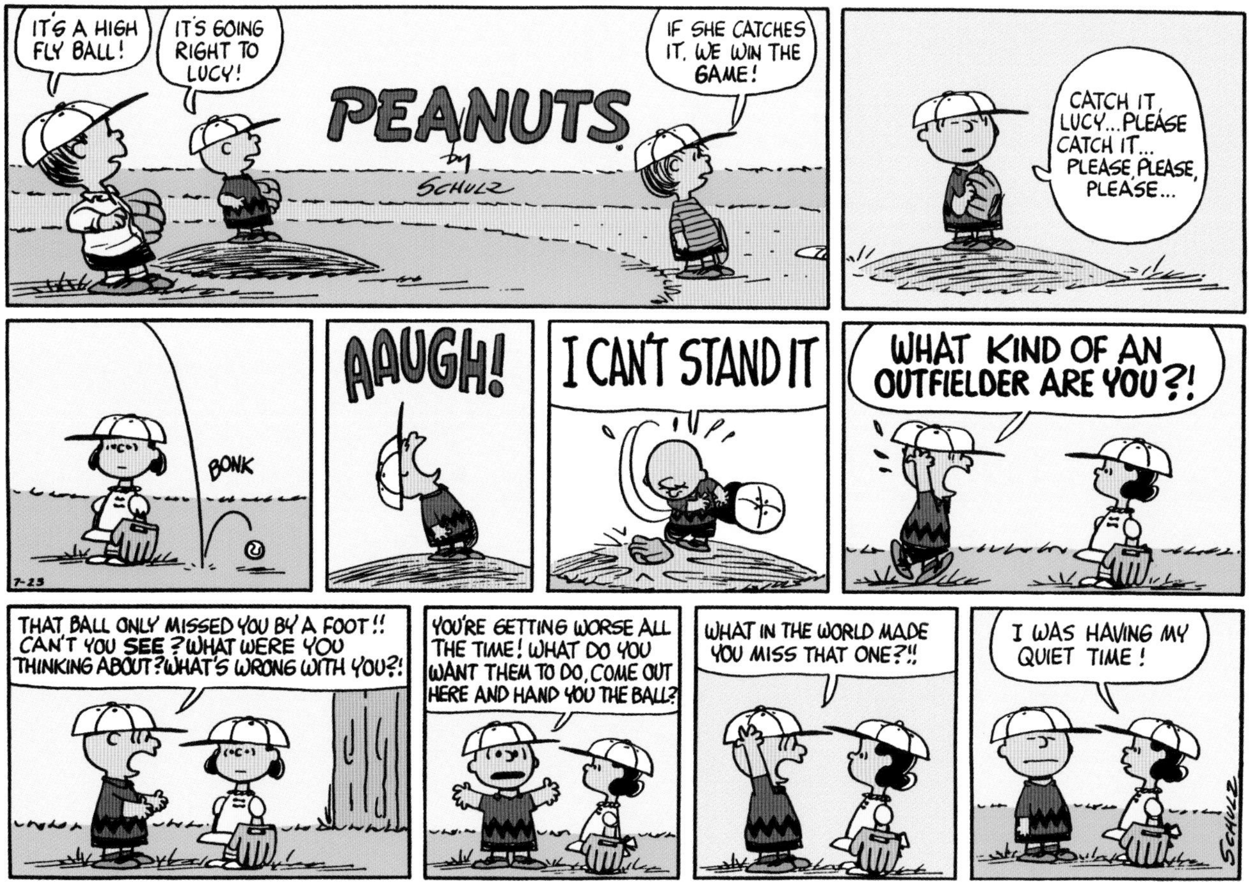

IT'S A HIGH FLY BALL!
IT'S GOING RIGHT TO LUCY!
PEANUTS
by SCHULZ
IF SHE CATCHES IT, WE WIN THE GAME!
CATCH IT, LUCY...PLEASE CATCH IT... PLEASE, PLEASE, PLEASE...
BONK
7-25
AAUGH!
I CAN'T STAND IT
WHAT KIND OF AN OUTFIELDER ARE YOU?!
THAT BALL ONLY MISSED YOU BY A FOOT!! CAN'T YOU SEE? WHAT WERE YOU THINKING ABOUT? WHAT'S WRONG WITH YOU?!
YOU'RE GETTING WORSE ALL THE TIME! WHAT DO YOU WANT THEM TO DO, COME OUT HERE AND HAND YOU THE BALL?
WHAT IN THE WORLD MADE YOU MISS THAT ONE?!!
I WAS HAVING MY QUIET TIME!
SCHULZ

# THE BOY AND HIS DOG

Charlie Brown loves Snoopy unconditionally. Snoopy, on the other hand, is a complicated, independent dog who doesn't always remember his owner's name and seems to appreciate Charlie Brown's ability to fill a supper dish more than his other qualities. Deep down, he loves his faithful owner, even if he won't openly admit it.

"Snoopy is a very contradictory character," observed Charles Schulz. "In a way, he's quite selfish. He likes to think of himself as independent, and he has dreams of doing great things. Without Charlie Brown he couldn't survive, but Snoopy won't even give Charlie Brown the love and affection he deserves. That's part of the humor."

> "There's always something that keeps me home . . . something that makes me stay . . . That ol' supper dish!" —Snoopy

Charles M. Schulz
PEANUTS
SCHULZ

THE COLLECTED STRIPS
SUPPERTIME!
CHARLES M. SCHULZ
A PEANUTS DIGITAL EDITION

PEANUTS
THESE ARE THE PLANS FOR SNOOPY'S NEW HOME...
IT'S A BIT MUCH, ISN'T IT? AFTER ALL, HE'S ONLY A STUPID DOG!
9-30
BOOT!
NOW, HERE IS WHERE WE'LL BE USING THE CERAMIC TILE, AND THIS STAIRWAY IS THE ONE I WAS TELLING YOU ABOUT..
I LOVE LOOKING AT HOUSE PLANS!
SCHULZ

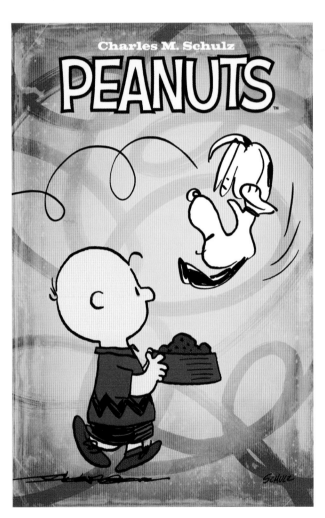

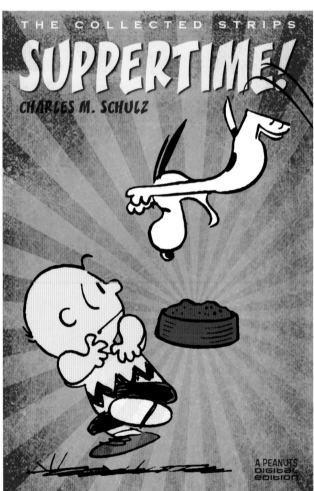

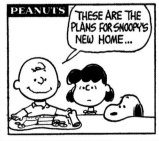

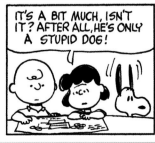

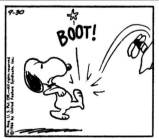

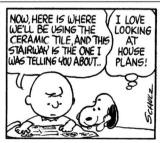

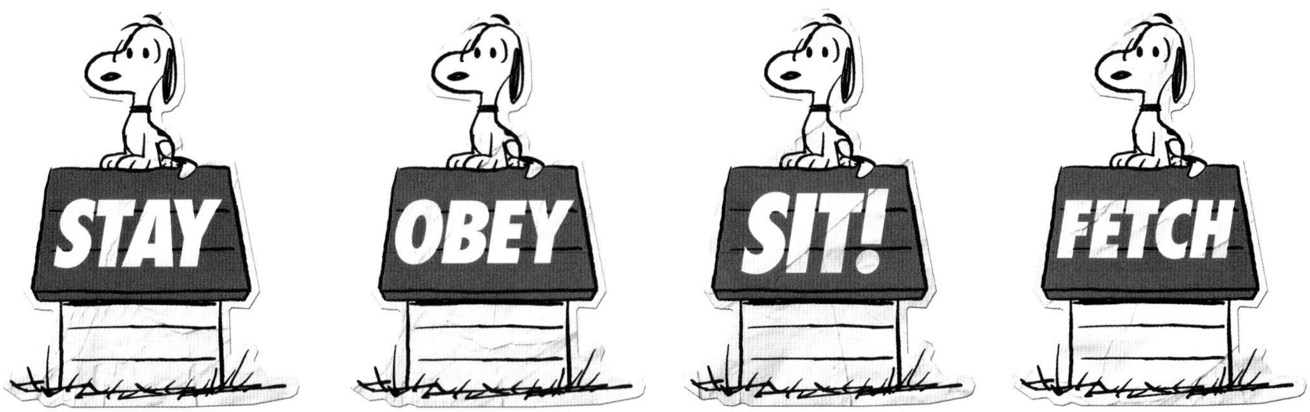
STAY
OBEY
SIT!
FETCH

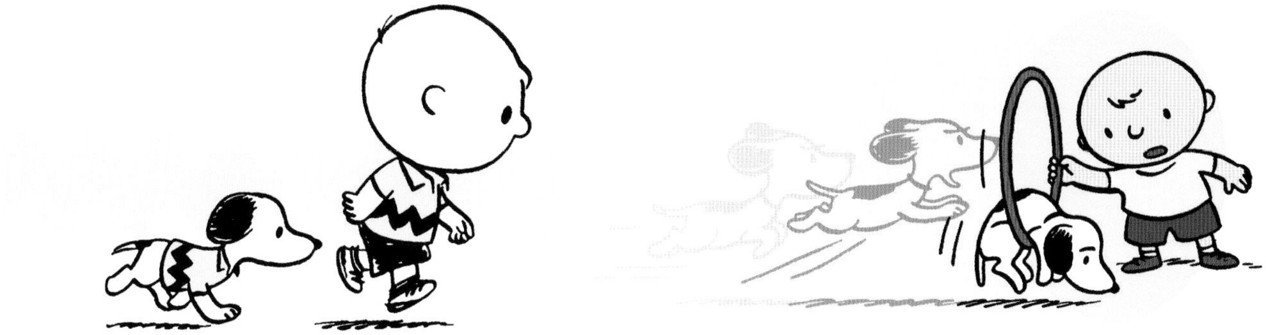

"Having a dog for a friend can make an ordinary life a beautiful life." —Charlie Brown

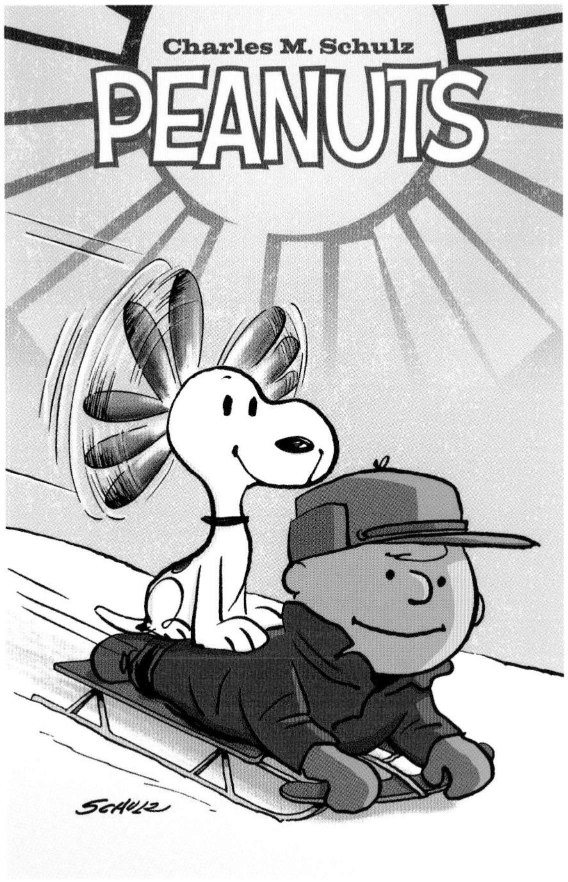
Charles M. Schulz
PEANUTS

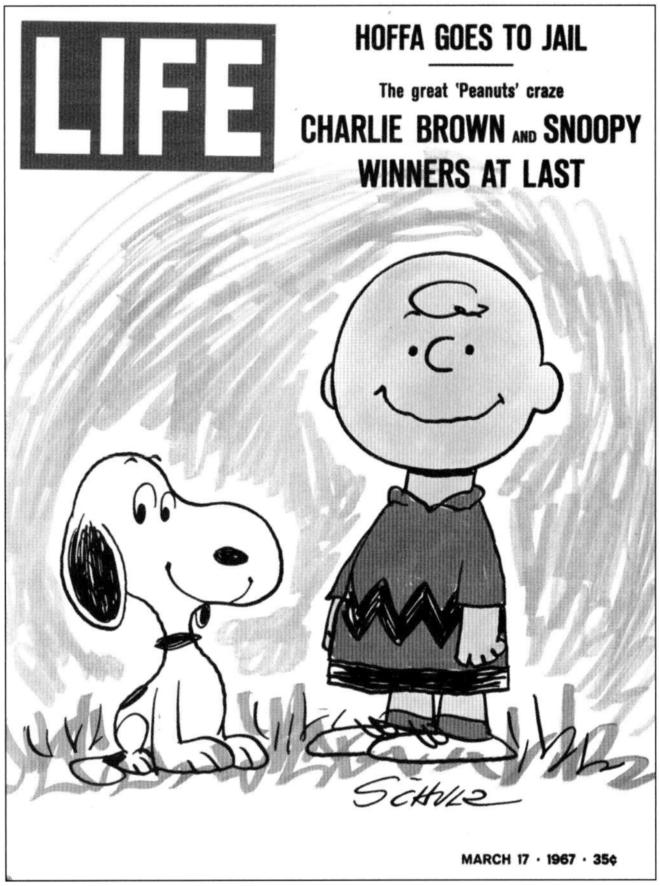
LIFE
HOFFA GOES TO JAIL
The great 'Peanuts' craze
CHARLIE BROWN AND SNOOPY
WINNERS AT LAST
MARCH 17 · 1967 · 35¢

OPPOSITE, LEFT: Peanuts, *Issue #9, Boom! Studios comic book covers – CSCA* | OPPOSITE, RIGHT: Suppertime, Peanuts *Digital Edition – CSCA*
TOP: *Style Guide art, 2011 – CSCA* | CENTER: *Style Guide art, 2011 – CSCA* | BOTTOM LEFT: Peanuts, *Issue #1, Boom! Studios comic book cover – CSCA*
| BOTTOM RIGHT: LIFE® *magazine cover, March 17, 1967 – CMSM*

# THE LOVABLE LOSER

Charlie Brown rarely comes out on top, but he never stops trying. When he strikes out with the bases loaded in the bottom of the ninth inning, misspells the word "beagle" in the spelling bee, and fails to get even a single piece of candy when he's trick-or-treating, we can all relate, even if our own failures pale in comparison to Charlie Brown's.

Charles Schulz drew from personal experience when creating tales of Charlie Brown's comic mishaps, but often exaggerated the results. "Charlie Brown is a caricature," he observed. "We all know what it's like to lose, but Charlie Brown keeps losing outrageously. It's not that he's a loser; he's really a decent little sort. But nothing seems to work out right."

"PEANUTS"
SIGH
WHAT'S THE MATTER, CHARLIE BROWN?
I'M A LONESOME COWBOY
WHY ARE YOU SO LONESOME?
Tm. Reg. U. S. Pat. Off.—All rights reserved
Copr. 1953 by United Feature Syndicate, Inc.
ALL THE OTHER KIDS ARE PLAYING "SPACEMAN"
7-24
SCHULZ

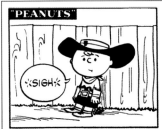

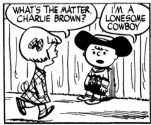

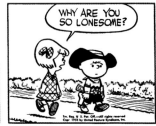

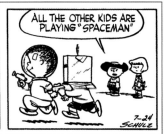

"As soon as I get up in the morning, I feel I'm in over my head" –Charlie Brown

ASTRONAUT SNOOPY
PEANUTS
CREATED BY SCHULZ
#9
CANNY CANINE OF THE COSMOS
SAY SOMETHING "MARTIAN", CHARLIE BROWN
?

THE MAN FROM O.U.T.E.R. S.P.A.C.E.
BASED ON THE CHARACTERS CREATED BY CHARLES M. SCHULZ
SNOOPY, THE WORLD FAMOUS ASTRONAUT
CHARLIE BROWN
LUCY VAN PELT
PATRICIA REICHARDT AND MARCIE
SCHROEDER
CSCA
SCHULZ

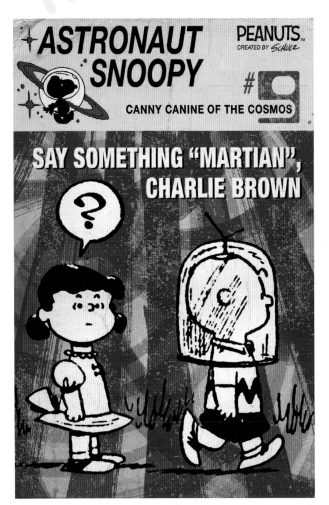

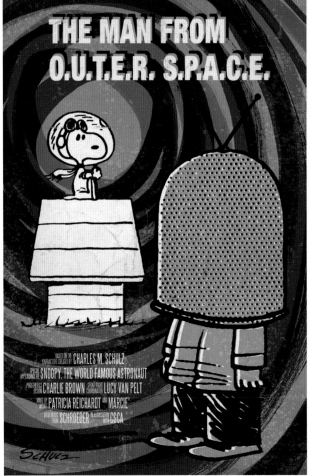

ABOVE LEFT: *Style Guide art, 2012 - CSCA* | ABOVE RIGHT: *Comic-Con postcard, 2013 - CSCA* | OPPOSITE: *Style Guide art - CSCA*

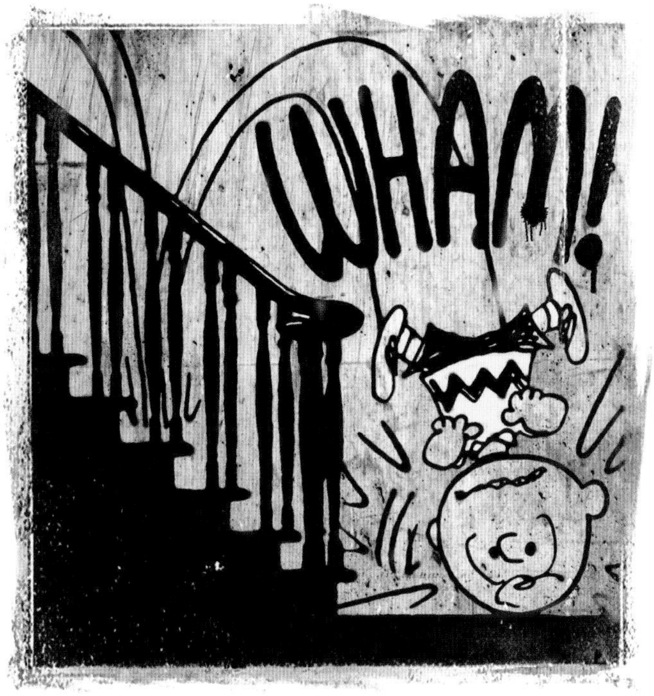
WHAM!!

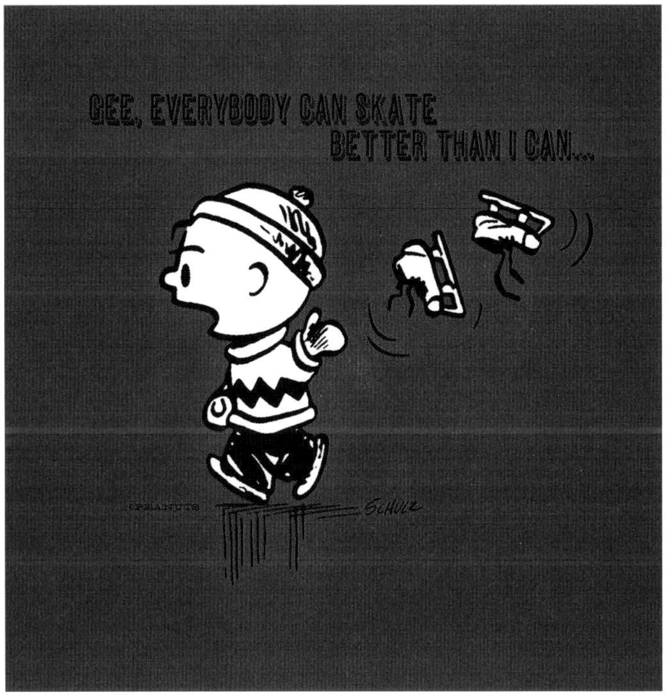
GEE, EVERYBODY CAN SKATE
BETTER THAN I CAN...
SCHULZ

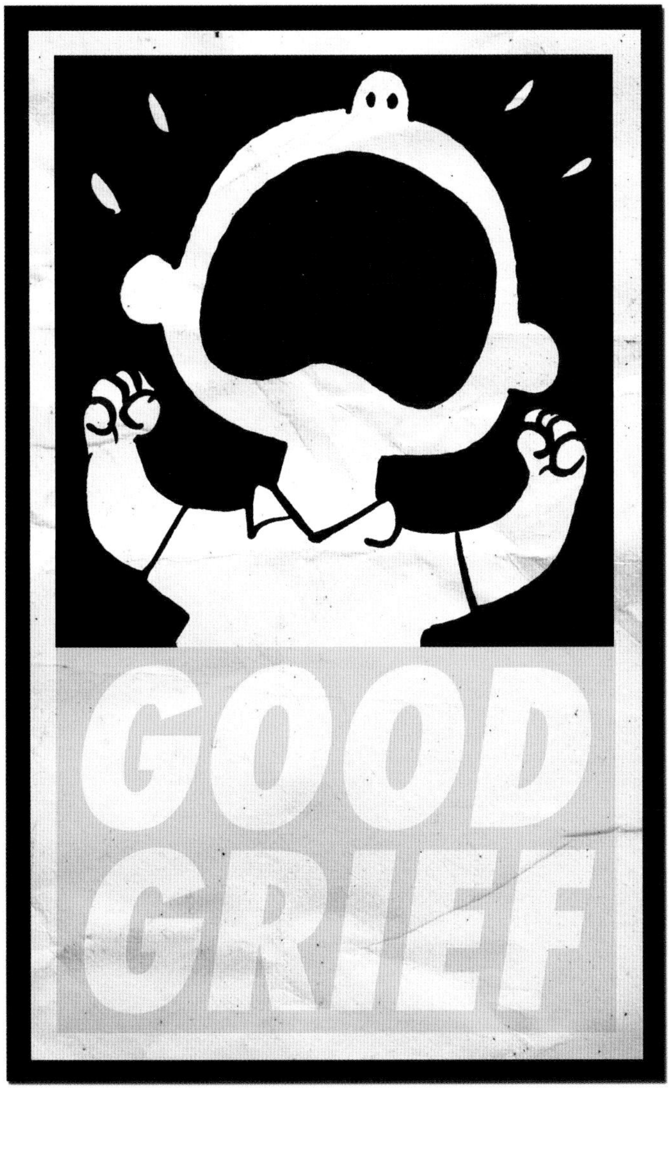
GOOD
GRIEF

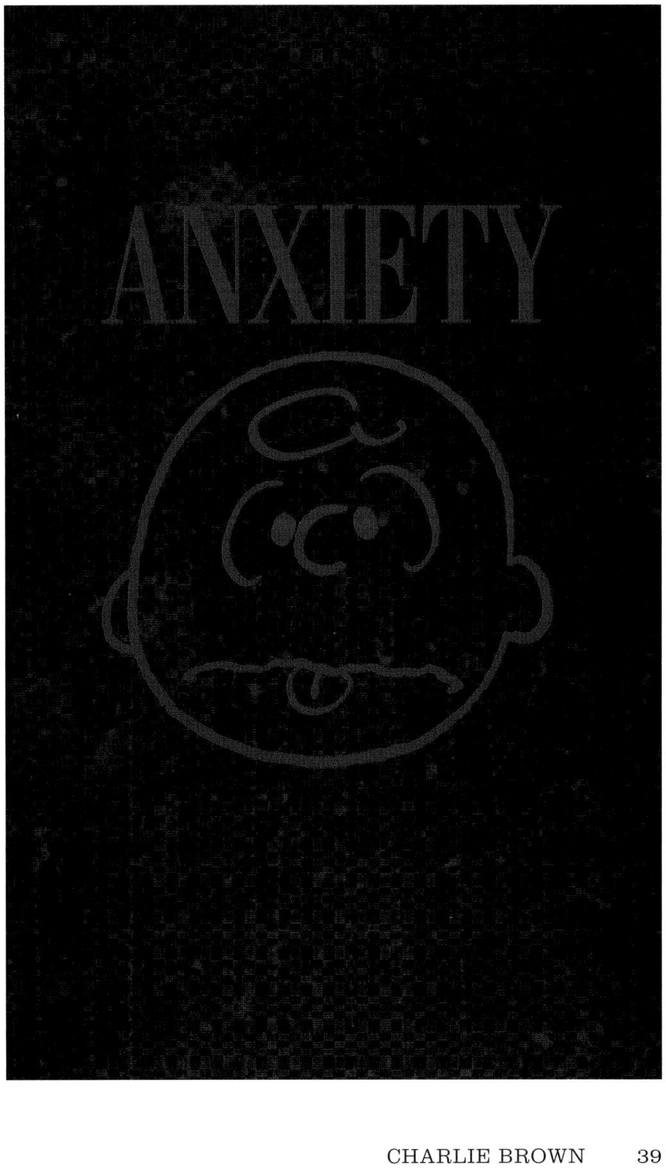
ANXIETY

# YOU'RE A GOOD MAN, CHARLIE BROWN

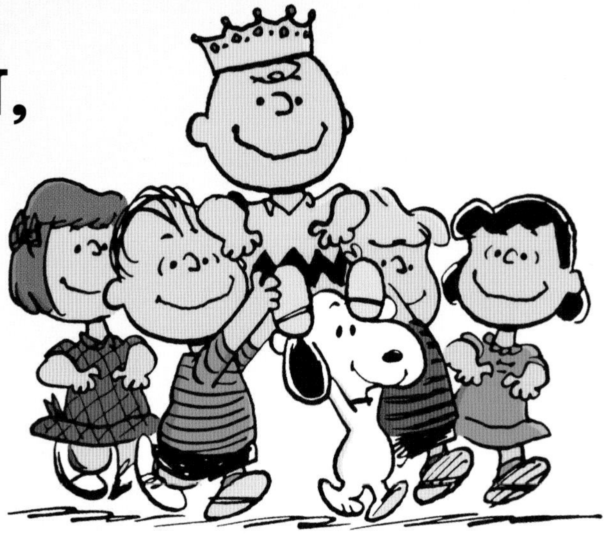

In 1967, the musical comedy *You're a Good Man, Charlie Brown*, featuring music and lyrics by Clark Gesner, debuted. A loving tribute to *Peanuts*, the beloved musical has been performed worldwide in venues from New York's Broadway to London's West End, and remains a popular stage production to this day.

Charles Schulz counted himself among the musical's biggest fans. "[*You're a good Man, Charlie Brown* has] become the most performed musical in the history of American theatre . . . every school and church and high school and grade school and kindergarten you can think of has put this thing on and it had taken a terrible beating but it survives. And, of course, the music is good and it's not cute. That was the main thing. It was incredible that they could have made so many mistakes putting it together, but everything just fell right into place just right and that's very gratifying. I used to go down to the theatre in San Francisco and it was a great pleasure to stand out in the lobby when the show was over and seeing the families coming out and everybody smiling because they had had a good time."

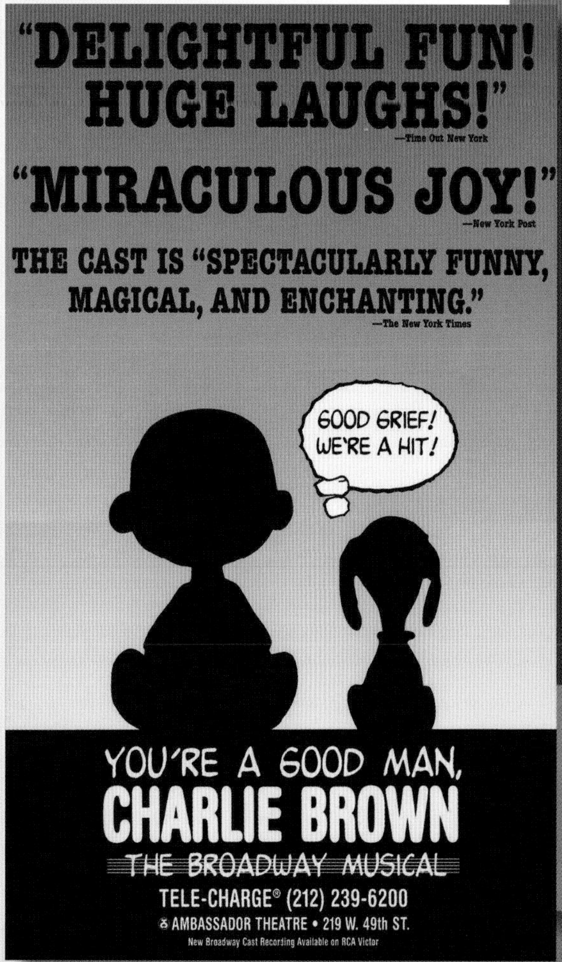
"DELIGHTFUL FUN! HUGE LAUGHS!"
—Time Out New York
"MIRACULOUS JOY!"
—New York Post
THE CAST IS "SPECTACULARLY FUNNY, MAGICAL, AND ENCHANTING."
—The New York Times
GOOD GRIEF! WE'RE A HIT!
YOU'RE A GOOD MAN, CHARLIE BROWN
THE BROADWAY MUSICAL
TELE-CHARGE® (212) 239-6200
AMBASSADOR THEATRE • 219 W. 49th ST.
New Broadway Cast Recording Available on RCA Victor

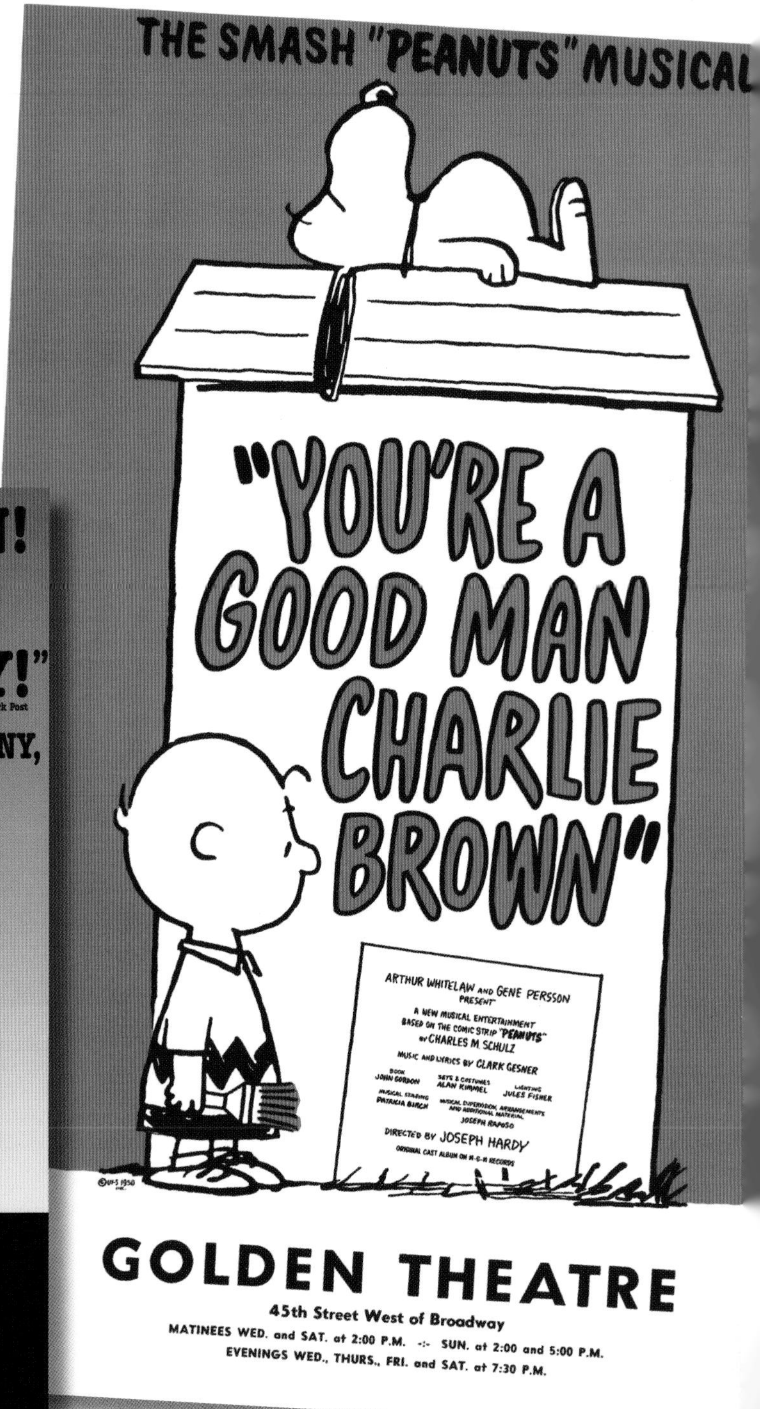
THE SMASH "PEANUTS" MUSICAL
"YOU'RE A GOOD MAN CHARLIE BROWN"
ARTHUR WHITELAW AND GENE PERSSON PRESENT
A NEW MUSICAL ENTERTAINMENT BASED ON THE COMIC STRIP "PEANUTS" BY CHARLES M. SCHULZ
MUSIC AND LYRICS BY CLARK GESNER
BOOK JOHN GORDON
SETS & COSTUMES ALAN KIMMEL
LIGHTING JULES FISHER
MUSICAL STAGING PATRICIA BIRCH
MUSICAL SUPERVISION, ARRANGEMENTS AND ADDITIONAL MATERIAL JOSEPH RAPOSO
DIRECTED BY JOSEPH HARDY
ORIGINAL CAST ALBUM ON M-G-M RECORDS
GOLDEN THEATRE
45th Street West of Broadway
MATINEES WED. and SAT. at 2:00 P.M. -:- SUN. at 2:00 and 5:00 P.M.
EVENINGS WED., THURS., FRI. and SAT. at 7:30 P.M.

TOP: *Style guide art – CSCA* | LEFT AND RIGHT: *Theater posters for* You're a Good Man, Charlie Brown, *performed at the Ambassador Theatre, New York City, 1999, and the Golden Theatre, New York City, 1971 – CMSM* | OPPOSITE: *Original Schulz mockup of* You're a Good Man, Charlie Brown *theater production, c. 1990 – CMSM*

proudly presents

# "You're a good man, CHARLIE BROWN"

Based on the comic strip... "PEANUTS" by Charles M. Schulz

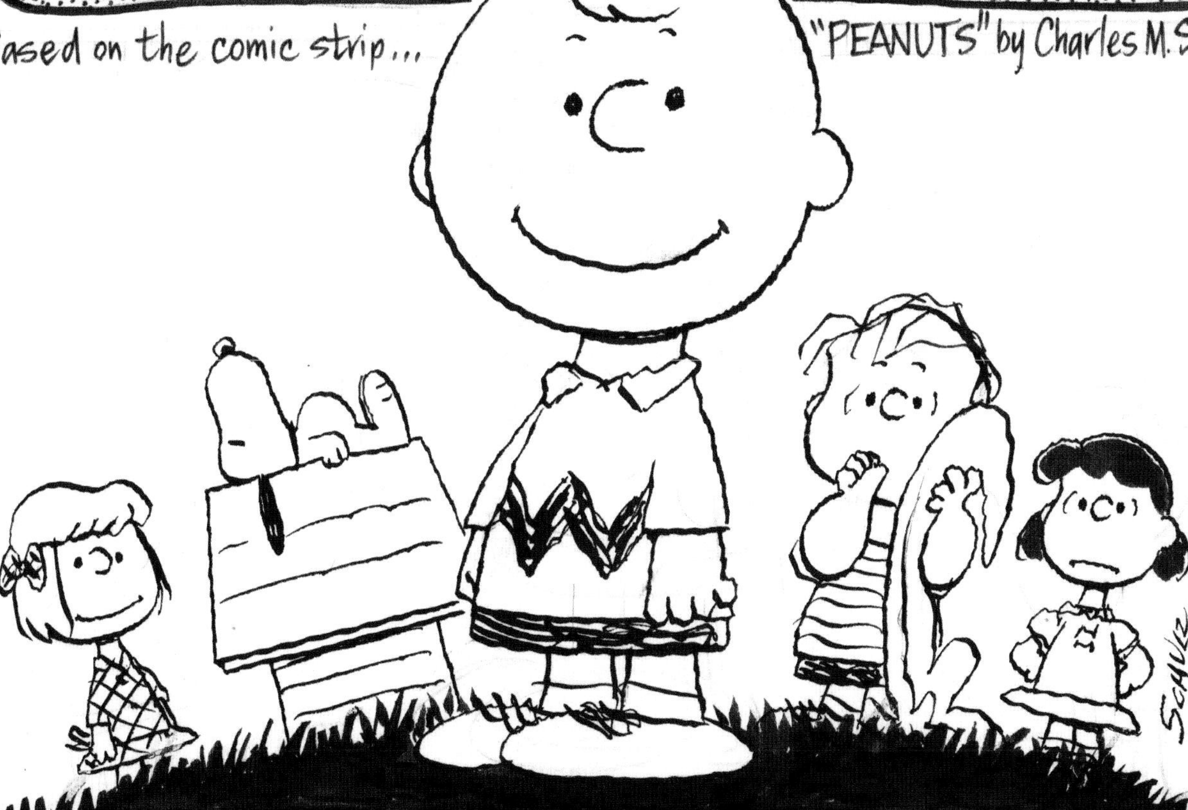
SCHULZ



BOOK, MUSIC AND LYRICS BY CLARK GESNER

**SEPT. 27 to NOV. 16**

PLEASE CALL BOX OFFICE FOR RESERVATIONS

# VALENTINE'S DAY

FIRST OBSERVED
02/14/1952

Valentine's Day is a bittersweet holiday for most of the gang. Charlie Brown can't work up the nerve to give a valentine to the Little Red-Haired Girl, Lucy never receives a valentine from Schroeder, Peppermint Patty and Marcie don't receive valentines from Charlie Brown, and Sally never gets a card from her "Sweet Babboo," Linus. As Charlie Brown observes each year, "Nothing echoes like an empty mailbox." Snoopy, however, always seems to receive more valentines than he can handle and spends the holiday enjoying a steady stream of cards from his many admirers.

Valentine's Day is, in many ways, one of the saddest days of the year in *Peanuts*. Charles Schulz noted many times that the cruelty of children is one of the strip's most poignant recurring themes. "Nothing in life ends with a pow! And aren't all kids egotists? And brutal? Children are caricatures of adults. We grown-ups don't change so much, except on the surface, because we get along better that way. Maybe I have the cruelest strip going."

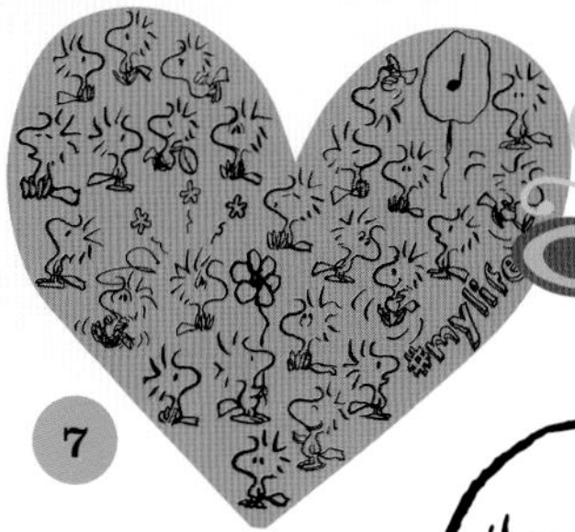

7

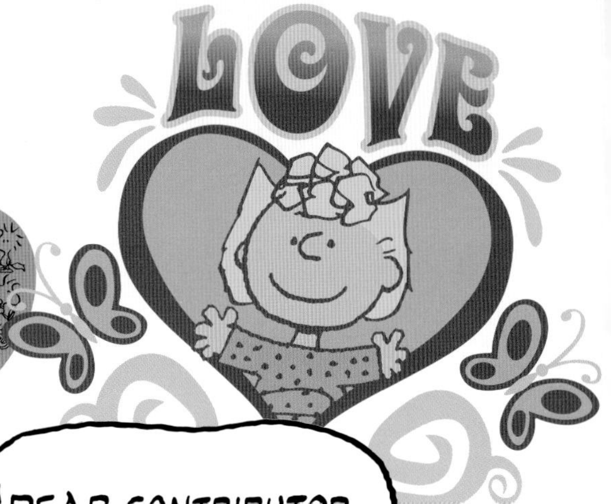
LOVE

8

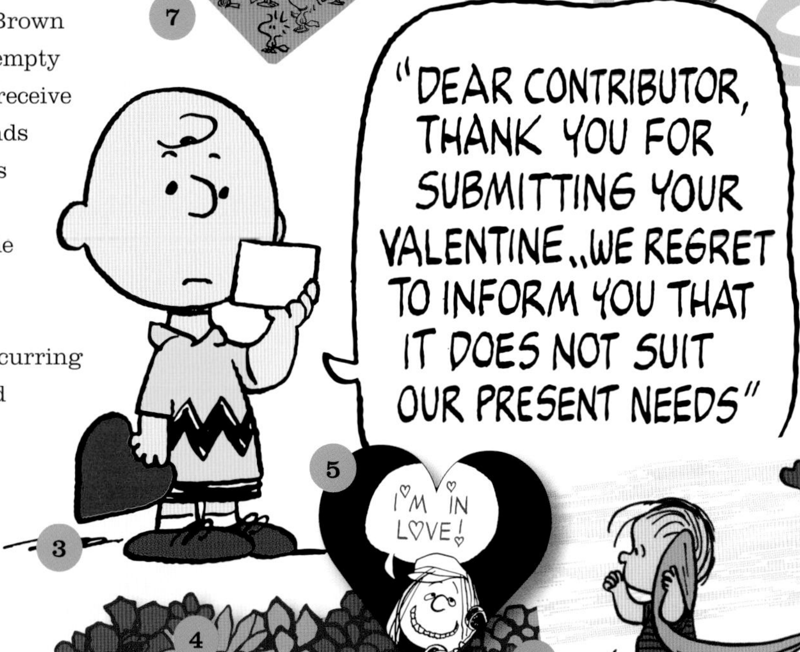
"DEAR CONTRIBUTOR, THANK YOU FOR SUBMITTING YOUR VALENTINE..WE REGRET TO INFORM YOU THAT IT DOES NOT SUIT OUR PRESENT NEEDS"

3

I'M IN LOVE!

5

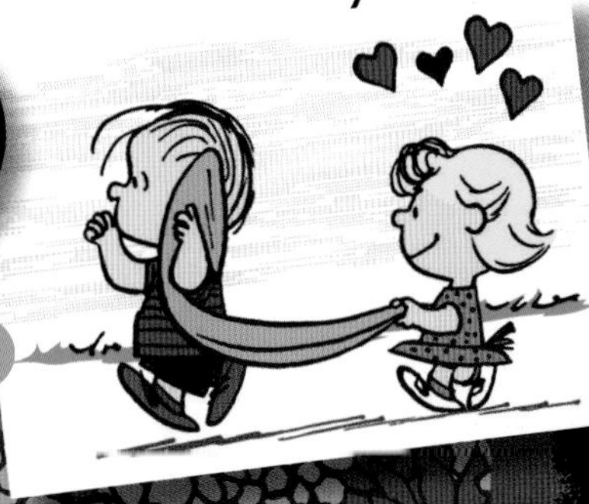

6

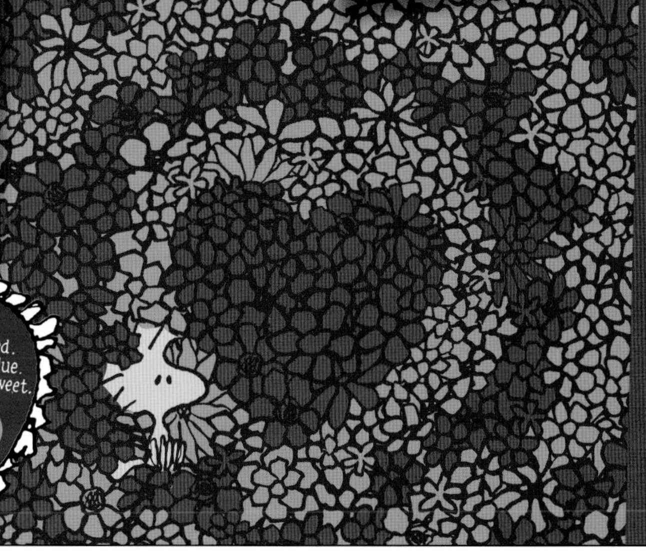

4

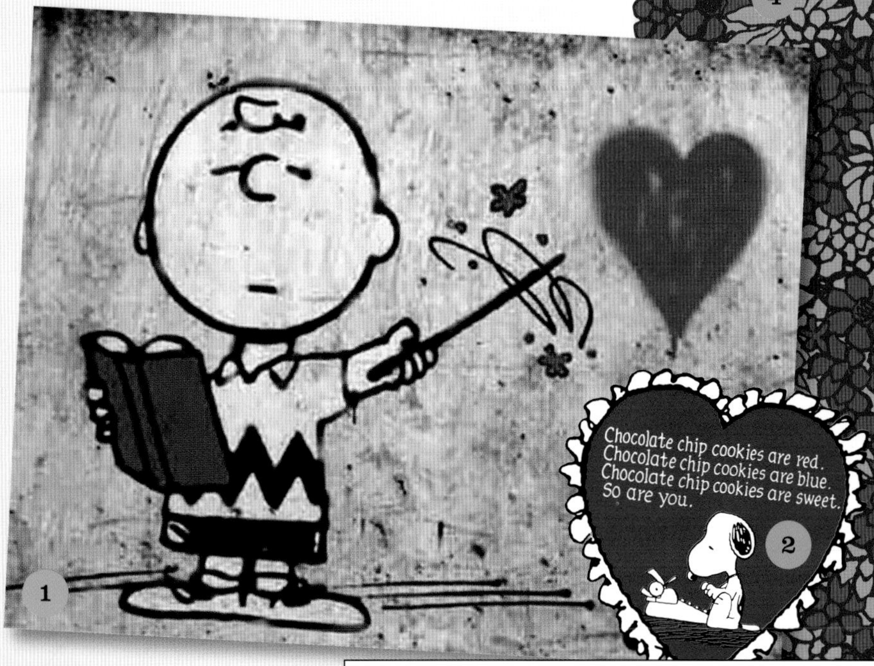

1

Chocolate chip cookies are red.
Chocolate chip cookies are blue.
Chocolate chip cookies are sweet.
So are you.

2

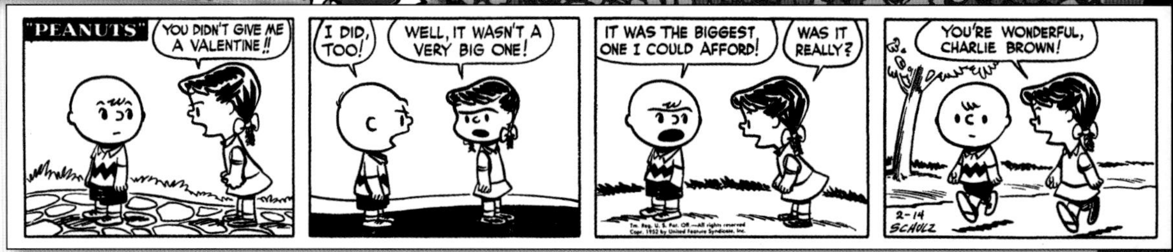
"PEANUTS"
YOU DIDN'T GIVE ME A VALENTINE!!
I DID, TOO!
WELL, IT WASN'T A VERY BIG ONE!
IT WAS THE BIGGEST ONE I COULD AFFORD!
WAS IT REALLY?
YOU'RE WONDERFUL, CHARLIE BROWN!
2-14
SCHULZ

*1–8: Style Guide art – CSCA; 9:* Waiting for Valentines, *Parts One and Two,* Peanuts *Digital Edition – CSCA; 10:* Be My Valentine, Charlie Brown; *Artist: Jayson Weidel; Limited Edition Print; Courtesy: Dark Hall Mansion; 11:* Snoopy Love; *Artist: Laurent Durieux; Limited Edition Print; Courtesy: Dark Hall Mansion*

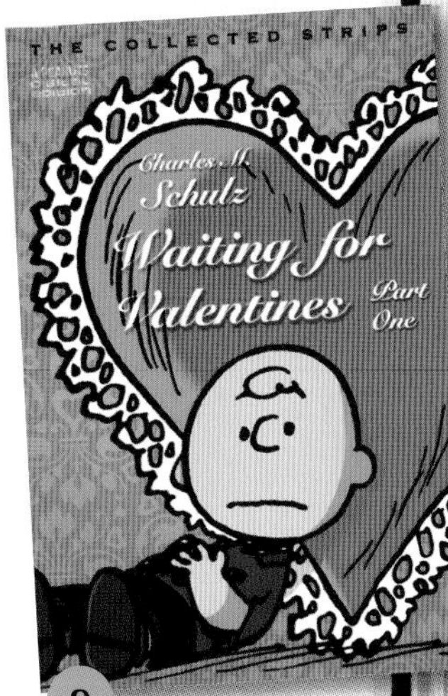
THE COLLECTED STRIPS
Charles M. Schulz
Waiting for Valentines
Part One

9

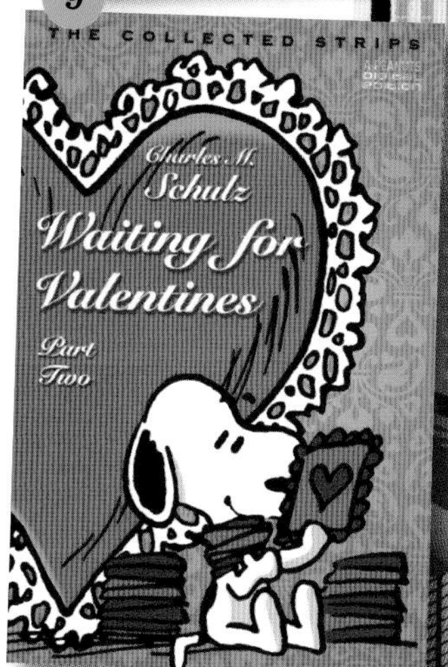
THE COLLECTED STRIPS
Charles M. Schulz
Waiting for Valentines
Part Two

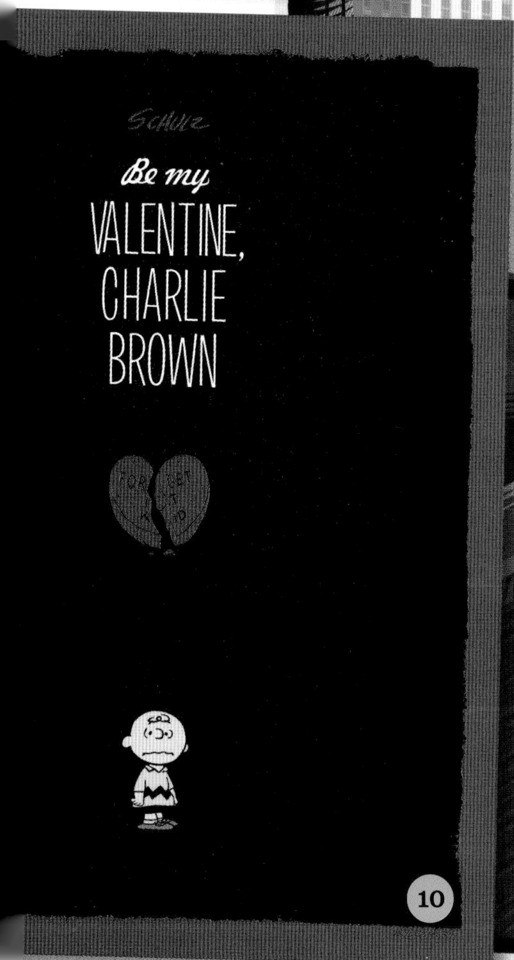
SCHULZ
Be my
VALENTINE,
CHARLIE
BROWN

10

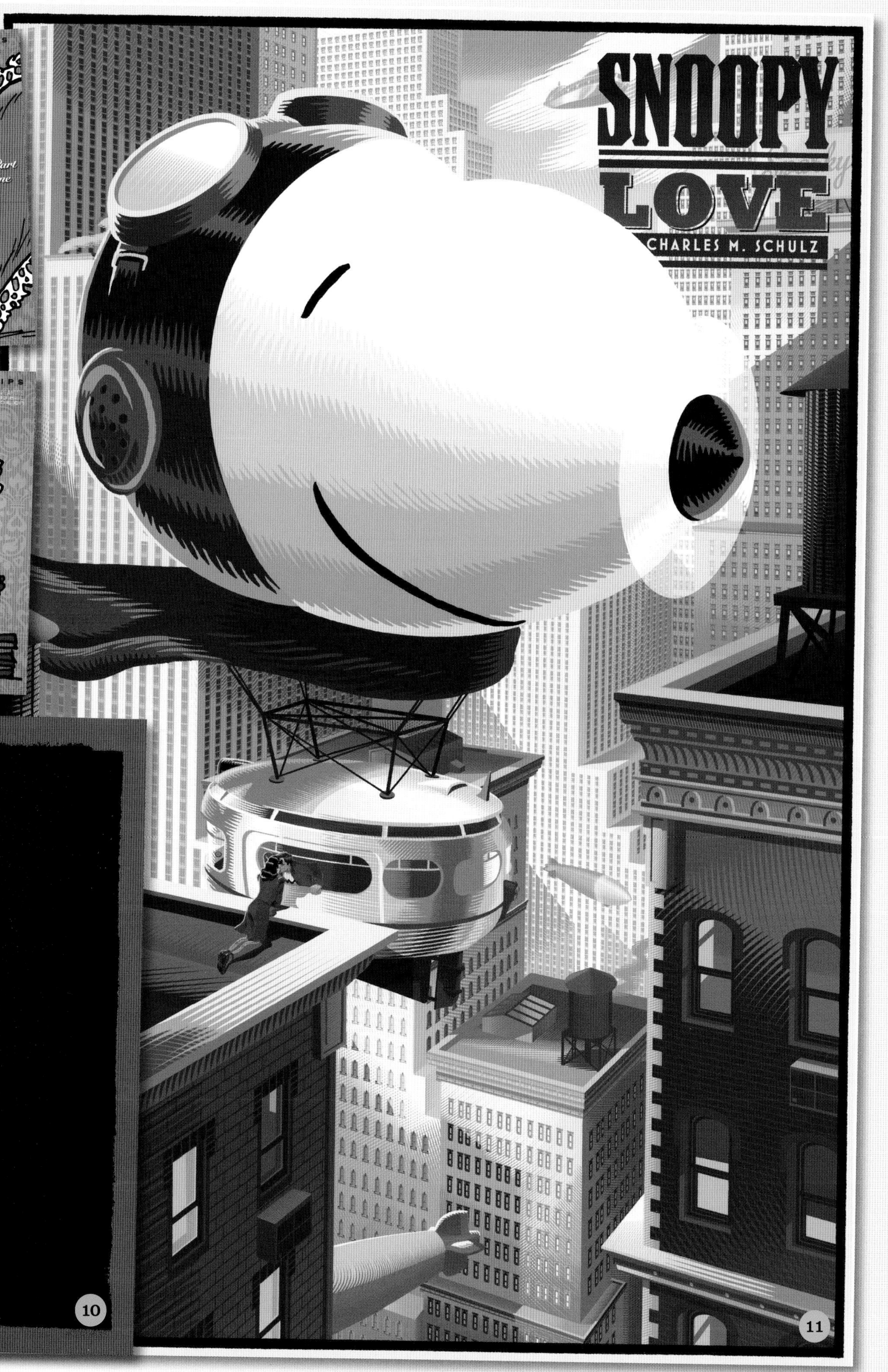
SNOOPY
LOVE
CHARLES M. SCHULZ

11

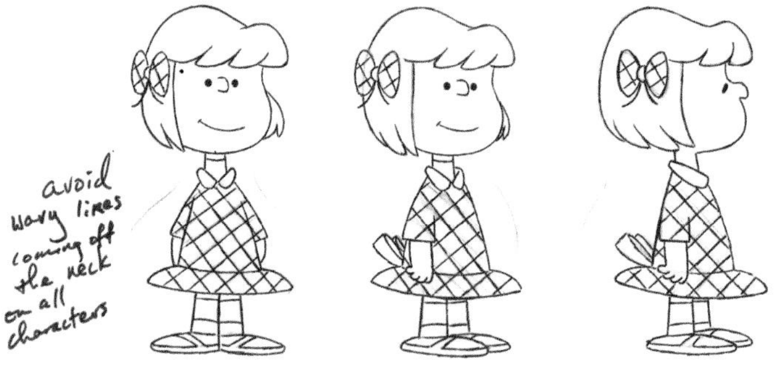
avoid wavy lines coming off the neck on all characters

ABOVE: *Patty model sheet, 2010 – CSCA* | BELOW: *Style Guide art – CSCA*

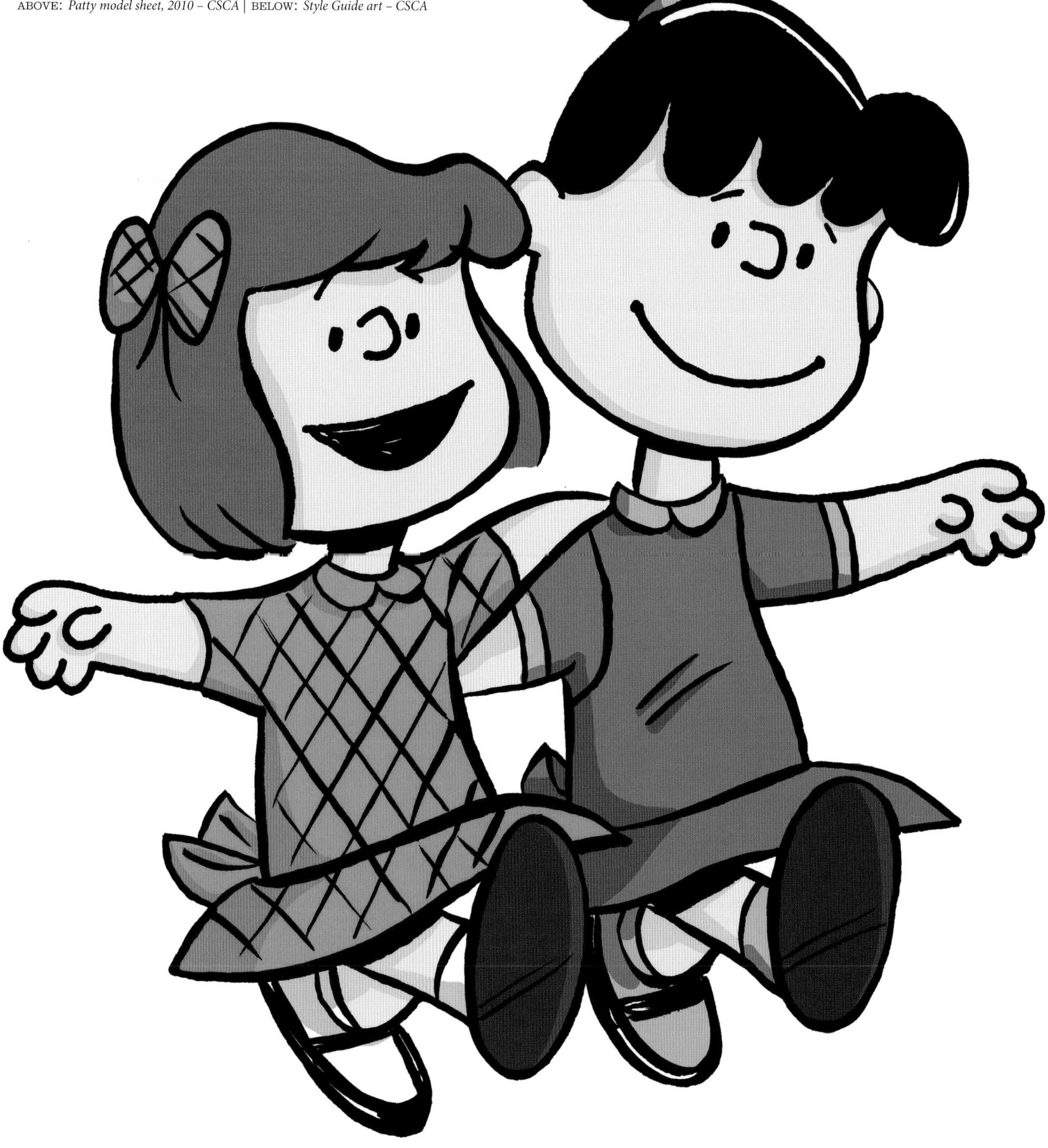

LITTLE GIRLS ARE MADE OF SUGAR AND SPICE....
..AND EVERYTHING NICE...
?
WHOP
THAT'S WHAT LITTLE GIRLS ARE MADE OF!
SCHULZ

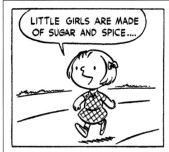

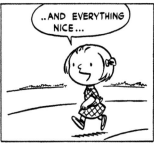

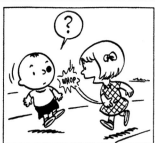

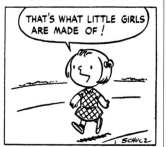

# PATTY

FIRST APPEARANCE
10/02/1950

Patty grew up in the same neighborhood as Charlie Brown and Shermy, and the trio—plus Snoopy—were inseparable in their early childhood days. Like many girls in the neighborhood, she has a complex relationship with Charlie Brown, happily playing house with him one day, mercilessly teasing him the next.

When another girl finally moves to their block, Patty is thrilled, and Violet joins their circle of friends. The two have many mutual interests, from dolls and records to taunting Charlie Brown, and become best friends right away. As more kids move to their part of town, Patty and Violet spend less and less time alone with Charlie Brown, but they all remain friends and continue to play outfield on his baseball team.

Patty's presence in the strip was in decline by the mid-1960s, but the introduction of Peppermint Patty cemented Patty's status as a background character. Schulz narrowed the core cast of the strip over the years, and there just wasn't room for two different girls named "Patty."

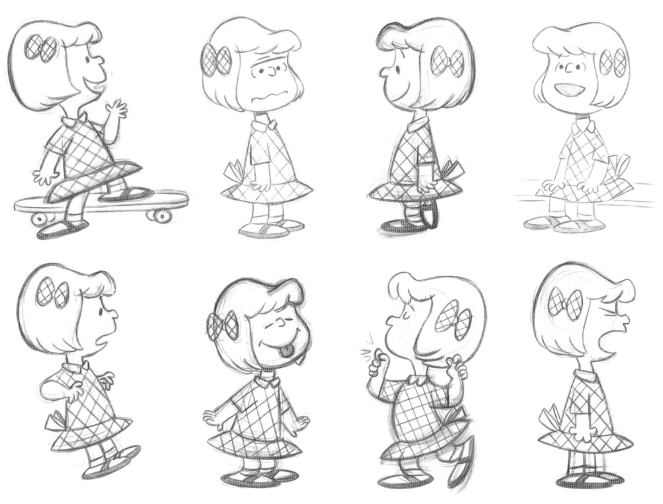

ABOVE: *Patty model sheet – CSCA*

RAIN, RAIN, RAIN, RAIN...
RAIN, RAIN, RAIN, RAIN...
SCHULZ

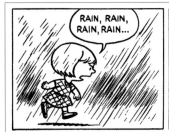

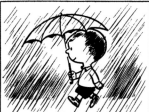

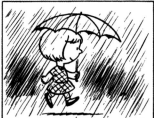

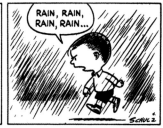

# SHERMY

FIRST APPEARANCE
10/02/1950

One of Charlie Brown's oldest friends, Shermy is always ready to jump in and join a game of catch, go to the movies, or enjoy a nice stroll around the block. His even temper and affability make him one of the most reliable kids in the neighborhood, and you can always count on him to join your baseball team or lend a hand.

Because of Shermy's reserved demeanor, however, he seems to fade into the background when new kids like Lucy and Linus move into the neighborhood. As Charles Schulz noted, Shermy's role diminished over time, and he soon appeared only when the cartoonist "needed a character with very little personality."

Shermy's last official appearance was on June 15, 1969, and his expression and single word of dialogue ("Really?") seemed to indicate that he knew his time was up. Lest it be forgotten, though, Shermy was there from the beginning and was the only character to speak in the very first strip, on October 2, 1950. His introduction of the strip's star set the tone for everything that followed: "Good ol' Charlie Brown . . . How I hate him!"

WIN-LESS BASEBALL CARDS
SHERMY
FIRST BASE & DH

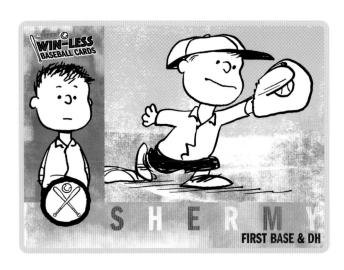

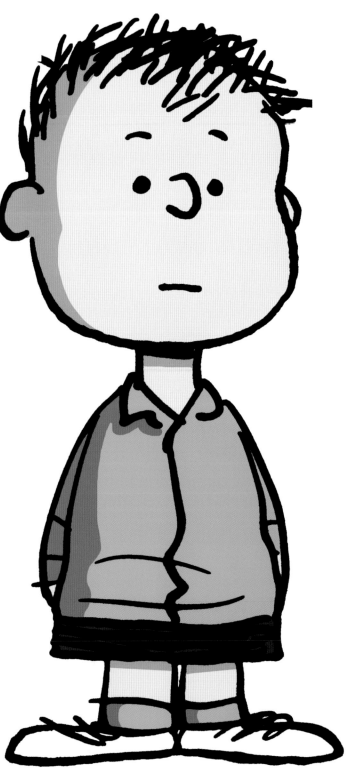

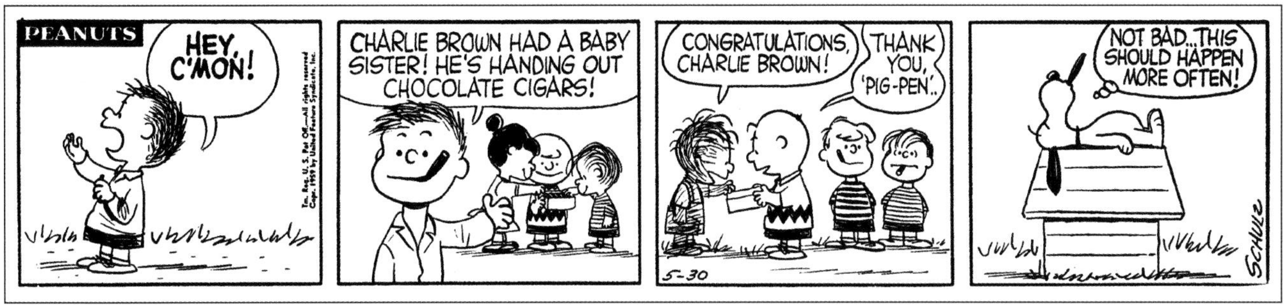
PEANUTS
HEY, C'MON!
CHARLIE BROWN HAD A BABY SISTER! HE'S HANDING OUT CHOCOLATE CIGARS!
CONGRATULATIONS, CHARLIE BROWN!
THANK YOU, 'PIG-PEN'..
NOT BAD...THIS SHOULD HAPPEN MORE OFTEN!
5-30
SCHULZ

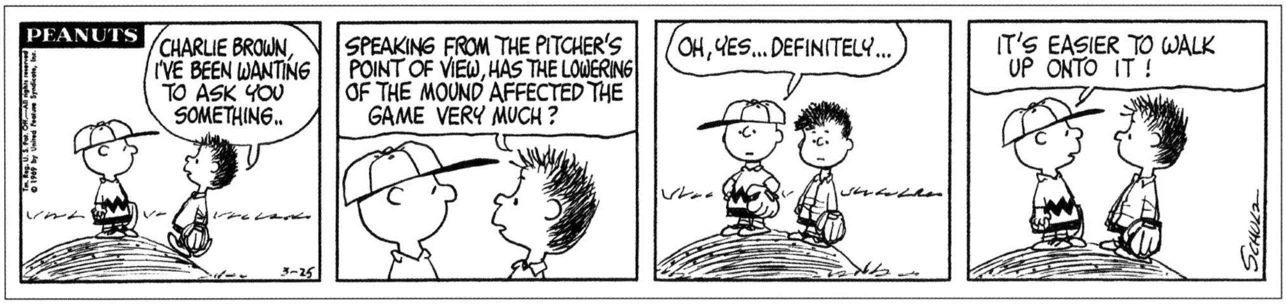
PEANUTS
CHARLIE BROWN, I'VE BEEN WANTING TO ASK YOU SOMETHING..
SPEAKING FROM THE PITCHER'S POINT OF VIEW, HAS THE LOWERING OF THE MOUND AFFECTED THE GAME VERY MUCH?
OH, YES...DEFINITELY...
IT'S EASIER TO WALK UP ONTO IT!
3-25
SCHULZ

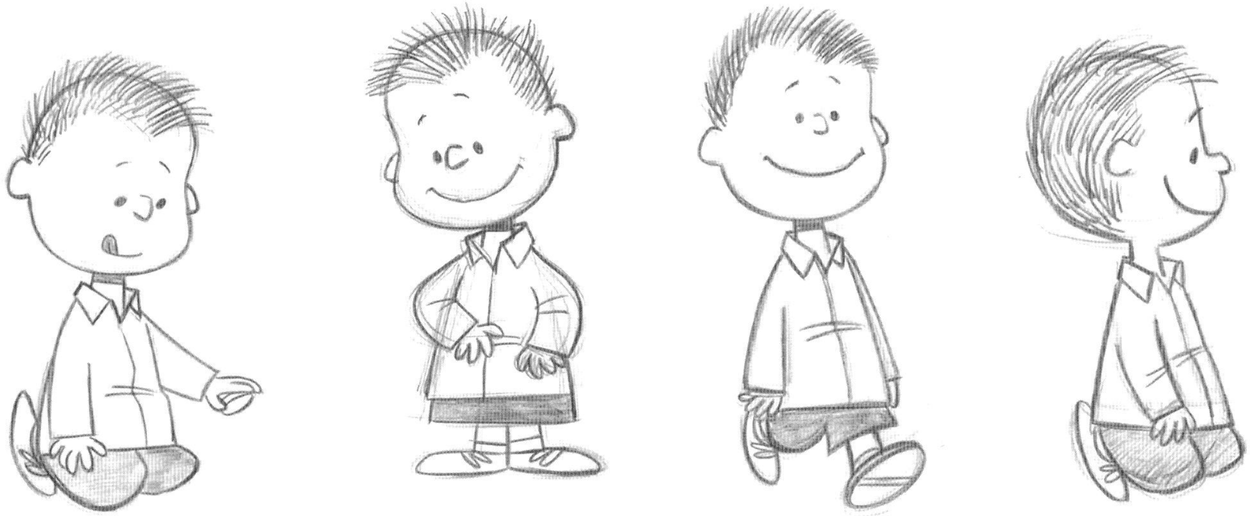

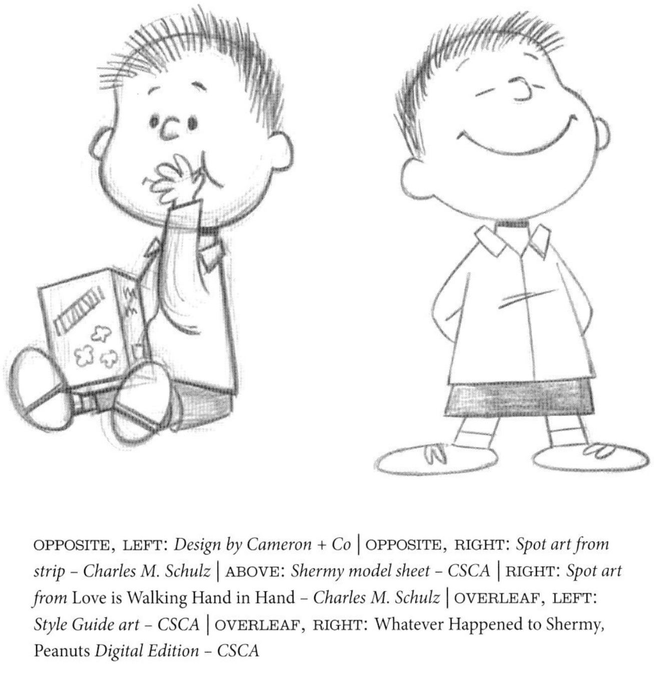

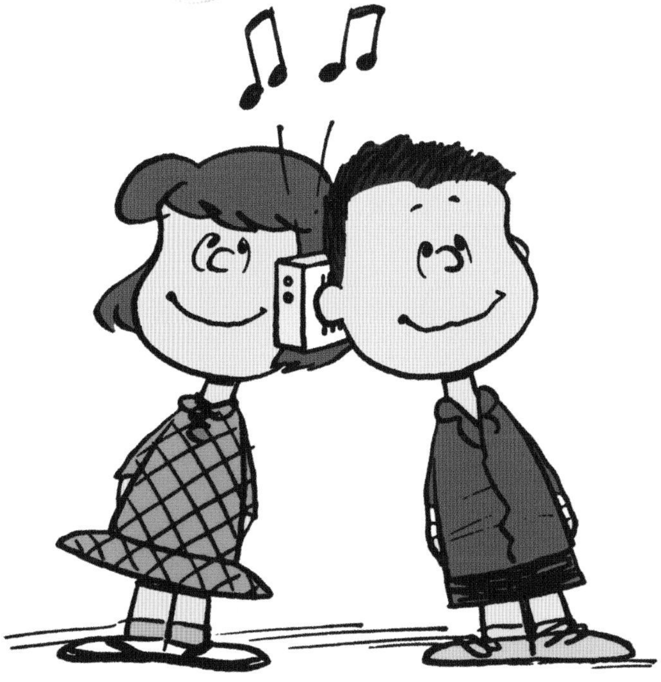

OPPOSITE, LEFT: *Design by Cameron + Co* | OPPOSITE, RIGHT: *Spot art from strip – Charles M. Schulz* | ABOVE: *Shermy model sheet – CSCA* | RIGHT: *Spot art from* Love is Walking Hand in Hand *– Charles M. Schulz* | OVERLEAF, LEFT: *Style Guide art – CSCA* | OVERLEAF, RIGHT: Whatever Happened to Shermy, Peanuts *Digital Edition – CSCA*

# ASTRONAUT SNOOPY

PEANUTS
CREATED BY *Schulz*

**# 2**

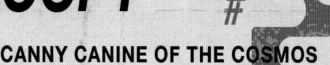

## CANNY CANINE OF THE COSMOS

## THE KIDS ARE PLAYING SPACEMAN AGAIN!

THE COLLECTED STRIPS

# Whatever Happened to Shermy?

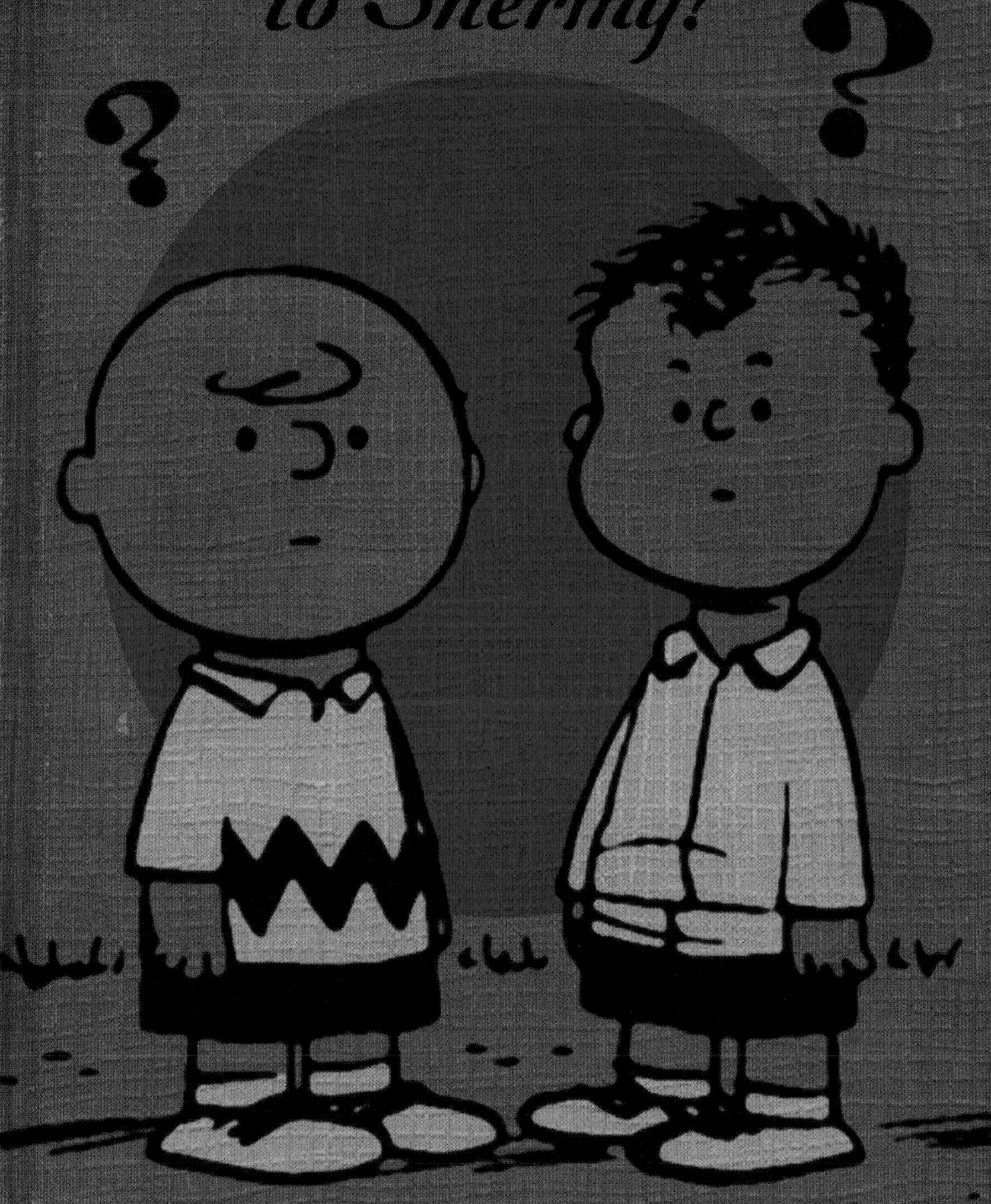

Charles M. Schulz

A PEANUTS DIGITAL EDITION

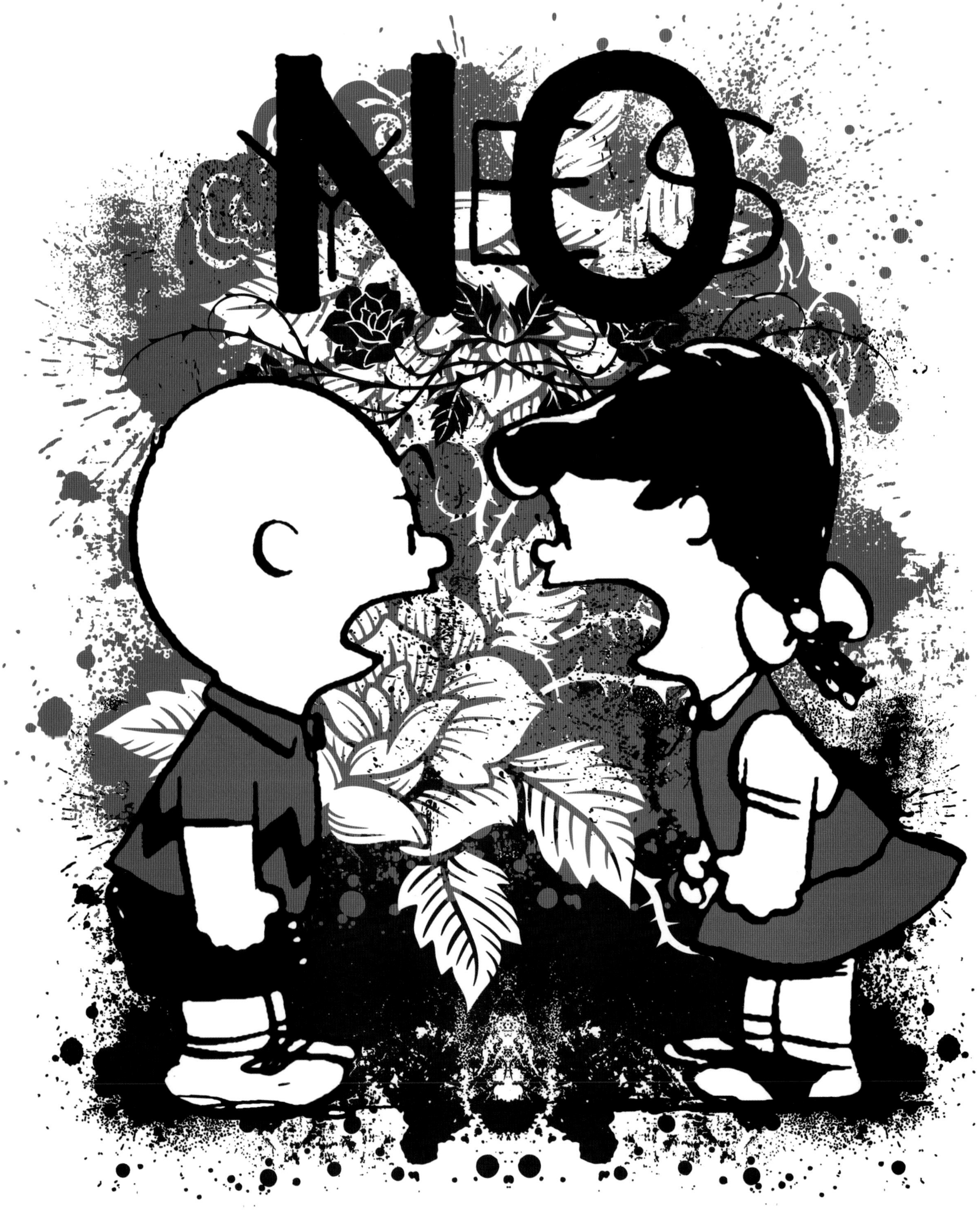
NO

OPPOSITE AND ABOVE: *Style Guide art – CSCA*

"PEANUTS"
WELL, HELLO, THERE!
?
YOU DON'T KNOW ME, DO YOU? MY NAME IS "VIOLET"
*AHEM*
YOU'RE REAL CUTE...
AHEM!!
WELL, WHY DIDN'T YOU INTRODUCE ME ?!
2-7
SCHULZ

# VIOLET

FIRST APPEARANCE
02/07/1951

Violet Gray is the second girl to move into Charlie Brown's neighborhood. She and Patty hit it off right away, and the two become best friends almost immediately—much to Charlie Brown's chagrin, as he is often on the receiving end of their criticism.

Violet comes from an affluent family and can be a bit pretentious at times. One of her favorite activities is organizing parties with Patty and deciding which kids should be excluded from the festivities. All the same, she's happy to join her friends in all their activities, whether playing house, making mudpies, or playing leftfield on Charlie Brown's baseball team.

As with her friend Patty, Violet's role declined over time. As new characters were introduced, she was relegated to the background or made to deliver the setup for other character's punchlines. "Some characters just don't seem to have enough personality to carry out ideas," Charles Schulz observed of Violet and his other early cast members. "They're just almost born straight men."

POW!

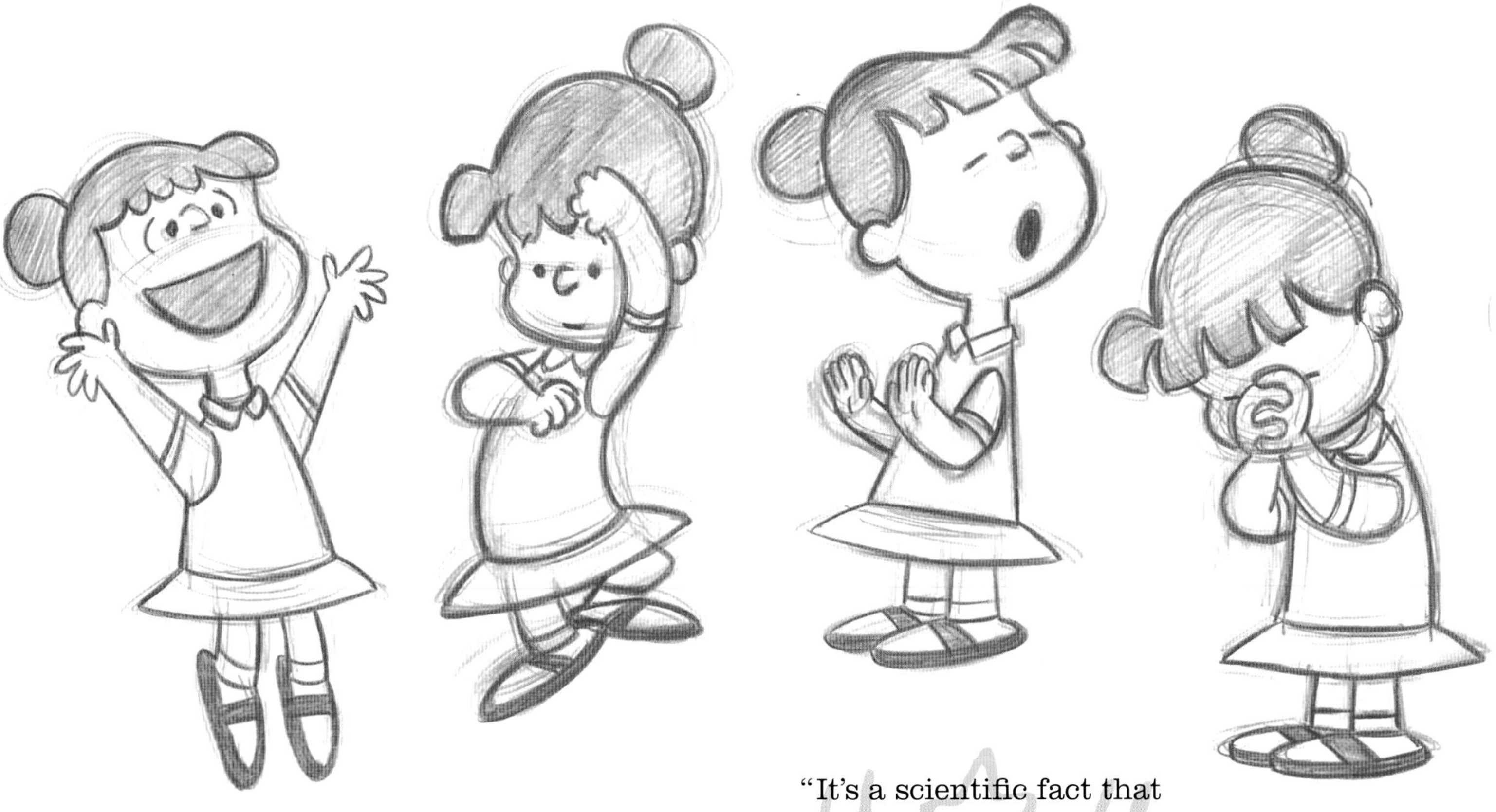

"It's a scientific fact that
at our age girls are
smarter than boys!"

—Violet

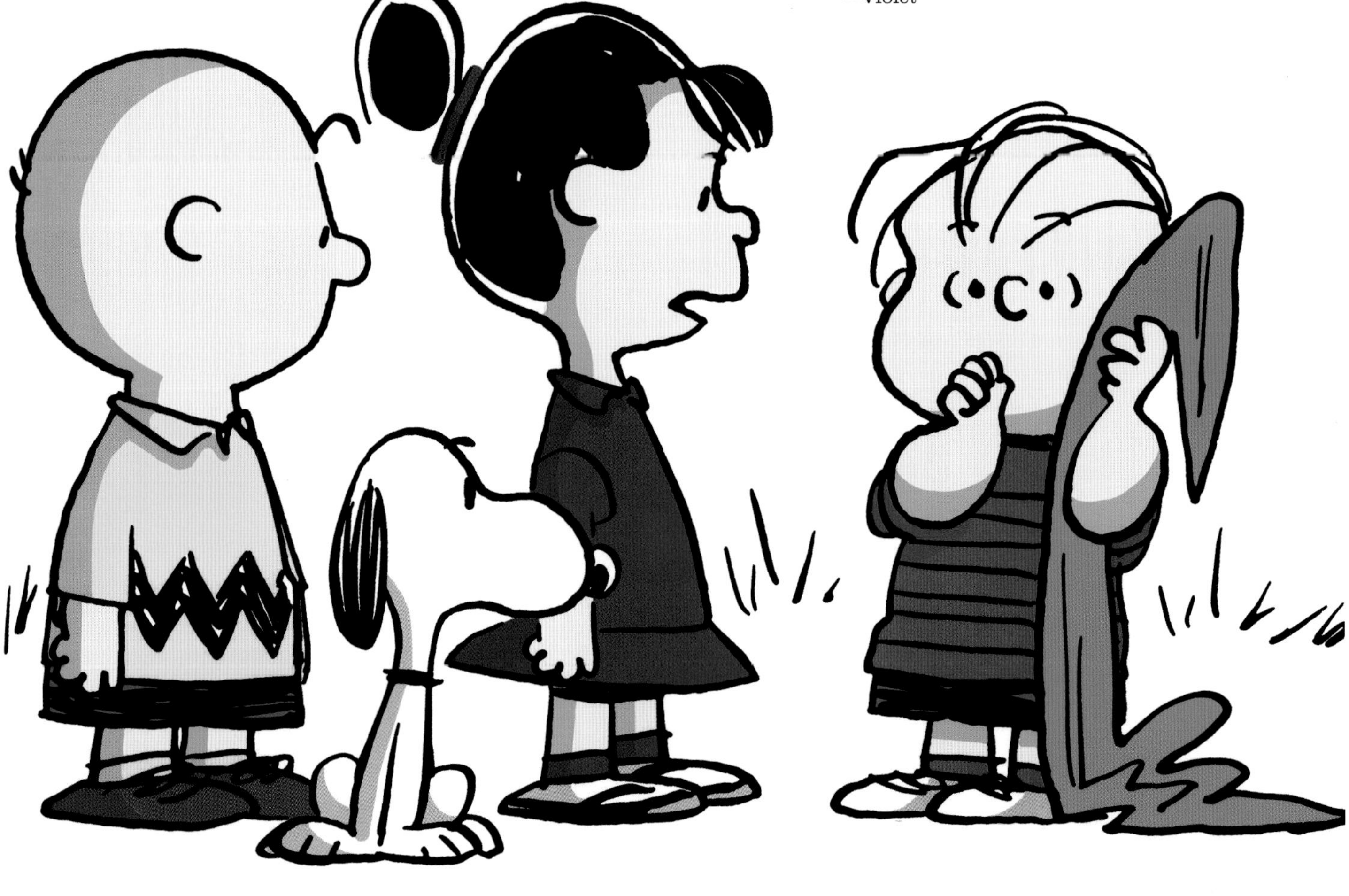

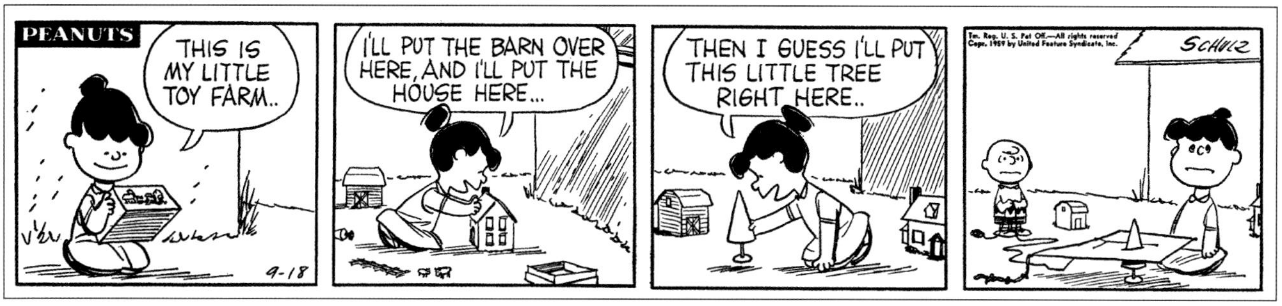
PEANUTS
THIS IS MY LITTLE TOY FARM..
I'LL PUT THE BARN OVER HERE, AND I'LL PUT THE HOUSE HERE...
THEN I GUESS I'LL PUT THIS LITTLE TREE RIGHT HERE..
SCHULZ
9-18

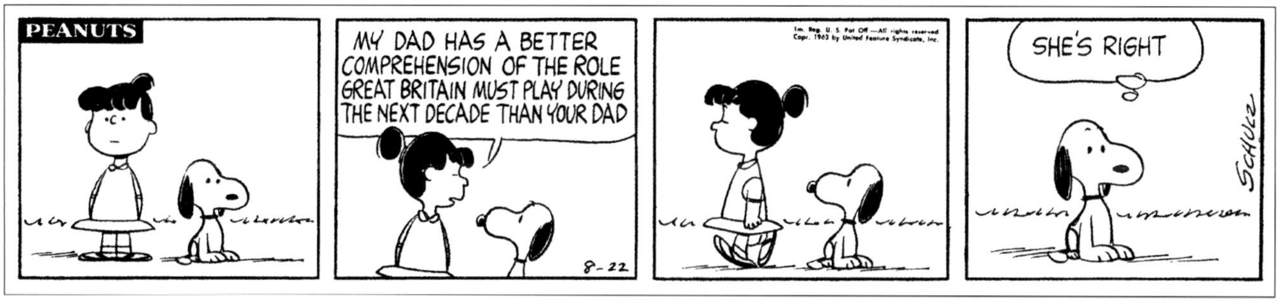
PEANUTS
MY DAD HAS A BETTER COMPREHENSION OF THE ROLE GREAT BRITAIN MUST PLAY DURING THE NEXT DECADE THAN YOUR DAD
SHE'S RIGHT
SCHULZ
8-22

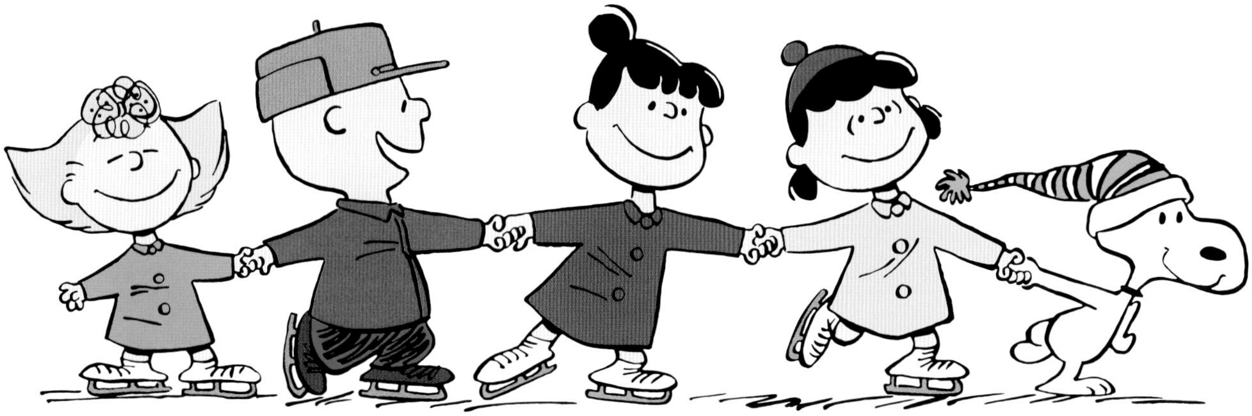

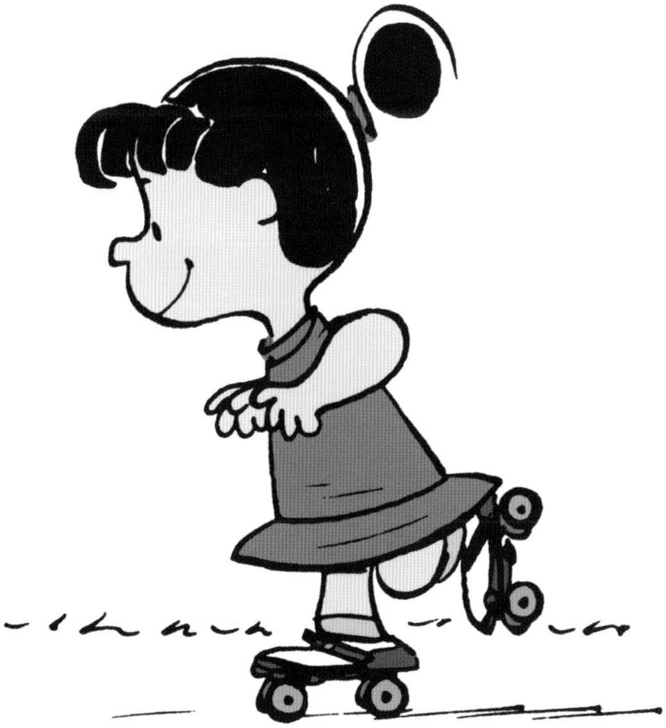

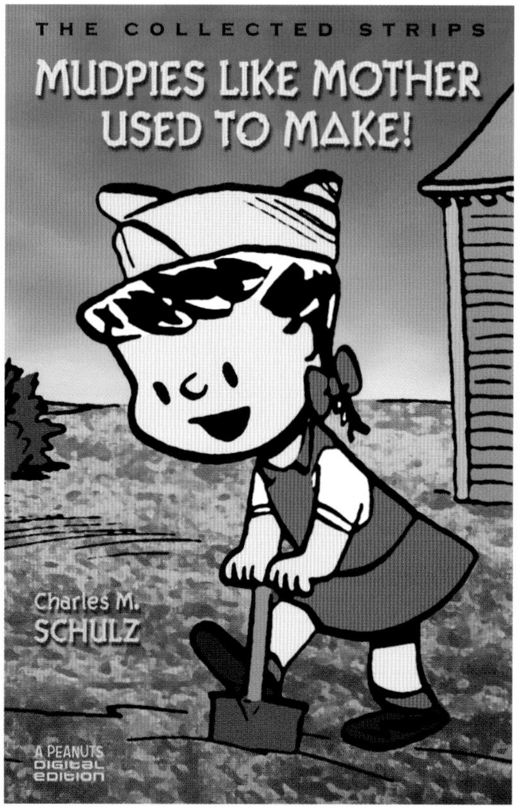
THE COLLECTED STRIPS
MUDPIES LIKE MOTHER USED TO MAKE!
Charles M. SCHULZ
A PEANUTS DIGITAL EDITION

OPPOSITE, TOP: *Violet model sheet – CSCA* | OPPOSITE, BOTTOM: *Spot art from strip – Charles M. Schulz* | ABOVE CENTER: *Style Guide art – CSCA* | ABOVE: *Spot art from* Happiness is a Warm Puppy *– Charles M. Schulz* | RIGHT: Mudpies Like Mother Used to Make, Peanuts *Digital Edition – CSCA*

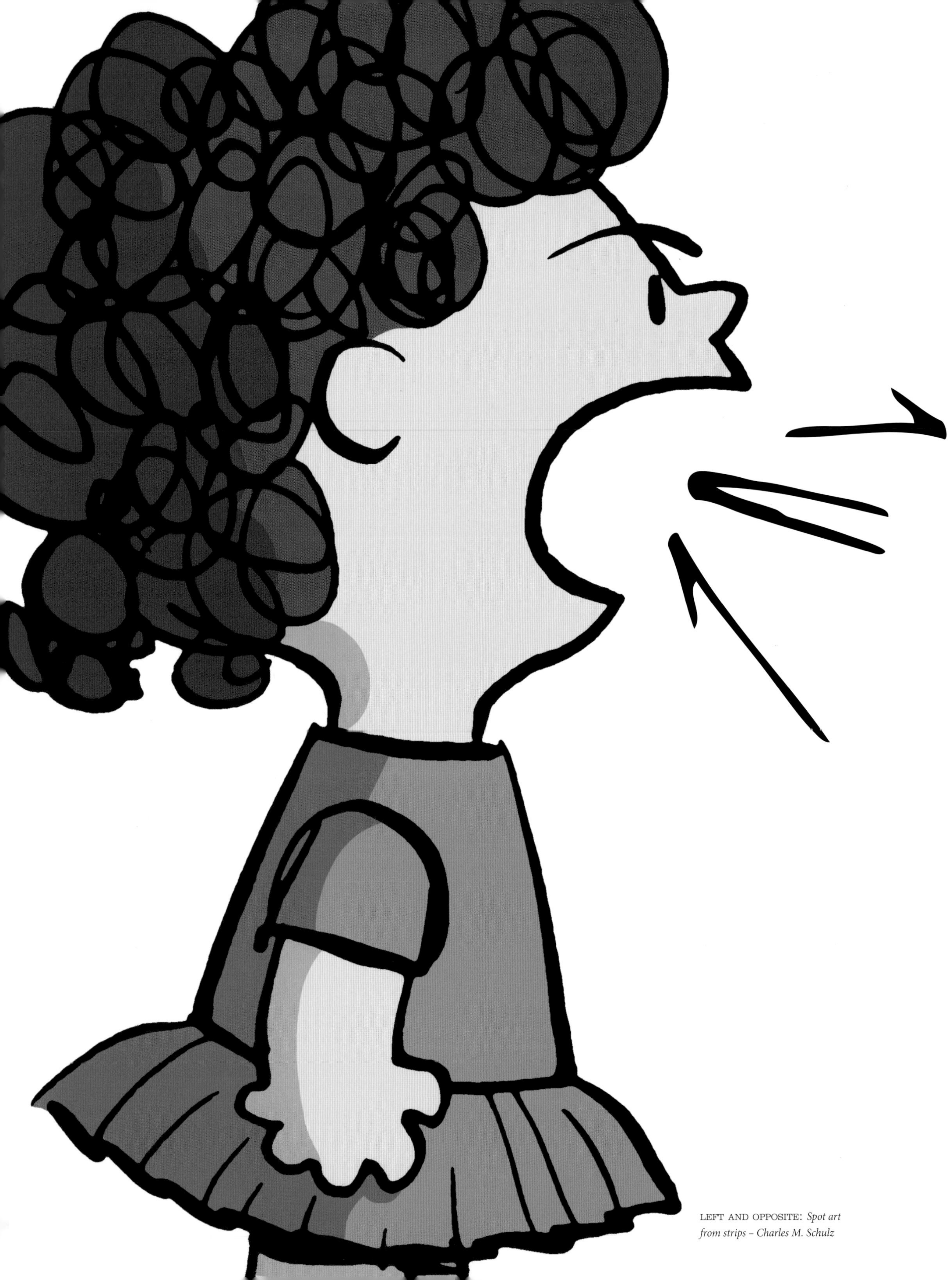

LEFT AND OPPOSITE: *Spot art from strips – Charles M. Schulz*

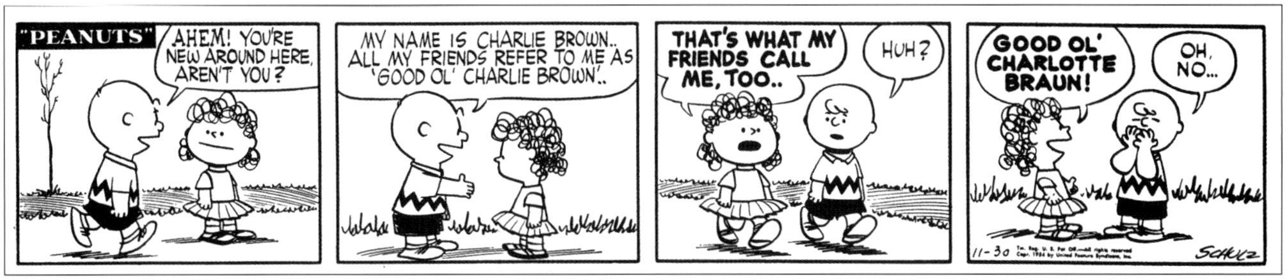
"PEANUTS"
AHEM! YOU'RE NEW AROUND HERE, AREN'T YOU?
MY NAME IS CHARLIE BROWN.. ALL MY FRIENDS REFER TO ME AS 'GOOD OL' CHARLIE BROWN'..
THAT'S WHAT MY FRIENDS CALL ME, TOO..
HUH?
GOOD OL' CHARLOTTE BRAUN!
OH, NO...
11-30
SCHULZ

# CHARLOTTE BRAUN

FIRST APPEARANCE
11/30/1954

What's in a name? Although Charlotte Braun's name is strikingly similar to Charlie Brown's, their personalities couldn't be more different. The brash, loud Charlotte Braun is everything that the wishy-washy Charlie Brown is not, and her abrasive nature failed to endear her to the gang—and to readers.

*Peanuts* fan Elizabeth Swaim was unimpressed with Charlotte Braun, an opinion she shared in a letter to Charles Schulz. Schulz wrote a personal response, and that letter is now part of the Library of Congress archives.

*Dear Miss Swaim,*

*I am taking your suggestion regarding Charlotte Braun and will eventually discard her. If she appears anymore it will be in strips that were already completed before I got your letter or because someone writes in saying that they like her. Remember, however, that you and your friends will have the death of an innocent child on your conscience. Are you prepared to accept such responsibility? Thanks for writing, and I hope that future releases will please you.*

*Sincerely,*

*Charles M. Schulz*

Charlotte made her final appearance on February 1, 1955, just a few months after this exchange.

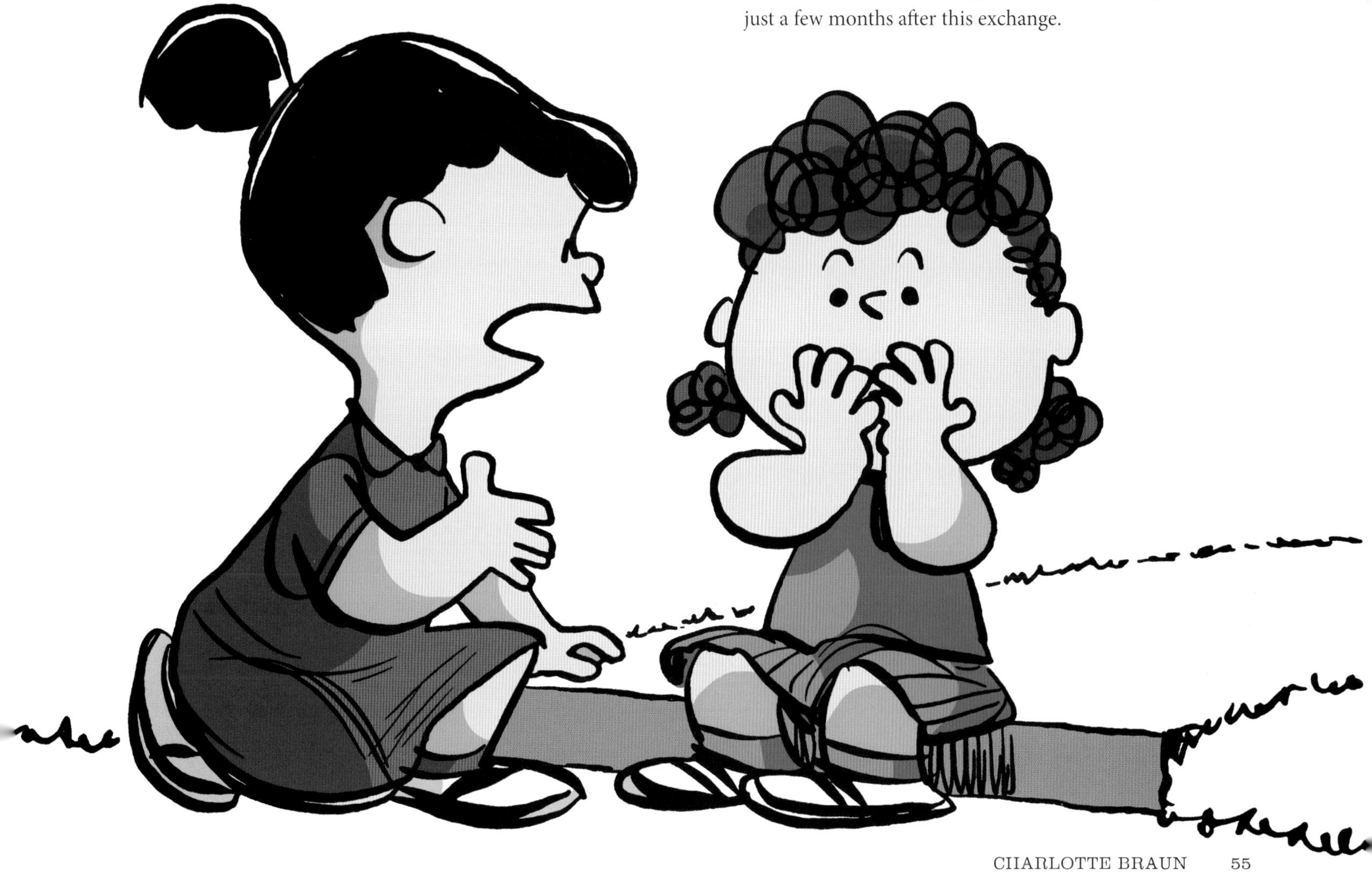

PEANUTS
DEAR PEN-PAL
RATS!
DEAR PEN-
RATS!
DE
RATS!
8-25
DEAR PENCIL-PAL,
SCHULZ

THE COLLECTED STRIPS
Not Even One Christmas Card!
A PEANUTS DIGITAL EDITION
Charles M. Schulz

ABOVE: Not Even One Christmas Card, Peanuts *Digital Edition – CSCA*

# Charlie Brown's Pen[cil] Pal

FIRST MENTIONED
08/25/1958

Charlie Brown strikes up a correspondence with his first Pen-Pal with the dual intentions of learning about his Pen-Pal's country and of practicing his penmanship with his nib pen and his inkwell. This proves to be much more difficult—and messy—than Charlie Brown

**"Nothing echoes like an empty mailbox."**
**—Charlie Brown**

expects, so he reluctantly agrees to begin with a Pencil-Pal instead. His friend certainly gets an interesting perspective on life in the United States, as Charlie Brown shares tales of his friends and family, from the birth of his sister to Snoopy's exploits, including the time that he thought he was a mountain lion.

Charlie Brown discovers a sympathetic ear in the form of his Pencil-Pal and finds that he can share his deepest fears and anxieties as well as his successes with his foreign friend. He develops a crush on his Scottish Pencil-Pal, Morag, and imagines their future together, but his hopes are dashed when he learns that she is corresponding with thirty other pen pals.

PEANUTS
WHAT DO YOU AND THIS PENCIL-PAL OF YOURS WRITE ABOUT?
OH, HE TELLS ME ABOUT HIS COUNTRY, AND I TELL HIM ABOUT OURS..
8-28
YOU SOUND LIKE A COUPLE OF SPIES TO ME!
SCHULZ

CHARLIE BROWN! WHERE HAVE YOU BEEN?
I'VE BEEN DOING THE HOKEY-POKEY WITH PATTY AND MARCIE..
LISTEN..THEY'RE PLAYING A FOX TROT..
www.snoopy.com
NOW I CAN ASK THE LITTLE RED HAIRED GIRL TO DANCE..
I THINK SOMEONE IS AHEAD OF YOU..
5-25
© 1998 United Feature Syndicate, Inc.
"DAISY AND GATSBY DANCED.. I REMEMBER HIS GRACEFUL CONSERVATIVE FOX TROT"

I'M ALWAYS THINKING ABOUT THAT LITTLE RED HAIRED GIRL, BUT I KNOW SHE DOESN'T THINK OF ME
SHE DOESN'T THINK OF ME BECAUSE I'M A NOTHING, AND YOU CAN'T THINK OF NOTHING!
5-30
YOU'RE NOT REALLY A NOTHING, CHARLIE BROWN
ALMOST
©1978 United Feature Syndicate, Inc.
DOES A GIRL EVER GO AROUND THINKING OF A .00001 ?!
SCHULZ

# THE LITTLE RED-HAIRED GIRL

FIRST MENTIONED
11/19/1961

Charlie Brown is head over heels in love with his classmate, the Little Red-Haired Girl, but she doesn't know he's alive. He spends many a lonely lunch hour thinking about how he'll introduce himself to her, but he can't work up the nerve to approach her.

Although he has several opportunities to meet the Little Red-Haired Girl, fate (and Charlie Brown's own wishy-washiness) always seems to get in the way. When they are paired together for a class science project, Charlie Brown avoids her until she joins another group. When a bully picks on her, Charlie Brown stands by indecisively as Linus springs into action and defends her. When he finally takes enough lessons so he feels he can impress her on the dance floor, he finds that Snoopy has already joined her for a fox trot.

The inspiration for the Little Red-Haired Girl came from an unrequited love in Charles Schulz's past. Never one to let a good idea go to waste, he used the grief of a rejected marriage proposal as the basis for Charlie Brown's heartbreak.

THE COLLECTED STRIPS
The Little Red-Haired Girl
Charles M. Schulz
A PEANUTS DIGITAL EDITION

ABOVE: The Little Red-Haired Girl, Peanuts *Digital Edition – CSCA*

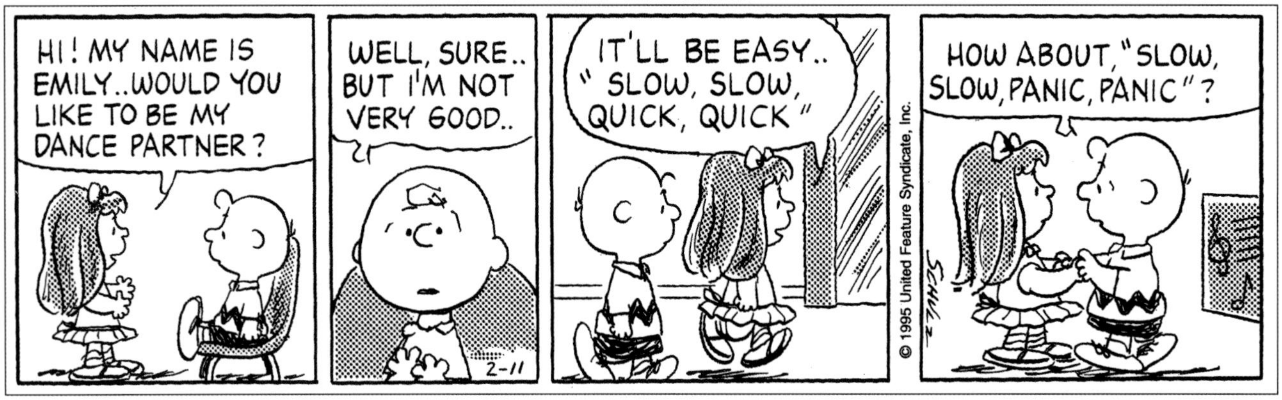
HI! MY NAME IS EMILY..WOULD YOU LIKE TO BE MY DANCE PARTNER?
WELL, SURE.. BUT I'M NOT VERY GOOD..
IT'LL BE EASY.. "SLOW, SLOW, QUICK, QUICK"
HOW ABOUT, "SLOW, SLOW, PANIC, PANIC"?
© 1995 United Feature Syndicate, Inc.
2-11
SCHULZ

# EMILY

FIRST APPEARANCE
02/11/1995

Emily takes an immediate liking to Charlie Brown and invites him to be her partner for their after-school dance class. The pair share what Charlie Brown describes as "an enchanted early afternoon" on the dance floor, and he spends the rest of the week eagerly anticipating their next lesson. When he returns to the classroom to see her again, however, his teacher claims that no one named Emily was enrolled in the class, and Charlie Brown's friends express skepticism that she really exists.

The two reunite eventually, though, and share an unforgettable evening at the Sweetheart Ball. They continue to pair up in dance classes—if she's real, that is.

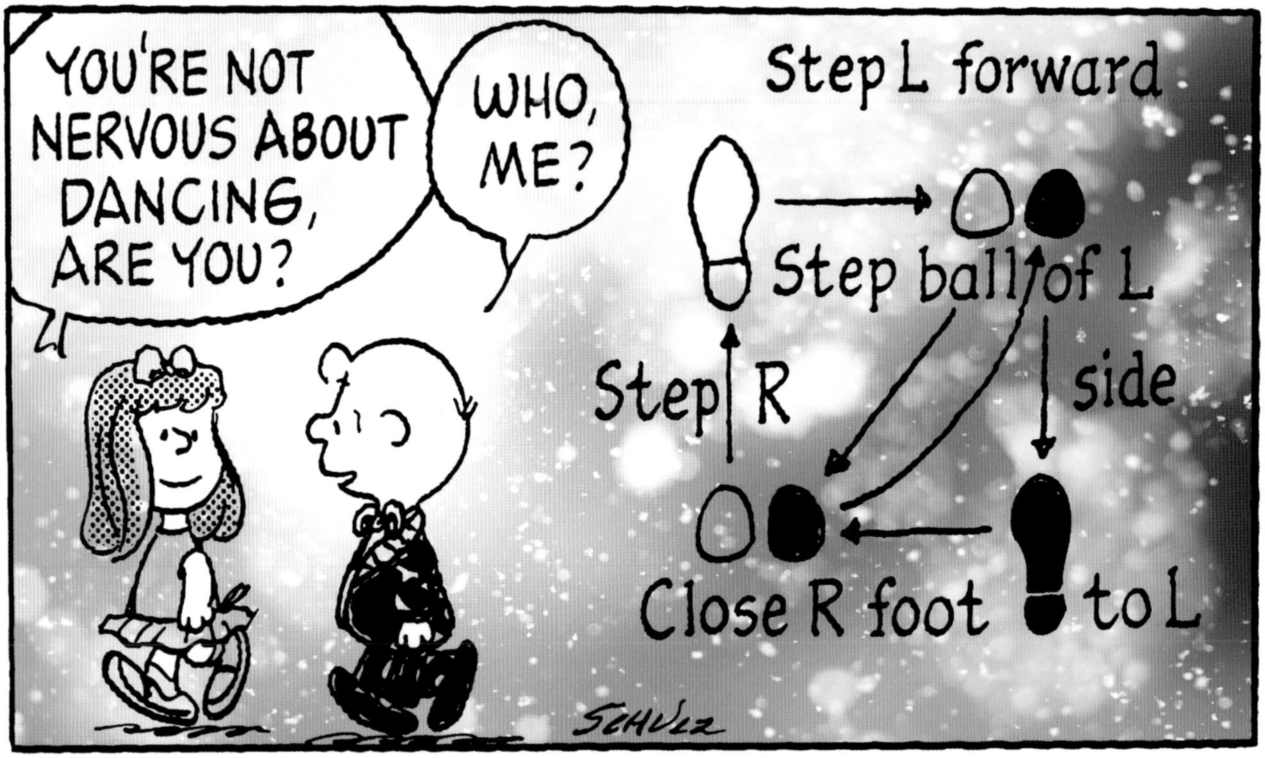
YOU'RE NOT NERVOUS ABOUT DANCING, ARE YOU?
WHO, ME?
Step L forward
Step ball of L
Step R
side
Close R foot to L
SCHULZ

ABOVE AND OPPOSITE: *Design by Cameron + Co*

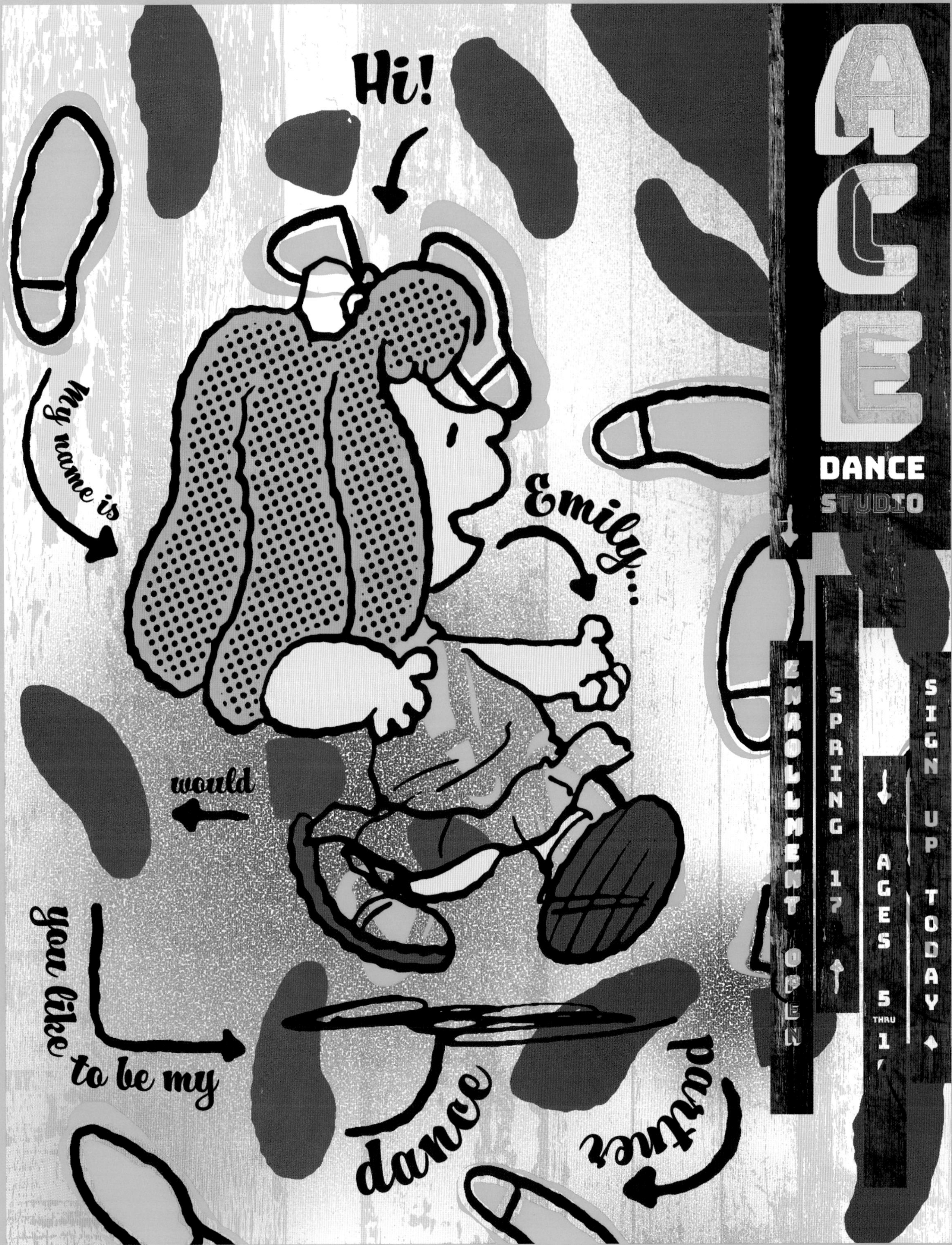
Hi!
My name is
Emily...
would
you like
to be my
dance
partner
ACE
DANCE
STUDIO
ENROLLMENT OPEN
SPRING 17
AGES 5 THRU 1
SIGN UP TODAY

"PEANUTS"
IN THE OLD DAYS IT WAS DIFFERENT
PEOPLE USED TO GO THROUGH THE WOODS TO GRANDMOTHER'S HOUSE
BUT NOT ANY MORE...
MY GRANDMOTHER LIVES IN THE APARTMENT RIGHT ABOVE US!
12-25
SCHULZ

# THE NEIGHBORHOOD WALL

FIRST APPEARANCE
12/25/1950

Charlie Brown always has a lot on his mind, and he spends a lot of time talking about his hopes and fears with his friends, often at the Neighborhood Wall. The conveniently placed waist-high brick wall is the perfect height for Charlie Brown to lean against when he's discussing theology with Linus, anxieties with Lucy, or sharing grandfather stories with Franklin.

*Peanuts* was always a very introspective strip, and the Neighborhood Wall served as the ideal venue for philosophy and thoughtful conversation. Although scholars and fans found *Peanuts* to be a very profound, deeply philosophical comic, Charles Schulz himself was very modest about the strip and its message. "I never thought of myself as having any writing ability at all. I never thought of myself as having any kind of philosophical approach. I really know nothing about psychology or psychiatry or philosophy or anything like that."

"PEANUTS"
BIG PEOPLE ARE ALWAYS ASKING ME WHAT I'M GOING TO BE WHEN I GROW UP..
HOW DO THEY EXPECT US TO KNOW?
DO YOU KNOW WHAT YOU'RE GOING TO BE WHEN YOU GROW UP, CHARLIE BROWN?
SURE
1-31
LONESOME!
SCHULZ

PEANUTS
HOW CAN YOU TELL IF YOU HAVE A BROKEN HEART?
WELL, FOR ONE THING, IF YOU HAVE A BROKEN HEART, YOU CAN'T SLEEP AT NIGHT..
WHEN YOU ROLL OVER IN BED, THE JAGGED EDGES POKE YOU IN THE SIDE
I'M GLAD I TALKED TO AN EXPERT
SCHULZ
8-28

ABOVE CENTER: *Style Guide art – PW* | OPPOSITE: *Style Guide art – CSCA*

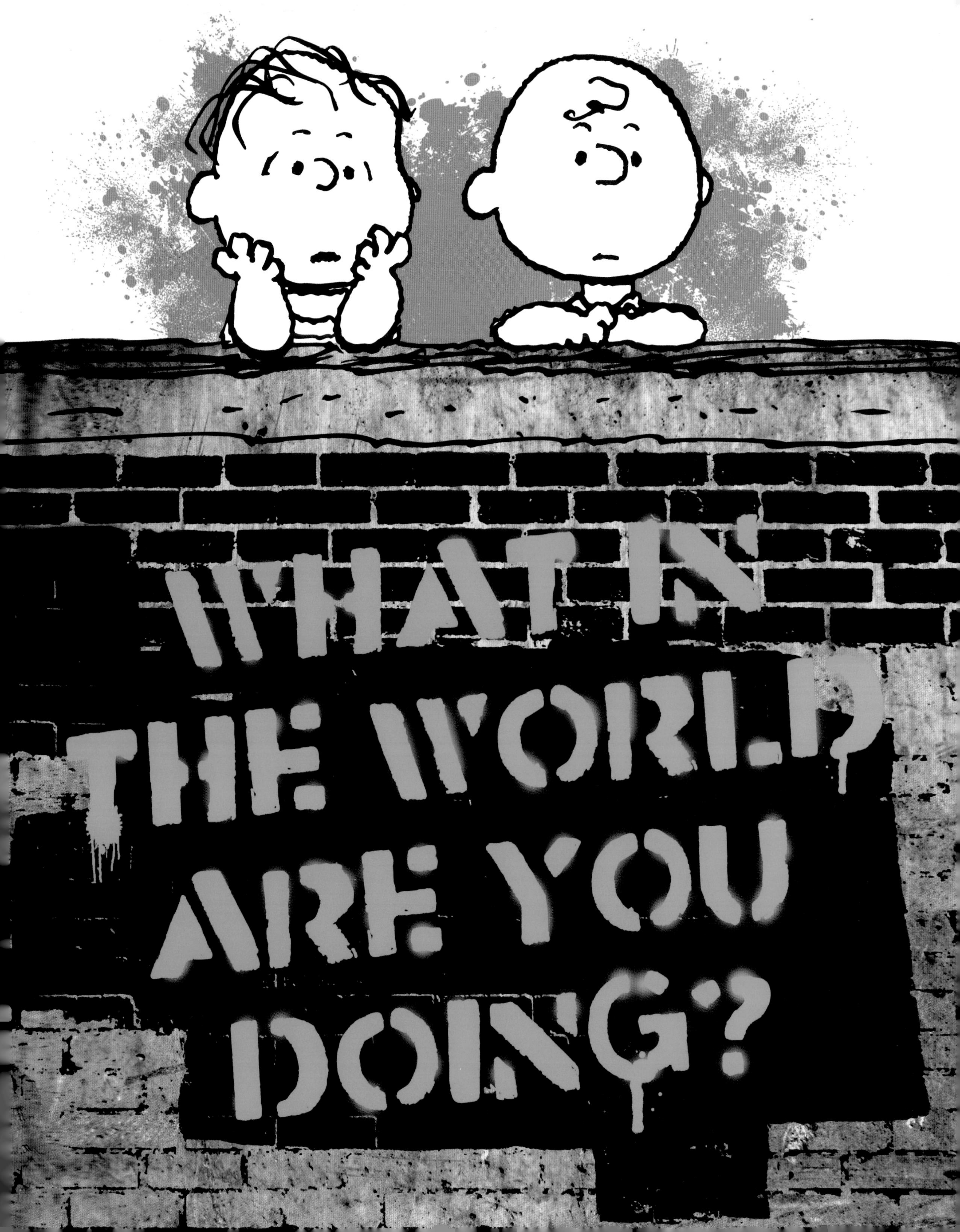
WHAT IN
THE WORLD
ARE YOU
DOING?

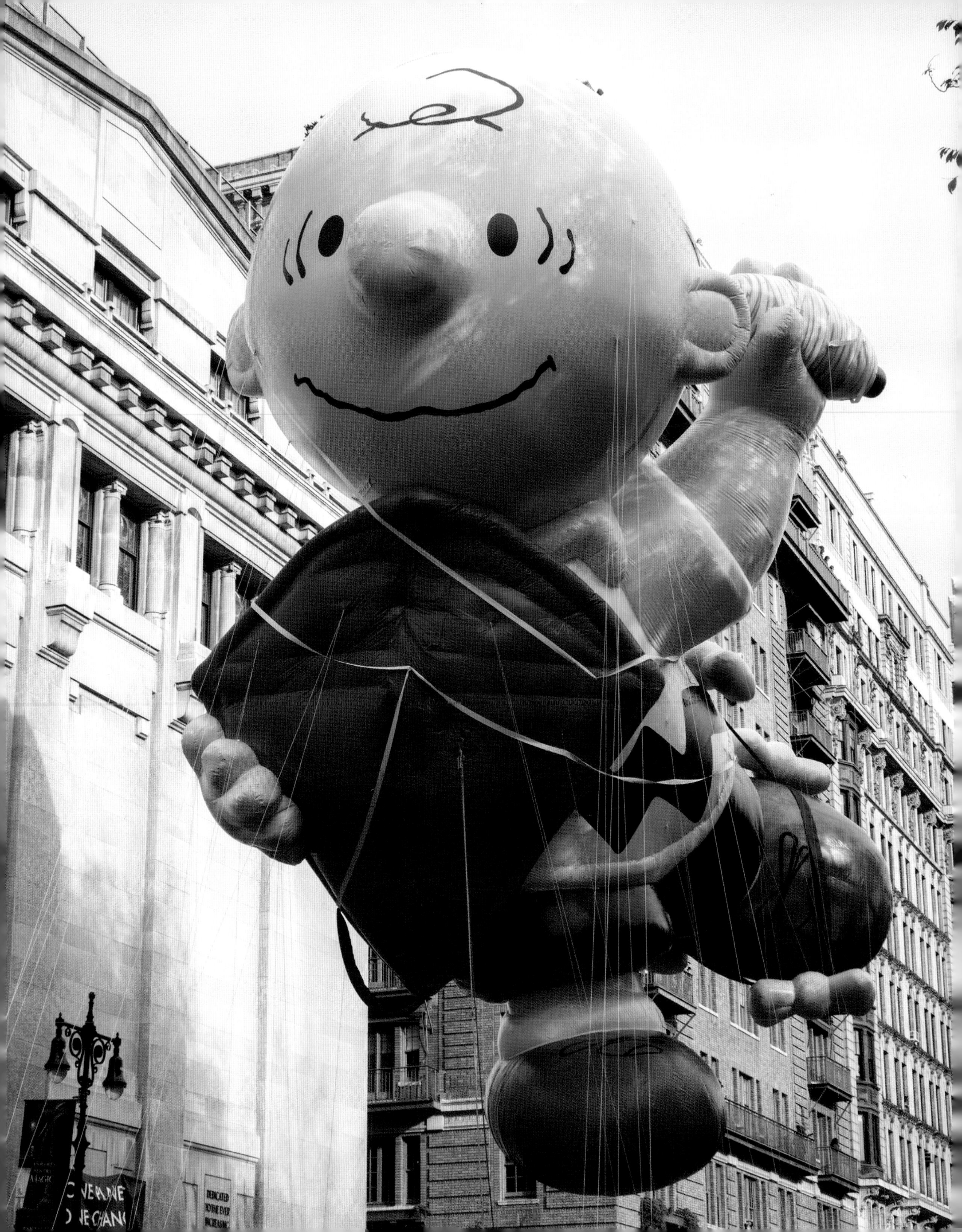
DEDICATED
TO THE EVER

"PEANUTS"
KITE CAUGHT IN THE TREE?
YUP!
CAN'T GET IT DOWN, HUH?
NOPE!
WHAT ARE YOU GOING TO DO ABOUT IT?
NOTHING..
I'M SO MAD I'M JUST GOING TO STAND HERE FOR THE REST OF MY LIFE!
SCHULZ
4-12

# THE KITE-EATING TREE

**FIRST APPEARANCE** 04/12/1956
**FIRST NAMED** 03/14/1965

The Kite-Eating Tree is native to the fields near Charlie Brown's home. Unlike other plants, the Kite-Eating Tree has a diet consisting entirely of kites flown by Charlie Brown. Although it seems to have a distinct preference for brand-new kites, it has been known to settle for used kites when necessary, and has even eaten raw toy pianos on very rare occasions (sorry, Schroeder).

Charlie Brown's lack of kite-flying prowess stems from Charles Schulz's own difficulties with the hobby. "I have never been a very successful kite flyer and have used the excuse that I never lived where there were good areas to fly kites. When I was growing up, we always lived in residential areas which had too many trees and too many telephone wires. Recollections of those handicaps inspired Charlie Brown's troubles with kite flying. As I grew older and tried to fly kites for my own children, I discovered that I still had the same problems. I observed that when a kite becomes caught in a tall tree, it is irretrievable and gradually disappears over a period of several weeks. Now obviously the kite had to go someplace, so it seemed to me that the tree must be eating it. This is how the series developed about Charlie Brown's violent battles with his local 'kite-eating tree.'"

THE COLLECTED STRIPS
Kites drive me crazy!
Part One
Charles M. Schulz
A PEANUTS DIGITAL EDITION

The One & Only
KITE-EATING TREE

OPPOSITE: *Charlie Brown at the Macy's Day Parade, New York* | ABOVE LEFT: Kites Drive Me Crazy, Peanuts *Digital Edition – CSCA* | ABOVE RIGHT: *Style Guide art – PW*

WELL, MOUND, THAT'S IT FOR ANOTHER YEAR
I GUESS IT WASN'T MUCH OF A SEASON FOR EITHER OF US...
MAYBE SOMEDAY WE'LL DO BETTER
MY MOTHER THINKS I'M IN YANKEE STADIUM
9-1
SCHULZ

# THE PITCHER'S MOUND

FIRST APPEARANCE
08/24/1951

Play ball! Every spring, Charlie Brown returns to the Pitcher's Mound to manage his baseball team through yet another losing season. The Pitcher's Mound is the site of many of Charlie Brown's most interesting conversations, including conferences with his catcher, Schroeder; theological debates with his second baseman, Linus; and long-distance arguments with his right fielder, Lucy.

**"If this pitcher's mound could talk, I bet it would have a lot of stories to tell." —Charlie Brown**

The Pitcher's Mound, the highest spot on the baseball diamond, is a literal port in the storm during torrential downpours. It is also the site of one of the first signs of spring every year—the first line drive that knocks Charlie Brown off the mound and scatters his glove, cap, clothes, and shoes across the infield!

LITTLE FOX THEATRE
PLAYBILL
the national magazine for theatregoers
"YOU'RE A GOOD MAN, CHARLIE BROWN"

ABOVE: *Theater program from* You're a Good Man, Charlie Brown, *produced at the Little Fox Theatre, San Francisco, 1967 – CMSM*

# CHARLIE BROWN'S BASEBALL GLOVE

FIRST APPEARANCE
03/01/1951

As soon as possible each spring, Charlie Brown retrieves his old, faithful baseball glove from his closet, as he readies himself for the coming baseball season. And each fall, after several months of activity, and occasionally catching a pop fly or a line drive, Charlie Brown rubs a little neat's-foot oil into his glove to ensure that it will be ready for action in time for that first day of spring training.

Charlie Brown's fondness for his mitt isn't reciprocated, however, as his glove resents Charlie Brown's inability to win a game, as well as being forced into hibernation for several months every year. Although their relationship is as one-sided as any of his games, Charlie Brown's glove will always be in good hands.

WELL, OL' FAITHFUL GLOVE, ANOTHER SEASON HAS COME AND GONE... I GUESS I'LL PUT YOU AWAY UNTIL NEXT SPRING...
10-15
SIGH THERE I WAS, A BEAUTIFUL PIECE OF GENUINE LEATHER...
SO WHAT HAPPENS? I END UP AS A BASEBALL GLOVE FOR A STUPID KID WHO LOSES EVERY GAME HE PITCHES!
OF COURSE, IT MIGHT HAVE BEEN WORSE... I COULD HAVE BEEN A PAIR OF GOALIE PADS AND GOT HIT BY PUCKS ALL WINTER...
SCHULZ
© 1983 United Feature Syndicate, Inc.

PEANUTS
5-7
OH, NO!
OTHER KIDS' BASEBALL HEROES HIT HOME RUNS...MINE GETS SENT DOWN TO THE MINORS!
SCHULZ

# JOE SHLABOTNIK

**FIRST MENTIONED** 05/07/1963
**FIRST NAMED** 08/18/1963

It's no surprise that Charlie Brown's baseball hero, Joe Shlabotnik, never seems to catch a break on or off the field. Charlie Brown's faith in Shlabotnik is unwavering, even when Shlabotnik's low batting average and lackluster fielding earn him a demotion from the majors down to the Green Grass League. Charlie Brown even sneaks out of summer camp to attend Shlabotnik's only game as manager of the Waffletown Syrups. He's fired immediately after the game due to his questionable in-game strategy, but Charlie Brown chases after the team bus and manages to shout some words of encouragement to his long-suffering idol.

Charlie Brown is easily the world's biggest Joe Shlabotnik fan and may very well be the world's only Joe Shlabotnik fan. He is so devoted to his hero that he once bought 500 packs of baseball cards in an attempt to get his bubblegum card, but he came up empty-handed. Lucy, ironically, can't seem to get any players but Joe Shlabotnik when she opens a pack of cards. Good grief!

PEANUTS
by SCHULZ
JOE SHLABOTNIK?
REALLY?
YOU HAVE A JOE SHLABOTNIK? YOU HAVE A JOE SHLABOTNIK BUBBLE GUM CARD?
HE'S MY FAVORITE PLAYER! I'VE BEEN TRYING TO GET HIM ON A BUBBLE GUM CARD FOR FIVE YEARS! YOU WANNA TRADE?
HERE...I'LL GIVE YOU WHITEY FORD, MICKEY MANTLE, ROBIN ROBERTS, LUIS APARICIO, BILL MONBOUQUETTE, DICK STUART AND JUAN PIZARRO!
NO, I DON'T THINK SO...
HOW ABOUT NELLIE FOX, DICK DONOVAN, WILLIE KIRKLAND, FRANK LARY, AL KALINE, ORLANDO PENA, JERRY LUMPE, CAMILO PASCUAL, HARMON KILLEBREW, BOB TURLEY AND ALBIE PEARSON?
NO, I DON'T WANT TO TRADE...I THINK JOE SHLABOTNIK IS KIND OF CUTE..
I'LL GIVE YOU TOM CHENEY, CHUCK COTTIER, WILLIE MAYS, ORLANDO CEPEDA, MAURY WILLS, SANDY KOUFAX, FRANK ROBINSON, BOB PURKEY, BILL MAZEROSKI, HARVEY HADDIX, WARREN SPAHN, HANK AARON, TONY GONZALES, ART MAHAFFEY, ROGER CRAIG, DUKE SNIDER, DON NOTTEBART, AL SPANGLER, CURT SIMMONS, STAN MUSIAL, ERNIE BANKS AND LARRY JACKSON!
NO, I DON'T THINK SO..
FOR FIVE YEARS I'VE BEEN TRYING TO GET A JOE SHLABOTNIK! MY FAVORITE BASEBALL PLAYER, AND I CAN'T GET HIM ON A BUBBLE GUM CARD... FIVE YEARS! MY FAVORITE PLAYER...
HE'S NOT AS CUTE AS I THOUGHT HE WAS!
SCHULZ
TRASH
8-18

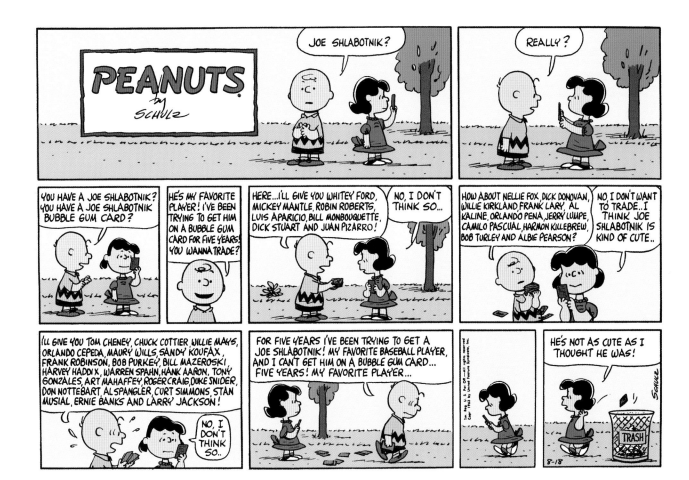

THIS IS NOT A BAD LOOKING NEIGHBORHOOD..
I WONDER WHERE I AM...
BONK!
I THINK YOU KILLED HIM, RUBY!
MAYBE NOT...SOMETIMES OLDER PEOPLE TAKE NAPS IN THE MIDDLE OF THE DAY...
© 1977 United Feature Syndicate, Inc.
SCHULZ
3-11

# THE GOOSE EGGS

**FIRST APPEARANCE** Austin and Ruby, 03/11/1977; Leland, 03/17/1977; Milo, 03/18/1977

Although the Goose Eggs are the smallest baseball team around, they never back down from a challenge. When Charlie Brown runs away from home, he is knocked out by a foul ball hit by the pint-size slugger Ruby. Obviously in need of some additional instruction, she and her teammate Austin invite Charlie Brown to become their new manager.

Under the guidance of Charlie Brown, whom they respectfully address as "Charles," the team learns the fundamentals of the game, from stealing bases to laying down bunts. When Ruby asks Charlie Brown about baseball terminology, she learns that "goose egg" means zero and is used when your team fails to score in an inning. She proudly announces that their team will be called "The Goose Eggs!"

Charlie Brown's brief tenure with the team is a rousing success, as the Goose Eggs win an impressive 100 percent of their games. Technically speaking, their lone win occurs when Lucy chooses to forfeit rather than compete against the tenacious toddlers, but this accomplishment marks one of the longest winning streaks in Charlie Brown's career.

The Goose Eggs
Season highlights
POW!
Leland
Austin
Milo
STRIKE ONE!
STRIKE TWO!
STRIKE THREE!
Ruby

ABOVE: *Poses from Boom! comic book, 2015 (CSCA); design of this piece, 2017 (Cameron + Co)*

ARE YOU THE KID WHO HIT THE HOME RUN OFF ME YESTERDAY?
WELL, I HOPE YOU'RE SATISFIED! YOU RUINED MY WHOLE LIFE!
YOU CAME CLEAR OVER HERE TO TELL ME THAT?
NO, I WAS JUST KIND OF CURIOUS TO SEE WHERE YOU LIVE..YOU PROBABLY HAVE A DOG, TOO, DON'T YOU?
SORT OF..
WHAT DO YOU MEAN, SORT OF?
© 1993 United Feature Syndicate, Inc.
4-1
SCHULZ

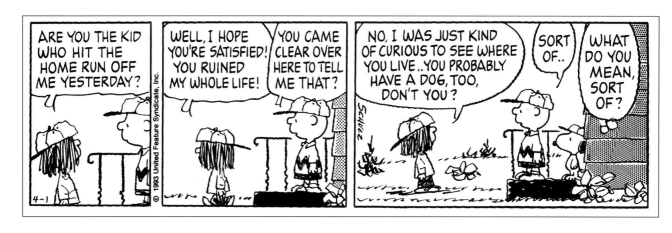

# ROYANNE HOBBS

FIRST APPEARANCE
04/01/1993

A natural talent on the baseball diamond, Royanne Hobbs claims to be the granddaughter of baseball legend Roy Hobbs, the hero of Bernard Malamud's acclaimed novel *The Natural*. Royanne is on the pitcher's mound when Charlie Brown hits his first-ever game-winning home run, an event that she claims "ruined [her] whole life!" Later that summer, Royanne gives up an inside-the-park home run to Charlie Brown, earning his team a rare multiple-win season.

Still later that summer, over chocolate sundaes at the local ice-cream parlor, Royanne confesses to Charlie Brown that she could have struck him out, but because she likes him, she allowed him to get those game-winning home runs. A dejected Charlie Brown informs her that Roy Hobbs is a fictional character, a revelation that causes her once again to exclaim, "My life is ruined." It's a complicated relationship.

ROYANNE
WIN-LESS
CATCHER

ABOVE: *Design by Cameron + Co*

# SUMMER DAYS

School's out! Summer is always a special time of year for Charlie Brown and his friends. It's time for family vacations, the county fair, trips to the beach and the circus, baseball, and summer camp!

Many of the neighborhood kids spend at least two weeks each year at summer camp, where they meet new friends, learn new skills, and develop new anxieties. Despite his reluctance to attend camp each summer, Charlie Brown has many unforgettable experiences and makes several lasting friendships, including Roy, who later introduces him to Peppermint Patty; Peggy Jean, his summer girlfriend; and his irritable bunkmate, whose only comment is, "Shut up and leave me alone!"

Much like his characters, Charles Schulz often dreaded his annual visit to summer camp. "Another reflection of my emotions are all of the summer camp ideas which I have drawn. They are a result of my having absolutely no desire as a child to be sent away to a summer camp. To me that was the equivalent of being drafted. When World War II came along, I met it with the same lack of enthusiasm."

*1 and 2: Boom! Studios cover, Issue #25 and #6 – CSCA; 3:* Your Beach Ball Just Left for Hawaii, Charlie Brown! Peanuts *Digital Edition – CSCA; 4, 5, 7, 8, and 9: Style Guide art – PW; 6: Style Guide art – CSCA*

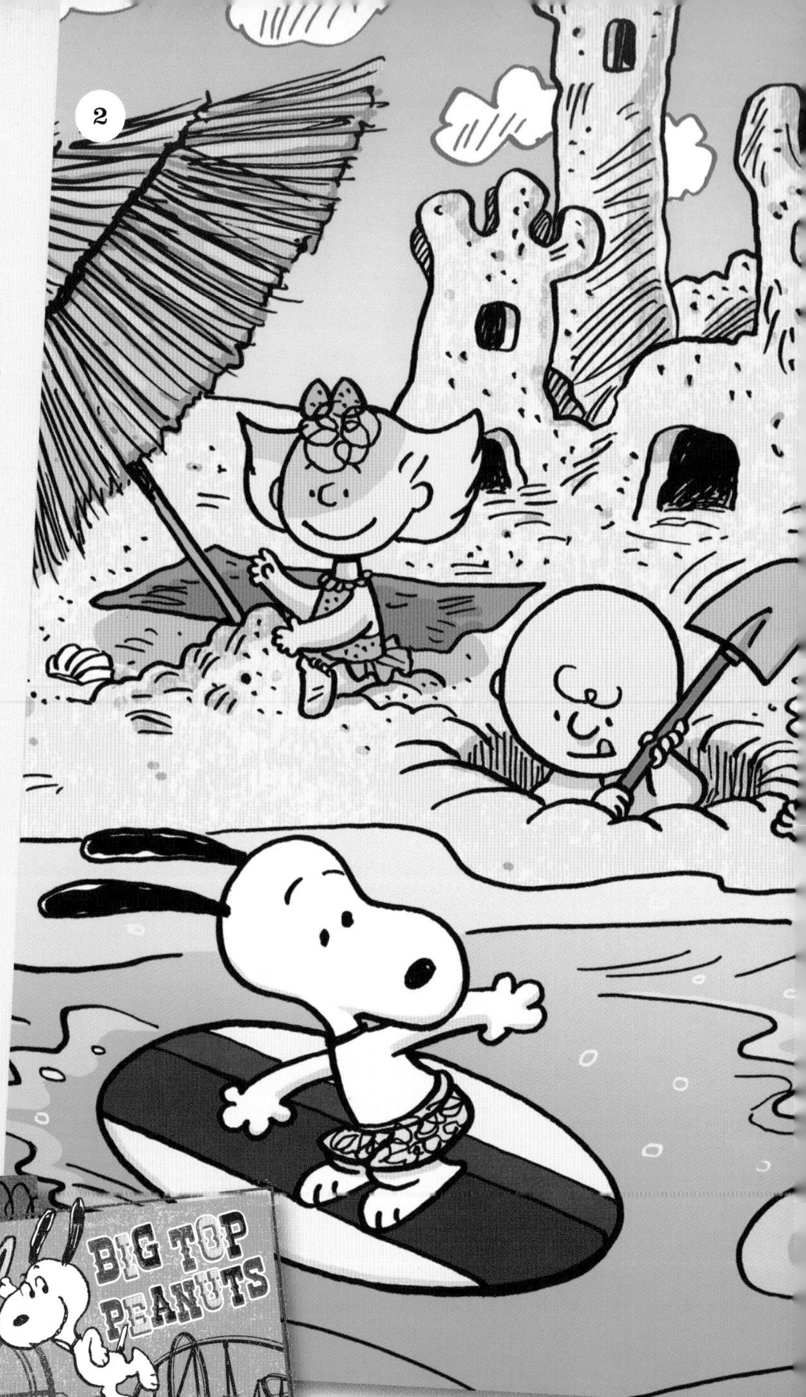
2

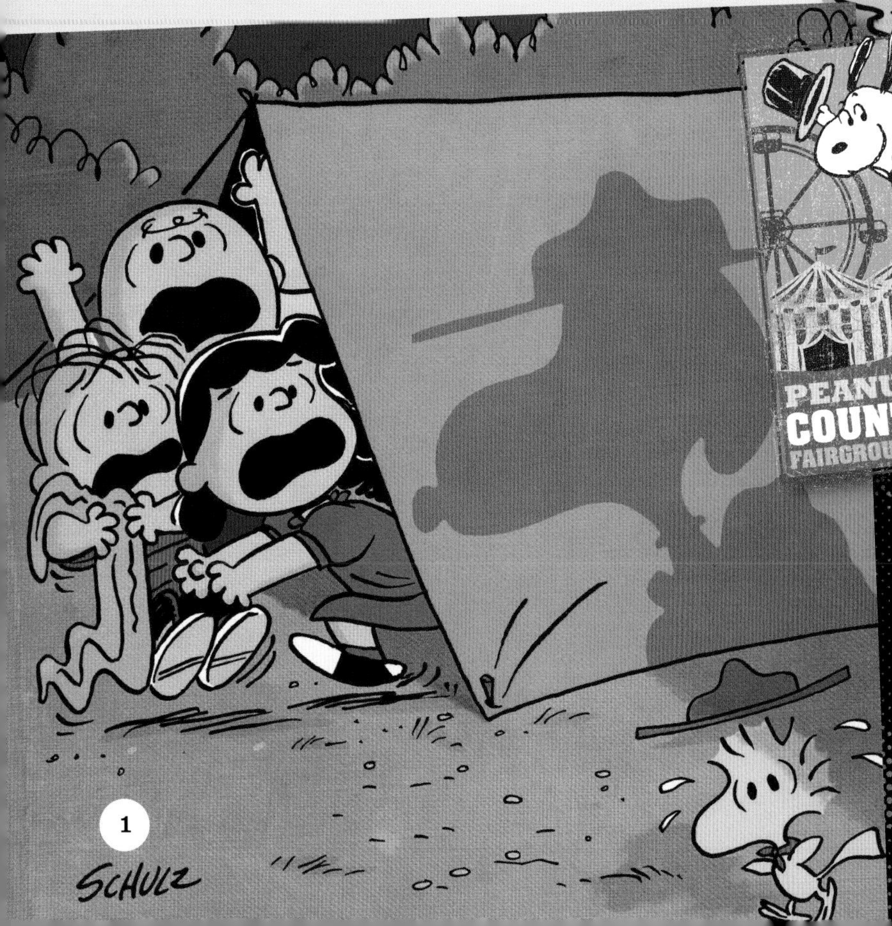
SCHULZ
1

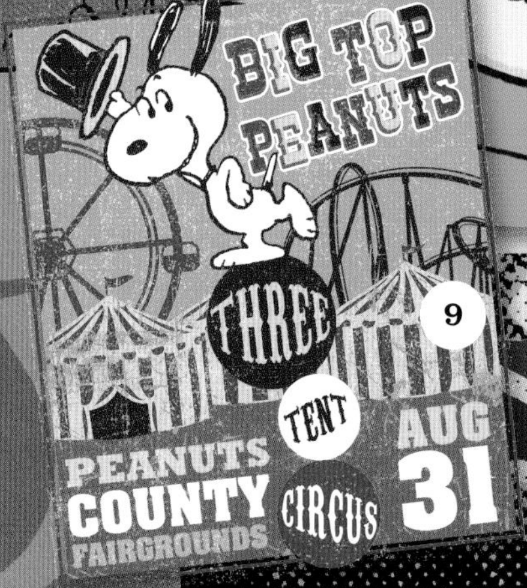
BIG TOP PEANUTS
THREE
TENT
CIRCUS
PEANUTS COUNTY FAIRGROUNDS
AUG 31
9

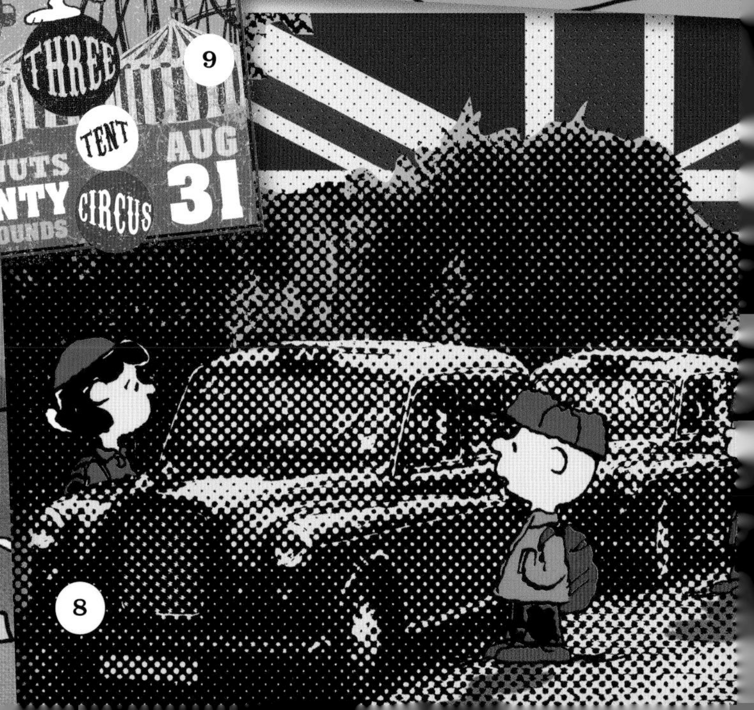
8

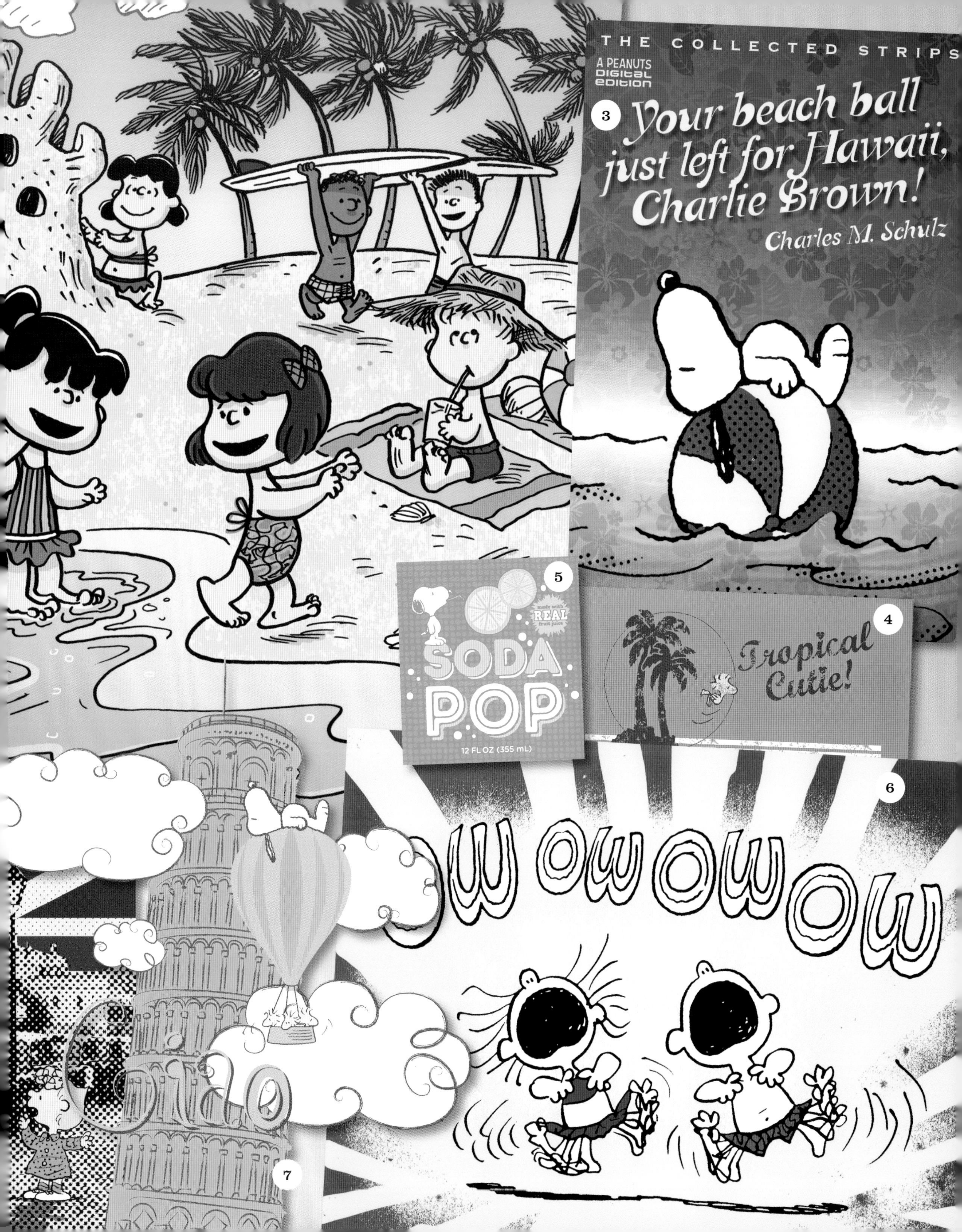
THE COLLECTED STRIPS
A PEANUTS DIGITAL EDITION
3
Your beach ball just left for Hawaii, Charlie Brown!
Charles M. Schulz
5
made with REAL fruit juices
SODA POP
12 FL OZ (355 mL)
4
Tropical Cutie!
6
WOWOWOW
Ciao
7

PEANUTS
YES, MA'AM, I HAVE AN APPOINTMENT TO SEE THE DOCTOR..
WELL, IT ALL STARTED ONE NIGHT WHEN I COULDN'T SLEEP, AND I SAW THE SUN COME UP, ONLY IT WASN'T THE SUN...IT WAS A BASEBALL!
WHY DO I HAVE THIS SACK OVER MY HEAD? WELL, I'VE ALSO DEVELOPED THIS RASH OR SOMETHING, YOU SEE, AND...
MA'AM, DO WE HAVE TO DISCUSS THIS IN FRONT OF THE WHOLE OFFICE?
6-16
SCHULZ

# MR. SACK

FIRST APPEARANCE
06/16/1973

When Charlie Brown wakes up one late spring morning, he's startled to see that the sun has been replaced by a huge baseball. He visits Lucy at her Psychiatric Booth and tells her that he's worried that he's cracking up, and that he feels alone, but she dismisses these concerns because she wants to hear more about his baseball hallucination. Soon, every round object reminds him of a baseball, whether it's the full moon or a scoop of ice cream.

Baseball seems to be on his mind all the time, to the point that his head breaks out in a rash resembling a baseball's stitches. Embarrassed by this rash, Charlie Brown covers his head with a grocery bag when he visits his doctor, who advises him to go to summer camp to forget about baseball for a while.

With his new, mysterious persona, Charlie Brown immediately becomes the most popular kid at camp and is elected Camp President. "Mr. Sack" is respected and admired by everyone at camp, and as Charlie Brown tells his parents in a letter to home, "Life here in camp is wonderful."

After a couple of weeks of rest and relaxation, Charlie Brown realizes that his head doesn't itch anymore. Even though it may cost him his position as Camp President, he doffs his sack on the evening of July 4 and decides to face the sunrise to learn if he's been cured of his baseball fixation. The next morning, alone in a field, he can barely stand the suspense as the sun moves into position. Fortunately for Charlie Brown, he doesn't see a baseball. Unfortunately, he sees MAD magazine's mascot, Alfred E. Neuman, along with his signature catchphrase, "What! Me Worry?"

Good grief!

ABOVE RIGHT: *Spot art from strip – Charles M. Schulz* | OPPOSITE: *Style Guide art – CSCA*

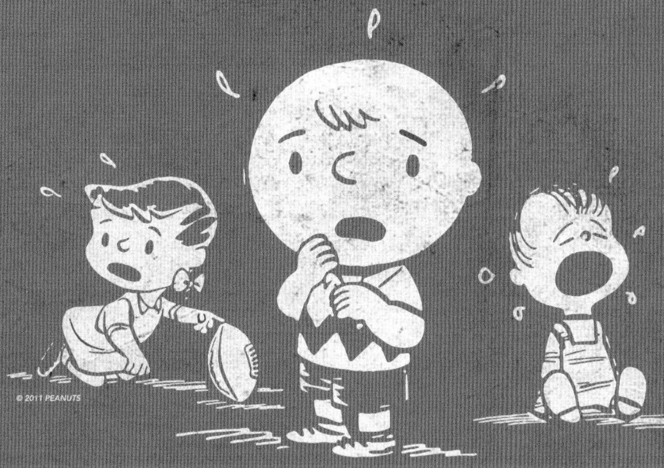
© 2011 PEANUTS

# KEEP
# CALM
# AND
# CARRY
# ON

PEANUTS
SNIF!
?
EXCUSE ME, BUT I COULDN'T HELP OVERHEARING YOU CRYING.. WHAT'S THE MATTER?
I DON'T KNOW... I GUESS I'M JUST LONESOME..
FRIEND!!
SCHULZ

# ROY

FIRST APPEARANCE
06/11/1965

Charlie Brown finds a kindred spirit in Roy when both are alone and in need of friendship at summer camp. The pair bond over loneliness and baseball. Charlie Brown is glad that his life experience is able to help Roy through a difficult time, and Roy is pleased that he makes "a good temporary friend" that summer.

Roy meets a homesick Linus at camp the following summer and relates the story of the round-headed kid who helped him get over his own anxieties, and they learn that they have a mutual friend in Charlie Brown. Roy reconnects with Charlie Brown later that summer when he visits the neighborhood and introduces Charlie Brown to another friend of his who enjoys baseball—Peppermint Patty!

Much like Charlie Brown and Roy, Charles Schulz often dreaded his annual visit to summer camp and the loneliness that he experienced there. "The three years I spent in the Army taught me all I need to know about loneliness, and my sympathy for the loneliness that all of us experience is dropped heavily upon poor Charlie Brown. I know what it is to have to spend days, evenings, and weekends by myself, and I also know how uncomfortable anxiety can be. I worry about almost all there is in life to worry about, and because I worry, Charlie Brown has to worry."

temporary friend.

RIGHT: *Design by Cameron + Co*

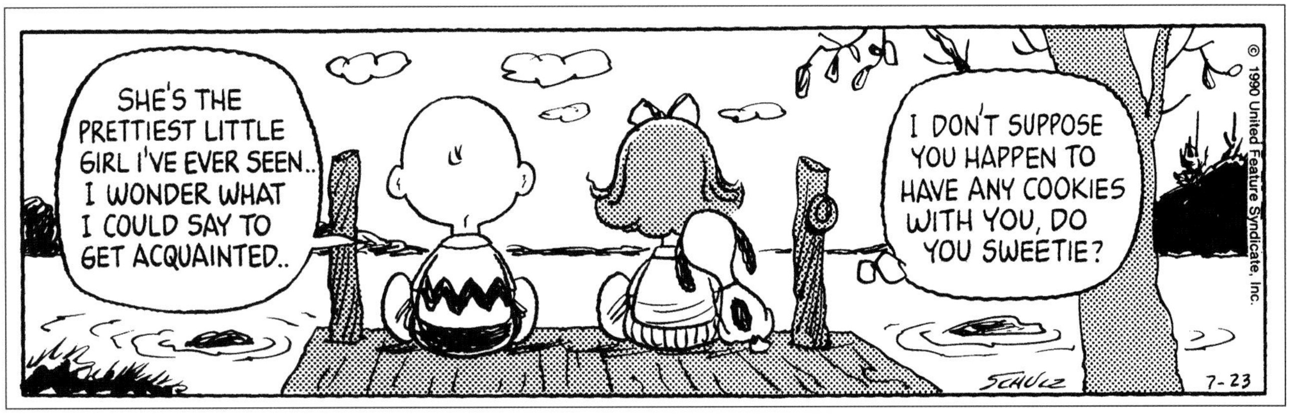
SHE'S THE PRETTIEST LITTLE GIRL I'VE EVER SEEN.. I WONDER WHAT I COULD SAY TO GET ACQUAINTED..
I DON'T SUPPOSE YOU HAPPEN TO HAVE ANY COOKIES WITH YOU, DO YOU SWEETIE?
© 1990 United Feature Syndicate, Inc.
SCHULZ
7-23

# PEGGY JEAN

FIRST APPEARANCE
07/23/1990

When Charlie Brown first meets Peggy Jean at summer camp, he gets so nervous that he introduces himself as "Brownie Charles." Fortunately, she finds this cute, and he never bothers to correct her. Their budding romance hits a snag when she challenges him to kick a football that she's holding and he can't bring himself to make the attempt. They soon reconcile and she gives Charlie Brown his first kiss when they leave camp at the end of the summer.

In a gesture of true love, Charlie Brown sells his comic book collection to earn enough money to buy Peggy Jean some nice gloves for Christmas. But when her mother buys her the exact same pair, a dejected Charlie Brown gives the gloves to Snoopy so that they don't go to waste. The next encounter of Charlie Brown and Peggy Jean is their last. They reunite at summer camp, and she mentions that she is late for a meeting with her new boyfriend. The heartbroken Charlie Brown, needing to hear a friendly voice, calls home that afternoon to talk to Snoopy.

Charlie Brown's relationship with Peggy Jean is bittersweet. Even though it ends in heartbreak, he can still look back fondly on their time together.

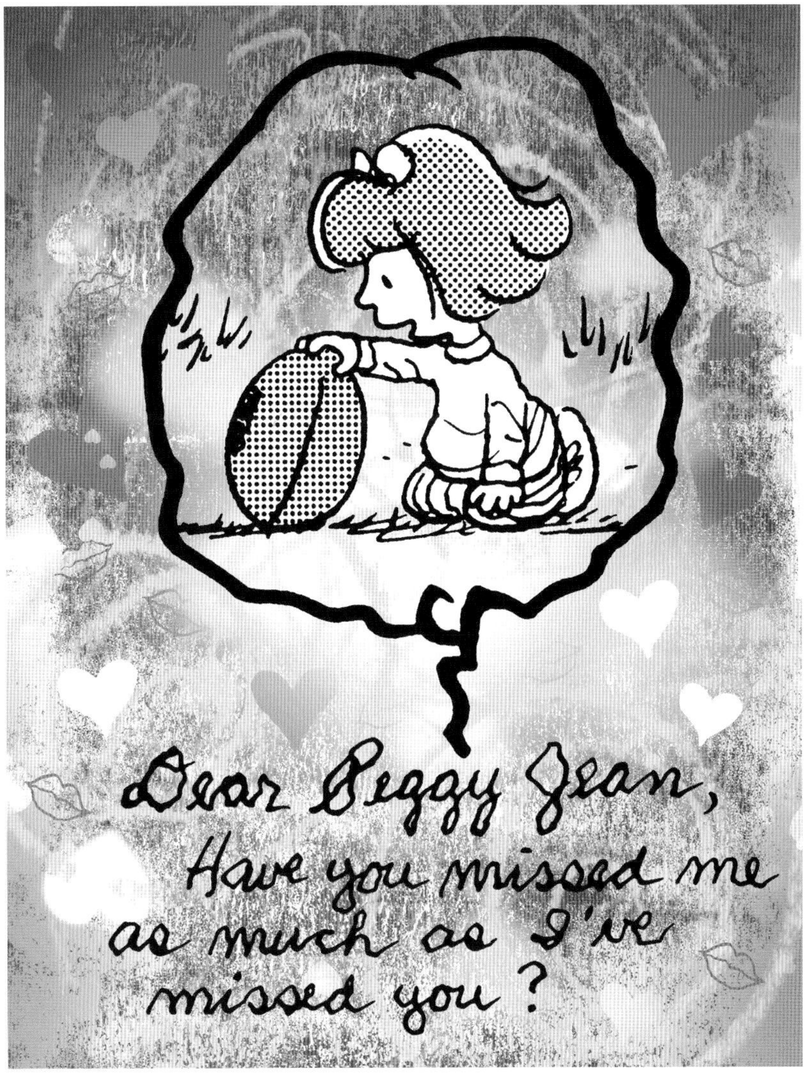
Dear Peggy Jean,
Have you missed me as much as I've missed you?

LEFT: *Design by Cameron + Co*

HI, MISTER BROWN... MY NAME IS CORMAC.. I'M YOUR SWIMMING BUDDY..
7-17
© 1992 United Feature Syndicate, Inc.
I ADMIT I DON'T KNOW MUCH ABOUT SWIMMING...
IS YOUR NOSE SUPPOSED TO GO ABOVE THE WATER OR BELOW THE WATER?
SCHULZ

I PLAN TO GROW..
SCHULZ

ABOVE: *Design by Cameron + Co*

# CORMAC

**FIRST APPEARANCE**
07/17/1992

In sharp contrast to his earliest trips to summer camp, Charlie Brown eventually achieves a sort of elder statesman status and serves as a mentor to younger campers such as his "swimming buddy," Cormac. From Charlie Brown, Cormac learns valuable skills such as floating in an inner tube and how to use a compass. Peppermint Patty and Marcie attend the same camp that summer, and not surprisingly, Cormac develops a crush on Marcie and suggests that she should be a model when she grows up.

**"I'm shorter than you now, but someday I'll be taller than you . . ." —Cormac**

Cormac is very self-confident. Unlike Charlie Brown, he finds it very easy to talk to girls, noting that he plans to be "smooth" when he grows up. This sense of bravado serves him well when he transfers to Sally's school the next fall and attempts to supplant Linus as her "Sweet Babboo."

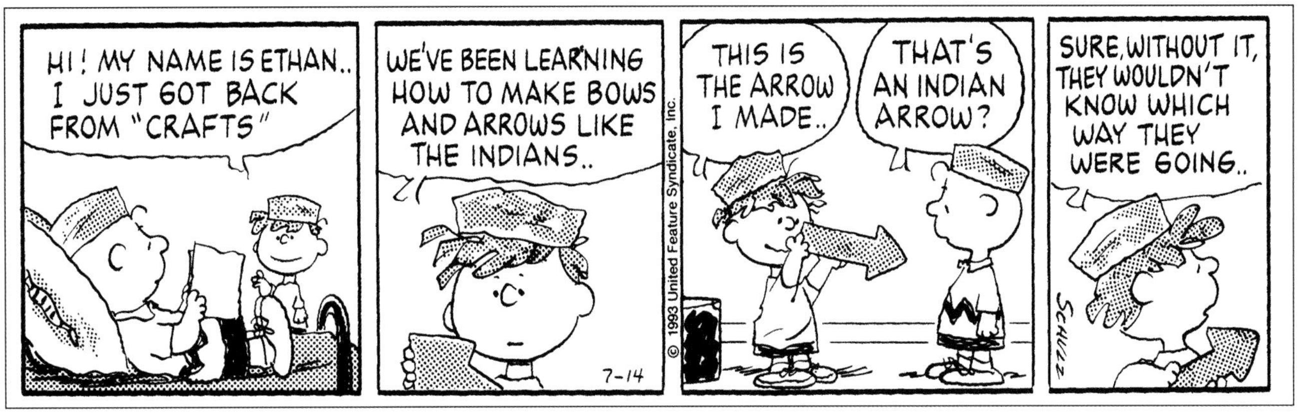
HI! MY NAME IS ETHAN.. I JUST GOT BACK FROM "CRAFTS"
WE'VE BEEN LEARNING HOW TO MAKE BOWS AND ARROWS LIKE THE INDIANS..
7-14
© 1993 United Feature Syndicate, Inc.
THIS IS THE ARROW I MADE..
THAT'S AN INDIAN ARROW?
SURE, WITHOUT IT, THEY WOULDN'T KNOW WHICH WAY THEY WERE GOING..
SCHULZ

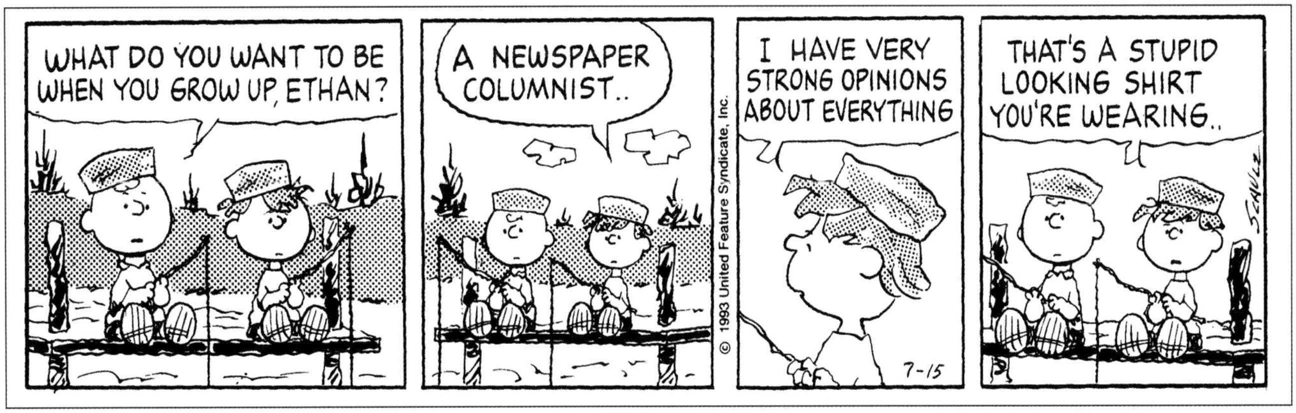
WHAT DO YOU WANT TO BE WHEN YOU GROW UP, ETHAN?
A NEWSPAPER COLUMNIST..
© 1993 United Feature Syndicate, Inc.
I HAVE VERY STRONG OPINIONS ABOUT EVERYTHING
7-15
THAT'S A STUPID LOOKING SHIRT YOU'RE WEARING..
SCHULZ

# ETHAN

**FIRST APPEARANCE**
07/14/1993

The strongly opinionated Ethan hopes to become a newspaper columnist when he grows up, so that he can share his viewpoints on every possible subject—such as his critique of Charlie Brown's "stupid looking shirt." Ethan also shows an aptitude for crafts, including the construction of "Indian arrows" to guide people around summer camp.

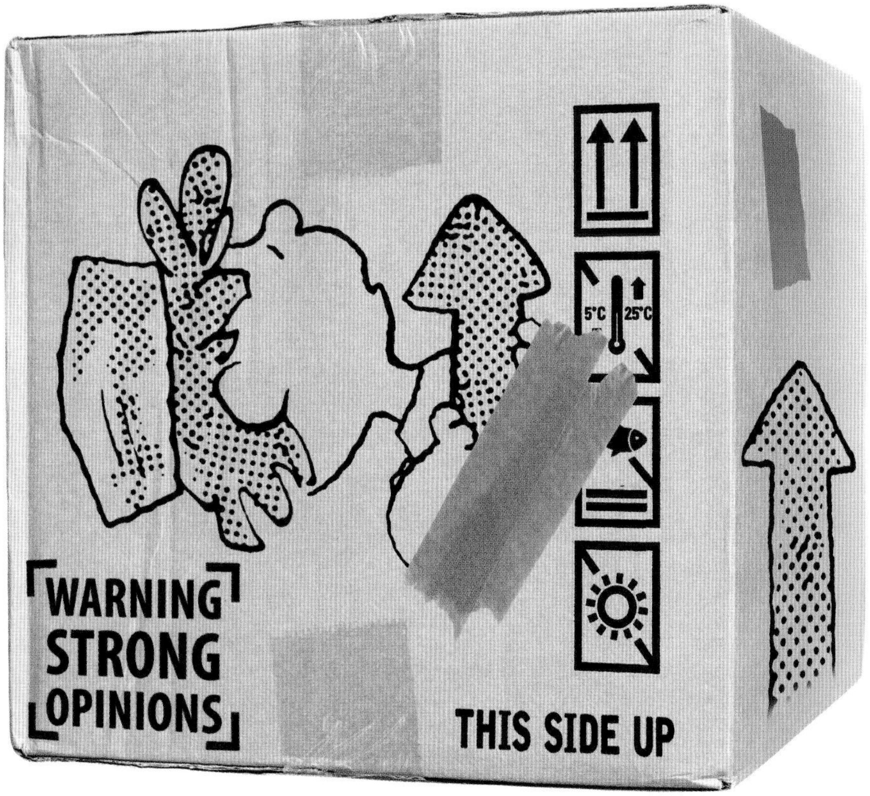
5°C
25°C
WARNING STRONG OPINIONS
THIS SIDE UP

ABOVE: *Design by Cameron + Co*

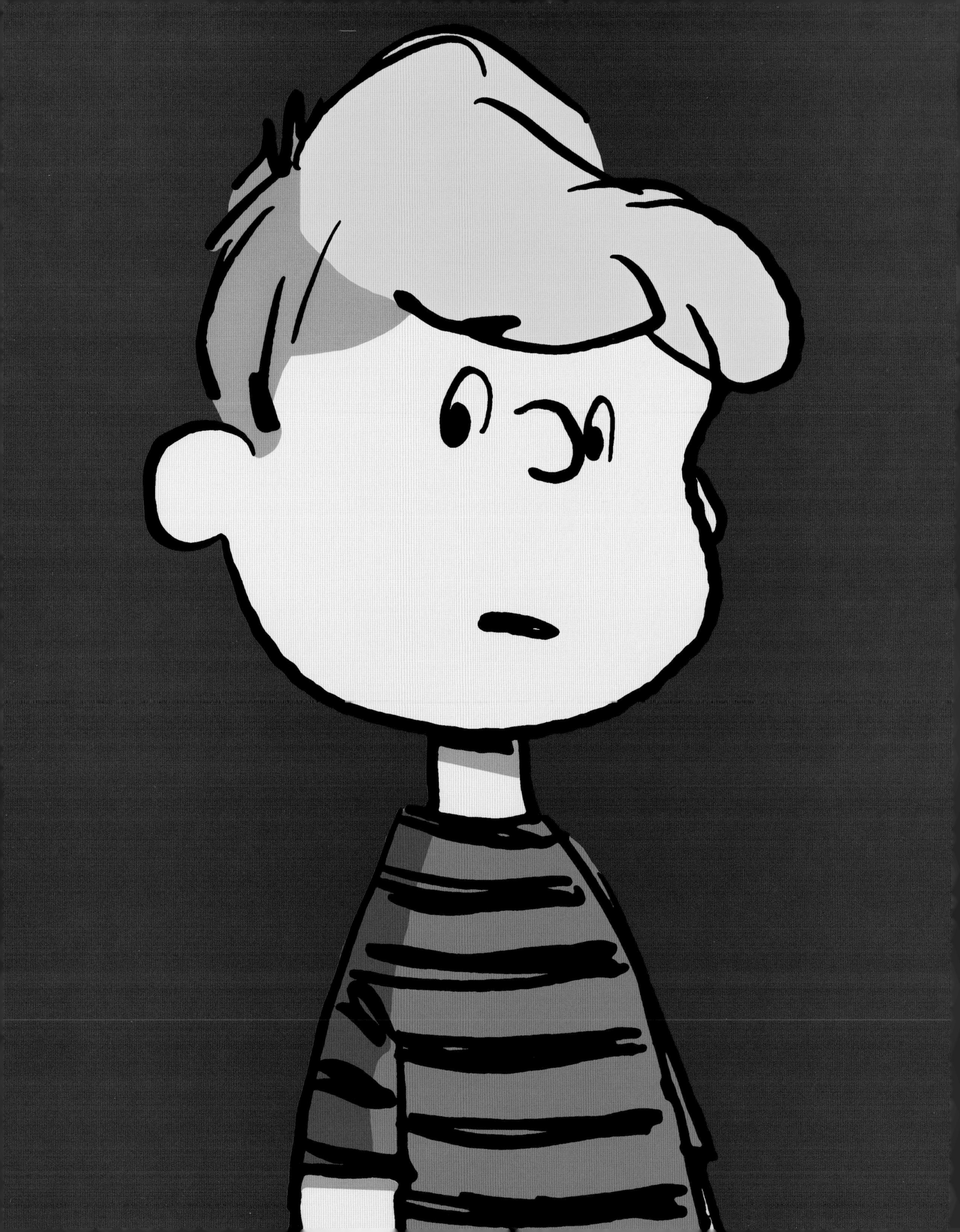

# SCHROEDER

FIRST APPEARANCE
05/30/1951

Much like his idol, Beethoven, Schroeder develops his love of the piano from childhood and devotes his life to his music. Charlie Brown, Patty, and Shermy first meet Schroeder when he is a baby and watch in fascination as the precocious child shows an innate skill with his toy piano and an endless fascination with the life and music of Ludwig van Beethoven, whose birthday, he gladly reminds you, occurs on December 16. While his friends don't share Schroeder's enthusiasm for Beethoven, they appreciate his talent and dedication.

Lucy, in particular, is very fond of Schroeder and spends countless hours perched beside his piano listening to music and speculating on what it would be like to be married to a famous musician. He tries his best to brush her off so that he can focus on his music, but deep down he enjoys her company—and knows that she might feed his piano to the Kite-Eating Tree if provoked. Snoopy, too, is a fan of Schroeder's music and expresses his enjoyment through dance.

When he's not practicing his piano, Schroeder can be found on the baseball diamond, playing catcher for Charlie Brown's team. The reliable backstop is a solid hitter and fielder and, more importantly, is always quick to offer words of encouragement to Charlie Brown, no matter how badly they're losing. Whether it's for his musical prowess or his work behind home plate, it's only a matter of time before Schroeder's face ends up on a bubblegum card.

"Schroeder? Well, in the first year I needed a baby," laughed Charles Schulz, when asked about the pint-sized pianist with an appreciation for classic music. "My own children were very small. I'd just bought a toy piano for my daughter Meredith. He had to do something so I had him grow up quickly and play Beethoven."

PEANUTS
by CHARLES M. SCHULZ

"PEANUTS"
HAVE YOU MET SCHROEDER YET, CHARLIE BROWN?
SCHROEDER?! WHO'S HE?
HE LIVES NEXT DOOR...C'MON, I'LL INTRODUCE YOU
HERE HE IS! SAY SOMETHING TO HIM
I DON'T KNOW WHAT TO SAY...
I ALWAYS FEEL SO UNCOMFORTABLE NEAR CHILDREN!
SCHULZ
5/30
Copr. 1951 by United Feature Syndicate, Inc.

PEANUTS
LOOK, SCHROEDER.. THE CATCHER IS SUPPOSED TO BE THE BACKBONE OF THE TEAM..
HOW ABOUT SHOWING A LITTLE SPIRIT? CAN'T YOU YELL A LITTLE OR WHISTLE?!
4-15
"NOCTURNE IN E FLAT MAJOR" BY CHOPIN
GOOD GRIEF!
SCHULZ

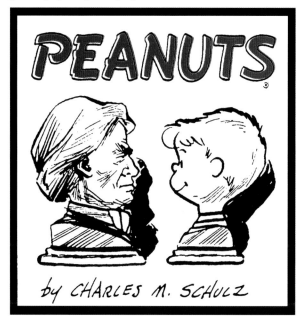

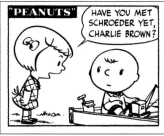

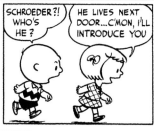

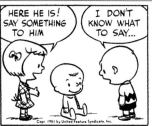

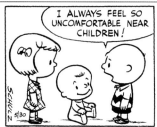

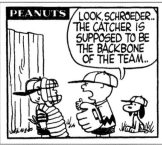

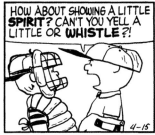

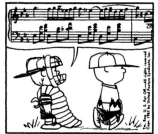

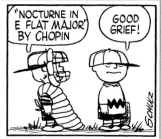

OPPOSITE: *Spot art from strip – Charles M. Schulz* | ABOVE RIGHT: *Spot art from strip – Charles M. Schulz*

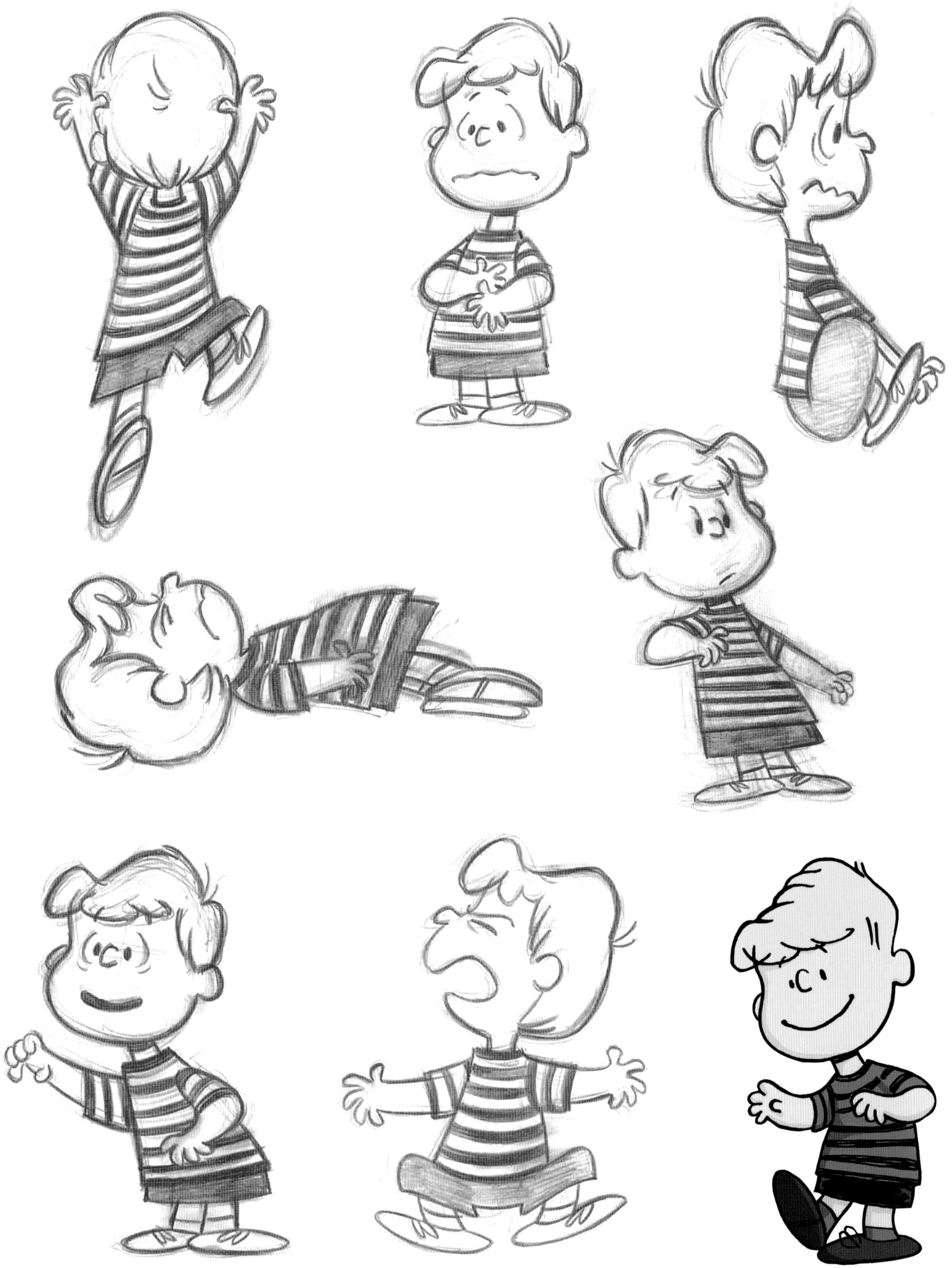

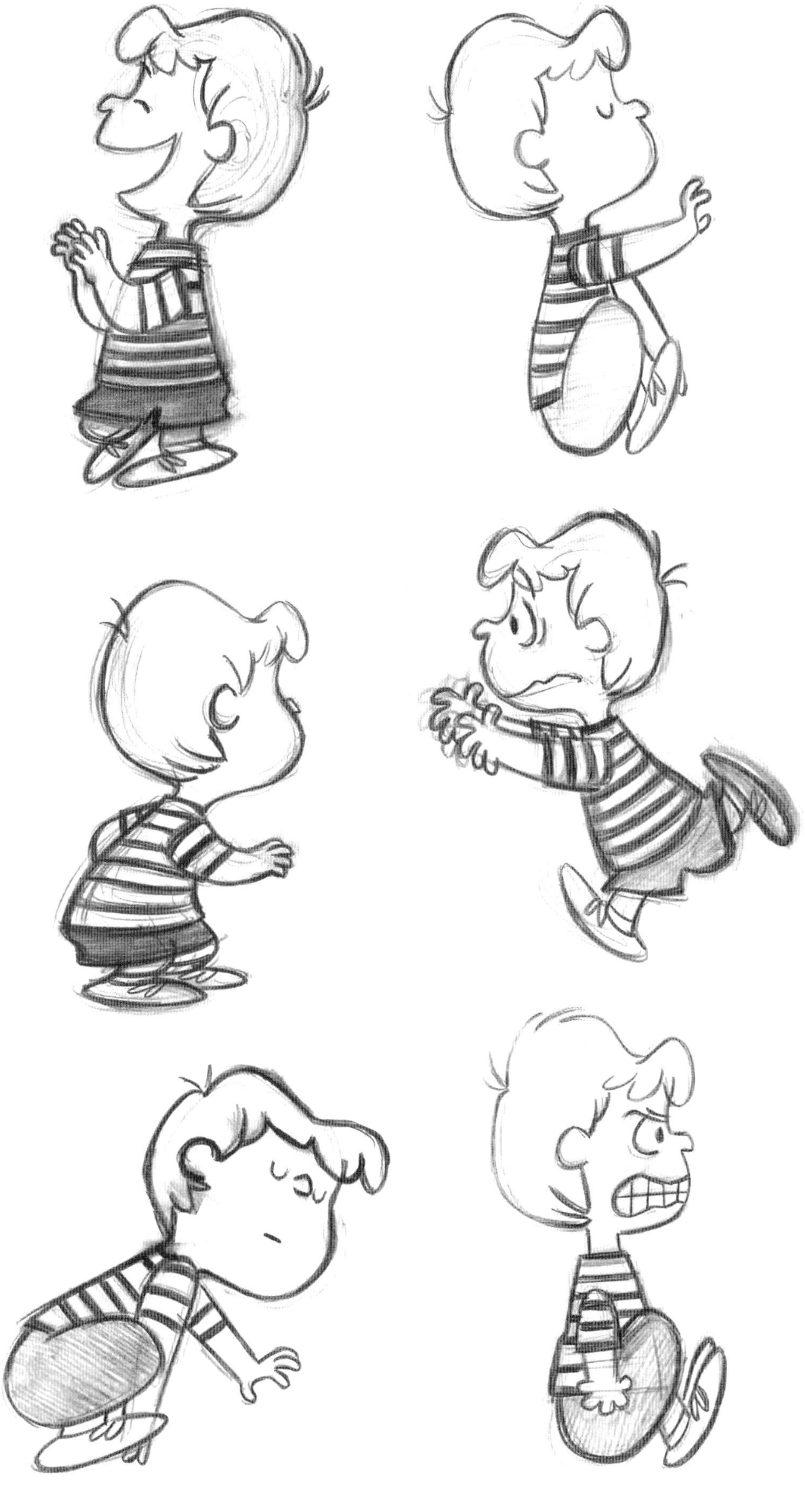

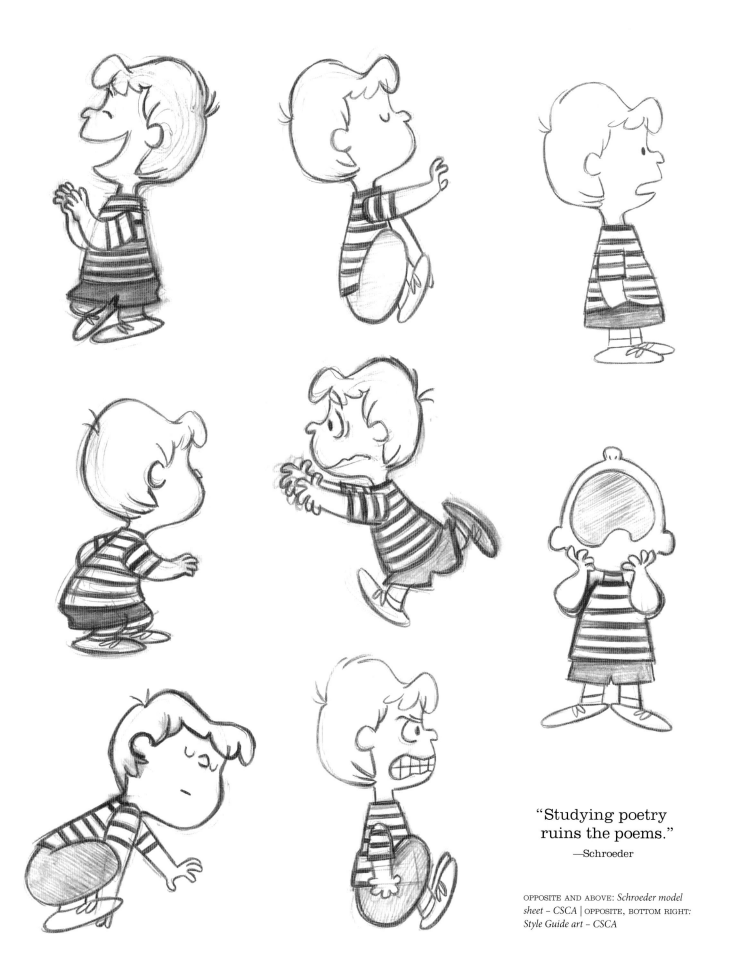

“Studying poetry ruins the poems.”

—Schroeder

OPPOSITE AND ABOVE: *Schroeder model sheet – CSCA* | OPPOSITE, BOTTOM RIGHT: *Style Guide art – CSCA*

# SCHROEDER'S PIANO

FIRST APPEARANCE
09/24/1951

Schroeder could play his piano before he could talk, and he was a gifted performer from day one—when Charlie Brown introduced him to his very first toy piano! It's rare to find the young musician away from his prized piano, which often sports an imposing bust of Schroeder's favorite composer, Ludwig van Beethoven.

**"Musicians have a hard life."**
**—Schroeder**

Schroeder's most ardent fans are Lucy, who is hopelessly in love with Schroeder and hopes to marry him one day, and Snoopy, who has been both moved to tears and inspired to dance by Schroder's music.

Sometimes the music that Schroeder plays takes on a life of its own—literally! The staff and musical notes emanating from his piano can support the weight of a full-grown beagle, can chase someone from the room, and can even be physically removed by Schroeder's listeners. Not even Beethoven could accomplish that!

Schroeder was an early favorite of Charles Schulz, but as the strip's cast expanded, Schulz scaled back on the young musician's appearances at his famed piano. "Well, you see, [Schroeder has been absent lately because] I don't listen to music as much as I used to. When I go to a symphony or a concert, though, I'll be inspired to do something about Schroeder. I kind of like Schroeder. He's fairly down to earth, but he has his problems, too. He has to play on painted black piano keys, and he thinks Beethoven was the first President of the United States."

2

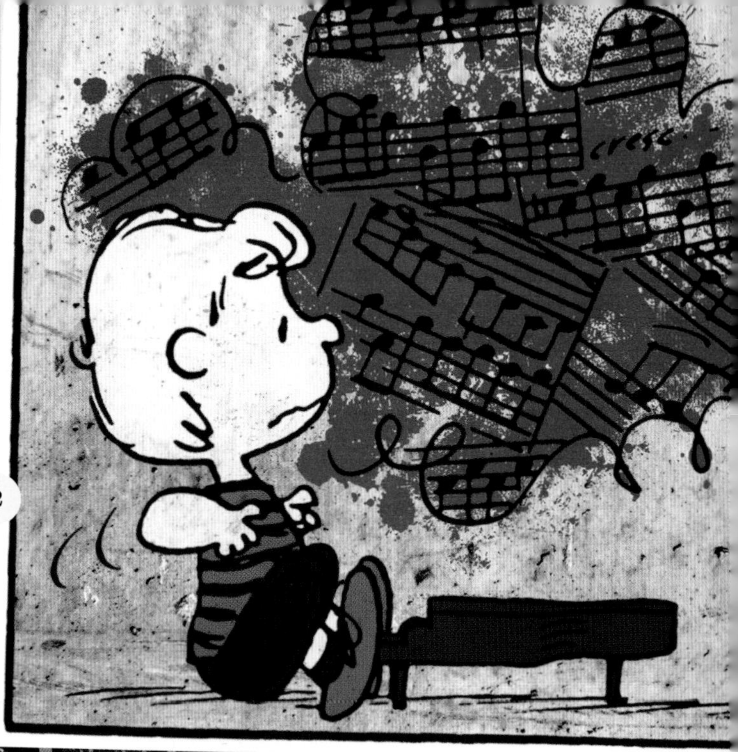

1

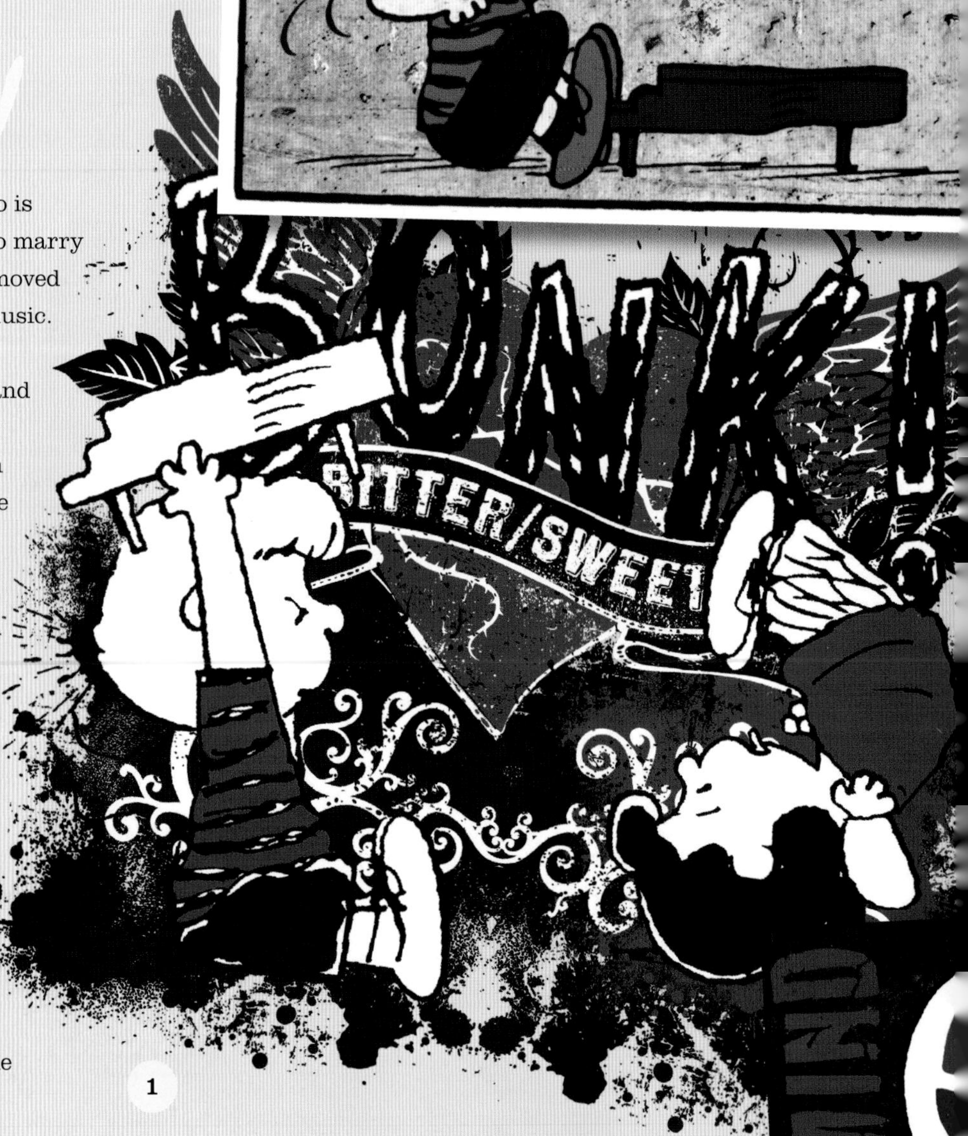

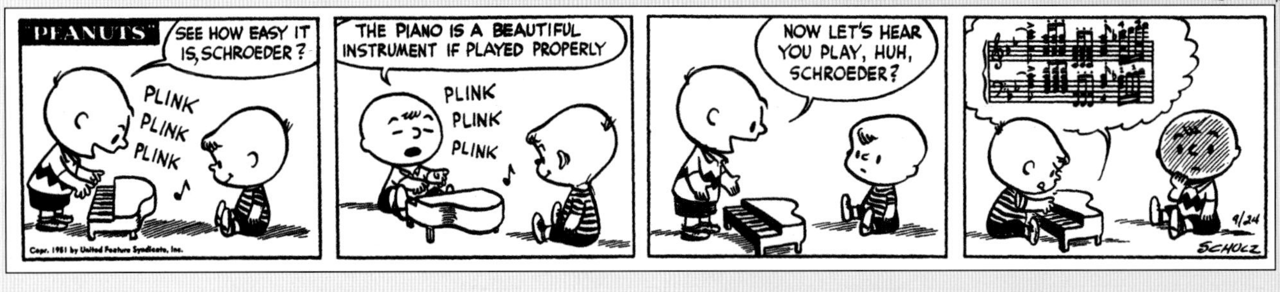
PEANUTS
SEE HOW EASY IT IS, SCHROEDER?
PLINK PLINK PLINK
Copr. 1951 by United Feature Syndicate, Inc.
THE PIANO IS A BEAUTIFUL INSTRUMENT IF PLAYED PROPERLY
PLINK PLINK PLINK
NOW LET'S HEAR YOU PLAY, HUH, SCHROEDER?
9/24
SCHULZ

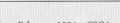

*1, 2, and 7: Style Guide art – CSCA; 3:* Electric Company *magazine cover, published by Children's Television Workshop, February 1984 – CSCA; 4, 5, and 6:* Lucy Loves Schroeder, Happy Beethoven's Birthday *and* Pomp and Circumstance, Peanuts *Digital Editions – CSCA*

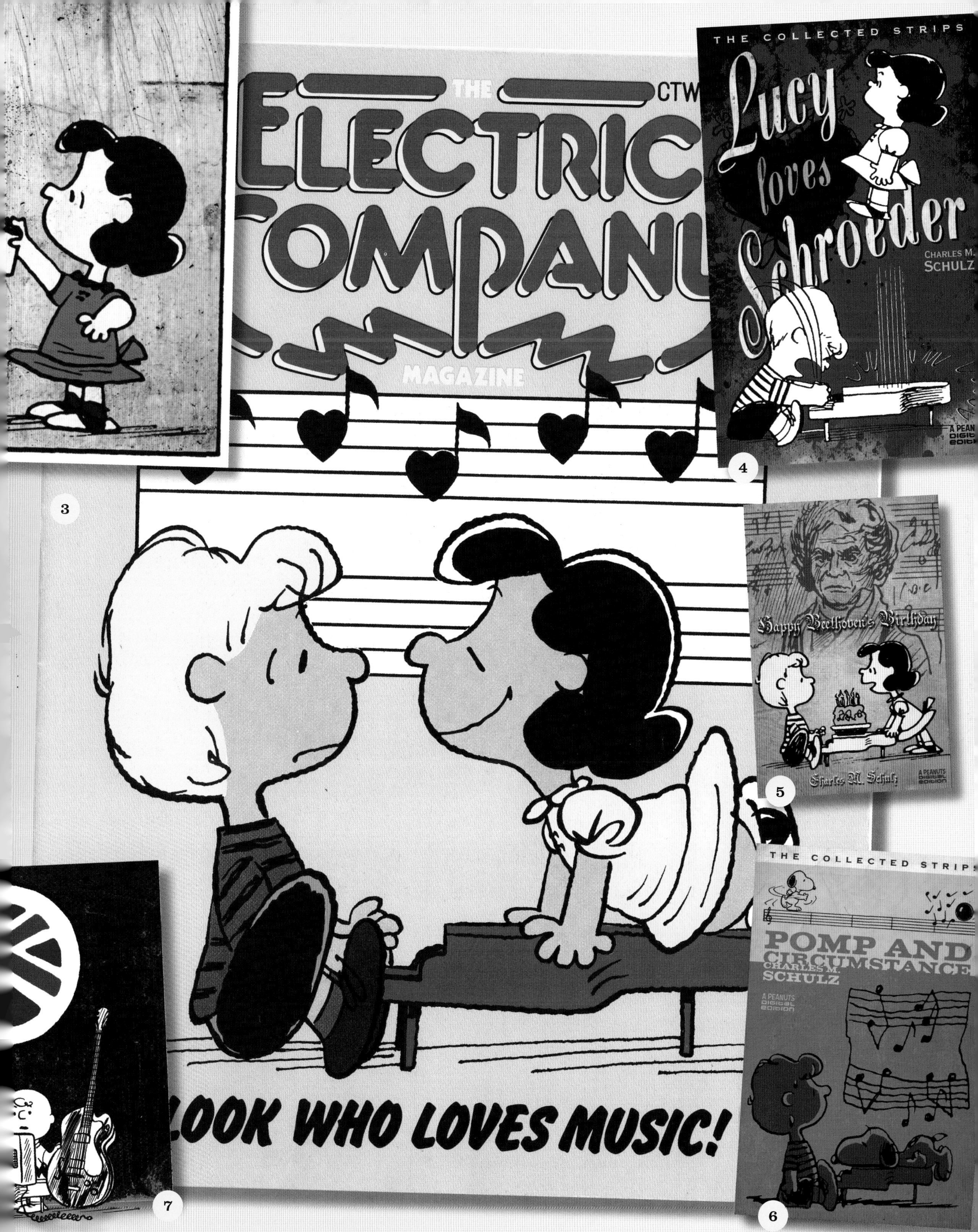
THE
CTW
ELECTRIC COMPANY
MAGAZINE
LOOK WHO LOVES MUSIC!
THE COLLECTED STRIPS
Lucy loves Schroeder
CHARLES M. SCHULZ
Happy Beethoven's Birthday
Charles M. Schulz
A PEANUTS DIGITAL EDITION
THE COLLECTED STRIPS
POMP AND CIRCUMSTANCE
CHARLES M. SCHULZ
A PEANUTS DIGITAL EDITION

3

4

5

6

7

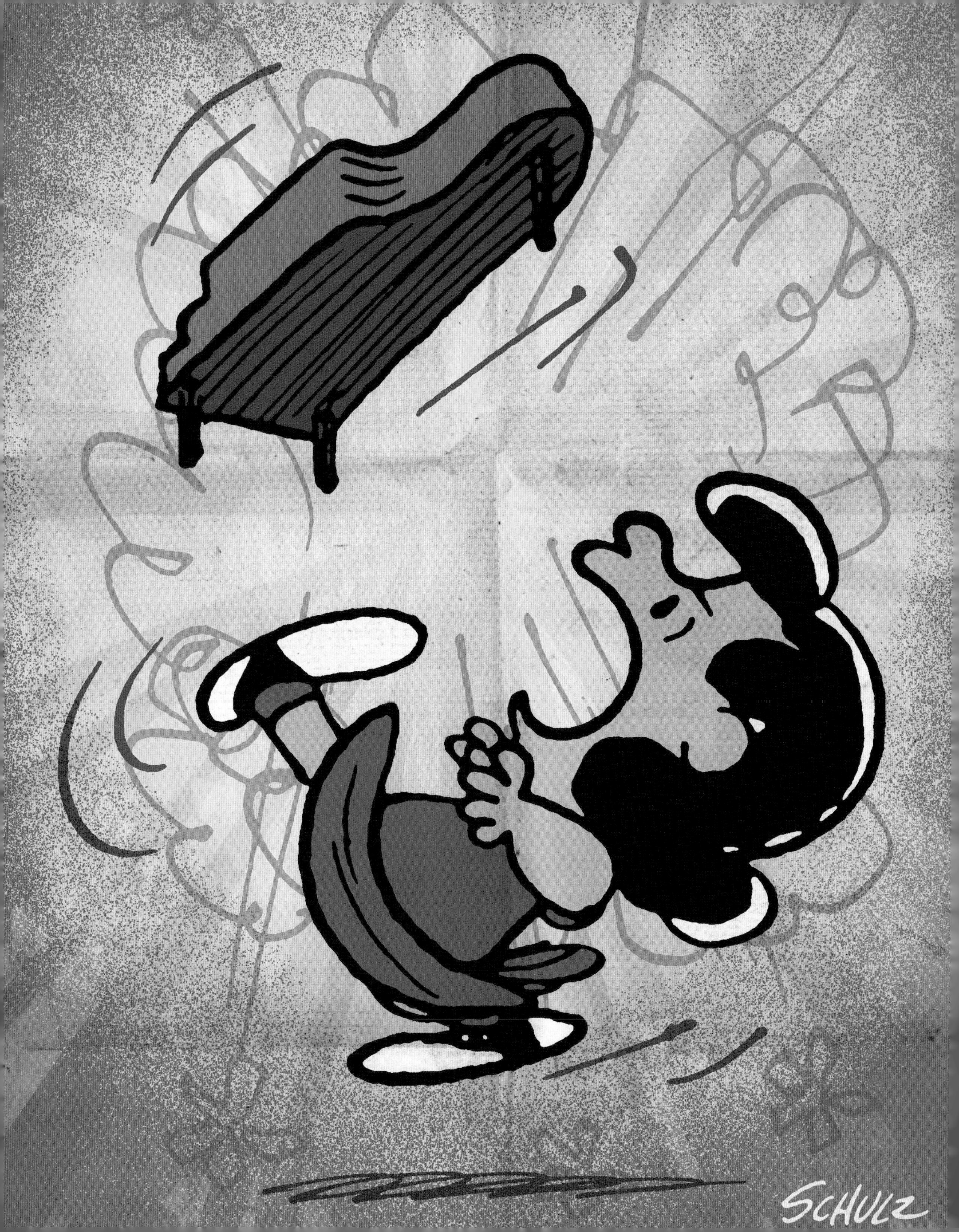
SCHULZ

# LUCY VAN PELT

FIRST APPEARANCE
03/03/1952

A natural-born fussbudget, Lucy Van Pelt is a real take-charge kind of girl. And if she's not in charge yet, just give her a few minutes.

Lucy is unwavering in her point of view and never hesitates to share it with anyone within earshot—and that's a long range, given Lucy's booming voice. She gladly offers an unsolicited, deep-seated opinion on any subject and is unwavering in her beliefs. While she gives these pronouncements freely, her more nuanced, insightful observations are reserved for the clients who visit her Psychiatric Booth, where she dispenses the best diagnosis a nickel can buy.

**"I oughta knock your block off!"**
**—Lucy**

Although Lucy is quick to point out the faults of others, she is not without her own foibles. As the right fielder on Charlie Brown's baseball team, she rarely pays attention to the game, unless she finds an opportunity to yell at Charlie Brown. The team's catcher, Schroeder, is the subject of Lucy's unrequited crush, and she is often seen perched beside his piano, hoping in vain to win his affection. Schroeder is one of the few people in Lucy's life who doesn't concede to her whims, which may explain her fascination with him.

Her closest friends are Patty, Violet, and Charlie Brown, even though they are often on the receiving end of her criticism. Lucy spends much of her free time in the company of her younger brothers, Linus and Rerun. She seems to give up on shaping Linus in her image, but still holds out hope for Rerun. After all, when she's Queen of the World, she'll need someone to help keep the castle in order. Within a few years of Lucy's introduction, Patty and Violet were relegated to supporting character status, and it was clear that Lucy provided the perfect counterpoint to Charlie Brown's wishy-washiness. While Charlie Brown shared many of Charles Schulz's neuroses, Lucy came from a very different part of his personality. "Lucy comes from that part of me that's capable of saying mean and sarcastic things, which is not a good trait to have, so Lucy gives me a good outlet. But each character has a weakness, and Lucy's weakness is Schroeder. With Schroeder, even Lucy has moments of sentimentality, like the time she asked him why he never sent her flowers and he said, 'Because I don't like you.' And she answered, 'The flowers wouldn't care.'"

LUCY
OF THE PEANUTS COMIC STRIP

"PEANUTS"
ONE, ONE, ONE,
?
ONE, ONE, ONE,
TWO, LUCY! TWO!
TWO, TWO, TWO...
3-3
SCHULZ

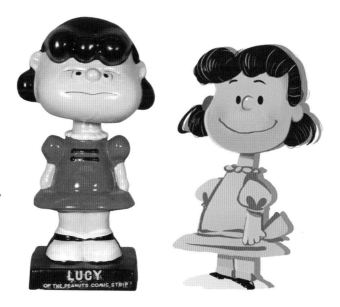

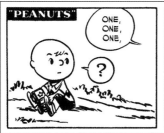

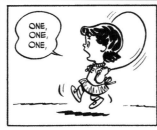

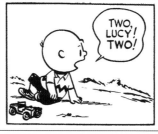

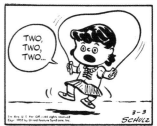

OPPOSITE: *Boom!* Peanuts, *Issue #30, Boom! Studios comic Book cover – CSCA* | ABOVE LEFT: *Lucy bobblehead produced by LEGO®, 1959 – CMSM;* ABOVE RIGHT: *Lucy art – CSCA*

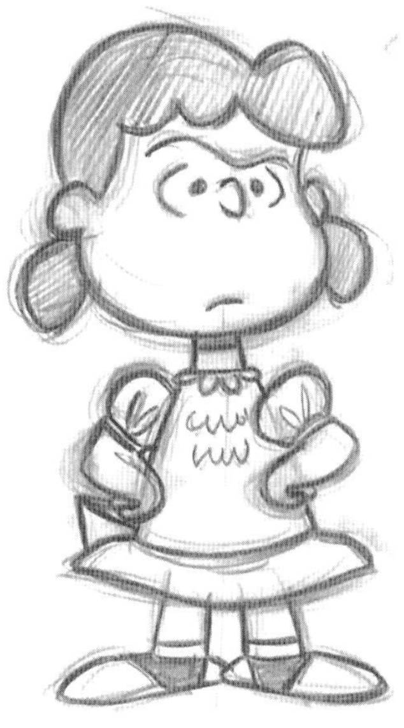

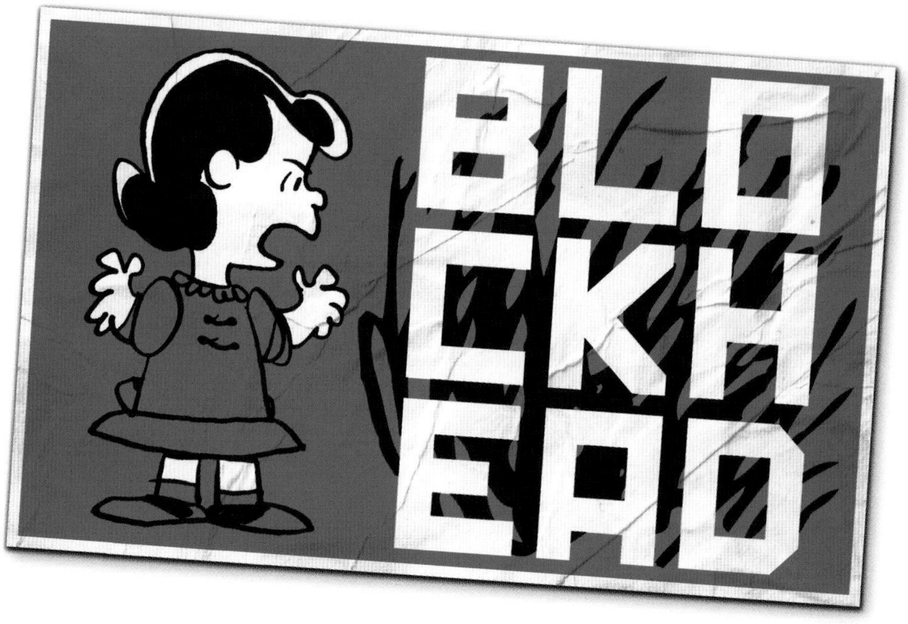
BLO
CKH
EAD

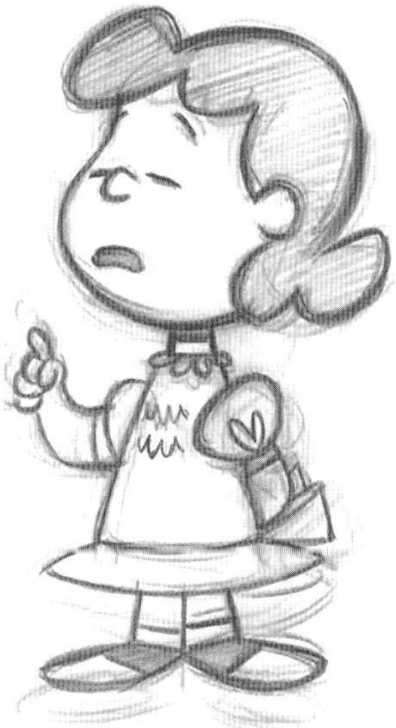

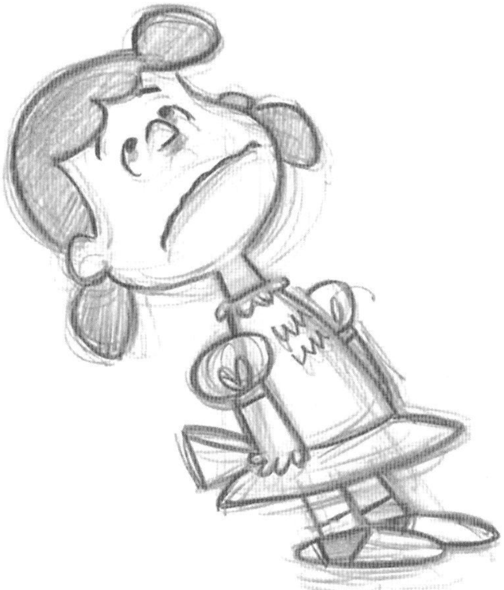

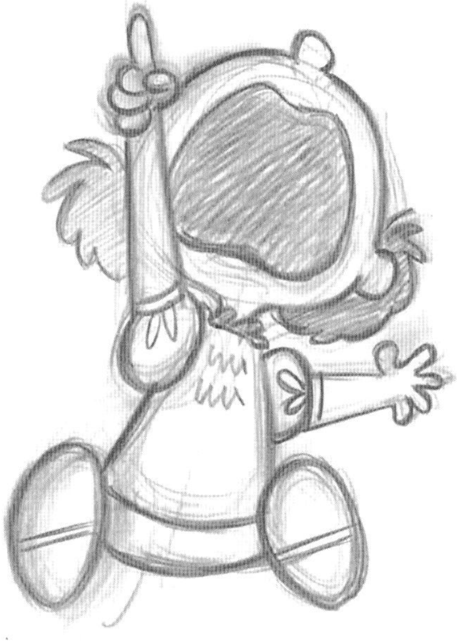

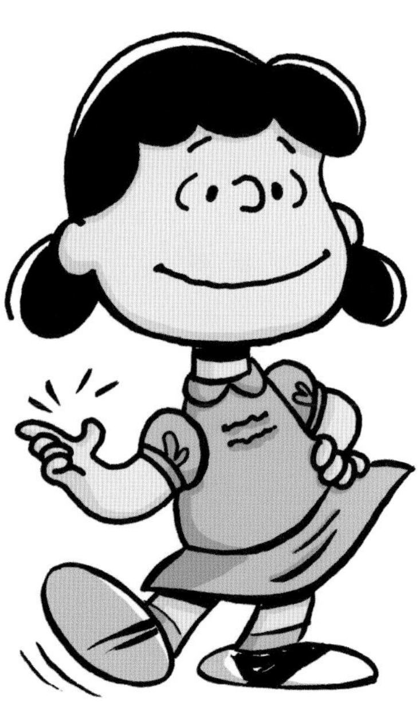

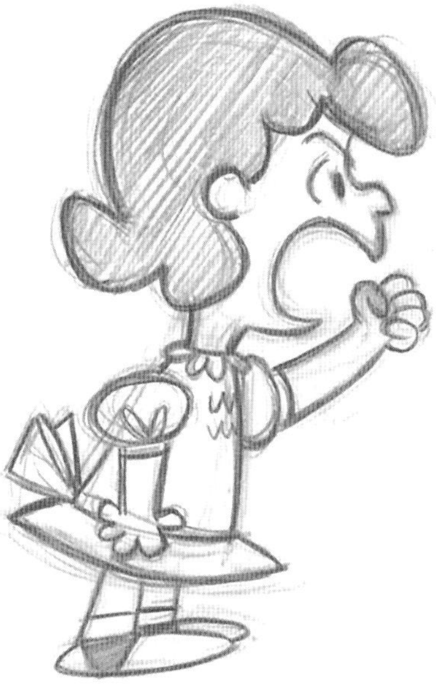

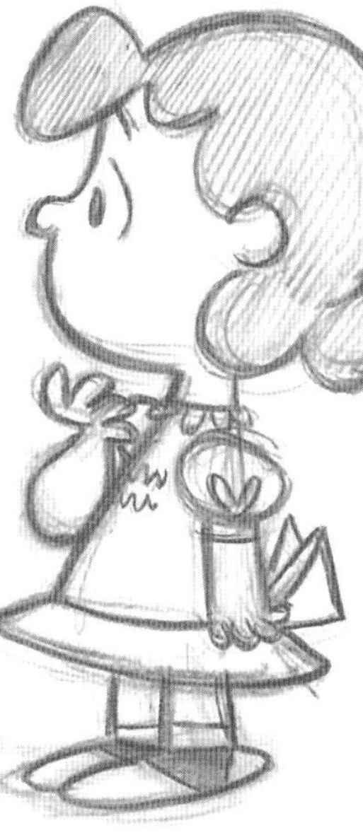

"A disarming smile doesn't stand a chance against my total-warfare frown!" —Lucy Van Pelt

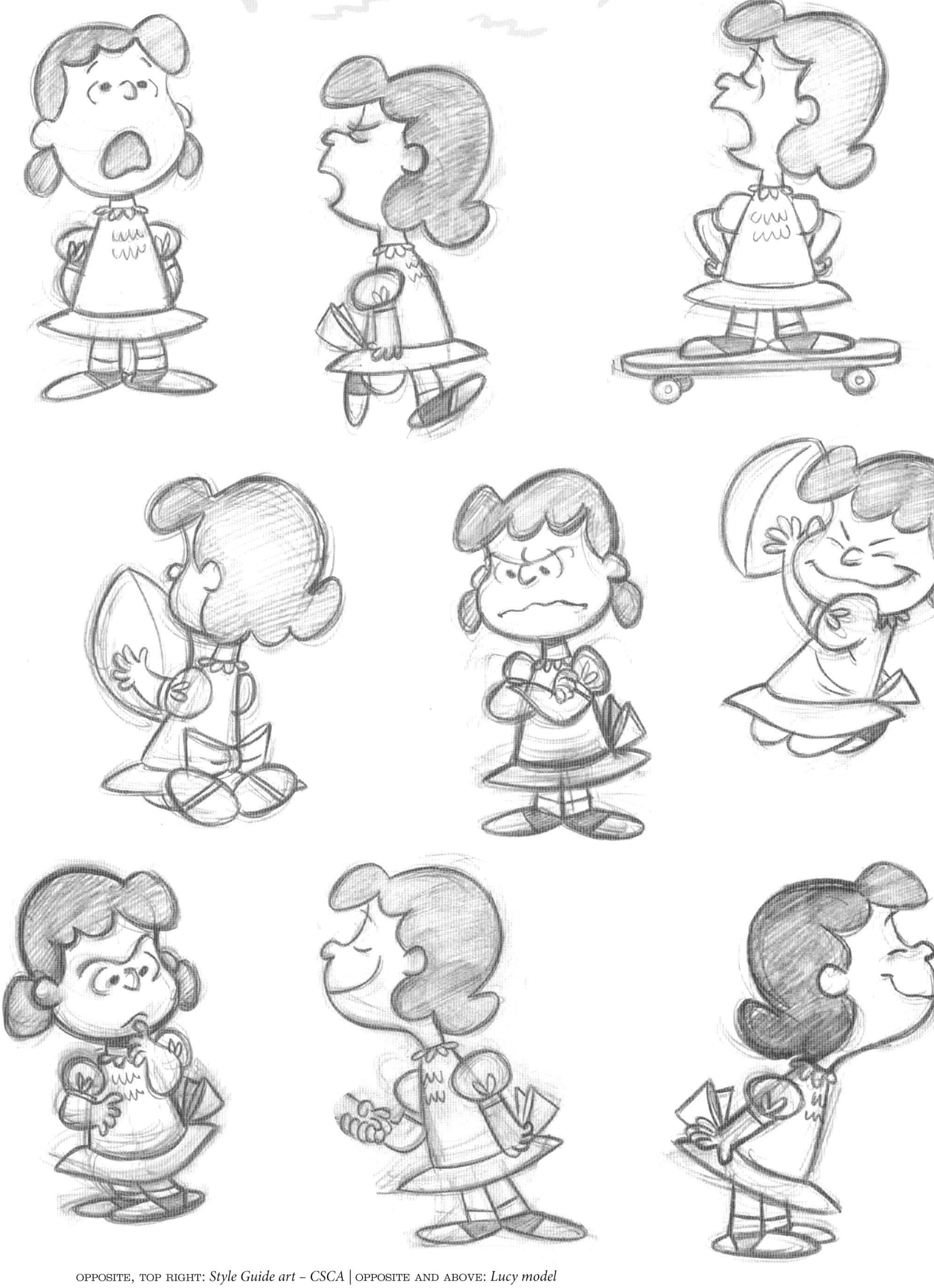

OPPOSITE, TOP RIGHT: *Style Guide art – CSCA* | OPPOSITE AND ABOVE: *Lucy model sheet – CSCA* | OPPOSITE, BOTTOM LEFT: *Style Guide art – CSCA*

# The Fussbudget

From the very beginning, Lucy has almost always gotten her way—but when she doesn't, look out! Lucy has raised tantrum-throwing and fussing to an art form, and has been named "Little Miss Fussbudget" by an expert panel of judges every single year that she's been in the running.

Her outspoken personality makes her a terror to her friends, but Charles Schulz admitted that her fussy ways provided him with endless story opportunities. "Linus, Charlie Brown, and Snoopy, and I like Lucy because of the fact that she provides me with so many ideas. I don't necessarily approve of her personality, but I really like Linus and Charlie Brown."

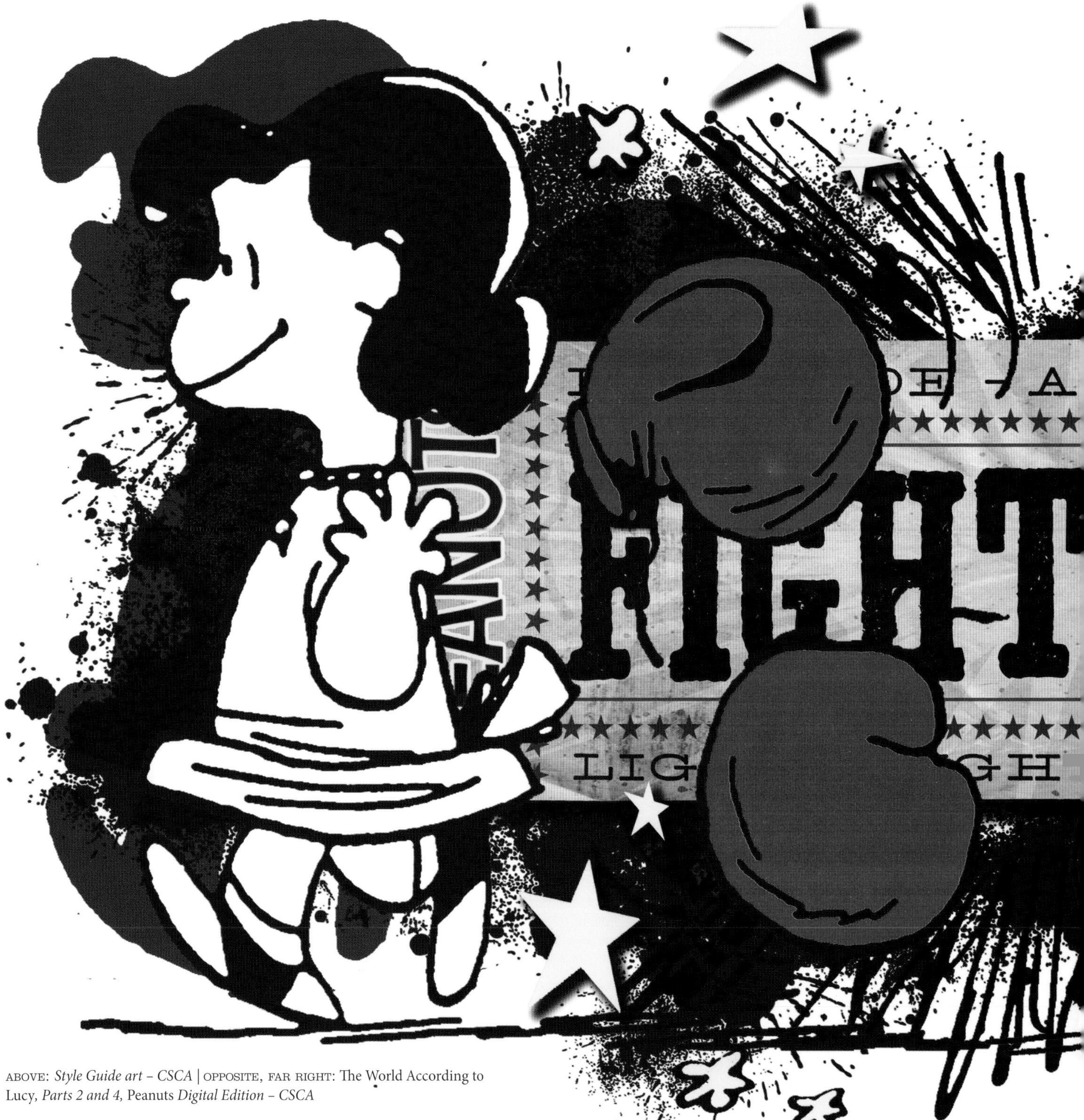

ABOVE: *Style Guide art – CSCA* | OPPOSITE, FAR RIGHT: The World According to Lucy, *Parts 2 and 4,* Peanuts *Digital Edition – CSCA*

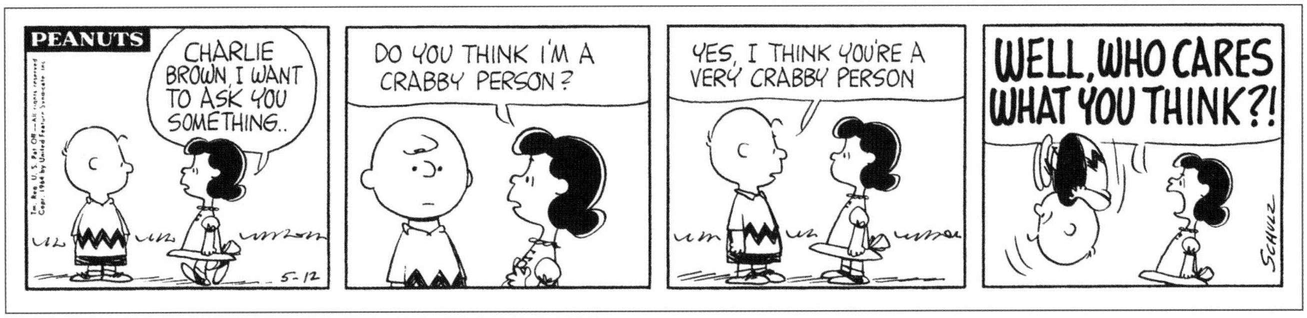
PEANUTS
CHARLIE BROWN, I WANT TO ASK YOU SOMETHING..
DO YOU THINK I'M A CRABBY PERSON?
YES, I THINK YOU'RE A VERY CRABBY PERSON
WELL, WHO CARES WHAT YOU THINK?!
SCHULZ

"By golly, nobody better get in my way today."

—Lucy Van Pelt

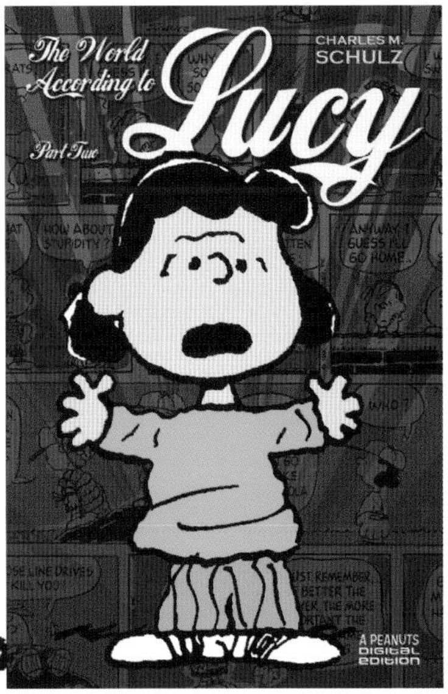
The World According to Lucy
Part Two
CHARLES M. SCHULZ
A PEANUTS DIGITAL EDITION

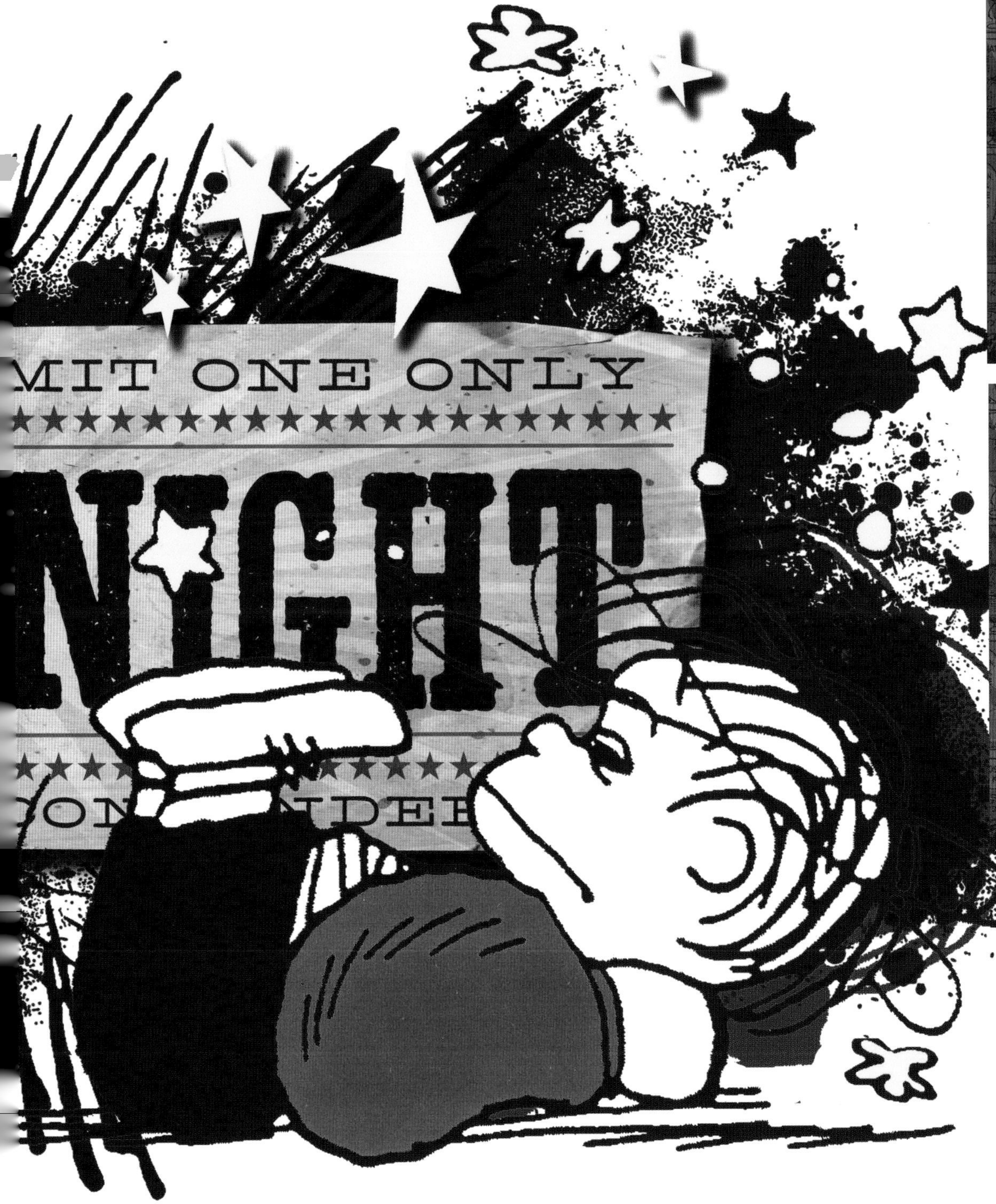
MIT ONE ONLY
NIGHT

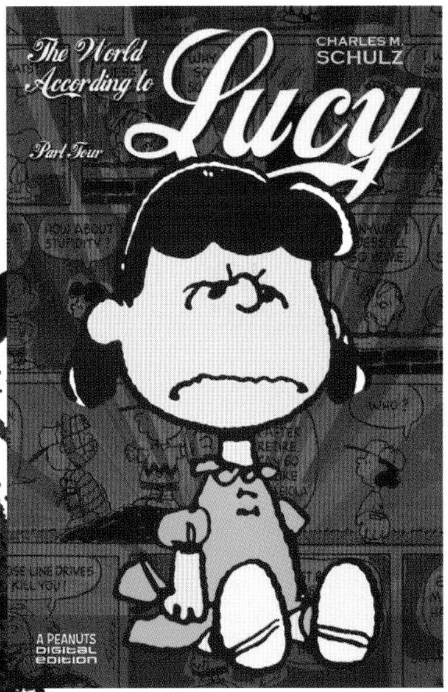
The World According to Lucy
Part Four
CHARLES M. SCHULZ
A PEANUTS DIGITAL EDITION

# THE QUEEN BEE

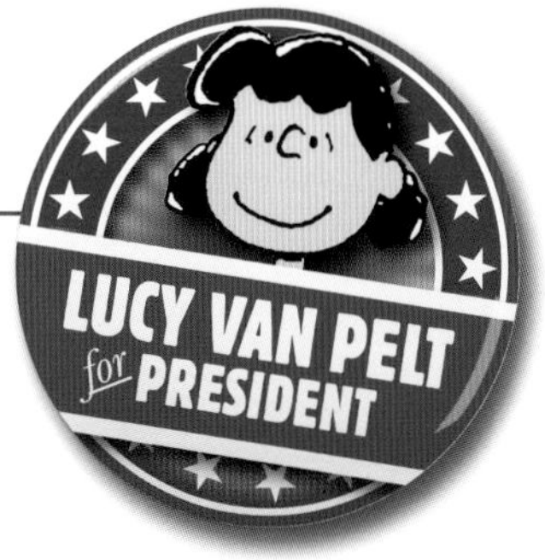
LUCY VAN PELT
for PRESIDENT

1

The world's a mess, but don't worry—Lucy's here to fix it! She may be starting small by bossing around her parents, little brothers, friends, and classmates, but someday Lucy plans to be Queen, so everyone had better get used to obeying her commands.

"Now about Lucy being so mean," said Charles Schulz. "She is mean first because it is funny, and because it just follows the standard comic-strip pattern—that the supposedly weak people in the world are funny when they dominate the supposedly strong people."

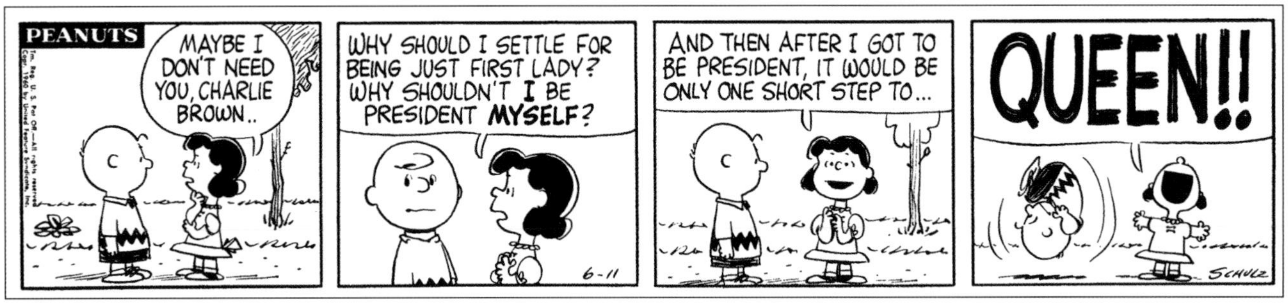
PEANUTS
MAYBE I DON'T NEED YOU, CHARLIE BROWN..
WHY SHOULD I SETTLE FOR BEING JUST FIRST LADY? WHY SHOULDN'T I BE PRESIDENT MYSELF?
6-11
AND THEN AFTER I GOT TO BE PRESIDENT, IT WOULD BE ONLY ONE SHORT STEP TO...
QUEEN!!
SCHULZ

2

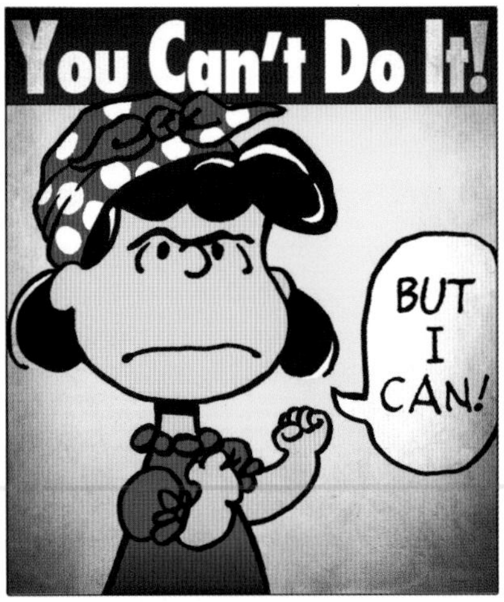
You Can't Do It!
BUT I CAN!

3

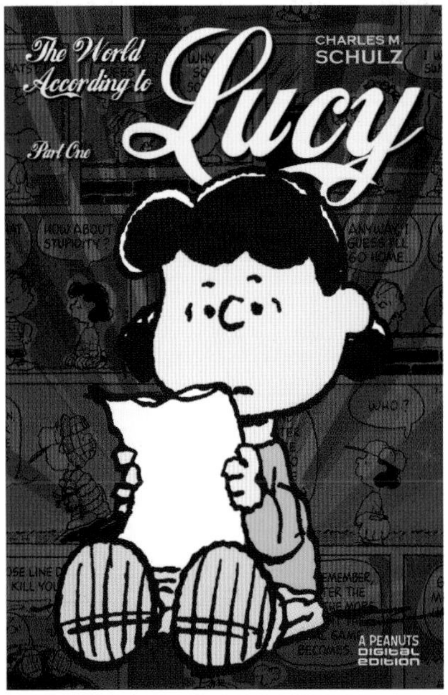
The World According to Lucy
CHARLES M. SCHULZ
Part One
A PEANUTS DIGITAL EDITION

4

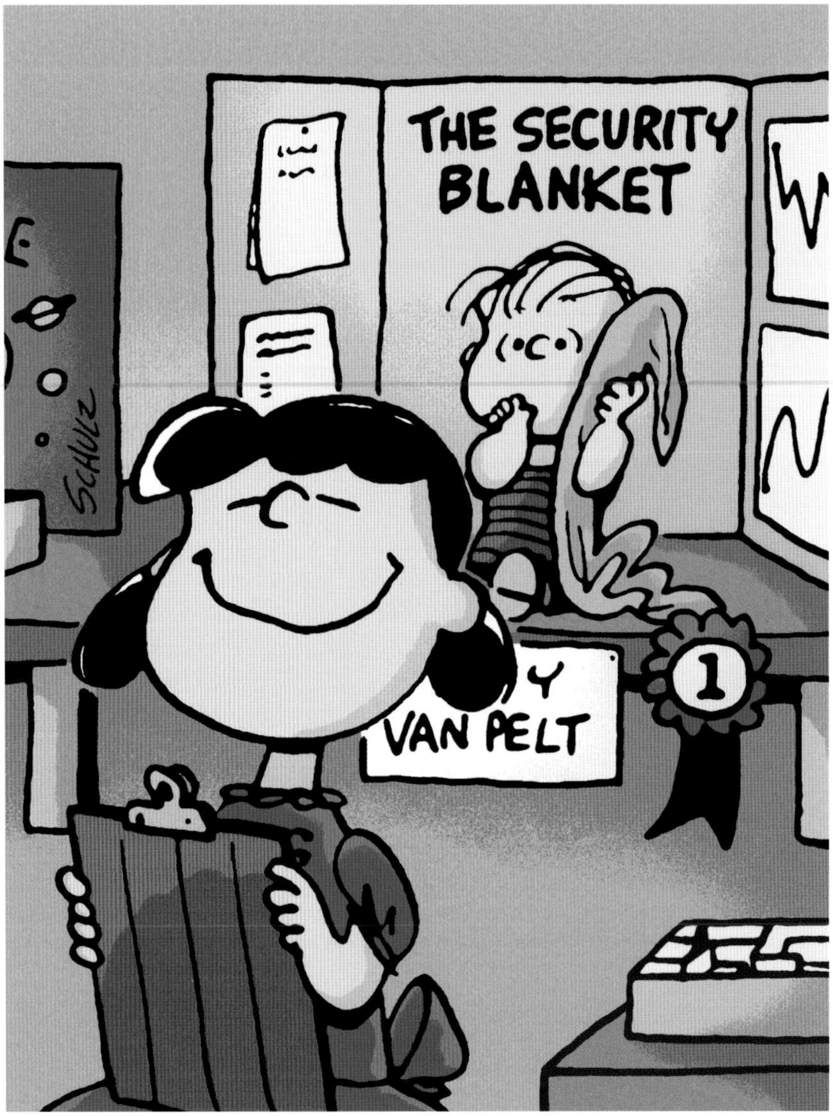
THE SECURITY BLANKET
VAN PELT
1
SCHULZ

*1: Style Guide art – PW; 2: Style Guide Art – CSCA; 3:* The World According to Lucy, *Part 1,* Peanuts *Digital Edition – CSCA; 4:* Peanuts, *Issue #24, Boom! comic book cover – CSCA | Opposite: Style Guide art – CSCA*

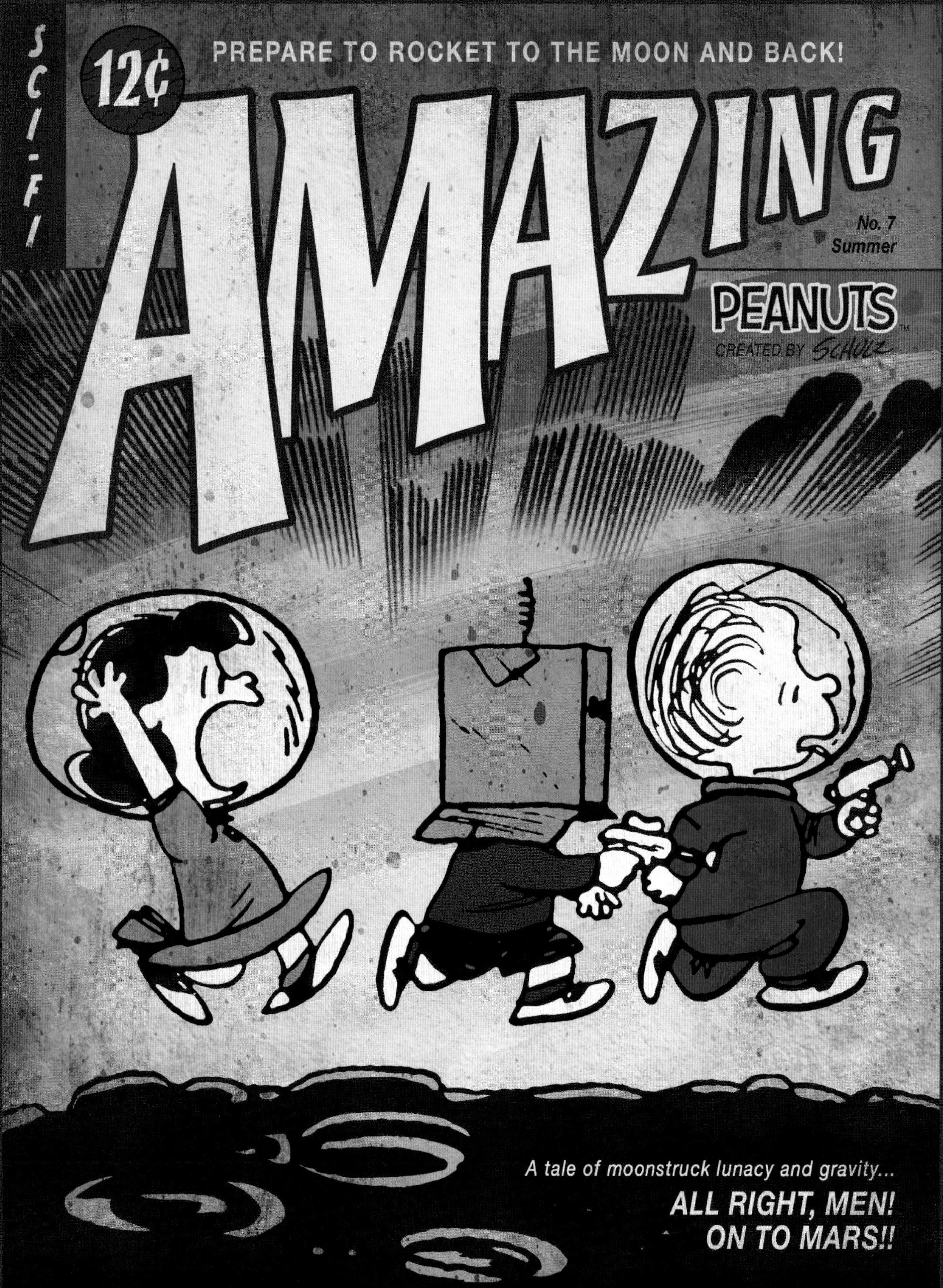
SCI-FI
12¢
PREPARE TO ROCKET TO THE MOON AND BACK!
AMAZING
No. 7
Summer
PEANUTS
CREATED BY SCHULZ
A tale of moonstruck lunacy and gravity...
ALL RIGHT, MEN!
ON TO MARS!!

# LUCY'S PSYCHIATRIC BOOTH

FIRST APPEARANCE
03/27/1959

Most kids have lemonade stands, but that's too pedestrian for the ambitious Lucy Van Pelt. Sensing a need for good, practical advice for the kids in her neighborhood, she opens her own Psychiatric Booth. For the very reasonable cost of five cents per session, she diagnoses her clients with ailments ranging from ailurophasia, the fear of cats, to pantophobia, the fear of everything.

Lucy's advice is occasionally thoughtful and profound, but for the most part, she offers very blunt, direct criticism of her clients. When Charlie Brown confesses that he is suffering from feelings of deep depression, the diagnosis is straight and to the point: "Snap out of it! Five cents, please."

**"I'm thinking of starting a discussion group . . . people would come from all over to listen to me."**
**— Lucy Van Pelt**

Charles Schulz didn't recall his exact inspiration for Lucy's famed Psychiatric Booth, but wasn't surprised that it resonated with his readers. "Five-cent psychiatry? I can't remember when I started Lucy doing that or why. Maybe it was because in our society we all need somewhere we can go and talk to somebody for an hour for just a nickel. There might be fewer dangerous people on the streets."

*1: Peanuts, Issue #16, Boom! Studios comic book cover – CSCA | 2, and 5: Psychiatric Help, Volumes One and Two, and The World According to Lucy, Peanuts Digital Editions – CSCA; 3: Ms. magazine cover, published by Ms. Magazine Corp., 1976 – CMSM; 4: Saturday Review magazine cover, published by Saturday Review Inc., 1969 – CMSM; 6: Lucy and the Flying Ace, lithograph drawing with water color added, by Charles M. Schulz – CMSM*

2

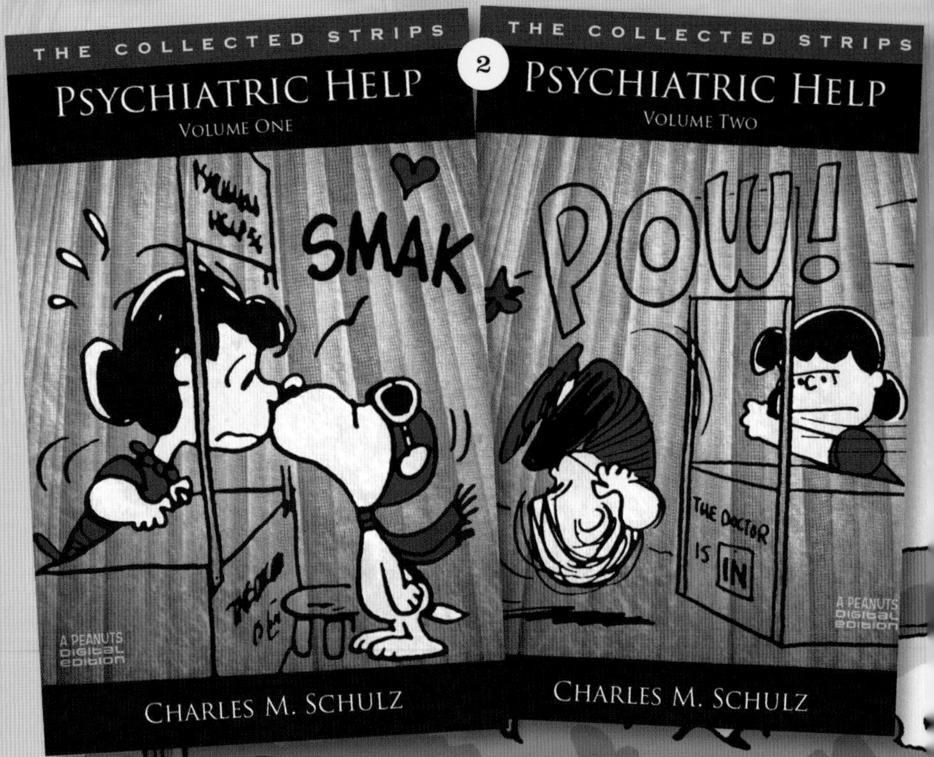
THE COLLECTED STRIPS
PSYCHIATRIC HELP
VOLUME ONE
SMAK
A PEANUTS DIGITAL EDITION
CHARLES M. SCHULZ
THE COLLECTED STRIPS
PSYCHIATRIC HELP
VOLUME TWO
POW!
THE DOCTOR IS IN
A PEANUTS DIGITAL EDITION
CHARLES M. SCHULZ

1

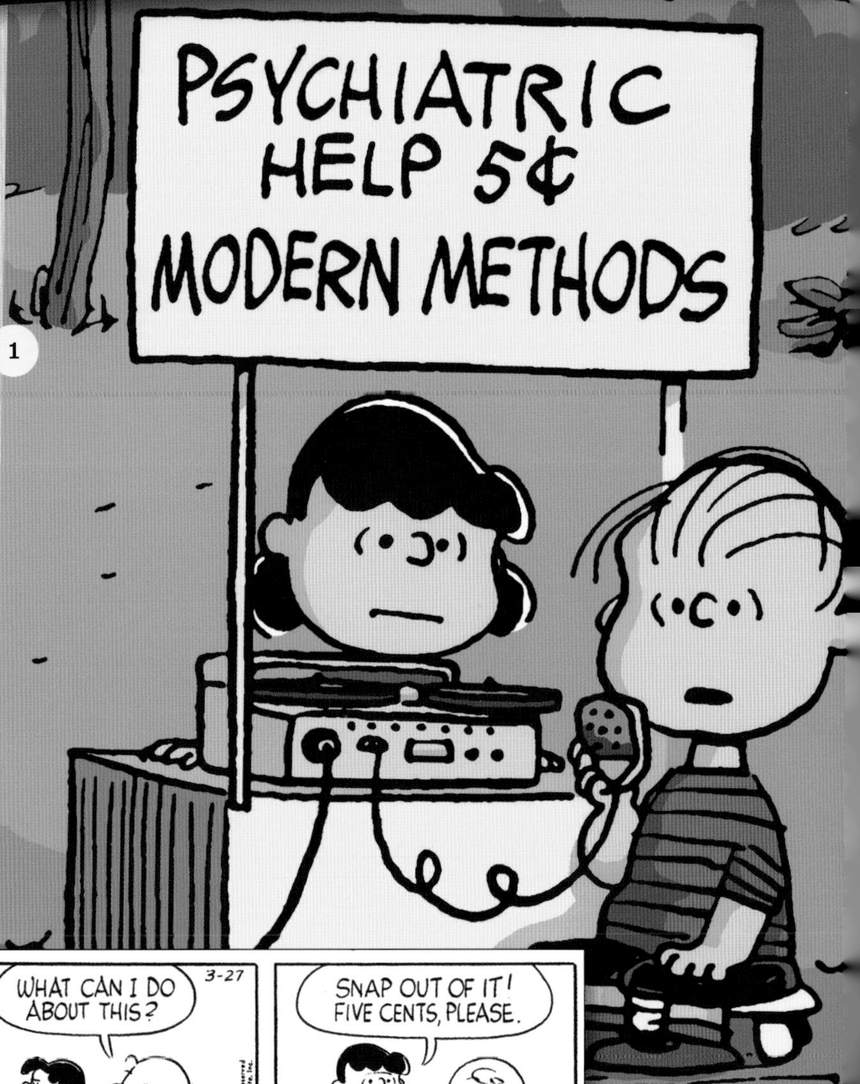
PSYCHIATRIC HELP 5¢
MODERN METHODS

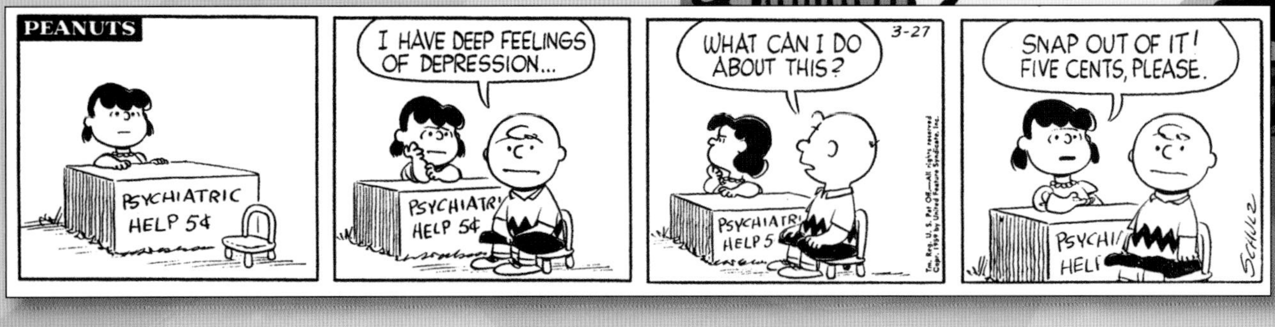
PEANUTS
PSYCHIATRIC HELP 5¢
I HAVE DEEP FEELINGS OF DEPRESSION...
3-27
WHAT CAN I DO ABOUT THIS?
SNAP OUT OF IT! FIVE CENTS, PLEASE.
SCHULZ

3

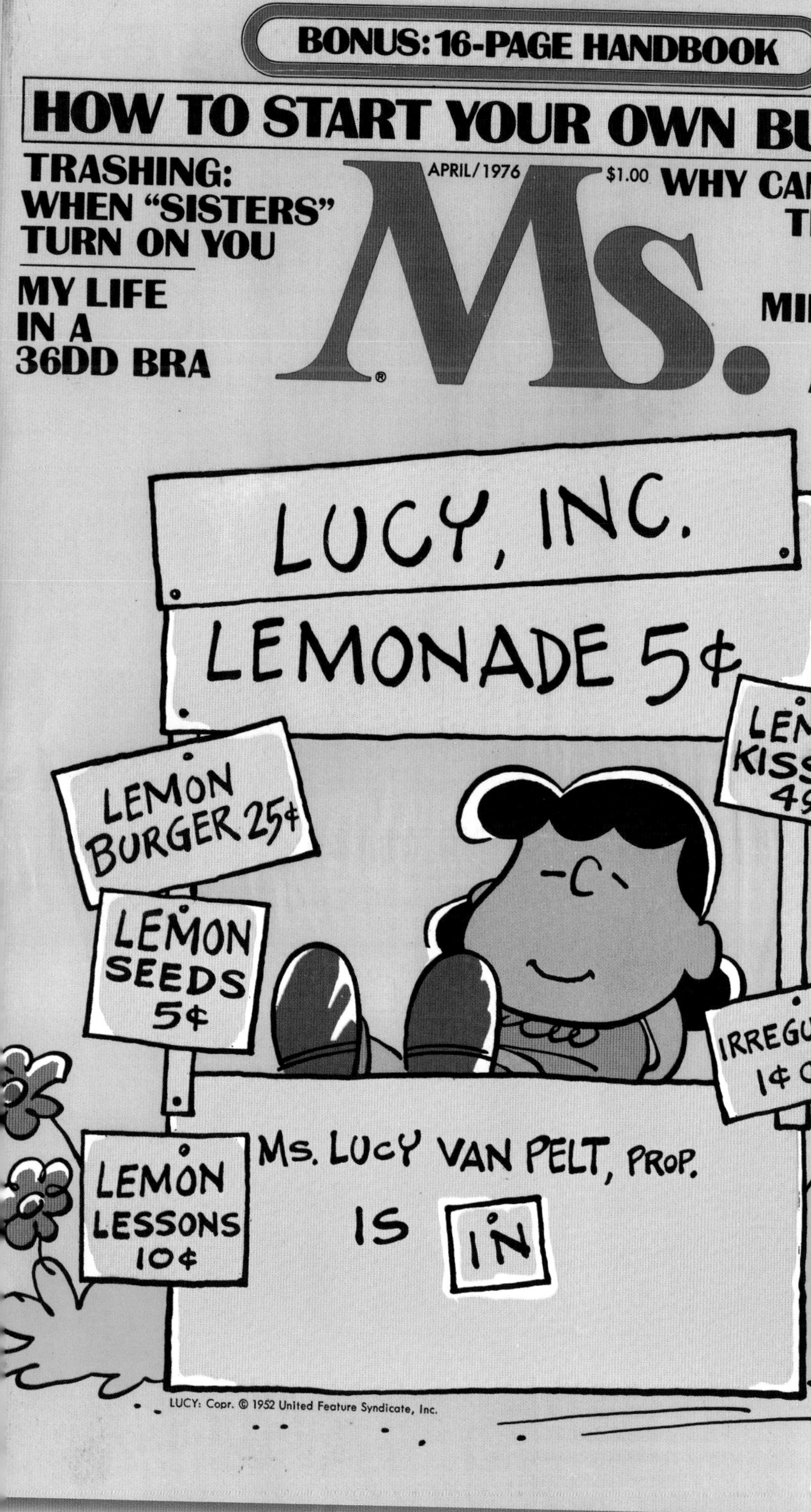
BONUS: 16-PAGE HANDBOOK
HOW TO START YOUR OWN BUS
TRASHING: WHEN "SISTERS" TURN ON YOU
MY LIFE IN A 36DD BRA
APRIL/1976
$1.00
Ms.
WHY CAN'T
THR
LI
MIDD
D
AN
LUCY, INC.
LEMONADE 5¢
LEMON BURGER 25¢
LEMON KISSES 49¢
LEMON SEEDS 5¢
IRREGULAR 1¢ OFF
LEMON LESSONS 10¢
Ms. LUCY VAN PELT, PROP.
IS IN
LUCY: Copr. © 1952 United Feature Syndicate, Inc.

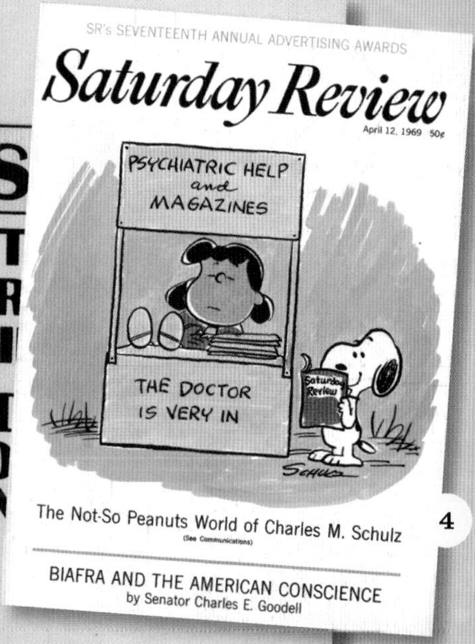
SR's SEVENTEENTH ANNUAL ADVERTISING AWARDS
Saturday Review
April 12, 1969 50¢
PSYCHIATRIC HELP and MAGAZINES
THE DOCTOR IS VERY IN
Saturday Review
SCHULZ
The Not-So Peanuts World of Charles M. Schulz
(See Communications)
BIAFRA AND THE AMERICAN CONSCIENCE
by Senator Charles E. Goodell

4

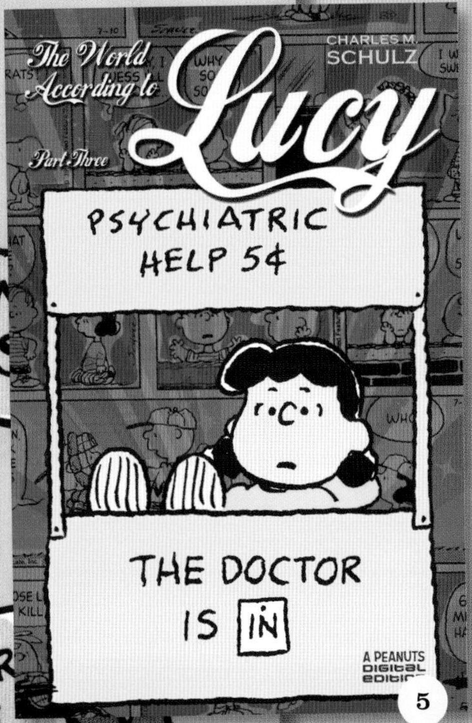
The World According to Lucy
Part Three
CHARLES M. SCHULZ
PSYCHIATRIC HELP 5¢
THE DOCTOR IS IN
A PEANUTS DIGITAL EDITION

5

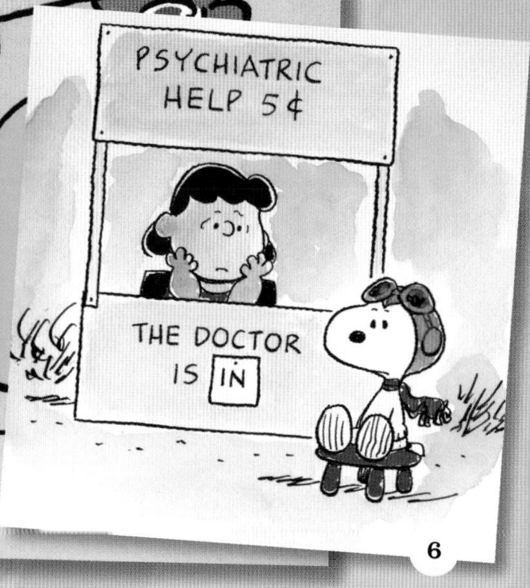
PSYCHIATRIC HELP 5¢
THE DOCTOR IS IN

6

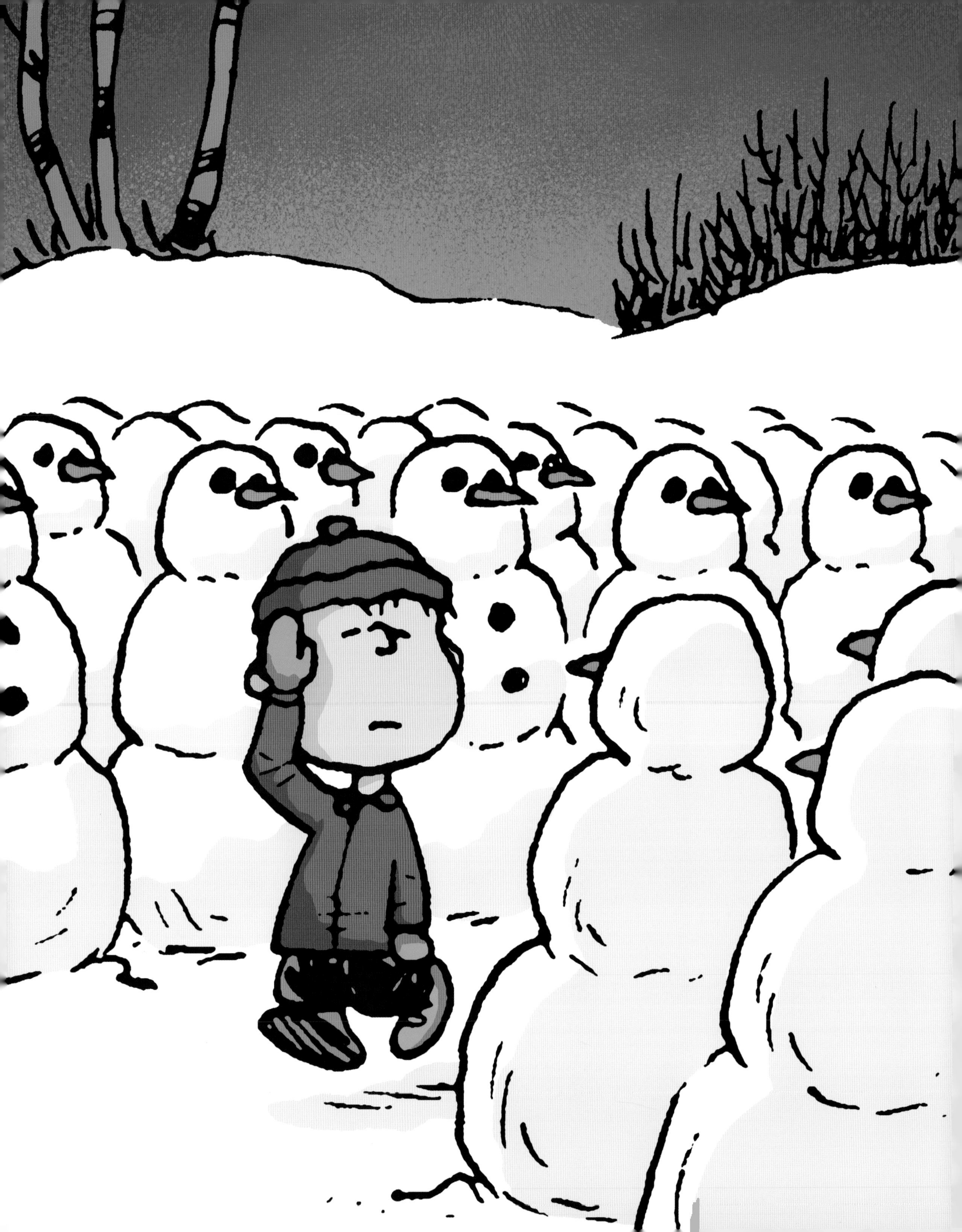

# LINUS VAN PELT

FIRST MENTIONED
07/14/1952

FIRST APPEARANCE
09/19/1952

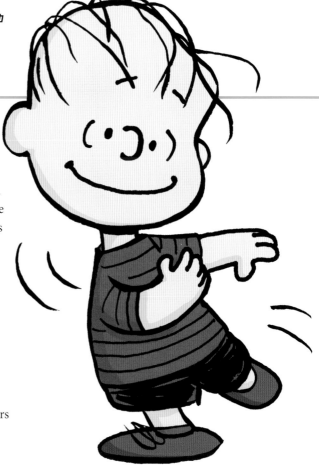

A philosopher at heart, Linus Van Pelt is the most thoughtful and articulate kid on the block. The younger brother of Lucy and older brother of Rerun, Linus is rarely seen without his trusted Security Blanket, which has been a source of great comfort to him over the years—and a source of great anxiety for his sister and his blanket-hating grandmother.

**"Cute isn't everything . . . I fall in love with any girl who smells like library paste." —Linus Van Pelt**

Linus is a voracious reader and can happily spend hours reading and discussing scripture and classic literature, although he's perfectly content to enjoy an evening watching whatever Lucy wants to see on television. He's no stranger to exercise, however, and he's a key member of Charlie Brown's baseball team. Linus at second base and Snoopy at shortstop form a dynamic (and quite unique) double-play combination.

Linus is easygoing, and he's a great listener, perhaps because his sister rarely lets him get a word in edgewise. He gets along well with nearly everyone in the neighborhood, especially Charlie Brown. Linus's relationship with Charlie Brown's sister Sally is a bit more complicated, as she adores him and calls him her "Sweet Babboo," a term of affection that he denies wholeheartedly.

Linus can also count Charles Schulz among his biggest supporters. "Linus is strong enough to carry a strip by himself. His biggest weakness, of course, is the blanket. But he's very bright. If I want to quote the Bible or say something profound, it comes best from Linus. But he's not a little intellectual. Linus's problem is that he's under the thumb of this dominating sister and a mother who puts notes in his lunch telling him to study harder. As Charlie Brown says, 'No wonder he carries that blanket.' I like to work with Linus. He's a neat character."

MY BABY BROTHER CAN SIT UP!
REALLY? ALL BY HIMSELF?
ALMOST... I ONLY HAD TO PROP HIM UP A LITTLE BIT
SCHULZ 9-19

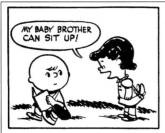

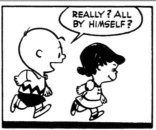

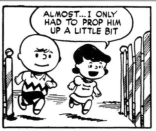

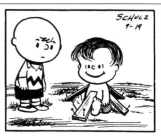

OPPOSITE: Peanuts, *Issue #14, Boom! Studios comic book cover – CSCA* | TOP RIGHT: *Style Guide art – CSCA*

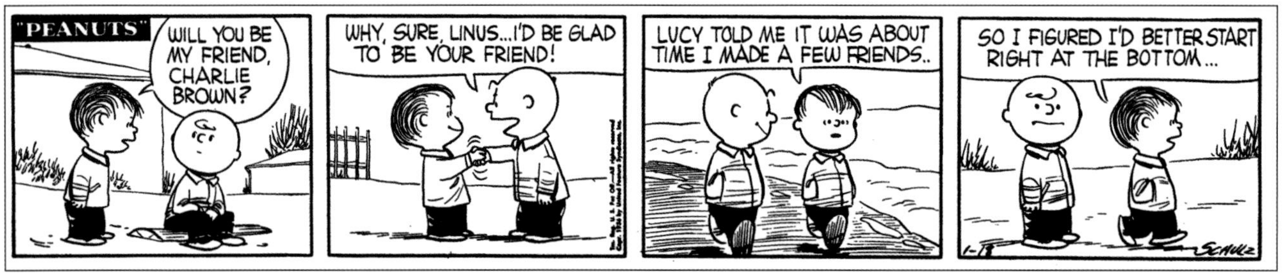
"PEANUTS"
WILL YOU BE MY FRIEND, CHARLIE BROWN?
WHY, SURE, LINUS...I'D BE GLAD TO BE YOUR FRIEND!
LUCY TOLD ME IT WAS ABOUT TIME I MADE A FEW FRIENDS..
SO I FIGURED I'D BETTER START RIGHT AT THE BOTTOM...
SCHULZ

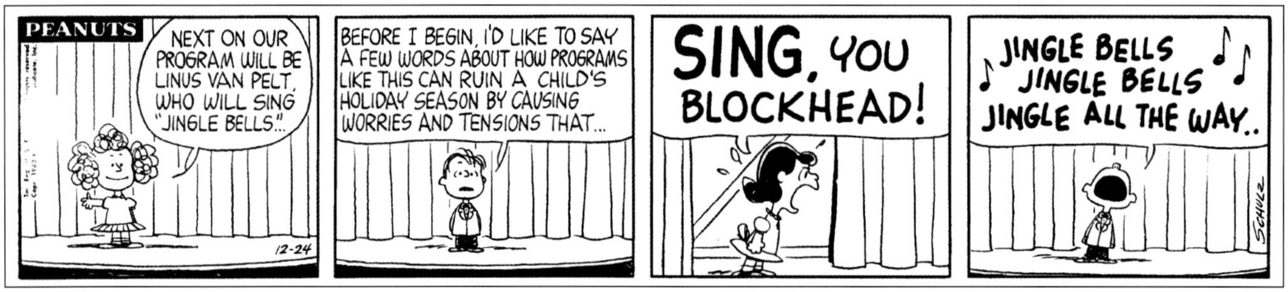
PEANUTS
NEXT ON OUR PROGRAM WILL BE LINUS VAN PELT, WHO WILL SING "JINGLE BELLS."
12-24
BEFORE I BEGIN, I'D LIKE TO SAY A FEW WORDS ABOUT HOW PROGRAMS LIKE THIS CAN RUIN A CHILD'S HOLIDAY SEASON BY CAUSING WORRIES AND TENSIONS THAT...
SING, YOU BLOCKHEAD!
JINGLE BELLS
JINGLE BELLS
JINGLE ALL THE WAY..
SCHULZ

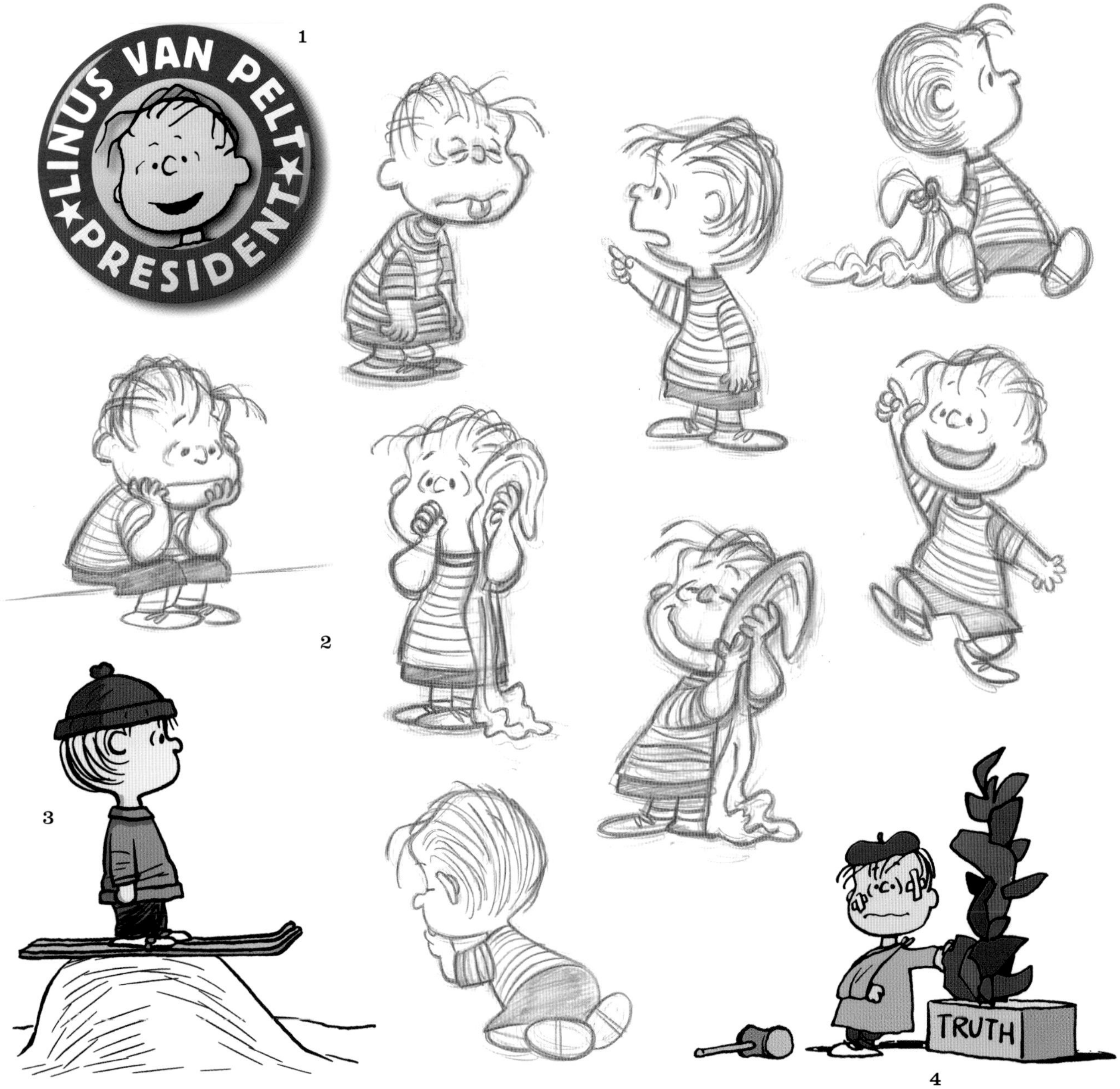
LINUS VAN PELT
PRESIDENT
TRUTH

1

2

3

4

*1: Style Guide Art – PW; 2: Linus model sheet – CSCA; 3 and 4: Spot art from strips – Charles M. Schulz*

"Sometimes there is no doubt in my mind that I'm a true artist."

—Linus Van Pelt

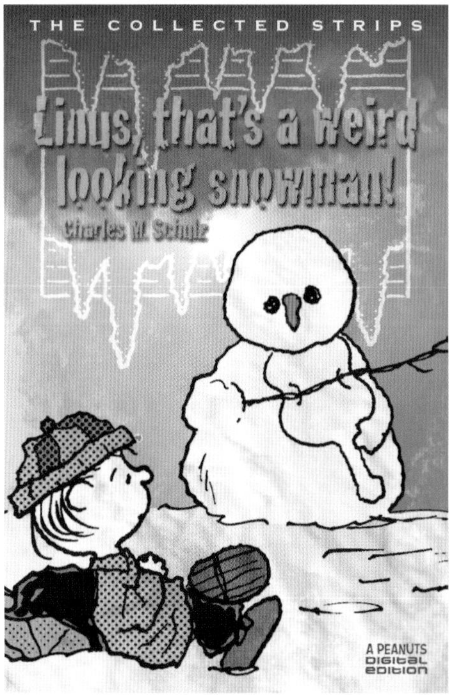
THE COLLECTED STRIPS
Linus, that's a weird looking snowman!
Charles M. Schulz
A PEANUTS DIGITAL EDITION

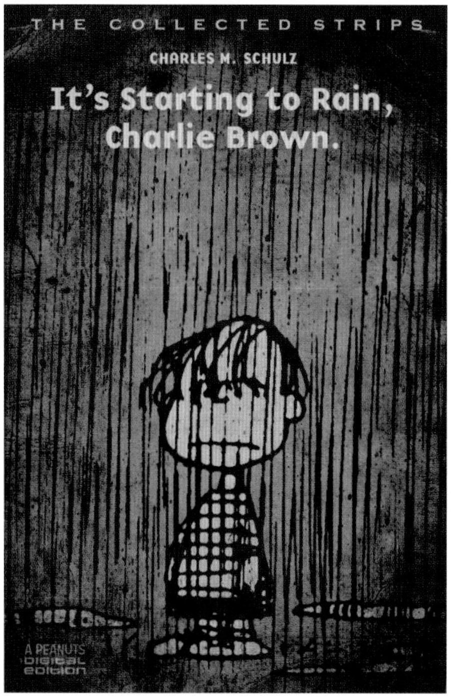
THE COLLECTED STRIPS
CHARLES M. SCHULZ
It's Starting to Rain, Charlie Brown.
A PEANUTS DIGITAL EDITION

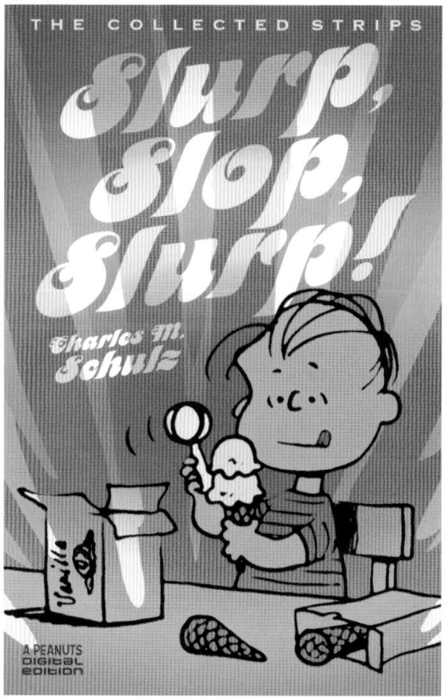
THE COLLECTED STRIPS
Slurp, Slop, Slurp!
Charles M. Schulz
Vanilla
A PEANUTS DIGITAL EDITION

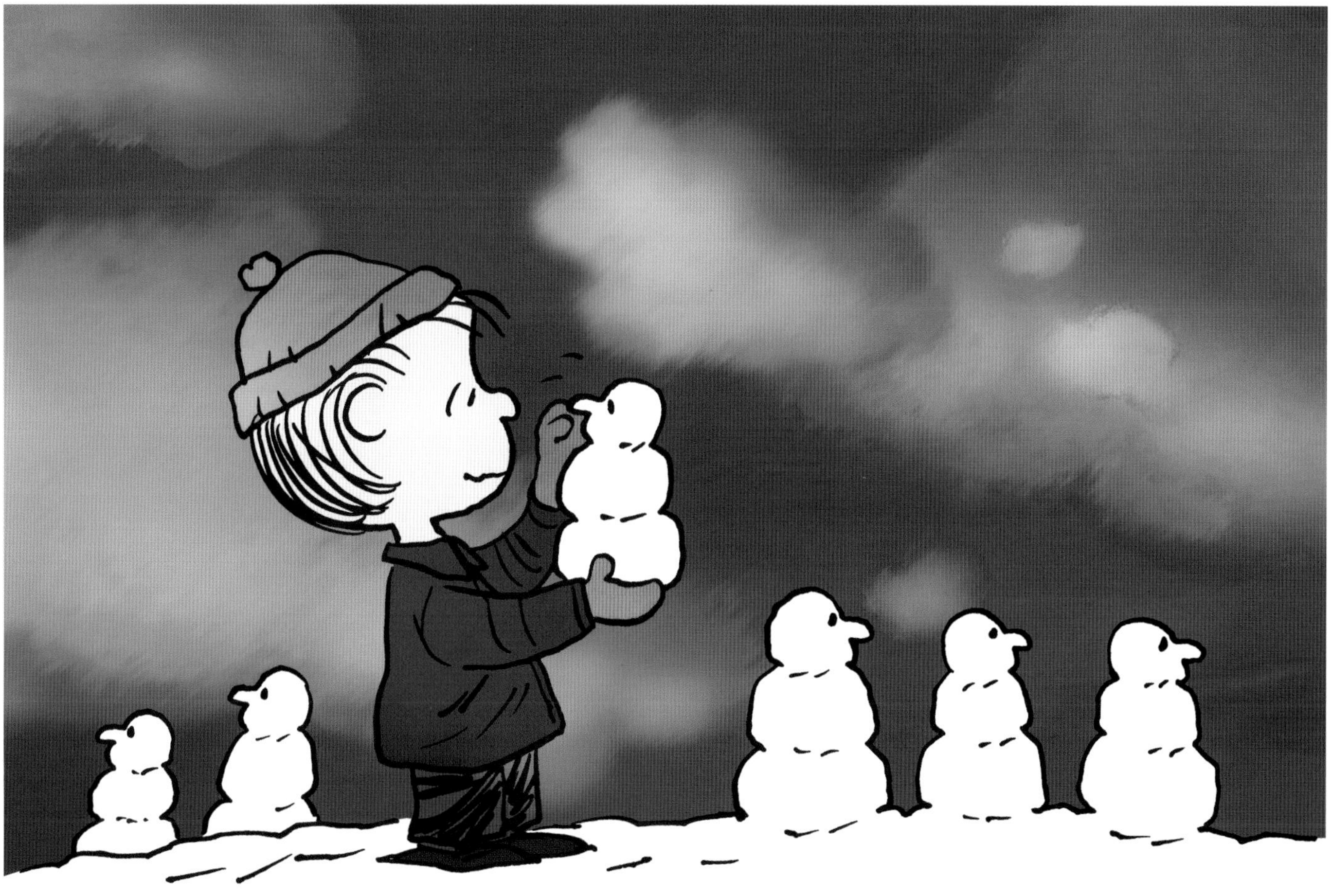

TOP: Linus, That's a Weird Looking Snowman; It's Starting to Rain, Charlie Brown; Slurp, Slop, Slurp; Peanuts *Digital Editions – CSCA* | ABOVE: *Spot art from strips – Charles M. Schulz*

# LINUS'S SECURITY BLANKET

FIRST APPEARANCE
06/01/1954

Although he is one of the most thoughtful and level-headed kids in the neighborhood, Linus is a nervous wreck whenever he's separated from his trusty security blanket. The light-blue blanket of "outing" flannel provides a sense of peace and tranquility to Linus when he has it, and a sense of panic and anxiety whenever he's deprived of it, usually through the machinations of his sister Lucy, his blanket-hating grandmother, or Snoopy, who enjoys snatching the blanket in his teeth and running away with it—often with Linus in tow!

The versatile blanket can be used for self-defense, as an offensive weapon, a parachute, a folded airplane, a hammock, and even as a pair of sportcoats for Snoopy and Woodstock, although that usage proved to be very traumatic for Linus.

Charles Schulz popularlized the phrase "security blanket" through his strip, and felt that people of all ages could sympathize with the need for comfort and reassurance. "Linus' affection for his blanket . . . is a symbol of the things we cling to . . . What I am getting at, of course, is the adult's inadequacy here the inability to give up habits which really should be given up. Not that I am completely against the idea that we have to cling to something! For once you accept Jesus it does not mean that all your problems are automatically solved, or that you will never be lonesome or unhappy again. How can you be happy all the time, if you are aware of the things that are going on around you? But some adult habits are ridiculous."

*1, 2, 4, and 5: Style Guide art – PW; 3:* Science Digest *magazine cover, published by Hearst Corporation, 1986 – CMSM; 6:* Peanuts, *Issue #8, Boom! Studios cover, 2014 – CSCA*

2

3

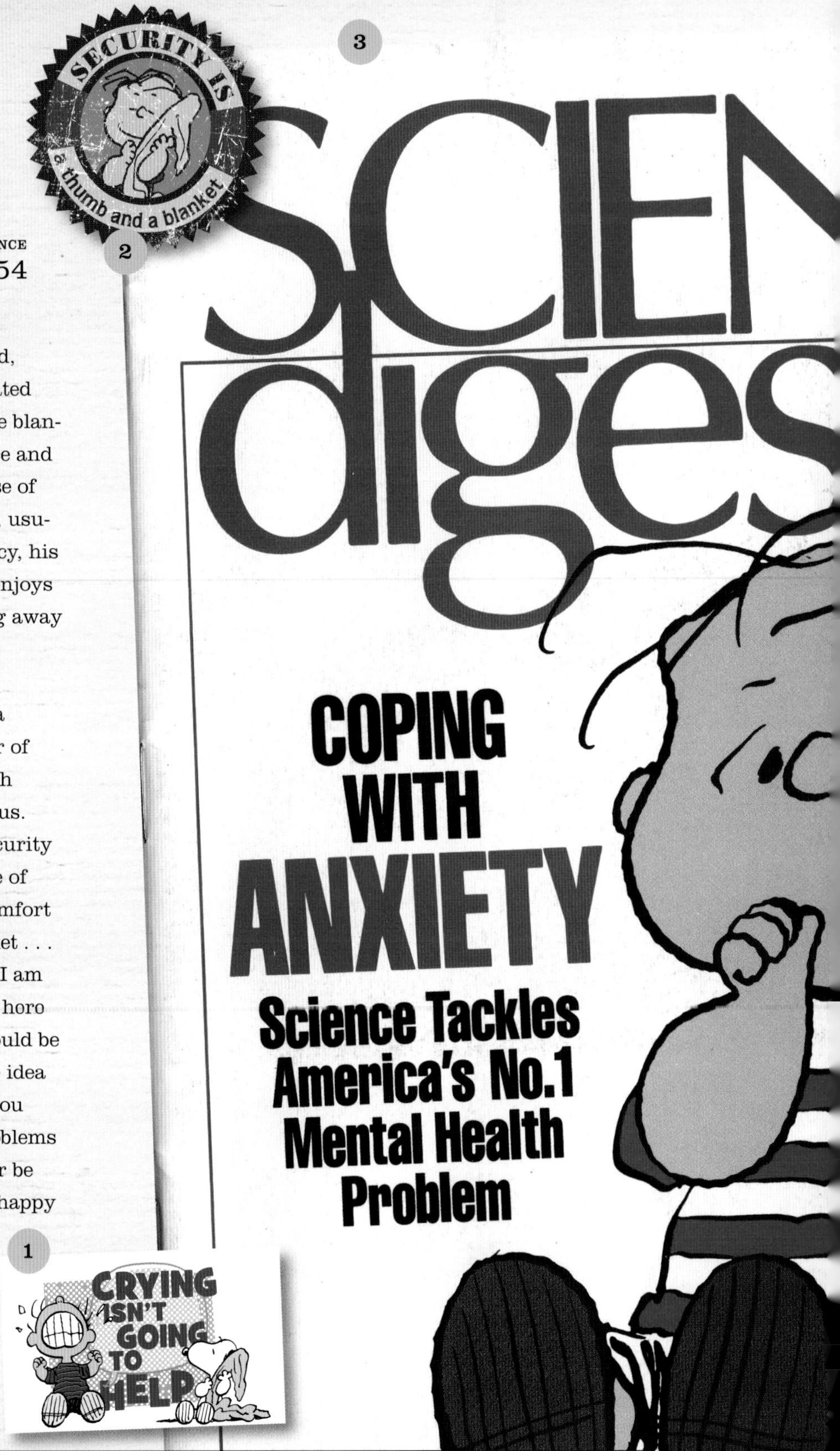
SECURITY IS
a thumb and a blanket
COPING WITH ANXIETY
Science Tackles America's No.1 Mental Health Problem
CRYING ISN'T GOING TO HELP

1

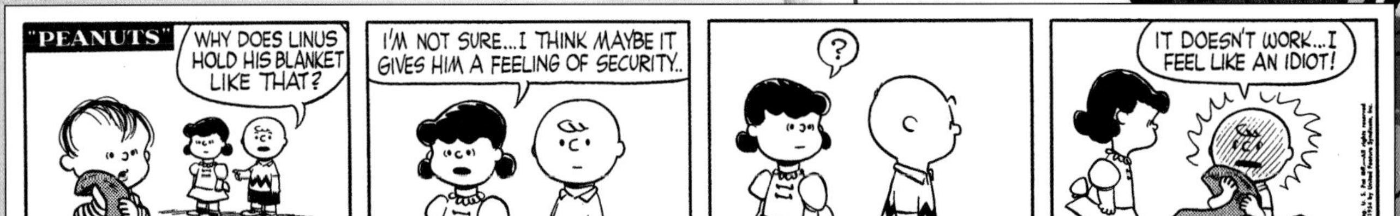
"PEANUTS"
WHY DOES LINUS HOLD HIS BLANKET LIKE THAT?
I'M NOT SURE...I THINK MAYBE IT GIVES HIM A FEELING OF SECURITY..
?
IT DOESN'T WORK...I FEEL LIKE AN IDIOT!
6-1
SCHULZ

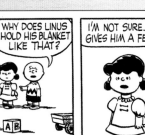

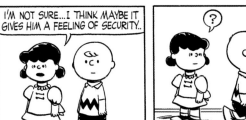

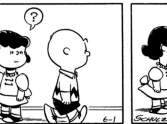

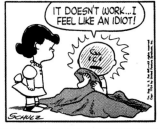

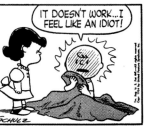

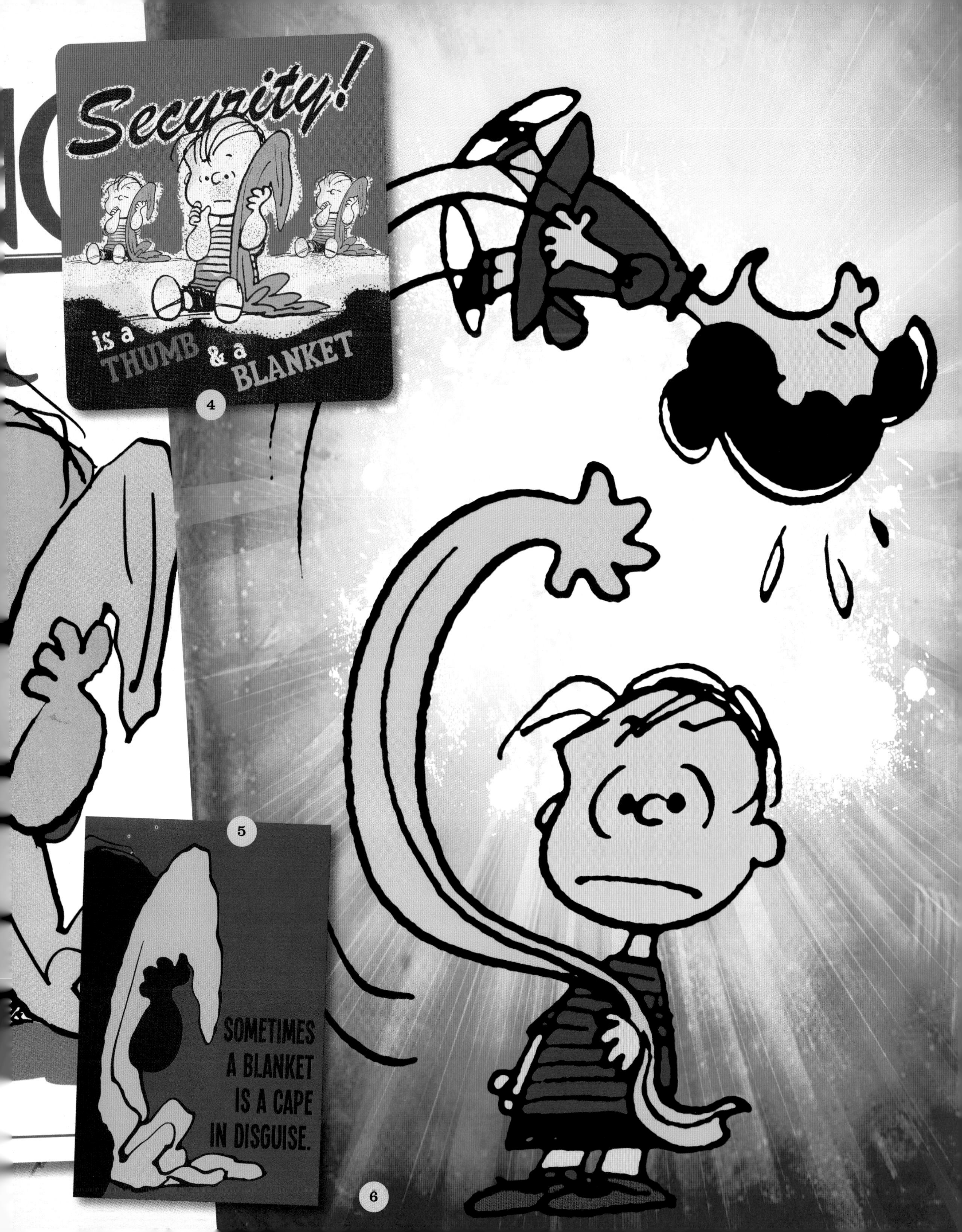

Secyrity!
is a THUMB & a BLANKET
4
5
SOMETIMES A BLANKET IS A CAPE IN DISGUISE.
6

# THE PHILOSOPHER

Linus is the most well-read kid in the neighborhood and loves to discuss philosophy, theology, and literature, even if his friends can't always follow along. Although many of his observations are thoughtful and profound, he's still a kid at heart, as anyone who's heard him speak about the Great Pumpkin can attest.

Much like Linus himself, Charles Schulz developed a reputation as a philosopher, although he wasn't sure that it was warranted. "When people say to me, 'I really admire your philosophy,' I literally and honestly do not know what they are talking about because I don't even know what my philosophy is."

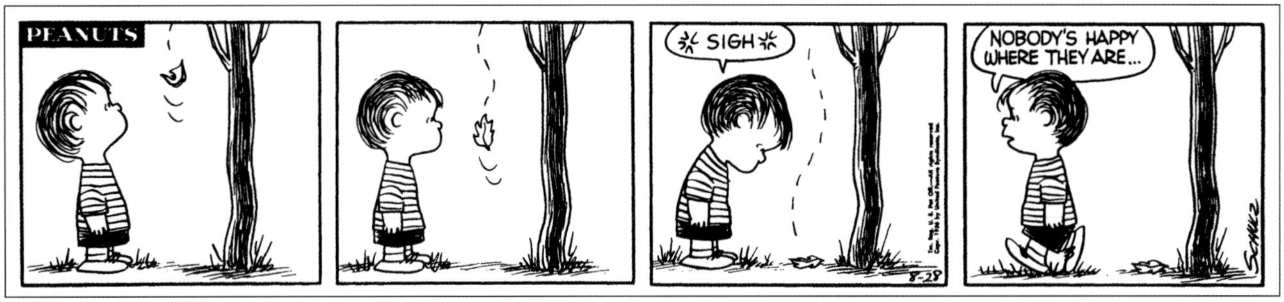
PEANUTS
SIGH
NOBODY'S HAPPY WHERE THEY ARE...

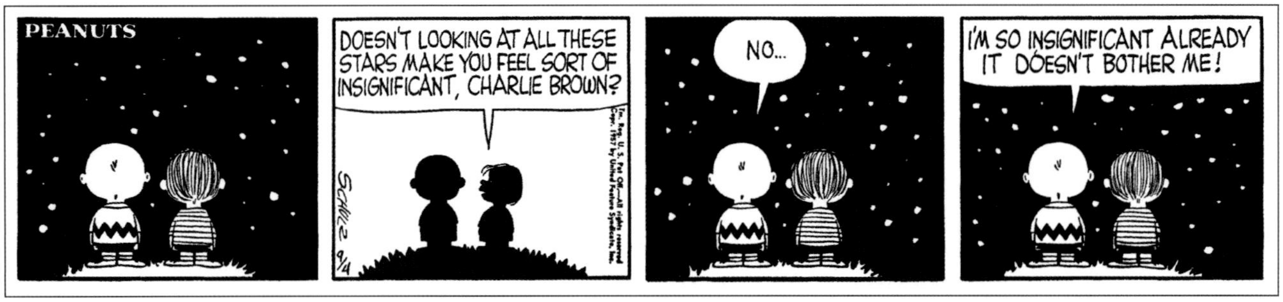
PEANUTS
DOESN'T LOOKING AT ALL THESE STARS MAKE YOU FEEL SORT OF INSIGNIFICANT, CHARLIE BROWN?
NO...
I'M SO INSIGNIFICANT ALREADY IT DOESN'T BOTHER ME!

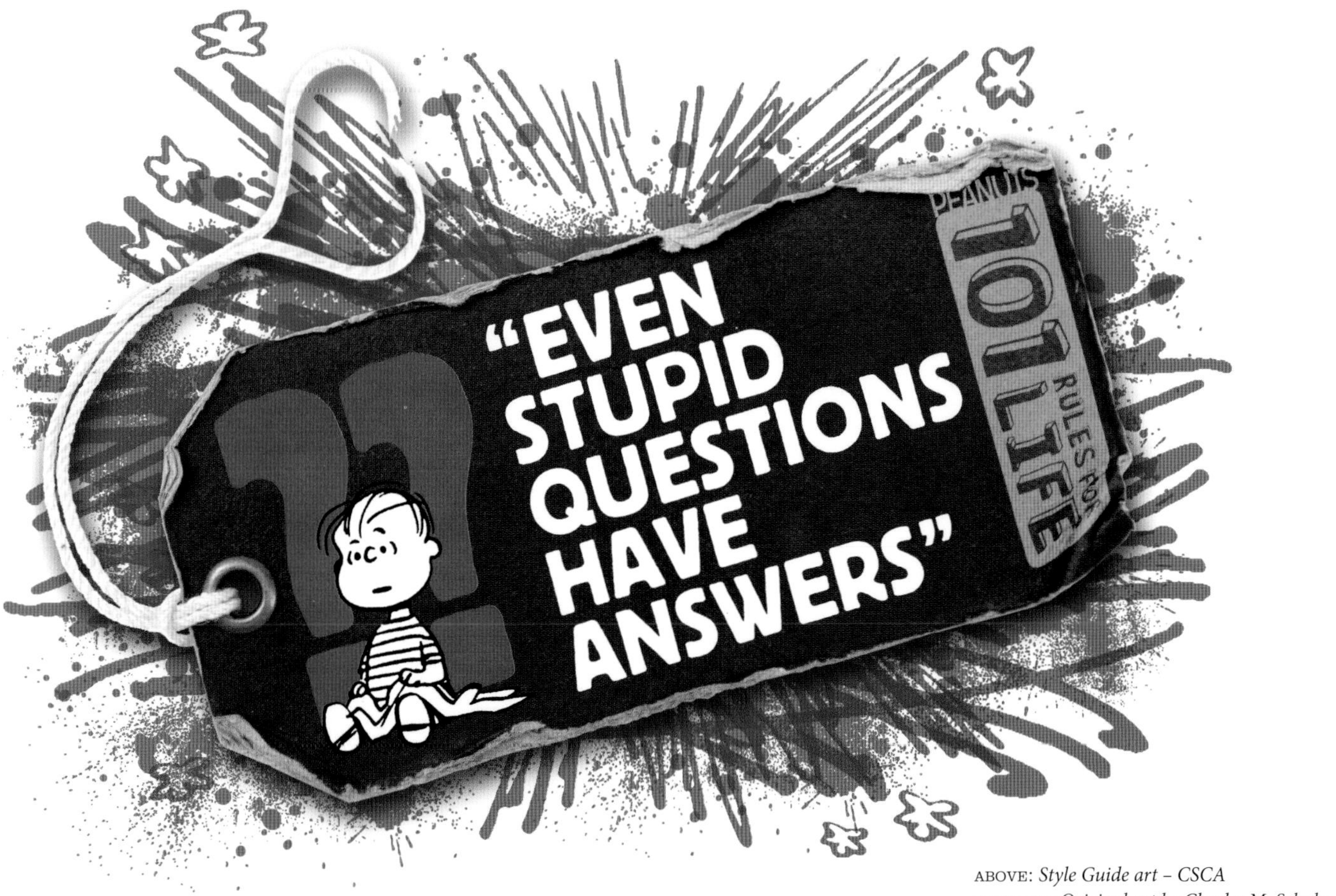
PEANUTS
101 RULES FOR LIFE
"EVEN STUPID QUESTIONS HAVE ANSWERS"

ABOVE: *Style Guide art – CSCA*
OPPOSITE: *Original art by Charles M. Schulz*

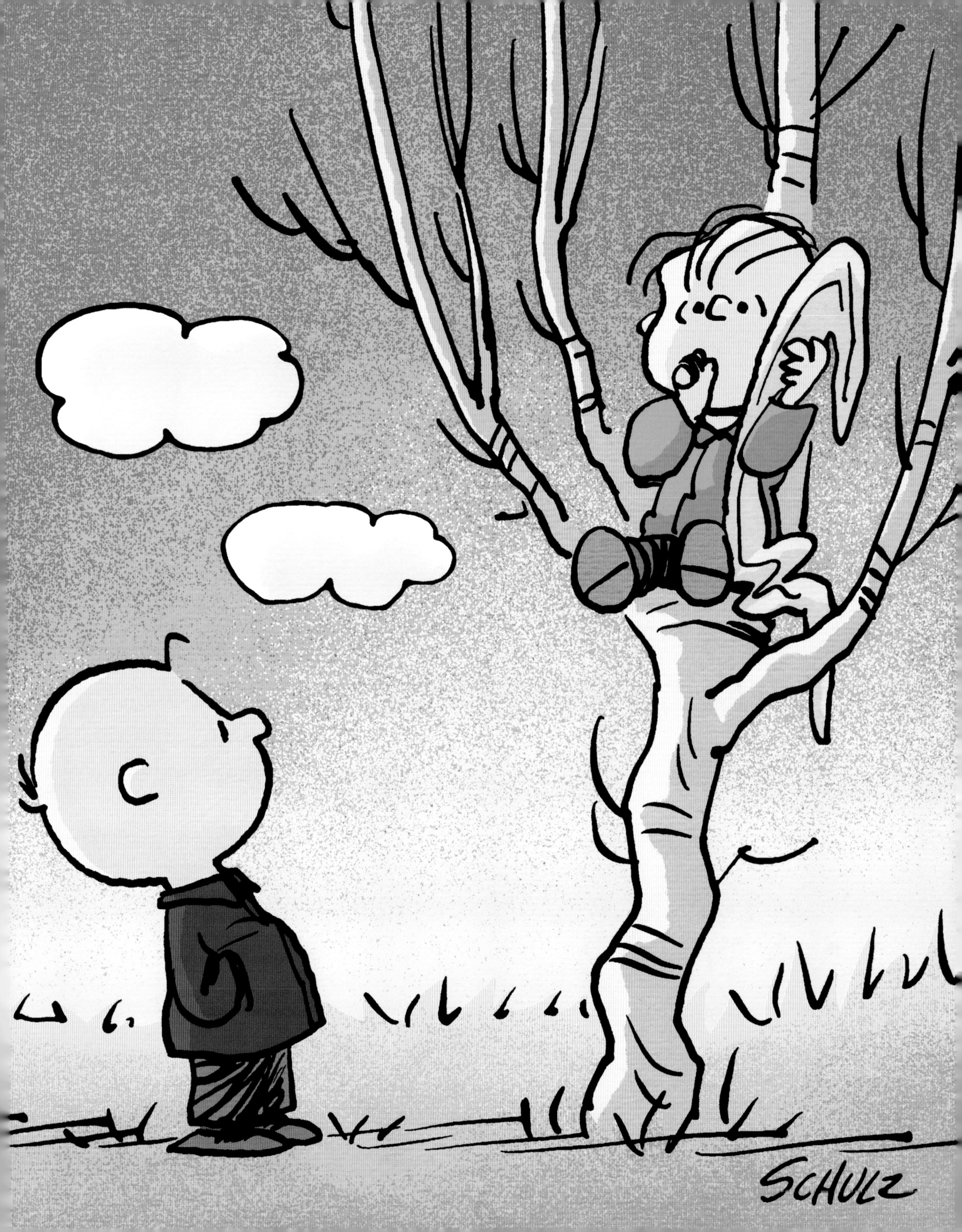
SCHULZ

# THE GREAT PUMPKIN

FIRST MENTIONED
10/26/1959

Each year, the Great Pumpkin rises out of the pumpkin patch that he thinks is the most sincere, and on Halloween night, he delivers toys to all good children everywhere.

That is the sincere belief of Linus Van Pelt, who spends the weeks leading up to Halloween spreading the gospel of the Great Pumpkin, despite mockery and bewilderment from his friends and neighbors. Although his beliefs are tested every year, and he is never visited by the Great Pumpkin, Linus's faith in the Halloween icon remains unwavering, even if his friends do not appreciate his beliefs.

As Linus grudgingly admits, "There are three things I have learned never to discuss with people: religion, politics, and the Great Pumpkin."

1, 5 *and* 6: *Style Guide art – CSCA;* 2: The Great Pumpkin, Peanuts *Digital Edition – CSCA;* 3: It's the Great Pumpkin, Charlie Brown; *Artist: Dave Perillo; Limited Edition Print; Courtesy: Dark Hall Mansion;* 4: *Style Guide art – PW;* 7: The Great Pumpkin, *poster – CSCA* | OVERLEAF, LEFT: It's the Great Pumpkin, Charlie Brown; *Artist: Michael De Pippo; Limited Edition Print; Courtesy: Dark Hall Mansion* | OVERLEAF RIGHT: It's the Great Pumpkin, Charlie Brown; *Artist: Tom Whalen; Limited Edition Print; Courtesy: Dark Hall Mansion*

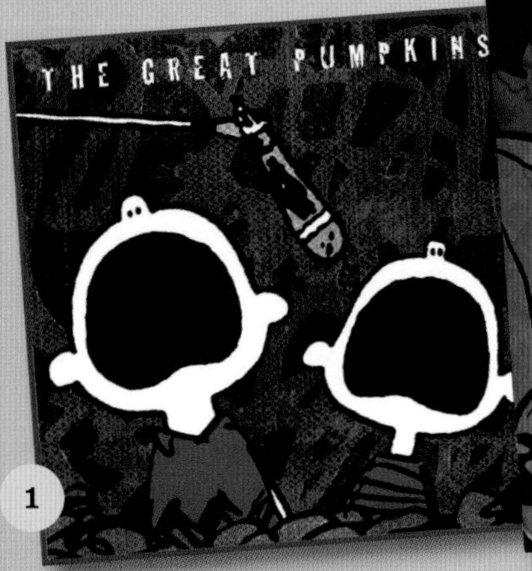
THE GREAT PUMPKINS

1

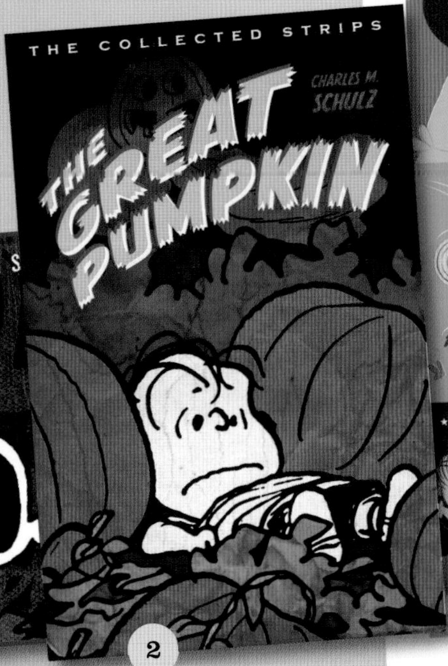
THE COLLECTED STRIPS
CHARLES M. SCHULZ
THE GREAT PUMPKIN

2

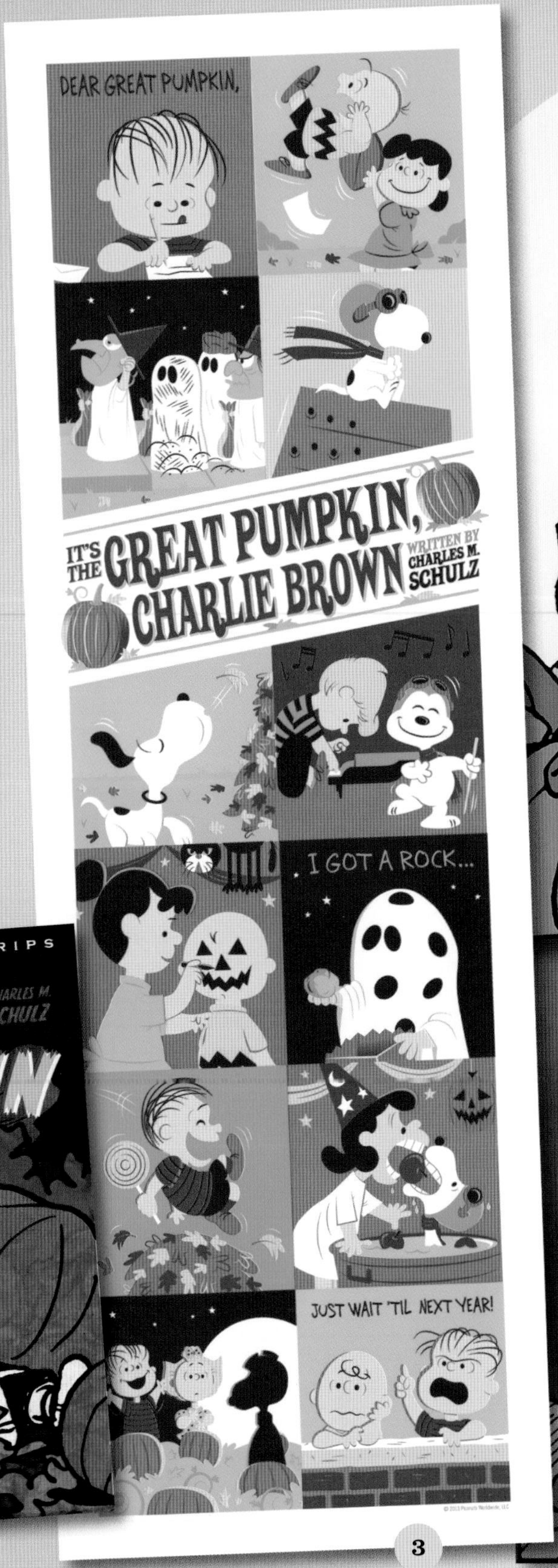
DEAR GREAT PUMPKIN,
IT'S THE GREAT PUMPKIN, CHARLIE BROWN
WRITTEN BY CHARLES M. SCHULZ
I GOT A ROCK...
JUST WAIT 'TIL NEXT YEAR!

3

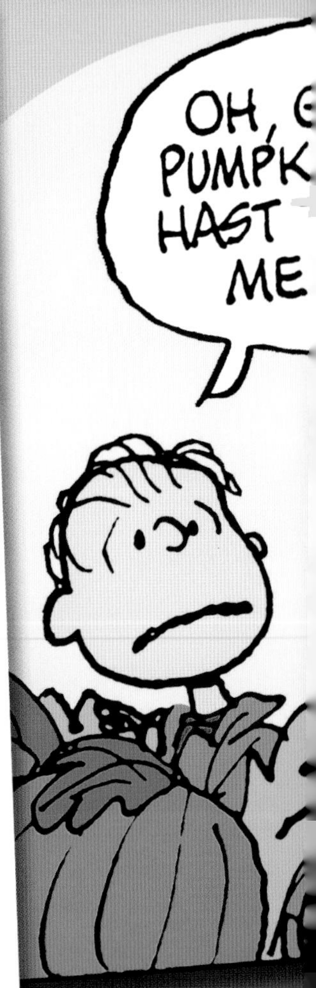
OH, G
PUMPK
HAST
ME

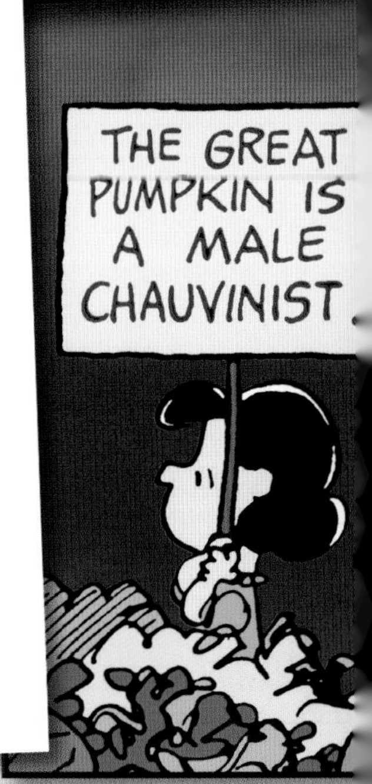
THE GREAT PUMPKIN IS A MALE CHAUVINIST

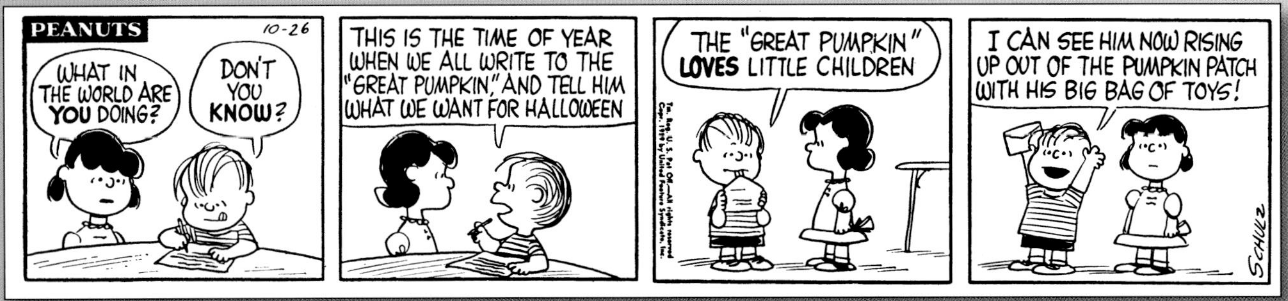
PEANUTS
10-26
WHAT IN THE WORLD ARE YOU DOING?
DON'T YOU KNOW?
THIS IS THE TIME OF YEAR WHEN WE ALL WRITE TO THE "GREAT PUMPKIN," AND TELL HIM WHAT WE WANT FOR HALLOWEEN
THE "GREAT PUMPKIN" LOVES LITTLE CHILDREN
I CAN SEE HIM NOW RISING UP OUT OF THE PUMPKIN PATCH WITH HIS BIG BAG OF TOYS!
SCHULZ

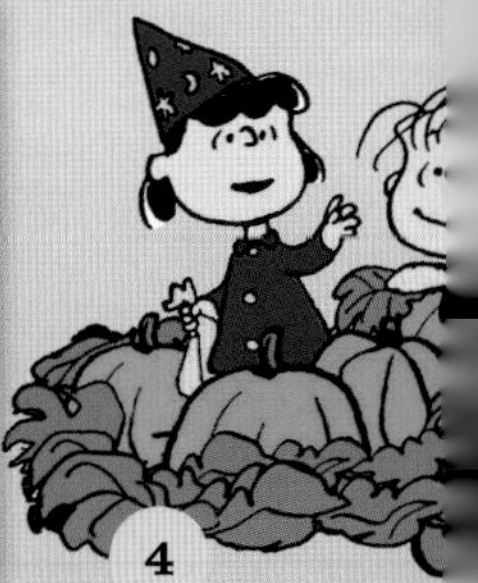

4

# PEANUTS

*by Schulz*

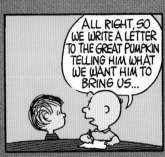

ALL RIGHT, SO WE WRITE A LETTER TO THE GREAT PUMPKIN TELLING HIM WHAT WE WANT HIM TO BRING US...

WHERE DO WE SEND IT?

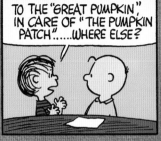

TO THE "GREAT PUMPKIN," IN CARE OF "THE PUMPKIN PATCH"......WHERE ELSE?

WHERE ELSE, INDEED?

TO: THE GREAT PUMPKIN C/O THE PUMPKIN PATCH

I DON'T SEE HOW THIS IS EVER GOING TO GET DELIVERED...

I'M SURPRISED AT YOU, CHARLIE BROWN!

10-27

YOUR LACK OF CONFIDENCE IN OUR POSTAL DEPARTMENT IS AN INSULT TO THE ENTIRE ORGANIZATION!

US MAIL

IF ANYONE HAD TOLD ME I'D BE OUT CRAWLING AROUND AMONG A BUNCH OF PUMPKINS ON HALLOWEEN NIGHT, I'D HAVE SAID THEY WERE CRAZY!

THIS IS FAR ENOUGH..

JUST THINK, CHARLIE BROWN... WHEN THE "GREAT PUMPKIN" RISES OUT OF THE PUMPKIN PATCH, WE'LL BE HERE TO SEE HIM!

IT JUST OCCURRED TO ME THAT THERE MUST BE TEN MILLION PUMPKIN PATCHES IN THIS COUNTRY.. WHAT MAKES YOU THINK WE'RE IN THE RIGHT ONE?

JUST A FEELING I HAVE, CHARLIE BROWN, ALTHOUGH I THINK THIS MUST BE THE KIND OF PUMPKIN PATCH HE WOULD PREFER...

I DOUBT IF HE LIKES LARGE PUMPKIN PATCHES...THEY'RE TOO COMMERCIAL..HE LIKES SMALL HOMEY ONES...THEY'RE MORE SINCERE...

SOMEHOW I'VE NEVER THOUGHT OF A PUMPKIN PATCH AS BEING SINCERE...

THERE HE IS! THERE HE IS!

IT'S THE 'GREAT PUMPKIN'! HE'S RISING UP OUT OF THE PUMPKIN PATCH

OH, OH!

KLUNK

WHAT HAPPENED? DID I FAINT? WHAT DID HE LEAVE US? DID HE LEAVE US ANY TOYS?

NO TOYS... JUST A USED DOG...

HE MUST BE WELL ON HIS WAY BY THIS TIME.. HAPPY JOURNEY, O, GREAT PUMPKIN! HAPPY JOURNEY!

"USED DOG"! GOOD GRIEF!

AT WHY U CAST F?

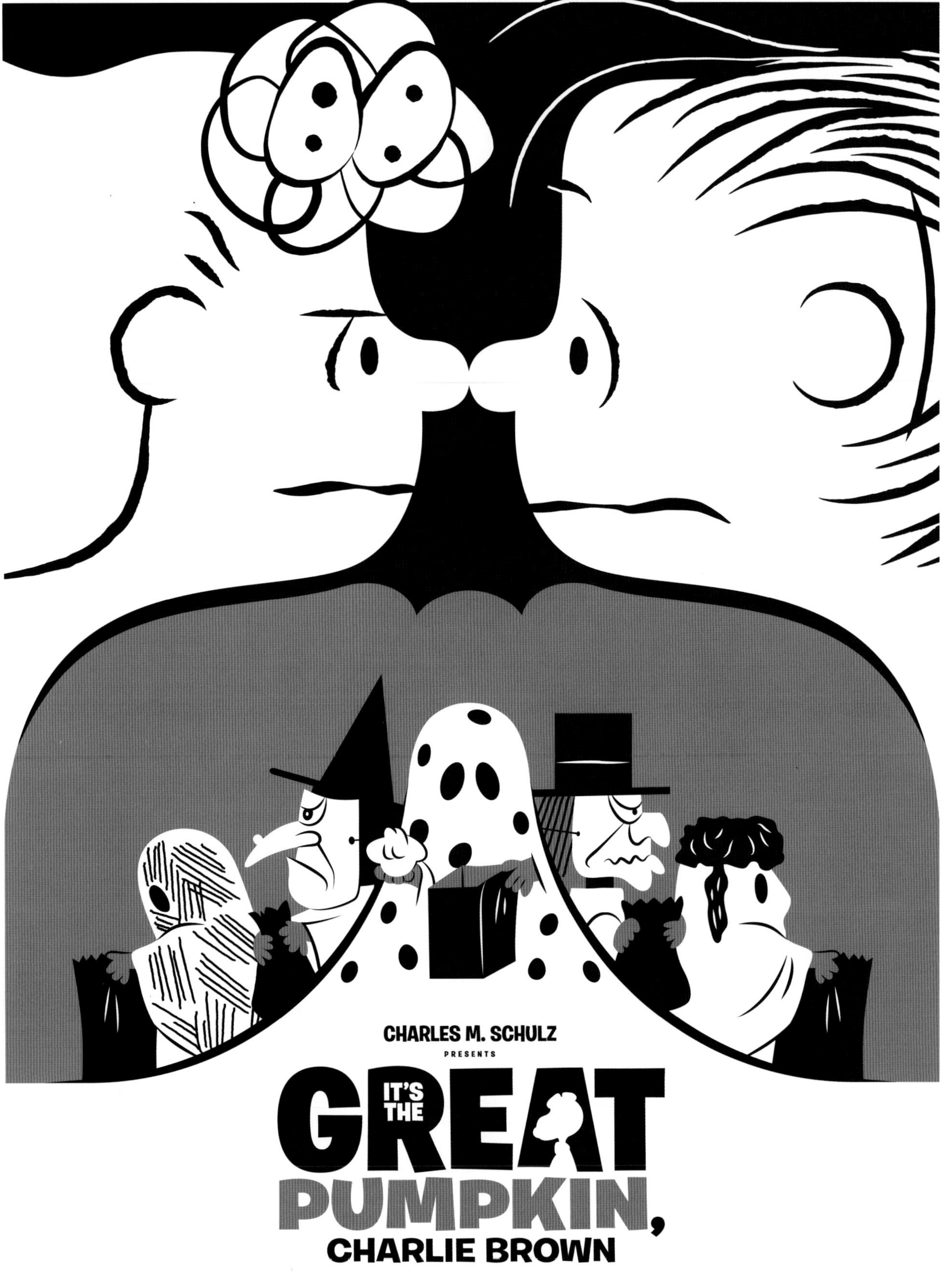
CHARLES M. SCHULZ
PRESENTS
IT'S THE
GREAT
PUMPKIN,
CHARLIE BROWN

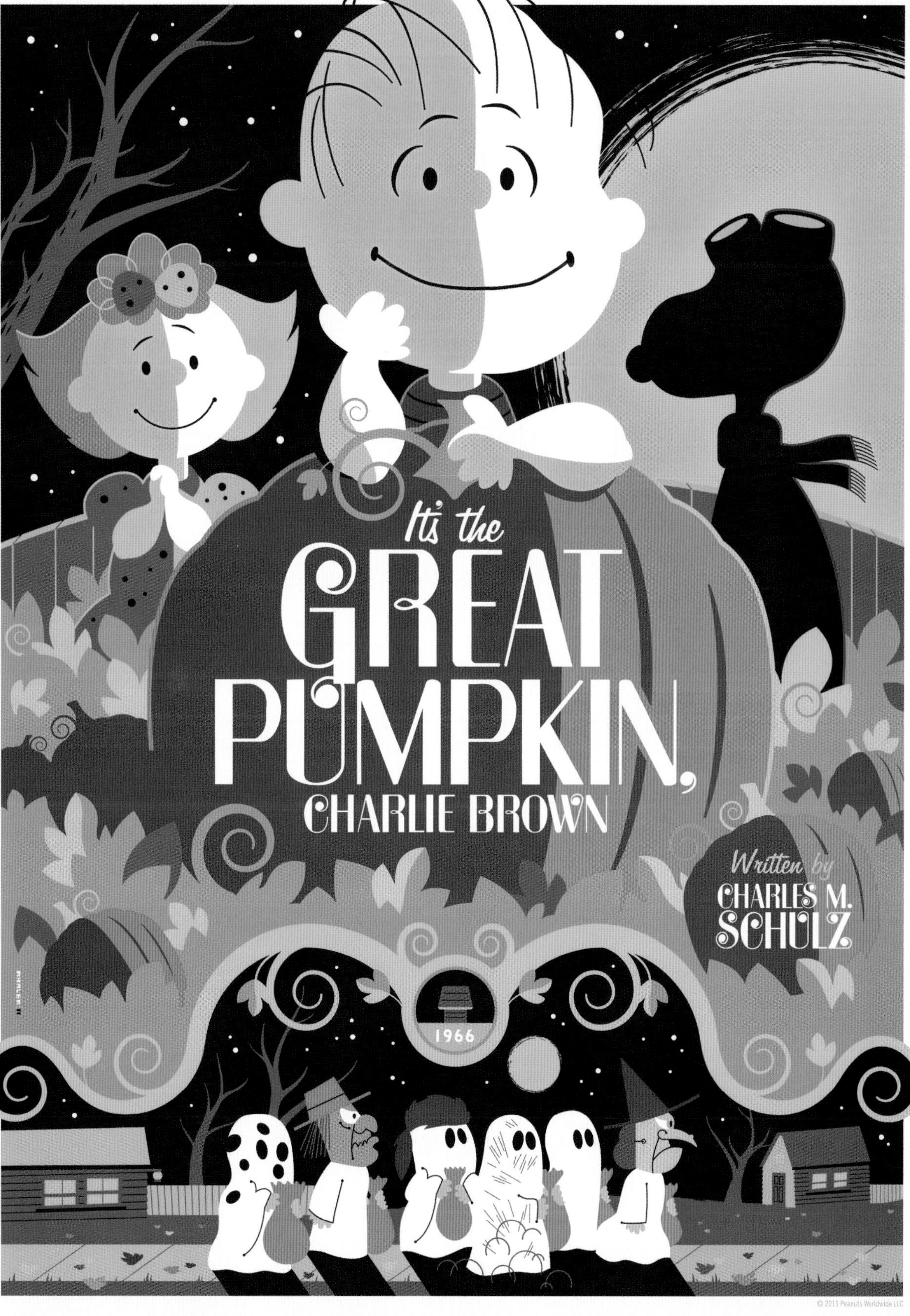
It's the
GREAT PUMPKIN,
CHARLIE BROWN
Written by
CHARLES M. SCHULZ
1966

PEANUTS
YOUR NAME IS WHAT?
MY NAME IS "5"!
MY DAD SAYS WE HAVE SO MANY NUMBERS THESE DAYS WE'RE ALL LOSING OUR IDENTITY..
HE'S DECIDED THAT EVERYONE IN OUR FAMILY SHOULD HAVE A NUMBER INSTEAD OF A NAME
CHARLIE BROWN, I'D LIKE TO HAVE YOU MEET 5!
OH, NO!
SCHULZ

# 5, 3 & 4

**5 FIRST APPEARANCE** 09/30/1963 **3 & 4 FIRST MENTIONED** 10/01/1963 **3 & 4 FIRST APPEARANCE** 10/17/1963

Date of birth. Identification number. Phone number. Height. Weight. Address. Some days, life feels like it's just one number after another, especially when your name is 555 95472, or 5, for short.

5's father is so overwhelmed by numbers that he changes his surname to 95472, the zip code for Sebastopol, California (which, at the time, was where Charles Schulz made his home). He takes it a step further and rechristens his son as 5, and his twin daughters are renamed 3 and 4.

Despite the supposed convenience, having a number for a name isn't as easy as you might think. Snoopy can't tell if 5 is pronounced like "five" or like the Roman numeral "V," and 5's teacher can't seem to pronounce his last name correctly, either—the accent is on the 4, not the 2, 5 helpfully notes.

ABOVE AND OPPOSITE: *5 model sheet – CSCA* | OPPOSITE, FAR RIGHT: *Spot art from strip – Charles M. Schulz*

PEANUTS
?
HI, BIG GIRL.. MY NAME IS 3, AND THIS IS MY SISTER...HER NAME IS 4...
OUR BROTHER'S NAME IS 5... I BELIEVE YOU'VE ALREADY MET HIM...OUR LAST NAME IS 95472
NUMBERS, NUMBERS AND MORE NUMBERS...
OUR DAD GETS UPSET EASILY LATELY...HE SAYS HIS HEAD HURTS
SCHULZ

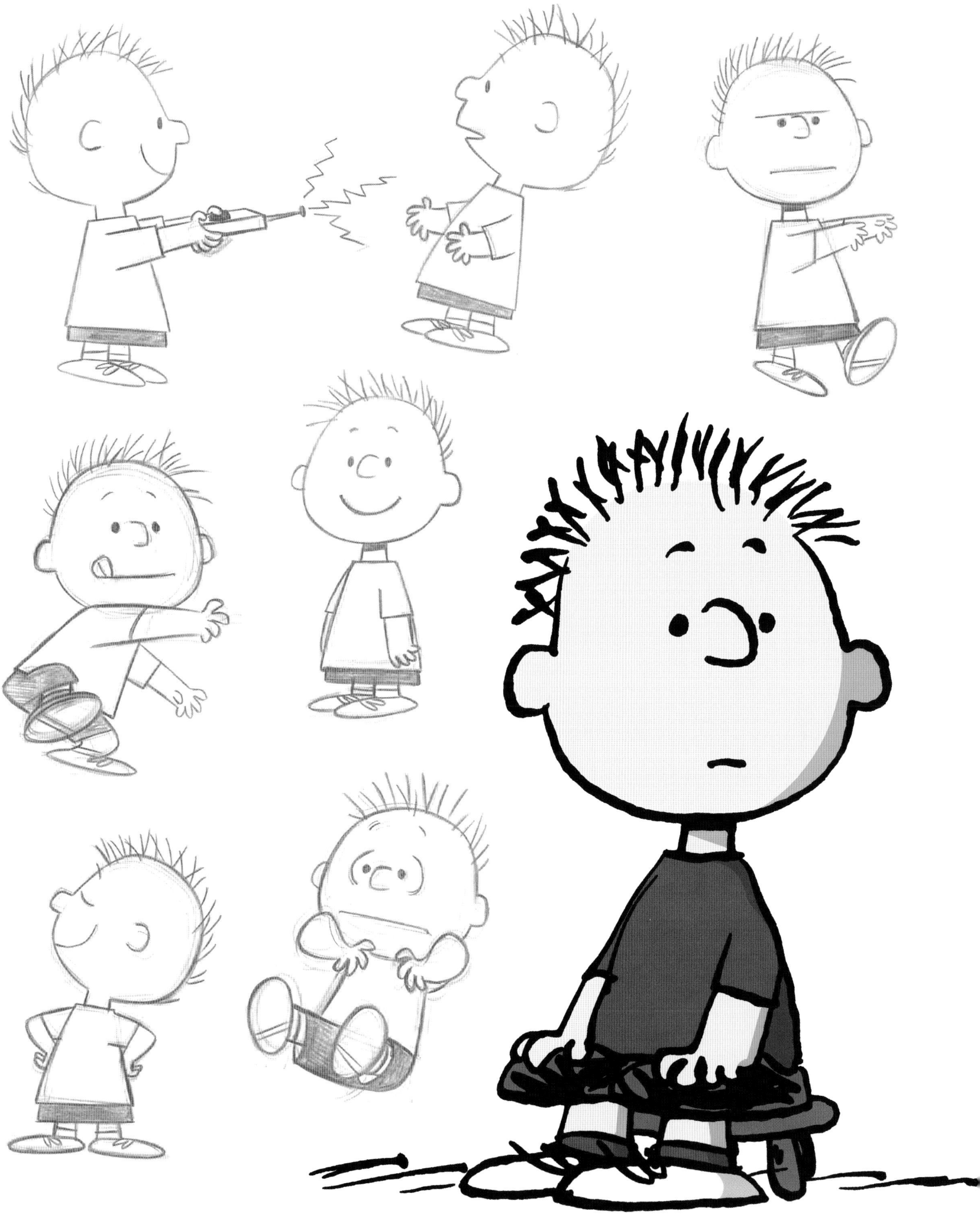

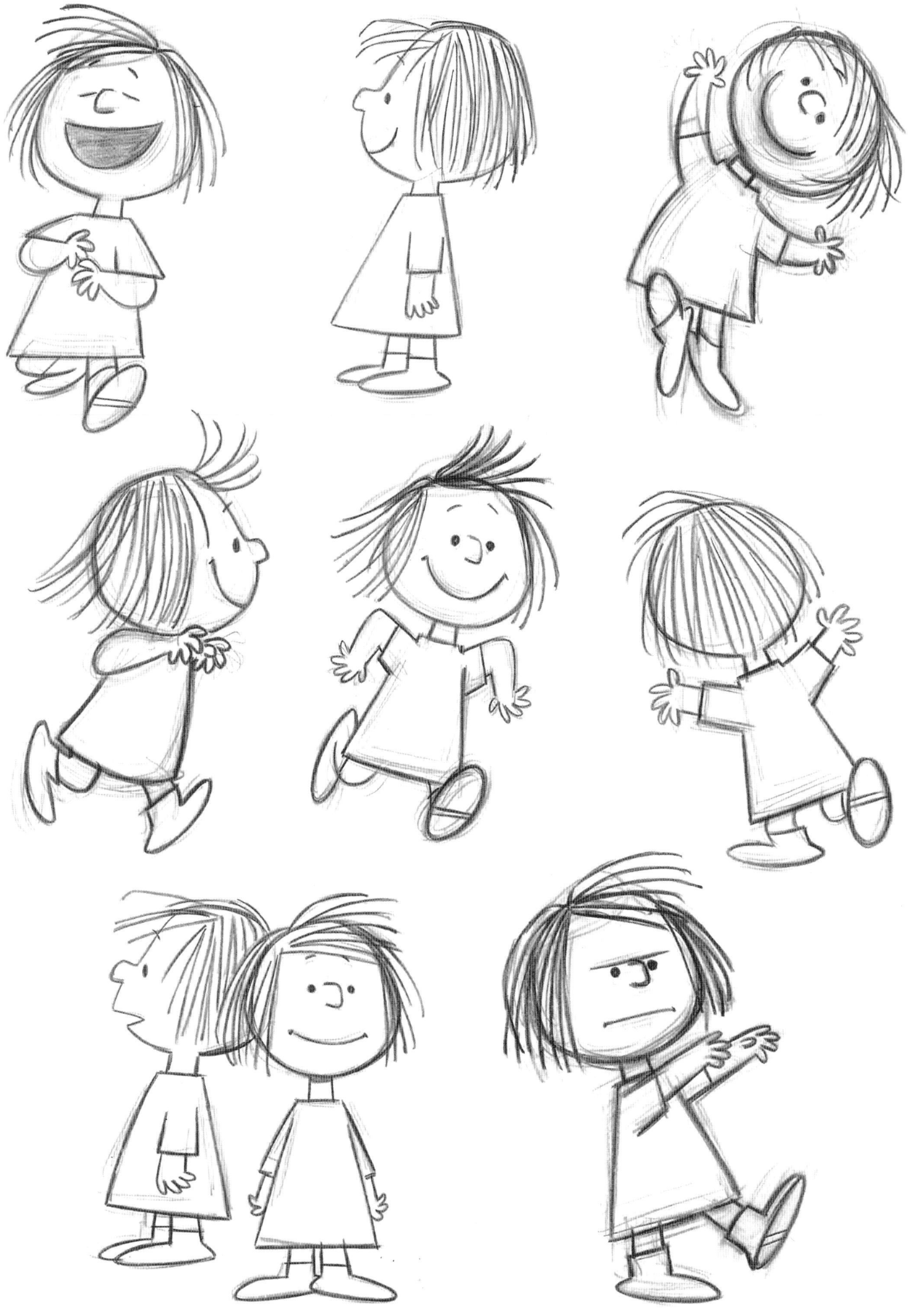

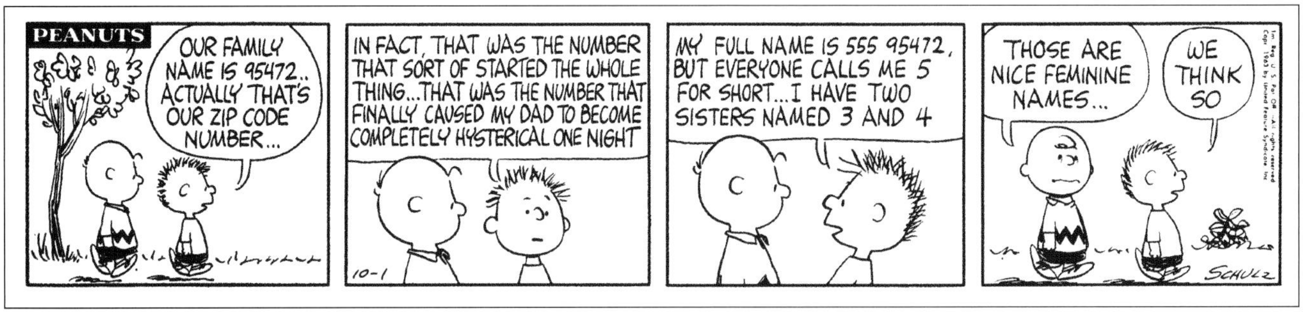
PEANUTS
OUR FAMILY NAME IS 95472.. ACTUALLY THAT'S OUR ZIP CODE NUMBER...
IN FACT, THAT WAS THE NUMBER THAT SORT OF STARTED THE WHOLE THING...THAT WAS THE NUMBER THAT FINALLY CAUSED MY DAD TO BECOME COMPLETELY HYSTERICAL ONE NIGHT
MY FULL NAME IS 555 95472, BUT EVERYONE CALLS ME 5 FOR SHORT...I HAVE TWO SISTERS NAMED 3 AND 4
THOSE ARE NICE FEMININE NAMES...
WE THINK SO
10-1
SCHULZ

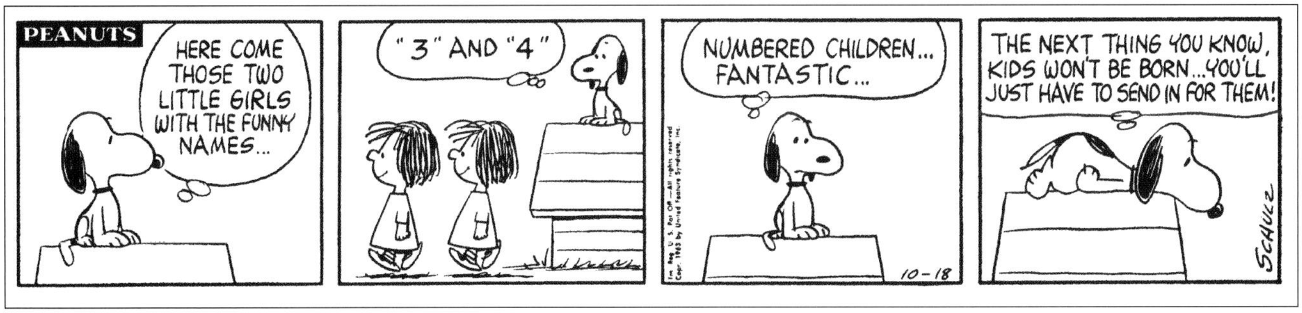
PEANUTS
HERE COME THOSE TWO LITTLE GIRLS WITH THE FUNNY NAMES...
"3" AND "4"
NUMBERED CHILDREN... FANTASTIC...
THE NEXT THING YOU KNOW, KIDS WON'T BE BORN...YOU'LL JUST HAVE TO SEND IN FOR THEM!
10-18
SCHULZ

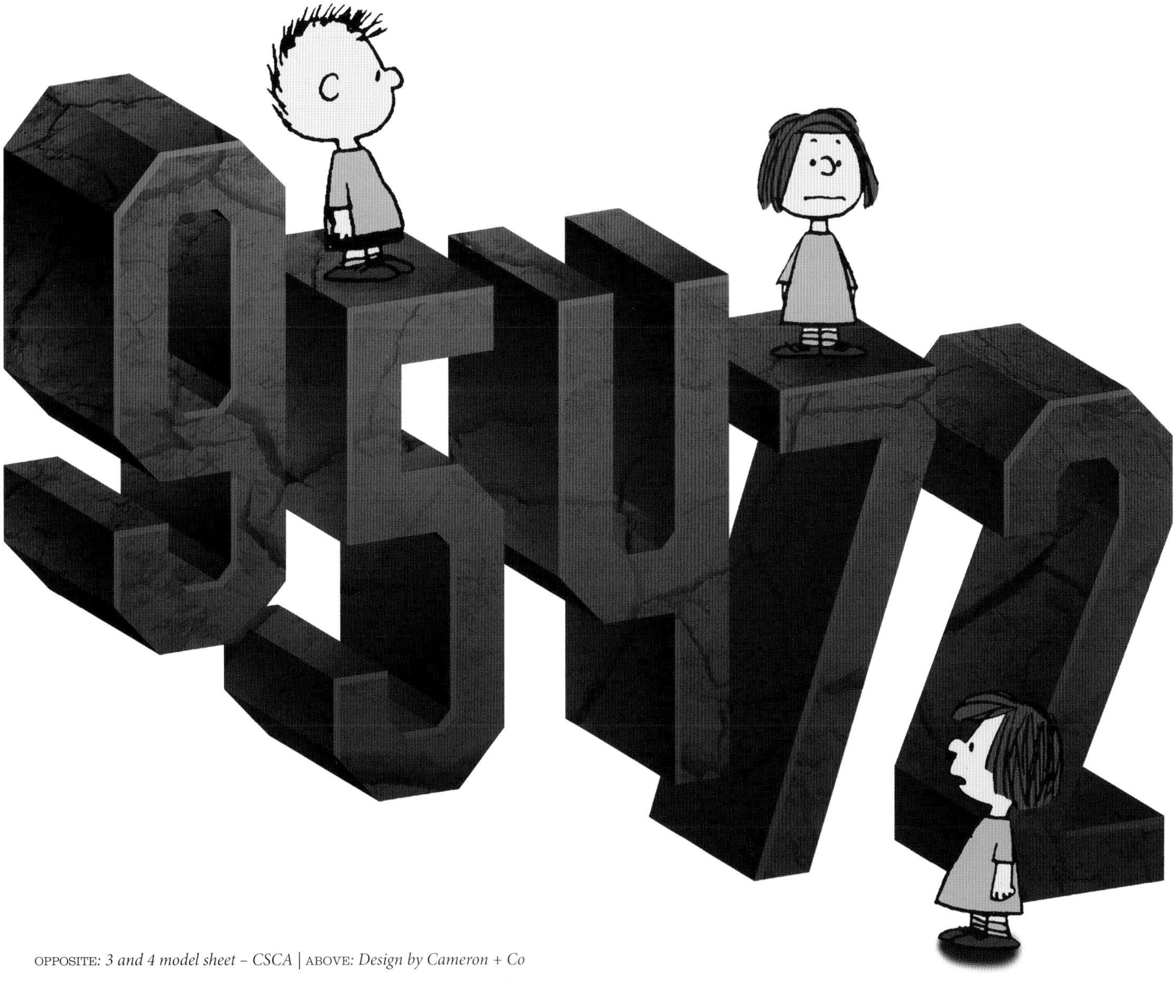

OPPOSITE: *3 and 4 model sheet – CSCA* | ABOVE: *Design by Cameron + Co*

HI! MY NAME IS LINUS..
MAY I SIT WITH YOU
AND EAT LUNCH?
©1986 United Feature Syndicate, Inc.
I DON'T
KNOW..WHEN
WERE YOU
BORN?
I WAS
BORN IN
OCTOBER..
6-9
I WAS BORN
IN DECEMBER
AREN'T YOU KIND OF
OLD FOR ME?
SCHULZ

# LYDIA

FIRST APPEARANCE
06/09/1986

"Aren't you kind of old for me?" asks Lydia upon learning that Linus's birthday is a full two months before hers. The question sets the tone for their entire relationship. The mercurial Lydia rarely goes by the same name twice, expects Christmas cards from Linus but won't tell him her address, and occasionally spends time with boys a full year older than her despite her unease with Linus's October birthdate.

These contradictions make Lydia the most frustrating and the most intriguing of Linus's classmates . . . even if he is kind of old for her.

Much of the humor in *Peanuts* is based on Charles Schulz's own experiences, and that's certainly true of Lydia's casual dismissal of Linus. "Every thought that I have, and every remembrance, goes into this strip. [Once] I was sitting at my desk at the art instruction school—I suppose I was 26—and nothing had been going right lately. I hadn't had any dates of any kind. I was lonely, and this very pretty young girl would come up with some letters to be signed. I'd see her walking around the room, day after day after day. It took me great courage, but I said, 'Would you be interested in going out for dinner and a movie?' and she said, 'Aren't you kind of old for me?' Oh boy, it would have been better if she had just reached over and punched me in the nose."

BEWARE
THE GIRL
WITH 1000 NAMES!
INTRODUCING
THE EVER-YOUTHFUL
LYDIA!
REBECCA
RACHEL
JEZEBEL
SUSAN
SARAH
MELISSA
SAMANTHA
ANNA
CLAUDIA
OPHELIA
POLLY
SNOWFLAKE

ABOVE: *Design by Cameron + Co*

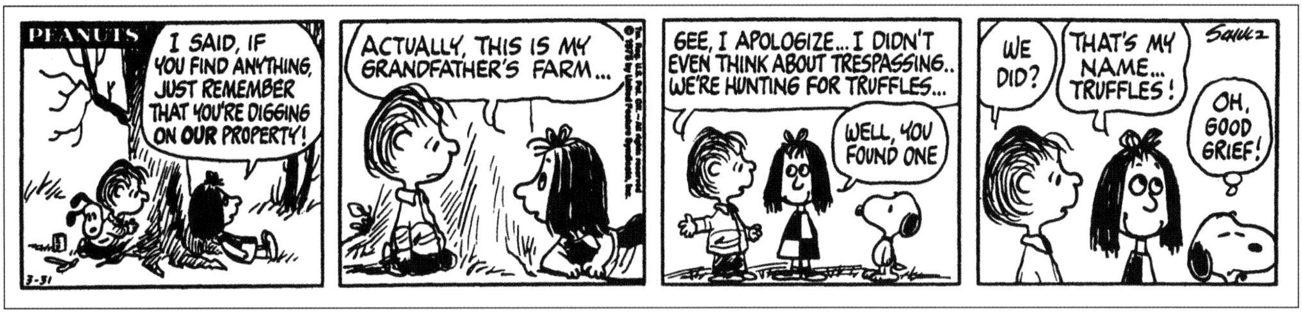
PEANUTS
I SAID, IF YOU FIND ANYTHING, JUST REMEMBER THAT YOU'RE DIGGING ON OUR PROPERTY!
ACTUALLY, THIS IS MY GRANDFATHER'S FARM...
GEE, I APOLOGIZE... I DIDN'T EVEN THINK ABOUT TRESPASSING.. WE'RE HUNTING FOR TRUFFLES...
WELL, YOU FOUND ONE
WE DID?
THAT'S MY NAME... TRUFFLES!
OH, GOOD GRIEF!

# TRUFFLES

FIRST APPEARANCE
03/31/1975

When Linus and Snoopy launch an expedition for truffles, their search fails to turn up the rare delicacy and, instead, leads them to the farmhouse of Truffles, so named by her grandfather because she's "as rare as a truffle." Linus and Snoopy both fall in love with Truffles, but only Snoopy is able to find his way back to her grandfather's farmhouse, leaving Linus heartbroken.

Truffles and Linus reunite during a school field trip, but a jealous Sally literally sends Linus up the roof, and it takes a Snoopy as a high-flying helicopter (piloted by Woodstock, who claims to have picked up this skill in Vietnam) to come to his rescue. Not surprisingly, Truffles never sees Linus again after Snoopy flies him to safety.

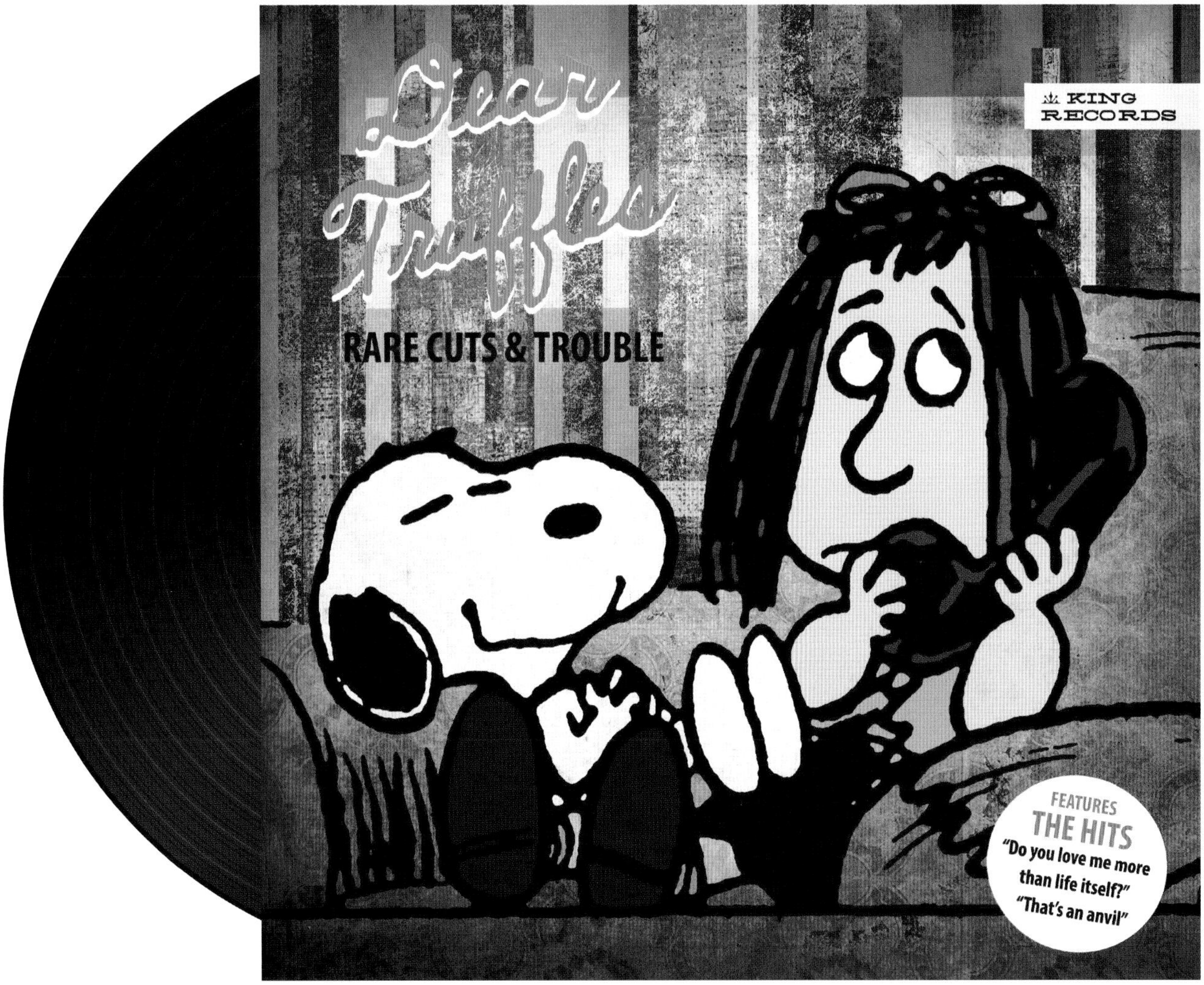
Dear Truffles
RARE CUTS & TROUBLE
KING RECORDS
FEATURES
THE HITS
"Do you love me more than life itself?"
"That's an anvil"

ABOVE: *Design by Cameron + Co*

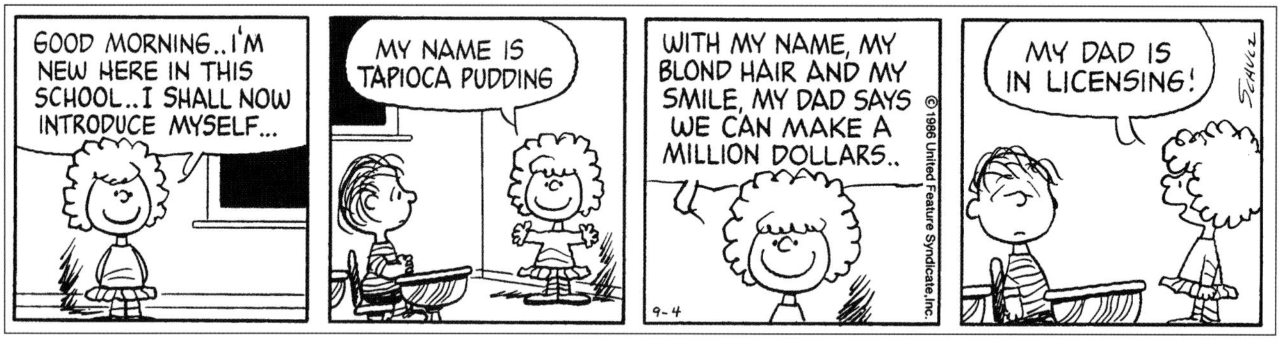
GOOD MORNING..I'M NEW HERE IN THIS SCHOOL..I SHALL NOW INTRODUCE MYSELF...
MY NAME IS TAPIOCA PUDDING
WITH MY NAME, MY BLOND HAIR AND MY SMILE, MY DAD SAYS WE CAN MAKE A MILLION DOLLARS..
© 1986 United Feature Syndicate, Inc.
9-4
MY DAD IS IN LICENSING!
SCHULZ

# Tapioca Pudding

FIRST APPEARANCE
09/04/1986

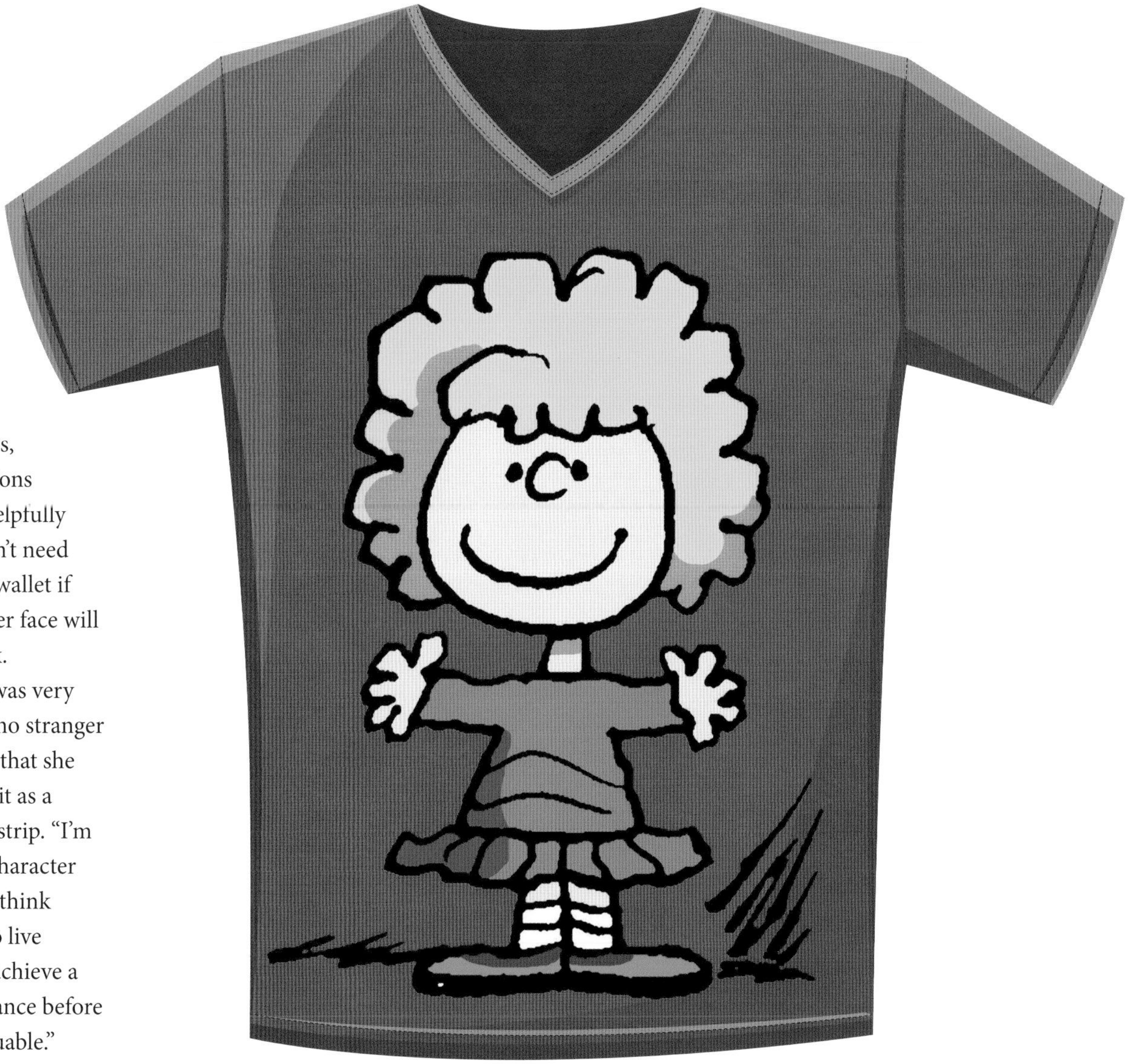

Tapioca Pudding is going to be a star—and she wants to make sure everyone knows it! Her father, who's in licensing, envisions his daughter as the cornerstone of a marketing empire, with her smiling face on T-shirts, greeting cards, and televisions everywhere. And, as she helpfully points out to Linus, he won't need to carry her picture in his wallet if she's his girlfriend, since her face will already be on his lunchbox.

Her tenure in *Peanuts* was very brief, and Charles Schulz, no stranger to licensing himself, knew that she simply wasn't going to cut it as a recurring character in the strip. "I'm not sure you can create a character specifically for licensing. I think the character almost has to live somewhere else first, and achieve a personality and an appearance before the character becomes valuable."

RIGHT: *Design by Cameron + Co* | OPPOSITE, TOP RIGHT: *Spot art from strip – Charles M. Schulz*

# MISS OTHMAR

**FIRST MENTIONED** 10/05/1959
**FIRST NAMED** 10/06/1959

"Wah, wah, wah, wah, wah,
wah, wah, wah, wah"

—Miss Othmar

"A gem among gems," Miss Othmar is the greatest teacher in the world, according to her star pupil, Linus. He develops a schoolboy crush on her almost immediately, but despite his devotion, he can never remember to bring eggshells from home for his big class project, to her eternal frustration.

Miss Othmar briefly retires when she marries Mr. Hagemeyer, but she misses teaching and soon returns to the classroom. Linus can't bring himself to address her by her married name, so continues to call her Miss Othmar.

Miss Othmar's voice was depicted as the sound of a trombone in television and film, and she was the first recurring adult character in *Peanuts*, which is surprising given young Charles Schulz's aversion to formal education. "I haven't always been too kind to teachers. I recall liking quite a few teachers in school, but I also remember being scared to death of more of them than I liked!"

PEANUTS
I HEAR YOU KIND OF LIKE YOUR NEW TEACHER, LINUS...
CHARLIE BROWN, I HAVE THE GREATEST TEACHER IN THE WHOLE WORLD! SHE'S A GEM AMONG GEMS!
SIGH
I NEVER REALIZED THAT THE NATIONAL EDUCATION ASSOCIATION TURNED OUT SUCH A FINE PRODUCT!
10-5
SCHULZ

PEANUTS
WHAT'S THIS ABOUT YOU AND A "MISS OTHMAR"? WHO IN THE WORLD IS MISS OTHMAR?
SHE'S MY TEACHER...SHE UNDERSTANDS ME!
10-6
EITHER SHE'S A GENIUS, OR SHE'S NEW ON THE JOB
SCHULZ

PEANUTS
SO YOU REALLY LIKE YOUR TEACHER, EH, LINUS?
SHE'S A GOOD TEACHER, CHARLIE BROWN...NO, SHE'S MORE THAN JUST A GOOD TEACHER..SHE'S A GREAT HUMAN BEING!
10/13
NO, SHE'S MORE THAN A GOOD TEACHER AND A GREAT HUMAN BEING...
MISS OTHMAR IS A GOOD TEACHER, A GREAT HUMAN BEING AND A LIVING DOLL!!
SCHULZ

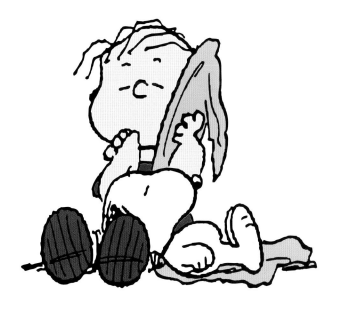

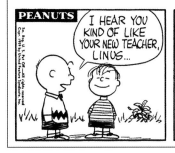

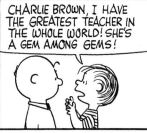

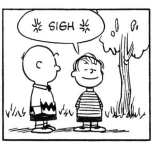

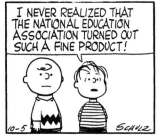

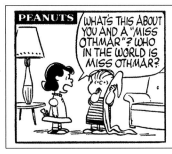

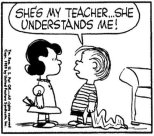

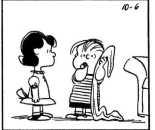

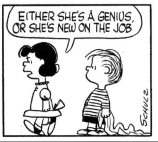

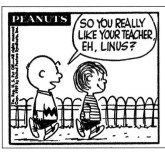

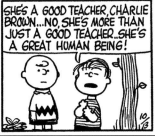

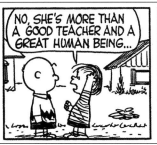

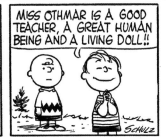

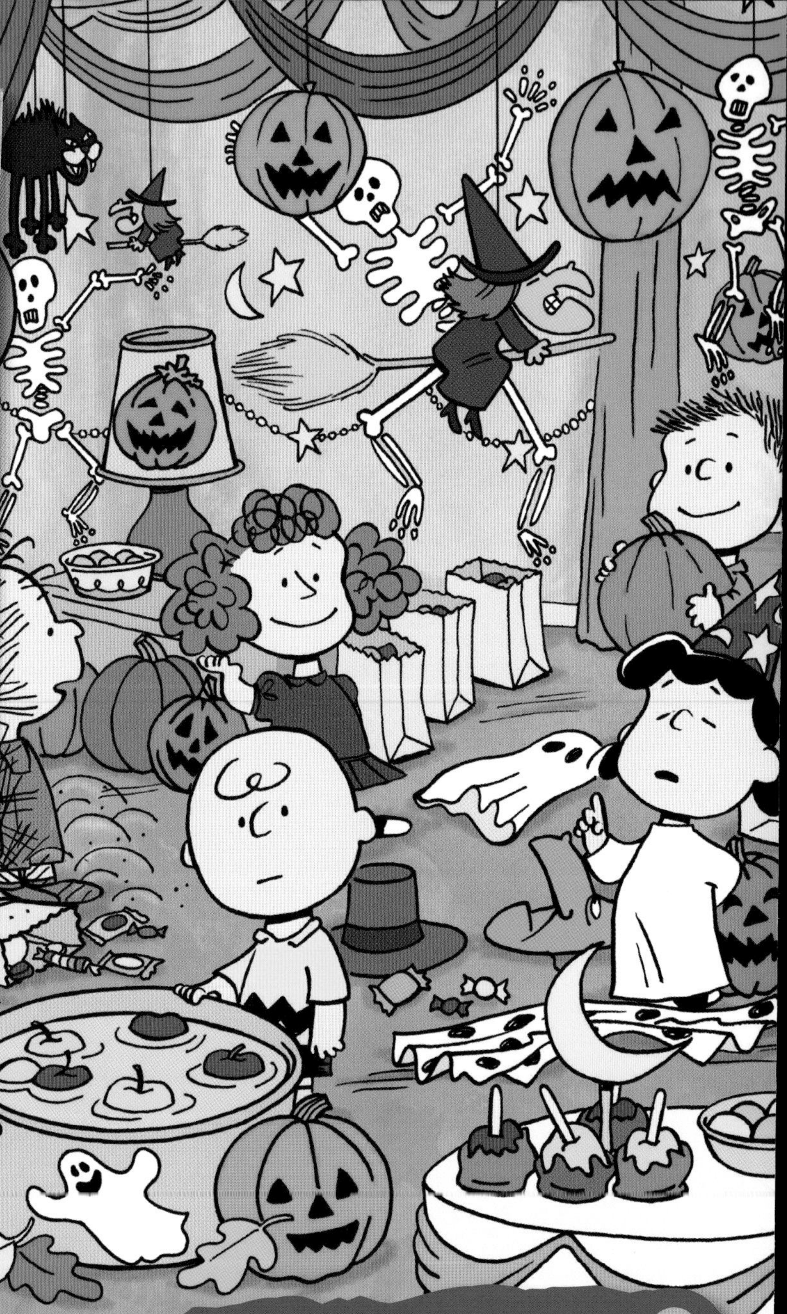

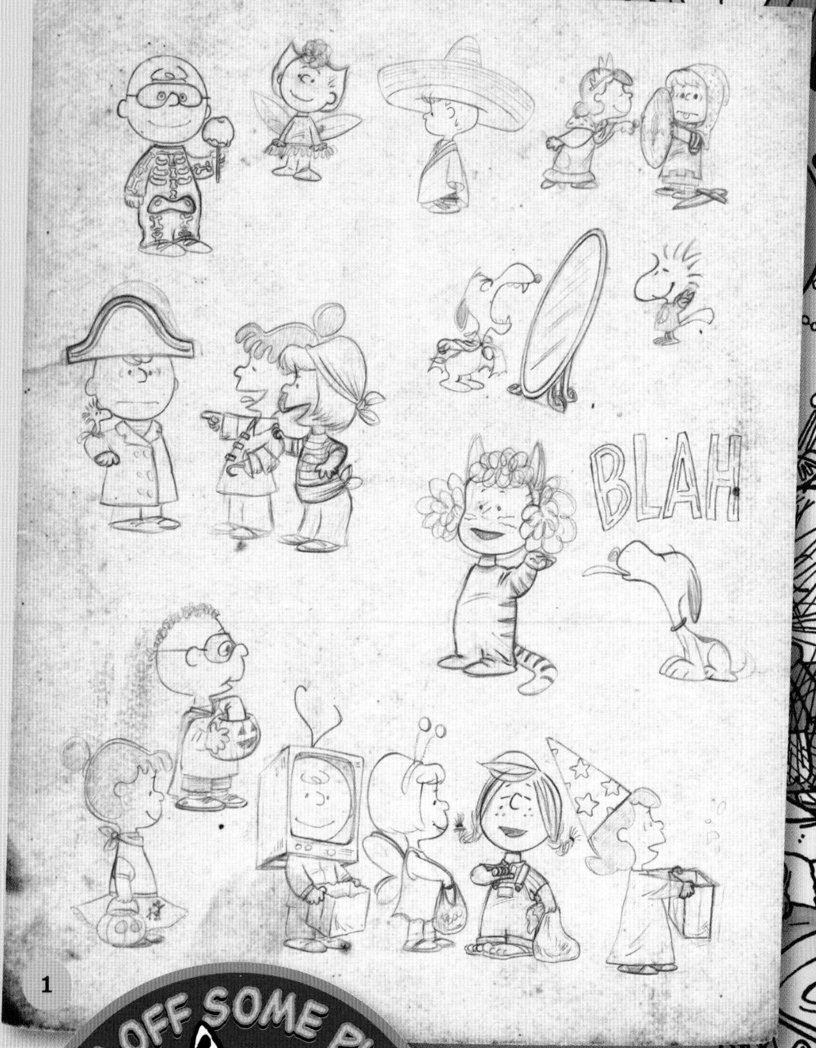
BLAH

1

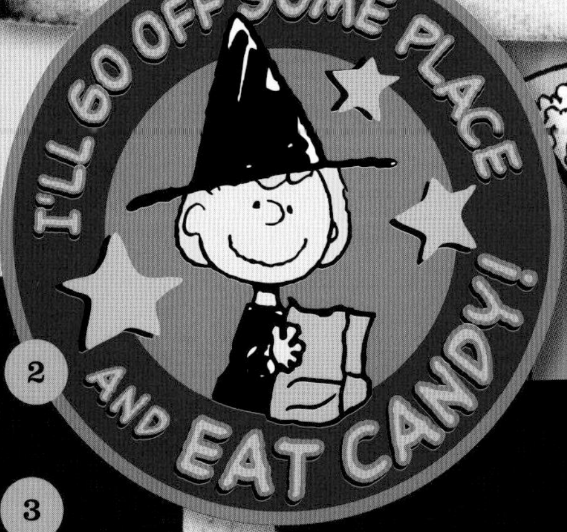
I'LL GO OFF SOME PLACE
AND EAT CANDY!

2

3

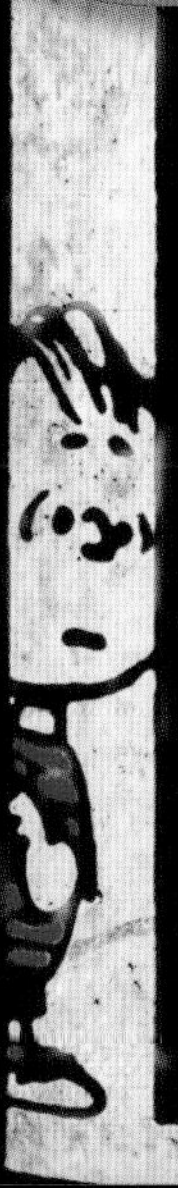

4

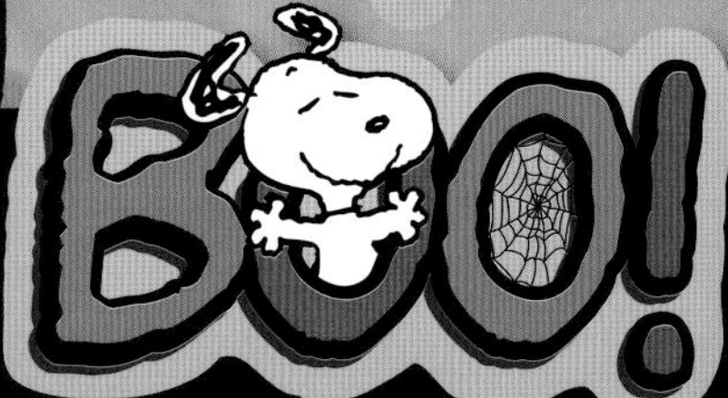
BOO!

5

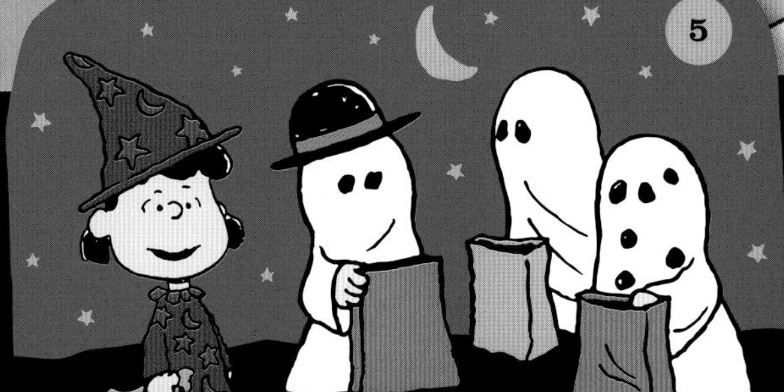

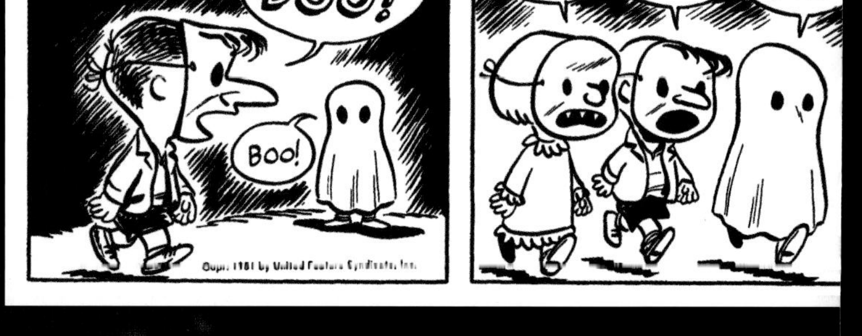
"PEANUTS"
BOO!
BOO!
BOO!
BOO!
BOO!

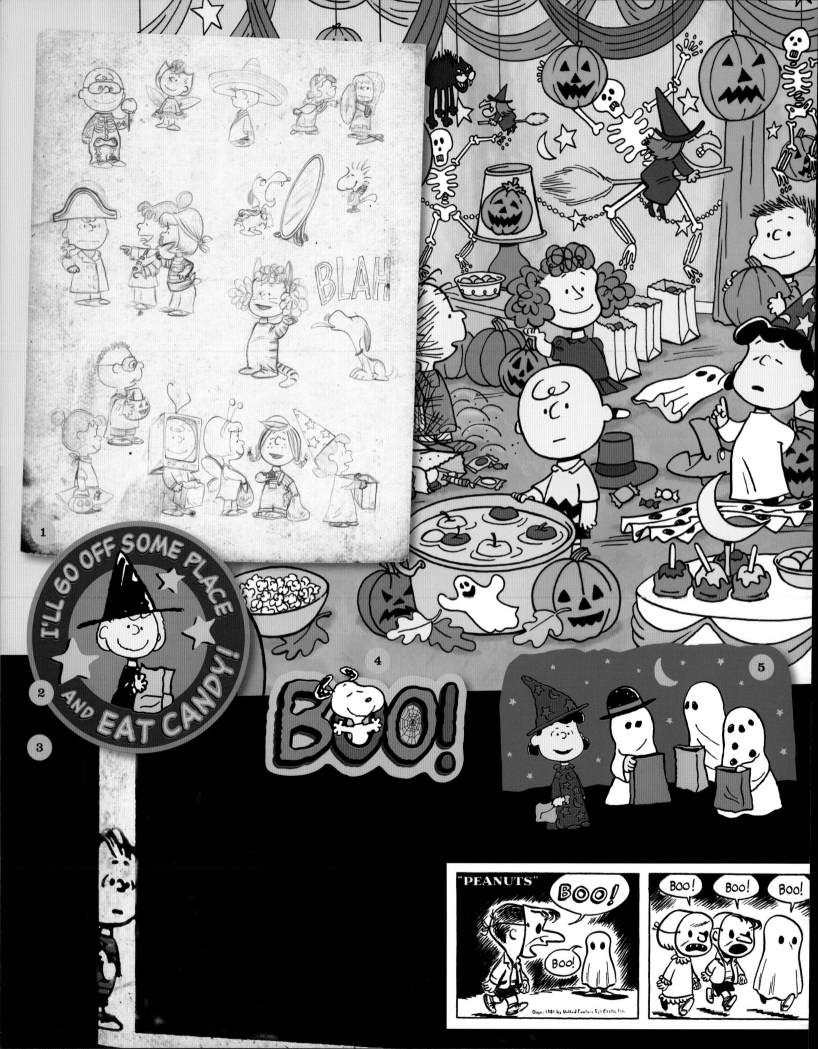

# HALLOWEEN

FIRST OBSERVED
10/31/1951

Each October 31, Charlie Brown and all of his friends dress up in costumes and go trick-or-treating from door to door before attending the big neighborhood Halloween party. All of his friends but one, since Linus spends each Halloween night in a quiet pumpkin patch, hoping to catch a glimpse of the Great Pumpkin, the mysterious holiday spirit who supposedly delivers presents to good children on Halloween night.

"I can't remember exactly [where the idea for the Great Pumpkin came from]," Charles Schulz told a reporter from *Psychology Today*. "I know I was drawing some Halloween strips about Linus, who is bright but very innocent, and he was confusing Halloween with Christmas because he was one holiday ahead of himself. Now the whole thing has become a parody of Christmas, and Linus gives the Great Pumpkin those qualities Santa Claus is supposed to have."

*1: Halloween costume preliminary designs – CSCA; 2: Style Guide art – CSCA; 3, 4, 5, 6, and 9: Style Guide art – PW; 7: Look & Find art – CSCA; 8: Got Milk ad – CSCA*

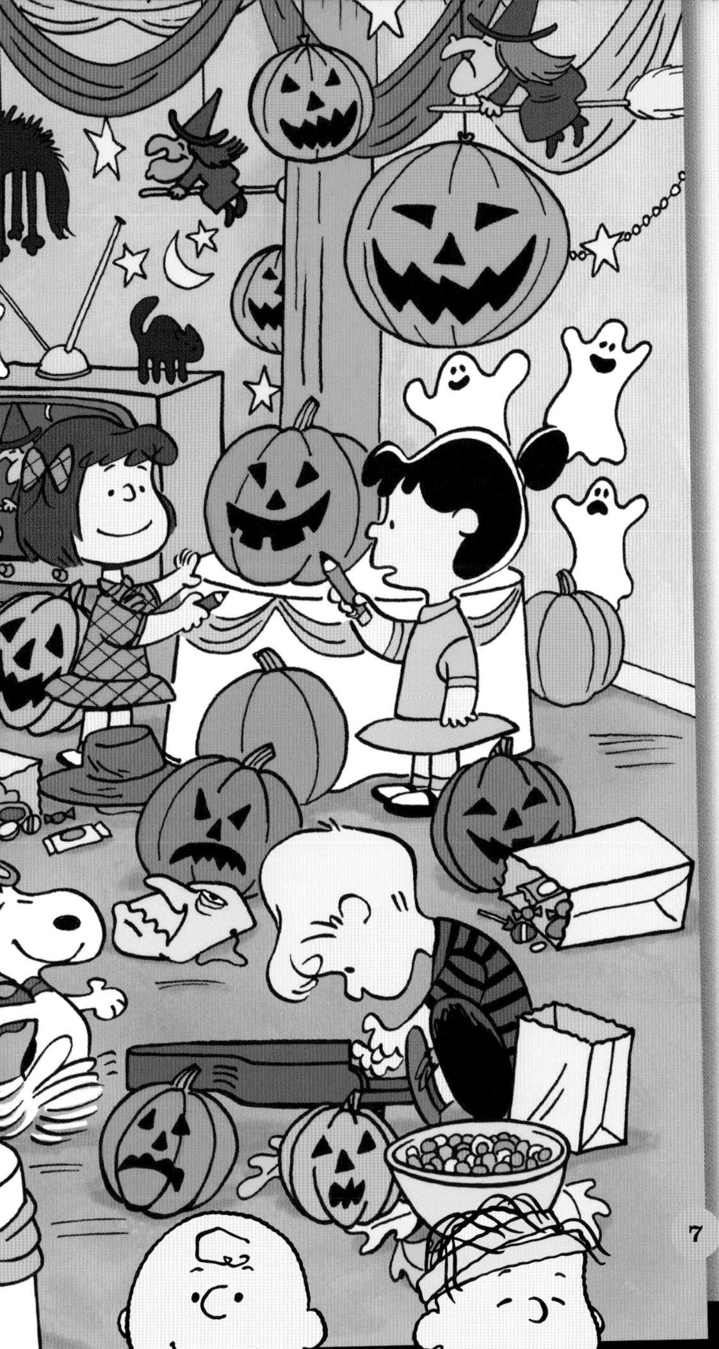

7

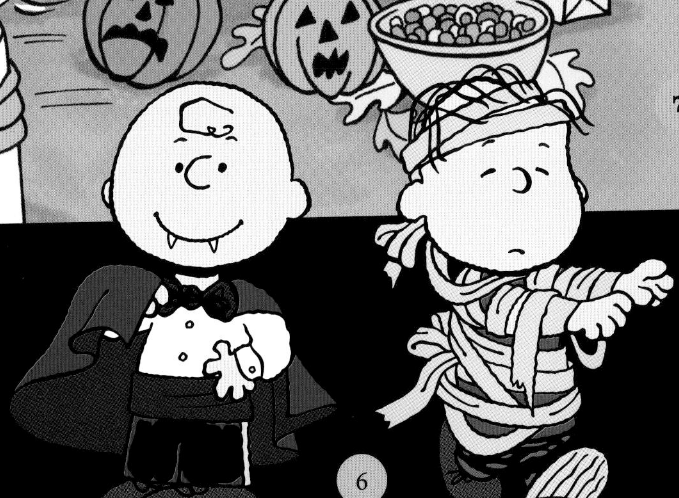

6

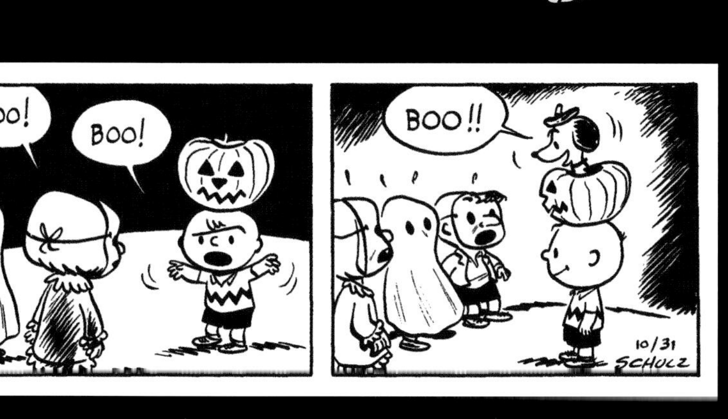

BOO!
BOO!!
10/31
SCHULZ


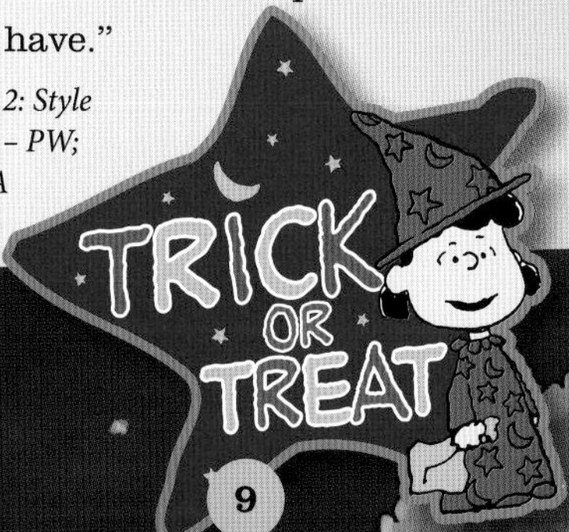

TRICK
OR
TREAT


9

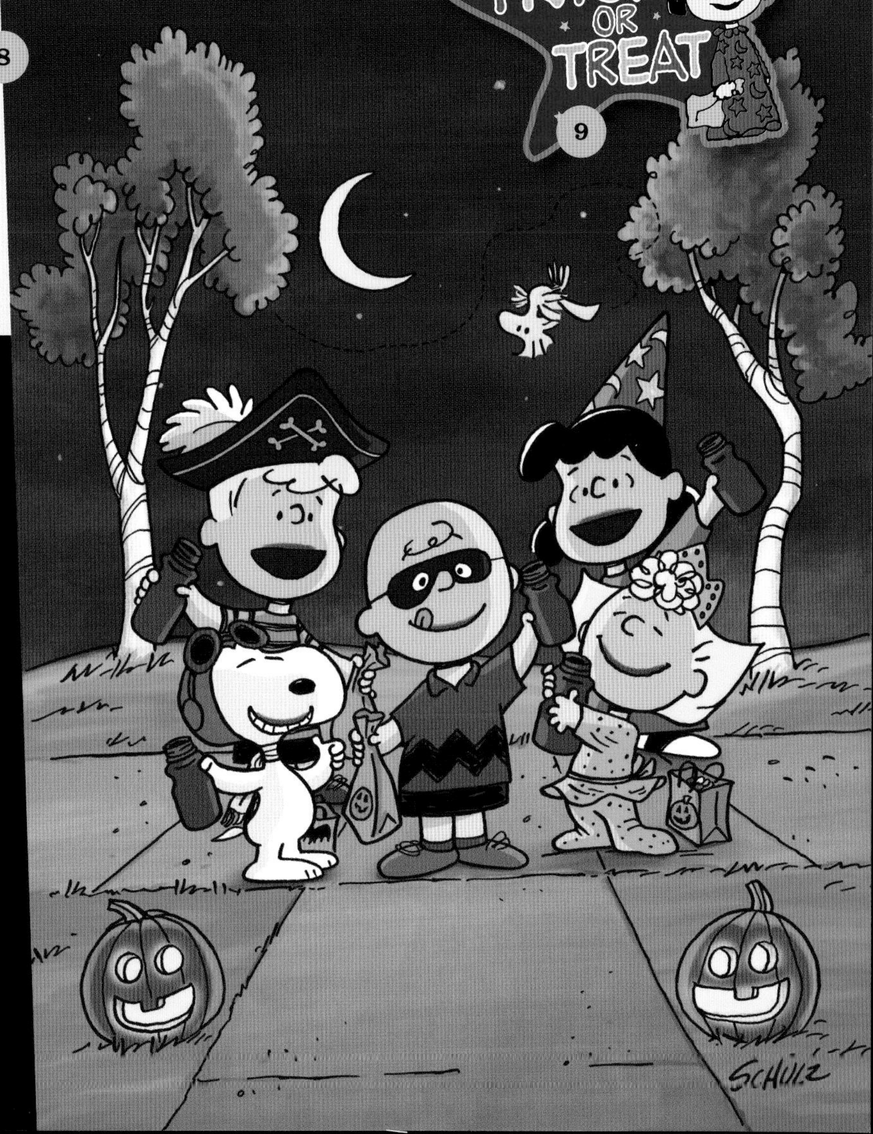

SCHULZ


8

# PIG-PEN

FIRST APPEARANCE
07/13/1954

With a cloud of dust accompanying him wherever he goes, Pig-Pen makes an unforgettable impression on everyone he meets—literally! Despite his (admittedly minimal) best efforts, Pig-Pen is a dust magnet and is rarely seen without his favorite overalls and several layers of dirt covering his clothes, face, and hands.

His friends learn to embrace his less-than-tidy appearance, and Charlie Brown is quick to defend Pig-Pen's dusty ways. As Charlie Brown explains to Patty, "Did it ever occur to you that 'Pig-Pen' might be carrying the dirt and dust of some past civilization? He could have on him some of the soil of ancient Babylon."

**"I have affixed to me the dirt and dust of countless ages . . . Who am I to disturb history?" —Pig-Pen**

Pig-Pen tries to clean himself up from time to time, but those efforts are always short-lived. Following his most successful attempt, he tries to attend a school dance but is turned away at the door, since his classmates don't recognize him! He embraces his unkempt appearance and accepts that it's just who he is. As he once explained to his mother while unsuccessfully trying to scrub his hands, "I think I've reached the point of no return!"

"I now have 20 characters, but there are really only six," noted Charles Schulz, when asked about the large cast of *Peanuts*. "I have not given the others depth enough to make them really useful. 'Pig-Pen,' for instance. He's only good when he's dirty. And I don't think about little boys who need a bath all that much."

RIGHT: *Spot art from strips – Charles M. Schulz* | OPPOSITE: *Style Guide art – CSCA*

HELLO THERE.. WHAT'S YOUR NAME?
I HAVEN'T GOT A NAME..PEOPLE JUST CALL ME THINGS..REAL INSULTING THINGS...
WHAT DO THEY CALL YOU MOST OF THE TIME?
I'LL TELL YOU IF YOU WON'T LAUGH...
'PIG-PEN'
7-13

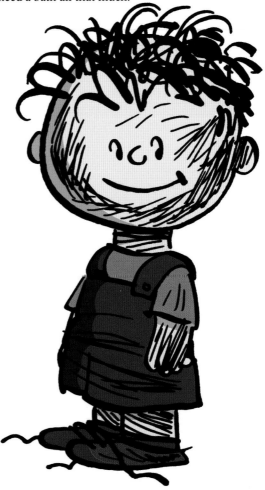

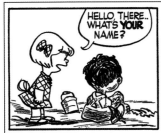

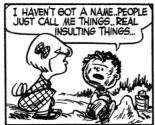

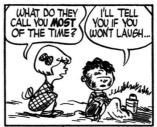

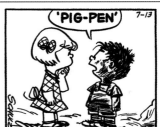

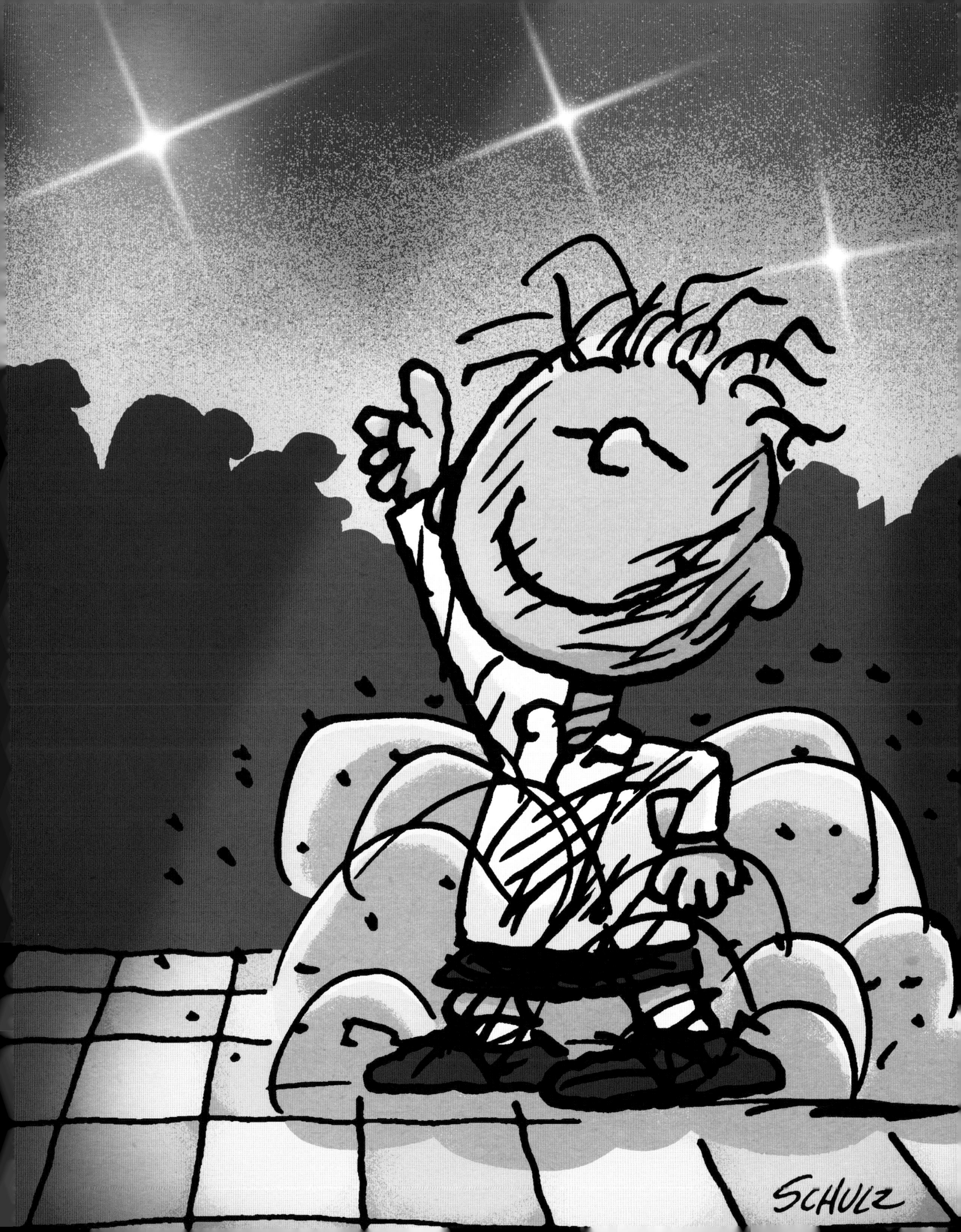
SCHULZ

"I'm perfectly clean now, but just let me step out of the house for one minute . . ." —Pig-Pen

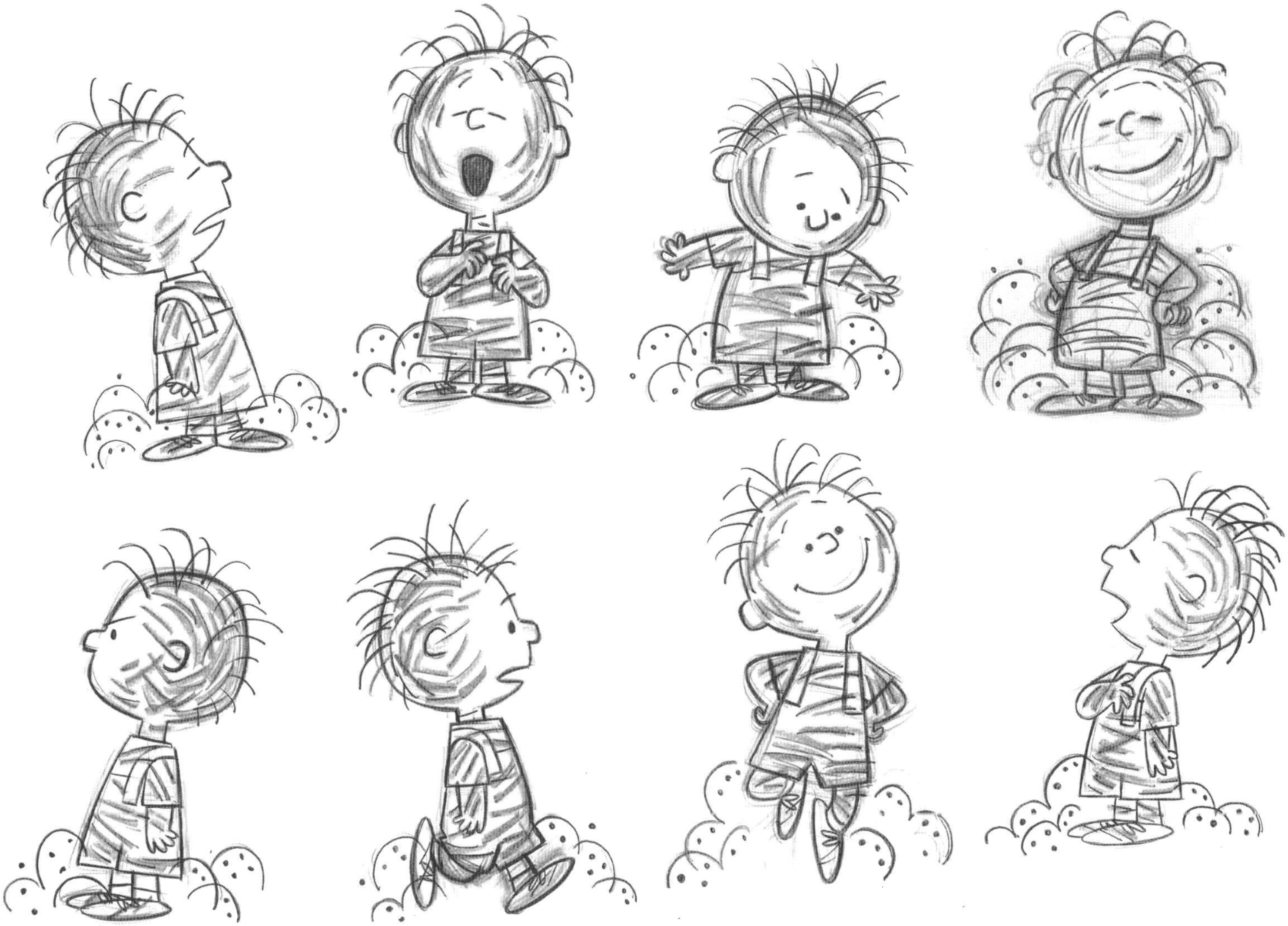

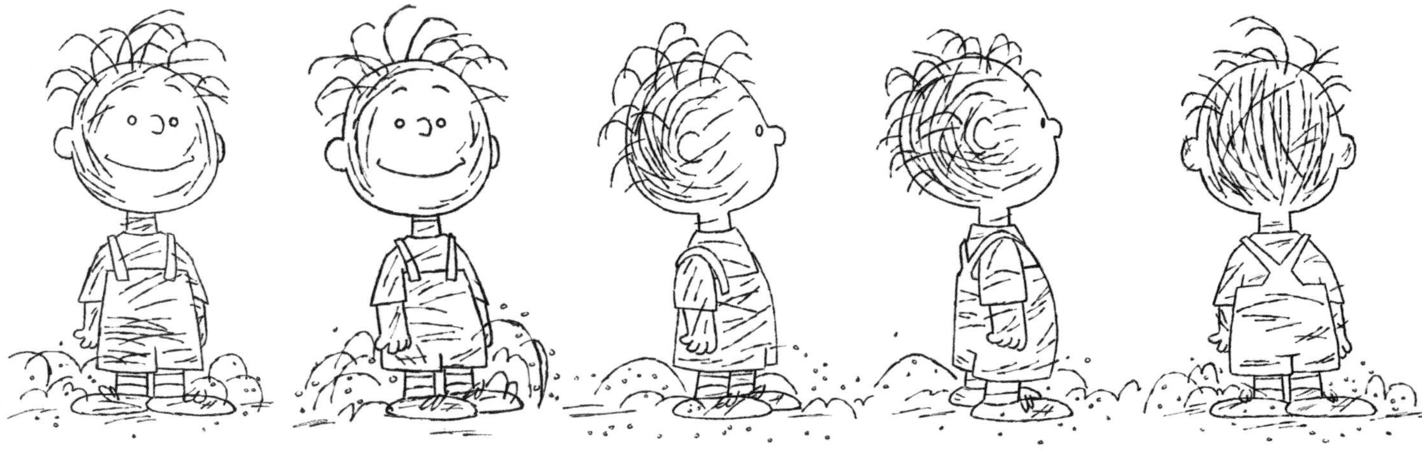

TOP AND ABOVE: *Pig-Pen model sheets – CSCA*

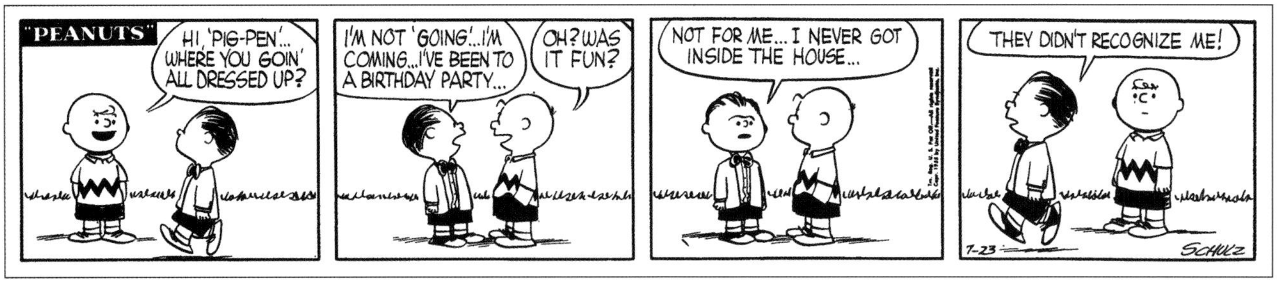
"PEANUTS"
HI, 'PIG-PEN'... WHERE YOU GOIN' ALL DRESSED UP?
I'M NOT 'GOING'...I'M COMING...I'VE BEEN TO A BIRTHDAY PARTY...
OH? WAS IT FUN?
NOT FOR ME... I NEVER GOT INSIDE THE HOUSE...
THEY DIDN'T RECOGNIZE ME!
7-23
SCHULZ

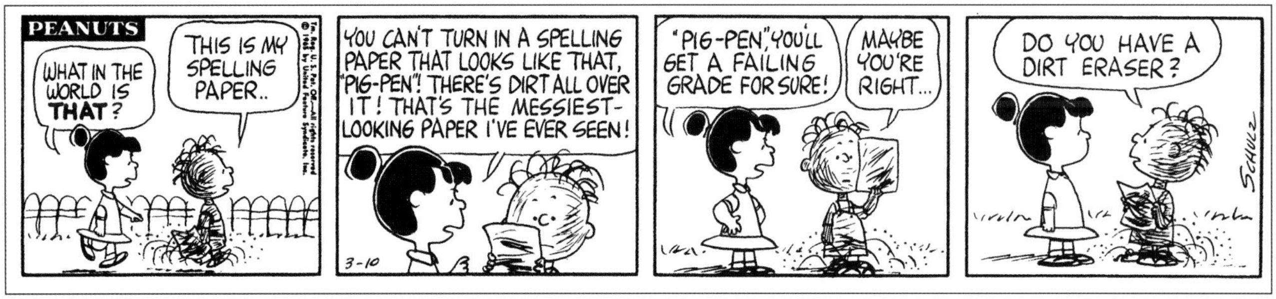
PEANUTS
WHAT IN THE WORLD IS **THAT**?
THIS IS MY SPELLING PAPER..
YOU CAN'T TURN IN A SPELLING PAPER THAT LOOKS LIKE THAT, "PIG-PEN"! THERE'S DIRT ALL OVER IT! THAT'S THE MESSIEST-LOOKING PAPER I'VE EVER SEEN!
3-10
"PIG-PEN," YOU'LL GET A FAILING GRADE FOR SURE!
MAYBE YOU'RE RIGHT...
DO YOU HAVE A DIRT ERASER?
SCHULZ

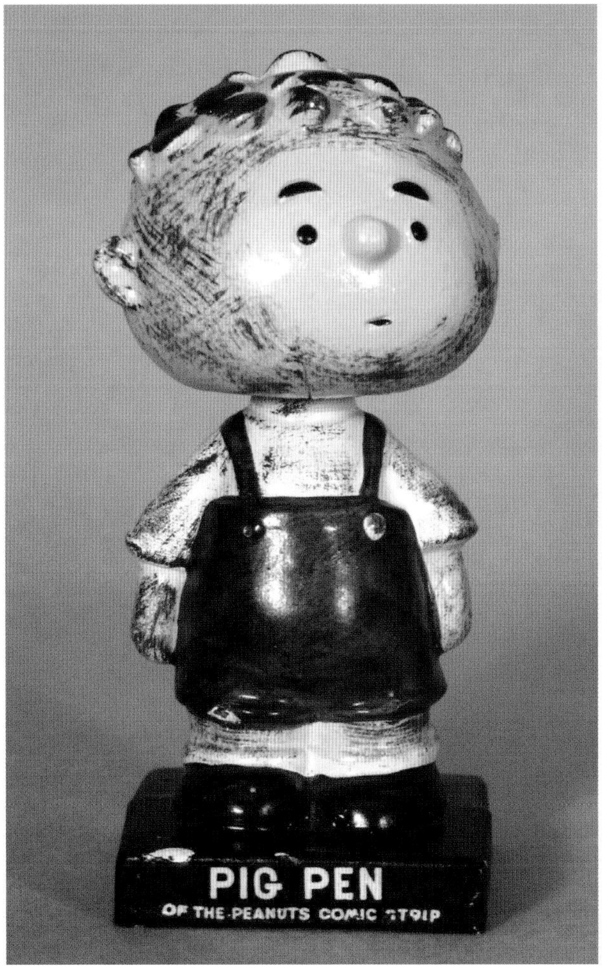
PIG PEN
OF THE PEANUTS COMIC STRIP

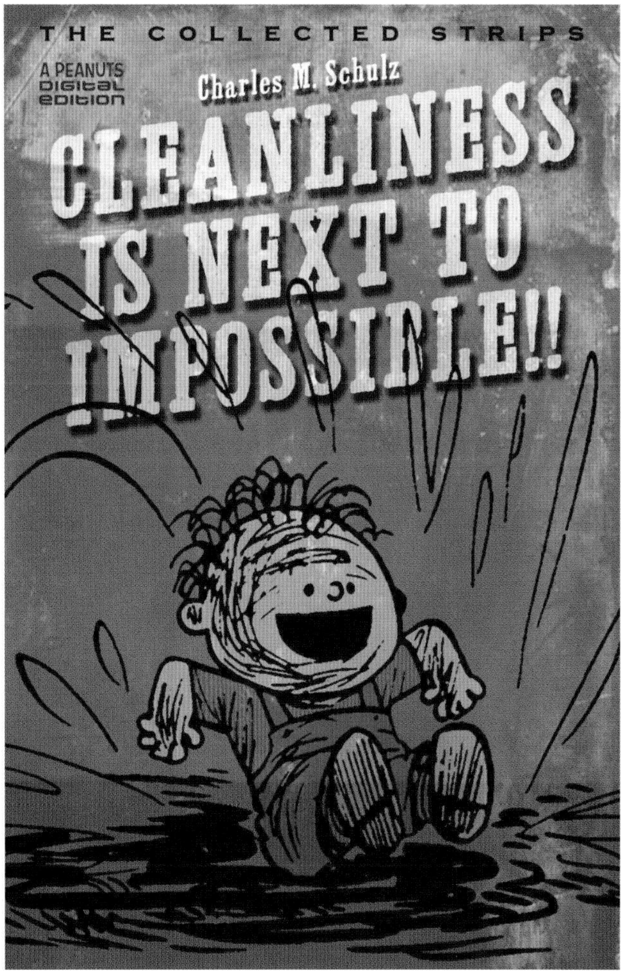
THE COLLECTED STRIPS
A PEANUTS DIGITAL EDITION
Charles M. Schulz
CLEANLINESS IS NEXT TO IMPOSSIBLE!!

ABOVE LEFT: *Pig-Pen bobblehead produced by LEGO®, 1959 – CMSM* | ABOVE RIGHT: Cleanliness Is Next to Impossible!!, Peanuts *Digital Edition – CSCA* | OVERLEAF, LEFT: *Comic book cover design concept – CSCA* | RIGHT: Peanuts, *#17 Boom! Studios comic book cover – CSCA*

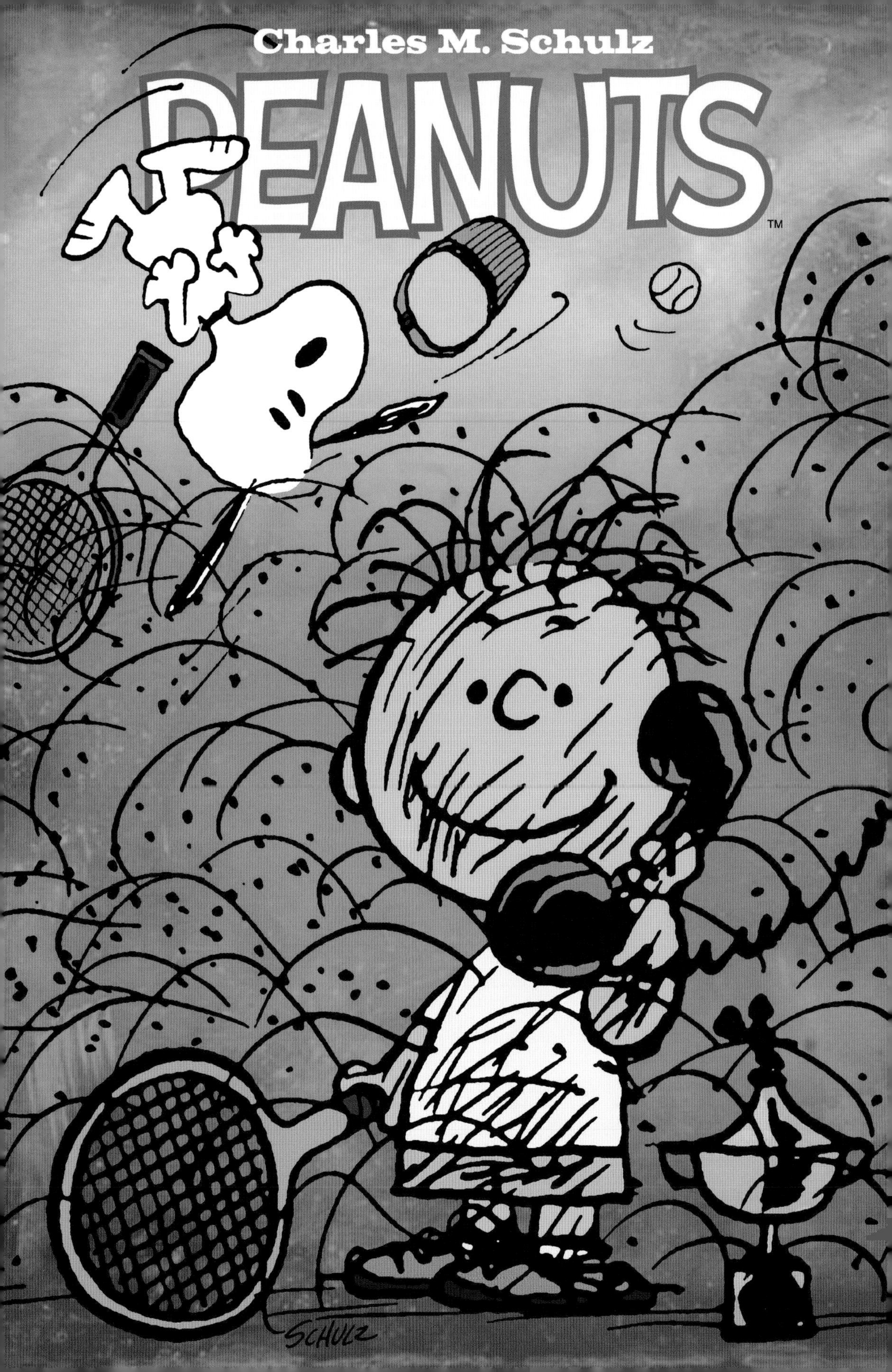
Charles M. Schulz
PEANUTS
SCHULZ

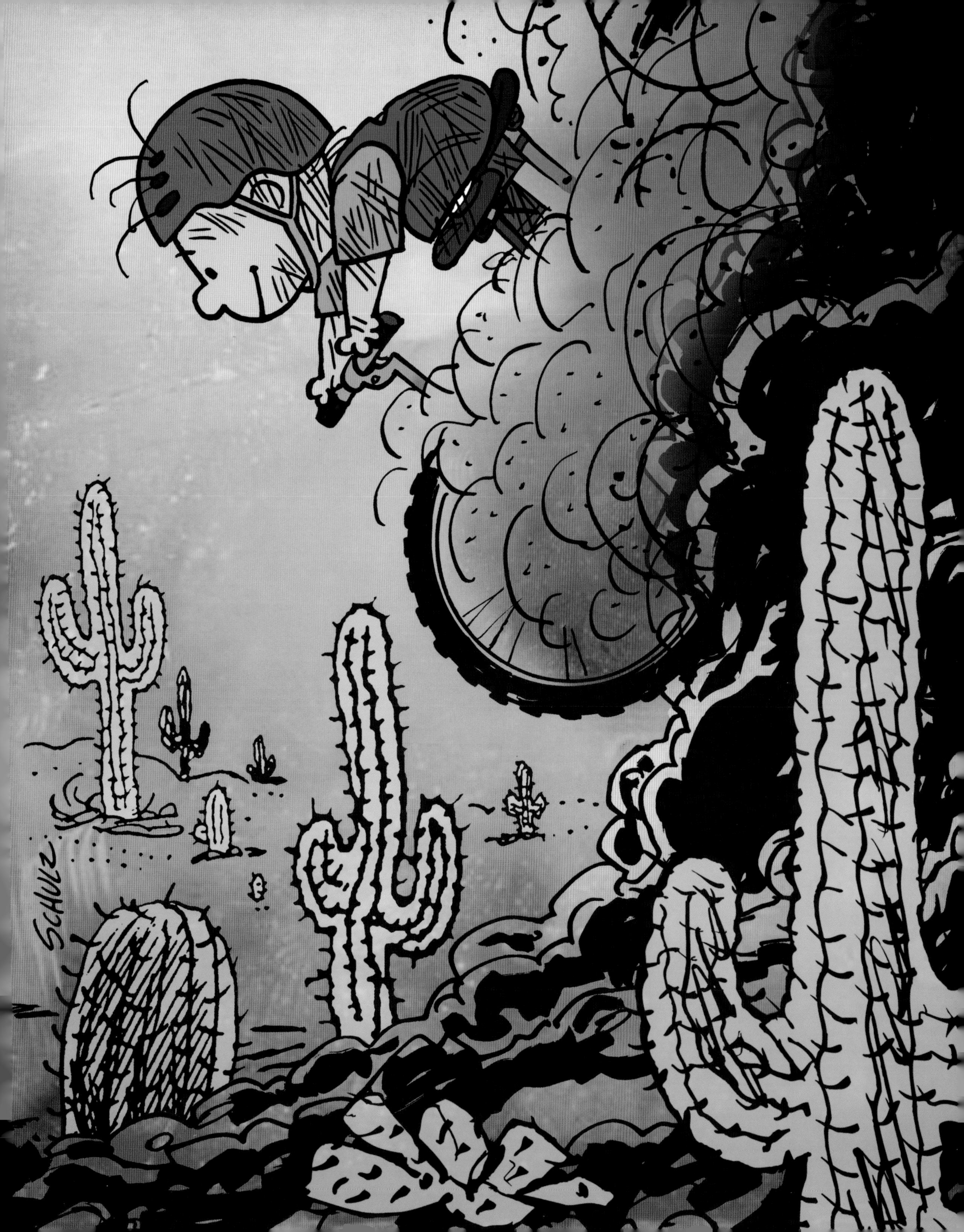
SCHULZ

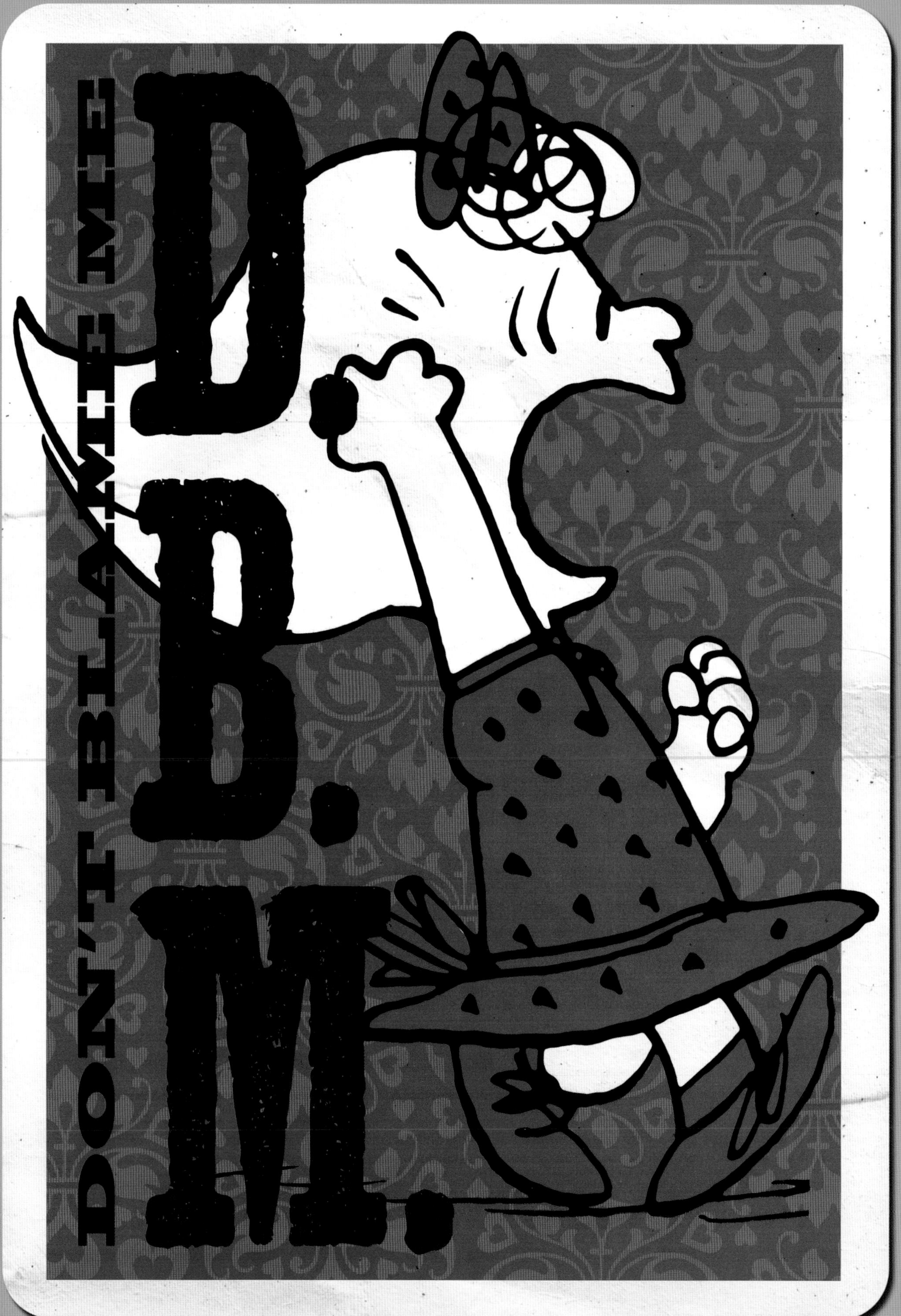
D.B.M.
DON'T BLAME ME

# SALLY BROWN

FIRST MENTIONED 05/26/1959
FIRST APPEARANCE 08/23/1959

Charlie Brown's younger sister, Sally, is the sweetest, kindest girl you'll ever meet. She's also the most cynical, shallow girl you'll ever meet. Her outlook on life is complex and full of contradictions, but her good nature always wins out in the end. Except when it doesn't.

Sally becomes disenchanted with school almost from the start and is skeptical of her teachers, her fellow students, and whether or not anything she learns will have any practical applications toward her future occupation as a hairstylist or housewife. To help her navigate school and her daily life, Sally adopts (and quickly abandons) a number of personal philosophies, including "What do I know?" "Don't blame me," and the classic "Who cares? How should I know? Do you think I'm out of my mind?"

She attempts to put as little effort as possible into her life, eschewing sports and once even enrolling in Beanbag Camp, where she watches TV and eats junk food all summer long. She does put more effort into wooing her "Sweet Babboo," Linus, who steadfastly rejects this pet name. Despite all these setbacks, Sally keeps on trying to do her best. Except when she doesn't.

"Sally . . . is the complete pragmatist," Charles Schulz noted, when asked about Charlie Brown's family. "I personally do not like her; she is rude to her big brother Charlie. I could easily become angry with her. Yet there is a certain charm when she fractures the language: 'By golly, if any centimeters come in this room, I'll step on them!'"

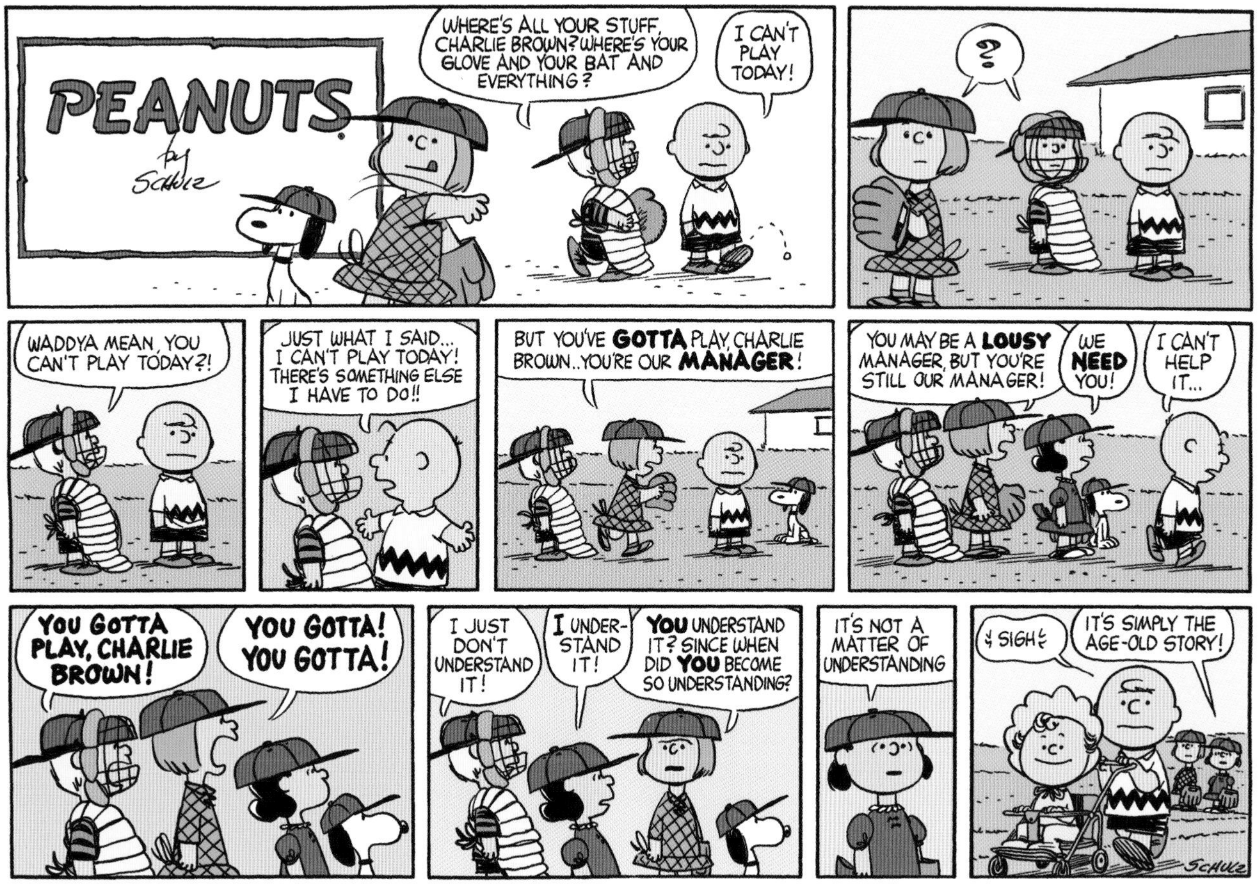
PEANUTS
by SCHULZ
WHERE'S ALL YOUR STUFF, CHARLIE BROWN? WHERE'S YOUR GLOVE AND YOUR BAT AND EVERYTHING?
I CAN'T PLAY TODAY!
?
WADDYA MEAN, YOU CAN'T PLAY TODAY?!
JUST WHAT I SAID... I CAN'T PLAY TODAY! THERE'S SOMETHING ELSE I HAVE TO DO!!
BUT YOU'VE GOTTA PLAY, CHARLIE BROWN.. YOU'RE OUR MANAGER!
YOU MAY BE A LOUSY MANAGER, BUT YOU'RE STILL OUR MANAGER!
WE NEED YOU!
I CAN'T HELP IT...
YOU GOTTA PLAY, CHARLIE BROWN!
YOU GOTTA! YOU GOTTA!
I JUST DON'T UNDERSTAND IT!
I UNDER-STAND IT!
YOU UNDERSTAND IT? SINCE WHEN DID YOU BECOME SO UNDERSTANDING?
IT'S NOT A MATTER OF UNDERSTANDING
SIGH
IT'S SIMPLY THE AGE-OLD STORY!
SCHULZ

OPPOSITE: *Style Guide art – CSCA*

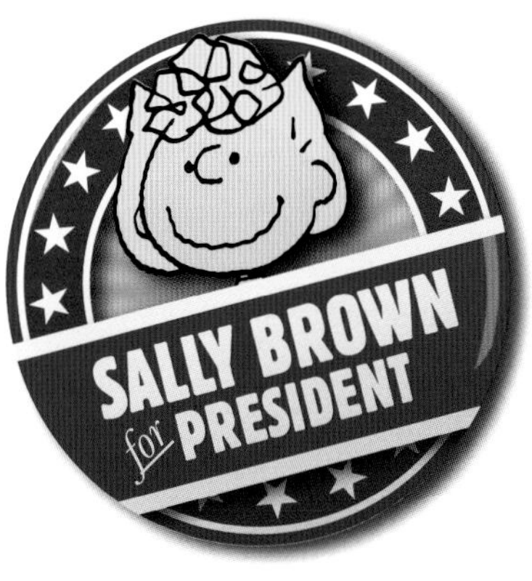
SALLY BROWN
for PRESIDENT

1

"If you'll help me with my homework, someday when I'm rich and famous, I'll talk to you."

—Sally Brown

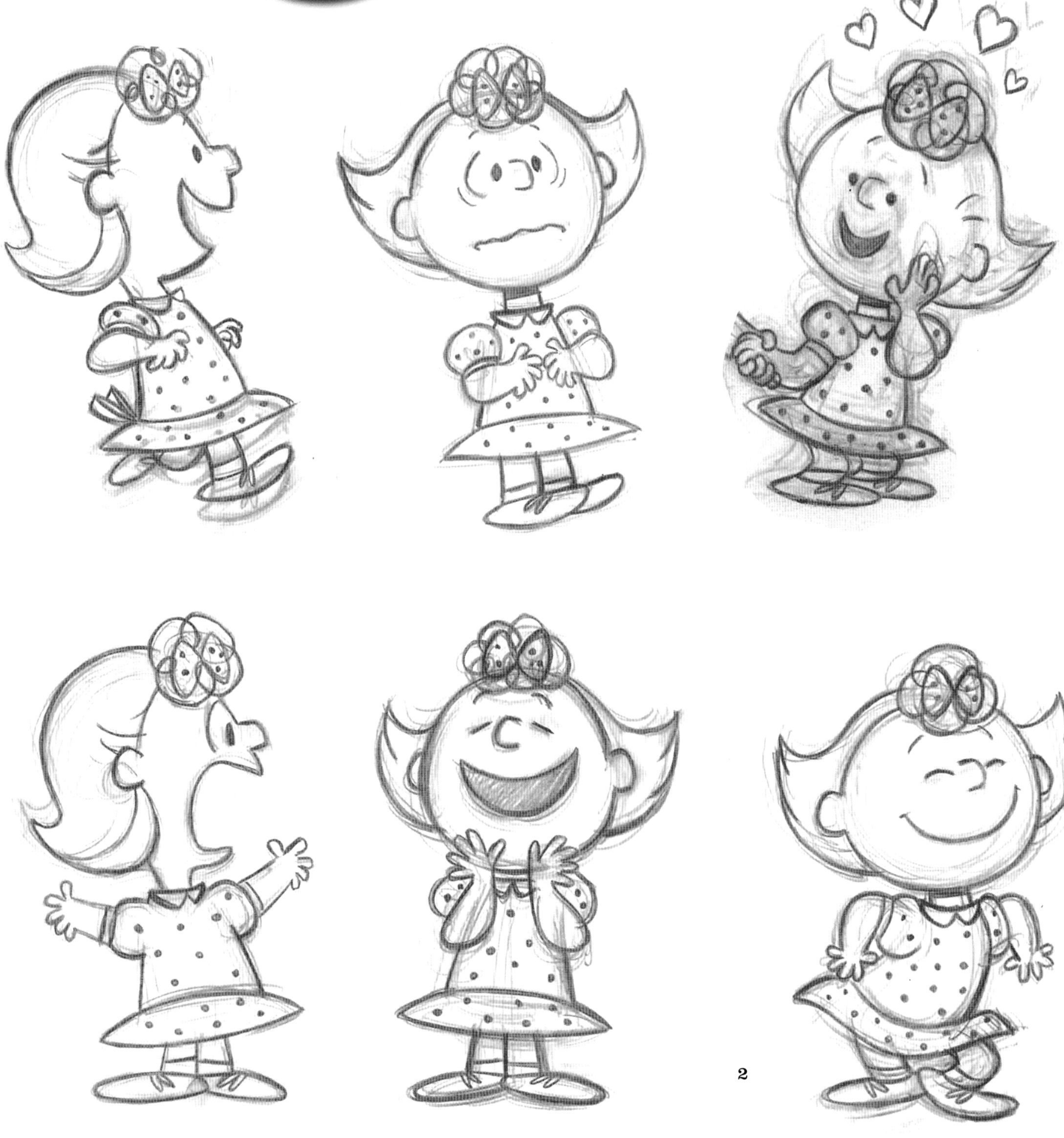

2

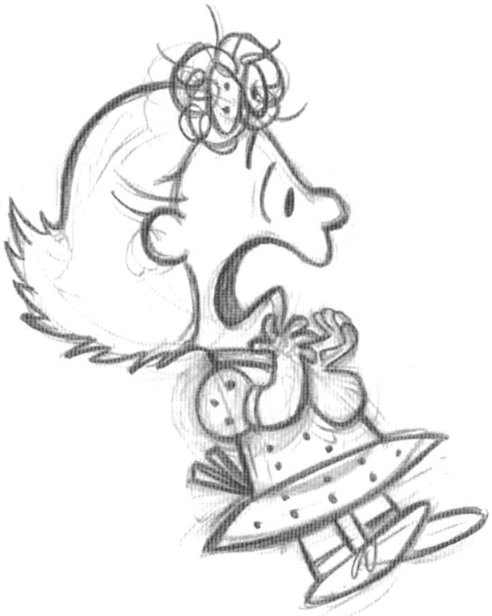

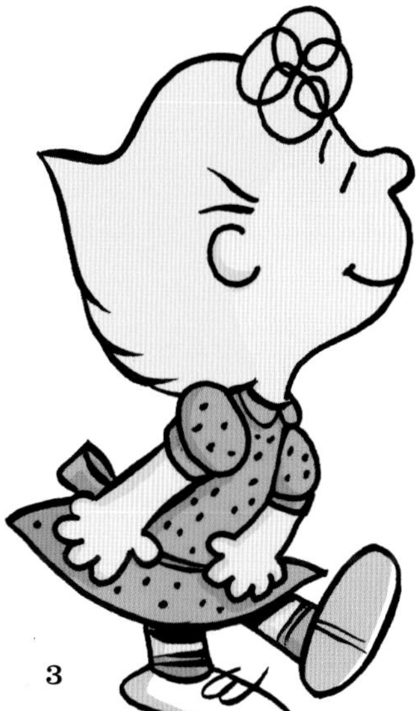

3

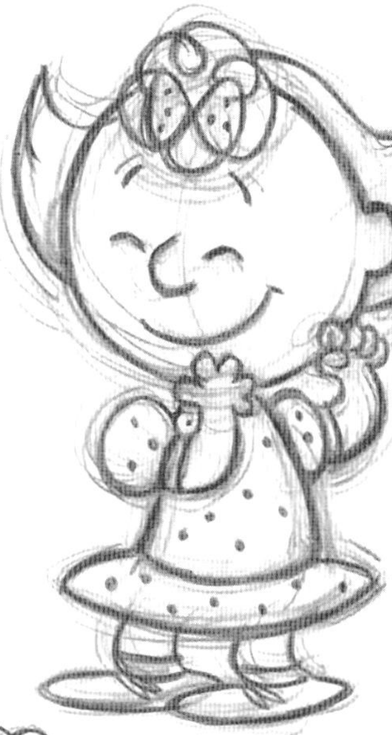

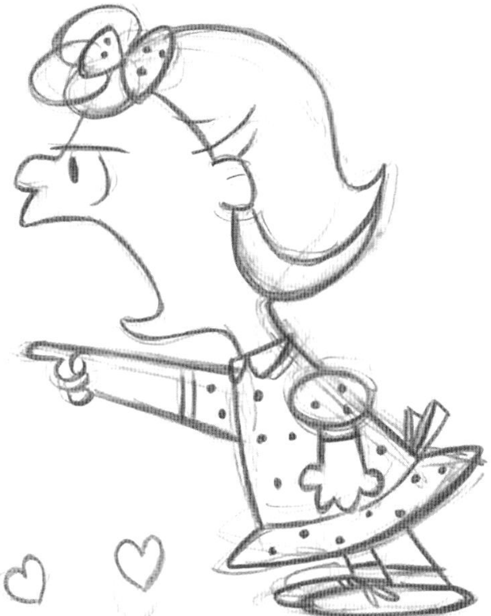

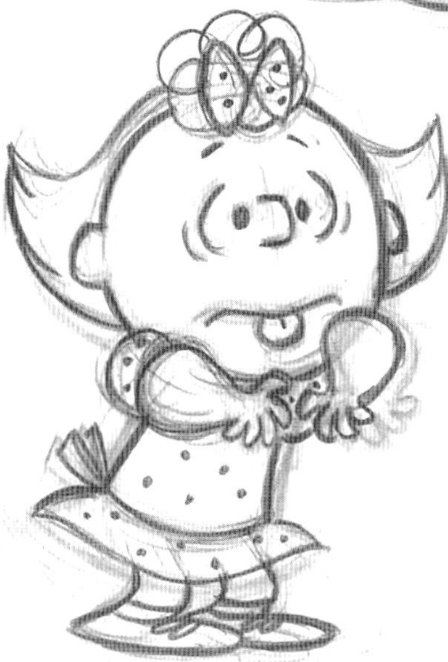

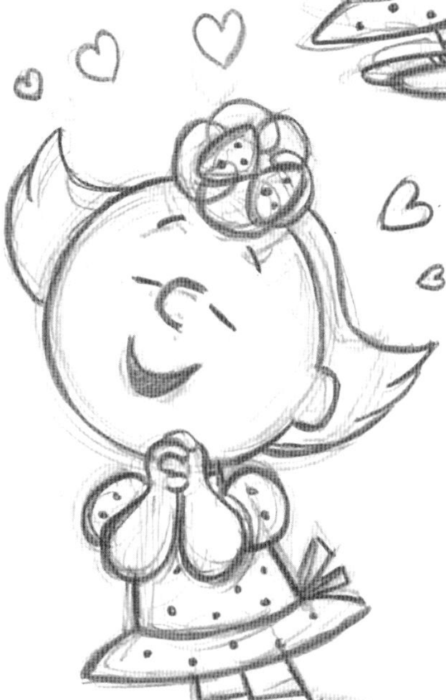

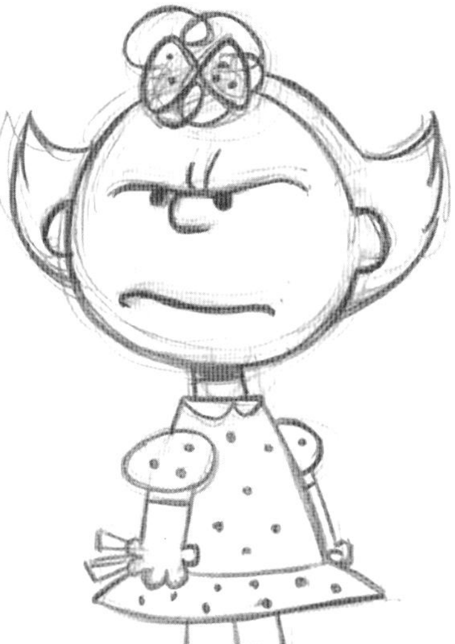

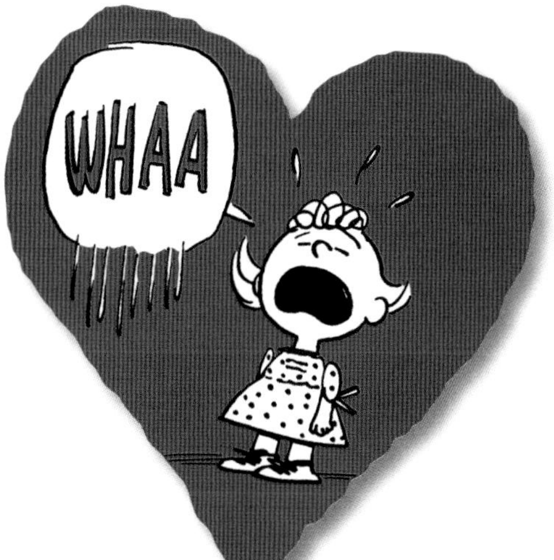
WHAA

4

*1: Style guide art – PW; 2: Sally model sheet – CSCA; 3 and 4: Style Guide art – CSCA*

## THE LITTLE SISTER

Sally Brown's personality is a sharp contrast to her big brother's. Where he's shy and introspective, she's boisterous and opinionated. She's quick to solicit his advice, and just as quick to ignore it. If he leaves the house for any length of time, whether it's a doctor's appointment or two weeks at summer camp, she attempts to claim his bedroom for herself.

But despite their differences, Sally loves Charlie Brown and knows that she can always count on him. Because after all, that's what big brothers are for.

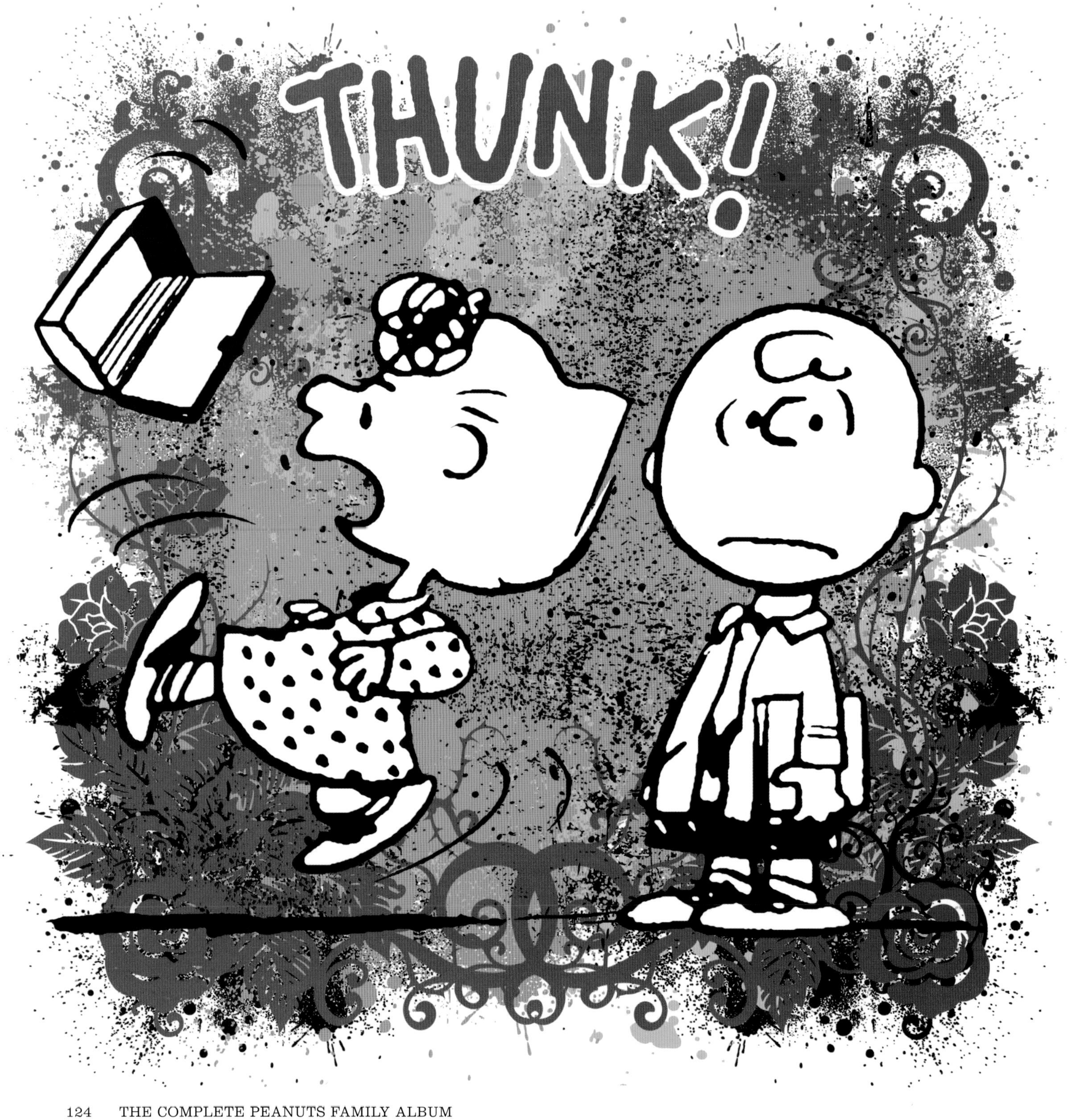
THUNK!

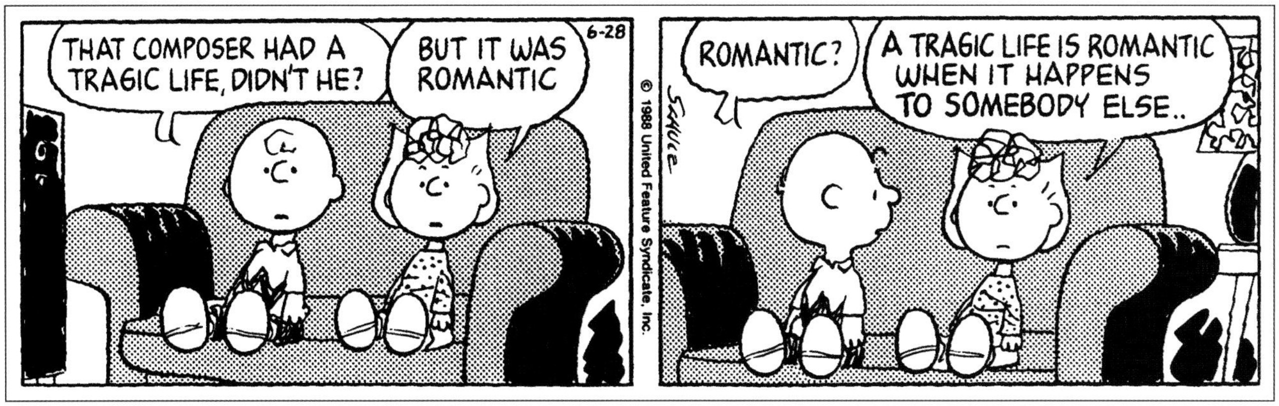
THAT COMPOSER HAD A TRAGIC LIFE, DIDN'T HE?
BUT IT WAS ROMANTIC
6-28
© 1988 United Feature Syndicate, Inc.
ROMANTIC?
A TRAGIC LIFE IS ROMANTIC WHEN IT HAPPENS TO SOMEBODY ELSE..

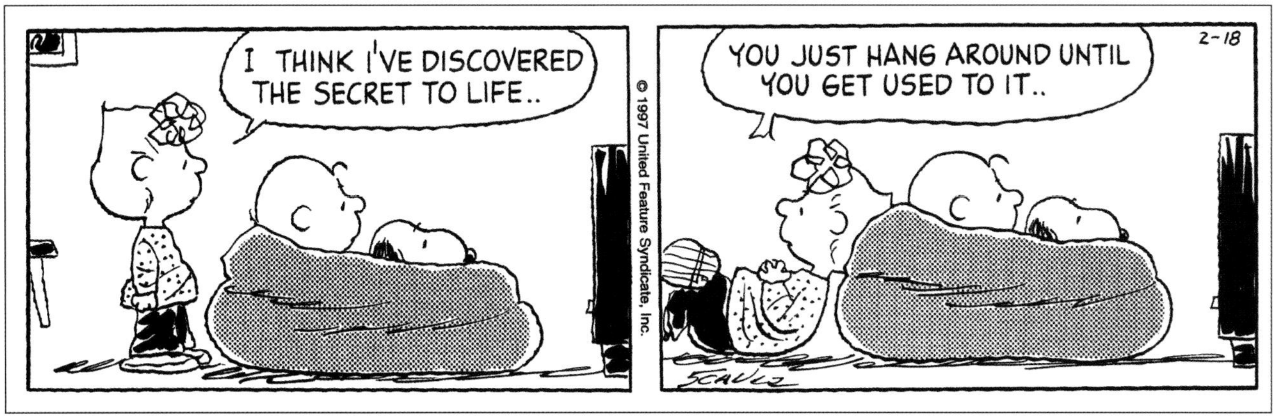
I THINK I'VE DISCOVERED THE SECRET TO LIFE..
© 1997 United Feature Syndicate, Inc.
YOU JUST HANG AROUND UNTIL YOU GET USED TO IT..
2-18

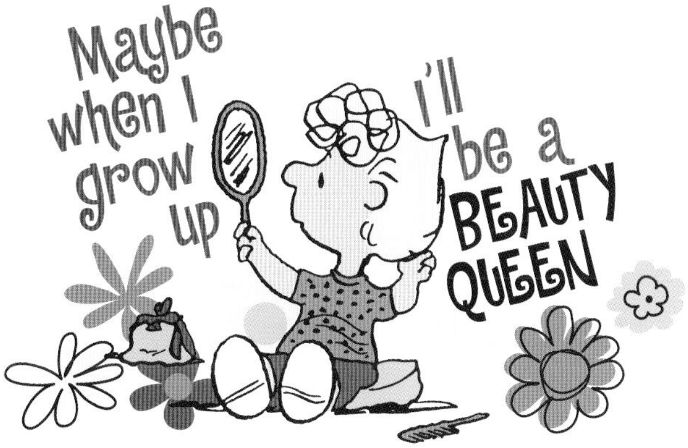
Maybe when I grow up I'll be a BEAUTY QUEEN

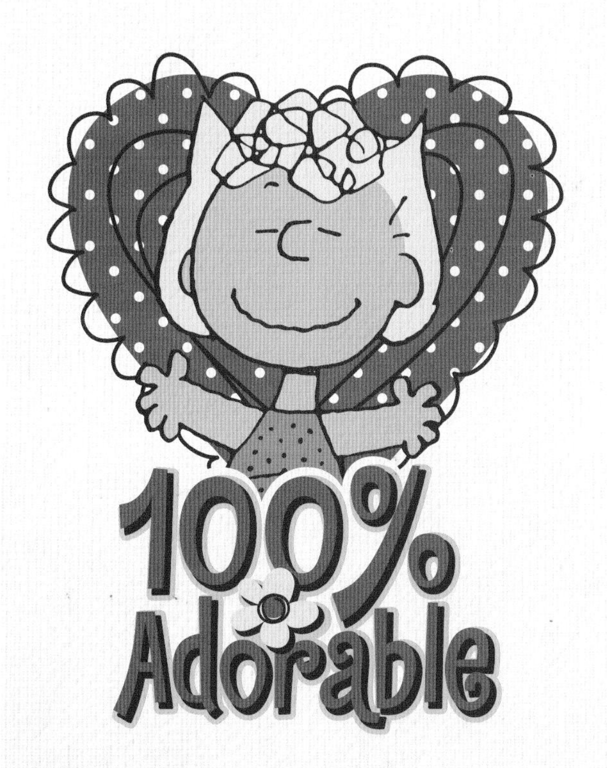
100% Adorable

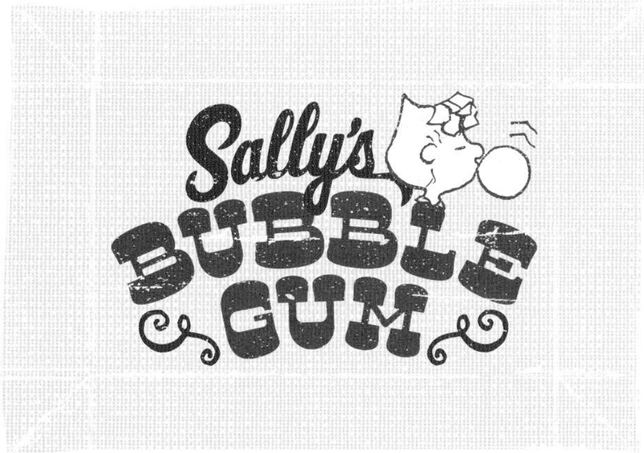
Sally's BUBBLE GUM

OPPOSITE: *Design by Cameron + Co* | ABOVE: *Style Guide art – PW*

"I've decided to try to be a better person . . . but not right away of course . . . maybe a few days from now . . ." —Sally

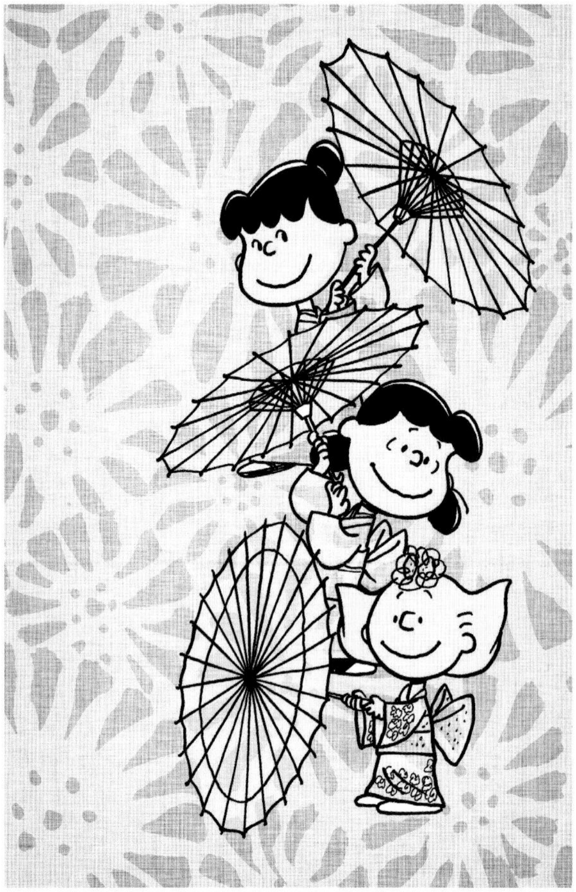

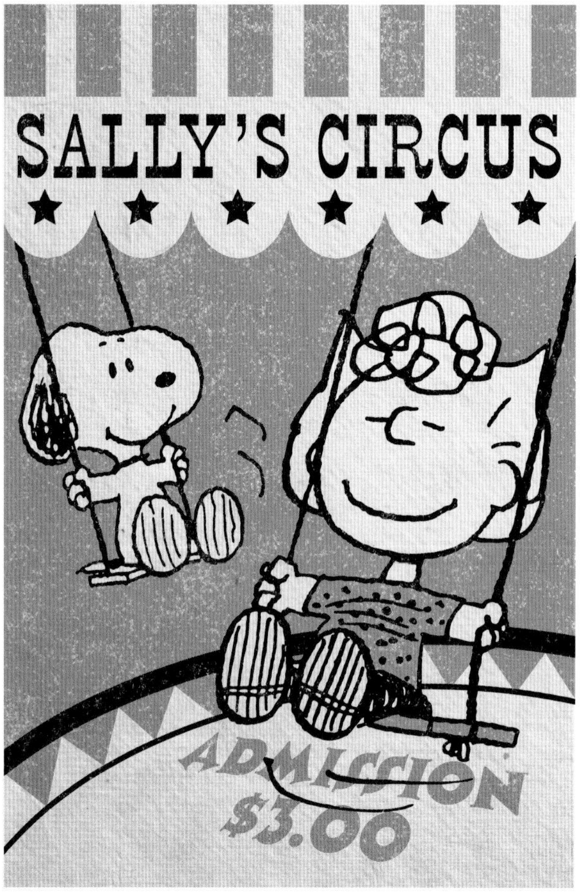
SALLY'S CIRCUS
ADMISSION
$3.00

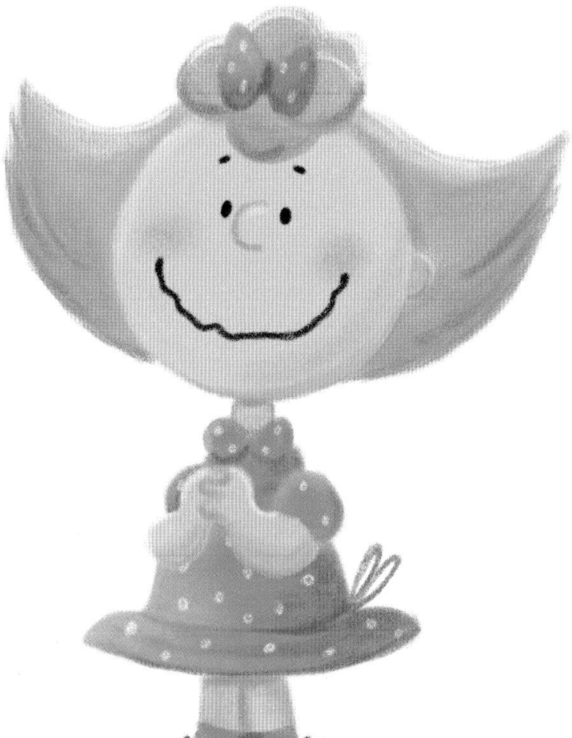

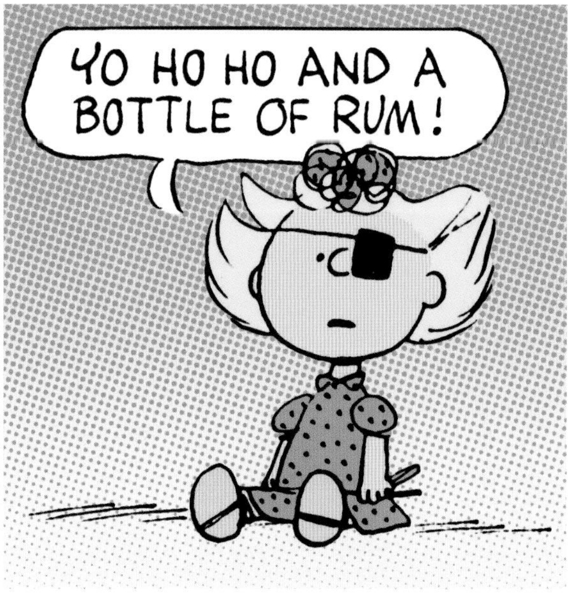
YO HO HO AND A BOTTLE OF RUM!

TOP LEFT: *Comic-Con postcard, 2013 – CSCA;* TOP RIGHT: *Style Guide art – PW;* LEFT AND ABOVE: *Style Guide art – CSCA*

"Why does everything have to be so complicated?" —Sally

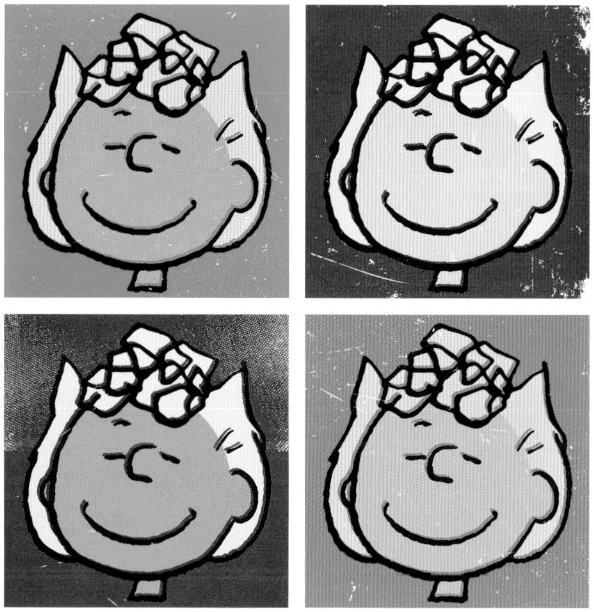

ABOVE AND RIGHT: *Style Guide art – PW;* BELOW: You Shouldn't Be Watching This Program *and* Circle the Zambonis, Peanuts *Digital Edition – CSCA*

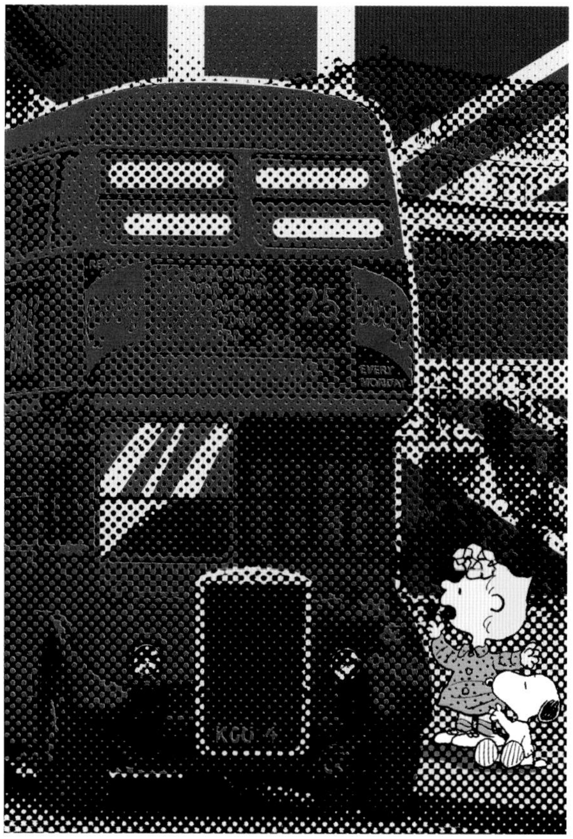

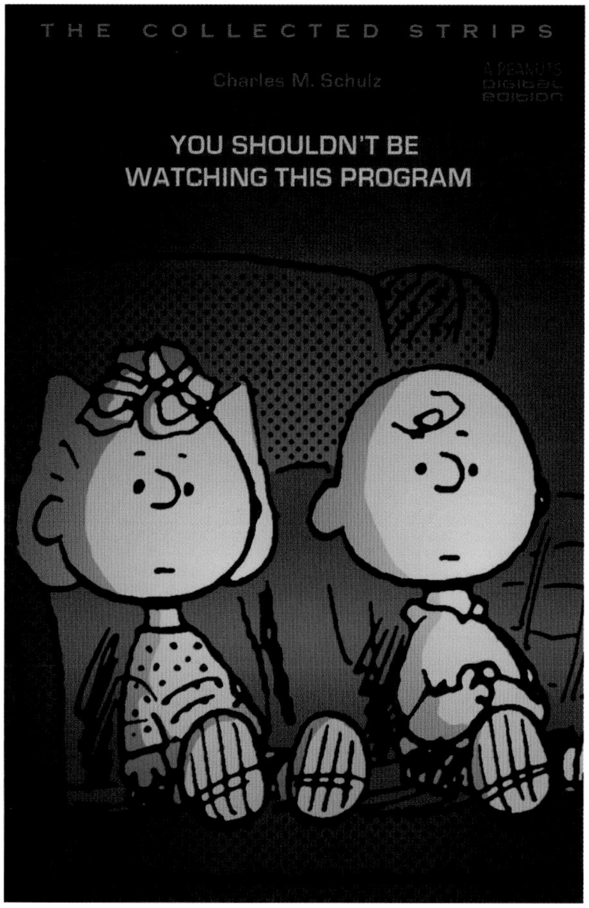
THE COLLECTED STRIPS
Charles M. Schulz
A PEANUTS DIGITAL EDITION
YOU SHOULDN'T BE WATCHING THIS PROGRAM

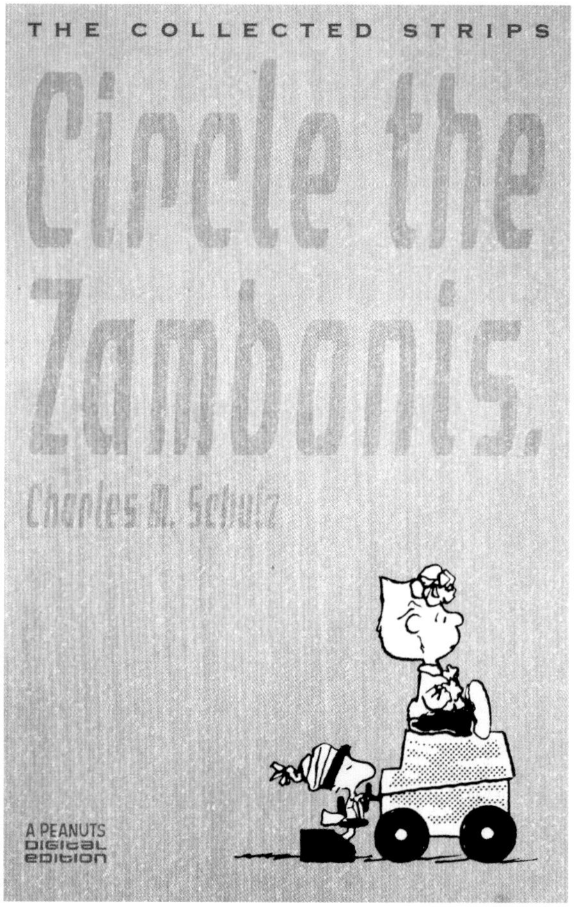
THE COLLECTED STRIPS
Circle the Zambonis.
Charles M. Schulz
A PEANUTS DIGITAL EDITION

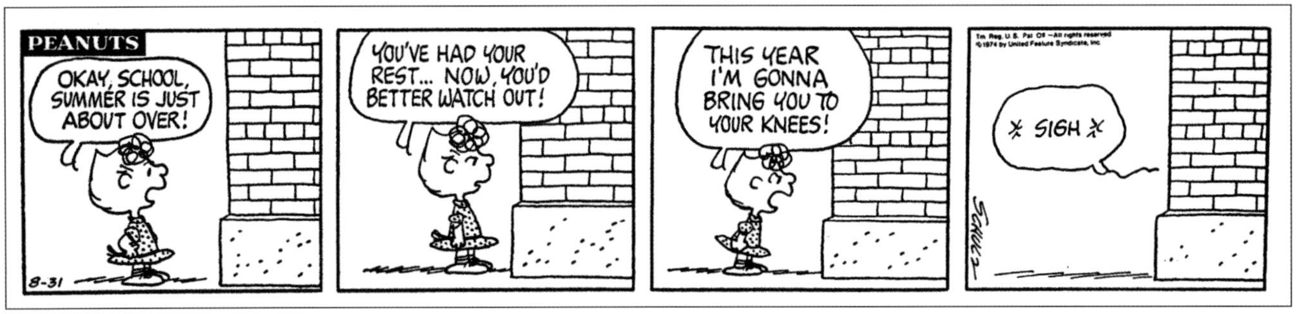
PEANUTS
OKAY, SCHOOL, SUMMER IS JUST ABOUT OVER!
YOU'VE HAD YOUR REST... NOW, YOU'D BETTER WATCH OUT!
THIS YEAR I'M GONNA BRING YOU TO YOUR KNEES!
* SIGH *
8-31

# THE SCHOOL

FIRST APPEARANCE
08/31/1974

Sally is not an enthusiastic student, and every year she dreads the end of summer and the start of another school year. She often voices her frustrations to the School itself, and the building is always ready to offer a sympathetic ear—or brick, as the case may be. The School is a philosophical building, and it often reflects on how its life might have been different if it had been an airline terminal or a disco.

Sally's first school collapses unexpectedly one night, possibly from nerves or exhaustion, and Sally and Charlie Brown have to enroll in another building on the other side of town. She immediately strikes up a friendship with her new school, even though Lucy and other kids don't understand why Sally talks to buildings. As the School itself says, "It's a living!"

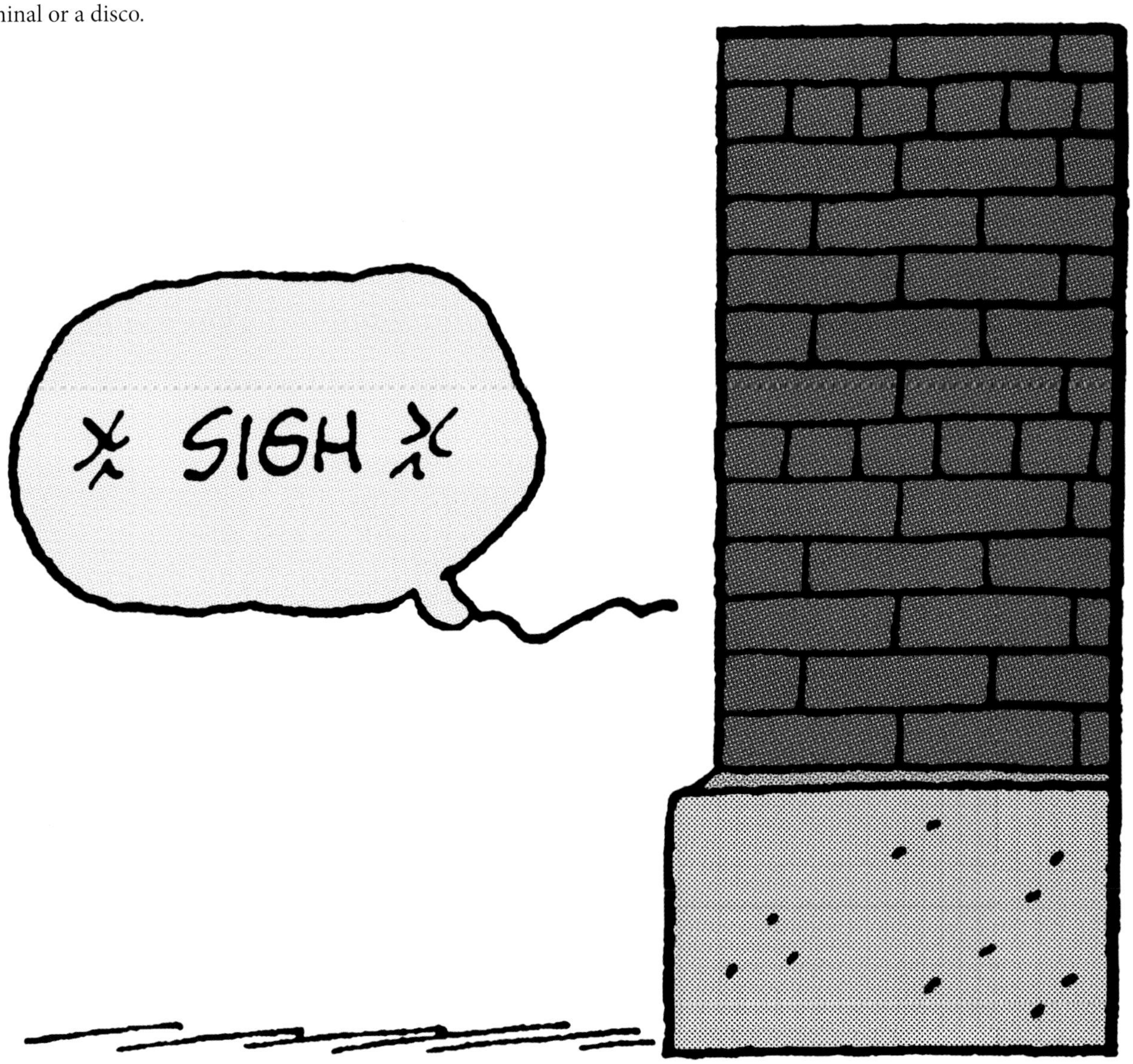
* SIGH *

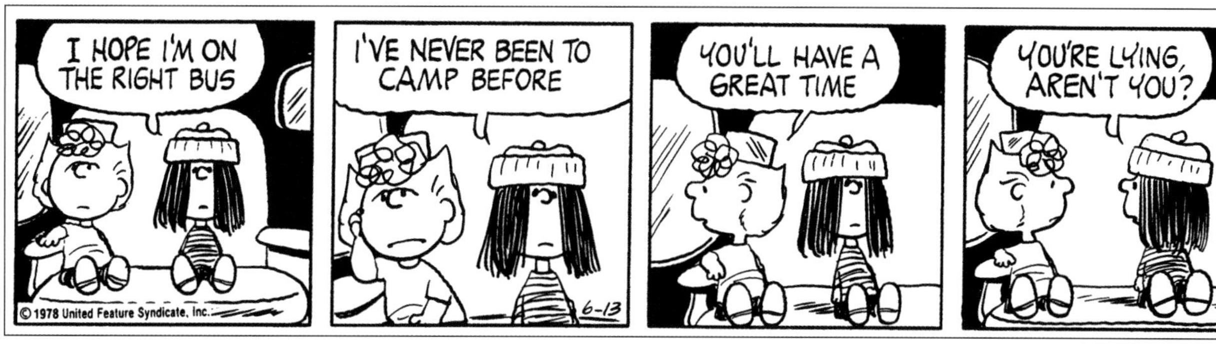
I HOPE I'M ON THE RIGHT BUS
I'VE NEVER BEEN TO CAMP BEFORE
YOU'LL HAVE A GREAT TIME
YOU'RE LYING, AREN'T YOU?
SCHULZ
6-13
© 1978 United Feature Syndicate, Inc.

# EUDORA

FIRST APPEARANCE
06/13/1978

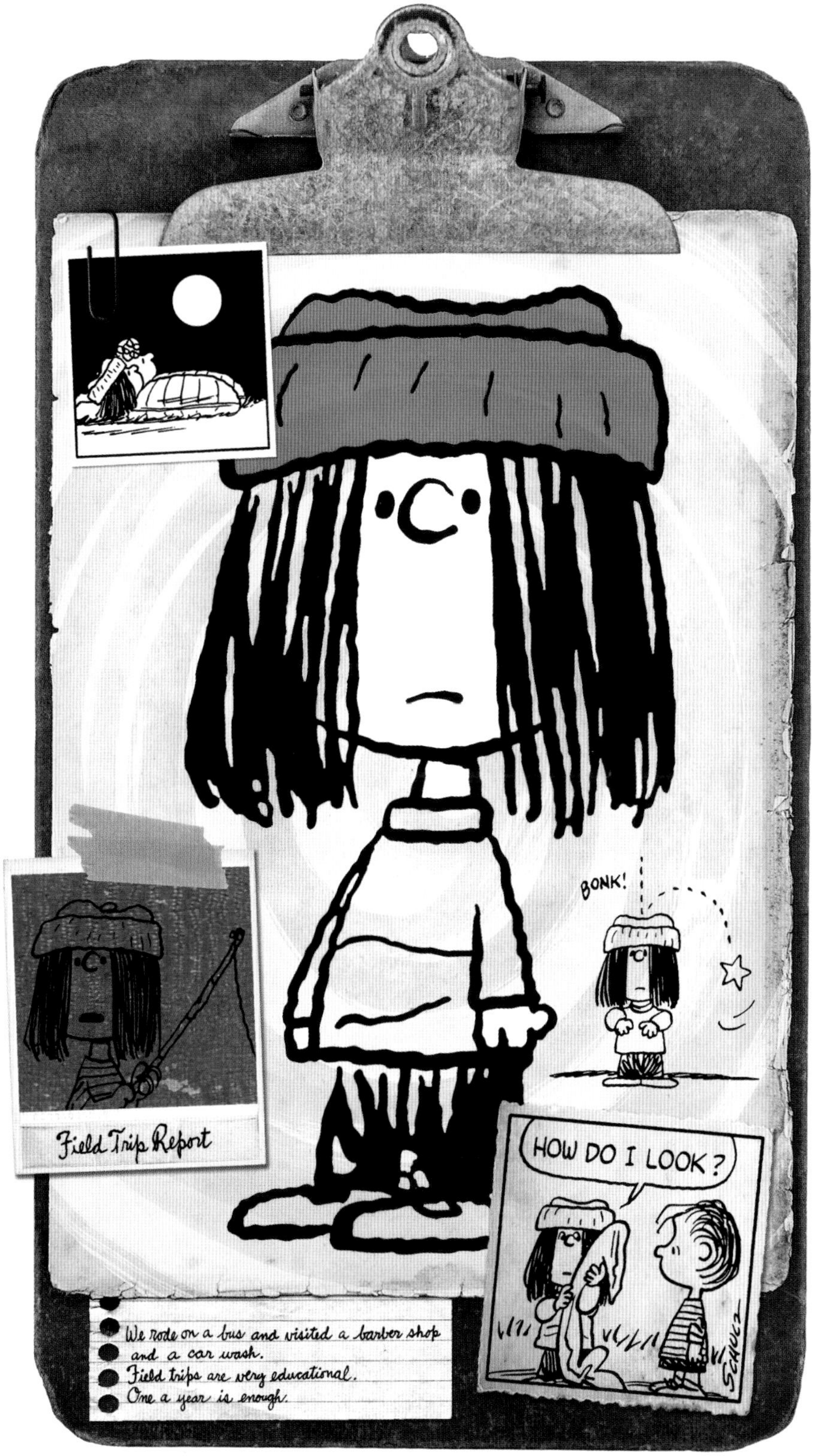
BONK!
Field Trip Report
HOW DO I LOOK?
SCHULZ
We rode on a bus and visited a barber shop
and a car wash.
Field trips are very educational.
One a year is enough.

Like her brother before her, Sally is sure that she isn't going to enjoy her time at summer camp, but a new friend makes the whole experience worthwhile. Eudora and Sally meet on the bus to summer camp, and they hit it off immediately thanks to their similar outlooks on life and their mutual lack

**"Saturday's the only day I never get anything wrong."**
**–Eudora**

of practical camping experience.

Eudora transfers to Sally's school that fall, and their friendship picks up right where it left off, with campouts, sleepovers, and frequent visits to the Brown household. Her easygoing nature wins over all of Sally's friends, too, and outside school, Eudora is just as likely to visit Charlie Brown, Snoopy, and Linus as Sally, but the two remain the best of friends for many years—although Sally can do without Eudora's fondness for her "Sweet Babboo" Linus.

OPPOSITE: *Spot art from strips – Charles M. Schulz* | LEFT: *Design by Cameron + Co*

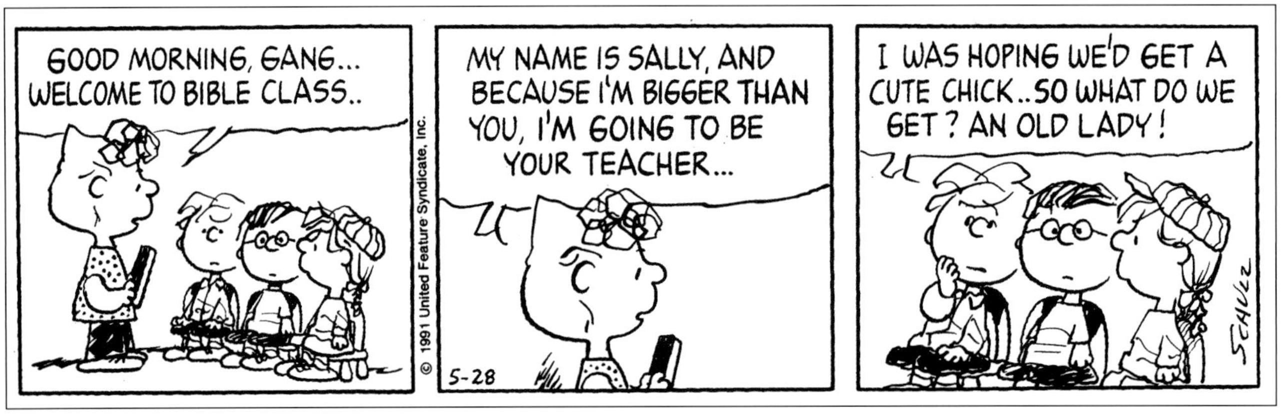
GOOD MORNING, GANG... WELCOME TO BIBLE CLASS..
MY NAME IS SALLY, AND BECAUSE I'M BIGGER THAN YOU, I'M GOING TO BE YOUR TEACHER...
© 1991 United Feature Syndicate, Inc.
5-28
I WAS HOPING WE'D GET A CUTE CHICK..SO WHAT DO WE GET ? AN OLD LADY !
SCHULZ

# LARRY

FIRST APPEARANCE
05/28/1991

Sally never fully appreciates her teachers until she meets Larry, the most vocal student in her Bible Class. His enthusiasm doesn't translate into practical knowledge of the Old Testament, however, as he insists that the characters from F. Scott Fitzgerald's classic novel *The Great Gatsby* were involved with events ranging from the parting of the Red Sea to the slaying of Goliath.

This youthful exuberance gets Larry ejected from Sally's class. Later that week, she learns that he is the minister's son. Embarrassed by his actions, he visits Sally's home to apologize and to reveal that he acted up because he fell in love with her. Despite being reprimanded by his father, he remains fixated on *The Great Gatsby*. As he departs Sally's home, he promises that whenever he thinks of her, he'll think of Gatsby and the green light at the end of Daisy's dock.

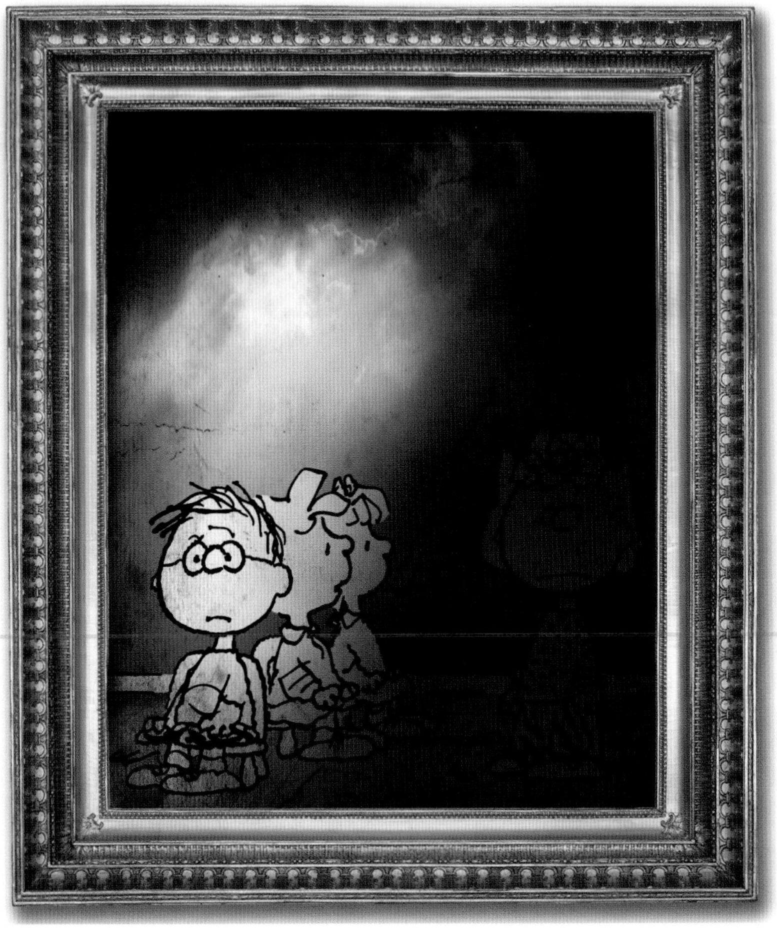

ABOVE: *Design by Cameron + Co*

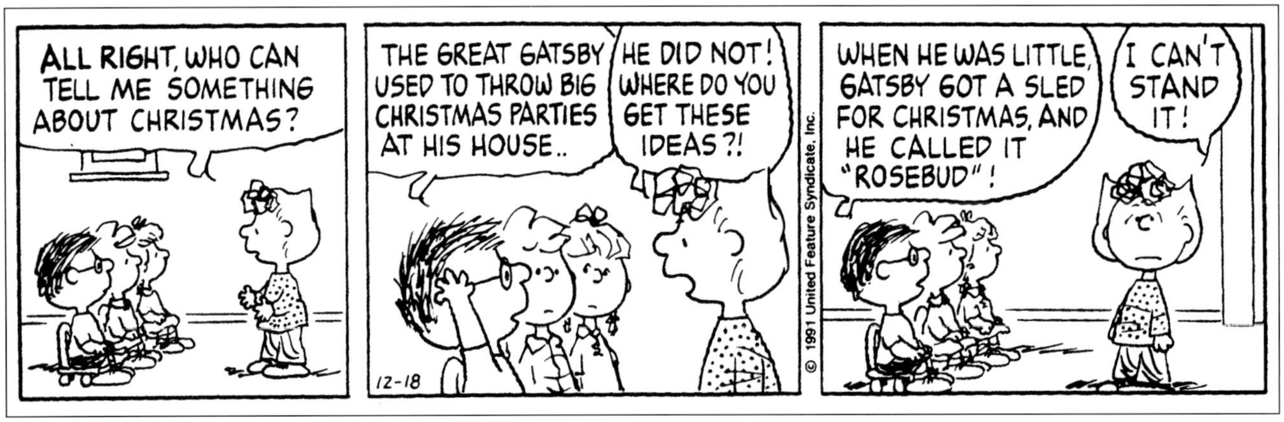
ALL RIGHT, WHO CAN TELL ME SOMETHING ABOUT CHRISTMAS?
THE GREAT GATSBY USED TO THROW BIG CHRISTMAS PARTIES AT HIS HOUSE..
HE DID NOT! WHERE DO YOU GET THESE IDEAS ?!
12-18
© 1991 United Feature Syndicate, Inc.
WHEN HE WAS LITTLE, GATSBY GOT A SLED FOR CHRISTMAS, AND HE CALLED IT "ROSEBUD" !
I CAN'T STAND IT !

SO FAR THIS HAS BEEN A GOOD CHRISTMAS PLAY, CHARLIE BROWN...
WHEN DOES YOUR SISTER COME ON?
© 1983 United Feature Syndicate, Inc.
12-21
RIGHT AFTER THE DANCING SHEEP...SHE STEPS OUT AND SAYS, "HARK!" AND THEN HAROLD ANGEL SINGS
HAROLD ANGEL?
ALL I KNOW IS WHAT SHE TOLD ME...

HARK
Love Duets
KING RECORDS
Harold Angel
FEATURES
THE HITS
"Is Sally Home?"
"A Glass of Water"
"Remember Me?"

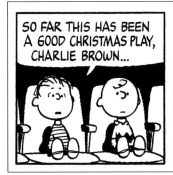

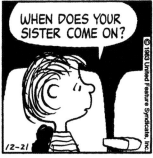

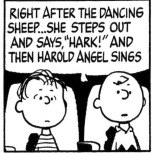

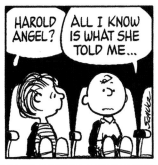

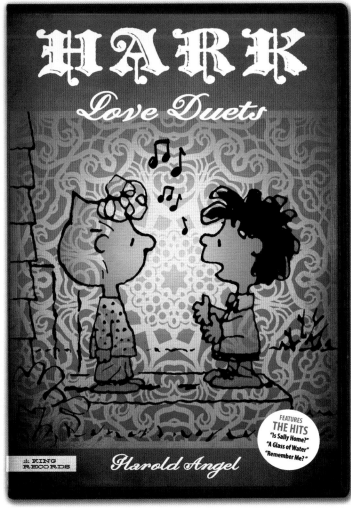

ABOVE: *Design by Cameron + Co*

# HAROLD ANGEL

FIRST MENTIONED 12/16/1983
FIRST APPEARANCE 12/24/1983

Parents may look forward to their children's Christmas pageants every year, but for the participants, this annual tradition is a source of great anxiety. Linus frets about memorizing his lines and reciting them in front of an audience; Peppermint Patty is dejected when Marcie is cast as Mary, while she's relegated to playing a sheep; and Sally manages to find her unique holiday problems each December.

"When the sheep are through dancing, I come out and say, 'Hark!'" Sally explains to her brother. "Then Harold Angel starts to sing." Charlie Brown and Linus are convinced that Sally has misunderstood her instructions for the Christmas play, as she often does. The day after Sally flubs her line and yells "Hockey stick!" during the play, however, Harold Angel himself pays Sally a visit, much to the surprise of Charlie Brown.

I DON'T KNOW...I DIDN'T SEE THE REST OF THE PLAY..AS SOON AS SALLY SAID, "HOCKEY STICK," AND EVERYONE LAUGHED, I LEFT
SHE GETS EVERYTHING MIXED UP...SHE EVEN THOUGHT SOMEONE NAMED "HAROLD ANGEL" WAS GOING TO SING!
12-24
EXCUSE ME, SOMEBODY'S AT THE DOOR...
© 1983 United Feature Syndicate, Inc.
HI, IS SALLY HOME? MY NAME IS HAROLD ANGEL..

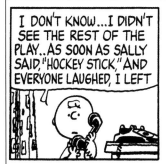

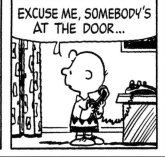

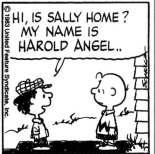

# CHRISTMAS

FIRST OBSERVED 12/25/1951

Christmas is always a special time of year. It's a time for Sally to compose a detailed wish list and finally to get around to writing thank-you cards for gifts that she received the previous year. It's a time for Christmas pageants and memorizing lines. It's a time for Snoopy to decorate his doghouse and dress up as Santa Claus. And it's a time for Charlie Brown and Linus to discuss theology and the true meaning of Christmas. Most of all, it's a time for friends and family.

Charlie Brown always found Christmas to be a bittersweet holiday, as did Charles Schulz. "To me Christmas is a lonesome season, and I try to put this over quite often in my strips. Christmas and a lot of holidays bring out the loneliness in us because we never seem to be able to come up to the joy the magazines tell us we're supposed to have. They show us illustrations of homes with packages and trees, and people smiling, but in real life it's never quite that way. And holidays bring out sadness. This is why Charlie Brown said he hated Valentine's Day so much. He said he knows that nobody likes him and he doesn't see why we have a holiday to emphasize it."

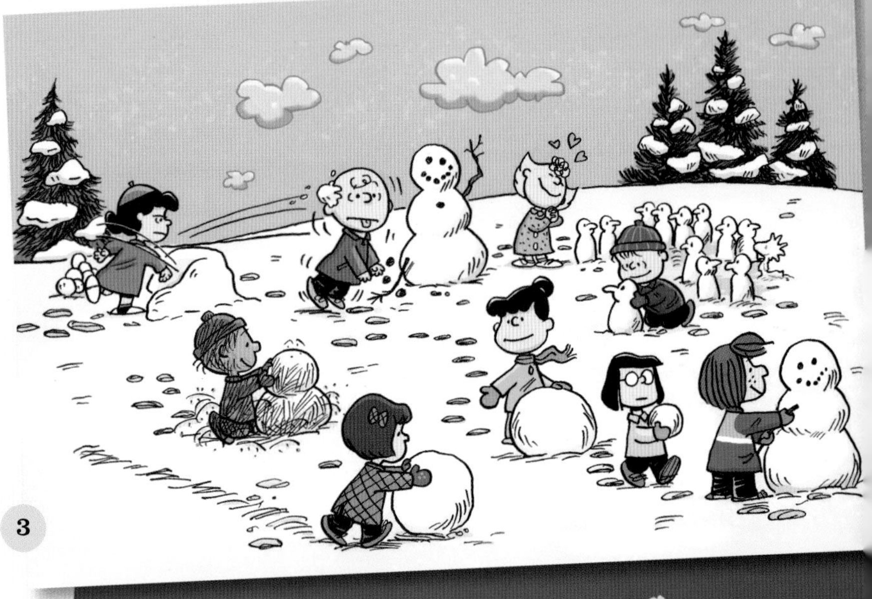

3

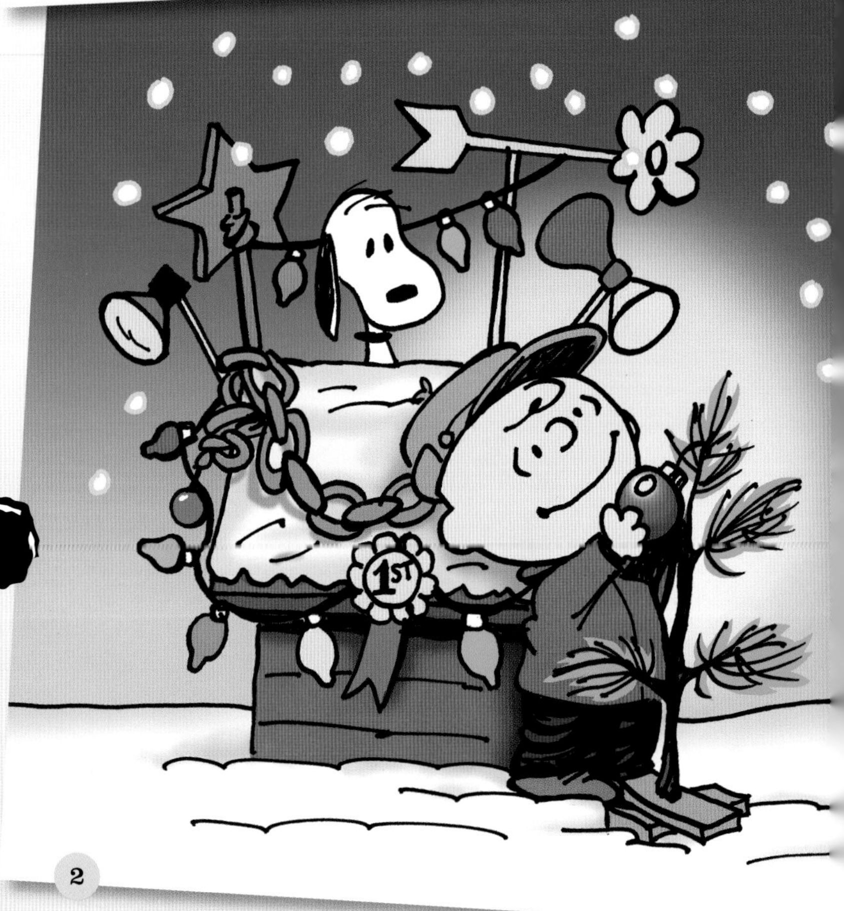
1ST

2

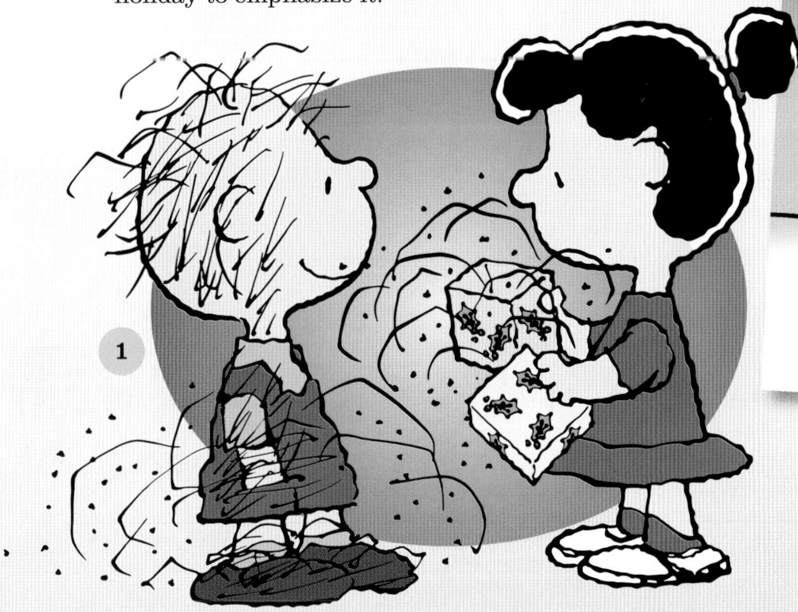

1

*1: Design by Cameron + Co; 2:* A Charlie Brown Christmas Story *book – CSCA; 3, 6 and 7: Style Guide art – CSCA; 4:* A Charlie Brown Christmas; *Artist: Tom Whalen; Limited Edition Print; Courtesy: Dark Hall Mansion; 5:* A Charlie Brown Christmas; *Artist: Laurent Durieux; Limited Edition Print; Courtesy: Dark Hall Mansion* | OVERLEAF: *1: Design by Cameron + Co; 2, 3, 4, and 5: Style Guide art – CSCA; 6:* A Charlie Brown Christmas Story *book – CSCA; 7:* A Charlie Brown Christmas; *Artist: Dave Perillo; Limited Edition Print; Courtesy: Dark Hall Mansion*

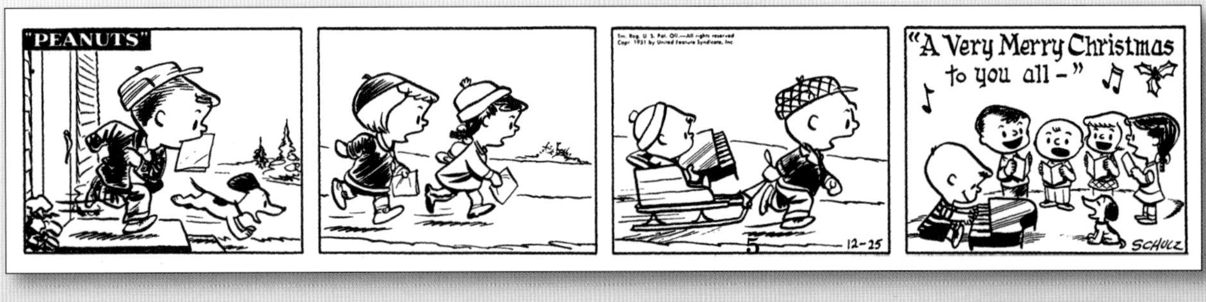
"PEANUTS"
"A Very Merry Christmas to you all –"
12-25
SCHULZ

7

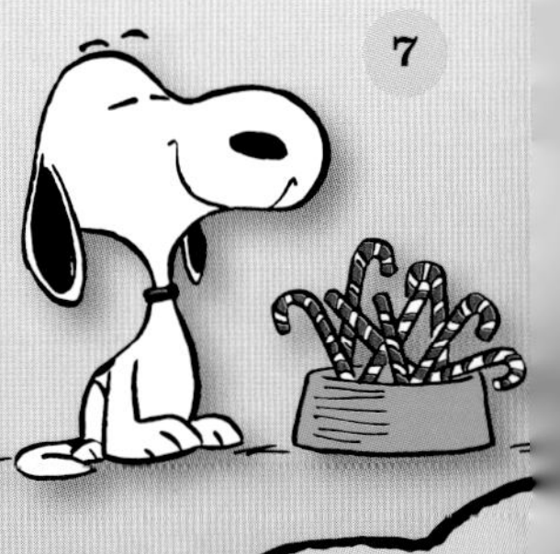

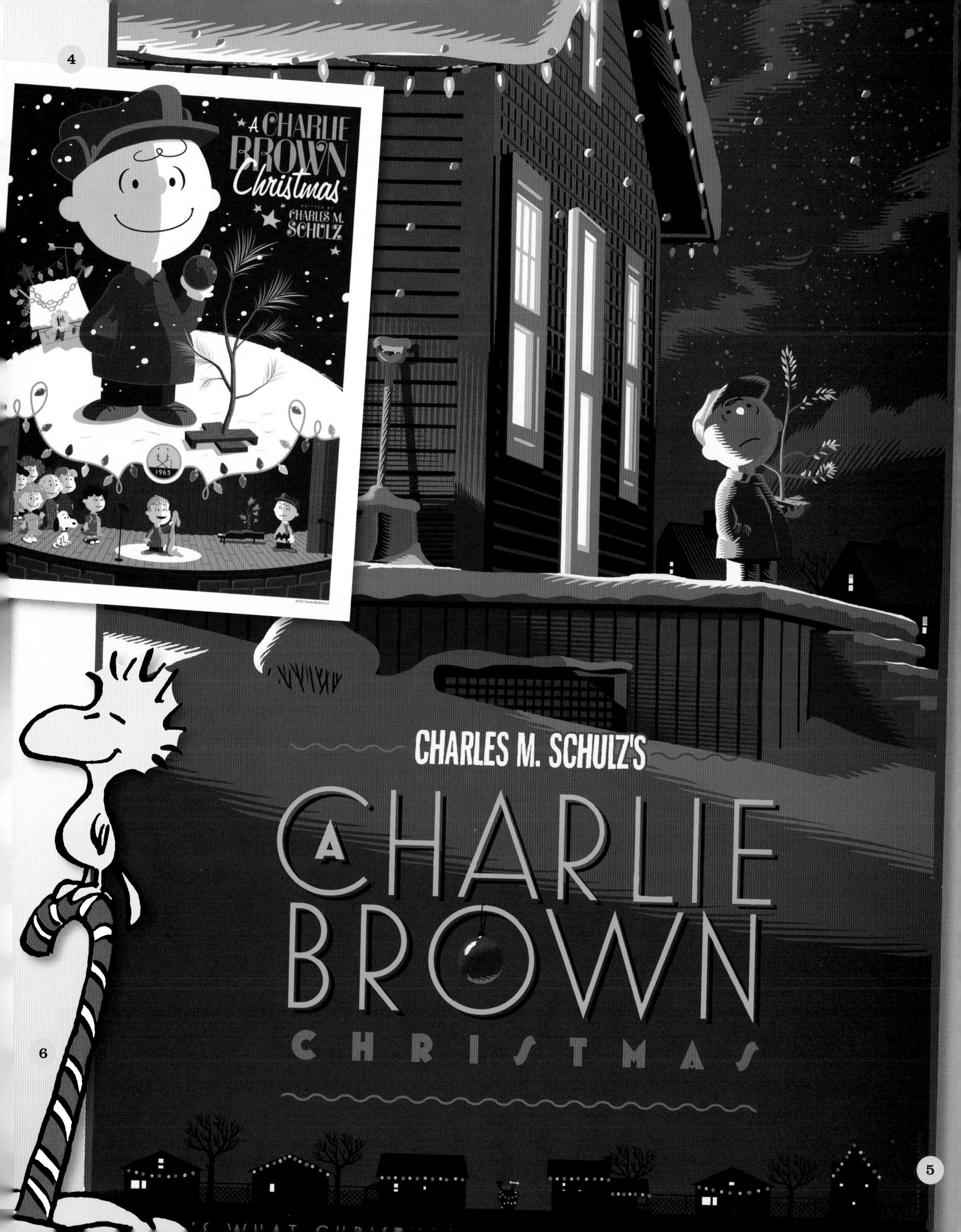
4
A CHARLIE BROWN Christmas
WRITTEN BY
CHARLES M. SCHULZ
1965
CHARLES M. SCHULZ'S
A CHARLIE BROWN
CHRISTMAS
6
5

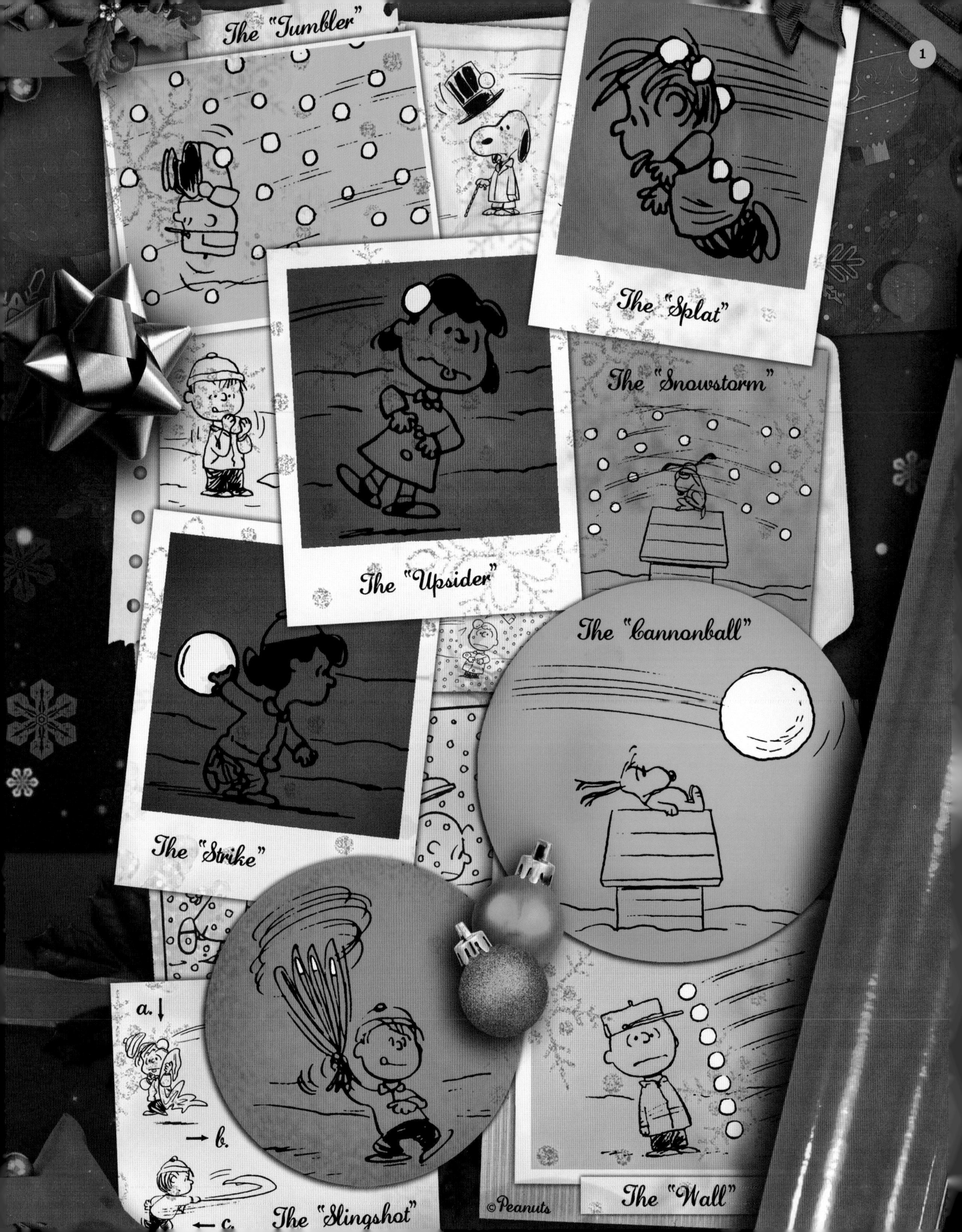
1
The "Tumbler"
The "Splat"
The "Snowstorm"
The "Upsider"
The "Cannonball"
The "Strike"
a.
b.
c.
The "Slingshot"
©Peanuts
The "Wall"

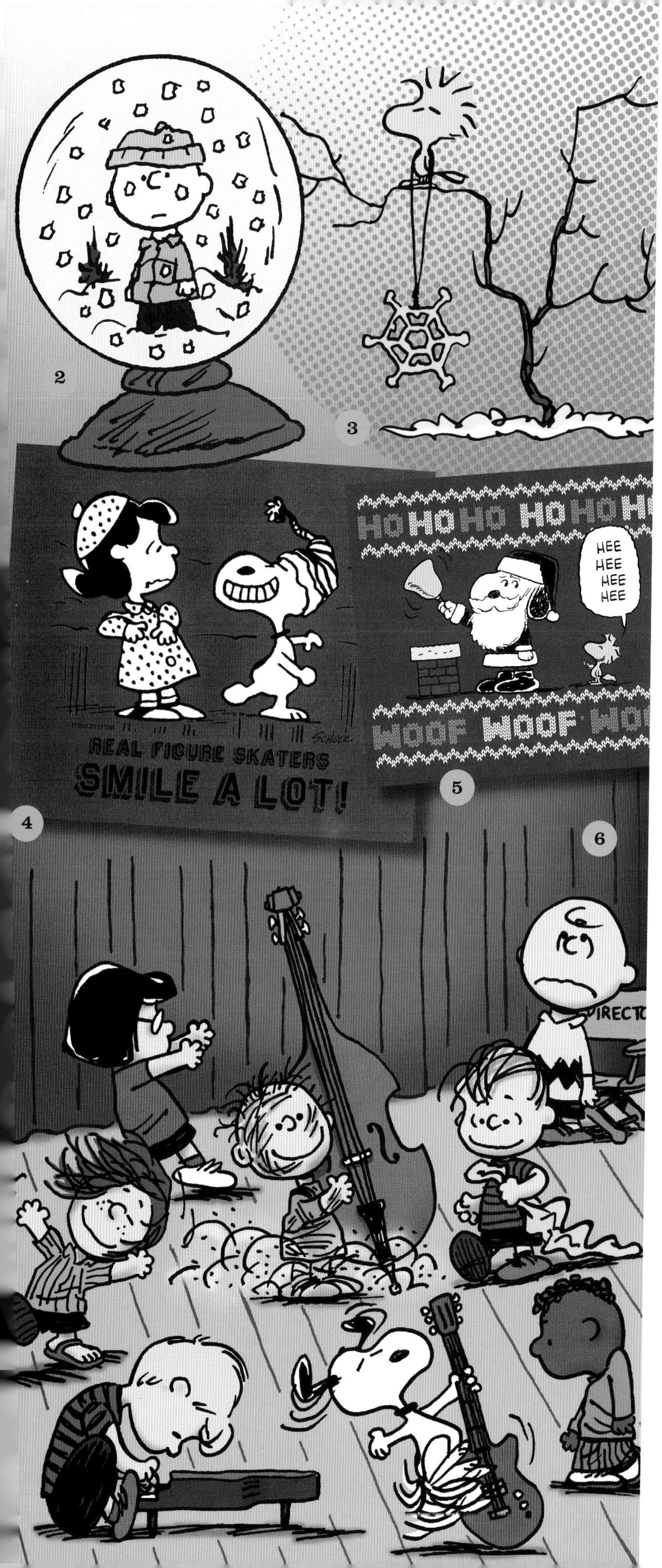
2
3
HOHOHO HOHOHO
HEE HEE HEE HEE
WOOF WOOF
SCHULZ
REAL FIGURE SKATERS
SMILE A LOT!
4
5
6

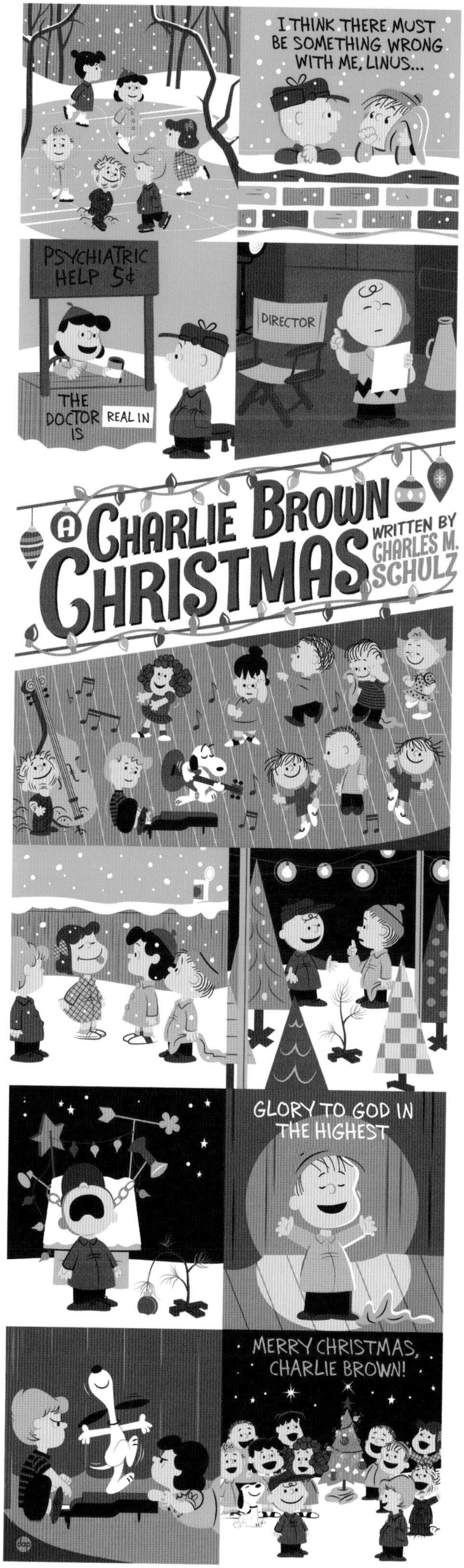
I THINK THERE MUST BE SOMETHING WRONG WITH ME, LINUS...
PSYCHIATRIC HELP 5¢
THE DOCTOR IS REAL IN
DIRECTOR
A CHARLIE BROWN CHRISTMAS
WRITTEN BY CHARLES M. SCHULZ
GLORY TO GOD IN THE HIGHEST
MERRY CHRISTMAS, CHARLIE BROWN!

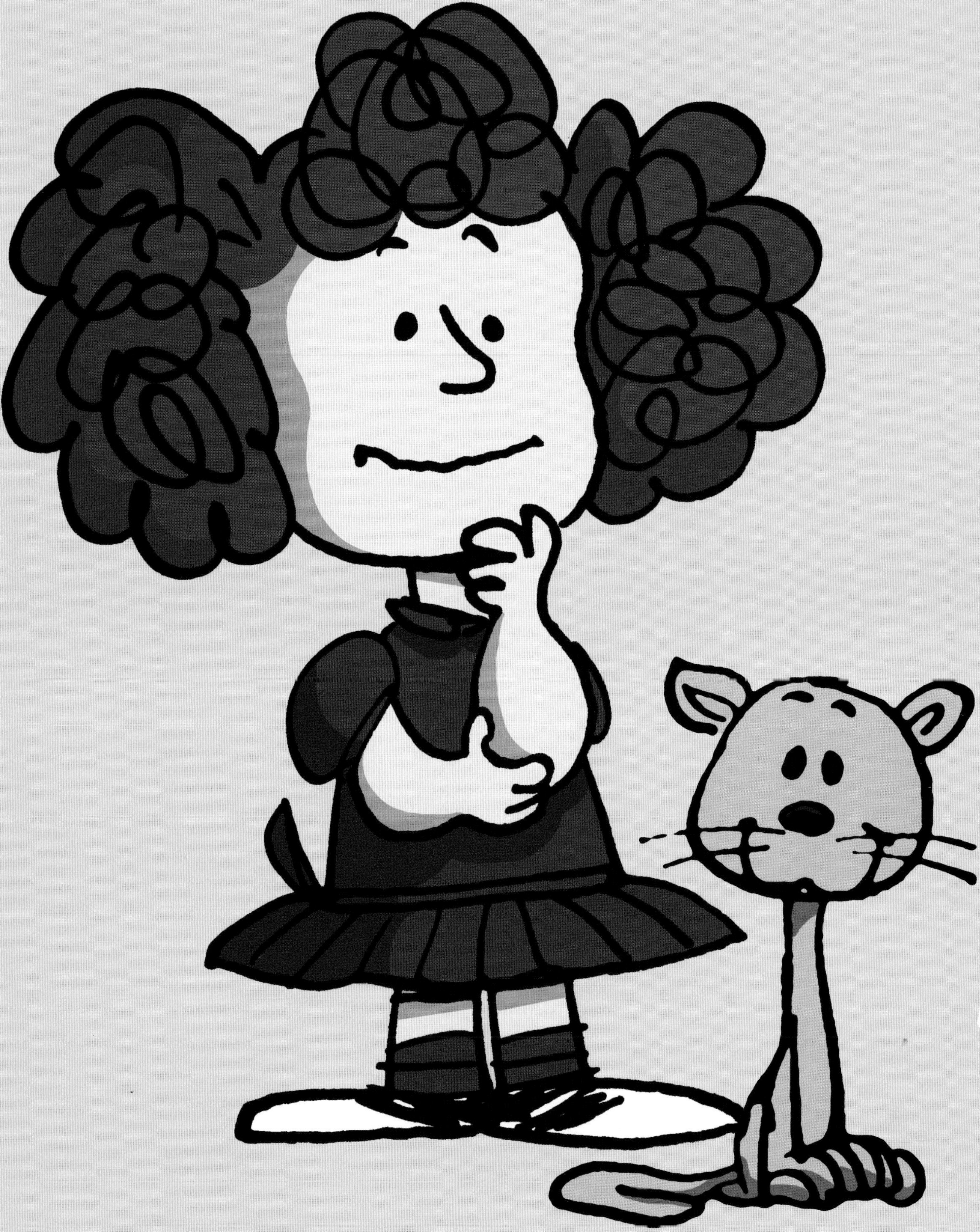

# Frieda (FIRST APPEARANCE 03/06/1961) & Faron (FIRST APPEARANCE 05/23/1961)

The first thing you notice about Frieda is her naturally curly hair. If you don't notice it, don't worry—she'll make sure to tell you all about it. When she's not talking about herself or her naturally curly hair, she can often be seen playing outfield for Charlie Brown's baseball team, planting flowers on his pitcher's mound, or admonishing Snoopy for lying on his doghouse instead of chasing rabbits.

Frieda's near boneless cat, Faron, is known for his complete and utter lack of motion, which may explain why Frieda is so keen on keeping Snoopy active.

"The cat [Faron] was a mistake," noted Charles Schulz. "First, I found I couldn't draw a cat very well. Second, he played off poorly against Snoopy, making the strip too 'cat-and-doggish.' It hurt in other ways as well, so I'm afraid Faron is gone forever. . . . He is now invisible, that 'cat next door'—and as such can play off better against Snoopy."

PEANUTS
?
CHARLIE BROWN, I WOULD LIKE VERY MUCH TO HAVE YOU MEET FRIEDA!
HOW DO YOU DO, FRIEDA..
HOW DO YOU DO, CHARLIE BROWN... I HAVE NATURALLY CURLY HAIR!
DO YOU FEEL THAT SPRING WILL BE HERE SOON? I BELONG TO TWELVE RECORD CLUBS! NOW THAT WE'RE GETTING A GOOD PICTURE ON OUR TV, THE PROGRAMS ARE LOUSY!
3-6
FRIEDA PRIDES HERSELF ON BEING A GOOD CONVERSATIONALIST!
SCHULZ

PEANUTS
by SCHULZ
NO! WHY SHOULD I?
NO!
NO! ABSOLUTELY NO! TAKE CARE OF YOUR OWN STUPID CAT!
BUT I'M GOING TO THE LIBRARY, AND THEY WON'T LET ME BRING FARON IN!
WELL, GET SOMEONE ELSE TO HOLD HIM! I'M NOT GOING TO DO IT!
WHO CAN I GET?
CHARLIE BROWN, I DON'T SUPPOSE YOU'D BE WILLING TO...
NO! GOOD GRIEF, NO!!
11-5
SIGH
HOW DO THINGS LIKE THIS HAPPEN?
SCHULZ

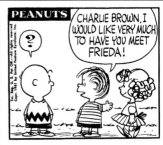

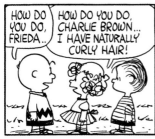

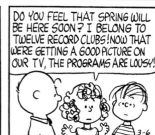

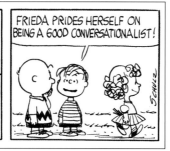

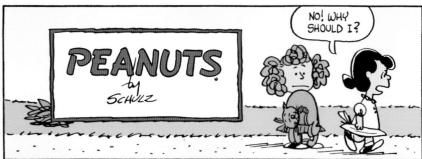

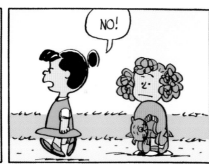

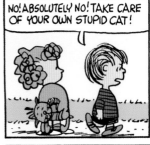

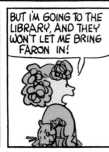

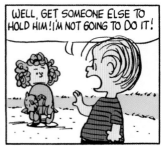

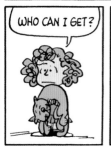

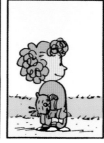

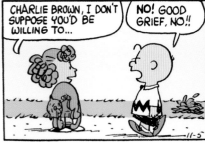

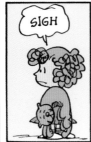

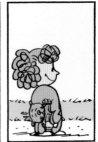

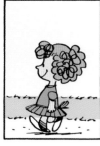

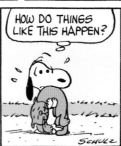

OPPOSITE: *Spot art from strip – Charles M. Schulz*

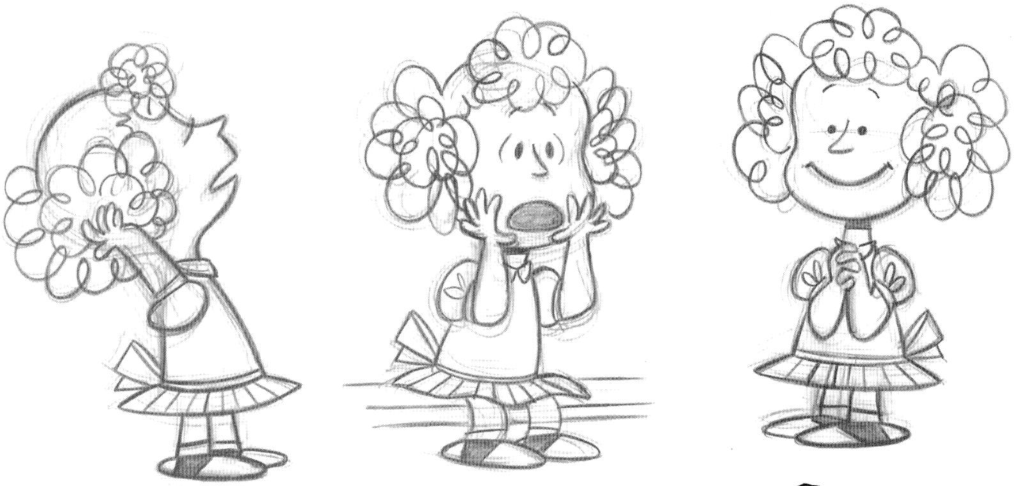

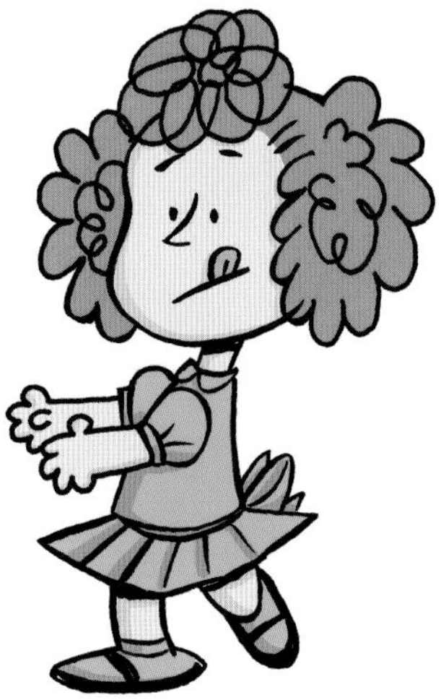

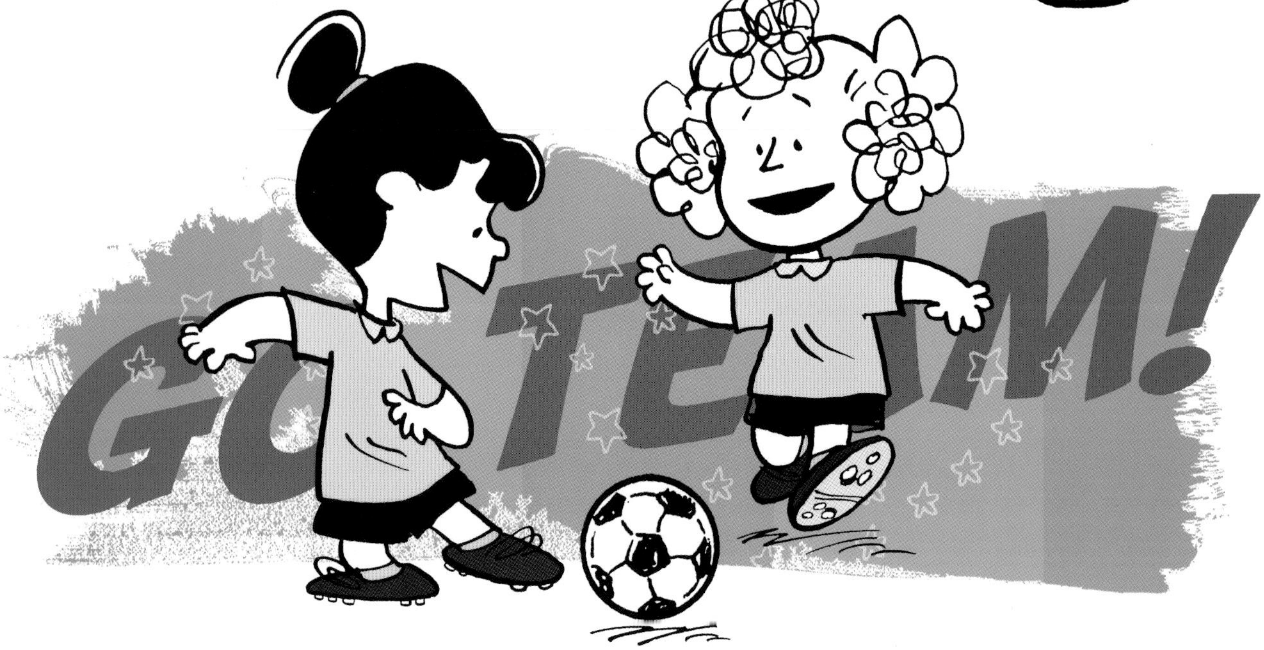

GO TEAM!

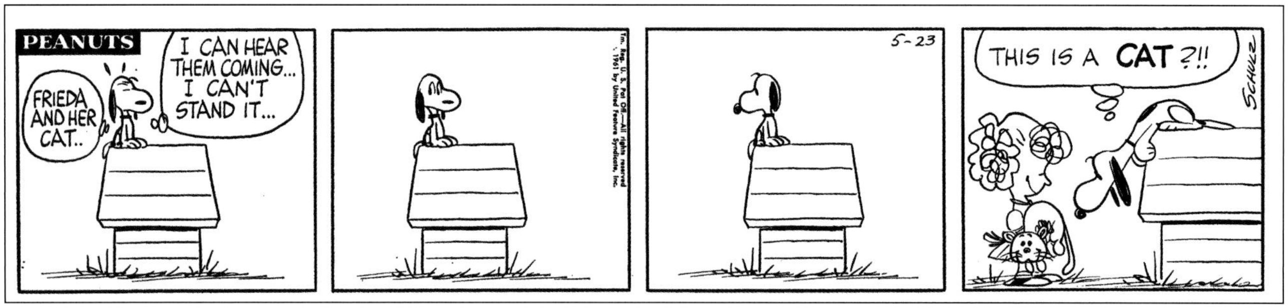

PEANUTS
I CAN HEAR THEM COMING... I CAN'T STAND IT...
FRIEDA AND HER CAT..
5-23
THIS IS A CAT?!!
SCHULZ

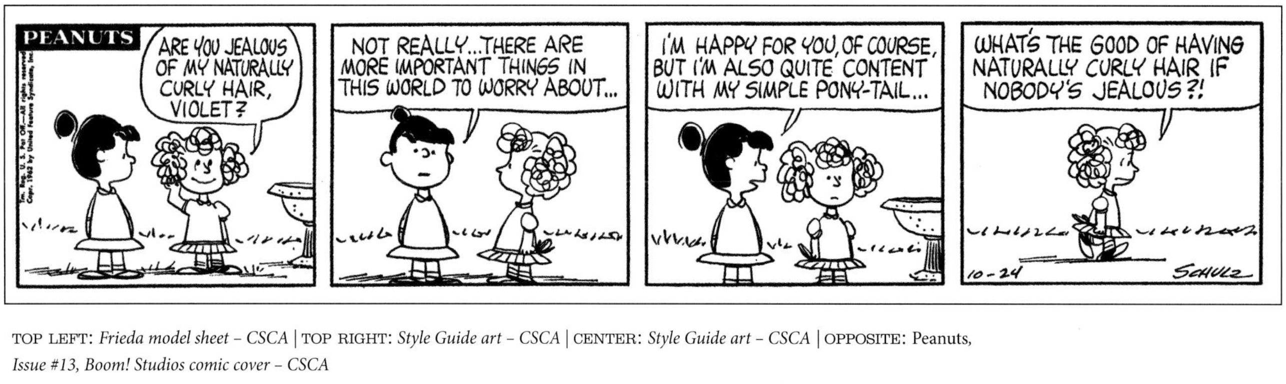

PEANUTS
ARE YOU JEALOUS OF MY NATURALLY CURLY HAIR, VIOLET?
NOT REALLY...THERE ARE MORE IMPORTANT THINGS IN THIS WORLD TO WORRY ABOUT...
I'M HAPPY FOR YOU, OF COURSE, BUT I'M ALSO QUITE CONTENT WITH MY SIMPLE PONY-TAIL...
WHAT'S THE GOOD OF HAVING NATURALLY CURLY HAIR IF NOBODY'S JEALOUS?!
10-24
SCHULZ

TOP LEFT: *Frieda model sheet – CSCA* | TOP RIGHT: *Style Guide art – CSCA* | CENTER: *Style Guide art – CSCA* | OPPOSITE: Peanuts, *Issue #13, Boom! Studios comic cover – CSCA*

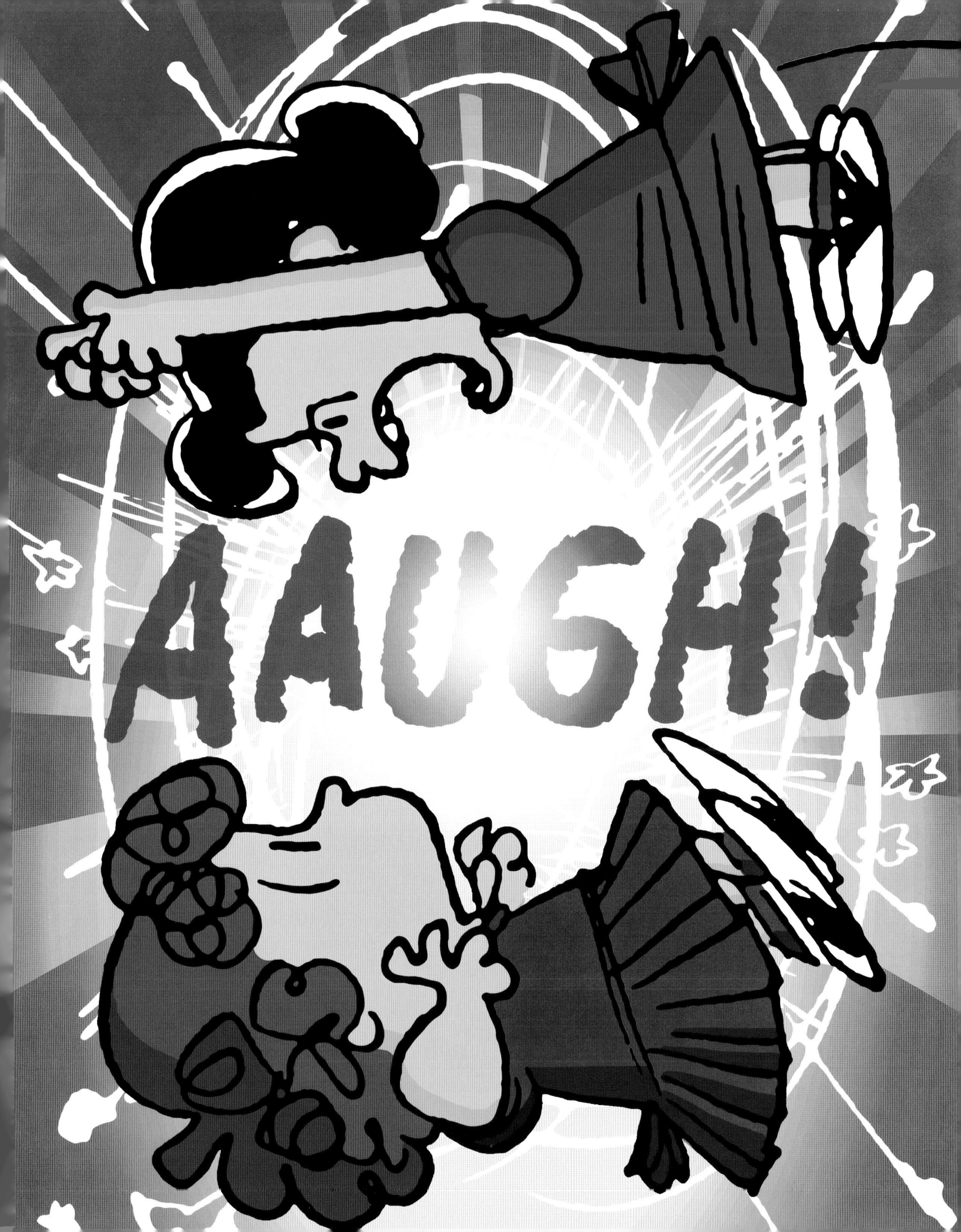
AAUGH!

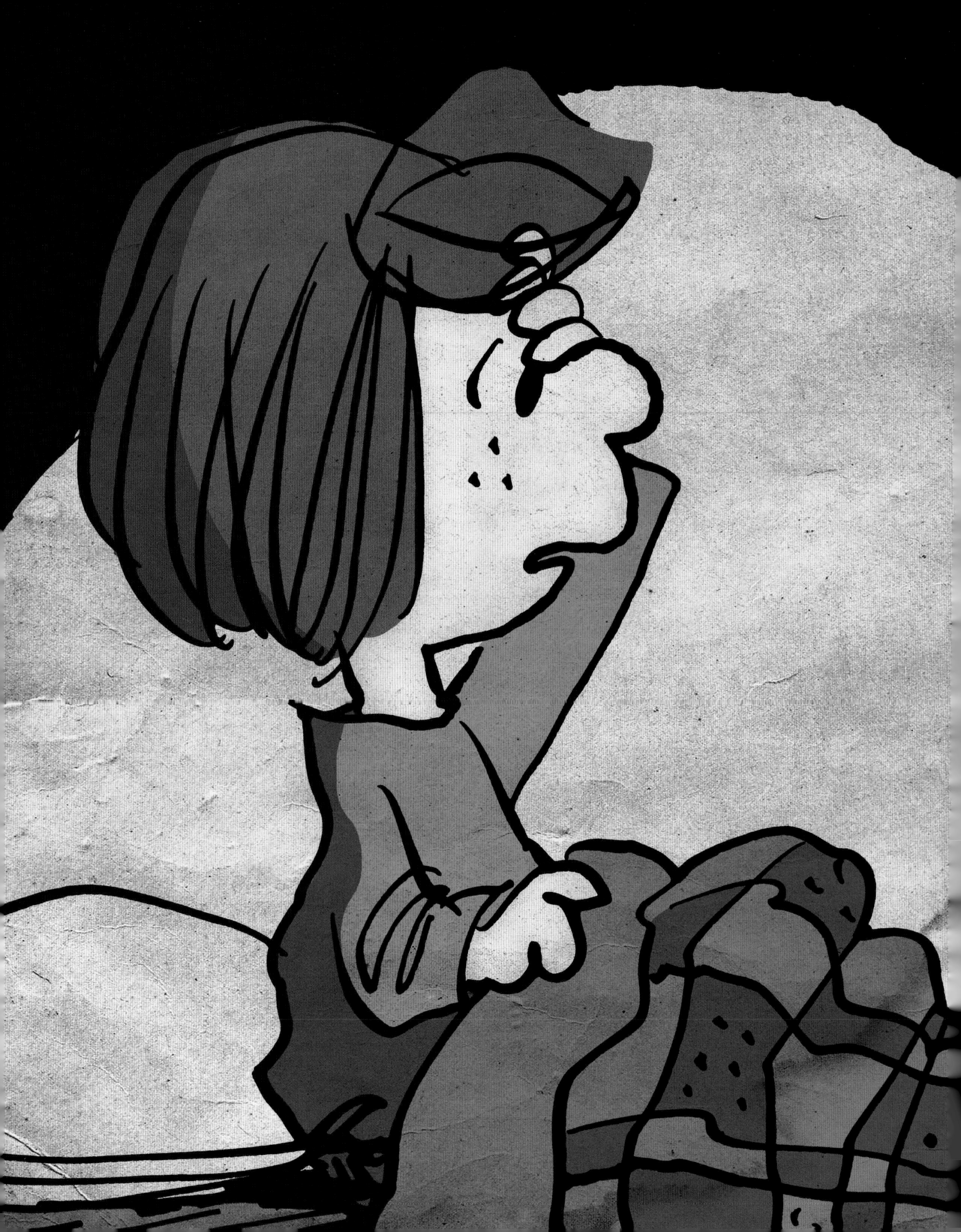

# PEPPERMINT PATTY

FIRST APPEARANCE
08/22/1966

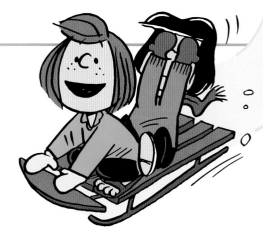

Patricia Reichardt, known as Peppermint Patty to her friends, is an all-star athlete, has a boisterous personality, and is enshrined in the D-Minus Hall of Fame for her less-than-stellar grades in school. Whatever she does on the field or in the classroom, however, she will always be her father's "Rare Gem" and Marcie's best friend.

Peppermint Patty is introduced to Charlie Brown through Roy, their mutual friend from summer camp the previous year. She invites herself to join Charlie Brown's team, but abruptly quits when she realizes that they aren't going to win any games no matter what, even if she hits a home run every time she's at the plate. She forms a baseball team in her own neighborhood soon after, but she and Chuck, as she calls Charlie Brown, still remain close friends.

**"If they ever lower the voting age to seven, look out!"**
**—Peppermint Patty**

Peppermint Patty excels at all sports, especially baseball, and she has long been a very vocal proponent of women's rights on and off the playing field. Her best friend, Marcie, also supports the cause, even if she isn't quite sure about the difference between baseball and hockey.

As naturally gifted as she is at athletics, Peppermint Patty is the exact opposite in school, as her classmates Marcie and Franklin can attest. Peppermint Patty lives in a single-parent home, and because she stays up late every night waiting for her father to come home, she often falls asleep in class and struggles to keep up.

Despite her outward bravado, Peppermint Patty is insecure about her looks and often feels awkward at social interaction. She has an unrequited crush on Charlie Brown, who, ironically enough, often complains to her that no one seems to like him. But through it all, she puts on a brave face and always tries her best at everything she does, which makes her a Rare Gem indeed.

"I tried to start up a little something with Peppermint Patty and her father," Charles Schulz noted. "Some college student wrote in and gave me his theories of what Peppermint Patty's father must be like, and his theory on her home life was that Peppermint Patty's mother must have died or was gone. It seemed this way to him. I like it that people can speculate on this. It makes it wonderful. It makes the off-stage characters much more real this way."

PEANUTS
HI, ROY... WHO YOU WRITIN' TO?
I'M WRITING TO A LITTLE KID NAMED LINUS THAT I MET AT CAMP SEVERAL WEEKS AGO
IS HE CUTE? IF HE IS, TELL HIM YOUR VERY GOOD FRIEND, "PEPPERMINT" PATTY SAYS, "HELLO"
TELL HIM WHAT A REAL SWINGER I AM...
8-22
PUT IN A GOOD WORD FOR ME, ROY, AND THE NEXT TIME WE INDIAN WRESTLE I'LL TRY NOT TO CLOBBER YOU!
SCHULZ

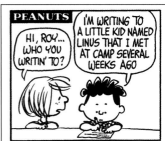

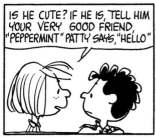

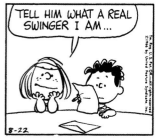

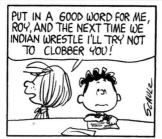

OPPOSITE: *Design by Cameron + Co* | TOP RIGHT: *Style Guide art – CSCA*

# ALL-STAR ATHLETE

Peppermint Patty is the best athlete in town, and she excels at every sport she plays. She especially enjoys baseball, even though there's not a team in the neighborhood that can provide her with decent competition.

"I like Peppermint Patty; she's a neat little girl," enthused Charles Schulz when asked about Patty. "She's quite athletic and not dumb about the world she knows. But she has blinders on. She is set in her ways."

"All right, who's next?"
—Peppermint Patty

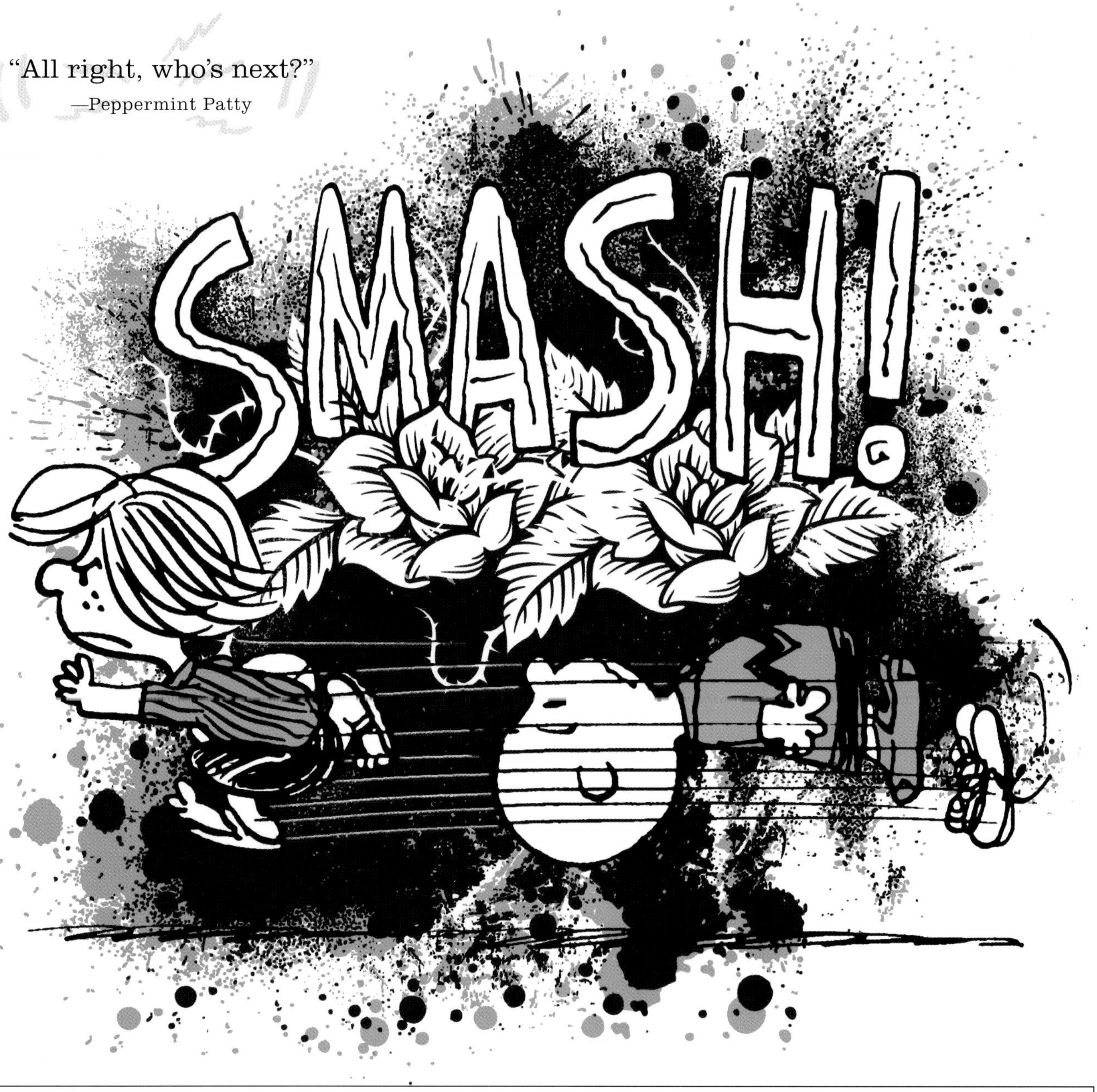

SMASH!


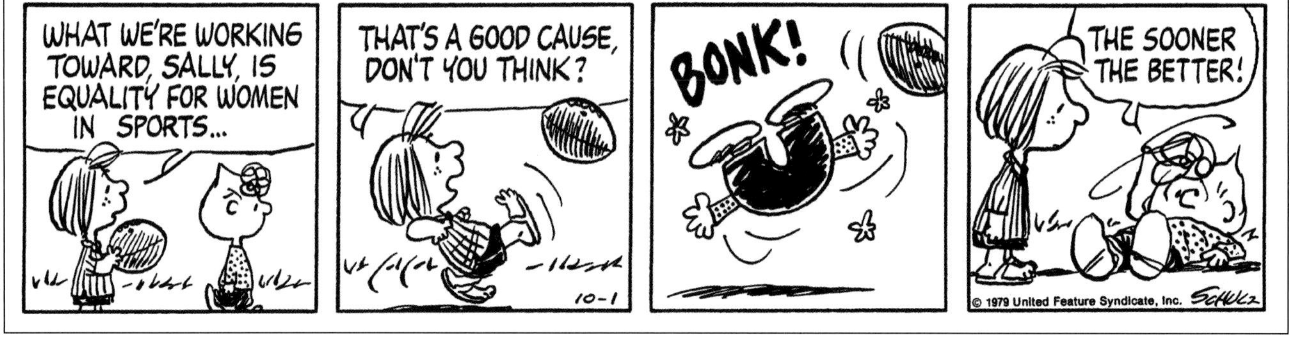

WHAT WE'RE WORKING TOWARD, SALLY, IS EQUALITY FOR WOMEN IN SPORTS...
THAT'S A GOOD CAUSE, DON'T YOU THINK?
10-1
BONK!
THE SOONER THE BETTER!
© 1979 United Feature Syndicate, Inc.
SCHULZ

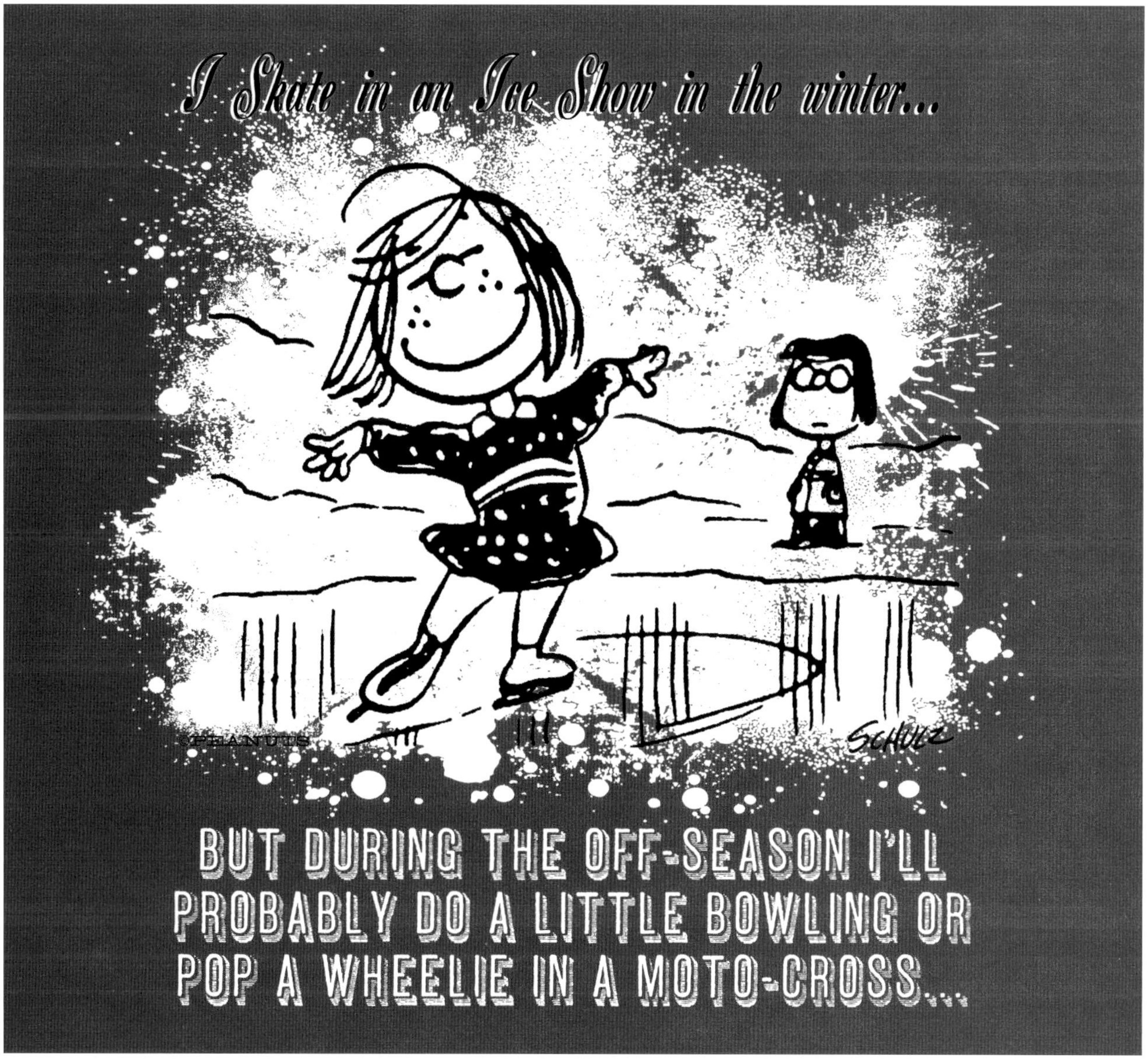
I Skate in an Ice Show in the winter...
©PEANUTS
SCHULZ
BUT DURING THE OFF-SEASON I'LL PROBABLY DO A LITTLE BOWLING OR POP A WHEELIE IN A MOTO-CROSS...

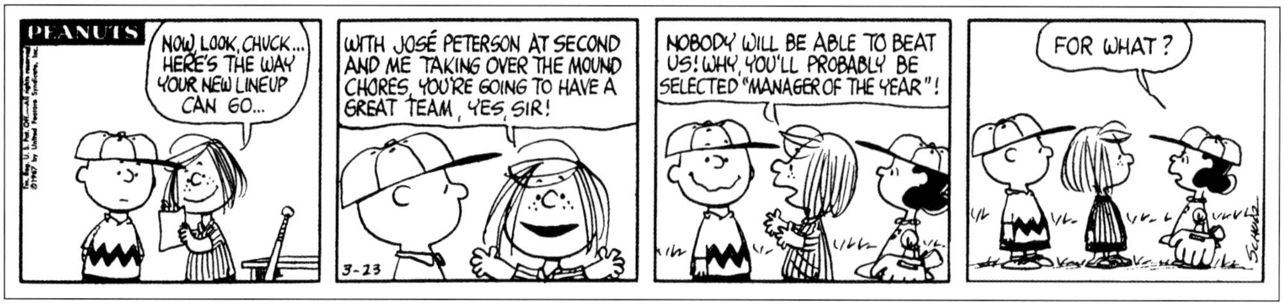
PEANUTS
NOW LOOK, CHUCK... HERE'S THE WAY YOUR NEW LINEUP CAN GO...
WITH JOSÉ PETERSON AT SECOND AND ME TAKING OVER THE MOUND CHORES, YOU'RE GOING TO HAVE A GREAT TEAM, YES, SIR!
3-23
NOBODY WILL BE ABLE TO BEAT US! WHY, YOU'LL PROBABLY BE SELECTED "MANAGER OF THE YEAR"!
FOR WHAT?
SCHULZ

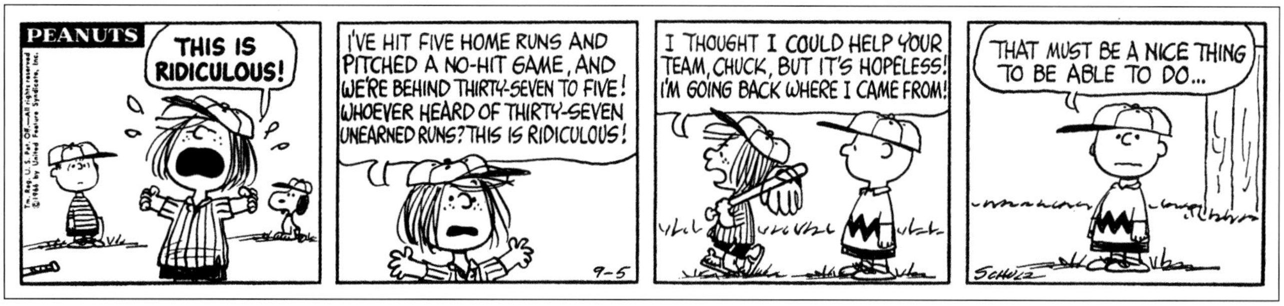
PEANUTS
THIS IS RIDICULOUS!
I'VE HIT FIVE HOME RUNS AND PITCHED A NO-HIT GAME, AND WE'RE BEHIND THIRTY-SEVEN TO FIVE! WHOEVER HEARD OF THIRTY-SEVEN UNEARNED RUNS? THIS IS RIDICULOUS!
9-5
I THOUGHT I COULD HELP YOUR TEAM, CHUCK, BUT IT'S HOPELESS! I'M GOING BACK WHERE I CAME FROM!
THAT MUST BE A NICE THING TO BE ABLE TO DO...
SCHULZ

OPPOSITE: *Design by Cameron + Co* | TOP: *Style Guide art – CSCA*

# THE HAPLESS STUDENT

Despite Peppermint Patty's quick wit and fantastic athletic skills, she's always had a hard time in school, and has the D-minus average to prove it. If she could put the same drive and ambition that she displays on the baseball diamond in the classroom, she'd become an "A" student overnight.

Charles Schulz could find inspiration for his characters everywhere—even a candy dish. "I thought of the name [Peppermint Patty] one day and thought it a good name for some kind of character—maybe even for a book of stories. But I was afraid somebody else would think of the name and so I just created the character and gave her the name so that no one else would steal it before I used it."

"History should always be studied in the morning . . . before anything else can happen."—Peppermint Patty

© 1978 United Feature Syndicate, Inc.

Z

I'M AWAKE! I'M AWAKE!

NO, MA'AM...I DON'T KNOW WHAT'S GOING ON

BUT I'M AWAKE!

2-20

HOW DO YOU THINK I'M DOING, MARCIE? CHECK THESE ANSWERS

YOU GOT THE FIRST NINE QUESTIONS WRONG, SIR..

OH, WELL..I LEARNED A LONG TIME AGO THAT IT'S NOT HOW YOU START, IT'S HOW YOU FINISH..

YOU GOT THE LAST ONE WRONG, TOO!

© 1994 United Feature Syndicate, Inc.

2/1

TOP LEFT: *Style Guide art – CSCA* | TOP CENTER: *Style Guide art – CSCA* | TOP RIGHT: *Spot art from strip – Charles M. Schulz* | OPPOSITE: *Design by Cameron + Co*

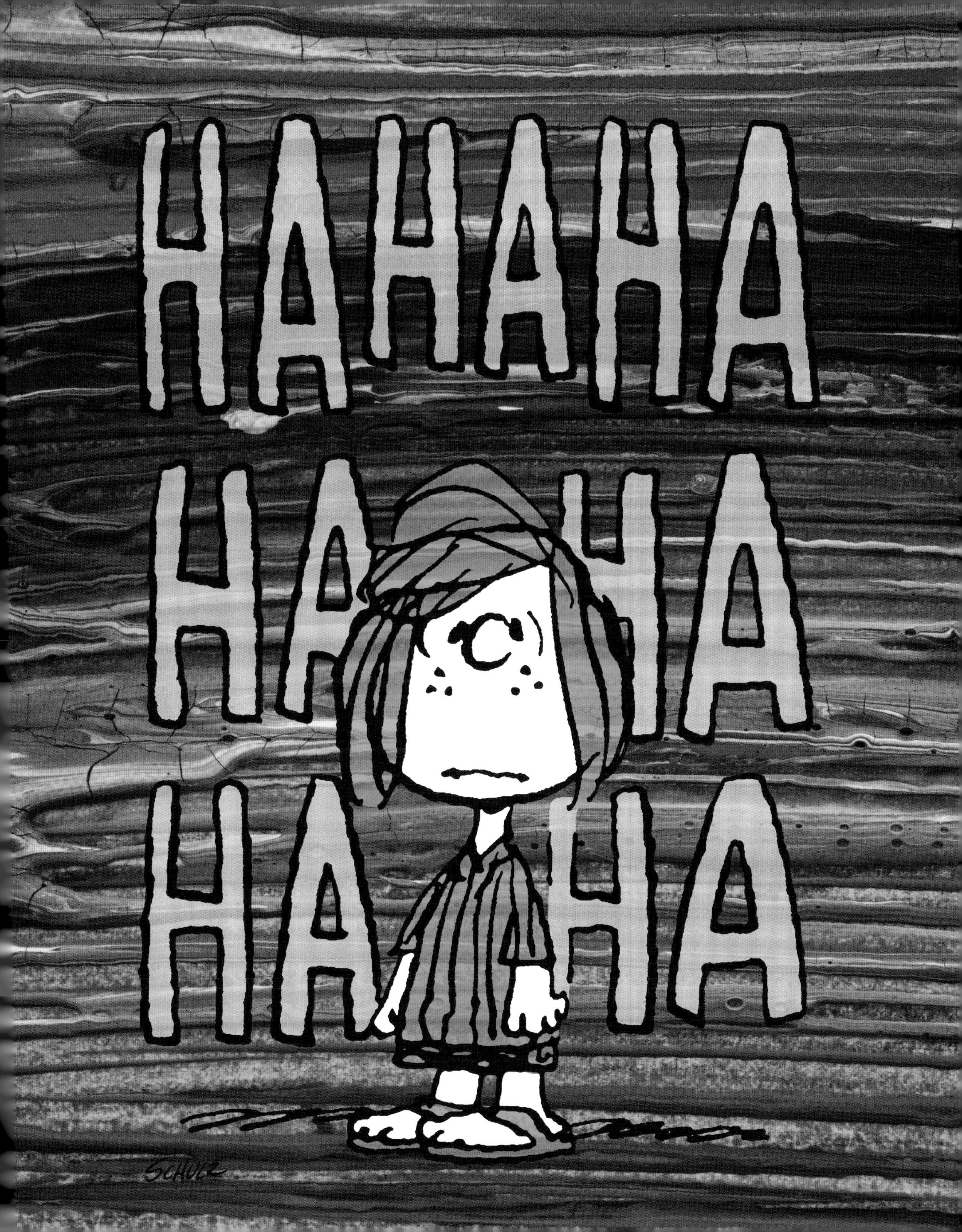
HAHAHA
HAHAHA
HAHAHA
SCHULZ

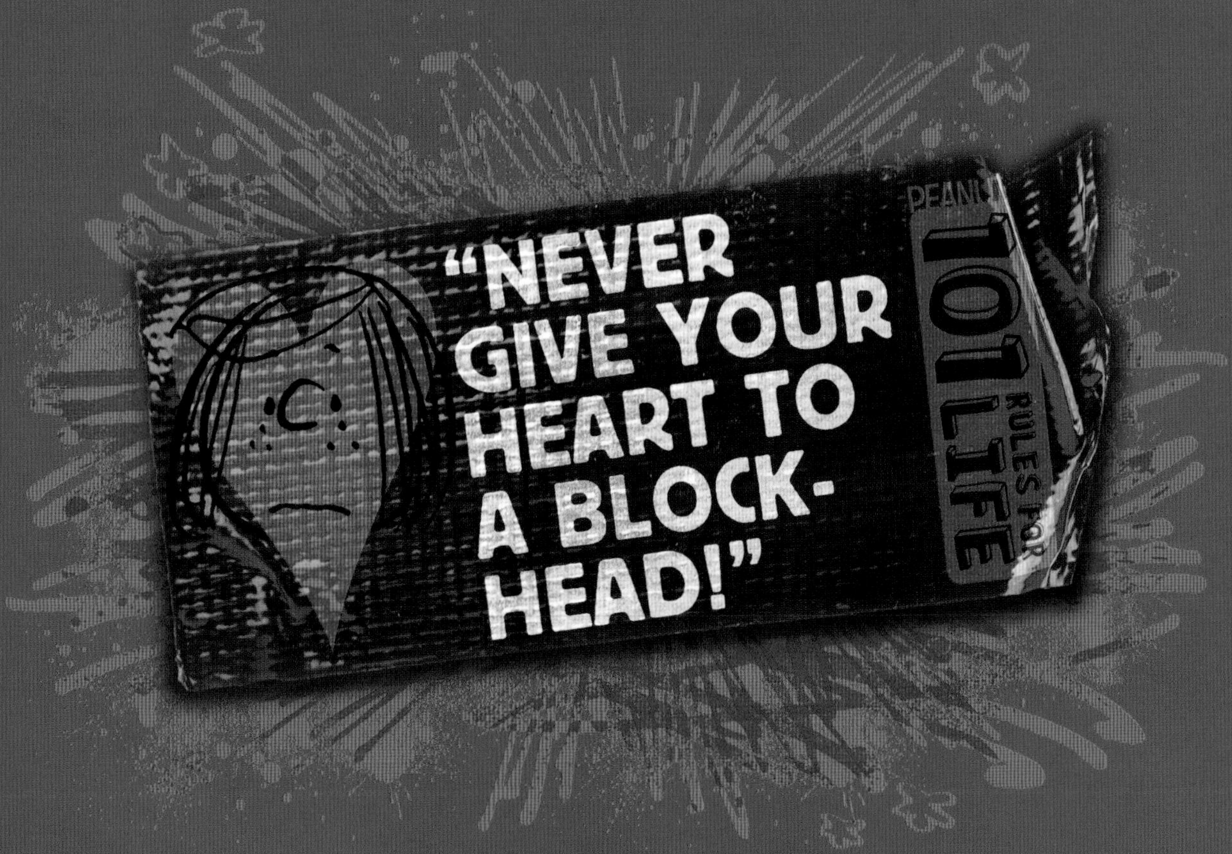
"NEVER GIVE YOUR HEART TO A BLOCK-HEAD!"
101 RULES FOR LIFE

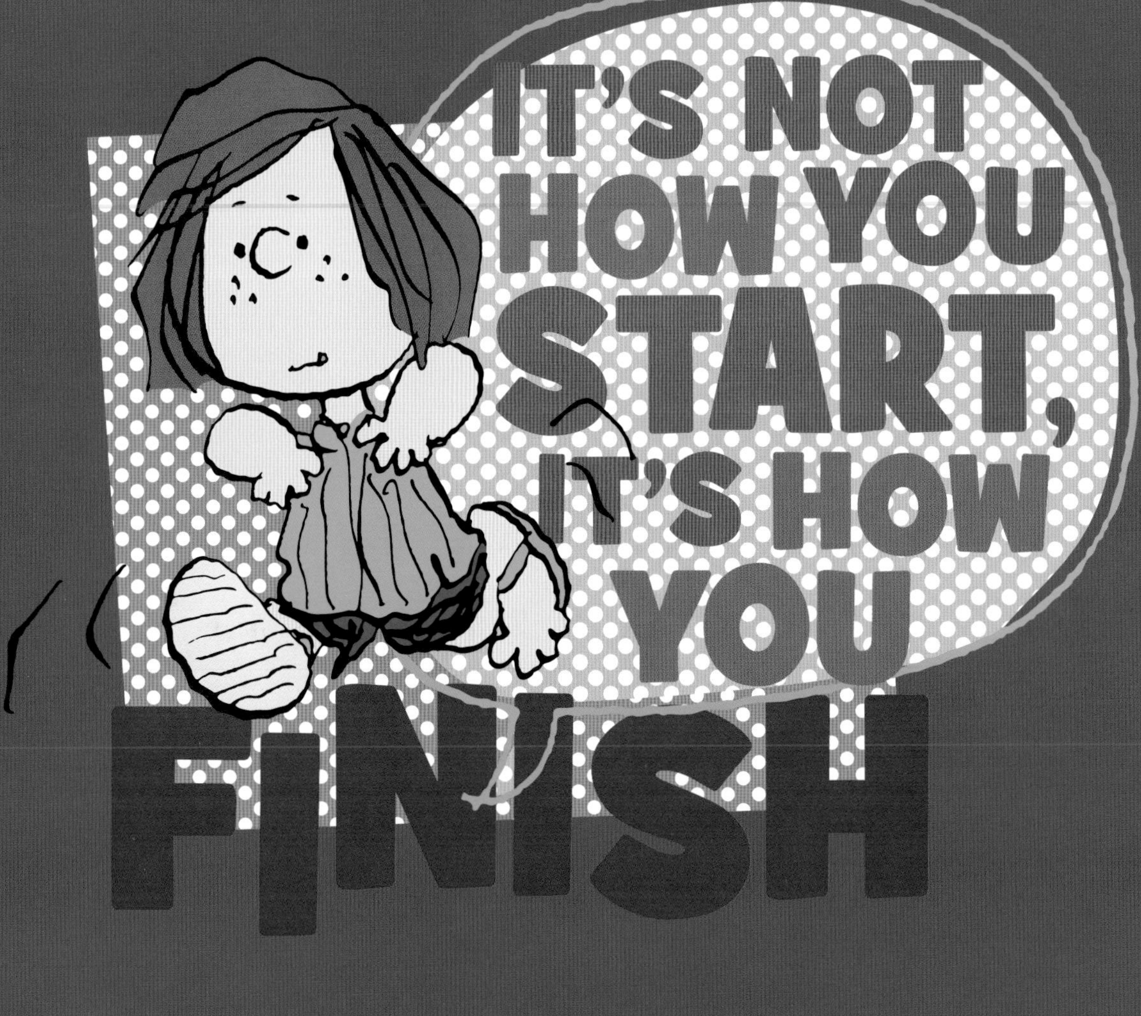
IT'S NOT HOW YOU START, IT'S HOW YOU
FINISH

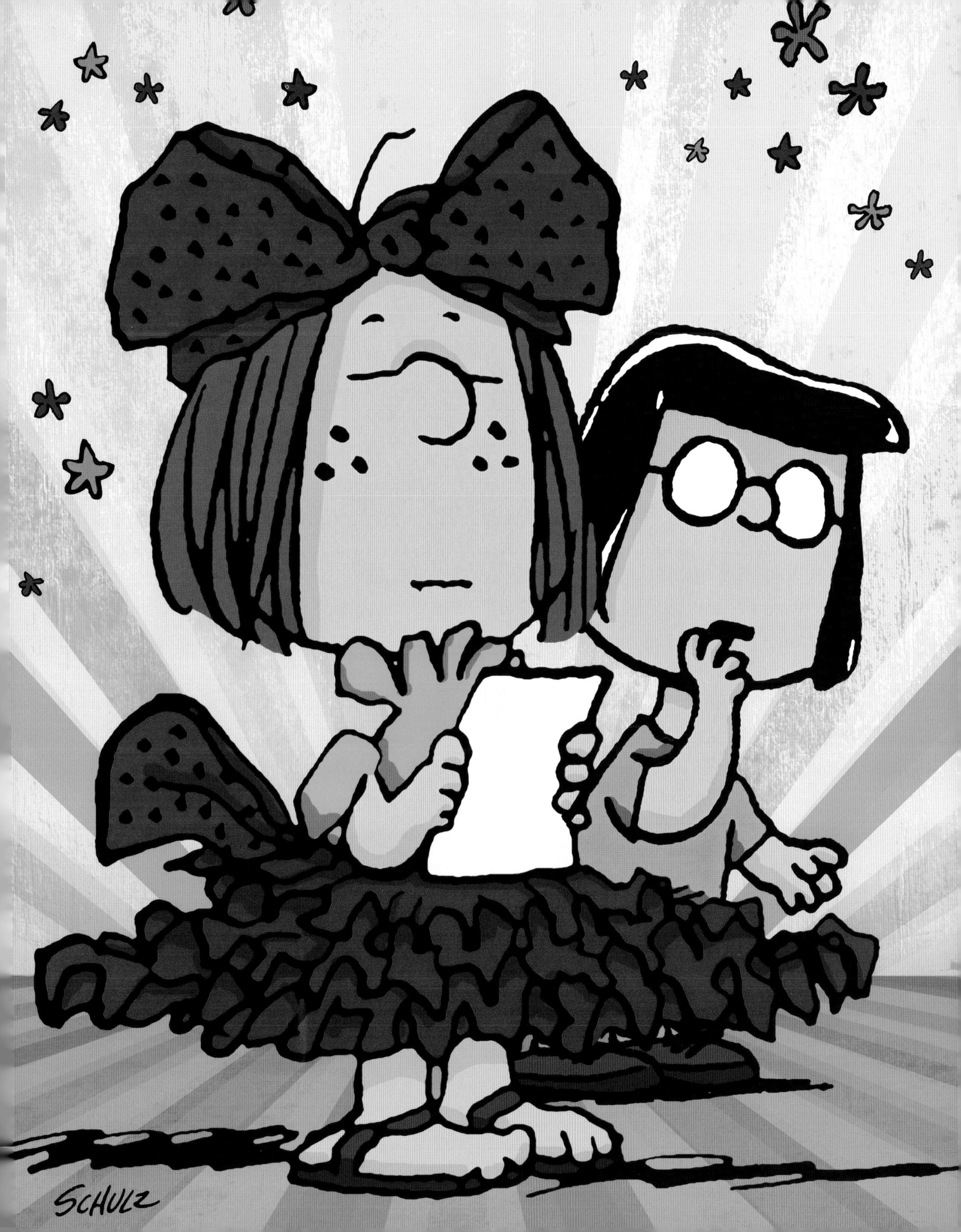
SCHULZ

PEANUTS
HELLO?
HELLO, CHUCK? THIS IS OL' PEPPERMINT PATTY! HAVE I GOT A SURPRISE FOR YOU! I'VE FOUND YOU A NEW BALL PLAYER....
3-20
THIS GUY IS TERRIFIC! HE'S NOT VERY BIG, BUT HE CAN REALLY PLAY! HIS NAME?
JOSÉ PETERSON!
SCHULZ

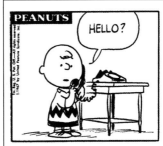

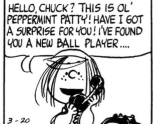

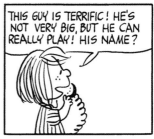

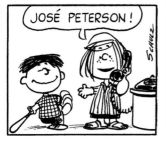

# José Peterson

FIRST APPEARANCE
03/20/1967

An all-star talent by way of New Mexico (batting average .640) and North Dakota (batting average .850), José Peterson naturally catches the attention of Peppermint Patty when he moves to her neighborhood at the start of baseball season. He is an excellent fielder, as well, and is the core of Peppermint Patty's planned overhaul of Charlie Brown's team.

But before Charlie Brown can clear room on his mantel for his "Manager of the Year" trophy, Peppermint Patty reassesses his team and opts to form a team with José in her own neighborhood. She encourages Charlie Brown to look into alternative sports, such as shuffleboard, while she and José make plans to enjoy a traditional meal at the Peterson household—tortillas and Swedish meatballs.

"I had a dream in which I dreamed a new character whose name was a combination of Mexican and Swedish," noted Charles Schulz, when asked about Peppermint Patty's latest teammate. "Why in the world I had such a dream and would think of such a name as José Peterson is a mystery to me. Most of the time things that are a complete riot when you are dreaming are not the least bit funny when you wake up. In this case, however, it seemed like a good idea, so I developed a story about the arrival of José Peterson in the neighborhood, and he has remained ever since, usually playing on Peppermint Patty's baseball team."

Rookie of the year
.850
José Peterson

PREVIOUS PAGES, TOP LEFT AND BOTTOM LEFT: *Style Guide art – PW*; RIGHT: Peanuts, *Issue #6, Boom! Studios comic book cover, 2011 – CSCA* | RIGHT AND OPPOSITE: *Design by Cameron + Co*

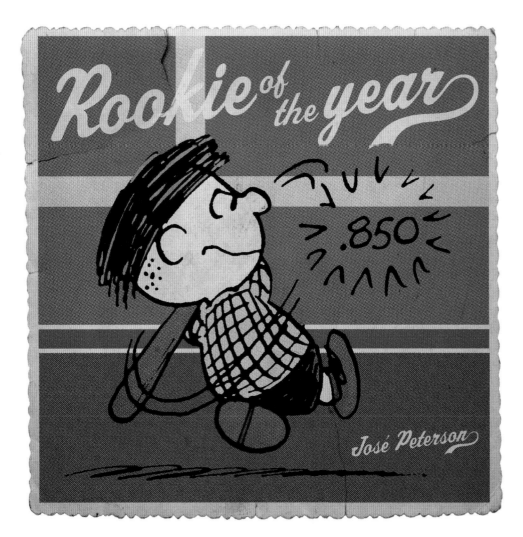

PEANUTS
HELLO, GIRLS... I'M "PEPPERMINT" PATTY, YOUR TENT MONITOR...
ACTUALLY, MY NAME REALLY ISN'T "PEPPERMINT" PATTY...THAT'S JUST A NICK-NAME MY DAD GAVE ME... HE ALSO CALLS ME HIS "RARE GEM"
6-18
NOW, WHAT ARE YOUR NAMES?
AFTER ALL THAT, WHAT CAN WE SAY?

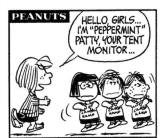

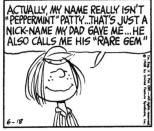

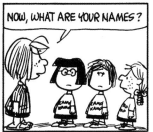

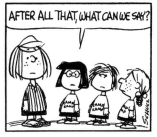

# Clara, Shirley & Sophie

FIRST APPEARANCE
06/18/1968

Fate—and summer camp—work in mysterious ways, as the inseparable trio of Clara, Shirley, and Sophie discover when Peppermint Patty is assigned as their tent monitor. Over the course of two short weeks, Peppermint Patty teaches them how to swim and how to make new friends at camp. Sophie is more homesick than the others, but a surprise visit from Snoopy in his guise as the World War I Flying Ace helps her get through her time away from home.

The trio is assigned to Peppermint Patty's tent again their next time at camp, and they are eager to learn new athletic skills from their experienced tent monitor. Sophie is a particularly enthusiastic diving student and hopes to apply her newfound skills during the next Summer Olympic Games.

The trio's names are derived from Charles Schulz's own family, including his grandmother Sophia, aunt Clara, and cousin Shirley.

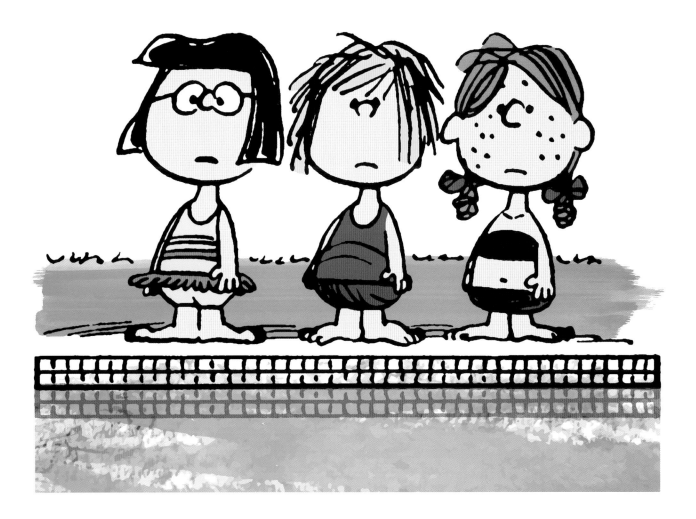

PEANUTS
GEE, CHUCK, WHERE'VE YOU BEEN? OUR GAME IS READY TO GO.. DID YOU BRING THE GLOVE? NICE SHOT!
HERE, GIVE IT TO THIBAULT... HE'S THE ONE WHO DOESN'T HAVE A GLOVE...
THIBAULT?
GET OUT THERE, THIBAULT, AND SHOW 'EM HOW IT'S DONE!
YOU CAN WATCH THE GAME FROM OVER THERE, CHUCK.. WISH US LUCK...
THIBAULT?

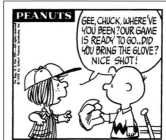

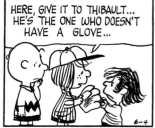

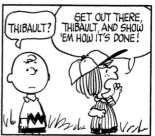

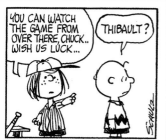

# THIBAULT

FIRST APPEARANCE
06/04/1970

Short of stature and short of temper, Thibault is one of the most pugnacious, argumentative kids in the neighborhood. Although he may not have a winning personality, he's a gifted athlete, which explains his continued presence on Peppermint Patty's baseball team.

Thibault is never one to back down from a fight, whether he's refusing to return Charlie Brown's baseball glove or scrapping with his teammates, including Peppermint Patty. His promising career at second base is cut short after his taunts earn him a punch right in the chops from Marcie—the next time he is seen on the baseball diamond, he is Peppermint Patty's catcher and is wearing as much protective gear as possible when he takes the field!

The aggressive Thibault is a rarity in *Peanuts*, as most of the strip's bullies only appear for a single storyline before exiting. Thibault never changes his misanthropic ways, but Peppermint Patty apparently can't afford to lose a talented baseball player.

WIN-LESS
BASEBALL CARDS
THIBAULT
SECOND BASE & CATCHER

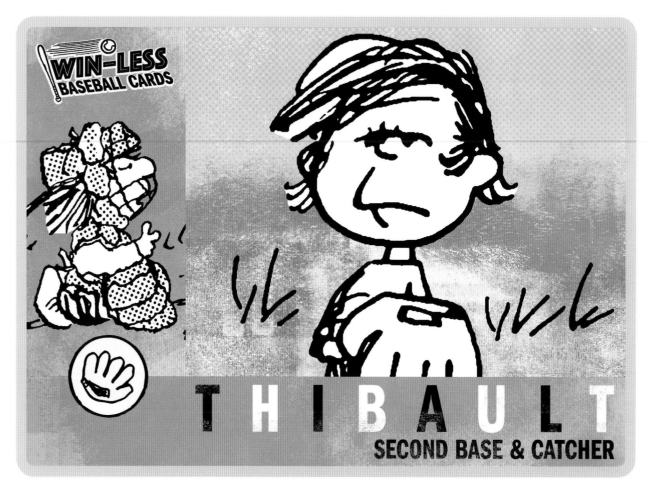

ABOVE AND OPPOSITE: *Design by Cameron + Co*

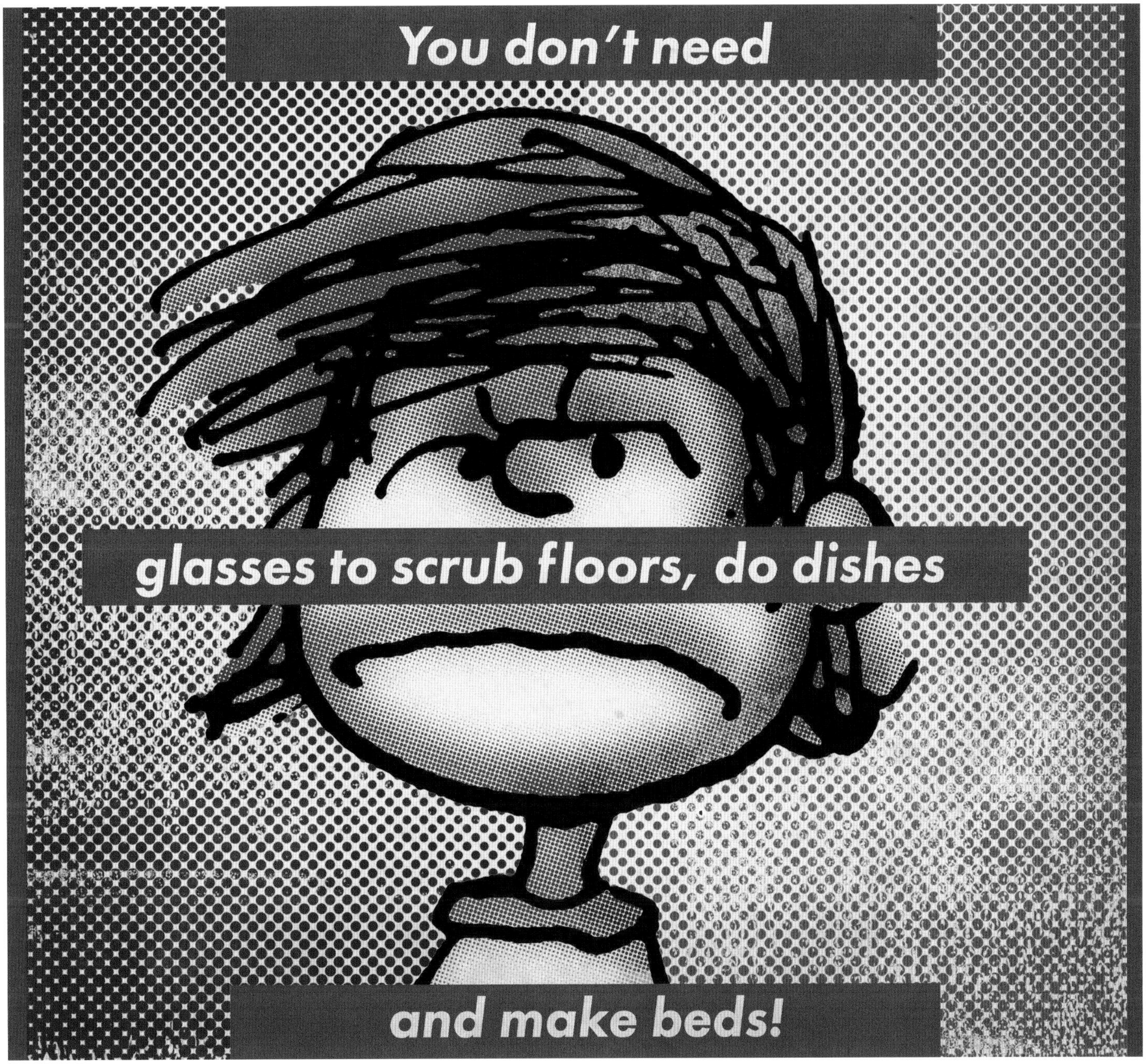
You don't need
glasses to scrub floors, do dishes
and make beds!

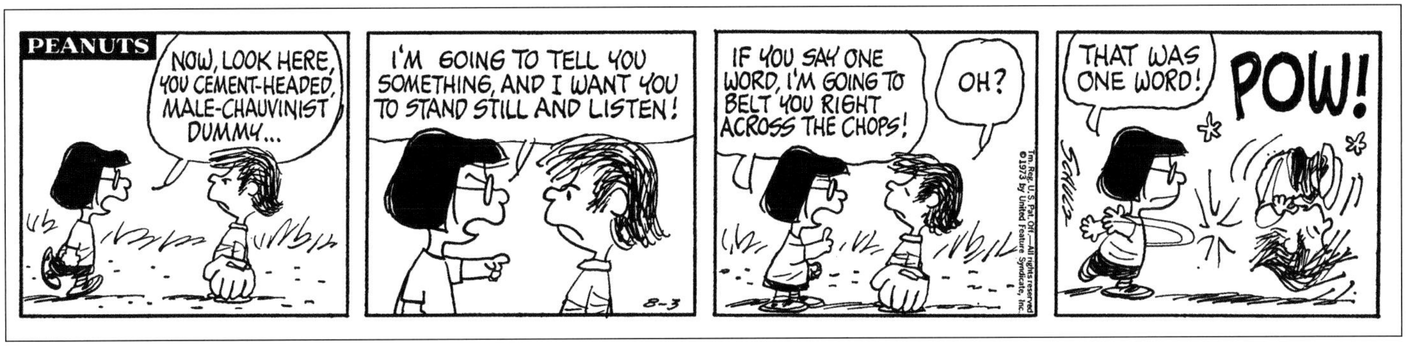
PEANUTS
NOW, LOOK HERE, YOU CEMENT-HEADED, MALE-CHAUVINIST DUMMY...
I'M GOING TO TELL YOU SOMETHING, AND I WANT YOU TO STAND STILL AND LISTEN!
8-3
IF YOU SAY ONE WORD, I'M GOING TO BELT YOU RIGHT ACROSS THE CHOPS!
OH?
Tm. Reg. U.S. Pat. Off.—All rights reserved
©1973 by United Feature Syndicate, Inc.
THAT WAS ONE WORD!
POW!

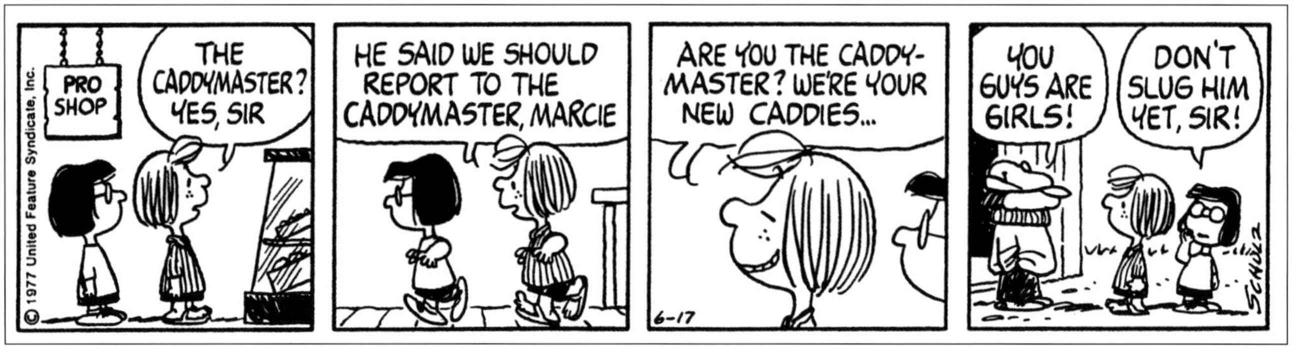
© 1977 United Feature Syndicate, Inc.
PRO SHOP
THE CADDYMASTER? YES, SIR
HE SAID WE SHOULD REPORT TO THE CADDYMASTER, MARCIE
ARE YOU THE CADDY-MASTER? WE'RE YOUR NEW CADDIES...
6-17
YOU GUYS ARE GIRLS!
DON'T SLUG HIM YET, SIR!
SCHULZ

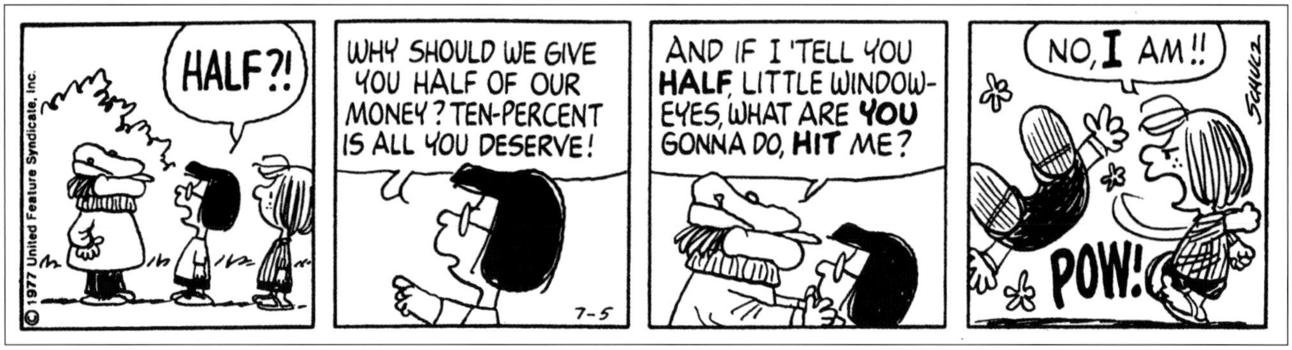
© 1977 United Feature Syndicate, Inc.
HALF?!
WHY SHOULD WE GIVE YOU HALF OF OUR MONEY? TEN-PERCENT IS ALL YOU DESERVE!
7-5
AND IF I TELL YOU HALF, LITTLE WINDOW-EYES, WHAT ARE YOU GONNA DO, HIT ME?
NO, I AM!!
POW!
SCHULZ

# THE CADDYMASTER

FIRST APPEARANCE
06/17/1977

The belligerent Caddymaster rules the pro shop at the Ace Country Club with an iron fist—or at least a nine-iron. When Peppermint Patty and Marcie apply for summer jobs at the club, the Caddymaster disparages them for being girls, then assigns them the difficult task of caddying for Mrs. Nelson and Mrs. Bartley, well known for their heavy golf bags and constant arguments.

Peppermint Patty and Marcie quit after four grueling holes, and the Caddymaster insists on receiving fifty percent of their day's pay. When he rejects their counteroffer of ten percent and threatens Marcie, Peppermint Patty slugs him, and the pair decide to leave their caddying ambitions behind them.

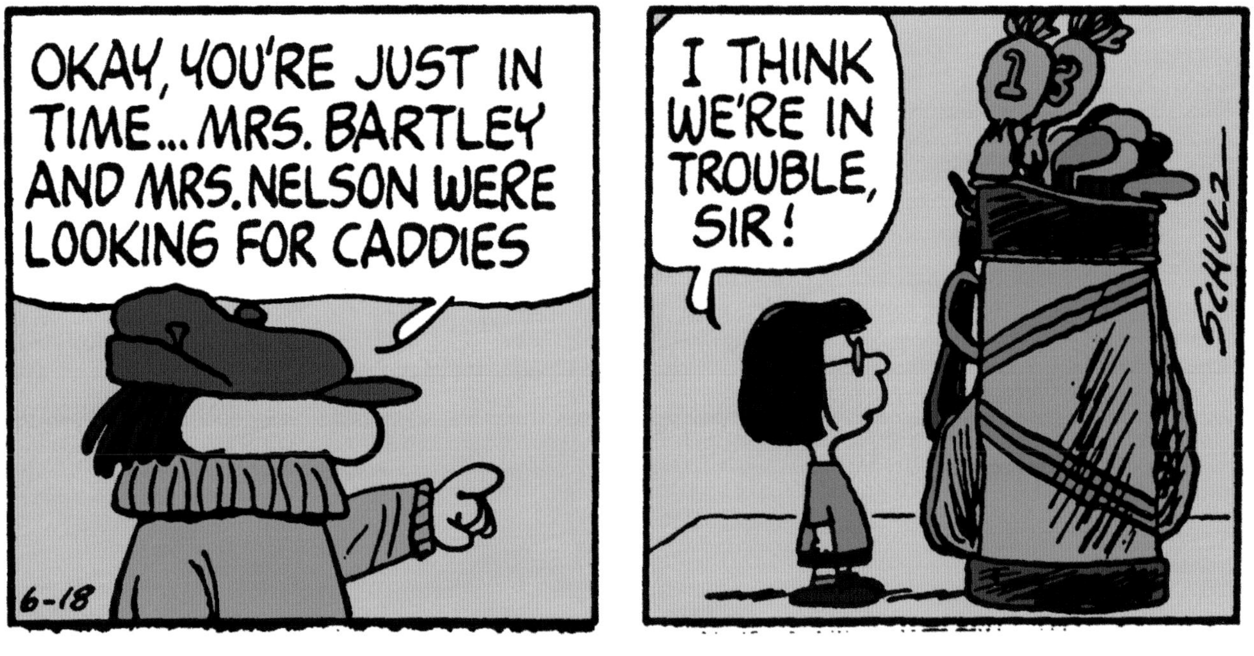
OKAY, YOU'RE JUST IN TIME... MRS. BARTLEY AND MRS. NELSON WERE LOOKING FOR CADDIES
6-18
I THINK WE'RE IN TROUBLE, SIR!
SCHULZ

ABOVE: *Spot art from strip – Charles M. Schulz* | OPPOSITE: *Design by Cameron + Co*

YEAH, MY DAD AND OUR TEACHER THINK MAYBE I NEED A TUTOR
WELL, YOU KNOW, TO HELP ME GET A BETTER START IN SCHOOL THIS YEAR..
7-21
© 1986 United Feature Syndicate, Inc.
WHOOPS! SOMEONE'S AT THE DOOR... IT'S PROBABLY MY TUTOR...
HI! ARE YOU THE DUMB ONE?
SCHULZ

WHAT DID YOU THROW ME OUT FOR?!
MARCIE SAYS YOU WERE GETTING PAID TO BE MY TUTOR! YOU SHOULD HAVE BEEN DOING IT OUT OF THE GOODNESS OF YOUR HEART!
7-29
"THE LABORER IS WORTHY OF HIS HIRE" LUKE 10:4
HE'S QUOTING SCRIPTURE, SIR
IS THAT FAIR?
© 1986 United Feature Syndicate, Inc.
SCHULZ

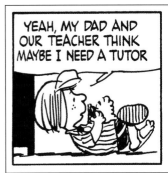

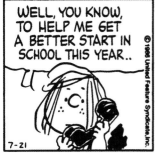

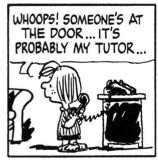

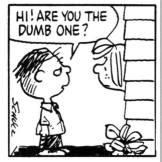

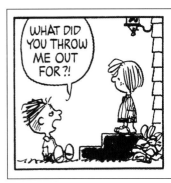

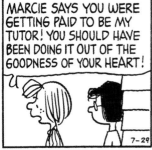

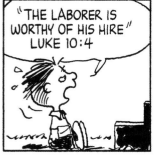

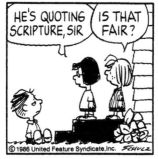

# MAYNARD

FIRST APPEARANCE 07/21/1986

In an effort to pull up Peppermint Patty's D-minus average in school, her father hires Marcie's cousin, Maynard, as her tutor. Maynard's condescending attitude and arrogance don't sit well with Peppermint Patty, who resents the implication that she needs help in school in the first place.

Their relationship gets off to a rocky start when Peppermint Patty insists on calling him "Joe Sarcasm" and "Captain Tutor." Their session ends abruptly when she realizes that he's being paid to help her, rather than offering assistance out of "the goodness of [his] heart."

Like Peppermint Patty, Charles Schulz also struggled in school, but his parents never thought to hire a tutor to help him out. "[My parents] never said anything to me. They were very nice people. They never got mad at me, and they never punished me for getting bad grades. The first time I was interviewed by *The Saturday Evening Post*, the writer and my father and I were sitting in a restaurant booth, and the writer asked how my Dad felt about my failing all those grades. And my Dad said: 'What do you mean? I always thought he did pretty well.'"

MAYNARD'S TUTORIAL GUIDE
GEOGRAPHY
MATHEMATICS
MODERN LANGUAGES
RELIGIOUS EDUCATION

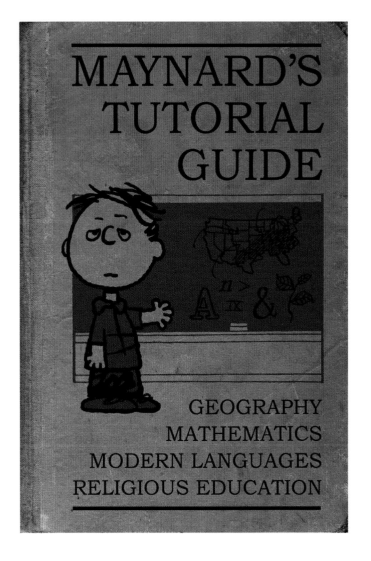

# THE SPORTING LIFE

The pitcher's mound, the hockey rink, the links, the football field—each is an ideal venue for Charlie Brown to exhibit uncanny ability to lose. As he wryly observes of his efforts on the baseball diamond, "We always seem to lose the first game of the season and the last game of the season . . . AND ALL THE STUPID GAMES IN-BETWEEN!"

Sports feature prominently throughout *Peanuts*, and Schulz has played with nearly all of them, from the mainstays of baseball, football, basketball, hockey, soccer, tennis, and golf to rowing, swimming, weight lifting, and wrestling.

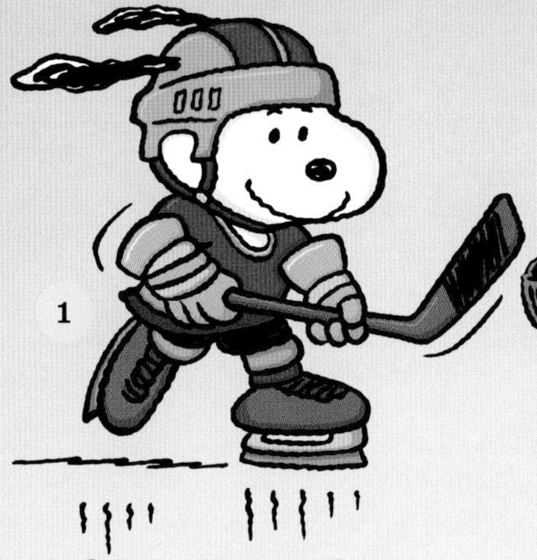
1

But to Schulz, the specific sport was not as important as the outcome. "Sports work well in my strips. They mirror the frustrations people have in their own lives. The games people play, the sports themselves aren't that important, but it's the winning and losing that people can identify with."

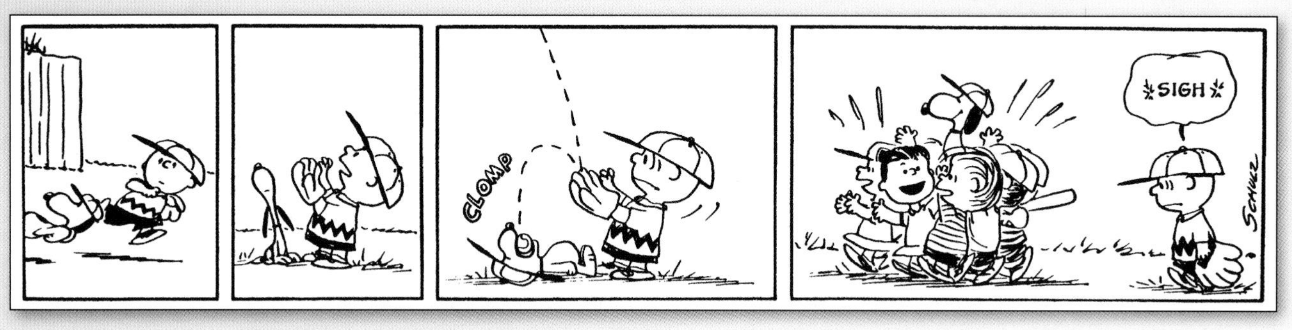

CLOMP
SIGH
SCHULZ


*1, 3, 6 and 8: Style Guide Art – PW; 2: Women's Sports Foundation poster – CMSM; 4: Style Guide art – CSCA; 5:* The Runner *magazine cover, published by CBS Magazines, 1986 – CMSM; ; 7:* It's Only Baseball, Charlie Brown, Peanuts *Digital Edition – CSCA*

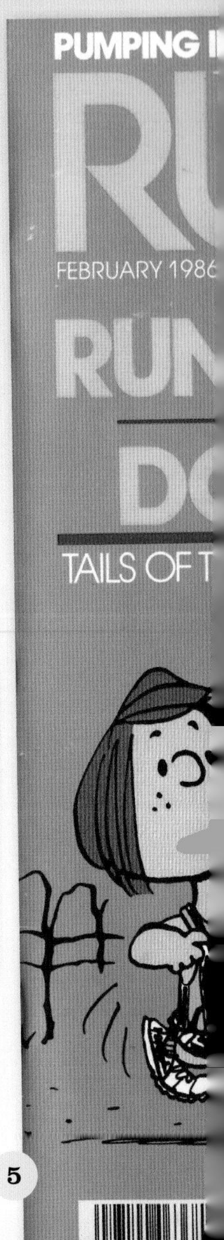

PUMPING I
FEBRUARY 1986
TAILS OF T

5

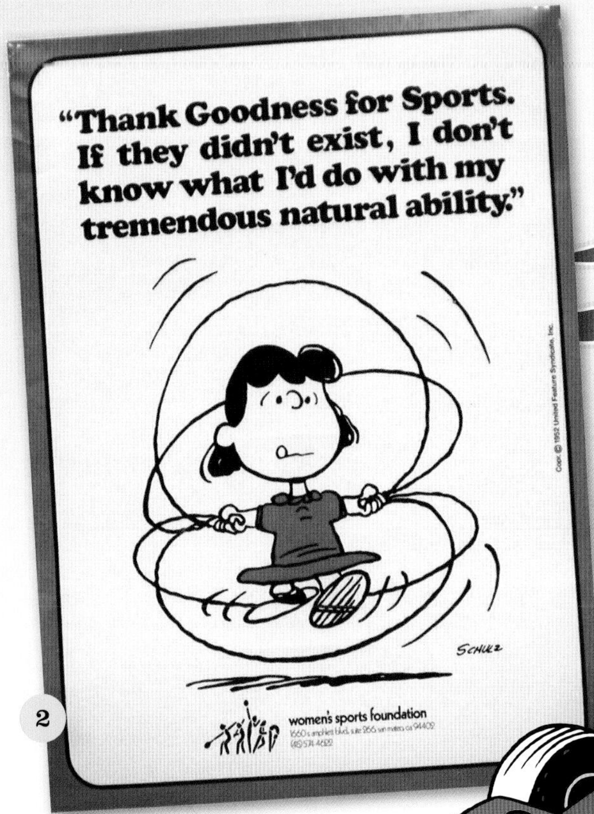

"Thank Goodness for Sports. If they didn't exist, I don't know what I'd do with my tremendous natural ability."
SCHULZ
women's sports foundation

2

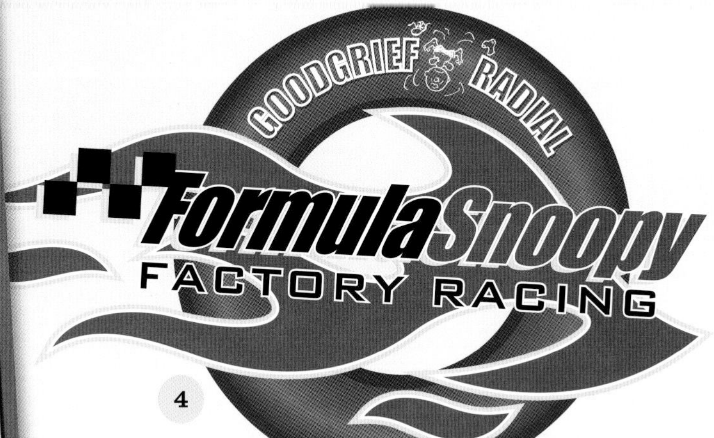

GOODGRIEF RADIAL
FormulaSnoopy
FACTORY RACING

4

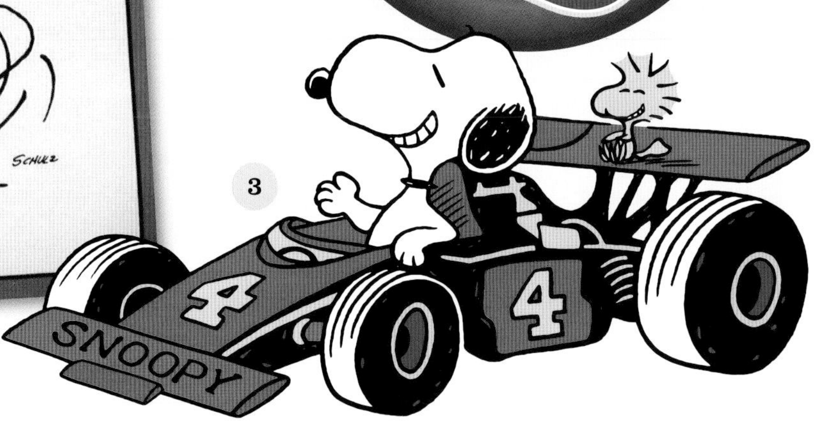

4
4
SNOOPY

3

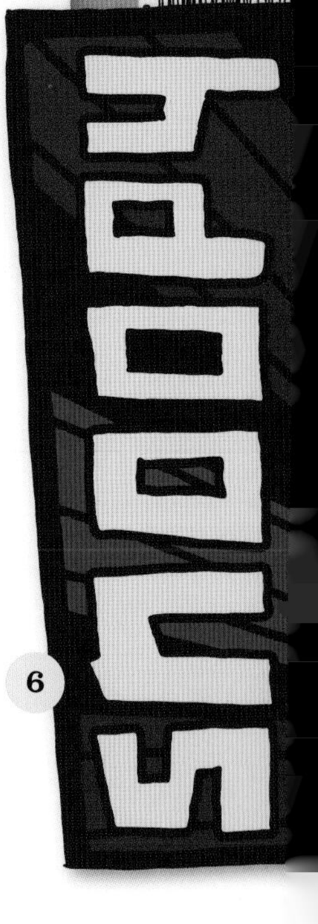

SNOOPY

6

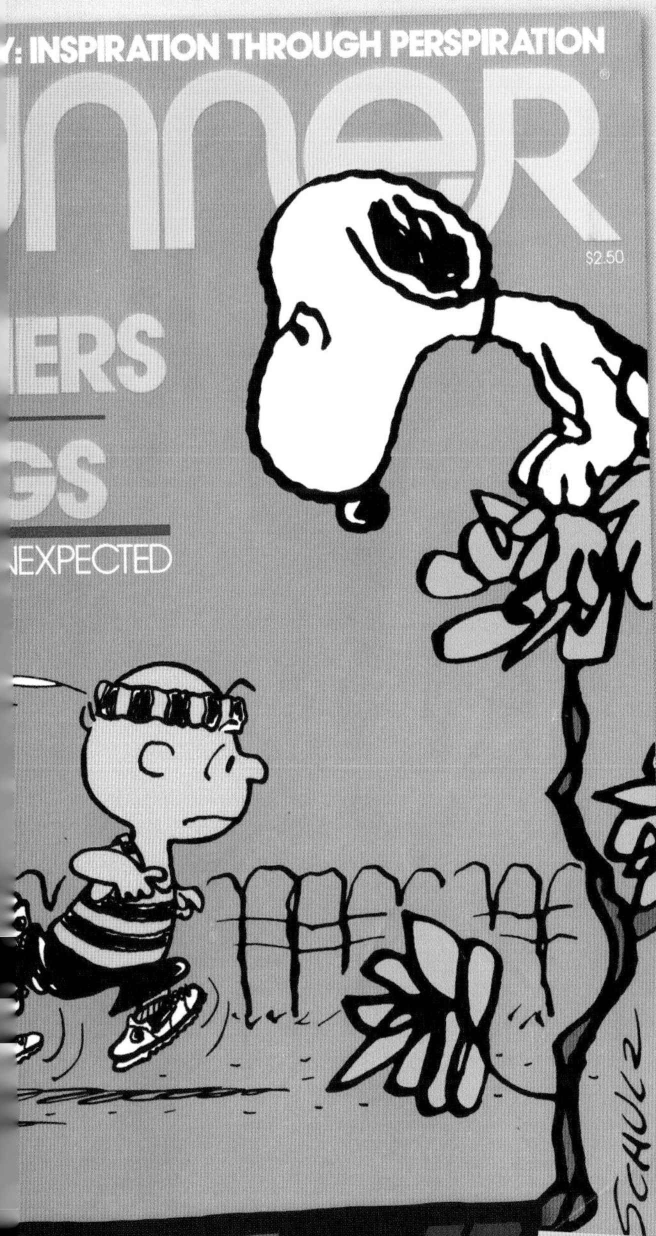
Y: INSPIRATION THROUGH PERSPIRATION
$2.50
NEXPECTED
SCHULZ

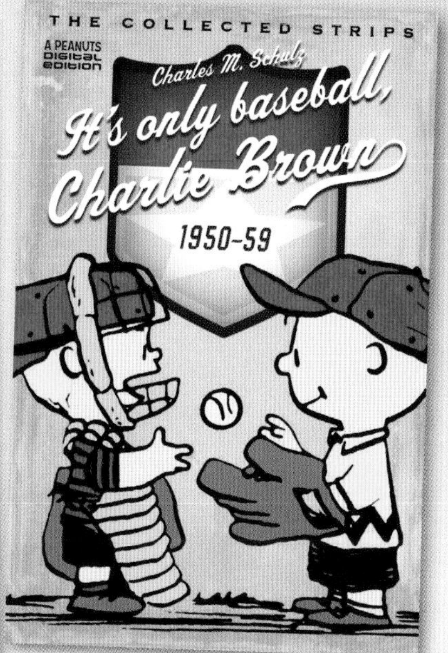
THE COLLECTED STRIPS
A PEANUTS DIGITAL EDITION
Charles M. Schulz
It's only baseball, Charlie Brown
1950–59

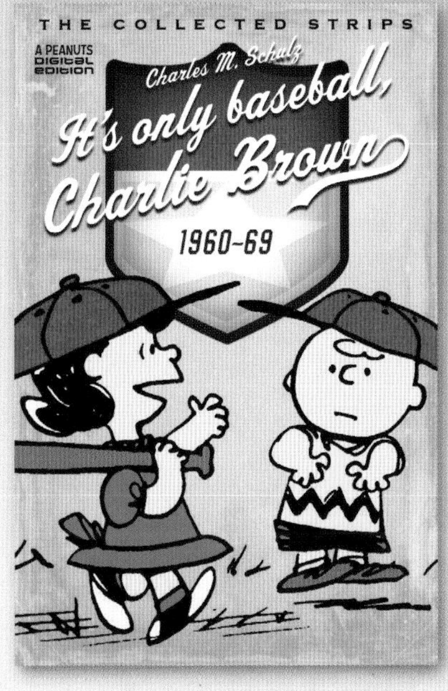
THE COLLECTED STRIPS
A PEANUTS DIGITAL EDITION
Charles M. Schulz
It's only baseball, Charlie Brown
1960–69

7

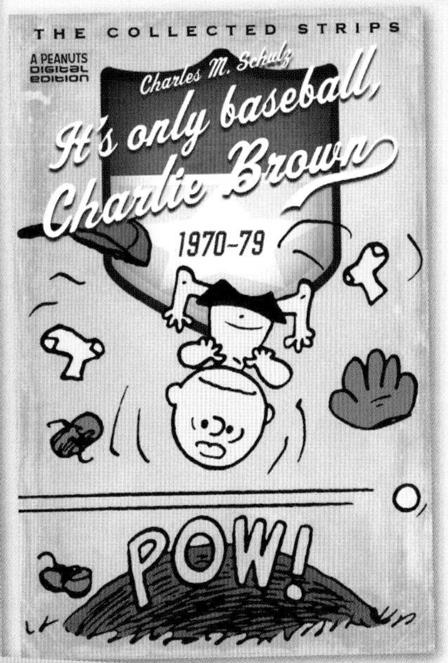
THE COLLECTED STRIPS
A PEANUTS DIGITAL EDITION
Charles M. Schulz
It's only baseball, Charlie Brown
1970–79
POW!

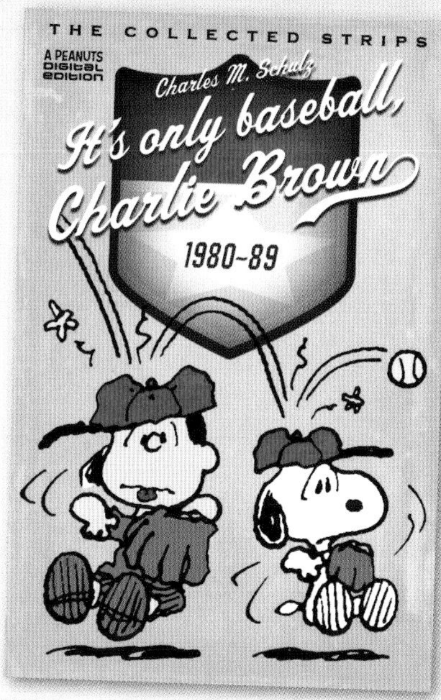
THE COLLECTED STRIPS
A PEANUTS DIGITAL EDITION
Charles M. Schulz
It's only baseball, Charlie Brown
1980–89

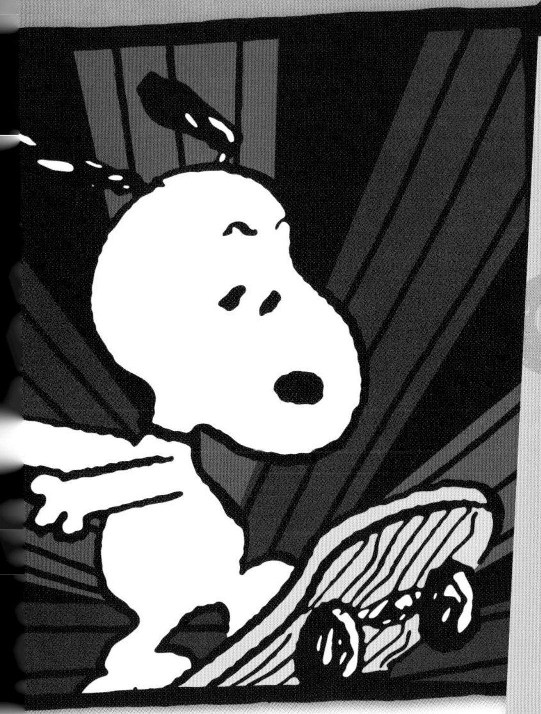

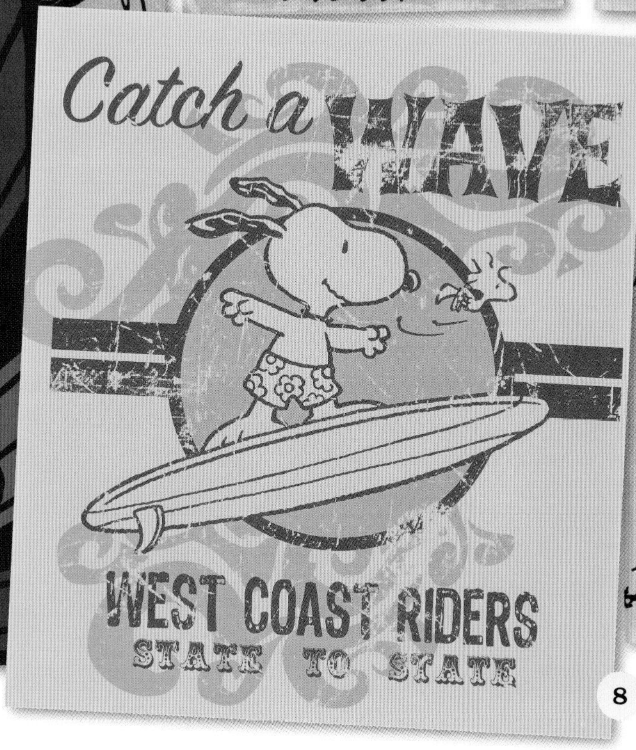
Catch a WAVE
WEST COAST RIDERS
STATE TO STATE

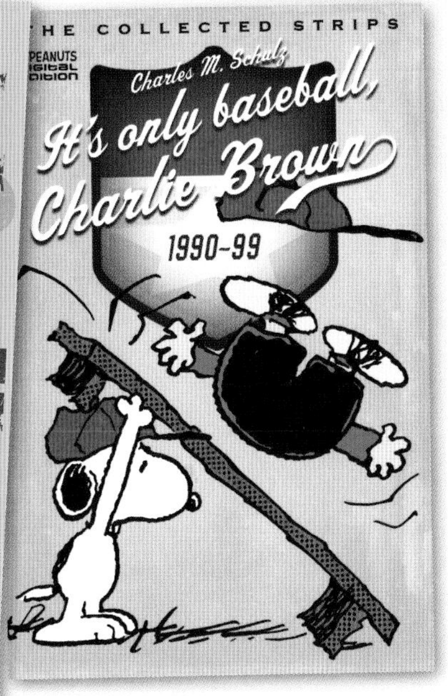
THE COLLECTED STRIPS
PEANUTS DIGITAL EDITION
Charles M. Schulz
It's only baseball, Charlie Brown
1990–99

8

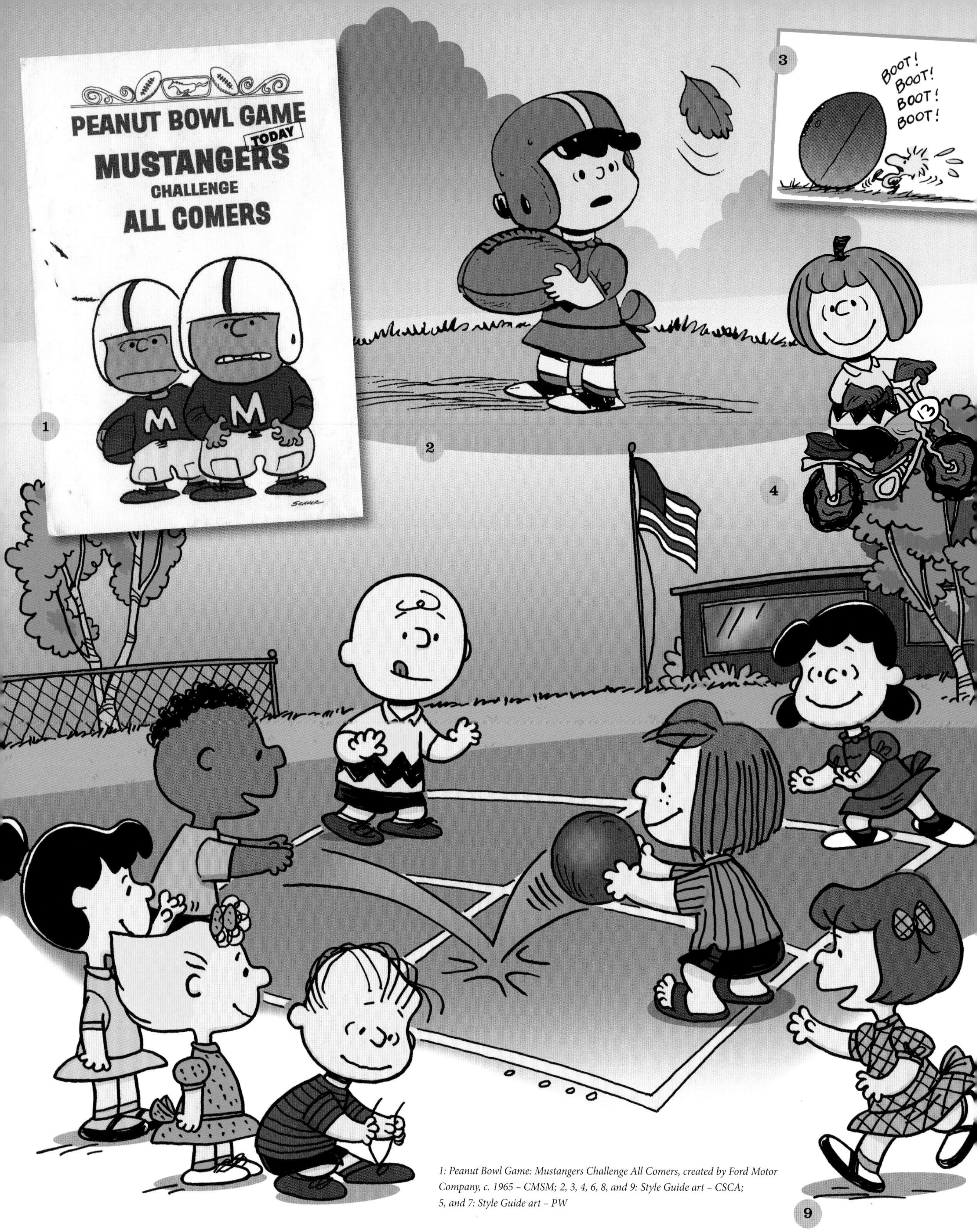
PEANUT BOWL GAME
TODAY
MUSTANGERS
CHALLENGE
ALL COMERS
M
M
1
2
3
BOOT!
BOOT!
BOOT!
BOOT!
13
4
9

*1: Peanut Bowl Game: Mustangers Challenge All Comers, created by Ford Motor Company, c. 1965 – CMSM; 2, 3, 4, 6, 8, and 9: Style Guide art – CSCA; 5, and 7: Style Guide art – PW*

5

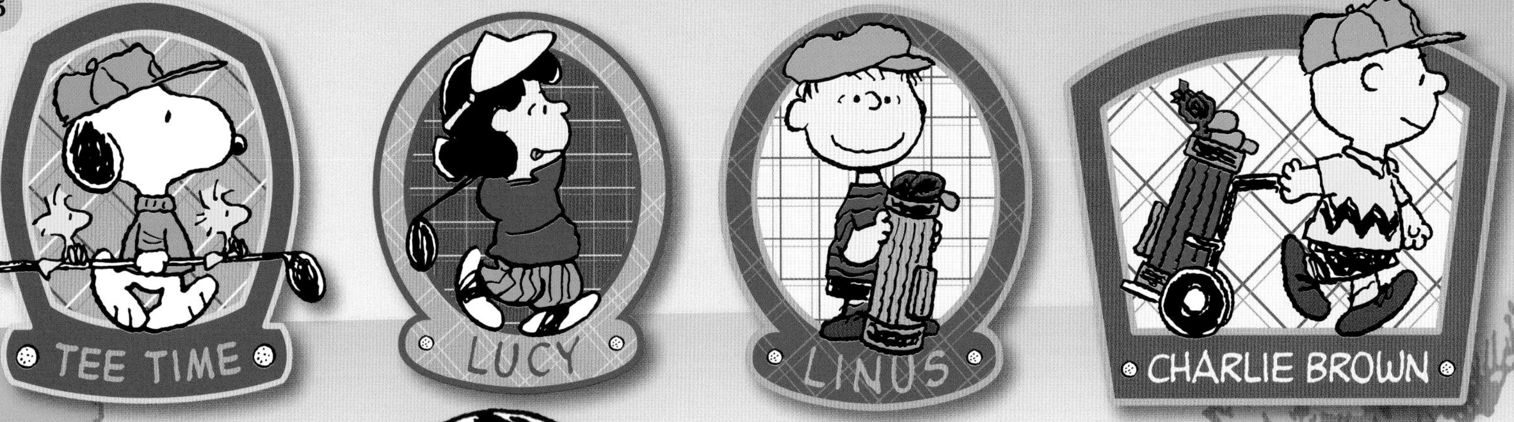
TEE TIME
LUCY
LINUS
CHARLIE BROWN

6

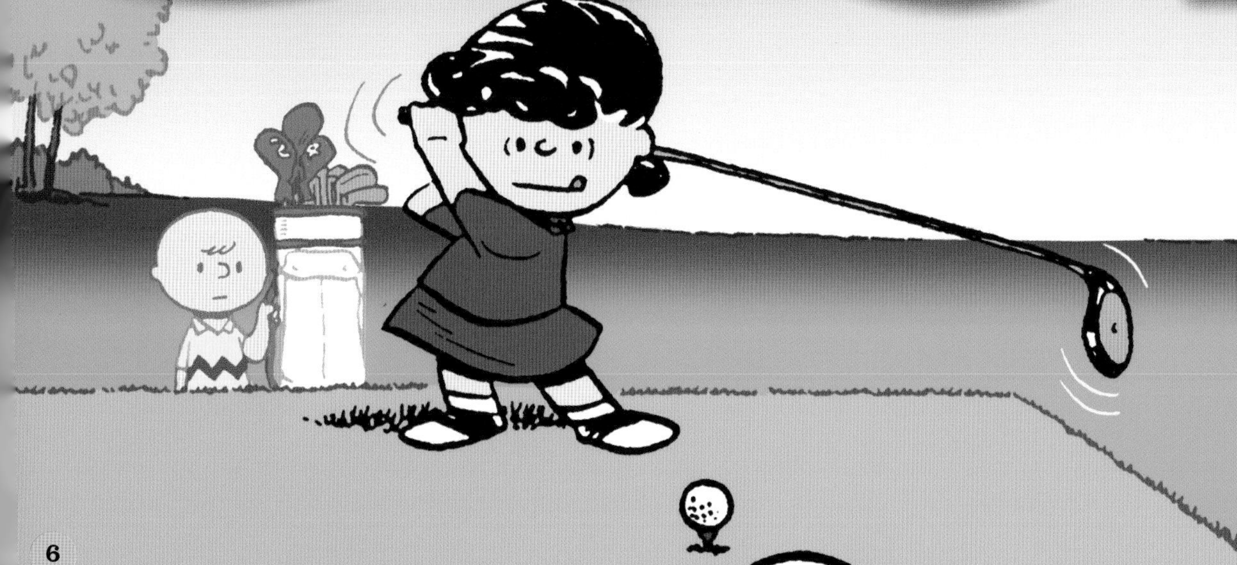

7

8

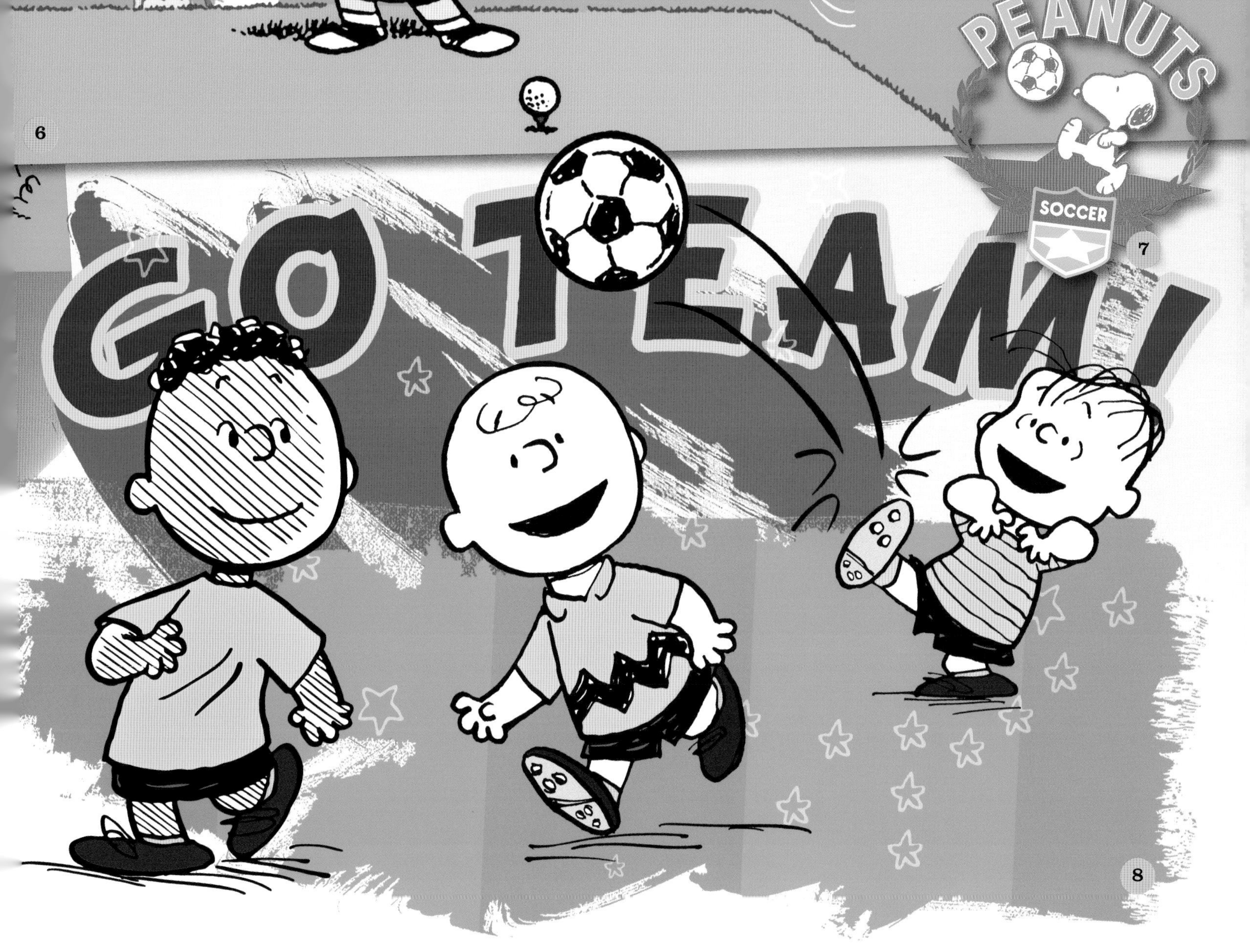
PEANUTS
SOCCER
GO TEAM!

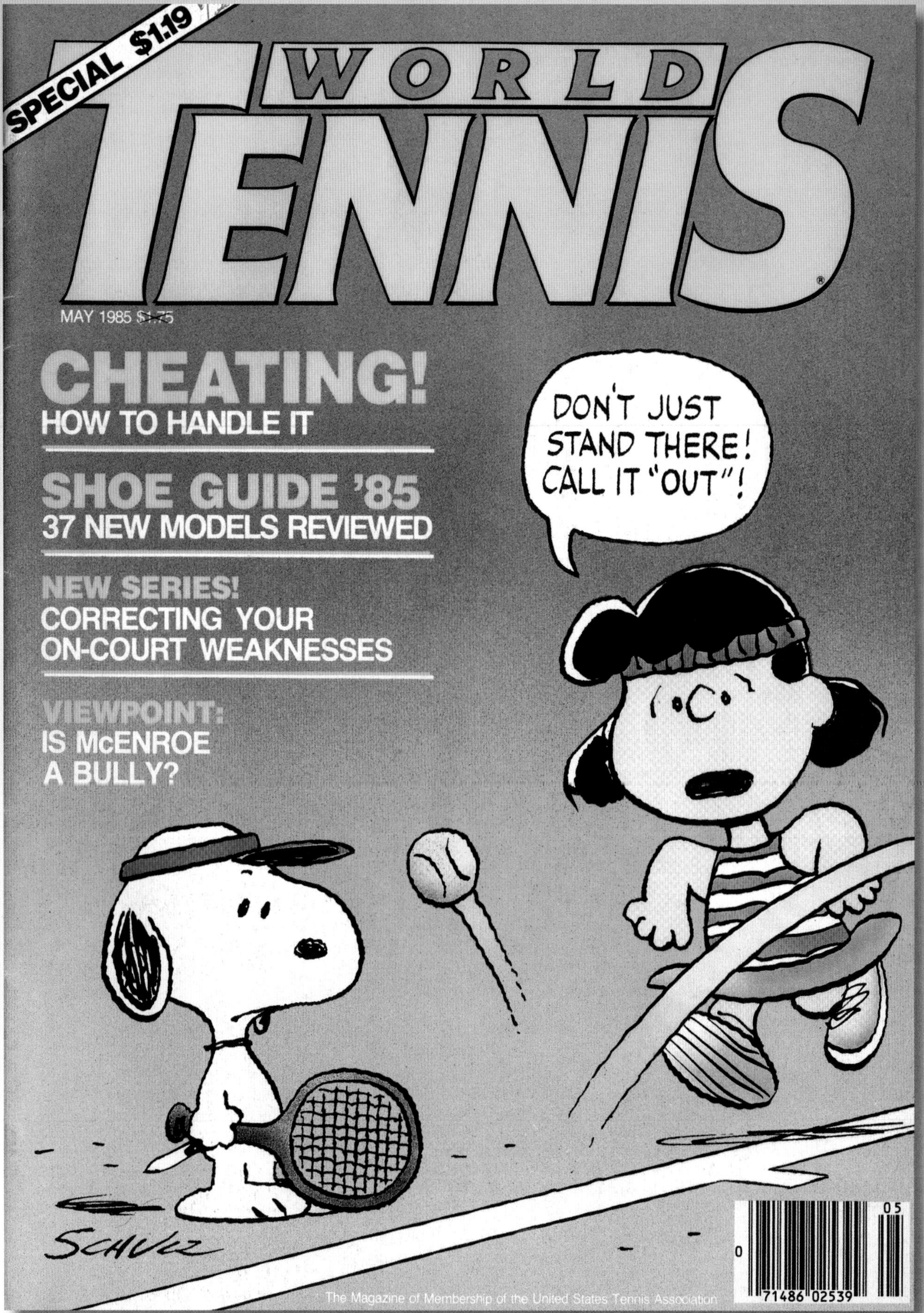
SPECIAL $1.19
WORLD
TENNIS
MAY 1985 $1.75
CHEATING!
HOW TO HANDLE IT
SHOE GUIDE '85
37 NEW MODELS REVIEWED
NEW SERIES!
CORRECTING YOUR
ON-COURT WEAKNESSES
VIEWPOINT:
IS McENROE
A BULLY?
DON'T JUST
STAND THERE!
CALL IT "OUT"!
SCHULZ
The Magazine of Membership of the United States Tennis Association

ABOVE: World Tennis *magazine cover, published by Family Media Inc., 1985 – CMSM* | OPPOSITE: *Design by Cameron + Co*

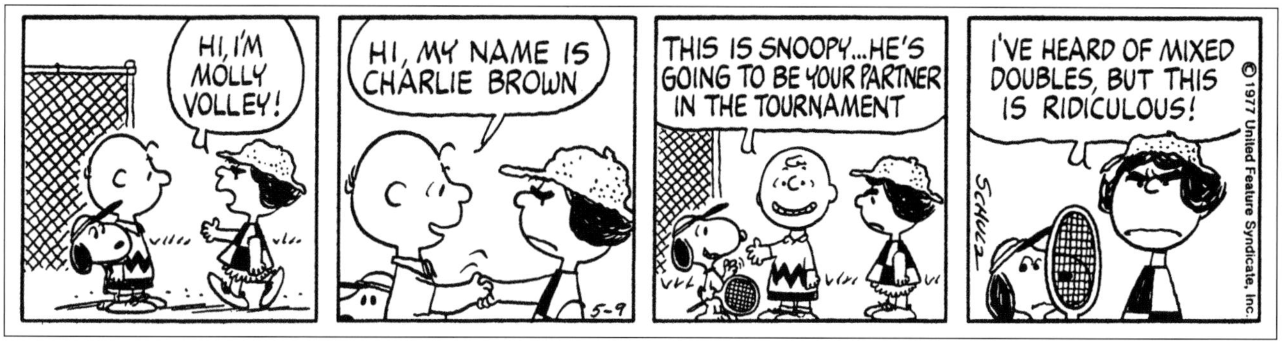
HI, I'M MOLLY VOLLEY!
HI, MY NAME IS CHARLIE BROWN
5-9
THIS IS SNOOPY...HE'S GOING TO BE YOUR PARTNER IN THE TOURNAMENT
I'VE HEARD OF MIXED DOUBLES, BUT THIS IS RIDICULOUS!
SCHULZ
© 1977 United Feature Syndicate, Inc.

# MOLLY VOLLEY

FIRST APPEARANCE
05/09/1977

The most talented—and by far the most competitive—tennis player around is Molly Volley. There's no such thing as a "friendly" game when the tennis ace takes the court, as Snoopy finds out when he is paired with her in a mixed doubles tournament. Her short temper ensures that the only "love" to be found when she's on the court is on her opponent's side of the scoreboard.

"Molly Volley is at once an offshoot of my own recent involvement in tennis and a caricature of human behavior on the court," observed Charles Schulz. "She is one tough cookie who embodies the widely held American belief that the only thing that matters is winning."

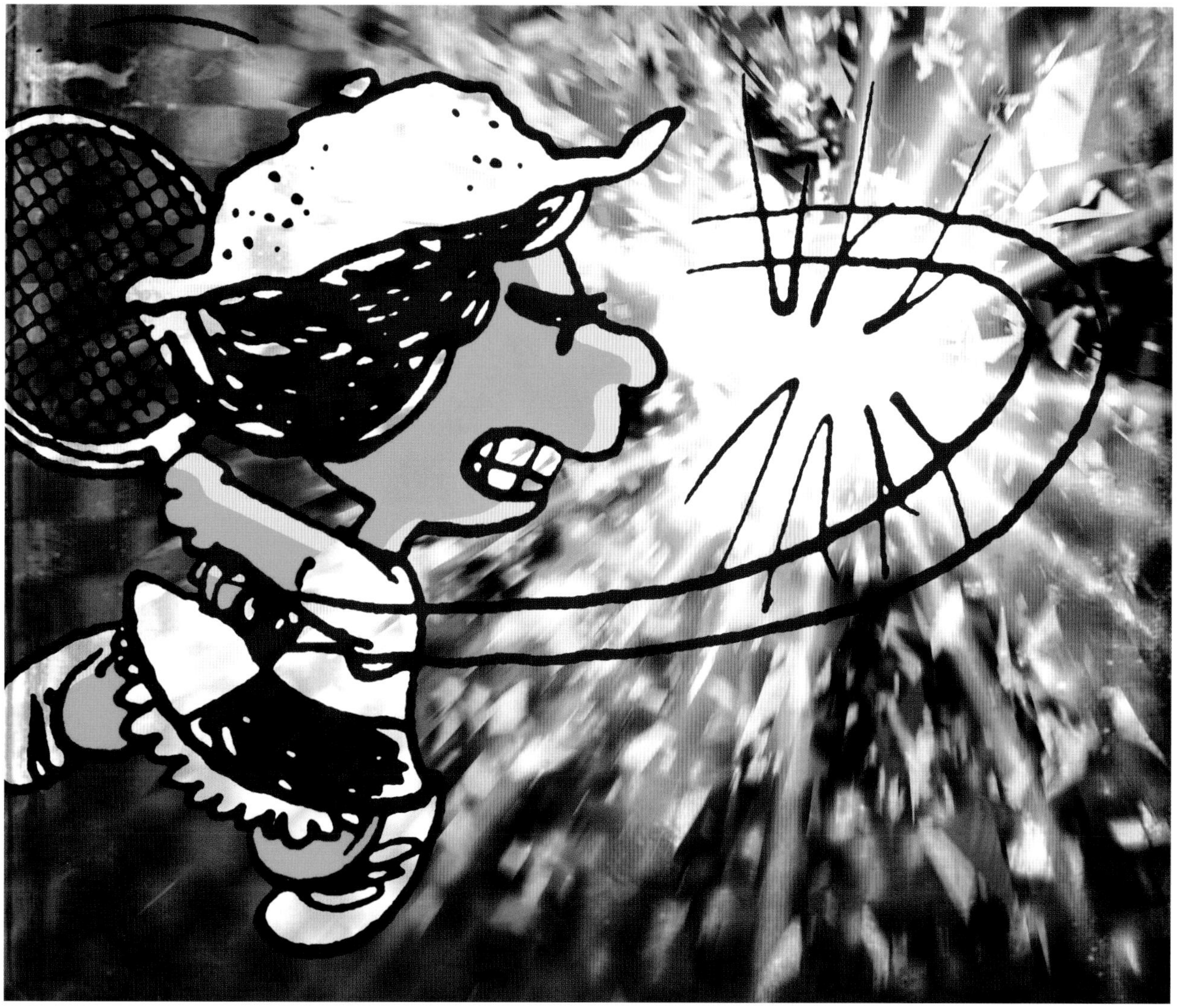

OKAY, WE'LL RECEIVE ON THIS SIDE
THAT'S NOT FAIR!
THAT MEANS WE HAVE THE SUN IN OUR EYES! WHY DO WE ALWAYS SERVE WITH THE SUN IN OUR EYES?!
7-5
SEE? DIDN'T I TELL YOU? "CRYBABY" BOOBIE COMPLAINS ABOUT EVERYTHING!
©1978 United Feature Syndicate, Inc.
I THINK THE NET IS TOO HIGH! THESE BALLS FEEL DEAD! I CAN'T PLAY ON A SLOW COURT! THESE BALLS ARE TOO LIVELY! I THINK THE NET IS TOO LOW!
SCHULZ

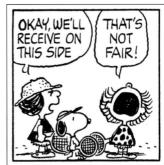

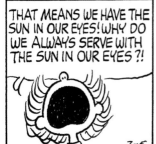

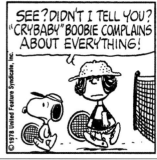

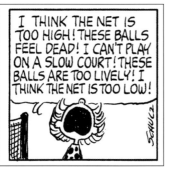

# "Crybaby" Boobie

FIRST MENTIONED 07/03/1978

FIRST APPEARANCE 07/05/1978

A terror on the tennis court (and just about everywhere else), "Crybaby" Boobie is Molly Volley's chief rival, as many a poor, unfortunate line judge can attest. Despite her skill, "Crybaby" plays nearly every match under protest—she manages to find fault with every aspect of every court, from the height of the net to the position of the sun. Her devoted mother attends every single one of "Crybaby's" matches, although she always watches from the safety of the family car.

Nearly every kid in the neighborhood takes part in at least one sporting activity, something that Charles Schulz felt was important to the development of his characters. "The challenges to be faced in sports work marvelously as a caricature of the challenges that we face in the more serious aspects of our lives. And when Charlie Brown has tried to analyze his own difficulties in life, he has always been able to express them best in sports terms."

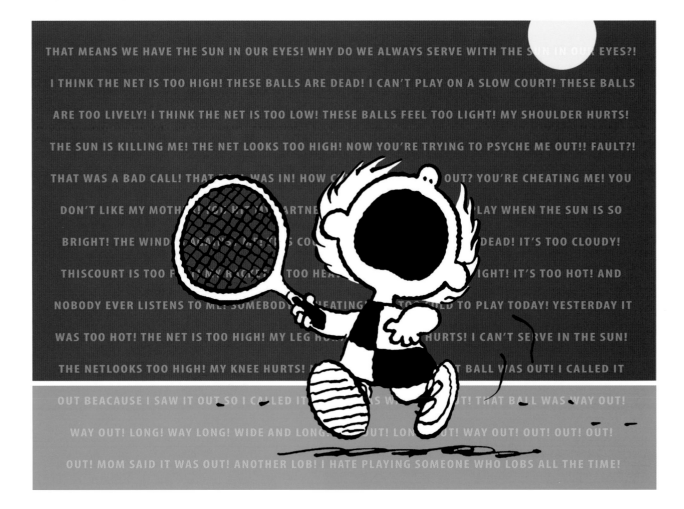

THAT MEANS WE HAVE THE SUN IN OUR EYES! WHY DO WE ALWAYS SERVE WITH THE
EYES?!
I THINK THE NET IS TOO HIGH! THESE BALLS ARE DEAD! I CAN'T PLAY ON A SLOW COURT! THESE BALLS
ARE TOO LIVELY! I THINK THE NET IS TOO LOW! THESE BALLS FEEL TOO LIGHT! MY SHOULDER HURTS!
THE SUN IS KILLING ME! THE NET LOOKS TOO HIGH! NOW YOU'RE TRYING TO PSYCHE ME OUT!! FAULT?!
THAT WAS A BAD CALL!
WAS IN!
OUT? YOU'RE CHEATING ME! YOU
LAY WHEN THE SUN IS SO
DEAD! IT'S TOO CLOUDY!
IGHT! IT'S TOO HOT! AND
TO PLAY TODAY! YESTERDAY IT
WAS TOO HOT! THE NET IS TOO HIGH! MY LEG
HURTS! I CAN'T SERVE IN THE SUN!
THE NETLOOKS TOO HIGH! MY KNEE HURTS!
BALL WAS OUT! I CALLED IT
OUT BEACAUSE I SAW IT OUT SO I CALLED IT
THAT BALL WAS WAY OUT!
WAY OUT! LONG! WAY LONG! WIDE AND LONG
WAY OUT! OUT! OUT! OUT!
OUT! MOM SAID IT WAS OUT! ANOTHER LOB! I HATE PLAYING SOMEONE WHO LOBS ALL THE TIME!

WHAT'S GOING ON?
IT'S THE FIRST ROUND OF THE MIXED DOUBLES TENNIS TOURNAMENT
SNOOPY AND MOLLY VOLLEY ARE PLAYING "CRYBABY" BOOBIE AND "BAD CALL" BENNY!
© 1982 United Feature Syndicate, Inc.
SEE? THEY'RE JUST INTRODUCING THEMSELVES NOW..I IMAGINE THEY'RE BEING VERY POLITE...
4-16
WELL, IF IT ISN'T "FAT LEGS" VOLLEY!!

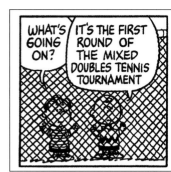

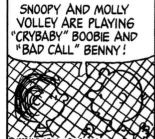

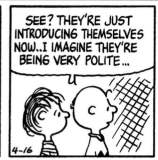

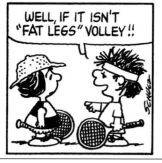

# "BADCALL" BENNY

FIRST MENTIONED 04/15/1982
FIRST APPEARANCE 04/16/1982

The abrasive brother of "Crybaby" Boobie, "Badcall" Benny is her most frequent doubles partner. They make one of the most fearsome duos in tennis when they pair up—thanks to "Crybaby's" tantrums and Benny's insistence on disputing every call from the line judge. "Badcall" is so skilled at causing conflict that he once argues that a can of tennis balls has been opened improperly—and wins!

Charles Schulz paid great attention to detail when he depicted tennis—or any other sport-in *Peanuts*. "I try to portray all the sports that I put the kids into authentically. If all you do is surface humor, such as somebody getting the ball stuck on their hand and sliding down the alley with the ball, I think that's disgusting. If you do something funny, but are still authentic, whether it's sports or a medical joke, you have a friend for life. If you do the subject well, the readers will stand by you."

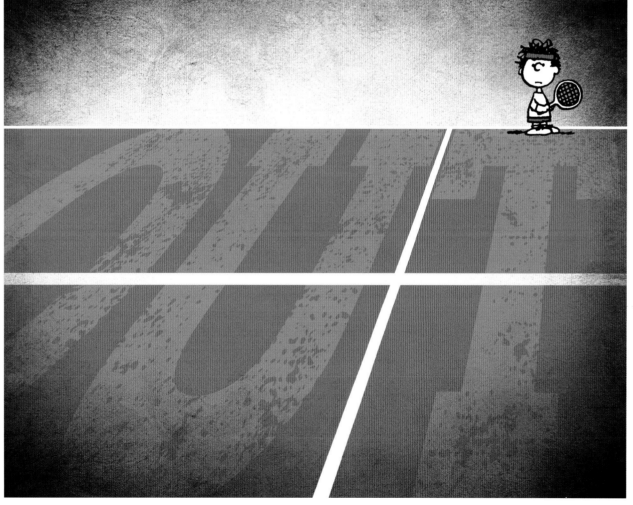

OPPOSITE AND ABOVE: *Design by Cameron + Co*

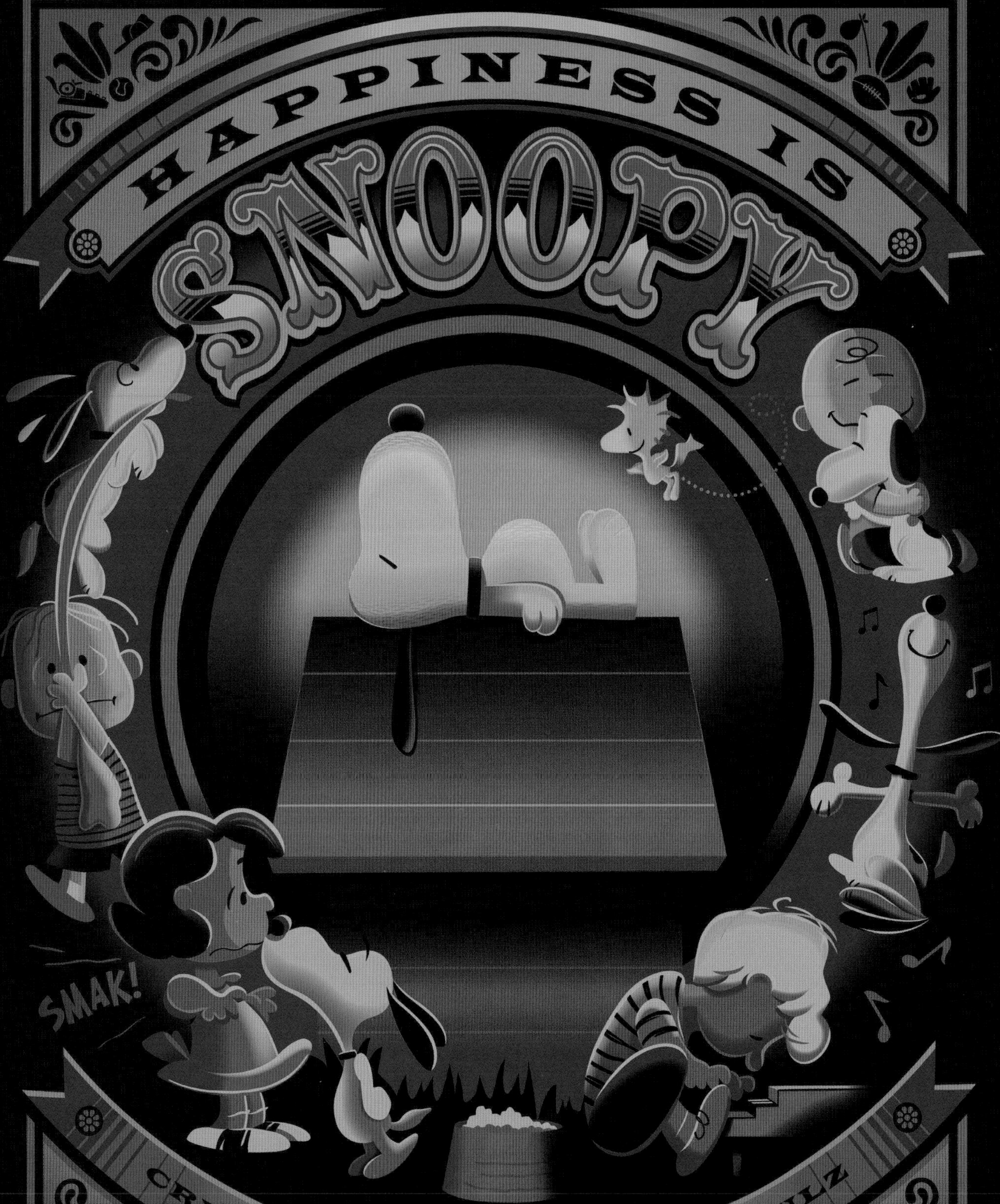
HAPPINESS IS
SNOOPY
SMAK!
CREATED BY CHARLES M. SCHULZ

# SNOOPY

FIRST APPEARANCE
10/04/1950

Snoopy is the pick of the litter when Charlie Brown adopts him from the Daisy Hill Puppy Farm, but he never suspects just how special Snoopy is when he first brings him home. The precocious beagle seems like a typical dog at first, but soon learns to walk on his hind legs, read and write, play bridge, dance, and do anything that any kid in the neighborhood can—only better!

Snoopy is supremely confident and never backs down from a challenge. A terrific athlete, he enjoys baseball, golf, tennis, and hockey, as well as more esoteric sports including badminton and shuffleboard. He is an avid reader and is particularly fond of Leo Tolstoy's epic novel *War and Peace,* a book that he savors by reading only one word per day.

The intrepid beagle is also a seasoned traveler. Snoopy flies—atop his doghouse—all over the world, from the Midwest to the Middle East to the moon to France in the early 1900s, always with his trusty supper dish close at hand.

No matter where his travels take him, Snoopy always comes back to Charlie Brown's backyard, because it's home. And, after all, that's where he keeps his unpublished manuscripts and his unrivaled modern art collection.

*Peanuts* became the world's most popular comic strip when Snoopy came into his own as a character. His rich fantasy life and bold personality amused and enthralled readers, and gave Charles Schulz endless inspiration for his adventures. "Snoopy is the most popular character in the strip. In fact, I think you could make a good case that he's the most popular cartoon character in the world. I supposed that's because what I've done with him is very original. I don't think there has been an animal character in a long time that has done the different things that Snoopy has done. He's an attorney. He's a surgeon. He's the World War I flying ace."

Snoopy's reality is just as important to the character as his fantasy life, however, and the contrast between those worlds makes Snoopy one of the most complex characters in popular fiction. "Snoopy is a very contradictory character. In a way he's quite selfish. He likes to think of himself as independent, and he has dreams of doing great things. Without Charlie Brown he couldn't survive, but Snoopy won't even give Charlie Brown the love and affection he deserves. That's part of the humor . . . I'll probably never draw Snoopy on all fours again. It's something that just happened. It evolved very gradually. But once you get to a certain point, you can't back up."

?
SCHULZ

"PEANUTS"
GO HOME, SNOOPY! GO HOME!!
GO HOME, I SAY! STOP FOLLOWING ME!!
?
HE'S NOT FOLLOWING YOU... HE LIVES IN THAT DIRECTION!
Copr. 1951 by United Feature Syndicate, Inc.
SCHULZ

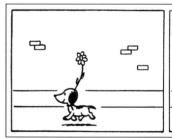

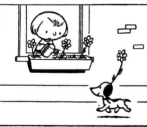

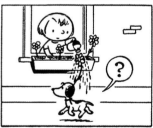

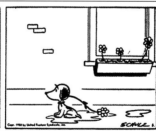

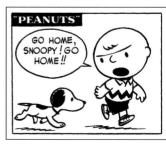

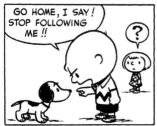

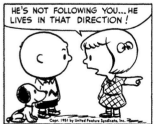

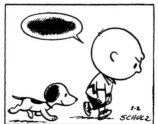

OPPOSITE: Happiness Is Snoopy; *Artist: Jeff Granito; Limited Edition Print; Courtesy: Dark Hall Mansion*

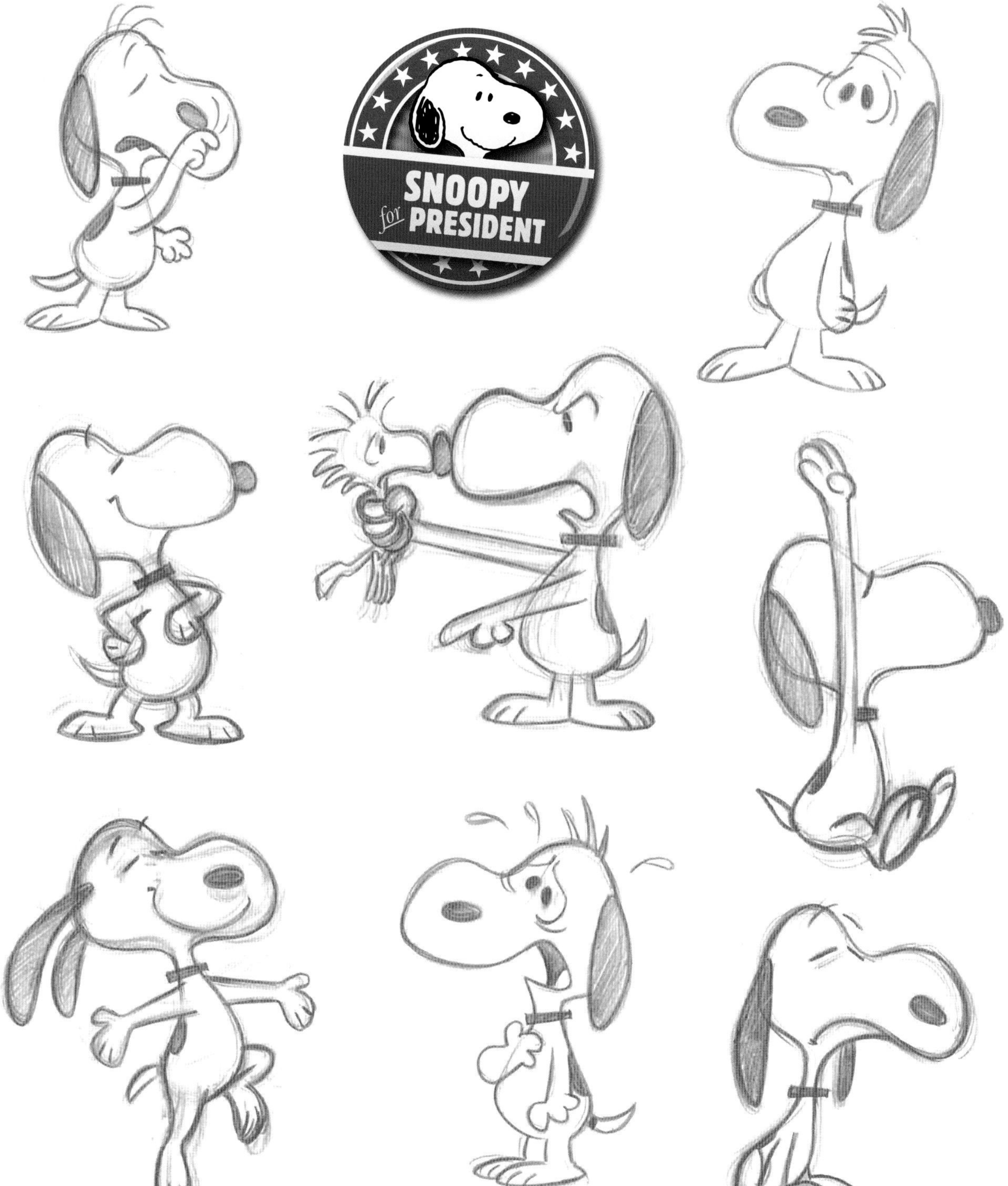
SNOOPY
for PRESIDENT

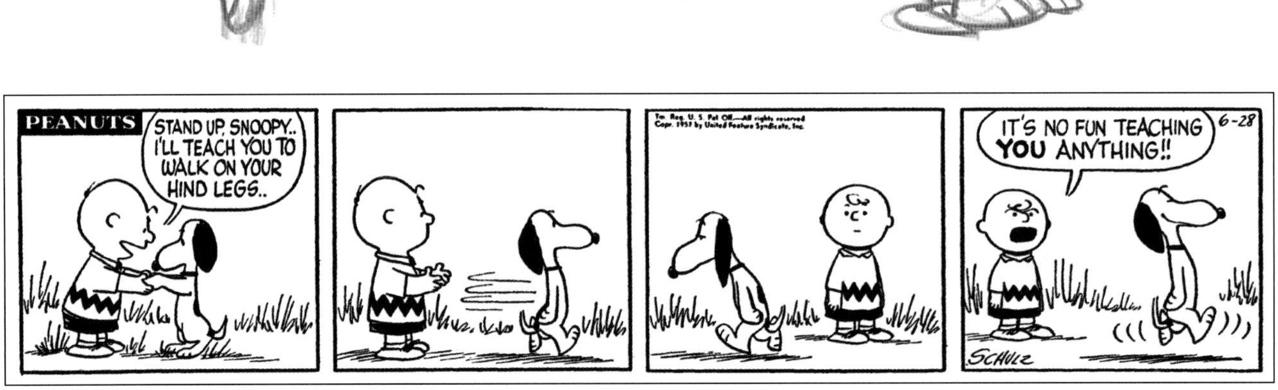
PEANUTS
STAND UP, SNOOPY.. I'LL TEACH YOU TO WALK ON YOUR HIND LEGS..
IT'S NO FUN TEACHING YOU ANYTHING!!
6-28
SCHULZ

"Never bug a beagle."

—Snoopy

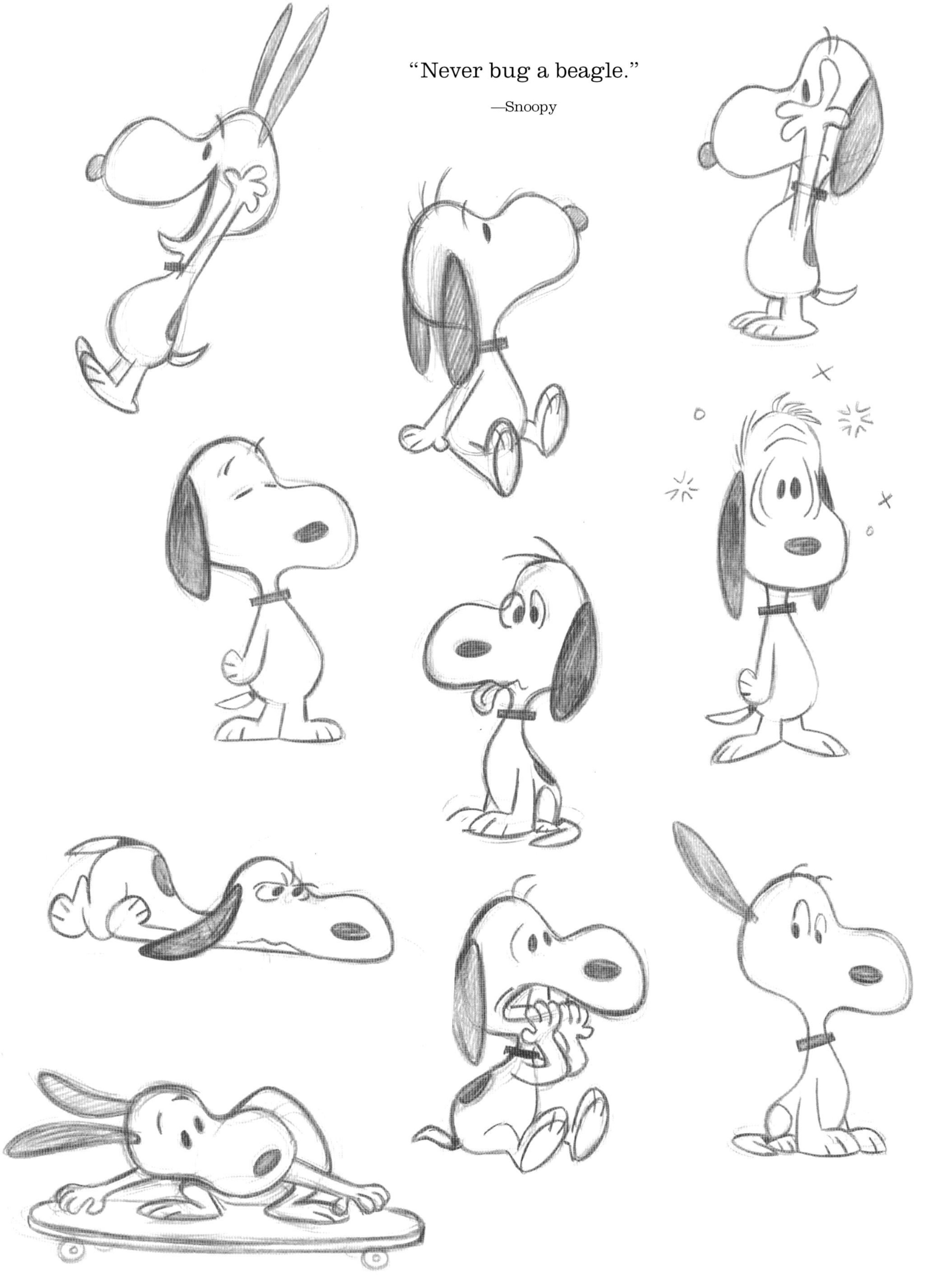

OPPOSITE, TOP CENTER: *Style Guide art – PW* | OPPOSITE AND ABOVE: *Snoopy model sheet – CSCA*

PEANUTS
THAT'S NOT A REAL BABY! THAT'S JUST A DOG DRESSED UP LIKE A BABY!
GOO!
SCHULZ
6-24

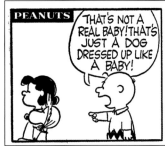

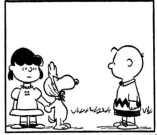

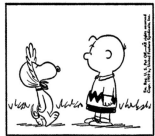

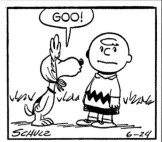

# MASTER OF DISGUISE

Snoopy is a master impressionist and has taken on dozens of roles over the years, from the smallest members of the animal kingdom to the most celebrated pro athletes of the era. He even imitates his own friends from time to time, although his subjects often disapprove. Early on, Snoopy favored animal impressions, but over time, his interest shifted toward "World Famous" professionals.

Snoopy demonstrates a range that would stagger even the most accomplished actor. Among his most unforgettable performances are shark, wolf, rhinoceros, snake, Violet, pelican, Lucy, moose, Beethoven, Mickey Mouse, giraffe, kangaroo, alligator, lion, python, elephant, polar bear, bird, mule, circus dog, sea monster, penguin, anteater, bald eagle, vulture, tiger, goat, bloodhound, cow, baby, cricket, mountain lion, TV antenna, helicopter, Dracula, dinosaur, rabbit, gorilla, calf, salmon, hood ornament, shepherd, gargoyle, teddy bear, weather vane, sheep, trapeze artist, skateboard champion, baby, bowling ace, surfer, WWI Army surgeon, piranha, leopard, secret agent, Easter Bunny, prairie dog, Easter Beagle, sheep dog, pirate, bat, owl, April Fool, scarecrow, rattlesnake, tennis players John McEnroe, Tracy Austin, and John Newcombe, Flashbeagle, Lone Beagle, Alistair Beagle, and Santa Claus himself! Whew!

1

スヌーピー

2

AARGHH

3

4

5

I
SPY

6

THE FIERCE GALE LASHES THE RAIN INTO THE FACE OF THE CAPTAIN AS HE STANDS ON DECK!

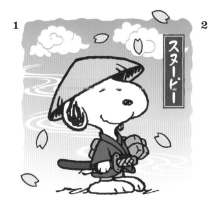

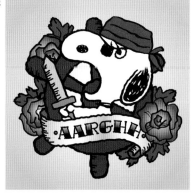

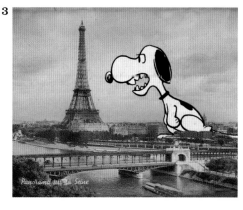

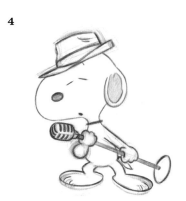

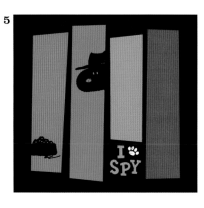

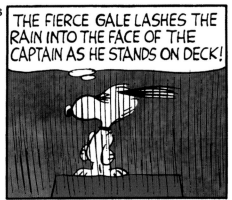

*1, 2, and 5: Style Guide art – PW; 3 and 4: Style Guide art – CSCA; 6: Spot art from strip – Charles M. Schulz* | OPPOSITE: *American Library Association poster, 2013 – CSCA*

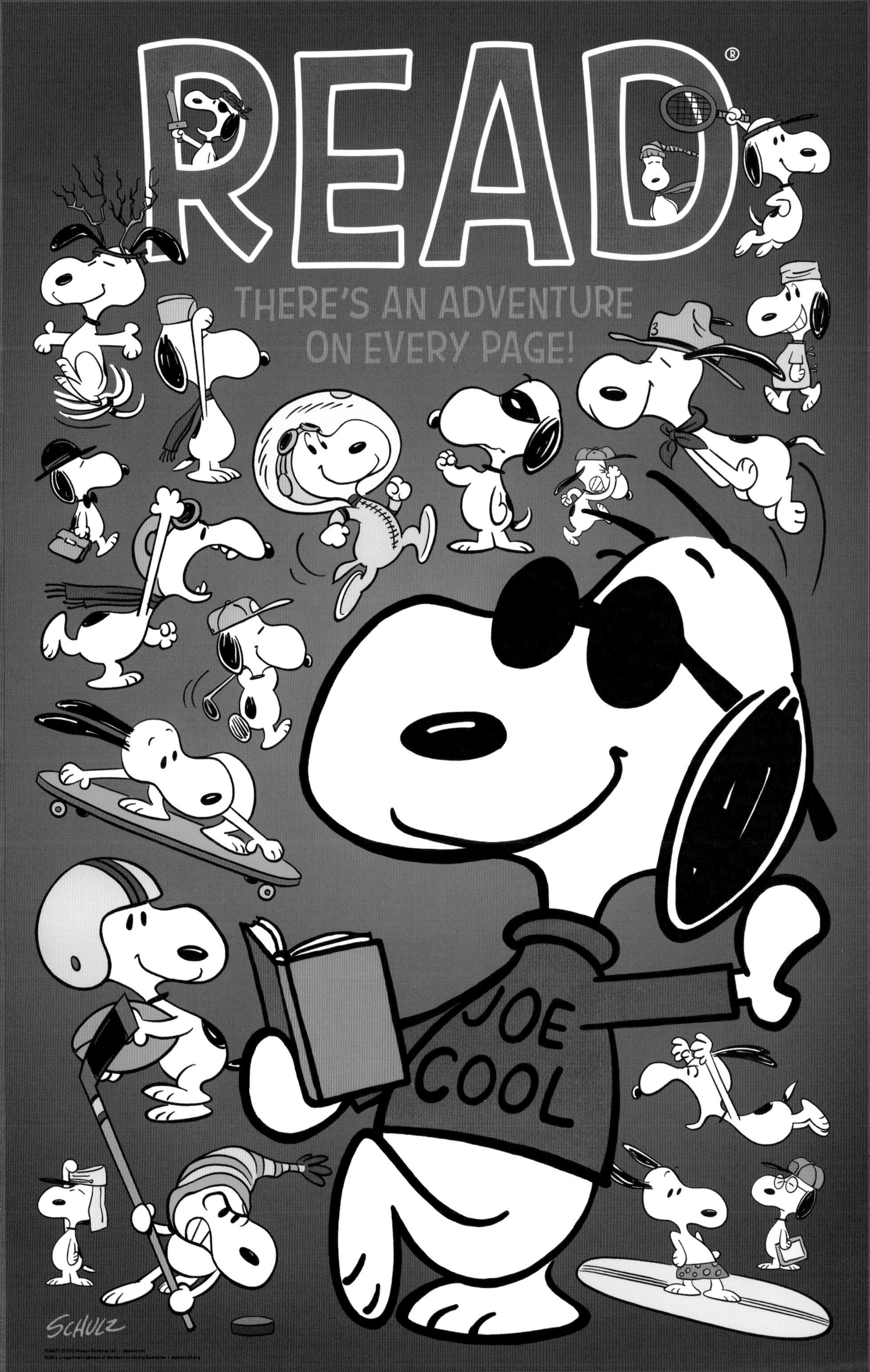
READ®
THERE'S AN ADVENTURE
ON EVERY PAGE!
JOE
COOL
SCHULZ

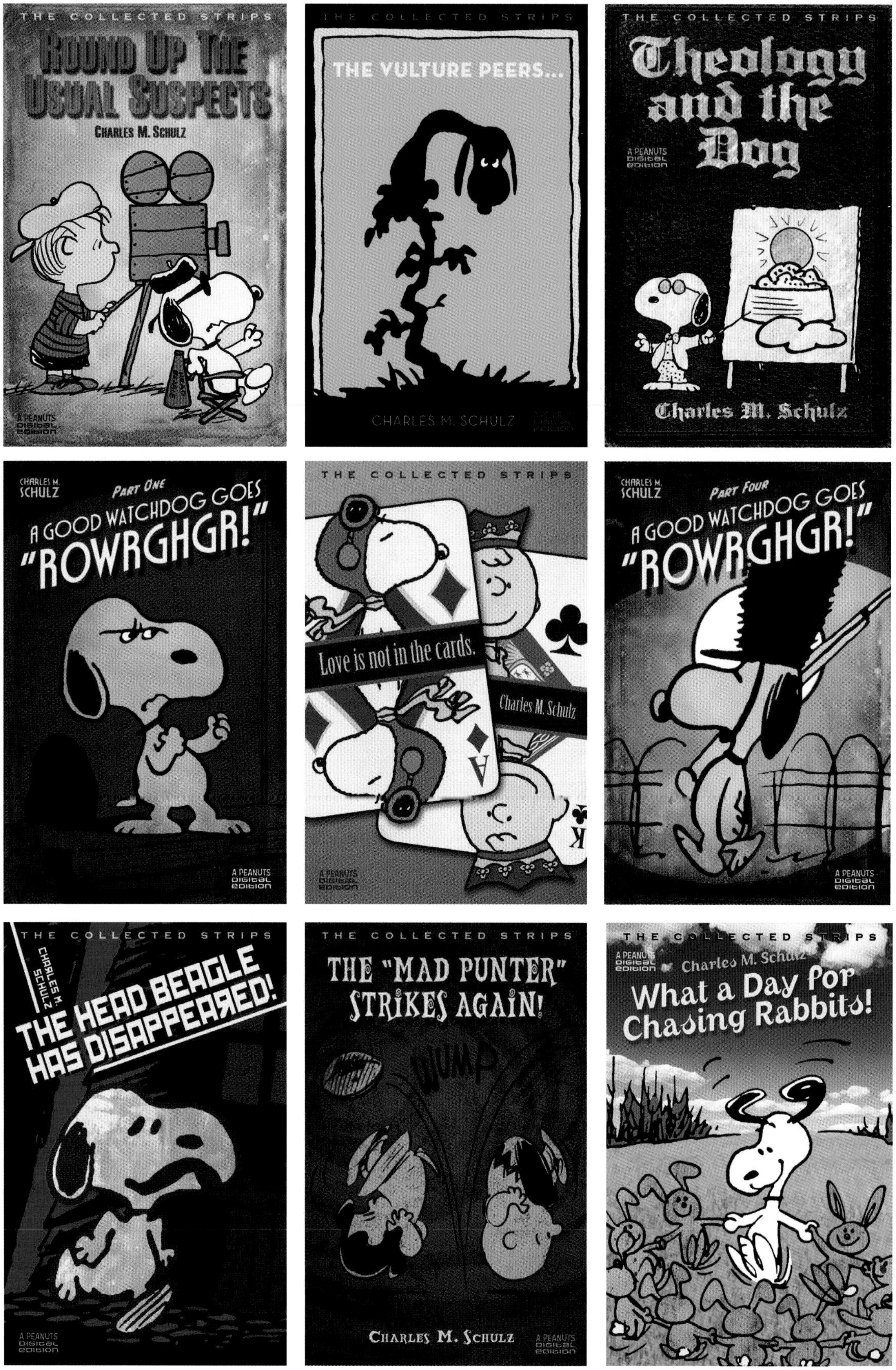
THE COLLECTED STRIPS
ROUND UP THE USUAL SUSPECTS
CHARLES M. SCHULZ
A PEANUTS DIGITAL EDITION
THE COLLECTED STRIPS
THE VULTURE PEERS...
CHARLES M. SCHULZ
THE COLLECTED STRIPS
Theology and the Dog
A PEANUTS DIGITAL EDITION
Charles M. Schulz
CHARLES M. SCHULZ
PART ONE
A GOOD WATCHDOG GOES "ROWRGHGR!"
A PEANUTS DIGITAL EDITION
THE COLLECTED STRIPS
Love is not in the cards.
Charles M. Schulz
A PEANUTS DIGITAL EDITION
CHARLES M. SCHULZ
PART FOUR
A GOOD WATCHDOG GOES "ROWRGHGR!"
A PEANUTS DIGITAL EDITION
THE COLLECTED STRIPS
CHARLES M SCHULZ
THE HEAD BEAGLE HAS DISAPPEARED!
A PEANUTS DIGITAL EDITION
THE COLLECTED STRIPS
THE "MAD PUNTER" STRIKES AGAIN!
WUMP
CHARLES M. SCHULZ
A PEANUTS DIGITAL EDITION
THE COLLECTED STRIPS
A PEANUTS DIGITAL EDITION
Charles M. Schulz
What a Day for Chasing Rabbits!

ABOVE: Peanuts *Digital Editions – CSCA* | OPPOSITE: A Charlie Brown Thanksgiving; *Artist: Tom Whalen; Limited Edition Print; Courtesy: Dark Hall Mansion* | OVERLEAF: *Snoopy alter-egos, design by Cameron + Co*

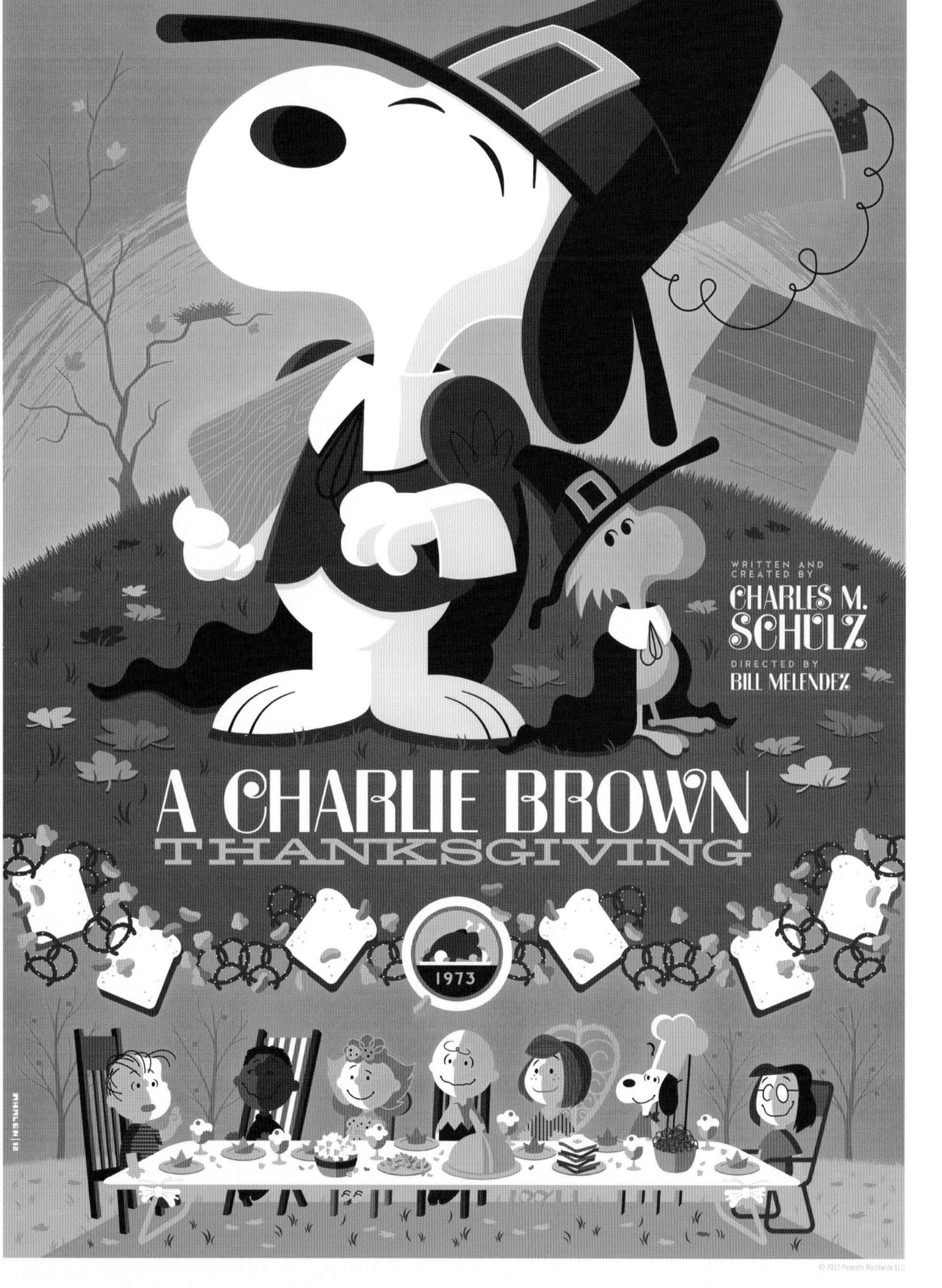
WRITTEN AND CREATED BY
CHARLES M. SCHULZ
DIRECTED BY
BILL MELENDEZ
A CHARLIE BROWN
THANKSGIVING
1973

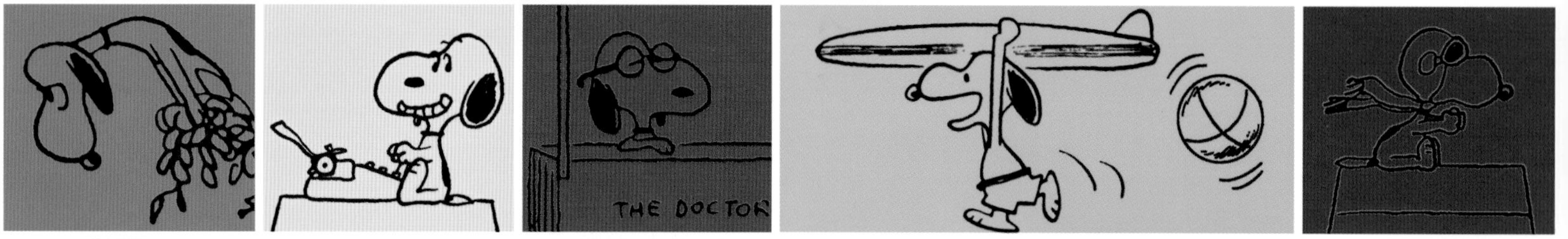
THE DOCTOR

VULTURE — AUTHOR — ASSISTANT PSYCHIATRIST — SURFER — WWI FLYING ACE

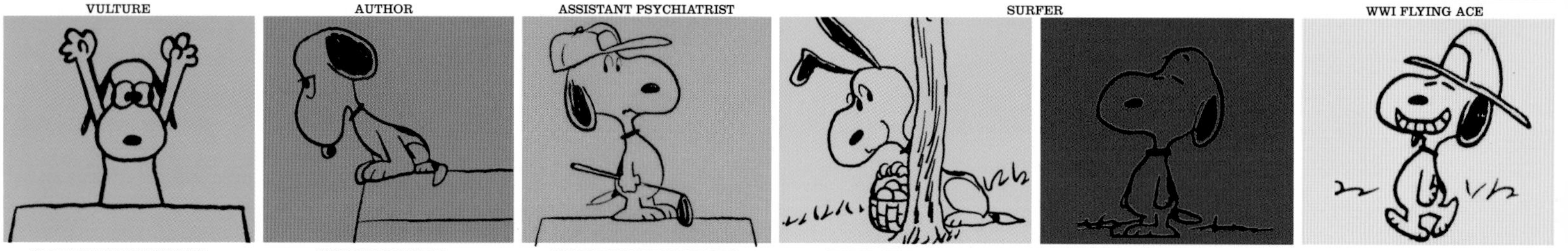

CREATURE FROM THE SEA — SCHOOL PRINCIPAL — WORLD FAMOUS GOLF PRO — THE EASTER BEAGLE — WARM PUPPY — CAPTAIN OF THE RESCUE SQUAD

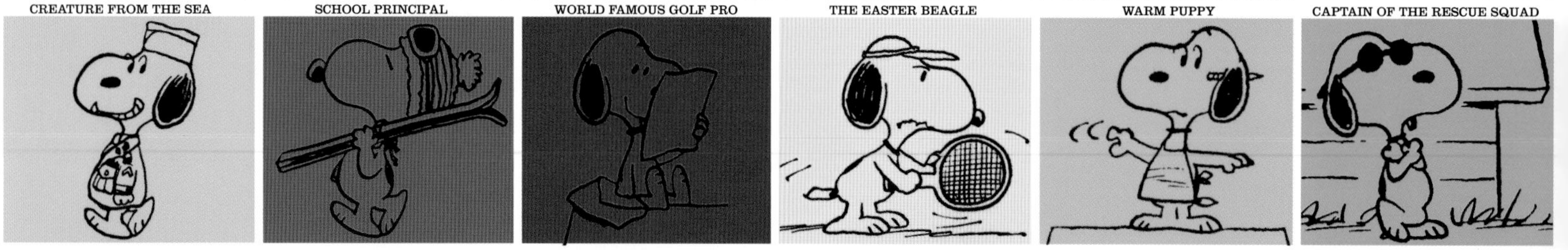

WWII VETERAN — WORLD FAMOUS SKIER — THE "HEAD BEAGLE" — WORLD FAMOUS TENNIS STAR — WORLD FAMOUS GROCERY CLERK — JOE COOL

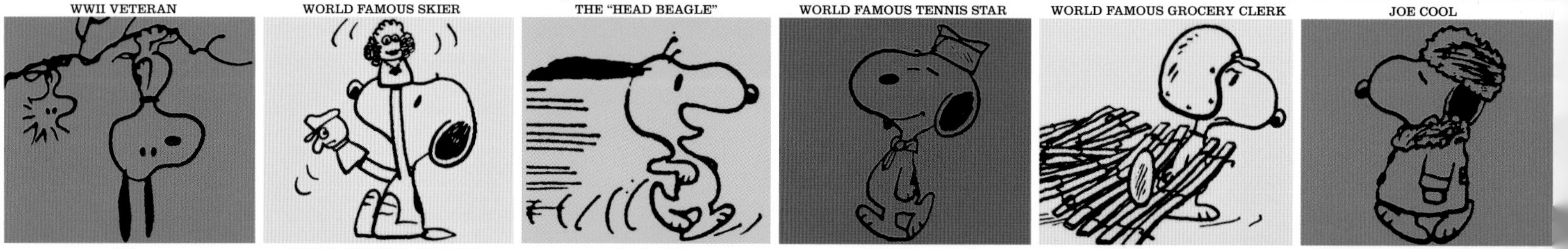

BAT — THE PAWPET THEATER HOST — STREAKER — THE BEAGLE SCOUT — JOE MOTORCROSS — WORLD FAMOUS CRABBY SKATING PR

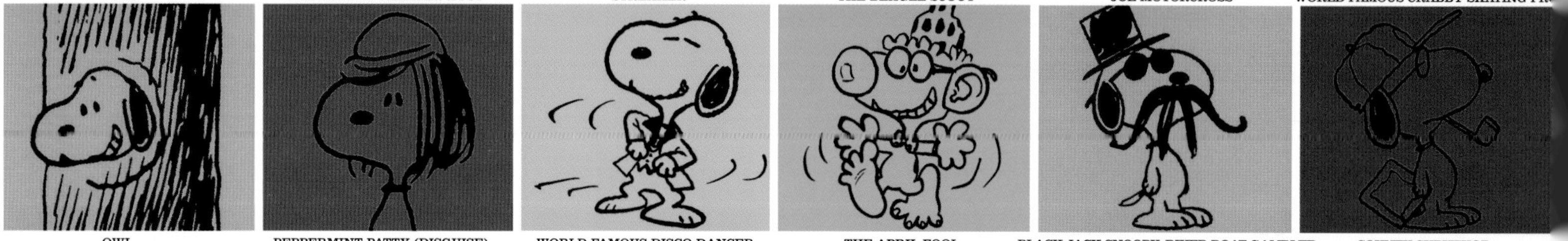

OWL — PEPPERMINT PATTY (DISGUISE) — WORLD FAMOUS DISCO DANCER — THE APRIL FOOL — BLACK JACK SNOOPY, RIVER BOAT GAMBLER — COUNTY SURVEYOR

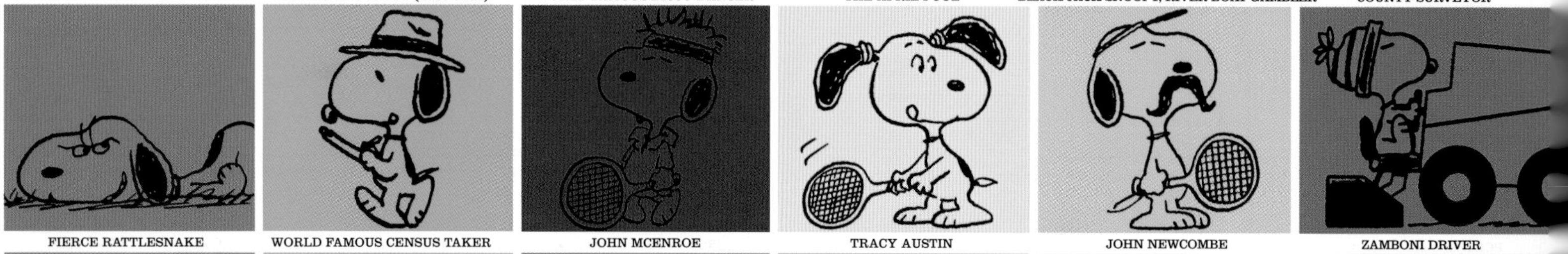

FIERCE RATTLESNAKE — WORLD FAMOUS CENSUS TAKER — JOHN MCENROE — TRACY AUSTIN — JOHN NEWCOMBE — ZAMBONI DRIVER

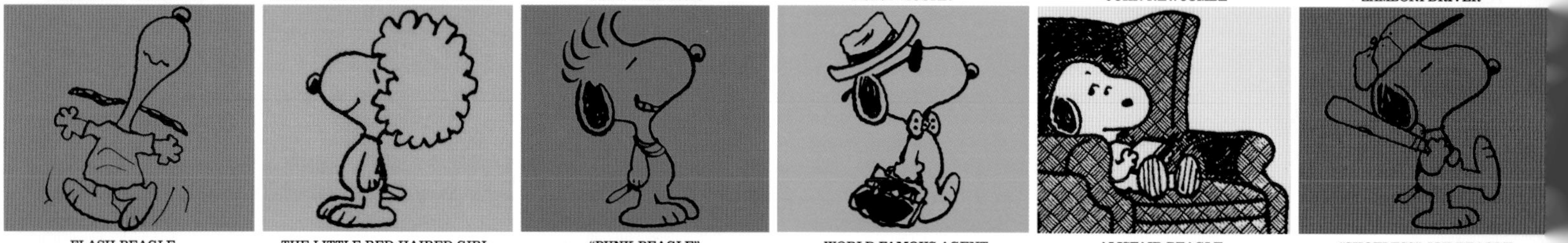

FLASH BEAGLE — THE LITTLE RED-HAIRED GIRL — "PUNK BEAGLE" — WORLD FAMOUS AGENT — ALISTAIR BEAGLE — "SHOELESS" JOE BEAGLE

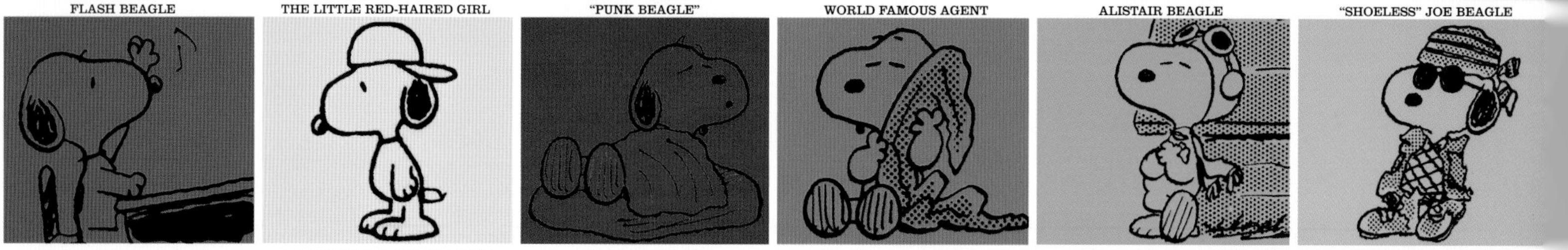

SCHOOL HONOR STUDENT — TRAINED SERVICE TECHNICIAN — WOUNDED SOLDIER — VENTRILOQUIST — PILOT FOR ACE AIRLINES — JOE GRUNGE

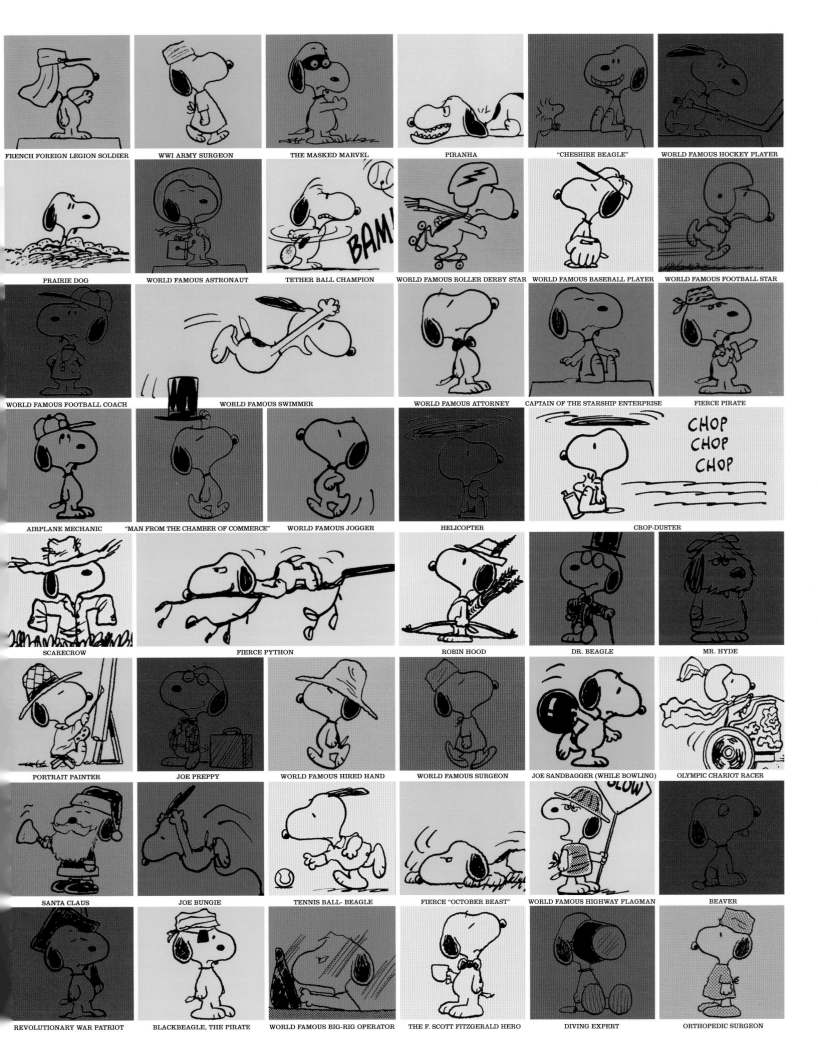

FRENCH FOREIGN LEGION SOLDIER | WWI ARMY SURGEON | THE MASKED MARVEL | PIRANHA | "CHESHIRE BEAGLE" | WORLD FAMOUS HOCKEY PLAYER

PRAIRIE DOG | WORLD FAMOUS ASTRONAUT | TETHER BALL CHAMPION | WORLD FAMOUS ROLLER DERBY STAR | WORLD FAMOUS BASEBALL PLAYER | WORLD FAMOUS FOOTBALL STAR

WORLD FAMOUS FOOTBALL COACH | WORLD FAMOUS SWIMMER | WORLD FAMOUS ATTORNEY | CAPTAIN OF THE STARSHIP ENTERPRISE | FIERCE PIRATE

AIRPLANE MECHANIC | "MAN FROM THE CHAMBER OF COMMERCE" | WORLD FAMOUS JOGGER | HELICOPTER | CROP-DUSTER

SCARECROW | FIERCE PYTHON | ROBIN HOOD | DR. BEAGLE | MR. HYDE

PORTRAIT PAINTER | JOE PREPPY | WORLD FAMOUS HIRED HAND | WORLD FAMOUS SURGEON | JOE SANDBAGGER (WHILE BOWLING) | OLYMPIC CHARIOT RACER

SANTA CLAUS | JOE BUNGIE | TENNIS BALL- BEAGLE | FIERCE "OCTOBER BEAST" | WORLD FAMOUS HIGHWAY FLAGMAN | BEAVER

REVOLUTIONARY WAR PATRIOT | BLACKBEAGLE, THE PIRATE | WORLD FAMOUS BIG-RIG OPERATOR | THE F. SCOTT FITZGERALD HERO | DIVING EXPERT | ORTHOPEDIC SURGEON

1

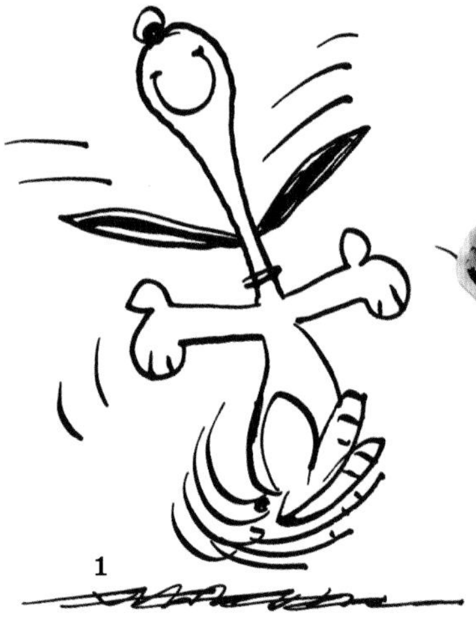

2

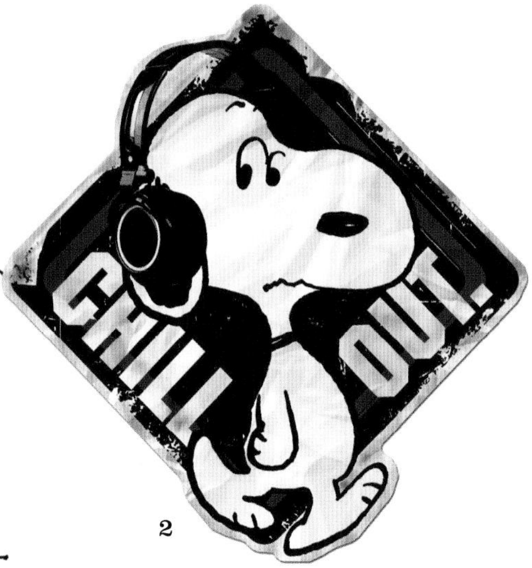

CHILL OUT.

3

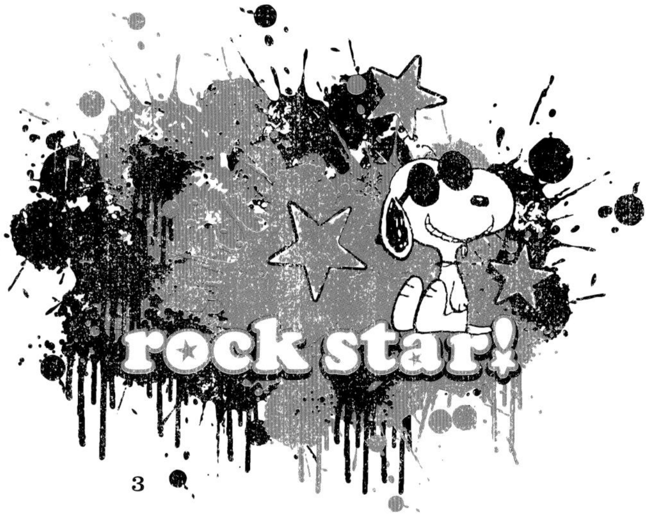

rock star!

"To those of us with real understanding, dancing is the only pure art form!" —Snoopy

4

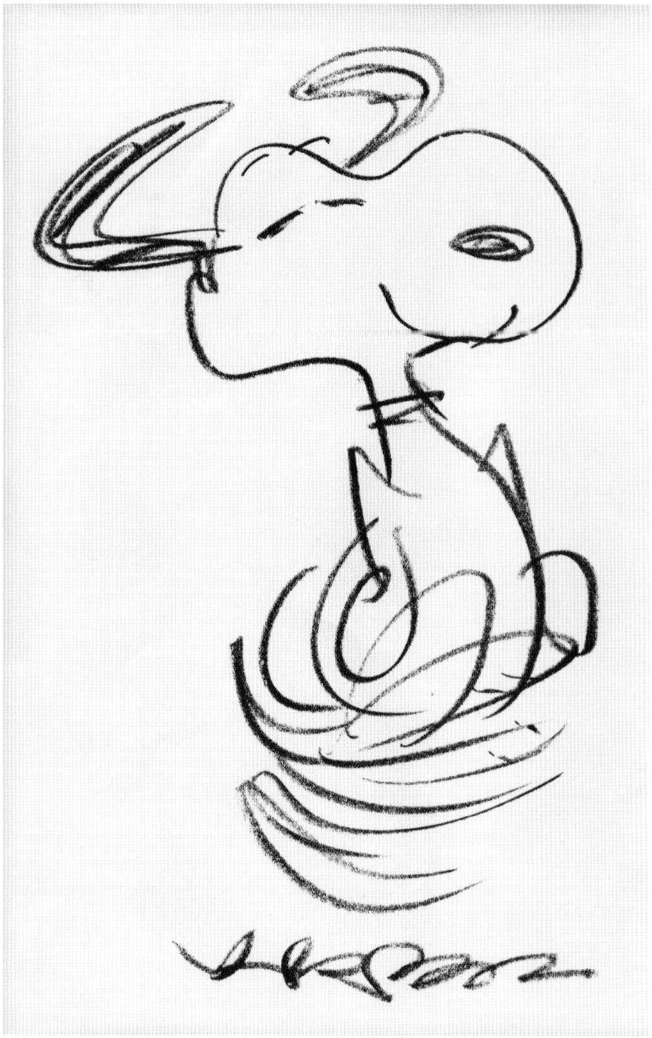

5

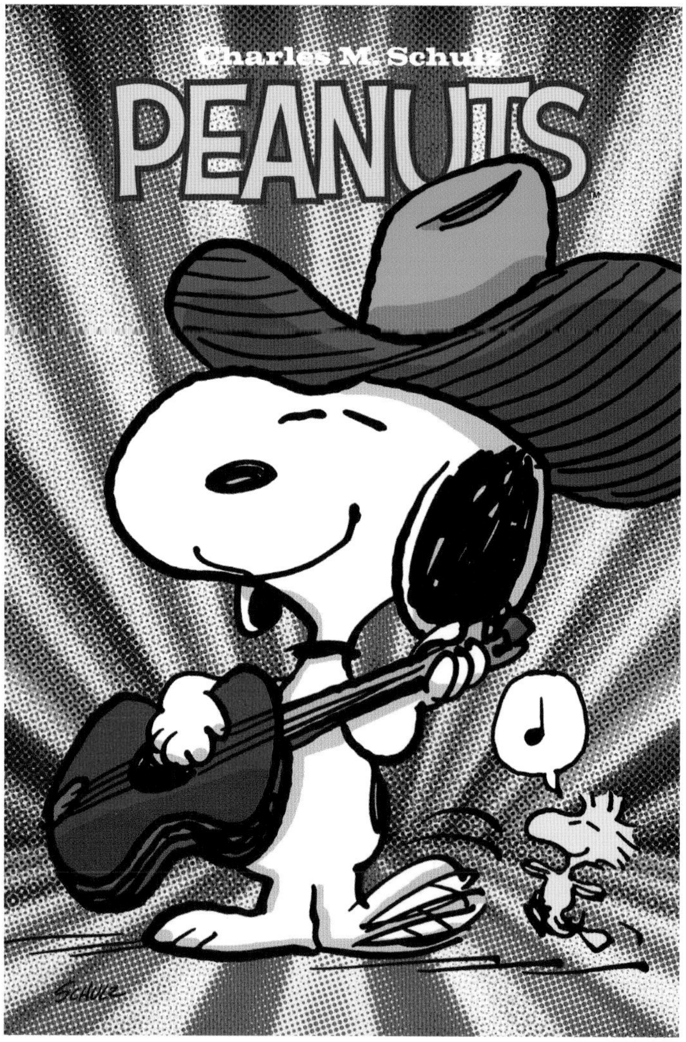

Charles M. Schulz
PEANUTS

*1: Spot art from strip – Charles M. Schulz; 2: Style Guide art – CSCA; 3: Style Guide art – PW; 4: Original sketch – Charles M. Schulz; 5:* Peanuts*, Issue #20, Boom! Studios – CSCA*

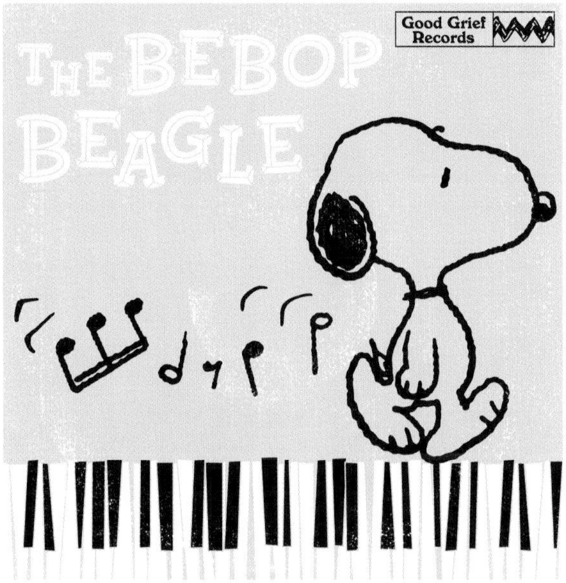
Good Grief Records
THE BEBOP BEAGLE

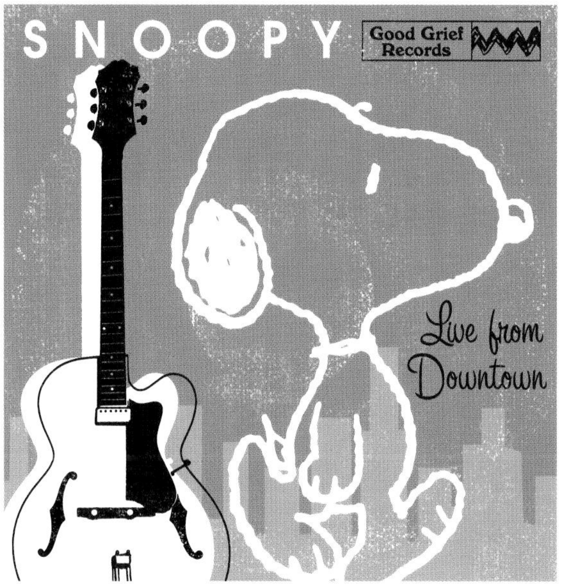
SNOOPY
Good Grief Records
Live from Downtown

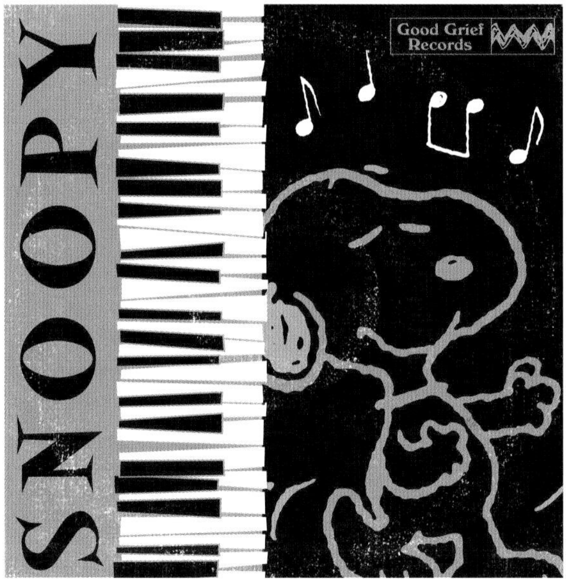
SNOOPY
Good Grief Records

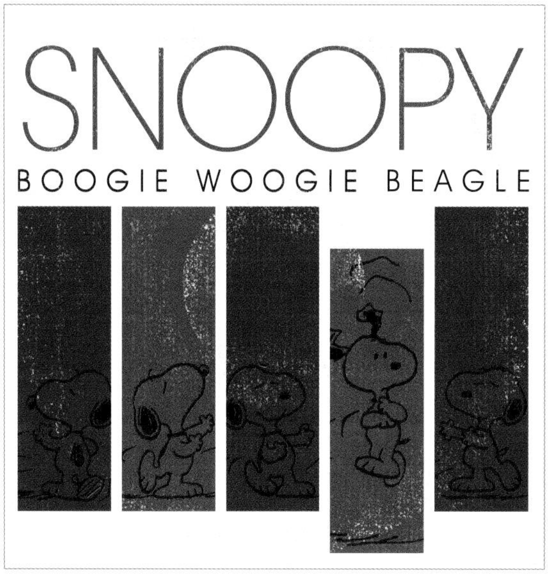
SNOOPY
BOOGIE WOOGIE BEAGLE

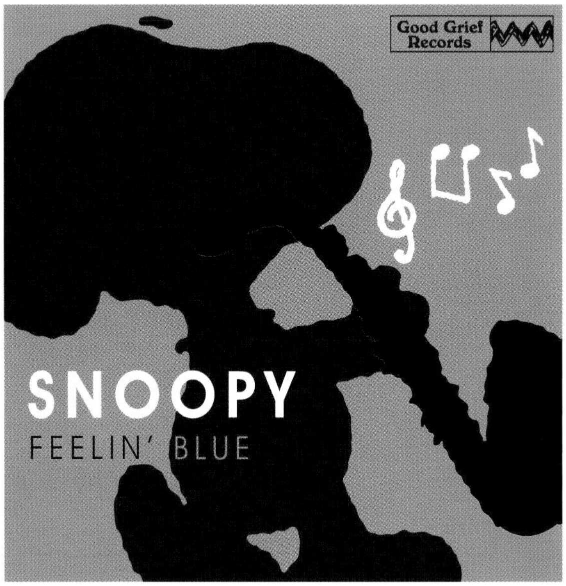
Good Grief Records
SNOOPY
FEELIN' BLUE

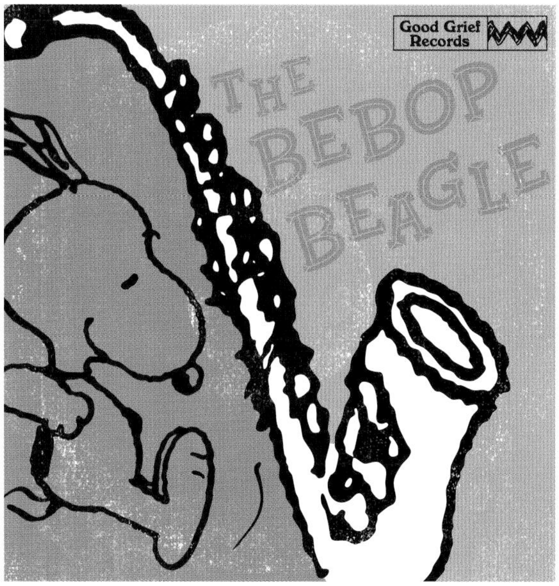
Good Grief Records
THE BEBOP BEAGLE

THIS PAGE: *Style Guide art – PW*

# SNOOPY'S DOGHOUSE

FIRST APPEARANCE 09/04/1951

Generally located in Charlie Brown's backyard, Snoopy's Doghouse is his home, his sanctuary, his place of rest, and his primary mode of transportation, among myriad other things. The interior houses Snoopy's modern art collection and his personal library, a rec room, a guest room, and a cedar closet, and can comfortably hold a beagle, several kids, and a flock of small birds.

Snoopy's Doghouse is durable, but not indestructible. A giant icicle, a housefire, and the Cat Next Door are among the catastrophes that destroy his home over the years, but you can't keep a good dog down, and Snoopy is always quick to rebuild his sanctuary.

Ironically, Charles Schulz noted that many of the most memorable characters and locales in *Peanuts* were never seen in the strip. "We can't [see the inside of Snoopy's doghouse]. It's too fantastic. No one could draw what we've said is down there. Also, Snoopy sits on the doghouse writing novels on his typewriter. If you look at the doghouse from a three-quarters view, the typewriter is going to fall off. But from the side, you can accept it. And you never see anything in the background; if you did, it would become too real, and then you no longer could have a dog typing out a novel."

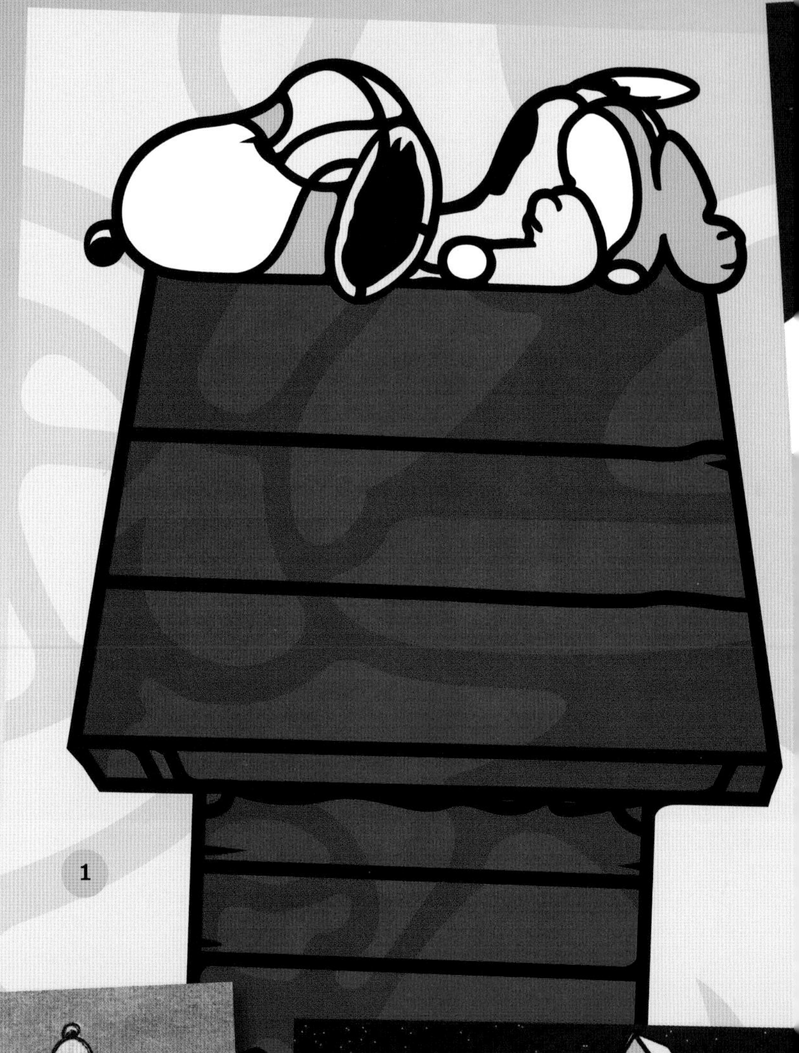

1

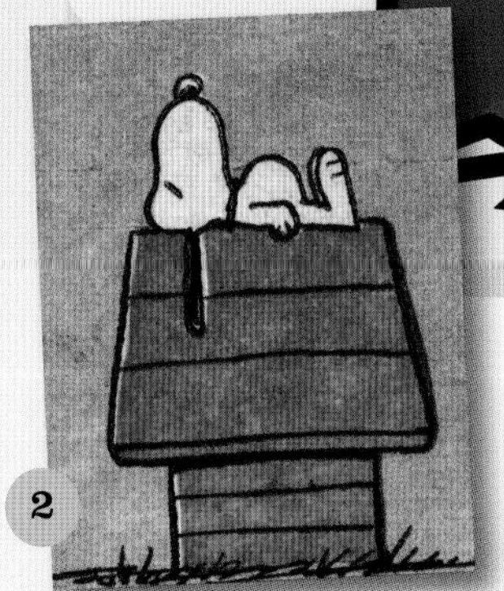

2

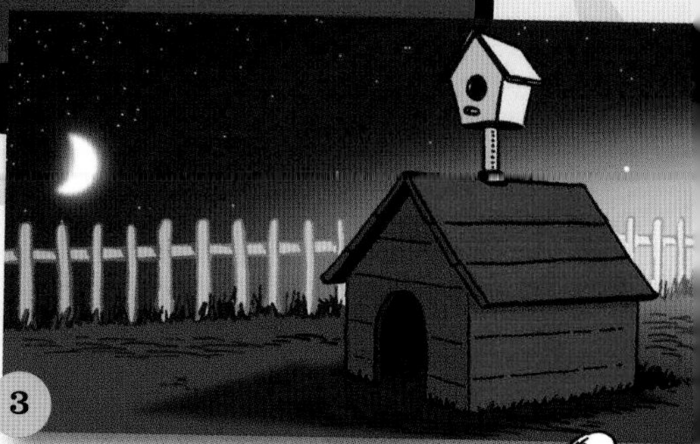

3

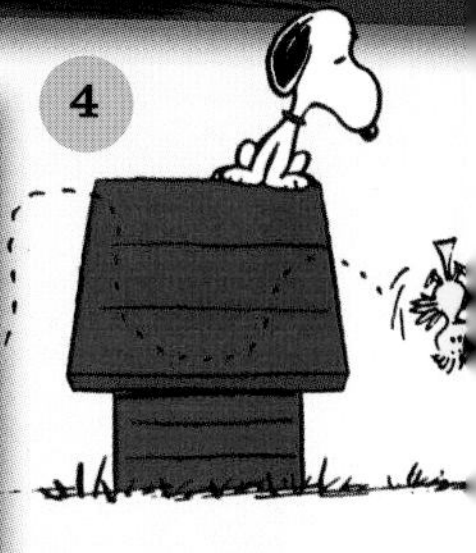

4

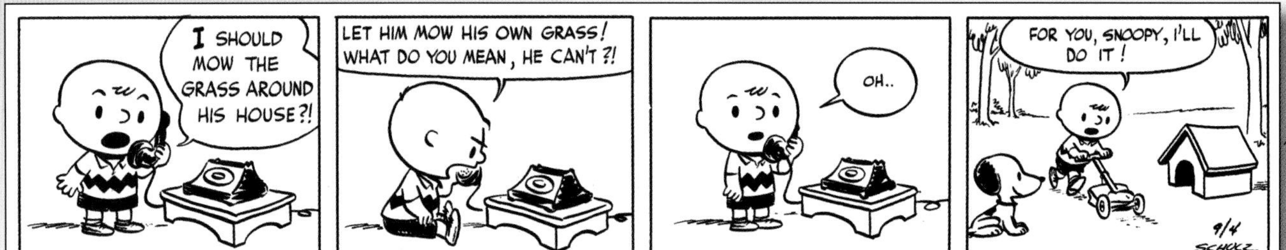
I SHOULD MOW THE GRASS AROUND HIS HOUSE?!
LET HIM MOW HIS OWN GRASS! WHAT DO YOU MEAN, HE CAN'T ?!
OH..
FOR YOU, SNOOPY, I'LL DO IT!
9/4
SCHULZ

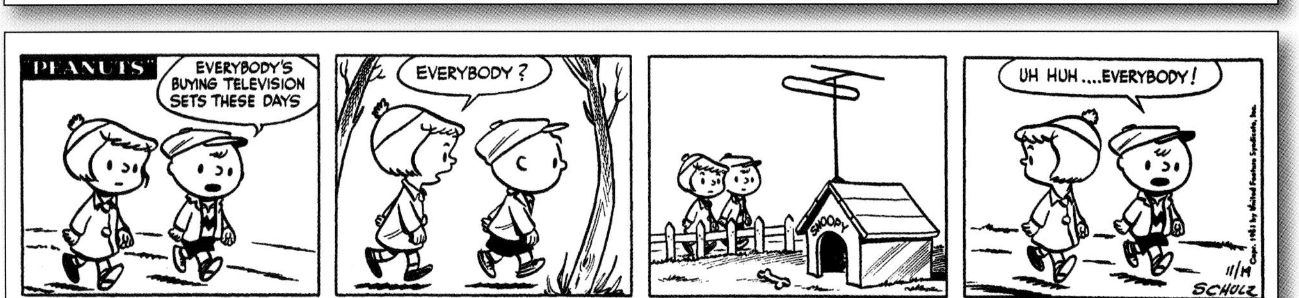
"PEANUTS"
EVERYBODY'S BUYING TELEVISION SETS THESE DAYS
EVERYBODY ?
SNOOPY
UH HUH ....EVERYBODY!
SCHULZ

*1: Snoopy; David Flores; Limited Edition Print; Courtesy: Dark Hall Mansion; 2 and 6: Spot art from strip – Charles M. Schulz; 3 and 5: Style Guide art – CSCA; 4: spot art from* Happiness Is on Top of a Doghouse *– Charles M. Schulz; 7:* Snoopy Just Married*; Artist: Laurent Durieux; Limited Edition Print; Courtesy: Dark Hall Mansion*

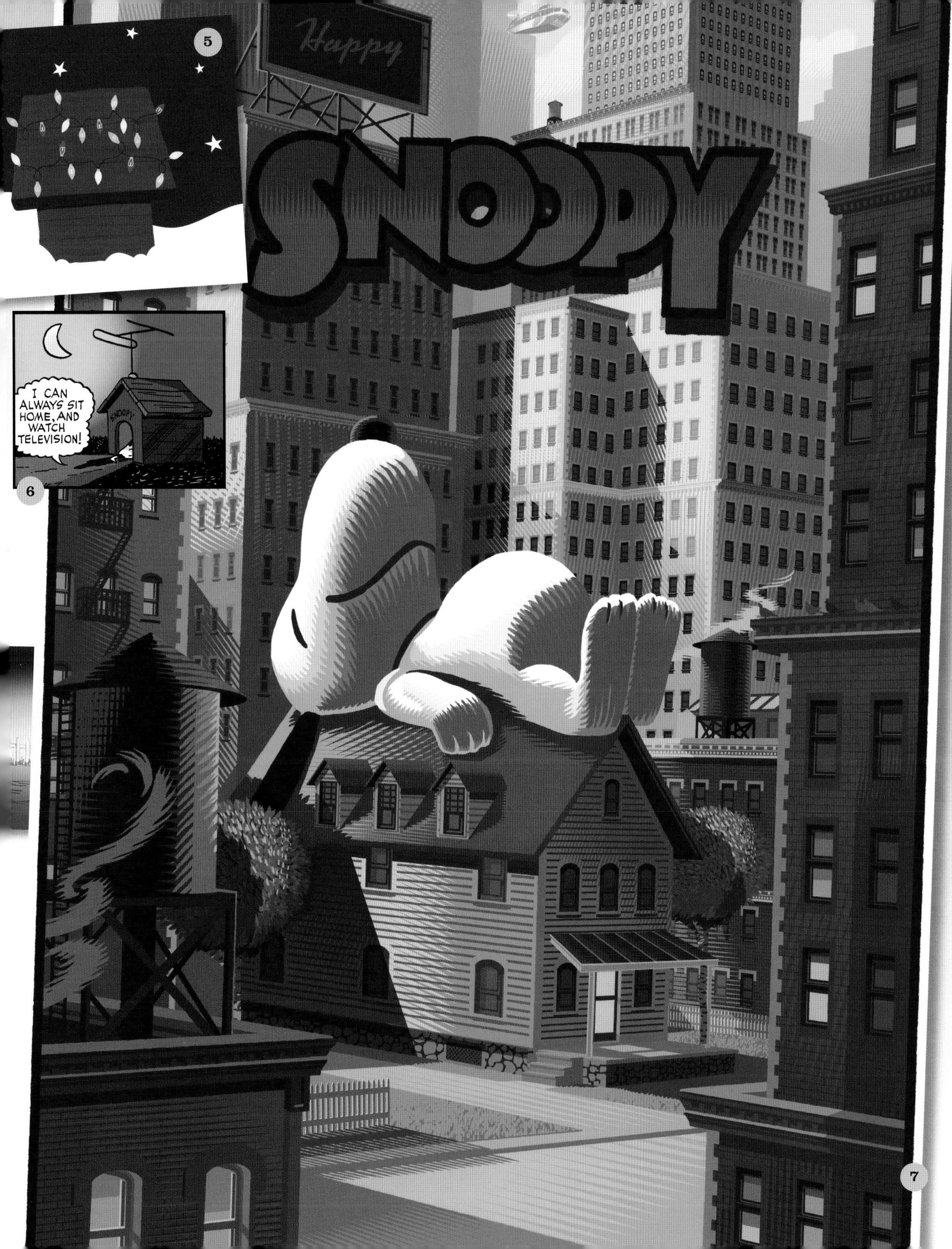
Happy
SNOOPY
I CAN ALWAYS SIT HOME, AND WATCH TELEVISION!
SNOOPY

# WORLD WAR I FLYING ACE

FIRST APPEARANCE
10/10/1965

Curse you, Red Baron! Sporting his trademark aviator helmet, goggles, and scarf, the World War I Flying Ace takes to the air in his Sopwith Camel, always ready for a dogfight with his famed German nemesis. Unfortunately for Snoopy, his skills are no match for the Red Baron's, and he invariably finds his doghouse riddled with bullets as he is forced to bring his plane in for an emergency landing.

Many of the World War I Flying Ace's adventures take place on the ground, after his Sopwith Camel crashes behind enemy lines. The brave soldier has an uncanny knack for finding the nearest tavern in any country and recuperates in the company of a young French lass (who bears a suspicious resemblance to Marcie) and a frosty mug of root beer.

Charles Schulz credited his family for Snoopy's decision to take to the skies while sitting atop his doghouse. "My son, Monte, was very interested in making World War I model airplanes. And one day I was just sitting at my drawing board like I am here now and he came in with his latest model plane. While we were talking about World War I planes, I just drew a little helmet on Snoopy and suddenly got the idea for it, and put him on top of the doghouse. I asked Monte to get one of his books about World War I planes he'd been reading. I thumbed through the book until we found the name—Sopwith Camel. That seemed to be the best. And that's how it all started. It really began as a parody of World War I movies. The line which I had originally thought I would use in the first page was the one which generally goes: 'But, Captain, surely you're not going to send young men up to die in crates like these!' But I never did use it."

PEANUTS
by SCHULZ
PILOTS! EMPTY YOUR POCKETS HERE!
GOOD MORNING, GROUND CREW!
HERE'S THE WORLD WAR I FLYING ACE POSING BESIDE HIS "SOPWITH CAMEL"...
10-10
CONTACT!
IT'S THE DAWN PATROL! WE'RE OUT TO HUNT DOWN THE RED BARON!
I CROSS OVER THE ENEMY LINES...I CAN SEE THE NETWORK OF TRENCHES BELOW...
SUDDENLY A "FOKKER TRIPLANE" APPEARS OUT OF THE CLOUDS! IT'S THE RED BARON!!
DIVING DOWN OUT OF THE SUN, ANTI-AIRCRAFT FIRE EXPLODING ALL AROUND ME, I CATCH HIM IN MY SIGHTS! I...
RAT A TAT TAT TAT TAT TAT TAT!
AAUGH!
MAYBE I CAN GET A JOB WITH A GOOD COMMERCIAL AIRLINE...
SCHULZ

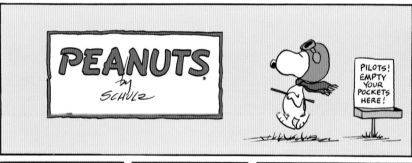

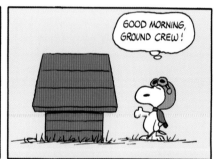

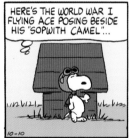

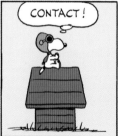

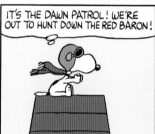

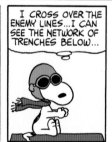

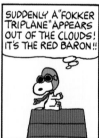

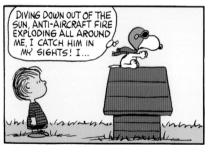

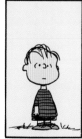

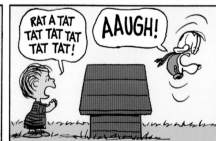

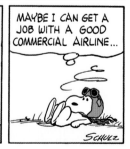

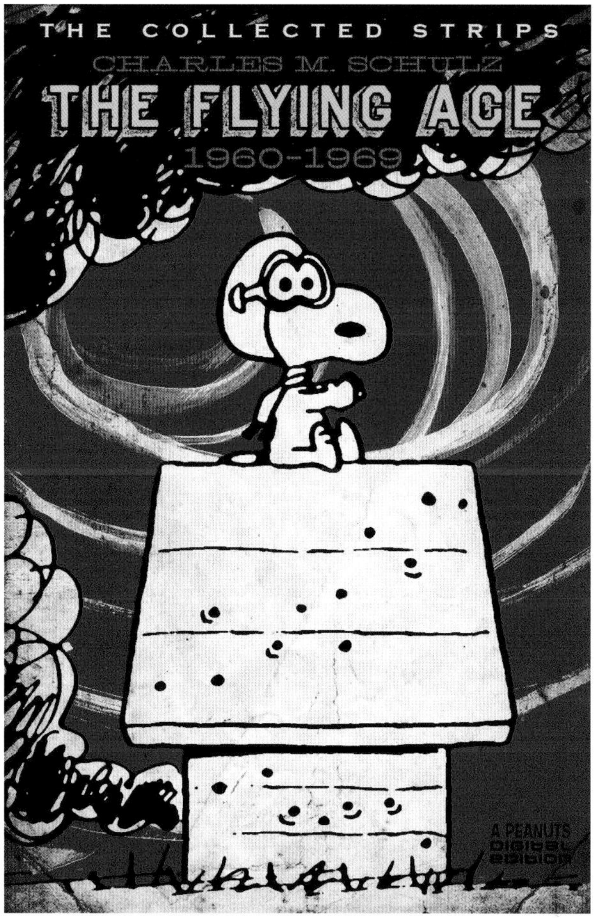
THE COLLECTED STRIPS
CHARLES M. SCHULZ
THE FLYING ACE
1960-1969
A PEANUTS
DIGITAL
EDITION

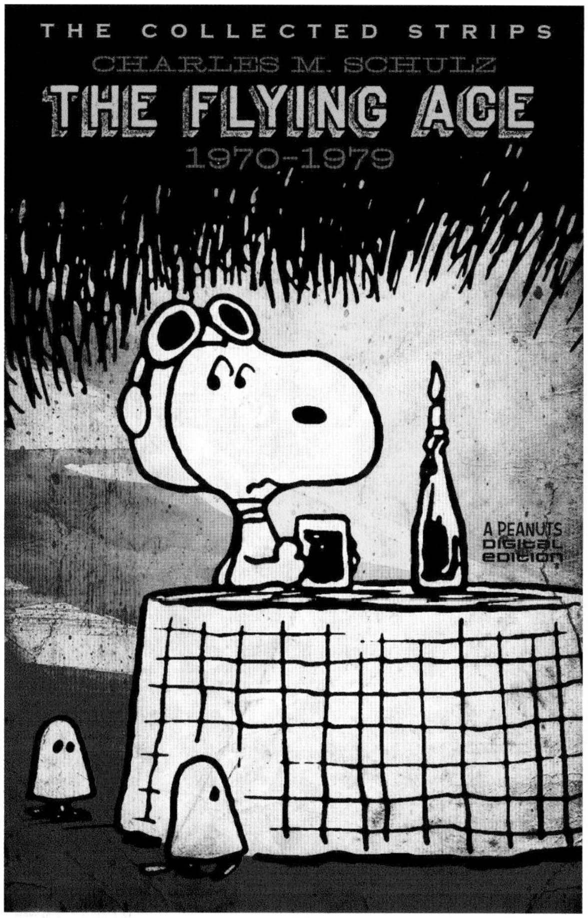
THE COLLECTED STRIPS
CHARLES M. SCHULZ
THE FLYING ACE
1970-1979
A PEANUTS
DIGITAL
EDITION

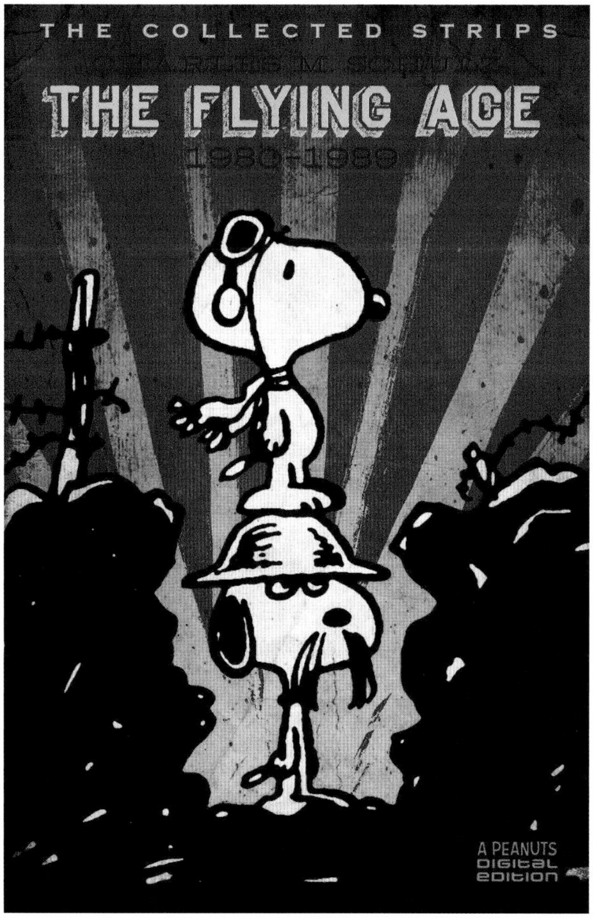
THE COLLECTED STRIPS
CHARLES M. SCHULZ
THE FLYING ACE
1980-1989
A PEANUTS
DIGITAL
EDITION

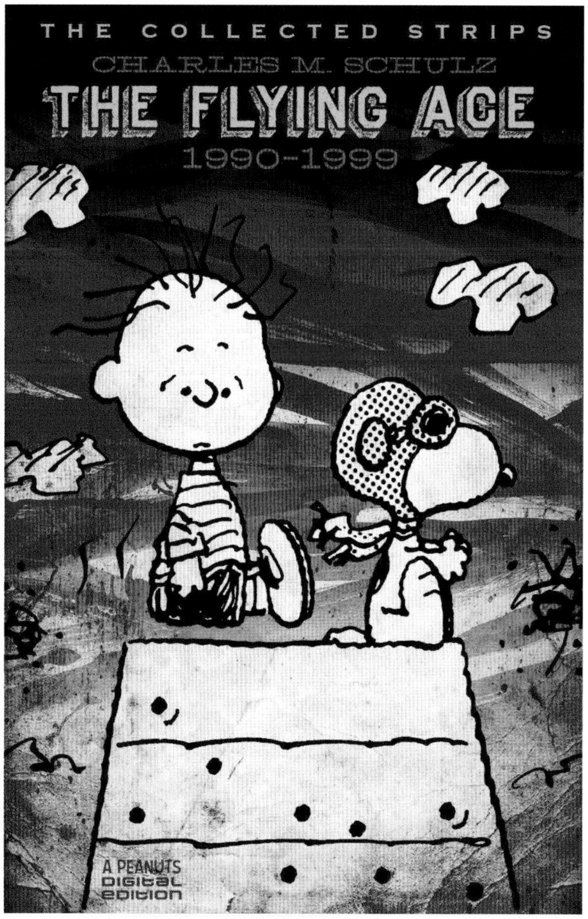
THE COLLECTED STRIPS
CHARLES M. SCHULZ
THE FLYING ACE
1990-1999
A PEANUTS
DIGITAL
EDITION

ABOVE: Peanuts *Digital Editions, 2011 – CSCA*

# THE RED BARON

FIRST MENTIONED 10/10/1965

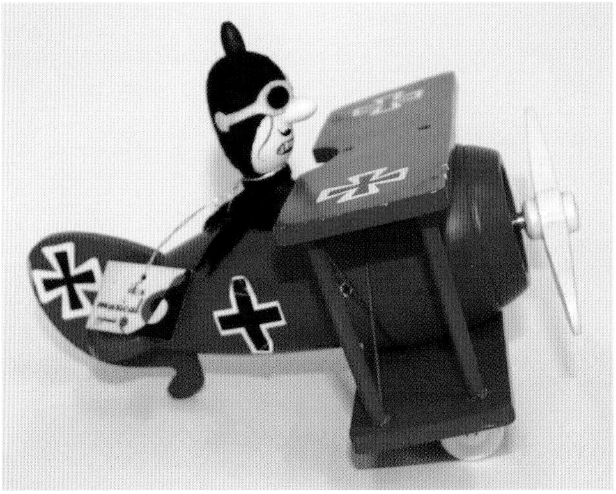

"Curse you, Red Baron!" is the familiar refrain of the World War I Flying Ace, the only pilot brave enough to face the dreaded German ace-of-aces. Snoopy and his Sopwith Camel are never able to defeat the Red Baron in a dogfight, but their aerial encounters give the World War I Flying Ace plenty of thrilling stories to share with anyone who treats him to a frosty mug of root beer.

Charles Schulz never knew when inspiration would strike, and some of his most enduring ideas came from very unlikely sources. His son Monte's collection of World War I model airplanes, including a replica of the plane piloted by the real Red Baron, Manfred Freiherr von Richthofen, led Schulz to reimagine Snoopy as a fighter pilot, and the rest was history. "I'm not sure how Snoopy got on top of the doghouse, but I'm glad he did, because it opened up whole new areas of fantasy for me."

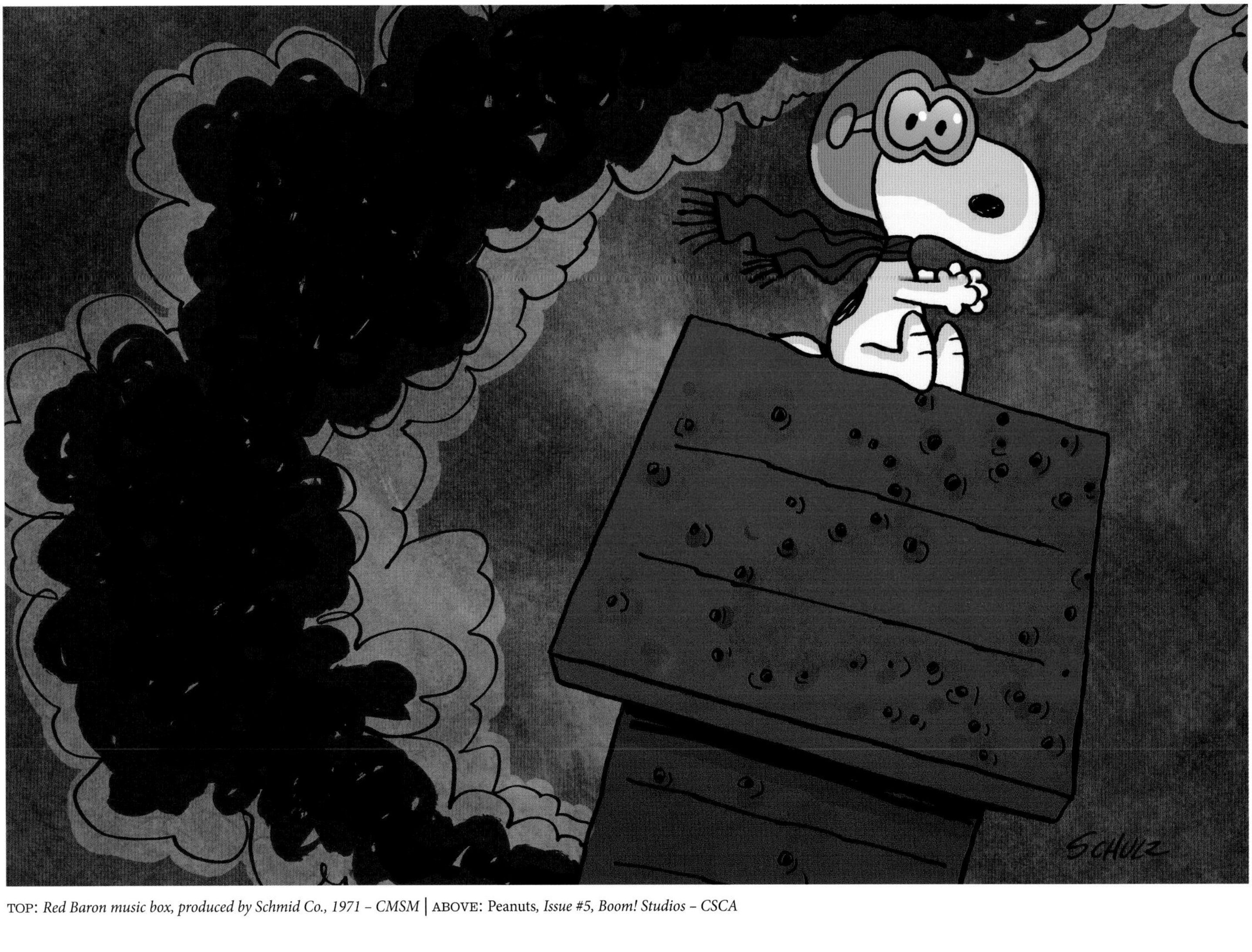
SCHULZ

TOP: *Red Baron music box, produced by Schmid Co., 1971 – CMSM* | ABOVE: Peanuts, *Issue #5, Boom! Studios – CSCA*

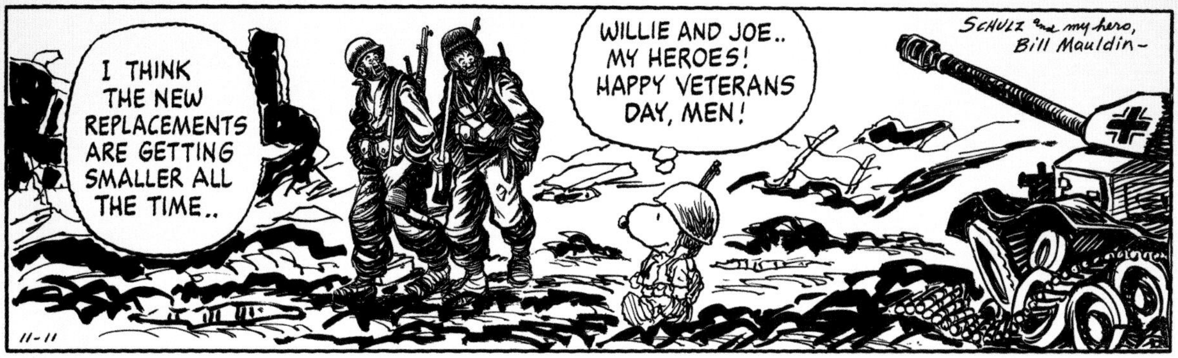
I THINK THE NEW REPLACEMENTS ARE GETTING SMALLER ALL THE TIME..
WILLIE AND JOE.. MY HEROES! HAPPY VETERANS DAY, MEN!
SCHULZ and my hero, Bill Mauldin-
11-11

# VETERAN'S DAY

FIRST OBSERVED
11/11/1969

Every Veteran's Day, Snoopy, often in the guise of the World War I Flying Ace, goes to Bill Mauldin's house "to quaff a few root beers." This tradition started on November 11, 1969, and nearly every year thereafter, Charles Schulz would pay tribute to Mauldin, whom he called "the greatest cartoonist to come out World War II."

Schulz, like many World War II veterans, followed Mauldin's Pulitzer Prize–winning "Willie and Joe" cartoons in the military newspaper Stars and Stripes. Mauldin served in the Army's 45th Infantry Division, and his cartoons depicted both the humor and the harsh reality of life on the front line, earning him admiration from his fellow soldiers as well as accolades from the press.

Mauldin holds the unique distinction as the only cartoonist to contribute to Schulz's daily comic strip. The 1998 Veterans Day installment of *Peanuts* depicts Snoopy meeting his heroes, Willie and Joe, as illustrated by Bill Mauldin, in a touching tribute to Schulz's hero.

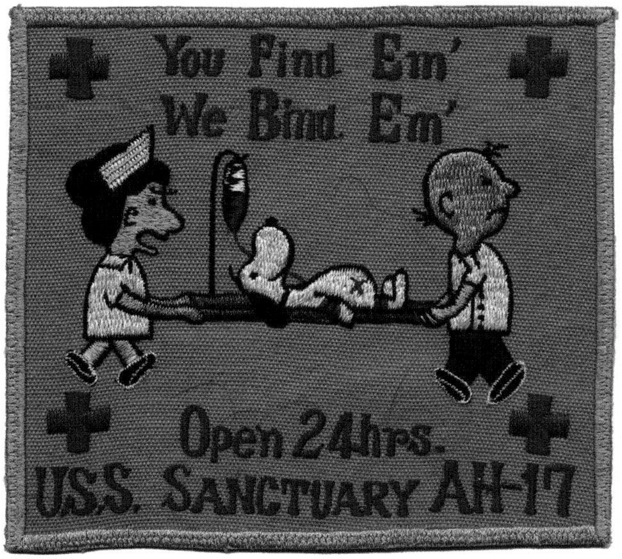
You Find Em'
We Bind Em'
Open 24hrs.
U.S.S. SANCTUARY AH-17

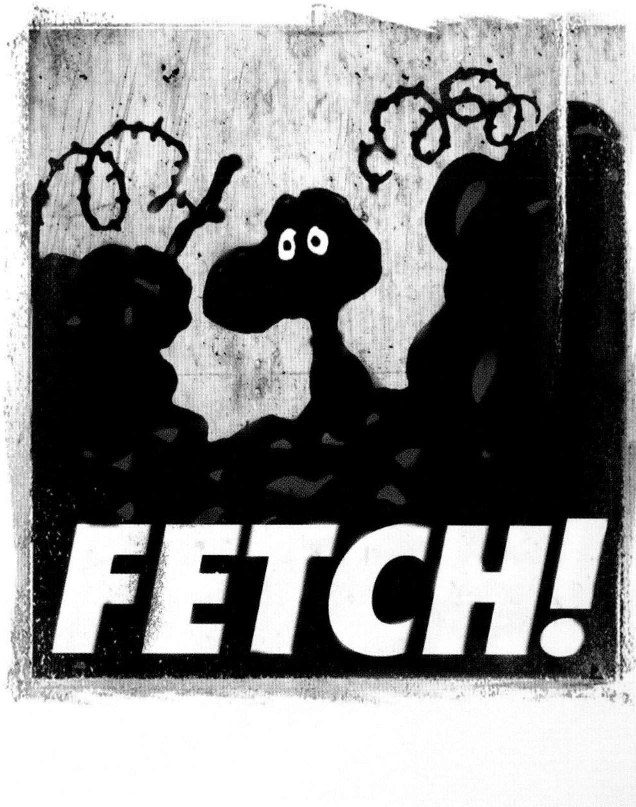
FETCH!

TOP RIGHT: U.S.S. Sanctuary *military patch, c. 1969 – CMSM* | RIGHT: *Style Guide art – CSCA*

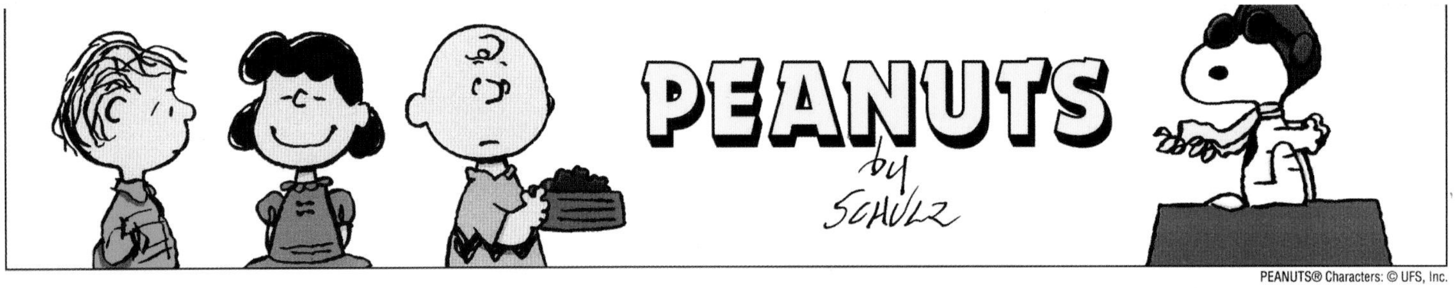
PEANUTS
by
SCHULZ



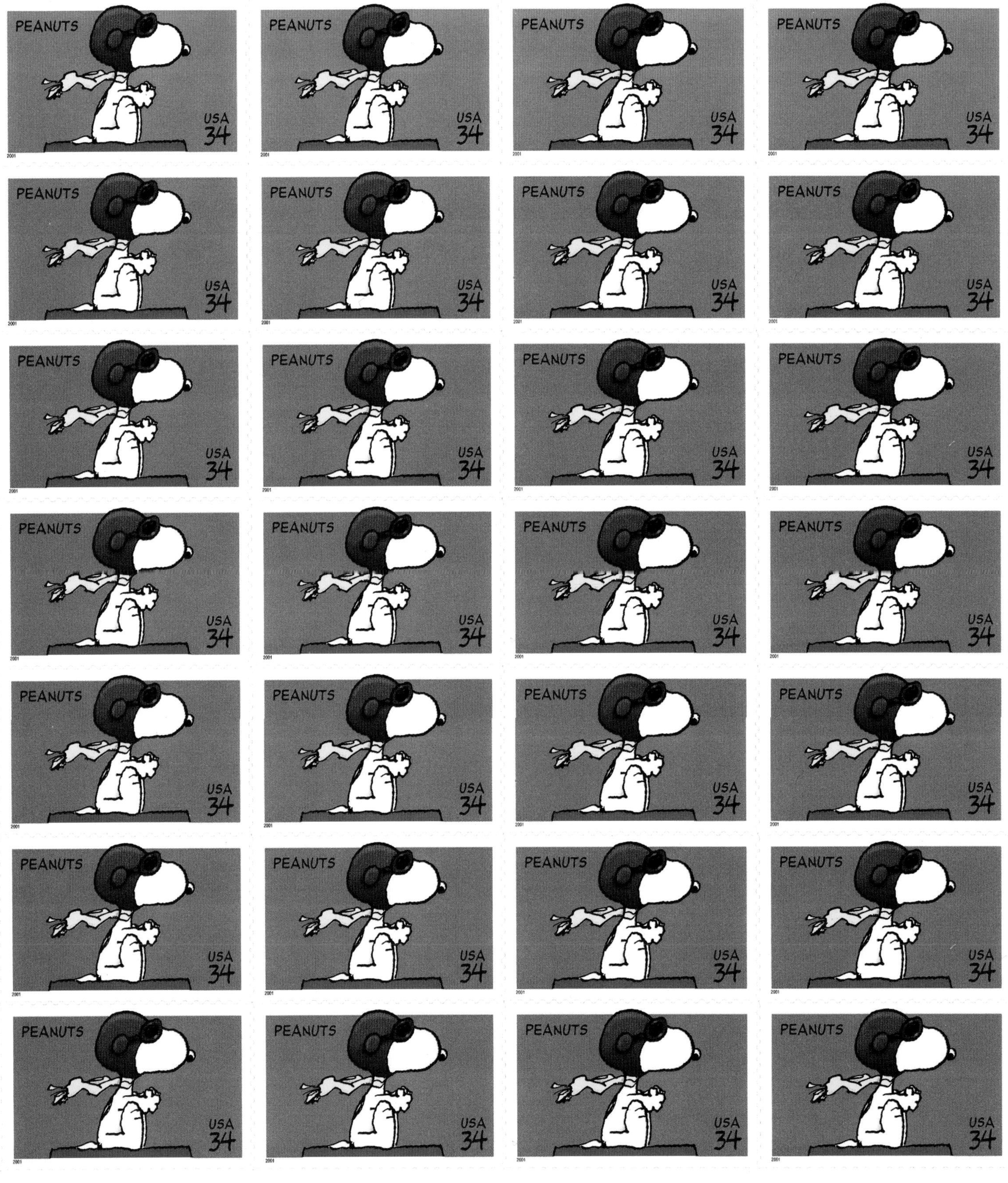
PEANUTS
USA
34
2001

# D-DAY

FIRST OBSERVED
06/06/1993

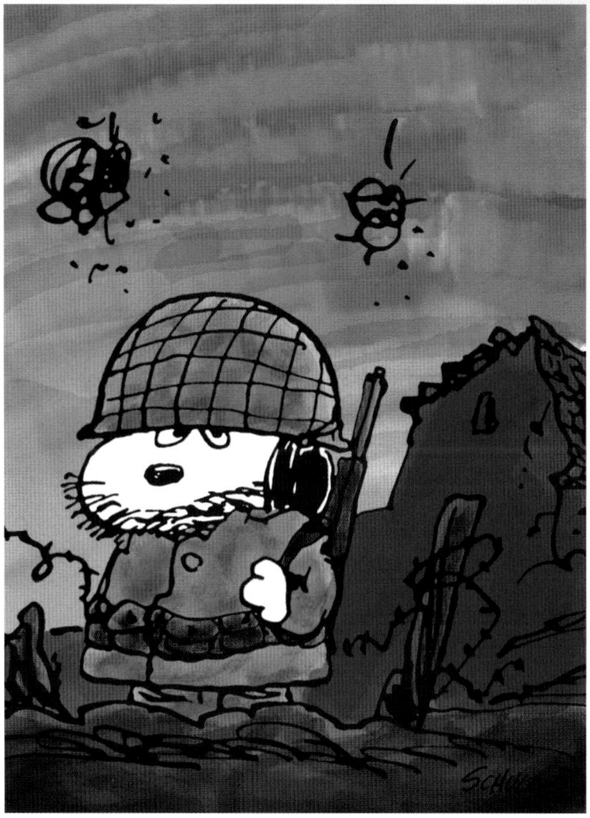

"I think any sensible person with a grasp of history would have to admit that D-Day was the most important day of our century," observed Charles Schulz in 1999. "Without D-Day it's possible that Europe could have remained for another 25 or 50 years in darkness. I'm glad I wasn't there, and yet my admiration for the people who were knows no bounds."

The Allied invasion of Normandy occurred June 6, 1944, and each June from 1993 to 1998 (with the exception of 1995), Schulz implored his readers "To Remember" the brave Allied soldiers and this turning point in World War II. In this poignant series of strips, he depicted Snoopy as a soldier on the front line, a solemn tribute to Schulz's fellow vets.

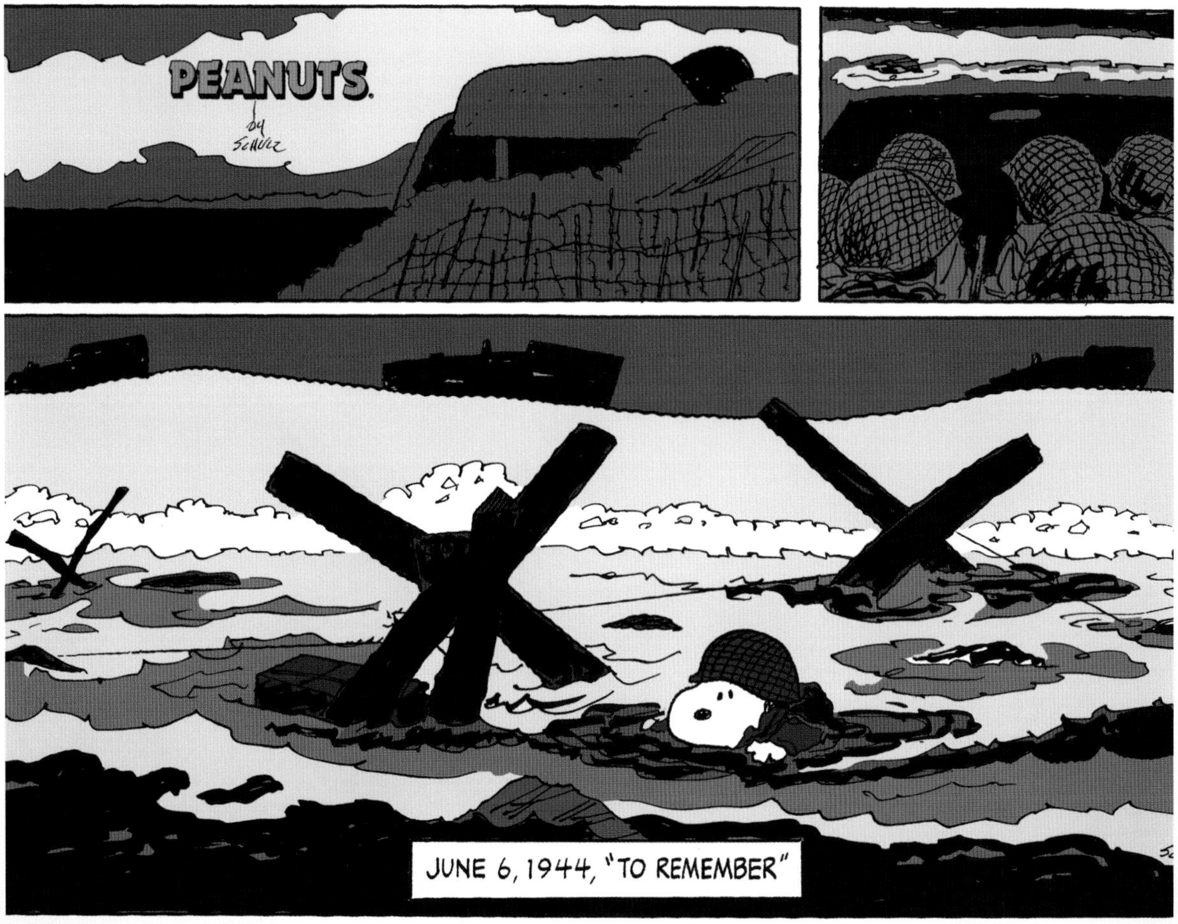
PEANUTS
by SCHULZ
JUNE 6, 1944, "TO REMEMBER"

OPPOSITE: *Snoopy as Flying Ace postage stamps, c. 2001 – CMSM* | OPPOSITE, TOP: *Style Guide art – CSCA*

PEANUTS
HERE'S JOE COOL HANGING AROUND THE STUDENT UNION
5-27
HI, JOE.. HOW'D YOU DO IN CHEMISTRY TODAY?
THAT CHEMISTRY IS A DRAG, MAN
JOE COOL CAN'T WORRY ABOUT CHEMISTRY WHEN HE'S BUSY HANGING AROUND THE STUDENT UNION
SCHULZ

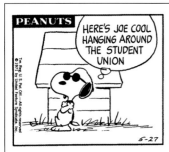

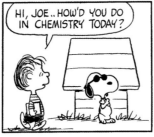

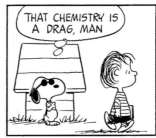

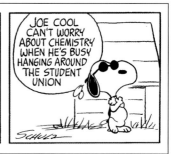

## JOE COOL FIRST APPEARANCE 05/27/1971

The Big Beagle on Campus, Joe Cool always knows where it's at. Whether he's scoping out the scene at the student union or just hanging out in his dorm, Joe is in a class by himself (especially since he rarely attends one). His ever-present dark sunglasses and relaxed attitude make him the coolest of the cool, and he knows it.

Joe is happy to join in a friendly game of Frisbee or take in a flick at the campus theater, as long as he doesn't have to exert himself, since that just wouldn't be cool. It isn't easy being the most popular beagle around, but somehow he manages. As Charles Schulz once observed, "Snoopy's philosophy is to try to look good at a distance."

Snoopy's not content to spend all of his free time lounging around on campus. He's been known to take part in off-road racing as Joe Motorcross, clean up his act as Joe Preppy, bowl a few frames as Joe Sandbagger, rock out as Joe Grunge, and play a few hands as Joe Blackjack, the World Famous Riverboat Gambler. No matter how he dresses, rest assured that Snoopy is no average Joe.

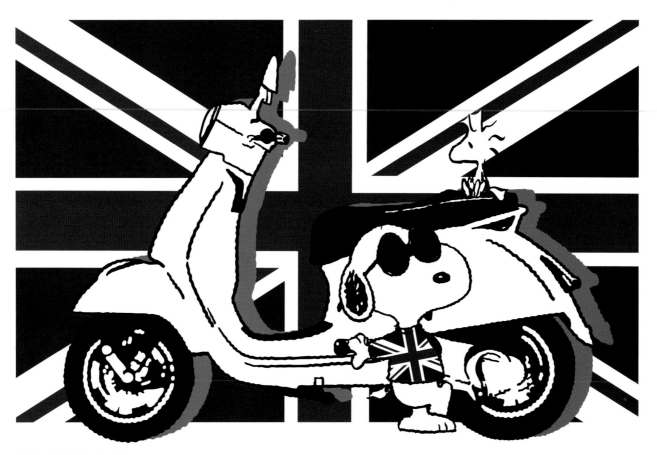

ABOVE: *Style Guide art – PW*

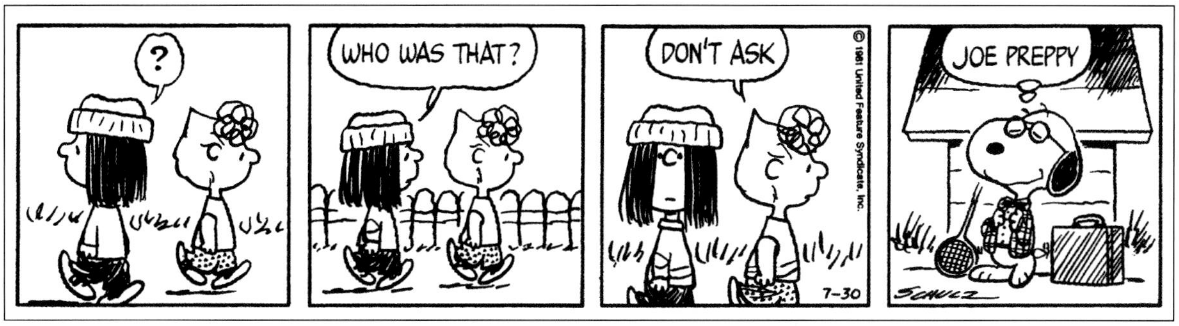
?
WHO WAS THAT?
DON'T ASK
© 1981 United Feature Syndicate, Inc.
7-30
JOE PREPPY

"Some of us prefer to sacrifice comfort for style." —Snoopy

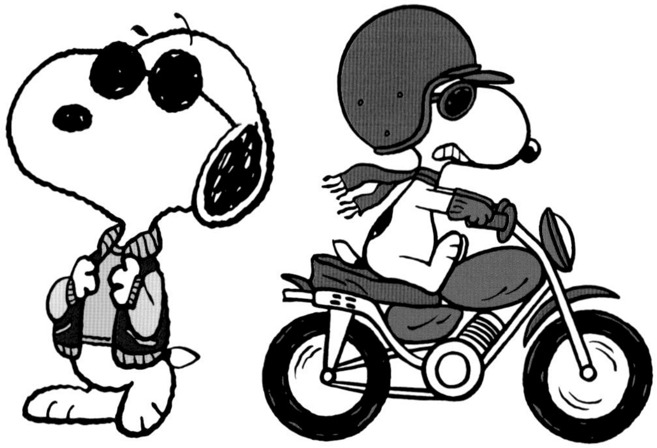

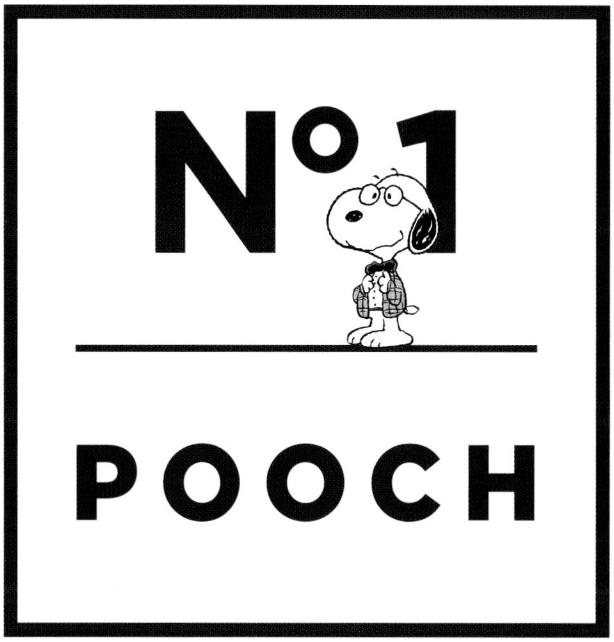
Nº1
POOCH

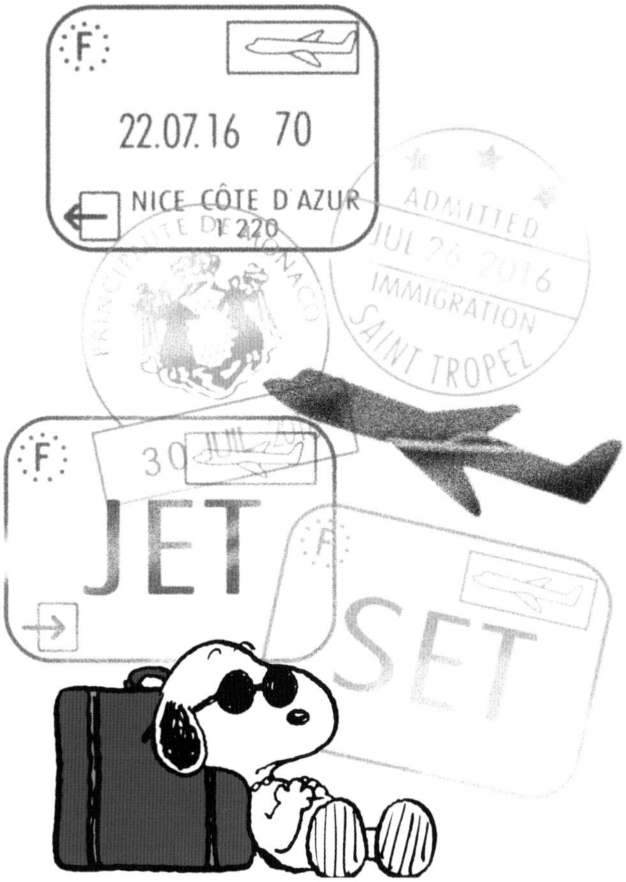
22.07.16 70
NICE CÔTE D'AZUR
F220
ADMITTED
JUL 26 2016
IMMIGRATION
SAINT TROPEZ
JET
SET

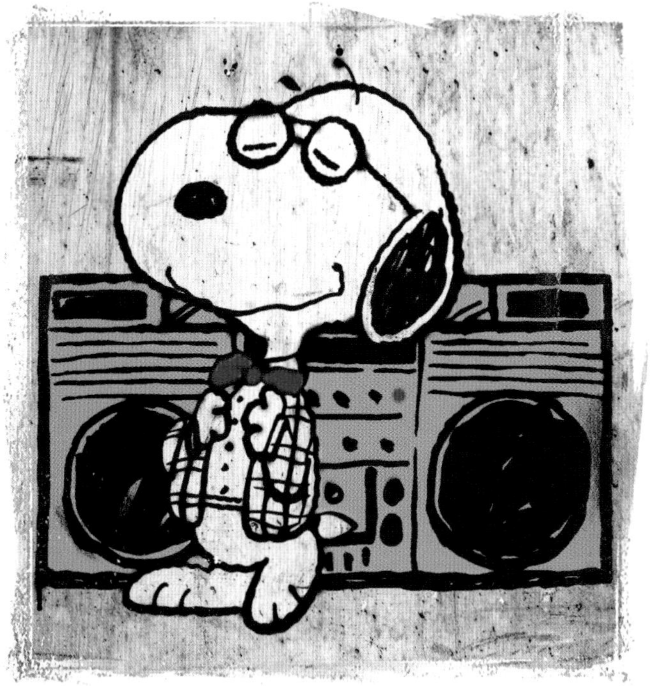

TOP LEFT AND BOTTOM RIGHT: *Style Guide art – CSCA* | TOP RIGHT AND BOTTOM LEFT: *Style Guide art – PW*

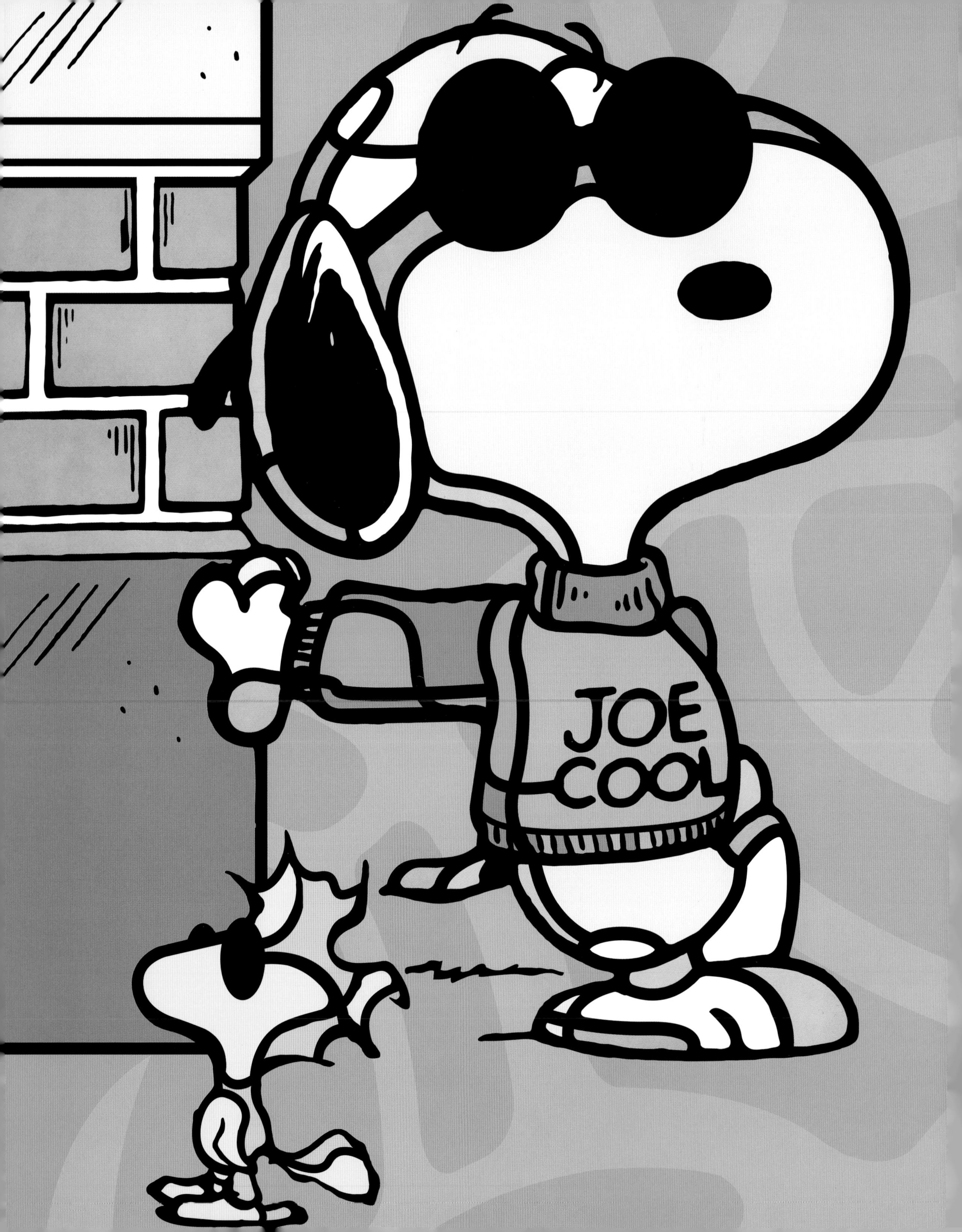
JOE
COOL

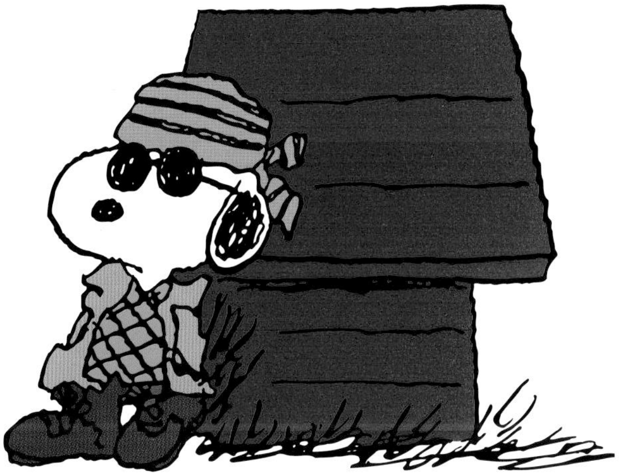

1

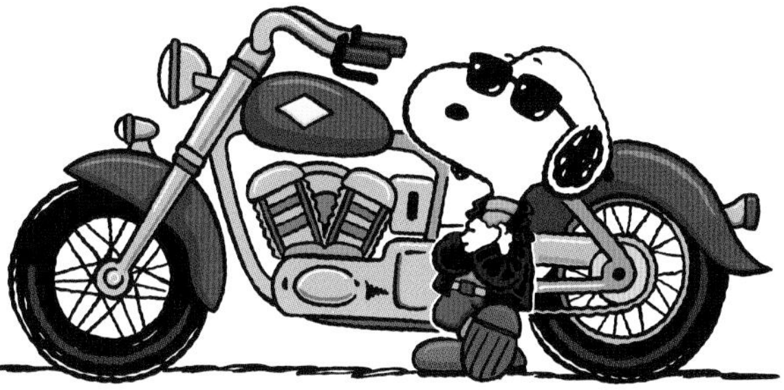

2

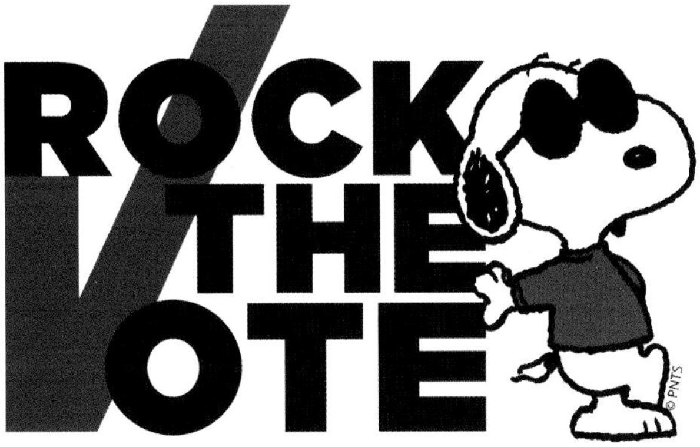

ROCK
THE
VOTE
© PNTS


3

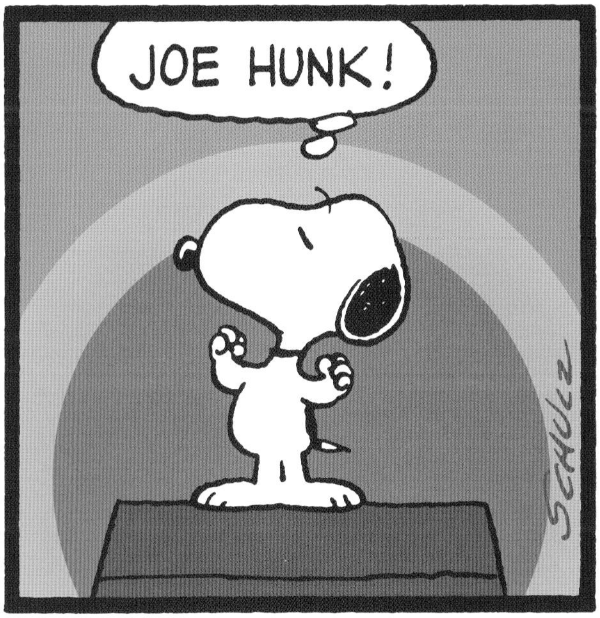

JOE HUNK!
SCHULZ


4

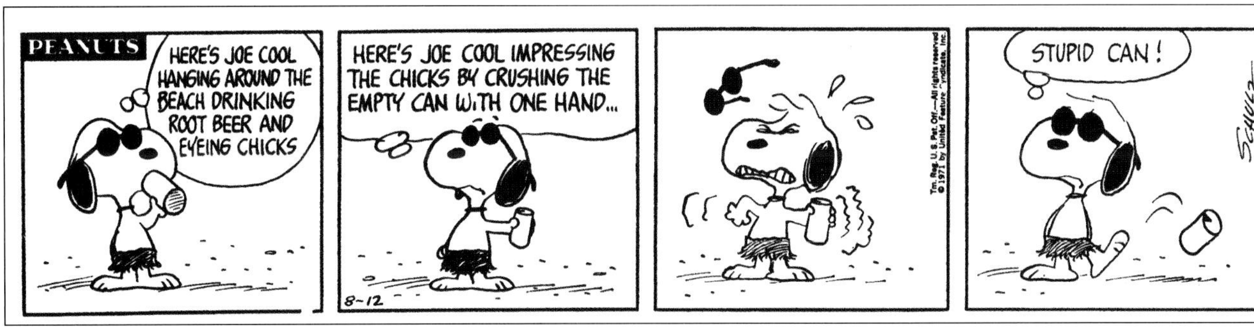

PEANUTS
HERE'S JOE COOL HANGING AROUND THE BEACH DRINKING ROOT BEER AND EYEING CHICKS
HERE'S JOE COOL IMPRESSING THE CHICKS BY CRUSHING THE EMPTY CAN WITH ONE HAND...
8-12
STUPID CAN!
SCHULZ


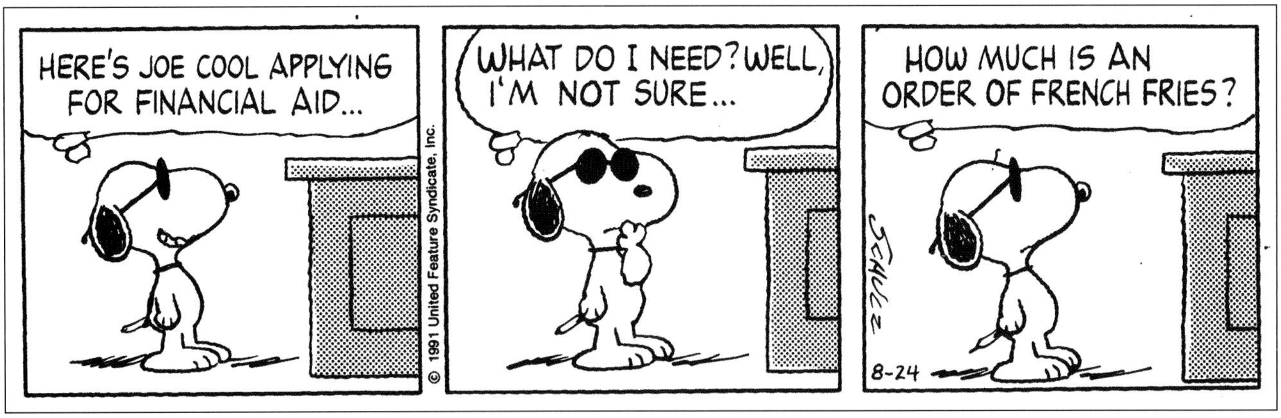

HERE'S JOE COOL APPLYING FOR FINANCIAL AID...
© 1991 United Feature Syndicate, Inc.
WHAT DO I NEED? WELL, I'M NOT SURE...
SCHULZ
HOW MUCH IS AN ORDER OF FRENCH FRIES?
8-24


OPPOSITE: Joe Cool and Woodstock; *David Flores; Limited Edition Print; Courtesy: Dark Hall Mansion* | THIS PAGE: *1 and 4: Spot art from strips – Charles M. Schulz; 2 and 3: Style Guide art – PW*

## “WORLD FAMOUS” SNOOPY

Obviously, Snoopy never settles for being second best at anything, so when he takes on a new profession, he assumes that he will rise to the top of his field.

At various times, he is “World Famous” at each of the following professions: hockey player, baseball manager, golf pro, astronaut, roller derby star, skier, tennis player, grocery clerk, swinger, football coach, swimmer, skater, member of the emergency rescue squad, crabby skating pro, truffle hound, disco dancer, river boat gambler, surveyor, census taker, advice columnist, hired hand, surgeon, agent, flagman, hockey coach, big-rig operator, and orthopedic surgeon.

World
Champion
(In the Making)
BASEBALL

SNOOPY
THE GREAT
KING
OF
CARDS

CHAMPION
EST. 1950
©PEANUTS
POND SKATER
SCHULZ

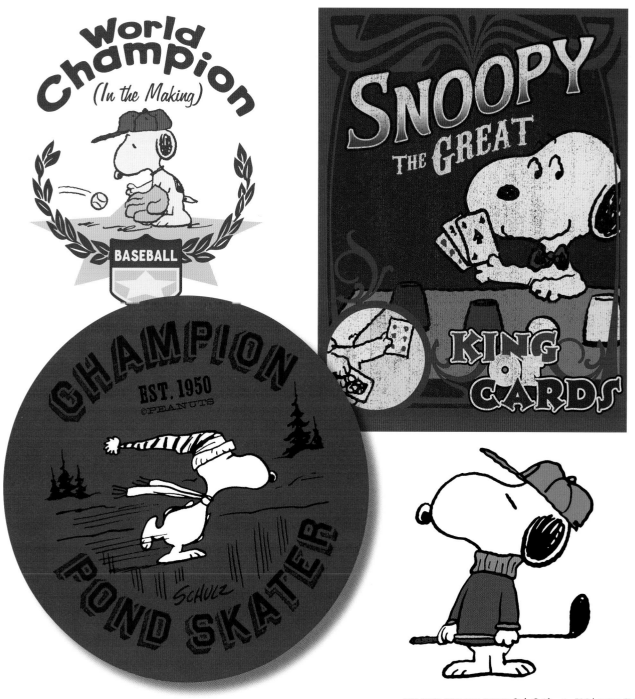

TOP LEFT AND TOP RIGHT: *Style Guide art – PW* | LEFT: *Style Guide art – CSCA* | ABOVE: *Spot art from Charles M. Schulz*

## THE WORLD FAMOUS ASTRONAUT

FIRST APPEARANCE 03/08/1969

One of Snoopy's greatest achievements was serving as NASA's official safety mascot, a designation earned when Al Chop, director of public affairs at the Manned Spacecraft Center, approached Charles Schulz about using his characters in a safety campaign designed especially for the space program. As Schulz recalled, "I suppose receiving the two Reubens [the highest honor awarded by his peers in the National Cartoonists Society] pleased me more than anything else, but I think having Snoopy go to the moon was the greatest triumph of all. This is because cartoonists have been sending their characters into space for years in their stories, but mine was the first character who really went to the moon. Snoopy lapel pins were carried by the astronauts into space."

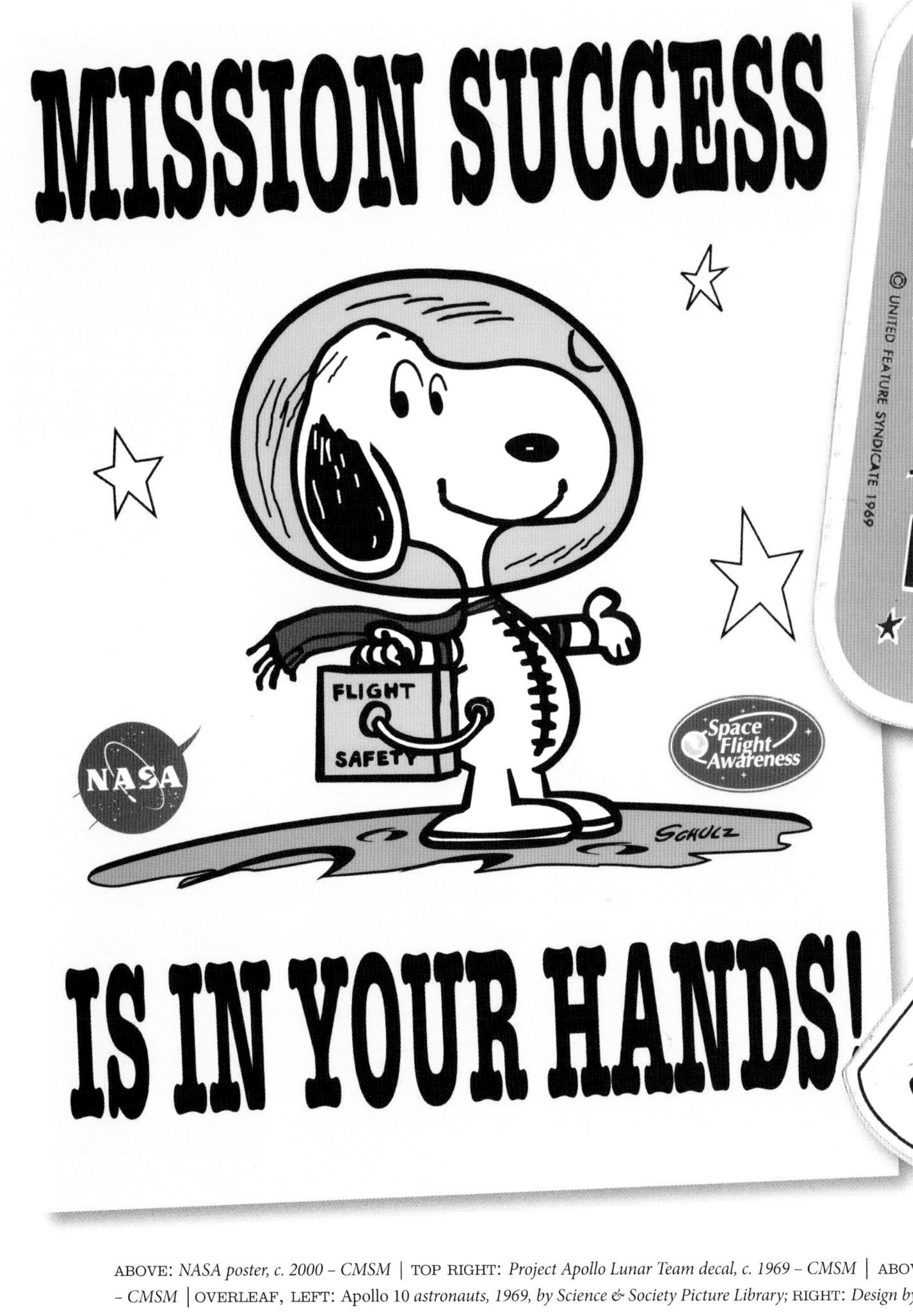
MISSION SUCCESS
FLIGHT SAFETY
NASA
Space Flight Awareness
SCHULZ
IS IN YOUR HANDS!

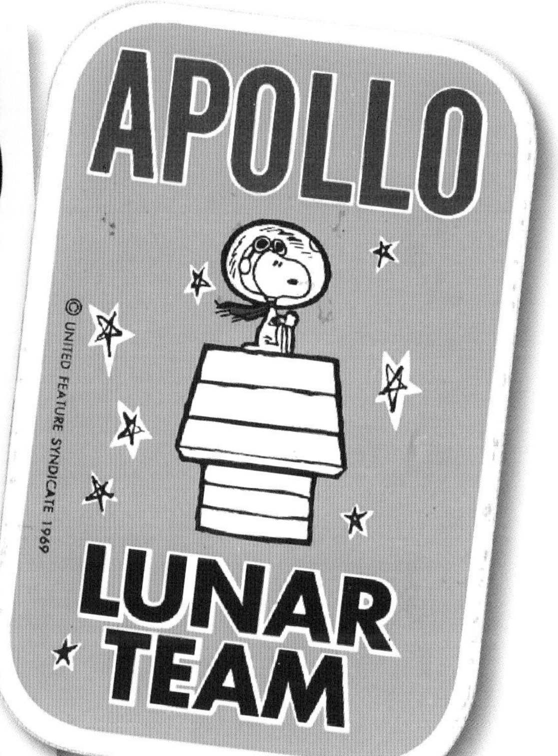
APOLLO
© UNITED FEATURE SYNDICATE 1969
LUNAR TEAM

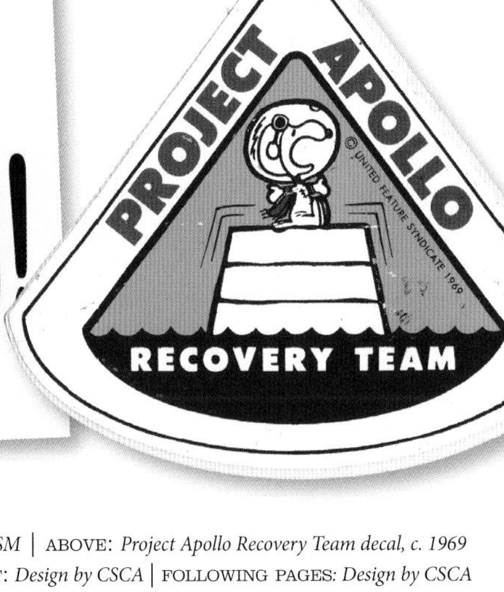
PROJECT APOLLO
© UNITED FEATURE SYNDICATE 1969
RECOVERY TEAM

ABOVE: *NASA poster, c. 2000 – CMSM* | TOP RIGHT: *Project Apollo Lunar Team decal, c. 1969 – CMSM* | ABOVE: *Project Apollo Recovery Team decal, c. 1969 – CMSM* | OVERLEAF, LEFT: Apollo 10 *astronauts, 1969, by Science & Society Picture Library;* RIGHT: *Design by CSCA* | FOLLOWING PAGES: *Design by CSCA*

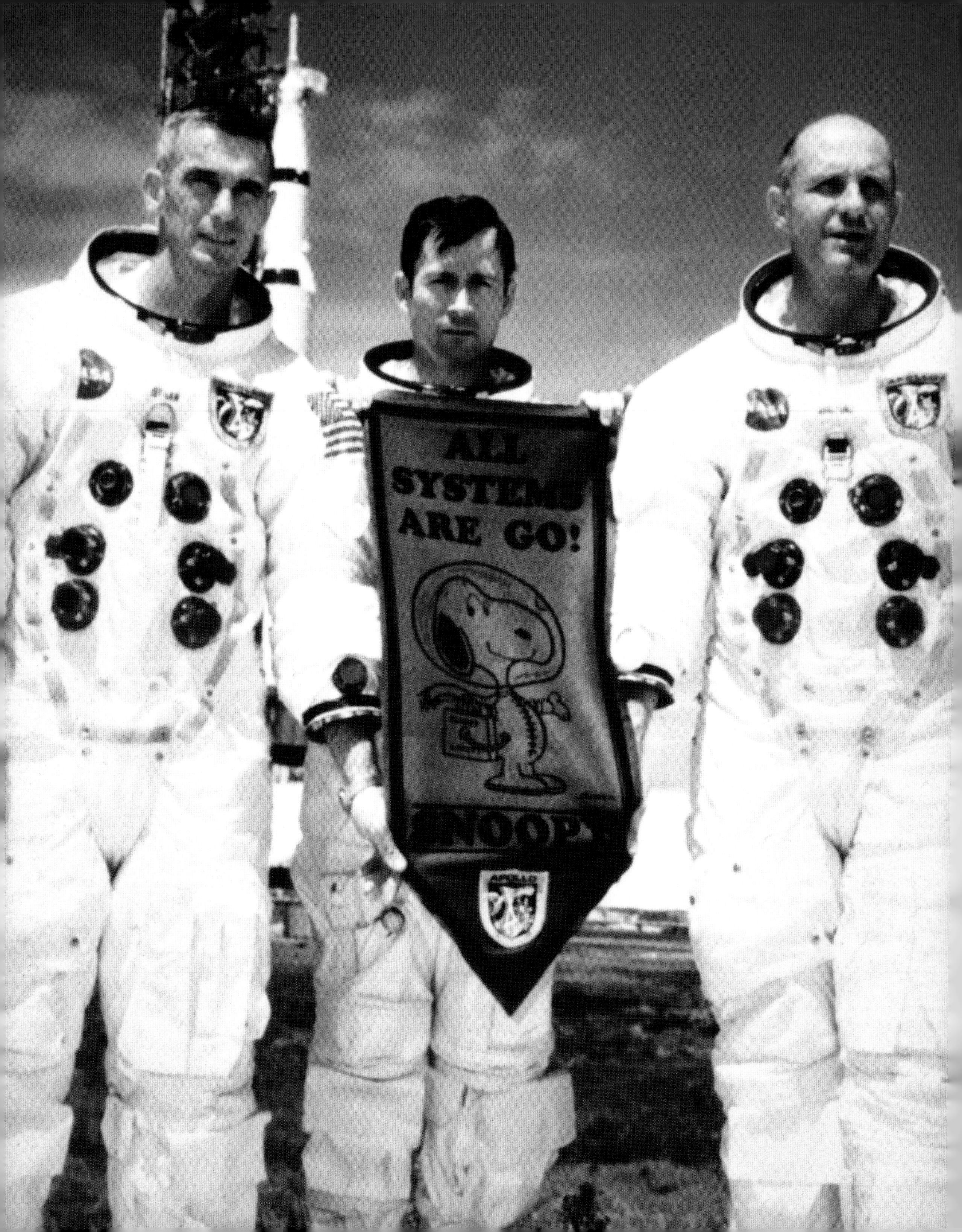
ALL SYSTEMS ARE GO!
SNOOPY

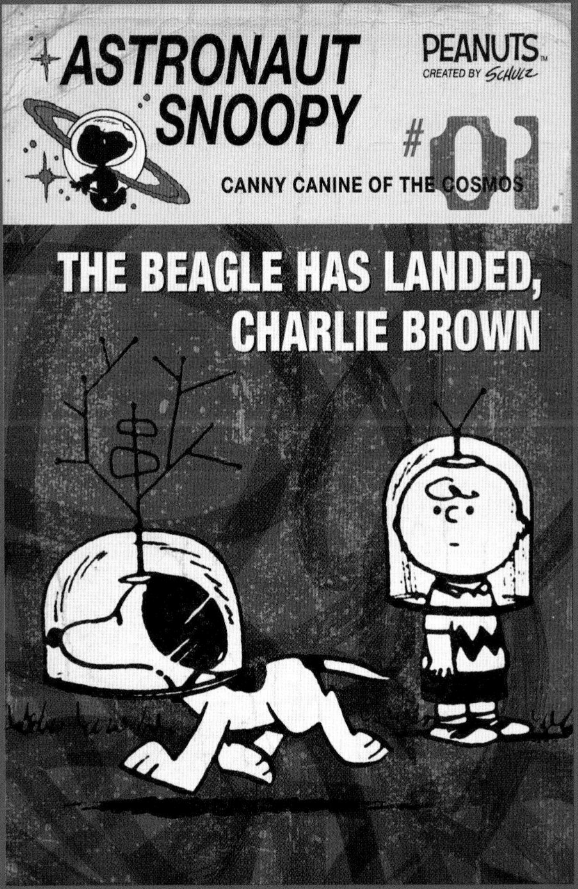
ASTRONAUT SNOOPY
PEANUTS
CREATED BY SCHULZ
#01
CANNY CANINE OF THE COSMOS
THE BEAGLE HAS LANDED, CHARLIE BROWN

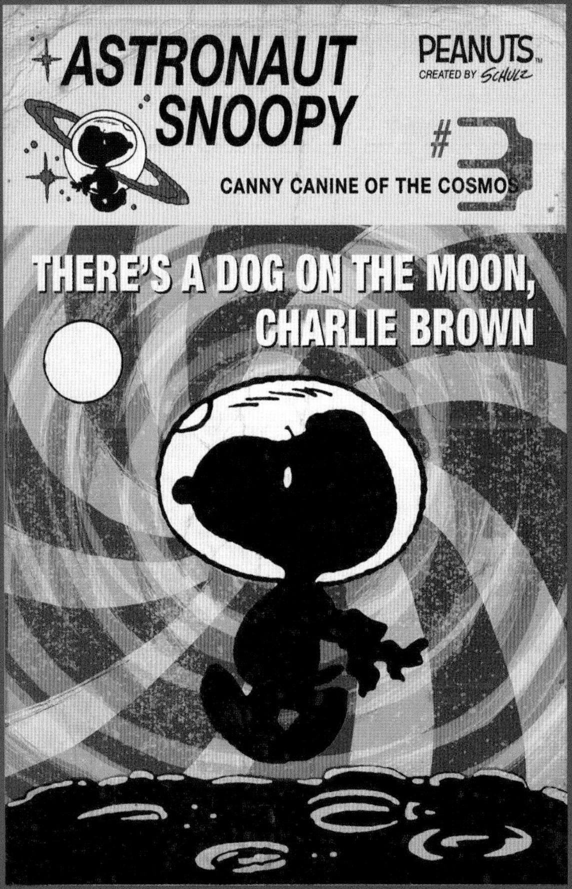
ASTRONAUT SNOOPY
PEANUTS
CREATED BY SCHULZ
#3
CANNY CANINE OF THE COSMOS
THERE'S A DOG ON THE MOON, CHARLIE BROWN

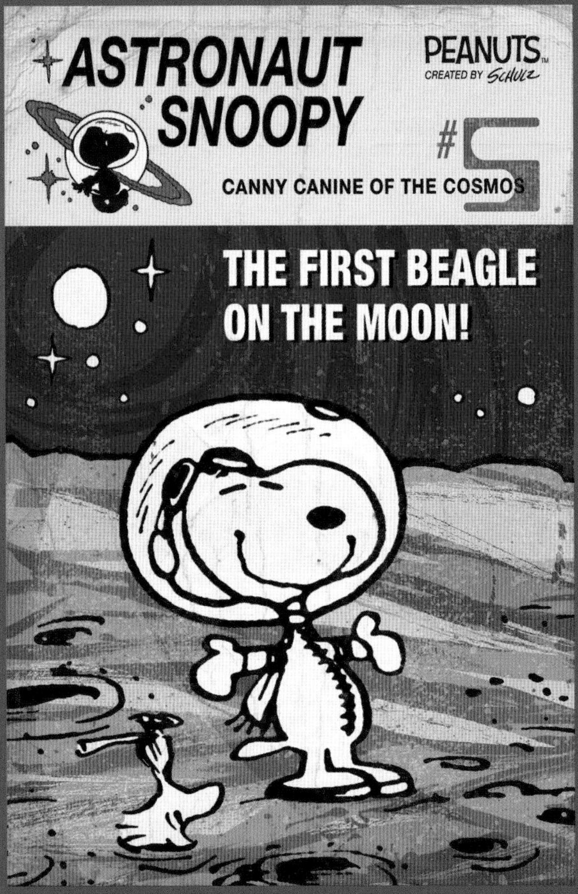
ASTRONAUT SNOOPY
PEANUTS
CREATED BY SCHULZ
#5
CANNY CANINE OF THE COSMOS
THE FIRST BEAGLE ON THE MOON!

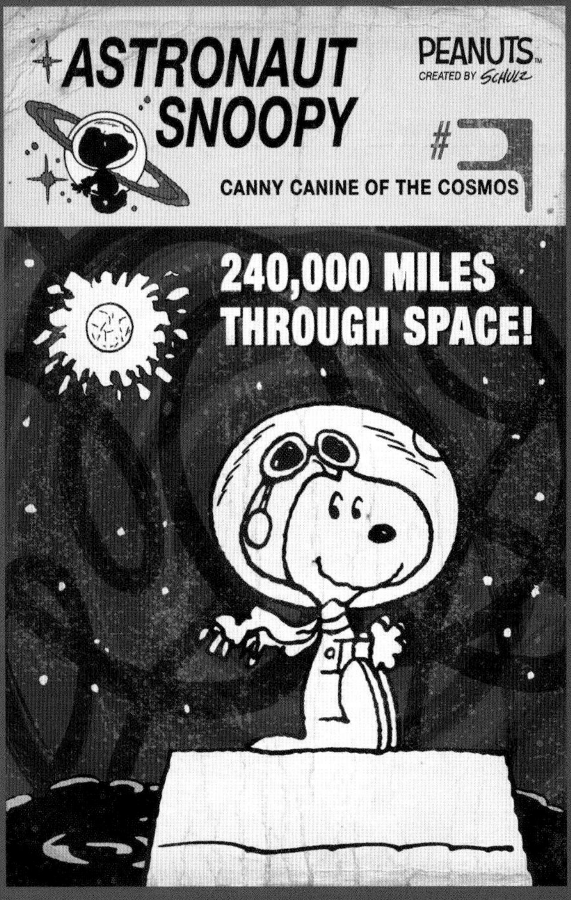
ASTRONAUT SNOOPY
PEANUTS
CREATED BY SCHULZ
#7
CANNY CANINE OF THE COSMOS
240,000 MILES THROUGH SPACE!

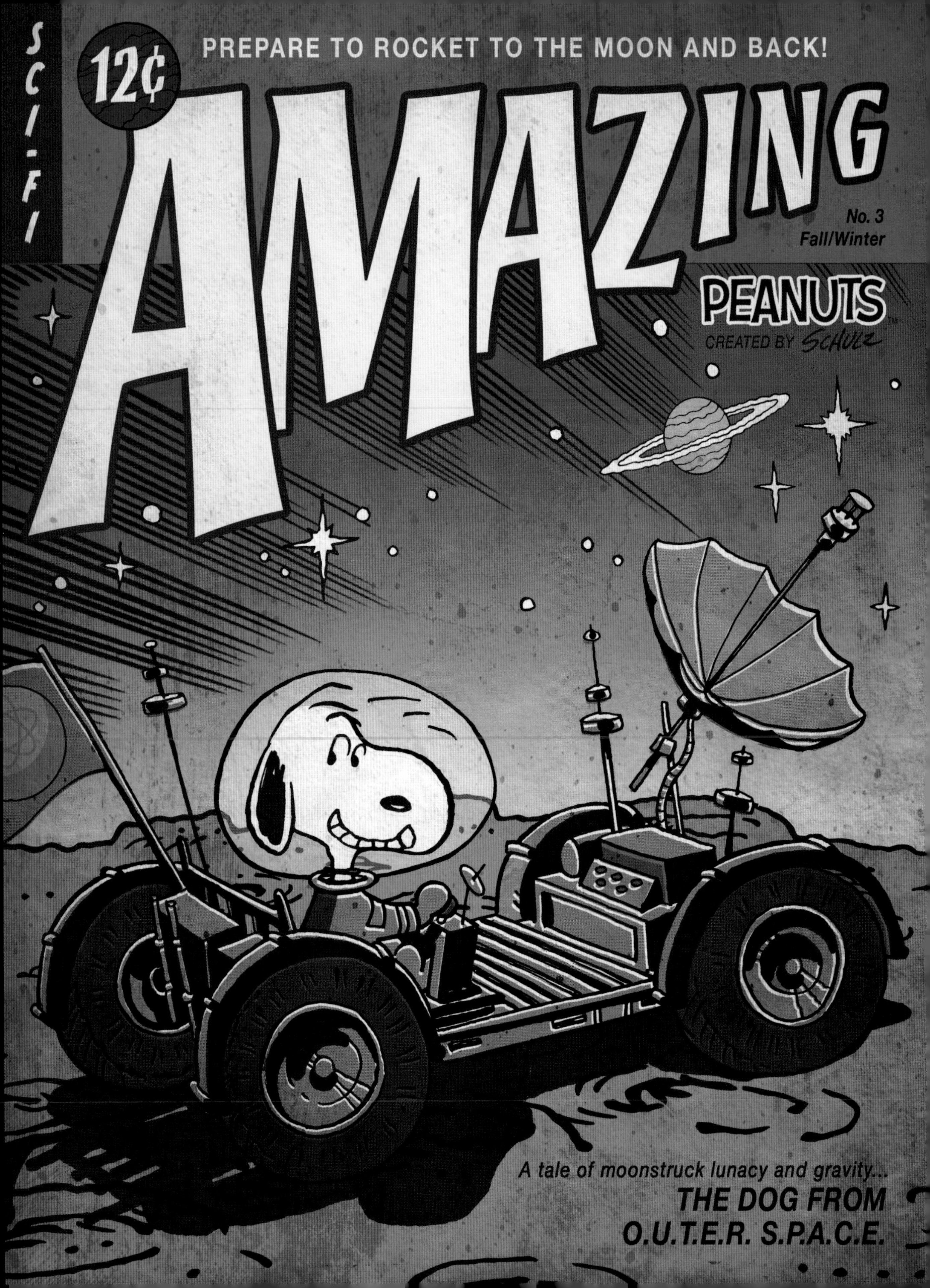
SCI-FI
12¢
PREPARE TO ROCKET TO THE MOON AND BACK!
AMAZING
No. 3
Fall/Winter
PEANUTS
CREATED BY SCHULZ
A tale of moonstruck lunacy and gravity...
THE DOG FROM
O.U.T.E.R. S.P.A.C.E.

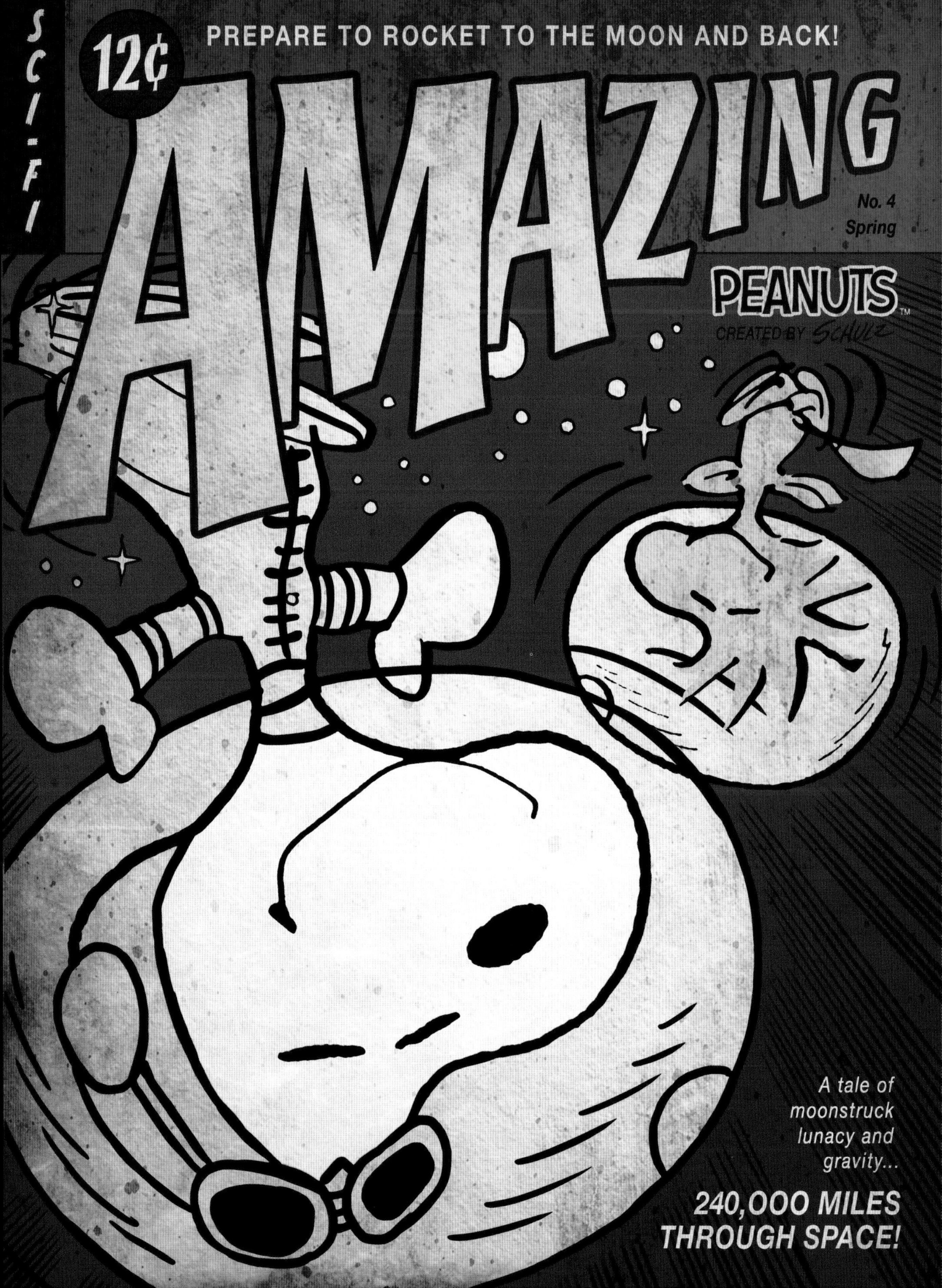
SCI-FI
12¢
PREPARE TO ROCKET TO THE MOON AND BACK!
AMAZING
No. 4
Spring
PEANUTS™
CREATED BY SCHULZ
A tale of moonstruck lunacy and gravity...
240,000 MILES THROUGH SPACE!

## THE WORLD FAMOUS SURGEON

FIRST APPEARANCE 07/12/1982

Prepare the operating room! The World Famous Surgeon is ready to perform the most complex medical procedures imaginable at a moment's notice—just as long as it doesn't conflict with his tee time.

Sporting a spotless surgical cap and gown, Snoopy is supremely confident in his abilities as a top-flight surgeon, whether he's operating on people or members of the animal kingdom. Lucy is considerably more skeptical of his prowess, however, noting that only about half of his patients seem to be satisfied with his performance, but Snoopy's not bothered by the naysayers, as he's "very easy going."

When Rerun falls and bumps his knee, Snoopy reveals himself as the World Famous Orthopedic Surgeon, and prepares to perform an emergency procedure on the youngest member of the Van Pelt family. Fortunately for Rerun, his knee is only bruised, which is just as well, since Snoopy can't find the emergency room anyway.

After a hard day's work, Snoopy likes to unwind with his fellow medical professionals on the golf course. He seems much more at home on the links than in the operating room—although his skill with a nine iron seem to be on par with his ability to use a scalpel.

ABOVE: *Spot art from strip – Charles M. Schulz*

HERE'S THE WORLD FAMOUS SURGEON ON HIS WAY TO THE OPERATING ROOM...
DOCTOR, IT SAYS HERE THAT AFTER SURGERY, FIFTY PERCENT OF YOUR PATIENTS FEEL PRETTY GOOD FOR HALF AN HOUR
DO THOSE STATISTICS BOTHER YOU?
NO, I'M VERY EASY GOING
©1982 United Feature Syndicate, Inc.
SCHULZ
7-12

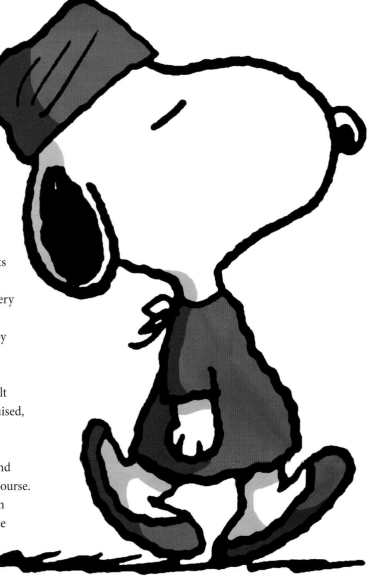

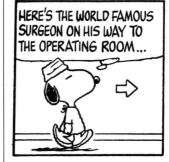

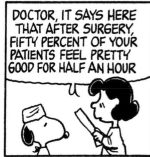

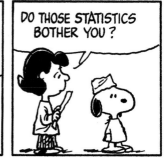

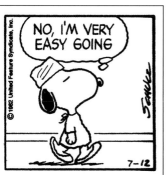

# THE WORLD FAMOUS SERGEANT-MAJOR OF THE FOREIGN LEGION

FIRST APPEARANCE
03/21/1966

Like many a wayward beagle before him, Snoopy joins the "Legion of Lost Souls" to forget a woman from his past. As the World Famous Sergeant-Major of the Foreign Legion, Snoopy leads Woodstock and a small regiment of birds across the desert in the hope of reclaiming Fort Zinderneuf for France. Their travels take them through beaches, golf courses, sandboxes, schools, and Snoopy's own backyard. Unlike the outcome of his literary inspiration, Beau Geste, they never seem to successfully accomplish their mission.

"Beau" Snoopy's regiment consists of the same group of birds that make up his Beagle Scout troop. The key difference is that the Beagle Scouts tend to favor camping in the woods, while the Foreign Legion's activities lead them into more hostile territories. So hostile that Snoopy once fired a cannon in an attempt to retake Fort Zinderneuf, only to demolish his own doghouse, Lucy's Psychiatric Booth, and Schroeder's piano in the process.

Snoopy considers all these problems to be minor setbacks in the grand scheme of things, however, and he vows that he will forget his lost love and will once again reclaim Fort Zinderneuf for the Legion.

THE COLLECTED STRIPS
RETAKE FORT ZINDERNEUF!
WRITTEN BY
CHARLES M. SCHULZ
STARRING
"BEAU" SNOOPY
A PEANUTS DIGITAL EDITION

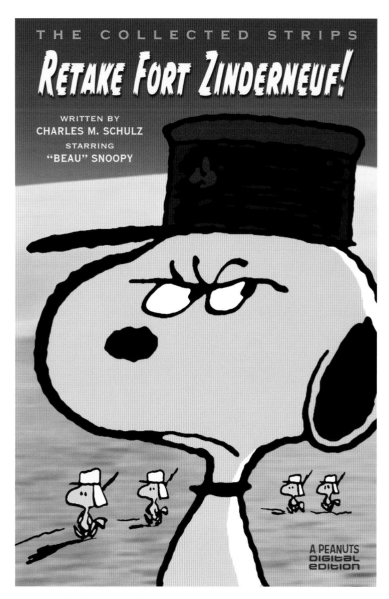

ABOVE: Retake the Zinderneuf! Peanuts *Digital Edition* – CSCA

PEANUTS
I THOUGHT I HAD A CLEAN WHITE HANDKERCHIEF IN HERE...
THERE'S A BLUE ONE... A GREEN ONE..ANOTHER BLUE ONE...
WHAT IN THE WORLD HAPPENED TO MY WHITE HANDKERCHIEF?
THERE IT IS, MEN... FORT ZINDERNEUF!!
3-21
SCHULZ

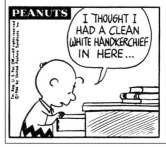

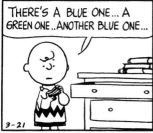

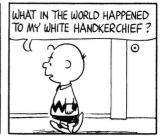

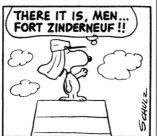

PEANUTS
7-12
It was a dark and stormy night.
SCHULZ

HERE'S THE WORLD FAMOUS AUTHOR ON HIS WAY TO MAIL HIS LATEST NOVEL TO THE PUBLISHER..
www.snoopy.com
!
4-30
© 1998 United Feature Syndicate, Inc.
I DIDN'T KNOW MAILBOXES COULD RUN..
SCHULZ

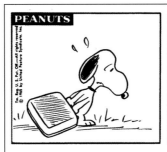

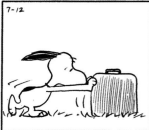

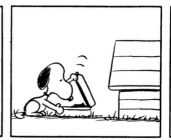

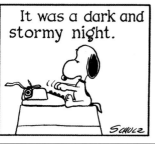

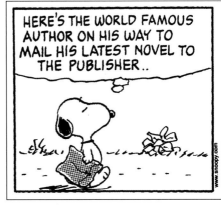

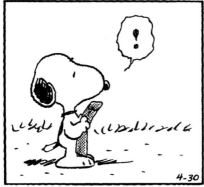

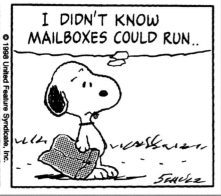

## THE WORLD FAMOUS AUTHOR FIRST APPEARANCE 07/12/1965

"It was a dark and stormy night." The World Famous Author starts every manuscript with that phrase, much to the chagrin of the publishers on Snoopy's mailing list.

Snoopy's writing career begins innocently enough, when he brings home a typewriter, perches it atop his doghouse, and starts crafting adventure stories, romance novels, and his memoirs. He sells the very first story that he writes, but enjoys minimal success as an author after that initial sale. Linus and Lucy offer friendly encouragement and advice to the struggling writer, but Snoopy has a tendency to ignore or misinterpret their advice. When Lucy suggests that "Once upon a time" might be a better way to open a story, Snoopy agrees and types the unforgettable introduction, "Once upon a time it was a dark and stormy night."

Editors waste little time reading and rejecting Snoopy's manuscripts, to the point that some prereject his yet-to-be-written stories. Woodstock, his friend of friends, is always supportive of Snoopy's writing career and makes him the best present an author could hope for—a quilt stitched together from his rejection slips!

It Was a Dark and Stormy Night
A NOVEL BY Snoopy

RIGHT: *Interior page from* It Was a Dark and Stormy Night, *1971 – CMSM* | OPPOSITE: *Spot art from strip – Charles M. Schulz*

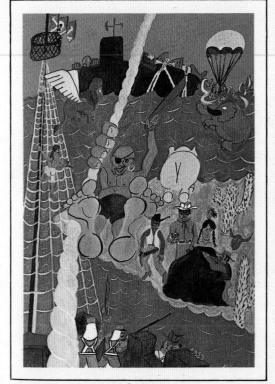

# THE WORLD FAMOUS ATTORNEY FIRST APPEARANCE 01/12/1972

Sporting a sharp, black bowtie and bowler hat, the World Famous Attorney is a model of professionalism when he saunters into court with his briefcase in hand. No case is too small for the intrepid lawyer, whose career begins when he unsuccessfully defends Peppermint Patty's right to challenge her school's dress code.

Snoopy loses several school-related cases over the course of his career and unsuccessfully argues cases involving air travel, homework, and counterfeit postage stamps. His impressive client list includes Sally Brown, Peter Rabbit, Little Red Riding Hood, and Alice from *Alice in Wonderland*.

The World Famous Attorney never wins a case and rarely bothers to learn anything about his client or his case before entering the courtroom. His rates, however, are very affordable, and he's always ready to take on a new case—if he can find the courtroom.

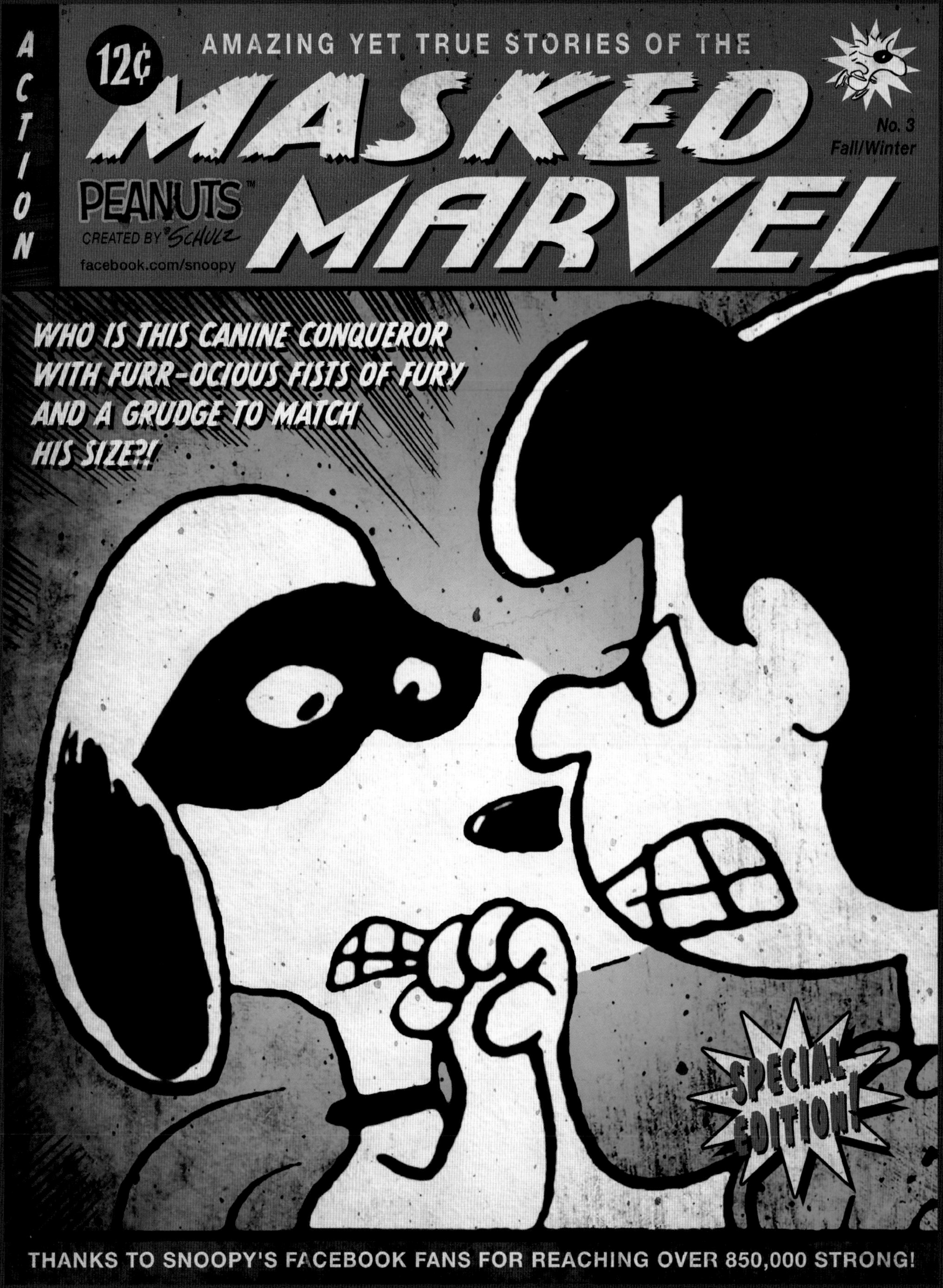
ACTION
12¢
AMAZING YET TRUE STORIES OF THE
MASKED MARVEL
PEANUTS™
CREATED BY SCHULZ
facebook.com/snoopy
No. 3
Fall/Winter
WHO IS THIS CANINE CONQUEROR
WITH FURR-OCIOUS FISTS OF FURY
AND A GRUDGE TO MATCH
HIS SIZE?!
SPECIAL EDITION!
THANKS TO SNOOPY'S FACEBOOK FANS FOR REACHING OVER 850,000 STRONG!

PEANUTS
YOU THINK YOU'RE THE "ARM WRESTLING" CHAMP, DON'T YOU?
OF COURSE, I'M THE CHAMP...I'VE BEATEN EVERYBODY AROUND HERE!
NOT EVERYBODY...
YOU'RE NOT THE CHAMPION UNTIL YOU'VE BEATEN THE "MASKED MARVEL"......
OH, GOOD GRIEF!
SCHULZ
2-9

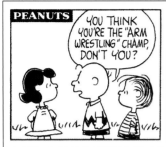

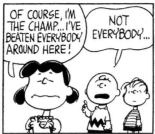

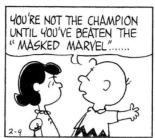

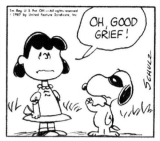

## THE MASKED MARVEL
FIRST APPEARANCE 02/09/1967

Everyone on the block fears Lucy, so when she declares herself to be the neighborhood's "arm wrestling" champ, no one can stand in her way. In short order, she defeats Charlie Brown and Linus, while Schroeder, not wanting to risk injury to his piano-playing fingers, declines to compete.

Snoopy is the only one brave enough—or foolish enough to wrestle Lucy. He doesn't want to risk losing face, however, so he adopts the persona of the Masked Marvel before throwing down the gauntlet, although his disguise doesn't seem to fool anyone. She initially declines his challenge, since she doesn't want to risk breaking "his paw or his arm or his shank or whatever it's called," but she accepts so that she doesn't look weak in front of Charlie Brown.

The Masked Marvel and Lucy wrestle to a standstill, and both are on the verge of collapse when Snoopy breaks the tie—and Lucy's grip—by planting a quick smooch on Lucy's nose. Lucy claims that the Masked Marvel cheated and announces that she is still the "arm wrestling" champ of the neighborhood. Charlie Brown and Linus visit Snoopy at his doghouse later that day to express their disappointment. Snoopy doesn't seem particularly bothered by his defeat, as he just wants to catch some sleep before moving on to his next adventure. "Sorry boys," he thinks to himself. "That's the way it goes."

POW

LEGENDARY

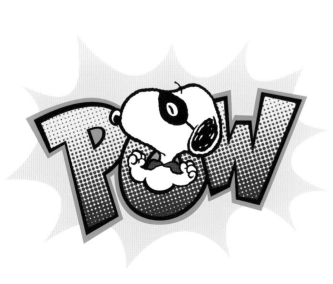

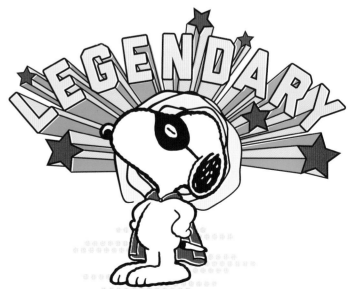

OPPOSITE: *Style Guide art – CSCA* | ABOVE: *Style Guide art – PW*

PEANUTS
WHAT IN THE WORLD IS THIS?
SNOOPY GOT A MESSAGE FROM THE HEAD BEAGLE... IT'S IN CODE...
WHAT DOES IT SAY?
IT SAYS, "THOMPSON IS IN TROUBLE!"
10-6
FOR A JOB LIKE THIS, I HAVE TO PUT ON MY FAMOUS DISGUISE...
THAT STUPID THOMPSON! THE LAST TIME THIS HAPPENED, HE ALMOST GOT US ALL KILLED...
SCHULZ

PEANUTS
THOMPSON ?
THOMPSON ?
HMM...THERE'S A LITTLE RESTAURANT THAT LOOKS FULL OF SHADY TYPES...
MAYBE THE WAITRESS KNOWS THOMPSON... I'LL GO IN, AND SLYLY STRIKE UP A CONVERSATION WITH HER...
10-9
HI, SWEETIE!
SCHULZ

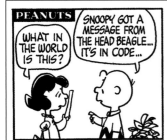

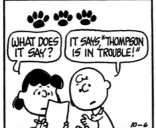

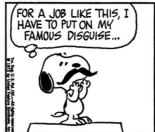

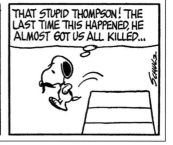

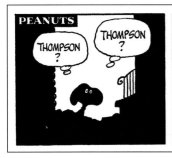

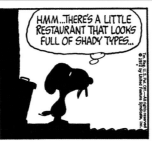

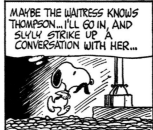

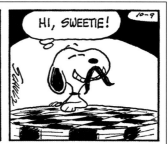

## THE SPY FIRST APPEARANCE 10/06/1972

"Thompson is in trouble!" When Snoopy receives that ominous message from the "Head Beagle," he dons a handlebar mustache and rushes to the aid of the mysterious agent Thompson. Snoopy's mission leads him to a restaurant full of shady characters, and he faces his most harrowing assignment since the nasty piece of business known as the "Moroccan Affair."

Snoopy finds his erstwhile comrade, but it's all for naught as ten thousand bunnies make Agent Thompson an offer he can't refuse. His mission for the Head Beagle comes to an unceremonious end—rabbit-tat-tat!

Snoopy's adventures often required him to disguise himself, and that was always a source of great fun for Charles Schulz. "I'm proud of the way he looks. I think he's well-drawn—not too cute in his appearance. His whole personality is a little bittersweet. But he's a very strong character. He can win or lose, be a disaster, a hero, or anything, and yet it all works out. I like the fact that when he's in real trouble, he can retreat into a fantasy and thereby escape."

ROOT BEER HALL?
No. 3
WHERE IS THE ?
THE HEAD BEAGLE HAS SPOKEN
MUST
OBEY!
No. 5
NUMBER 6
YOU HAVE BEEN SELECTED FOR A SPECIAL ASSIGNMENT
Number 6. (Beagle division)

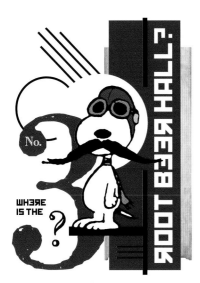

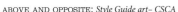

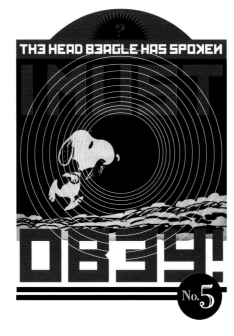

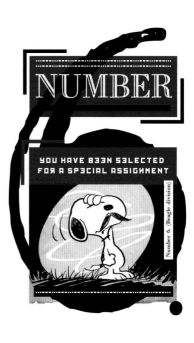

ABOVE AND OPPOSITE: *Style Guide art– CSCA*

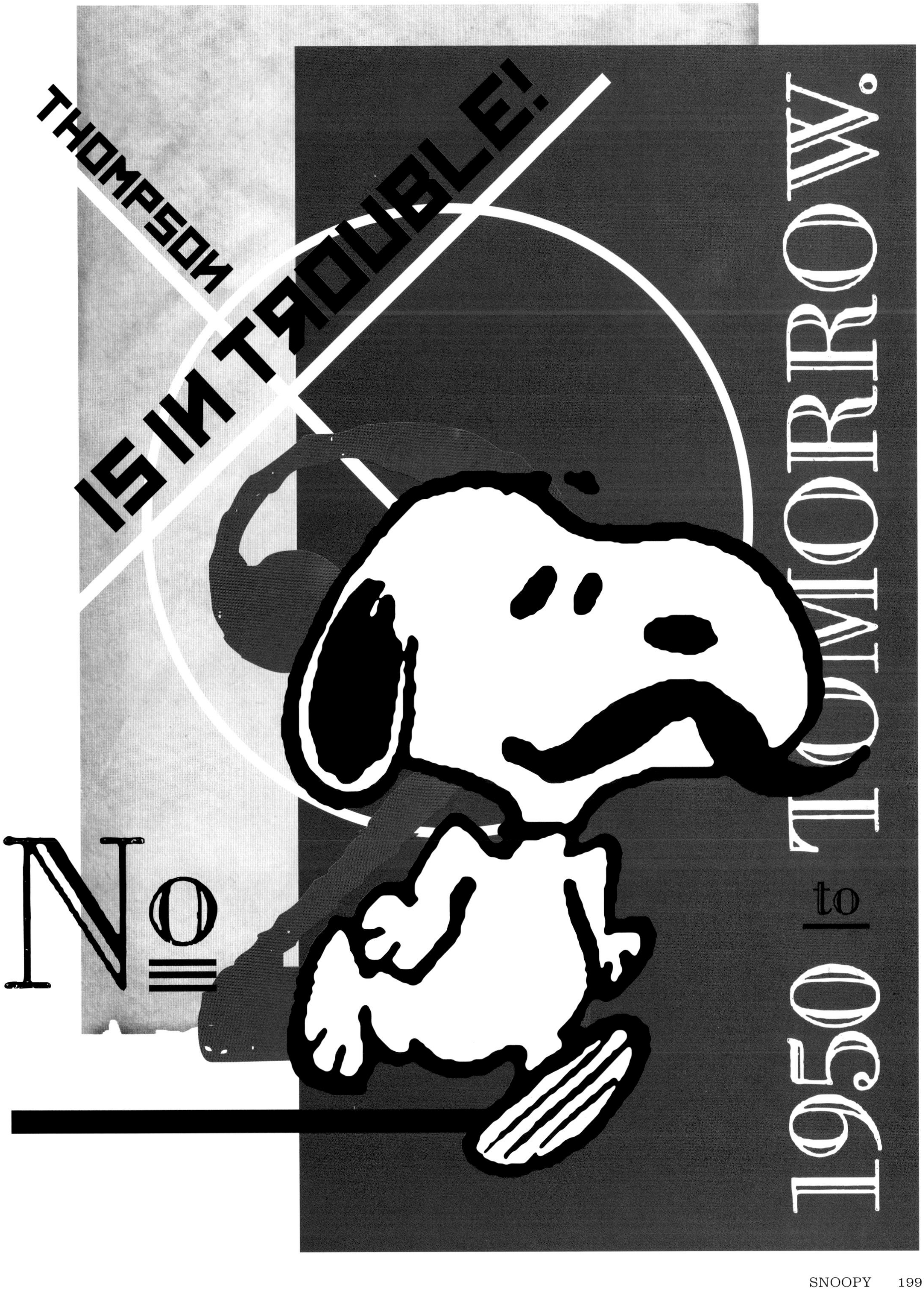
THOMPSON
IS IN TROUBLE!
No
1950 to TOMORROW.

PEANUTS
WOW! WHAT A BIG HOSPITAL!
IF ANY OF THE NURSES CATCH ME, THEY'LL KILL ME... THEY HATE BEAGLES IN HOSPITALS...
LILA?
SNOOPY!!
HI, SWEETIE!
SCHULZ
8-24

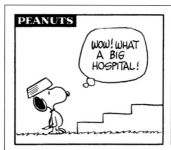

# LILA

FIRST MENTIONED 02/17/1968
FIRST (AND ONLY) APPEARANCE 08/24/1968

Shortly before he finds a home with Charlie Brown, Snoopy has a happy—but brief—stay with Lila, whose family adopts the beagle from the Daisy Hill Puppy Farm. Her family's apartment is too small for the boisterous pup, however, and they reluctantly give him up after a just a few weeks of living in the big city.

For years afterward, the mere mention of Lila's name is enough to put Snoopy through the emotional wringer. The pair finally reconcile when Lila finds herself in the hospital and in need of a good friend.

KING RECORDS
Lila
after all these years
FEATURES THE HITS
"Another letter!"
"Never bug a beagle"
"Lila needs me!"

ABOVE: *Design by Cameron + Co*

PEANUTS
And so, the six Bunny-Wunnies said good night, and went to sleep. Their adventure was over, and all had ended well. The End
THAT WAS THE MOST EXCITING NOVEL I'VE EVER READ... I THINK I'LL WRITE A FAN LETTER TO THE AUTHOR...
" MISS HELEN SWEETSTORY "
SOMEHOW, I HAVE THE FEELING THAT SHE'S A VERY NICE PERSON...
4-9
SCHULZ

PEANUTS
GUESS WHAT I FOUND...
IT'S A MAGAZINE PHOTO-STORY ABOUT YOUR FAVORITE AUTHOR... NOW, YOU'LL GET THE CHANCE TO SEE WHAT SHE LOOKS LIKE..
"MISS HELEN SWEETSTORY, AUTHOR OF THE BUNNY-WUNNIE SERIES, RELAXES HERE IN A PORCH SWING SURROUNDED BY HER TWENTY-FOUR PET.........
.....CATS"!
4-22
SCHULZ

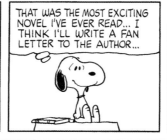

# MISS HELEN SWEETSTORY

FIRST MENTIONED 04/09/1971

Although Snoopy is a student of the classics, the aspiring novelist is well versed in modern literature as well. His favorite contemporary writer is Miss Helen Sweetstory, author of the beloved Bunny-Wunnies books, including *The Six Bunny-Wunnies Go to Long Beach*, *The Six Bunny-Wunnies Make Cookies*, *The Six Bunny-Wunnies Join an Encounter Group*, and the controversial *The Six Bunny-Wunnies Freak Out*, which was temporarily banned from the local school library.

Snoopy strikes up a correspondence with Miss Sweetstory, and although she seems only to respond with form letters, he remains a devoted fan—until he learns that she is the proud owner of twenty-four cats!

A CHARLES M. SCHULZ/HELEN SWEETSTORY COMEDY
Bonjour, Sweetie!
"...poor, sweet baby..." –L. VAN PELT, WDSTK
"...better than SIX BUNNY-WUNNIES: THE MOTION PICTURE..." –JOE SCHLABOTNIK, KPNTS
SCHULZ

ABOVE LEFT: *Spot art from strip – Charles M. Schulz* | ABOVE: Bonjour, Sweetie! Peanuts *Digital Edition – CSCA*

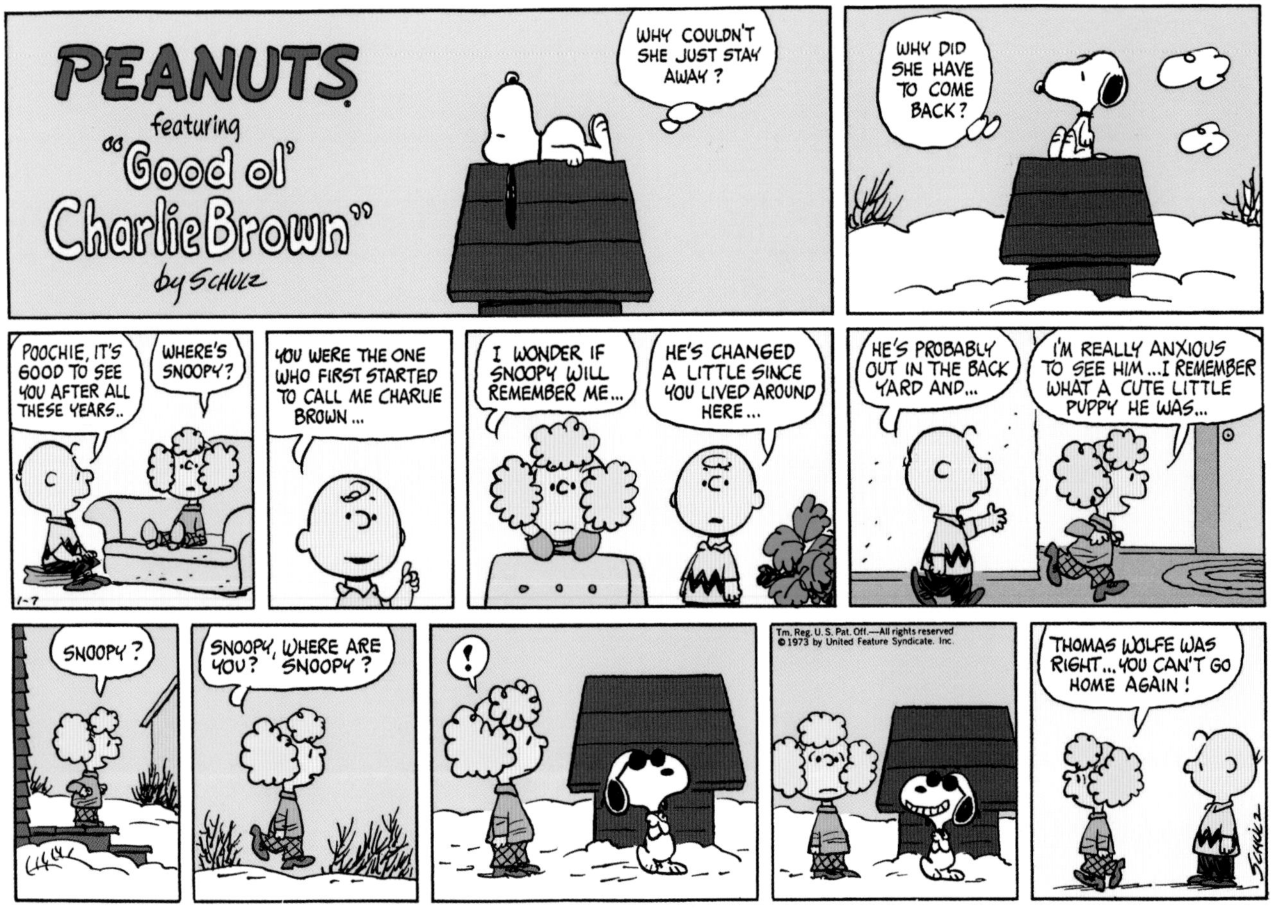
PEANUTS
featuring "Good ol' Charlie Brown"
by Schulz
WHY COULDN'T SHE JUST STAY AWAY ?
WHY DID SHE HAVE TO COME BACK?
POOCHIE, IT'S GOOD TO SEE YOU AFTER ALL THESE YEARS..
WHERE'S SNOOPY?
YOU WERE THE ONE WHO FIRST STARTED TO CALL ME CHARLIE BROWN...
I WONDER IF SNOOPY WILL REMEMBER ME...
HE'S CHANGED A LITTLE SINCE YOU LIVED AROUND HERE...
HE'S PROBABLY OUT IN THE BACK YARD AND...
I'M REALLY ANXIOUS TO SEE HIM...I REMEMBER WHAT A CUTE LITTLE PUPPY HE WAS...
SNOOPY ?
SNOOPY, WHERE ARE YOU? SNOOPY ?
!
Tm. Reg. U.S. Pat. Off.—All rights reserved
©1973 by United Feature Syndicate, Inc.
THOMAS WOLFE WAS RIGHT...YOU CAN'T GO HOME AGAIN !

# POOCHIE

FIRST MENTIONED 12/17/1972
FIRST (AND ONLY) APPEARANCE 01/07/1973

You never forget the girl next door, as hard as you might try. Poochie is responsible for one of Snoopy's earliest heartbreaks, when she cuts short a friendly game of fetch so that she can play with another dog. Poochie returns to the old neighborhood in an attempt to make amends, only to receive a casual dismissal from Snoopy in his "Joe Cool" persona. Confused and dejected, Poochie says farewell to Charlie Brown, noting that, "Thomas Wolfe was right . . . you can't go home again!"

As with many girls from his past, the mere mention of Poochie's name is enough to cause Snoopy indescribable heartache. Although he is a very affectionate and loving beagle, Snoopy can hold on to a grudge like no one else, and it can be very difficult for him to forgive someone who upsets him—especially if he's been rejected for another dog.

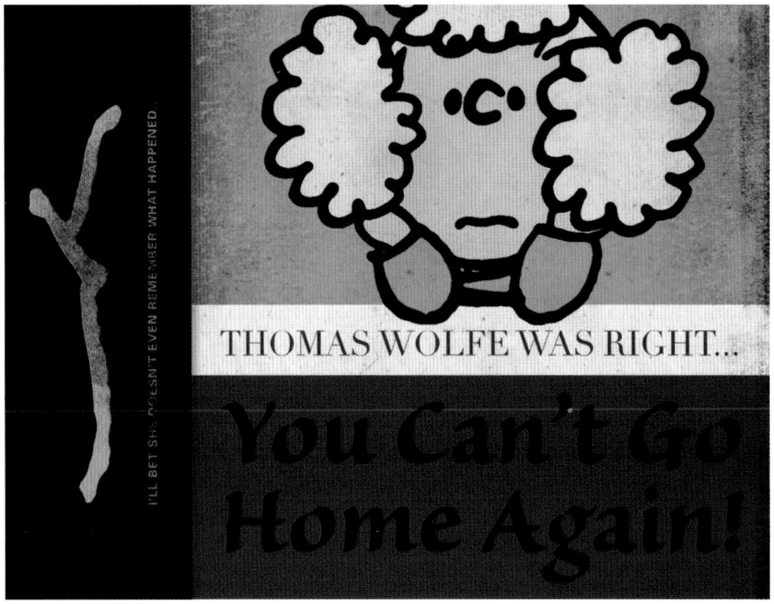
THOMAS WOLFE WAS RIGHT...
You Can't Go Home Again!

PEANUTS
I SEE SOMEONE!
IS IT A RESCUER? MAYBE IT'S SOMEONE COMING TO MUG ME! IT'S BAD ENOUGH BEING LOST WITHOUT GETTING MUGGED, TOO!
5-22
HE'S GETTING CLOSER! I'M TRAPPED! I'M DOOMED!!
HELLO! MY NAME IS LORETTA, AND I'M SELLING GIRL SCOUT COOKIES!
SCHULZ

PEANUTS
THAT'S MY DOG!
WHAT WAS MY DOG DOING HERE?
7-27
OH, EXCUSE ME...MY NAME IS CHARLIE BROWN, AND...
MY NAME IS LORETTA... WOULD YOU LIKE TO BUY SOME GIRL SCOUT COOKIES?
SCHULZ

# LORETTA

FIRST APPEARANCE 05/22/1974

Whether she is at the most happening party of the year or is hundreds of miles from civilization, Loretta always has a smile on her face, and she is always ready to sell you some Girl Scout Cookies. Although Charlie Brown is less than thrilled with her sales pitch, Snoopy puts up with just about anything if there 's even the slightest chance it will end with cookies.

7
4

OPPOSITE AND RIGHT: *Design by Cameron + Co*

PEANUTS
MY BROTHER HAS ARISEN!
EGGS BENEDICT FOR MY BROTHER, SPIKE!
I THINK YOU'D BETTER MAKE THAT TEN POUNDS OF BUFFALO STEAK...
8-13
SCHULZ

## SPIKE

FIRST APPEARANCE
08/13/1975

SPIKE
NEEDLES

Snoopy's older brother, Spike, does his best to keep himself occupied in the isolated desert on the outskirts of Needles, California, but his surroundings are a far cry from his carefree days at the Daisy Hill Puppy Farm. With only the minimal surrounding vegetation and wildlife to keep him company, Spike relies on his imagination and long philosophical discussions with random cacti to maintain his somewhat tenuous grasp on reality.

Due to the harsh conditions in the desert, Spike is rarely without his trademark fedora and, on occasion, a pair of comfortable yellow shoes supposedly gifted to him by Mickey Mouse. The slender, sleepy-eyed beagle doesn't leave his desert home very often, but sometimes makes the long cross-country trek to visit Snoopy and his family. Although several people have tried to adopt him over the years, the desert is his home, and he feels that it needs him as much as he needs it. After all, without him, who would run the Cactus Club's regular meetings?

One of the rare recurring characters who lives far away from the main cast, Spike, along with his desert home, is an indelible part of the *Peanuts* cast. "Spike, Snoopy's brother, is a beautiful example of images evoked by a location," observed Charles Schulz. "We know he lives with the coyotes outside Needles, and that's about all we know. There is about him, with his thin, faintly exotic mustache and soulful eyes, an air of mystery that is totally foreign to what Snoopy is. Our imagination takes over."

Charles M. Schulz
PEANUTS
SCHULZ

DID I EVER TELL YOU ABOUT WHAT HAPPENED TO ME ONE TIME WHEN I WAS IN LOUISVILLE?
WOULD YOU LIKE TO HEAR ABOUT IT?
Z
7-2
© 1984 United Feature Syndicate, Inc.
SCHULZ

LOOK, I GOT MYSELF A SLEEPING BAG..
I'M TIRED OF BEING COLD AT NIGHT
I WONDER WHO DESIGNS THESE THINGS..
2-11
© 1994 United Feature Syndicate, Inc.
SCHULZ

THE COLLECTED STRIPS
You're the Cactus Club President, Spike!
Charles M. Schulz
A PEANUTS DIGITAL EDITION

# JOE CACTUS

FIRST APPEARANCE 10/17/1983

"I guess we all just need someone to talk to," Spike writes Snoopy in a letter explaining his solitary life in the desert and his newfound friendship with Joe Cactus. Their conversations are very one-sided, but Spike is very appreciative of his prickly friend's listening skills and his reliability. When Spike wants a partner for basketball, bridge, or a footrace, he knows that he need look no further than his faithful cactus.

Spike includes the cactus in all of his celebrations, adorning it with Christmas lights and other festive decorations throughout the year. Snoopy worries about his brother's sanity at times, especially when he receives a Christmas card signed from both of them: Spike and Joe Cactus. No matter what anyone else thinks, Spike knows that his cactus will always be there for him.

OPPOSITE, TOP: *Spot art from strip – Charles M. Schulz* | OPPOSITE BOTTOM: Peanuts, *Issue #11, Boom! Studios – CSCA* | LEFT: You're the Cactus Club President! Peanuts *Digital Edition – CSCA*

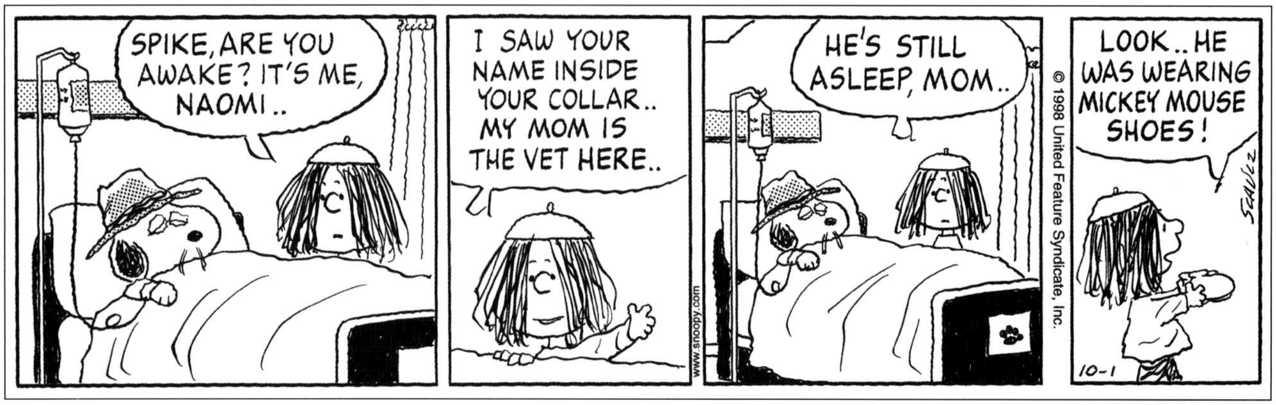
SPIKE, ARE YOU AWAKE? IT'S ME, NAOMI..
I SAW YOUR NAME INSIDE YOUR COLLAR.. MY MOM IS THE VET HERE..
www.snoopy.com
HE'S STILL ASLEEP, MOM..
© 1998 United Feature Syndicate, Inc.
LOOK.. HE WAS WEARING MICKEY MOUSE SHOES!
SCHULZ
10-1

# NAOMI

FIRST APPEARANCE
10/01/1998

A native of Needles, California, Naomi first meets Spike when he tires of life in the desert and ventures into the city to find "a nice Hollywood-type girl" to adopt him. When Naomi discovers him outside her mother's animal clinic, she bring him into the hospital for bedrest and tapioca pudding (the snack, not the aspiring movie star).

Naomi falls for the scruffy beagle during his hospital stay, but her mother asks her to return him to his desert home once he's well enough to be discharged. Although he's sad that he isn't able to find a permanent home with Naomi, Spike realizes that the desert will always be his home, and his cacti will always need him.

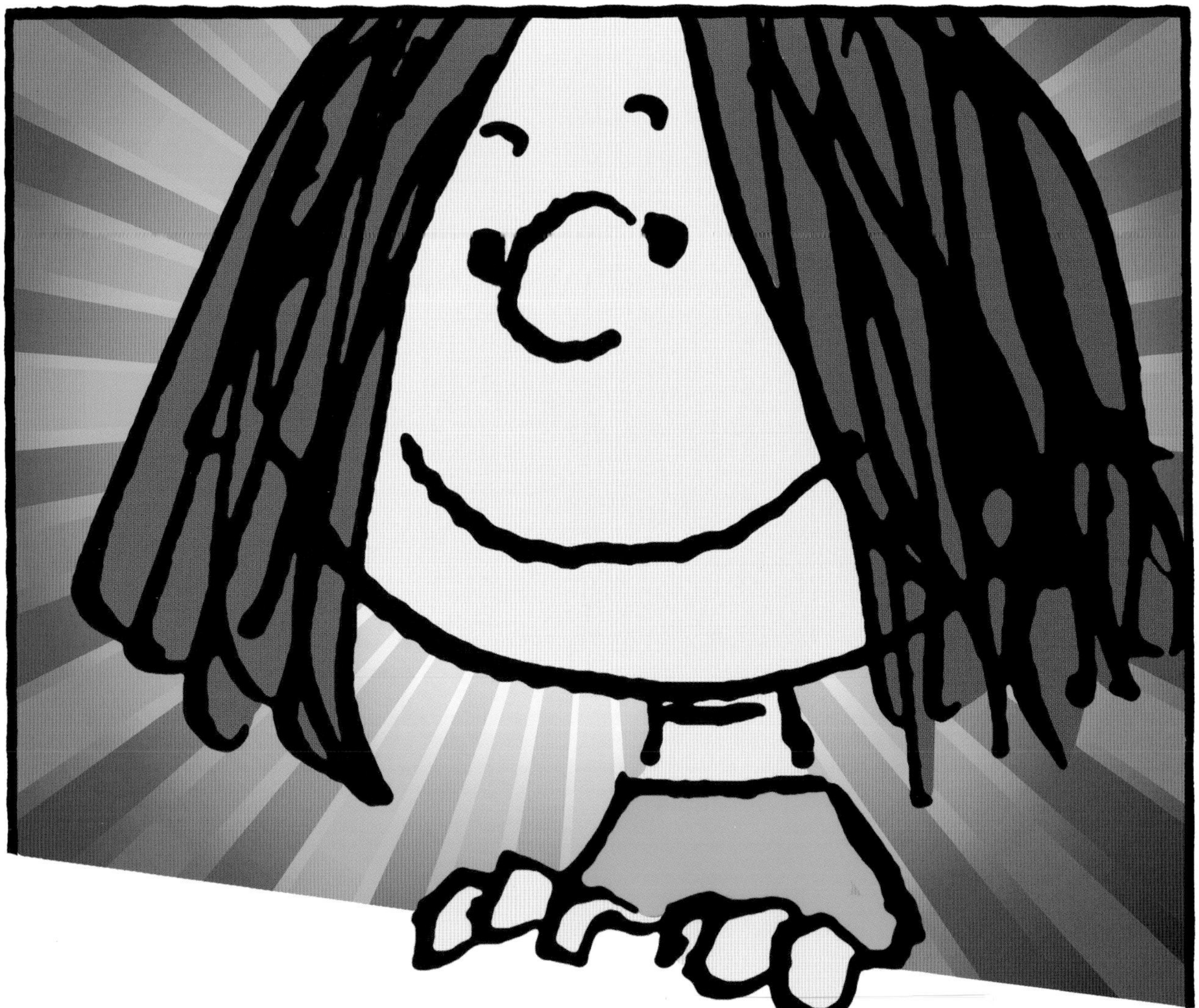

PEANUTS
I WONDER WHAT A DOG THINKS ABOUT WHEN HE SITS AND STARES LIKE THAT..
I CAN'T IMAGINE... THAT'S JUST ONE OF THOSE THINGS WE'LL NEVER KNOW...
5-4
SOMETIMES I MISS THE OL' PUPPY FARM!
SCHULZ

I DON'T KNOW WHEN MY BIRTHDAY IS, AND I DON'T KNOW HOW OLD I AM..
9-28
www.unitedmedia.com
AND THE DAISY HILL PUPPY FARM ISN'T THERE ANYMORE! EVERYTHING'S GONE!
© 1996 United Feature Syndicate, Inc.
NO, I'M STILL HERE..
SCHULZ

# DAISY HILL PUPPY FARM

FIRST MENTIONED 05/04/1965

Snoopy and his siblings were born at the Daisy Hill Puppy Farm, a scenic country home where puppies are bred and sold. Although Snoopy was only a few months old when he left, he has always taken pride in his upbringing as a Daisy Hill Puppy, and was once invited to return to his alma mater to deliver a speech to the young puppies in residence there. Unfortunately, Snoopy's visit was a tumultuous one, as a full-scale riot broke out before he could deliver his address.

Snoopy's next visit to the Daisy Hill Puppy Farm was even more traumatic, as he and Woodstock discovered that the entire farm had been paved over and replaced with a six-story parking garage. Snoopy briefly consoles himself that it may, in fact, have been a huge monument erected to mark the place of his birth, but Woodstock is quick to dispel that notion, and confirms that it was, in fact, a six-story parking garage. Maybe it is true that you can't go home again.

THE COLLECTED STRIPS
Charles M. Schulz
THE DAISY HILL PUPPIES
A PEANUTS DIGITAL EDITION

OPPOSITE: *Design by Cameron + Co*
RIGHT: Daisy Hill Puppies, Peanuts *Digital Edition – CSCA*

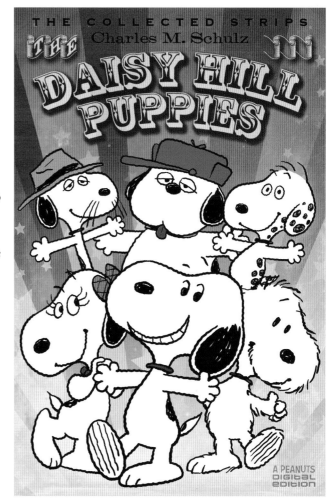

IF WE'RE A COUPLE OF FARM DOGS, OLAF, DON'T YOU THINK WE SHOULD BE DOING SOMETHING?
DON'T YOU THINK WE SHOULD BE USEFUL?
WE ARE USEFUL..
© 1994 United Feature Syndicate, Inc.
IF WE MOVE, THE BARN WILL FALL DOWN..
SCHULZ
5-2

## OLAF FIRST APPEARANCE 01/24/1989 & ANDY FIRST APPEARANCE 02/14/1994

Snoopy's brother Olaf comes back into his life when the local newspaper announces an Ugly Dog contest and Lucy is determined to find the winning canine. Charlie Brown shares Snoopy's family album, and they agree that his heavy-set brother, Olaf, should have no problem taking the top prize.

The self-conscious Olaf, cruelly nicknamed "Ugly Olaf" as a pup, arrives wearing a paper sack over his head. When he is unmasked, he is the judges' unanimous choice, earning Lucy a nice trophy and earning Olaf a nice bone. The trip gives him the opportunity to reconnect with Snoopy, at least, and the brothers share a fun week together before Olaf returns to his family's farm.

Years later, when Snoopy is hospitalized with a sudden illness, his brothers Spike, Olaf, and Andy rush to his bedside for an impromptu family reunion. The four reminisce, comfort each other, and, expectedly, help Snoopy eat his meals before suddenly disappearing. Charlie Brown is surprised by this behavior, but as the nonplused Snoopy observes, "Dogs don't say 'goodbye.'"

Following this visit, Spike returns to the desert while Andy and Olaf attempt to make their way back to their farm. The duo decide to visit Spike in Needles, California, but their poor navigation skills ("Two right turns and twenty-three wrong ones," Olaf notes) and questionable logic invariably lead them clear around the world, from the outskirts of Hollywood to the igloos of Alaska. No matter how far they roam, they always seem to find themselves back on Snoopy's doorstep.

Charles Schulz modeled Andy's shaggy appearance on his own dog, a wire-haired terrier named Andy. Snoopy's brother also holds the distinction of being the only *Peanuts* character to debut in animation before appearing in the strip. His first appearance was in the television special *Snoopy's Reunion*, which originally aired in 1991.

ABOVE: *Spot art from strip – Charles M. Schulz* | OPPOSITE: *Style Guide art – CSCA*

PEANUTS
?
HEY! THIS DOG LOOKS LIKE BELLE!
BELLE? YOU KNOW BELLE?
SEE? HE LOOKS JUST LIKE THAT BEAGLE IN THE NEXT BLOCK...
BEAGLE?
6-28
BELLE!!!
SCHULZ

# BELLE

FIRST APPEARANCE
06/28/1976

Snoopy's sister Belle lives in Kansas City, Missouri, with her teenage son, who bears a striking resemblance to the Pink Panther. Their family reunion takes place when Snoopy, who has been under the mistaken impression that the Wimbledon tennis tournament is held near Kansas City (and not, as Charlie Brown informs him, in England), decides to look up his sister, whom he hasn't seen since their childhood at the Daisy Hill Puppy Farm.

Their next visit, interestingly enough, takes place in France, when Snoopy—as the World War I Flying Ace—meets Belle, serving as a nurse for the Red Cross, in a small tavern near the front line. The pair are joined by Spike, who is serving in the infantry, and they enjoy a nice evening together reminiscing and sharing root beer and doughnuts. Snoopy sends a photograph of the joyous reunion to his parents, noting, "And that's the story of how two soldiers and their sister met in France during World War I. And I don't care if anyone believes me or not."

PEANUTS
"I SAID GOODBYE TO MY SISTER TODAY"
"WE HADN'T SEEN EACH OTHER FOR YEARS, AND MY VISIT WAS MUCH TOO SHORT"
7-1
"NEEDLESS TO SAY, OUR FAREWELL WAS TEARFUL"
SNIF
SCHULZ
Tm. Reg. U.S. Pat. Off.—All rights reserved © 1976 by United Feature Syndicate, Inc.

SO YOU'RE "MARBLES"
I KNOW YOUR WEIRD BROTHER
© 1982 United Feature Syndicate, Inc.
9/28
WELL, ANYWAY, HE AN' CHUCK ARE ON THEIR WAY OVER.. COME ON INSIDE, AND WAIT...
ANY CATS IN THERE ?
SCHULZ

# MARBLES

FIRST APPEARANCE
09/28/1982

Snoopy describes his brother Marbles, named for his speckled fur, as "the smart one in the family." Despite his intelligence, Marbles lacks the wit and imagination of his brother, as evidenced during one of their rare visits together. In his guise as the World War I Flying Ace, Snoopy invites his brother to ride with him atop his Sopwith Camel, but Marbles doesn't understand Snoopy's adventures and soon leaves for home, confused by his brother's antics. Marbles never really understands his brother, and the feeling seems mutual. Snoopy meets news of Marbles's departure with a shrug and an immediate return to his World War I Flying Ace persona.

"It's possible, I think, to make a mistake in the strip and without realizing it, destroy it," Charles Schulz noted, when reflecting on the expansion of his cast. "I realized it myself a couple of years ago when I began to introduce Snoopy's brothers and sisters. I realized that when I put Belle and Marbles in there it destroyed the relationship that Snoopy has with the kids, which is a very strange relationship."

SNOOPY! MARBLES!
AREN'T FAMILY REUNIONS SOMETHING, CHUCK? TWO BROTHERS, WHO HAVEN'T SEEN EACH OTHER FOR YEARS, ARE SUDDENLY REUNITED!
JUST THINK OF THE MILLIONS OF THINGS THEY HAVE TO TALK ABOUT
© 1982 United Feature Syndicate, Inc.
9-30
HOW'VE YOU BEEN?
FINE..HOW HAVE YOU BEEN?
SCHULZ

TOP: *Spot art from strip – Charles M. Schulz* | OPPOSITE: *Design by Cameron + Co*

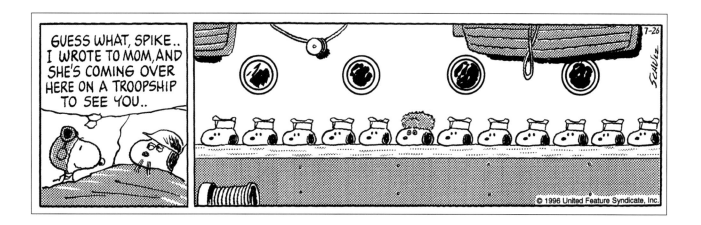

GUESS WHAT, SPIKE..
I WROTE TO MOM, AND
SHE'S COMING OVER
HERE ON A TROOPSHIP
TO SEE YOU..
7-26
SCHULZ
© 1996 United Feature Syndicate, Inc.

# SNOOPY'S FATHER & MOTHER

FIRST (AND ONLY) APPEARANCE 06/18/1989

FIRST (AND ONLY) APPEARANCE 07/26/1996

Snoopy's parents may live far away, but they're never far from his thoughts. Each Father's Day, he sends a card to his father in Florida—and one year he got all seven of his siblings to sign it, too!

Snoopy's Mother appears in the strip only once, in a World War I story related by Snoopy. When Spike is bedridden with the flu, he asks his brother, the World War I Flying Ace, to send word to their mother about his illness. She receives an urgent letter from Snoopy then travels overseas in a troopship to see her sons. Lucy finds the whole story implausible and wonders how Snoopy's mother returned home after her visit. The answer, Snoopy wistfully notes, is "Mom stayed in Paris after the War . . . but that's another story."

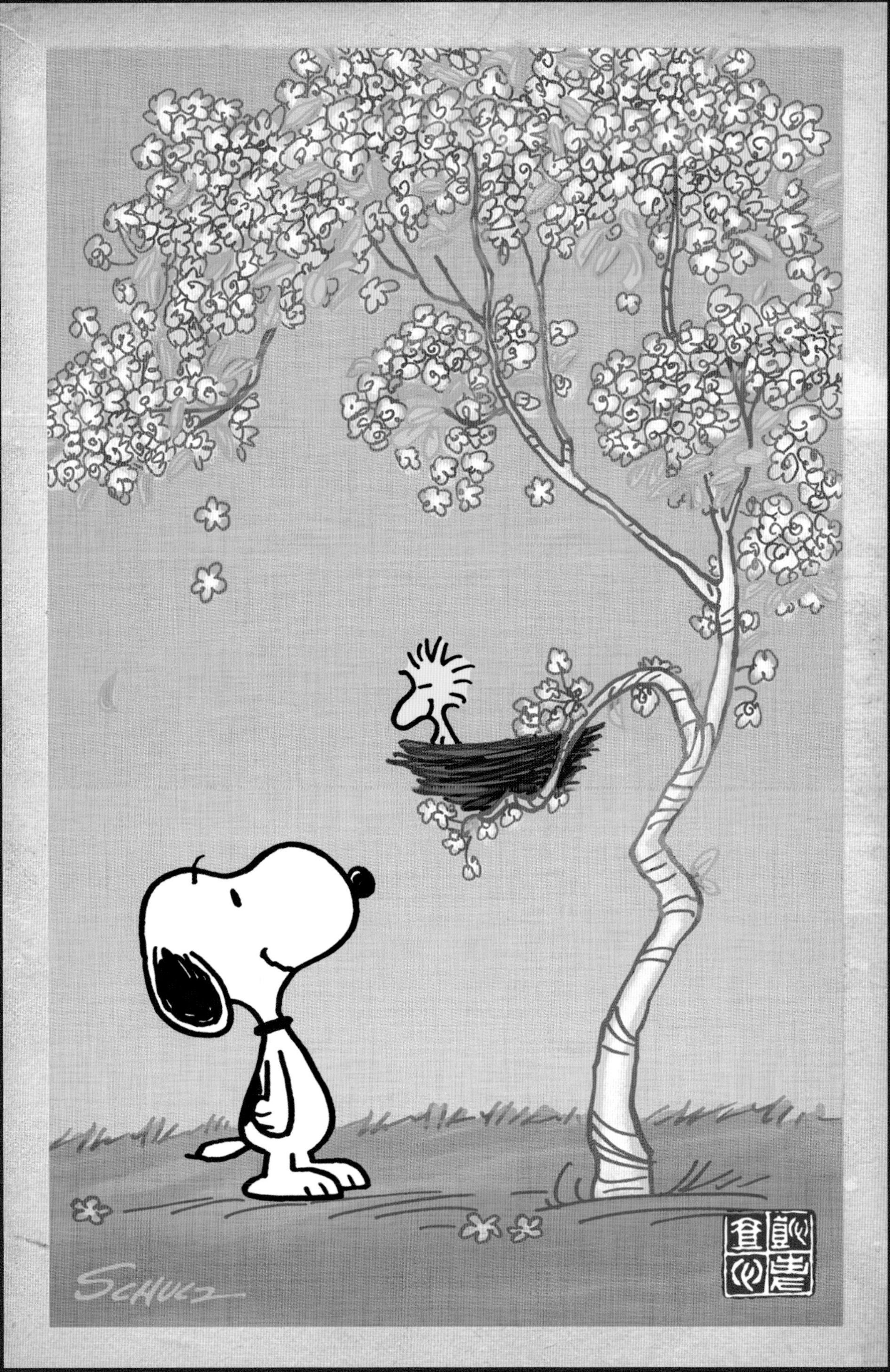
SCHULZ

# WOODSTOCK

FIRST APPEARANCE 04/04/1967
FIRST NAMED 06/22/1970

Woodstock, Snoopy's "Friend of Friends," first flitter-flutters into Snoopy's life after a long flight and settles in for a nap on top of his nose. Despite his unique topsy-turvy flying style and a questionable sense of direction, the World War I Flying Ace immediately recruits Woodstock as the official mechanic for his Sopwith Camel, and the pair have been best friends ever since. Oddly enough, they were friends for several years before Snoopy learned that his friend's name was "Woodstock," just like the 1969 summer music festival.

Woodstock may be small in stature, but he has a big heart and bristles with confidence, from his shaggy moptop to his oversized feet. He never shies away from one of Snoopy's adventures, whether he's piloting the fearless beagle as a helicopter, hiking through the woods with the Beagle Scouts, or downing root beers on New Year's Eve.

"Woodstock knows that he is very small and inconsequential indeed," related Charles Schulz. "It's a problem we all have. The universe boggles us. In the larger scheme, we suddenly realize, we amount to very little. It's frightening. Only a certain maturity will make us able to cope. The minute we abandon the quest for it we leave ourselves open to tragic results. Woodstock is a lighthearted expression of that idea."

眠
Sleepy

すぬーぴー

うっどすとっく

PEANUTS
!
flitter flutter flitter flutter flitter flutter
whew!
GASP GASP
Z
MUST HAVE BEEN A ROUGH FLIGHT
SCHULZ

OPPOSITE: *Comic-Con 2012 postcard – CSCA* | ABOVE: *Style Guide art – PW*

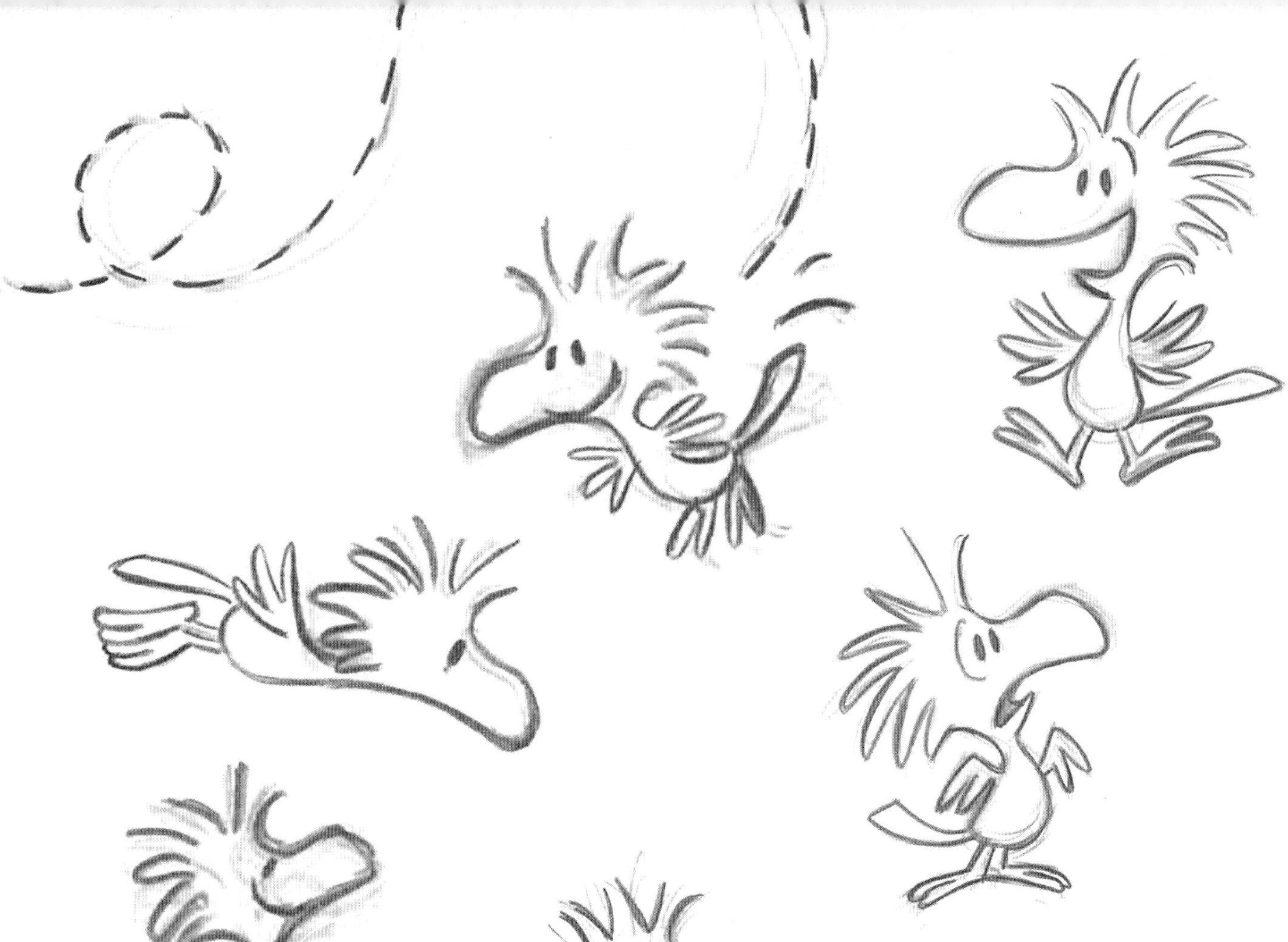

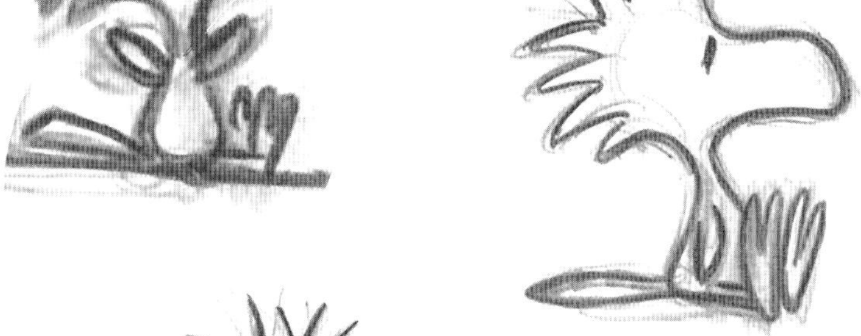

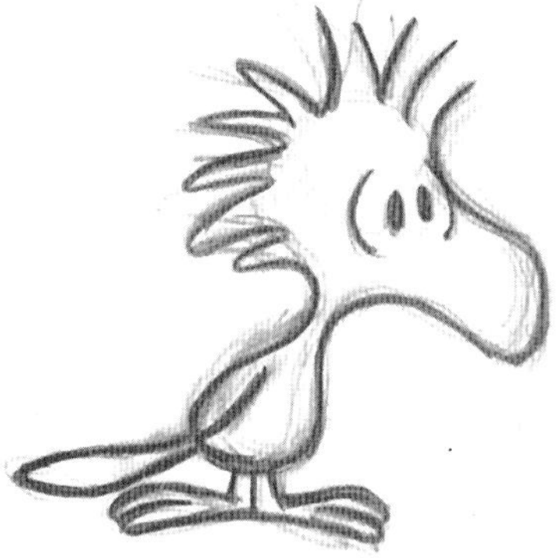

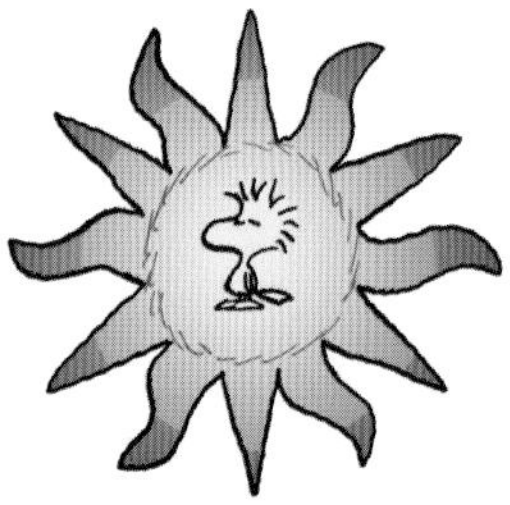

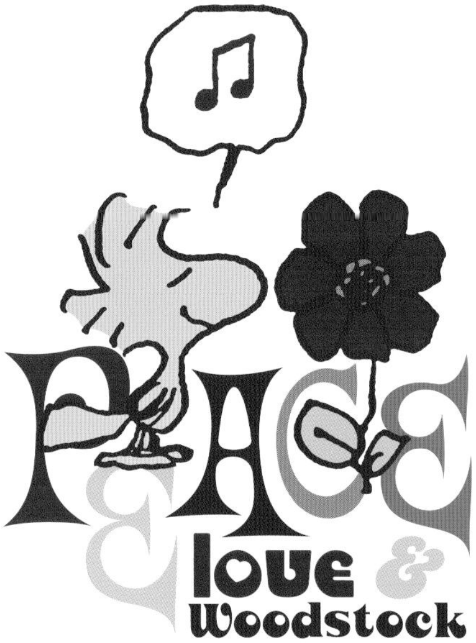
PEACE
love &
Woodstock

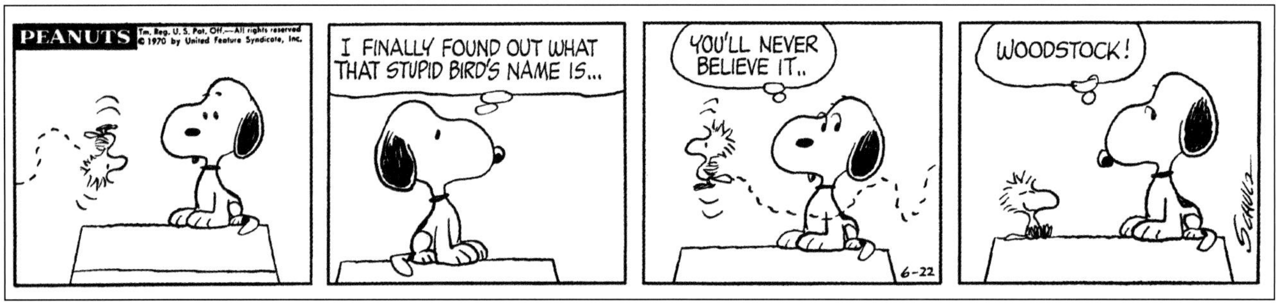
PEANUTS
Tm. Reg. U. S. Pat. Off.—All rights reserved © 1970 by United Feature Syndicate, Inc.
I FINALLY FOUND OUT WHAT THAT STUPID BIRD'S NAME IS...
YOU'LL NEVER BELIEVE IT..
6-22
WOODSTOCK!
SCHULZ

ABOVE LEFT: *Woodstock model sheet – CSCA* | ABOVE RIGHT: *Style Guide art – PW* | OPPOSITE: *Comic-Con poster – CSCA*

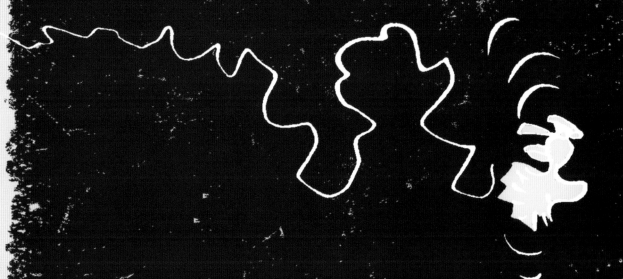

san diego comic-con® 2011

# far out

# THE BEST FRIEND

Woodstock and Snoopy have been friends from their first meeting, when the funny little bird fluttered onto Snoopy's nose and decided to set up a permanent residence near his beagle pal's doghouse. The pair have risked life an limb for each other, and each considers the other to be his "friend of friends."

Charles Schulz had drawn many little birds into the strip over the years, but one in particular stood out from the rest. "He appeared gradually as I discovered I was drawing this one little bird more and more. It seemed only natural to call him Woodstock. He's Snoopy's friend and confidant. He just worships Snoopy and would do anything for him, even type his letters for him."

SON
IC B
LAH

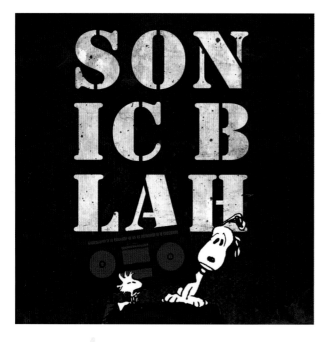

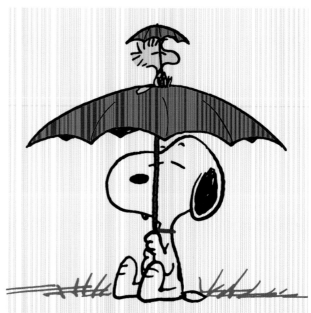

"Oh Woodstock, my little friend of friends . . . Don't you realize your heart is worth much much more than six dollars?!!" —Snoopy

PEANUTS
Tm. Reg. U. S. Pat. Off.—All rights reserved © 1972 by United Feature Syndicate, Inc.
3-11
!!!!
POOR WOODSTOCK...WORMS ARE ALWAYS PICKING ON HIM
!
SCHULZ

PEANUTS
HERE.. THIS CAME FOR YOU
1-26
AH! A LETTER FROM WOODSTOCK.. HE'S AWAY AT WORM SCHOOL...
WHAT A NICE WAY TO BEGIN A LETTER..
" DEAR FRIEND OF FRIENDS... "
SCHULZ

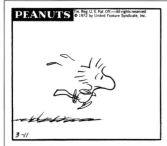

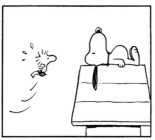

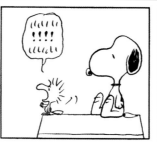

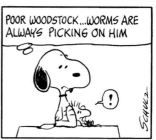

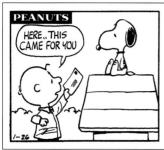

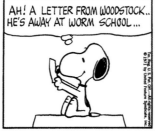

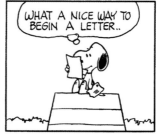

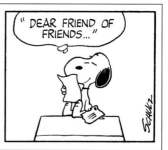

TOP, LEFT AND RIGHT: *Style Guide art - CSCA* | OPPOSITE: *Style Guide art - PW*

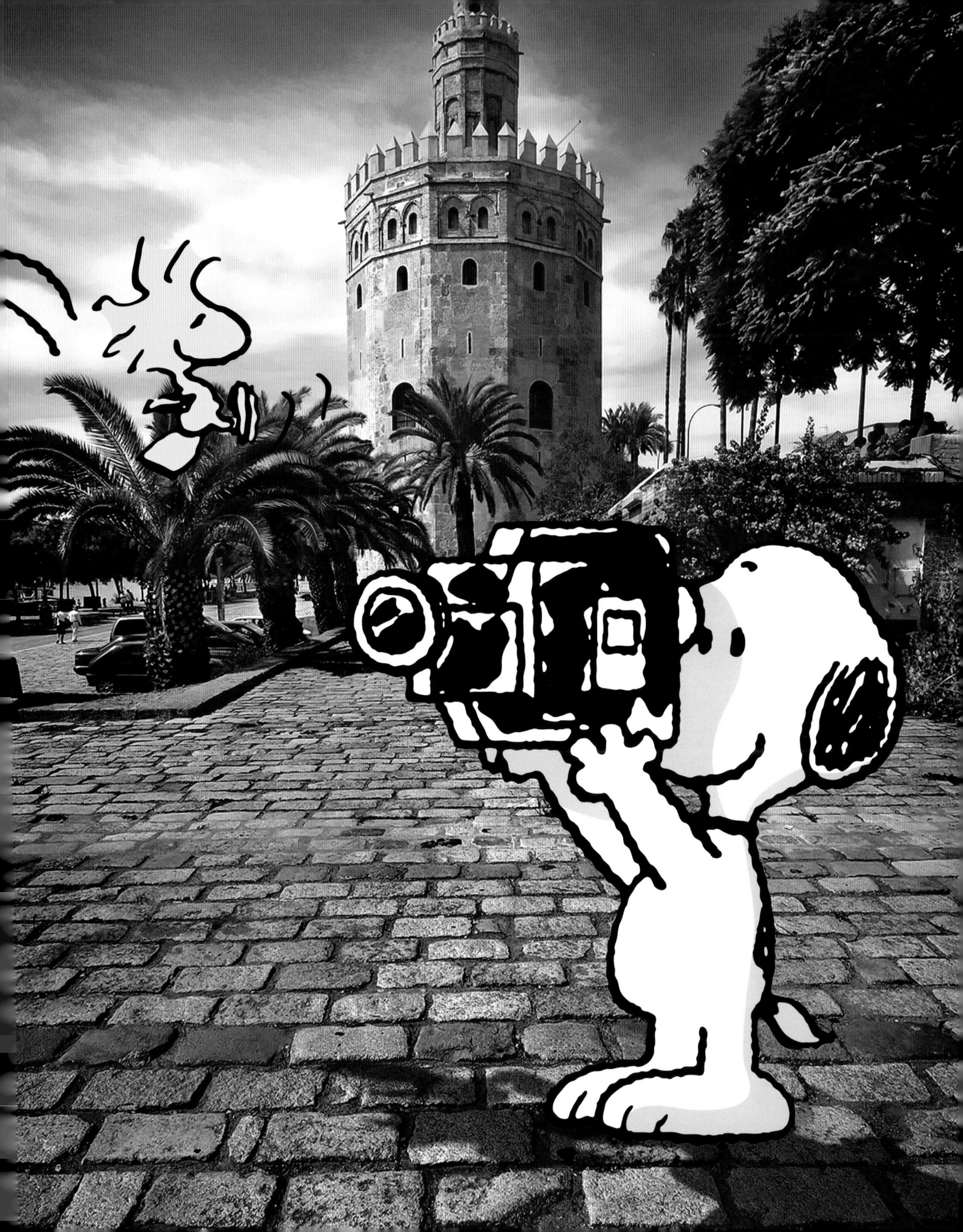

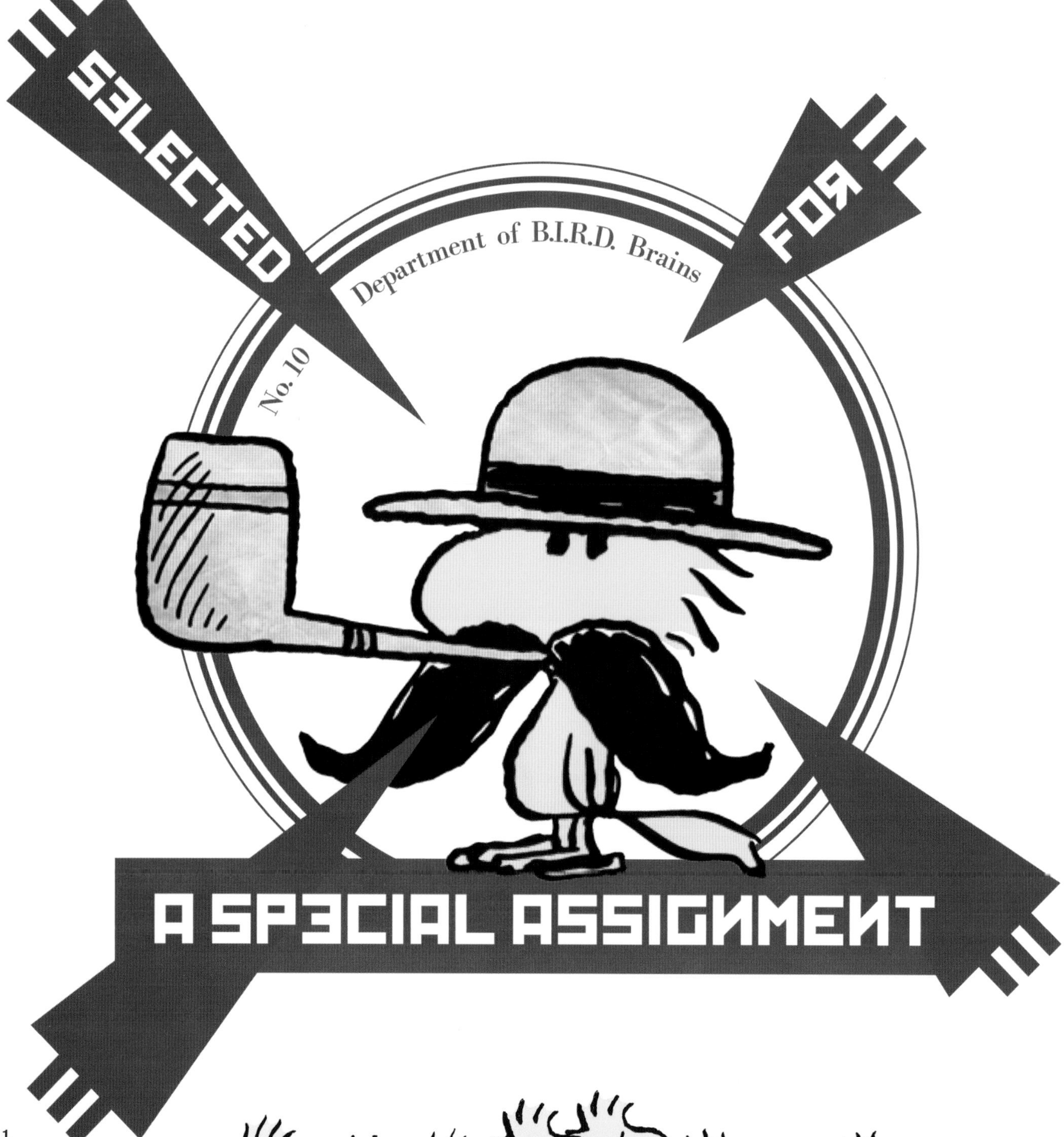
S∃LECTED
FOЯ
Department of B.I.R.D. Brains
No. 10
A SP∃CIAL ASSIGИMEИT

1

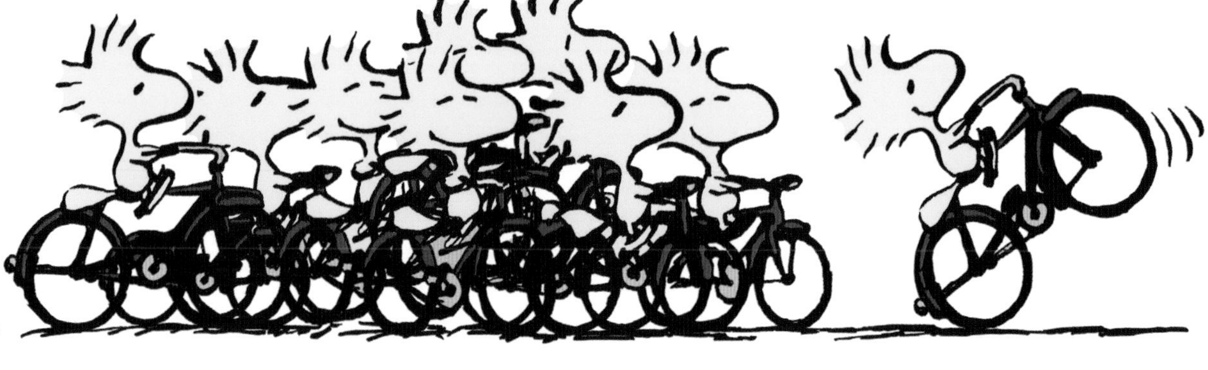

2

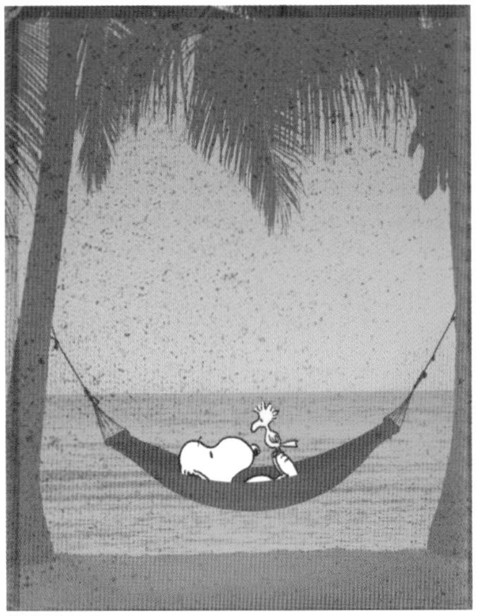

3

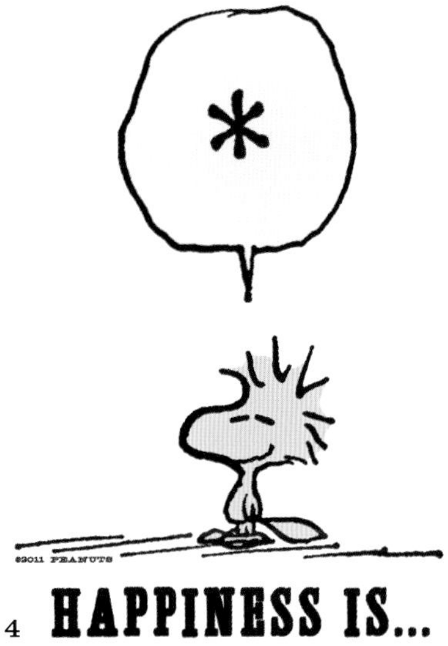
*
©2011 PEANUTS
HAPPINESS IS...

4

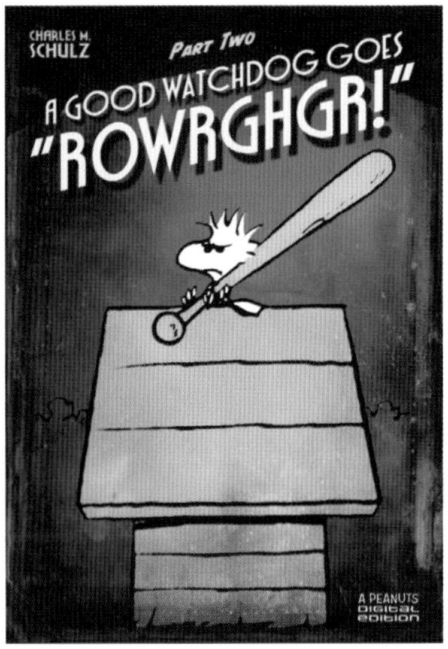
CHARLES M. SCHULZ
PART TWO
A GOOD WATCHDOG GOES
"ROWRGHGR!"
A PEANUTS DIGITAL EDITION

5

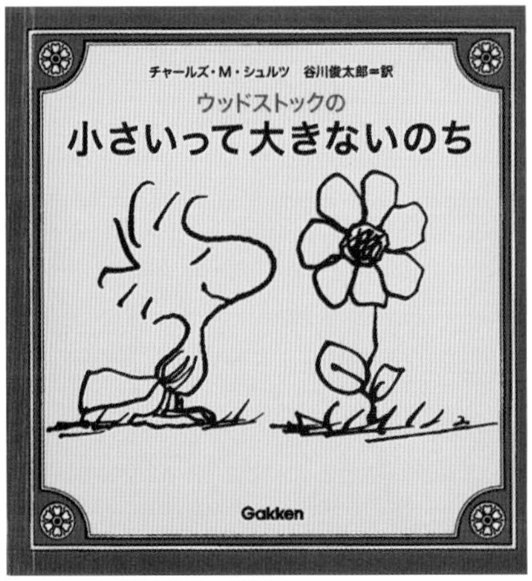
チャールズ・M・シュルツ　谷川俊太郎＝訳
ウッドストックの
小さいって大きないのち
Gakken

6

*1, 2, 4, 8: Style Guide art – CSCA; 3: Style Guide art – PW; 5:* A Good Watchdog Goes "ROWRGHGR!" Peanuts *Digital Edition – CSCA; 6: Cover for* Small is Beautiful *– Gakken; 7: Spot art from strip – Charles M. Schulz*

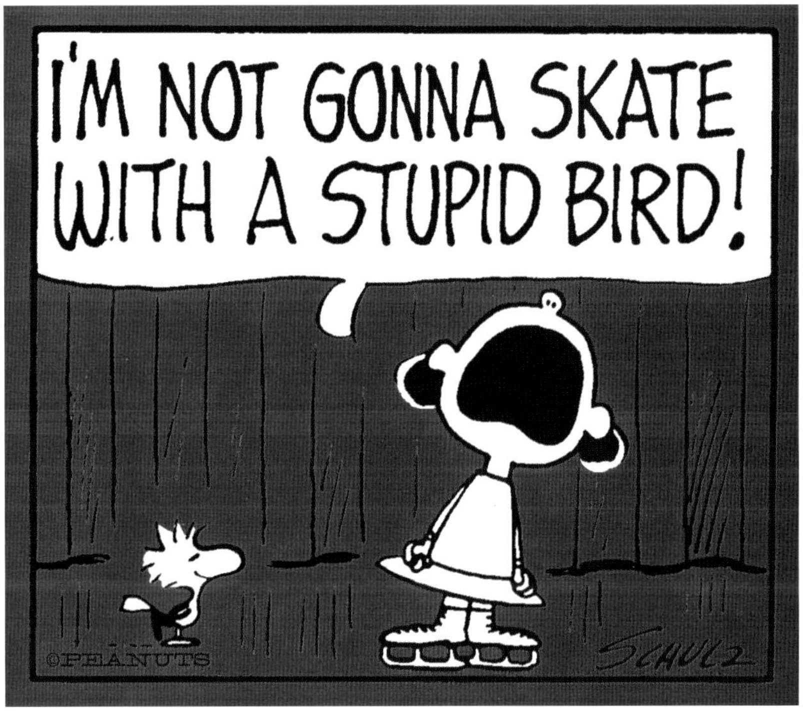
I'M NOT GONNA SKATE WITH A STUPID BIRD!
©PEANUTS
SCHULZ

7

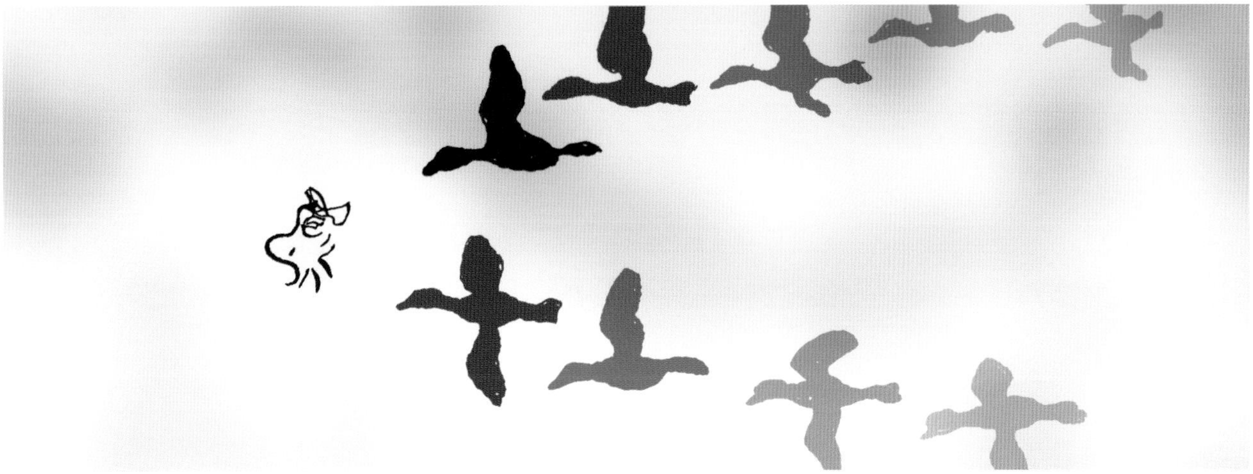

8

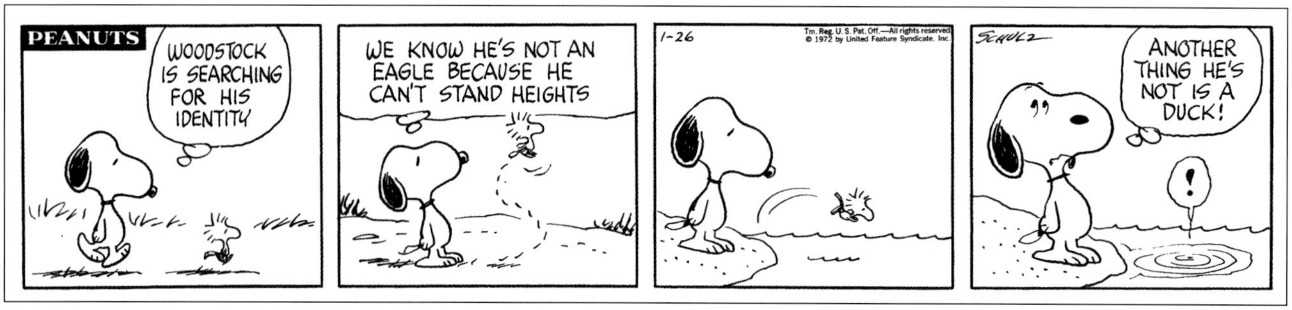
PEANUTS
WOODSTOCK IS SEARCHING FOR HIS IDENTITY
WE KNOW HE'S NOT AN EAGLE BECAUSE HE CAN'T STAND HEIGHTS
1-26
Tm. Reg. U.S. Pat. Off.—All rights reserved © 1972 by United Feature Syndicate, Inc.
SCHULZ
ANOTHER THING HE'S NOT IS A DUCK!
!

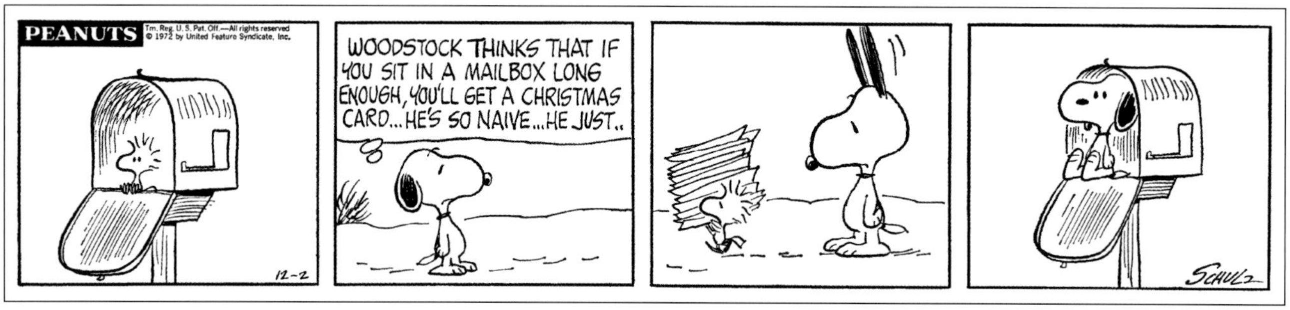
PEANUTS
Tm. Reg. U.S. Pat. Off.—All rights reserved © 1972 by United Feature Syndicate, Inc.
12-2
WOODSTOCK THINKS THAT IF YOU SIT IN A MAILBOX LONG ENOUGH, YOU'LL GET A CHRISTMAS CARD... HE'S SO NAIVE... HE JUST..
SCHULZ

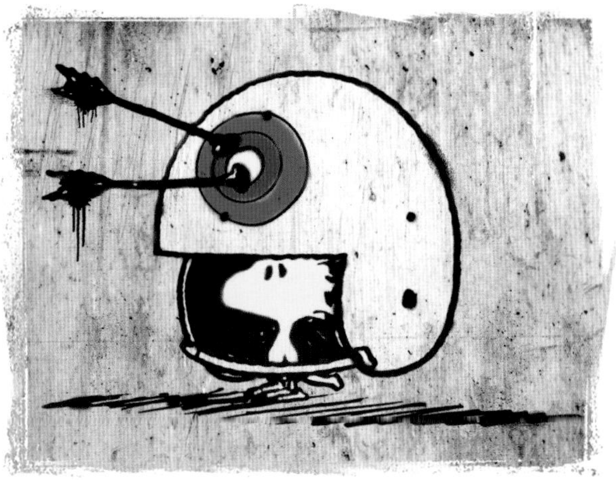

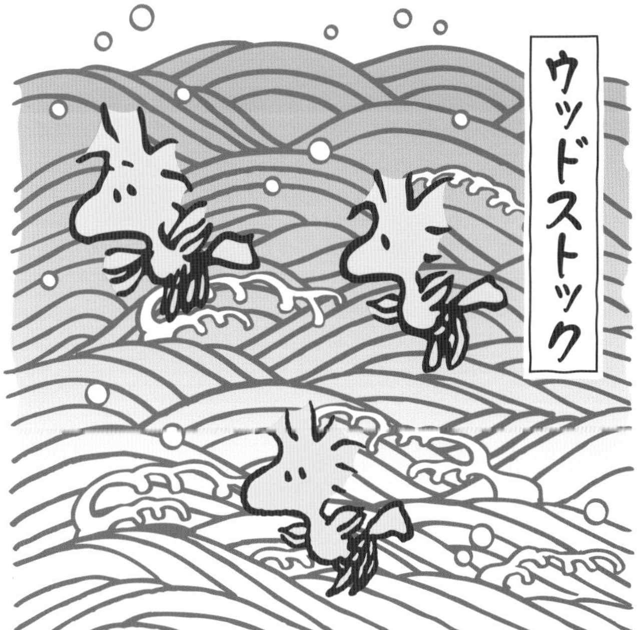
ウッドストック

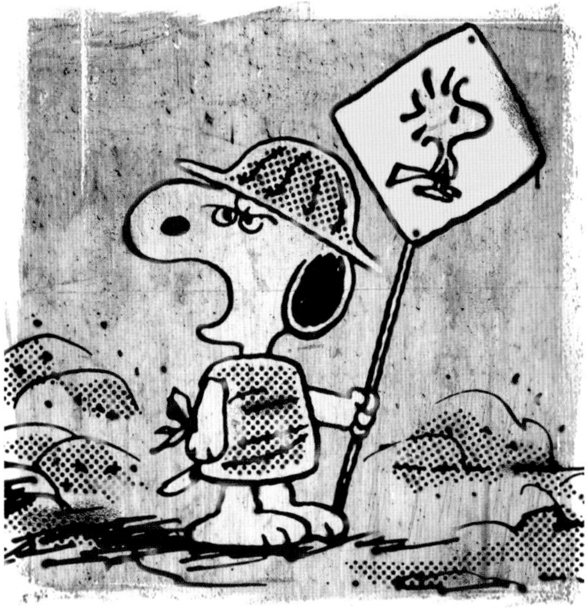

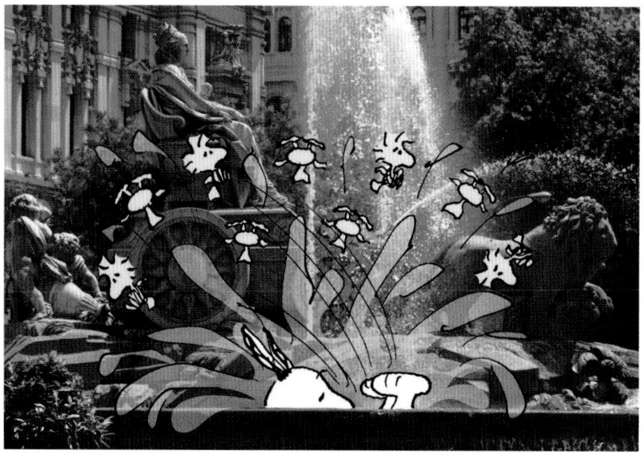

TOP AND BOTTOM LEFT: *Style Guide art – CSCA* | TOP AND BOTTOM RIGHT: *Style Guide art – PW* | OPPOSITE: *"Bend a Little, Pick Up a Lot" environmental poster, created by the US Department of the Interior, 1972 – CMSM*

Johnny Horizon
ENVIRONMENTAL
PROGRAM

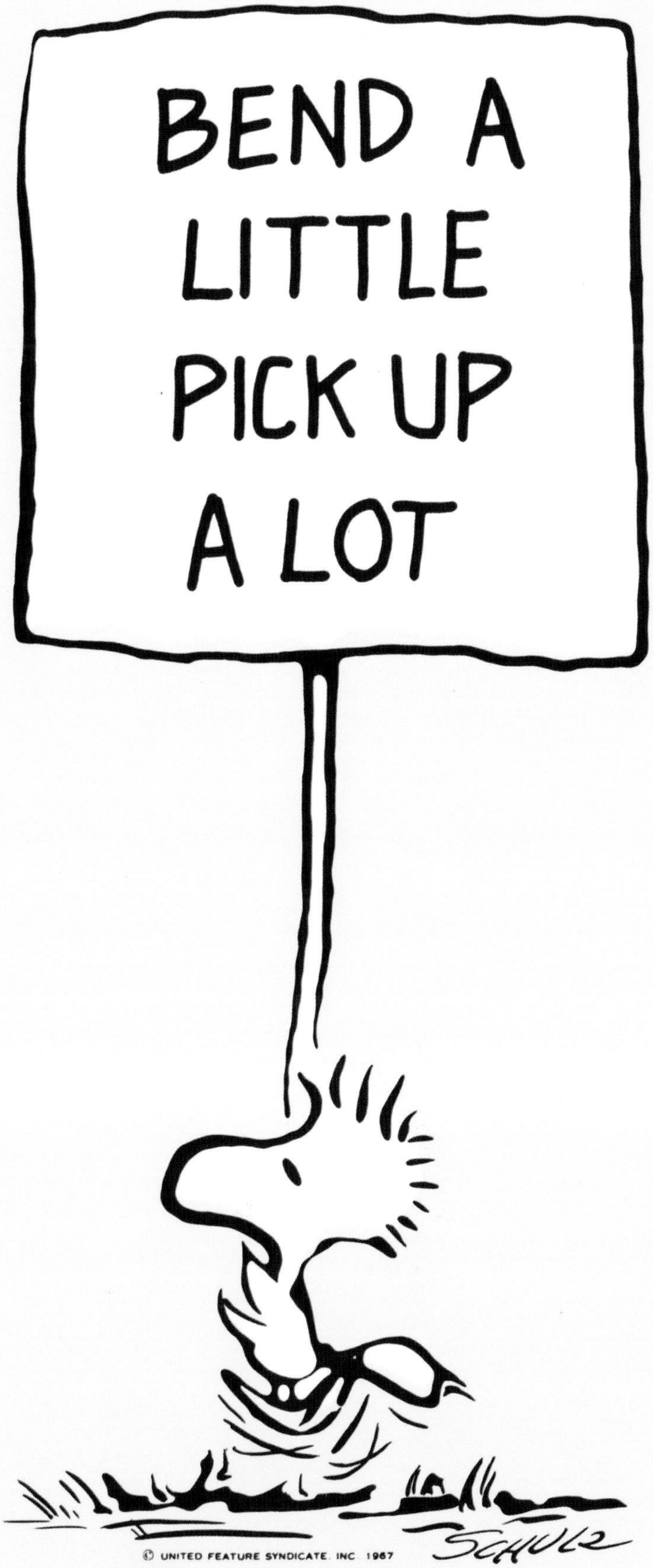
BEND A
LITTLE
PICK UP
A LOT
SCHULZ



U. S. DEPARTMENT OF THE INTERIOR

☆GPO 781-043

JH 62a (January 1972)

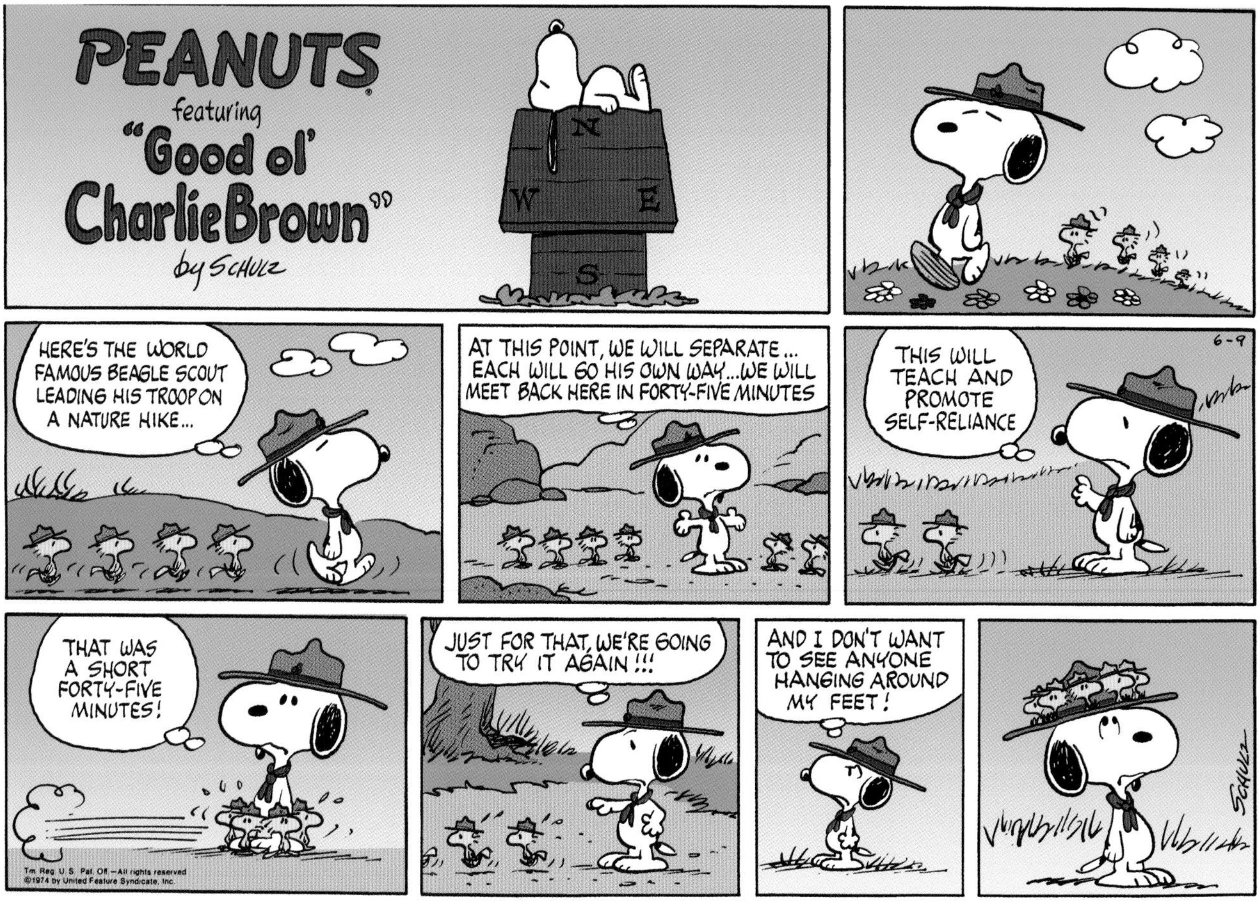
PEANUTS
featuring
"Good ol' CharlieBrown"
by SCHULZ
N
W
E
S
HERE'S THE WORLD FAMOUS BEAGLE SCOUT LEADING HIS TROOP ON A NATURE HIKE...
AT THIS POINT, WE WILL SEPARATE... EACH WILL GO HIS OWN WAY...WE WILL MEET BACK HERE IN FORTY-FIVE MINUTES
6-9
THIS WILL TEACH AND PROMOTE SELF-RELIANCE
THAT WAS A SHORT FORTY-FIVE MINUTES!
Tm Reg. U.S. Pat. Off.—All rights reserved
©1974 by United Feature Syndicate, Inc.
JUST FOR THAT, WE'RE GOING TO TRY IT AGAIN!!!
AND I DON'T WANT TO SEE ANYONE HANGING AROUND MY FEET!
SCHULZ

## THE BEAGLE SCOUTS

FIRST APPEARANCE
06/09/1974

Snoopy and his Beagle Scouts—with regulars Woodstock, Bill, Olivier, Harriet, Raymond, Fred, and Conrad, and with Roy and Wilson rounding out the ranks—are bold adventurers, always ready for a new expedition. On their long hikes, Snoopy is always ready to dispense sage advice, such as, "You can always tell which way is west, because the moon is always over Hollywood."

Although to the untrained eye these birds are generally indistinguishable from each other (with the exception of Raymond, whose purple feathers set him apart from his yellow companions), their faithful leader always seems to know who's who.

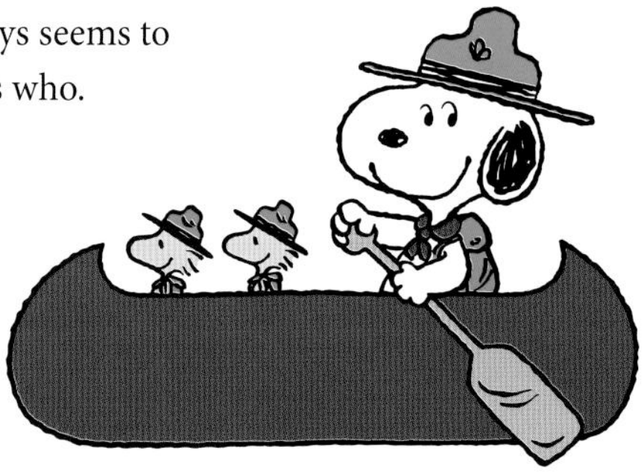

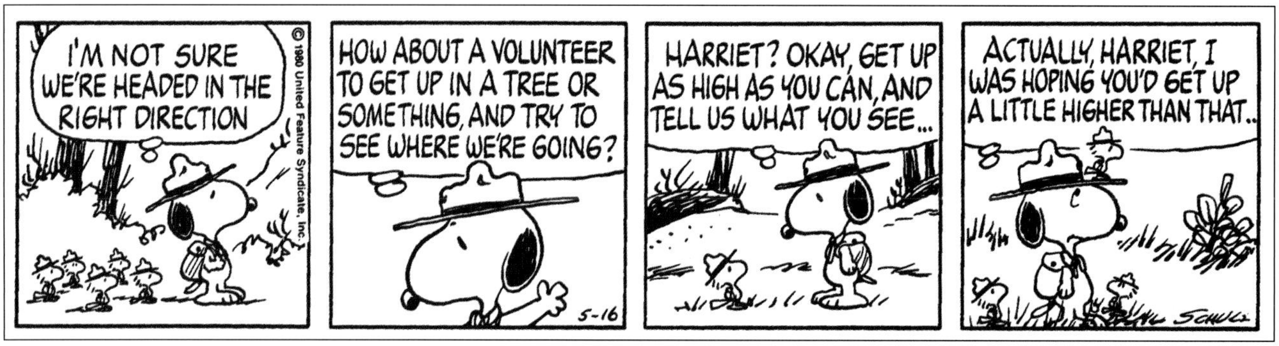
I'M NOT SURE WE'RE HEADED IN THE RIGHT DIRECTION
© 1980 United Feature Syndicate, Inc.
HOW ABOUT A VOLUNTEER TO GET UP IN A TREE OR SOMETHING, AND TRY TO SEE WHERE WE'RE GOING?
5-16
HARRIET? OKAY, GET UP AS HIGH AS YOU CAN, AND TELL US WHAT YOU SEE...
ACTUALLY, HARRIET, I WAS HOPING YOU'D GET UP A LITTLE HIGHER THAN THAT..
SCHULZ

CENTER: *Style Guide art – CSCA* | OPPOSITE: *Style Guide art – PW*

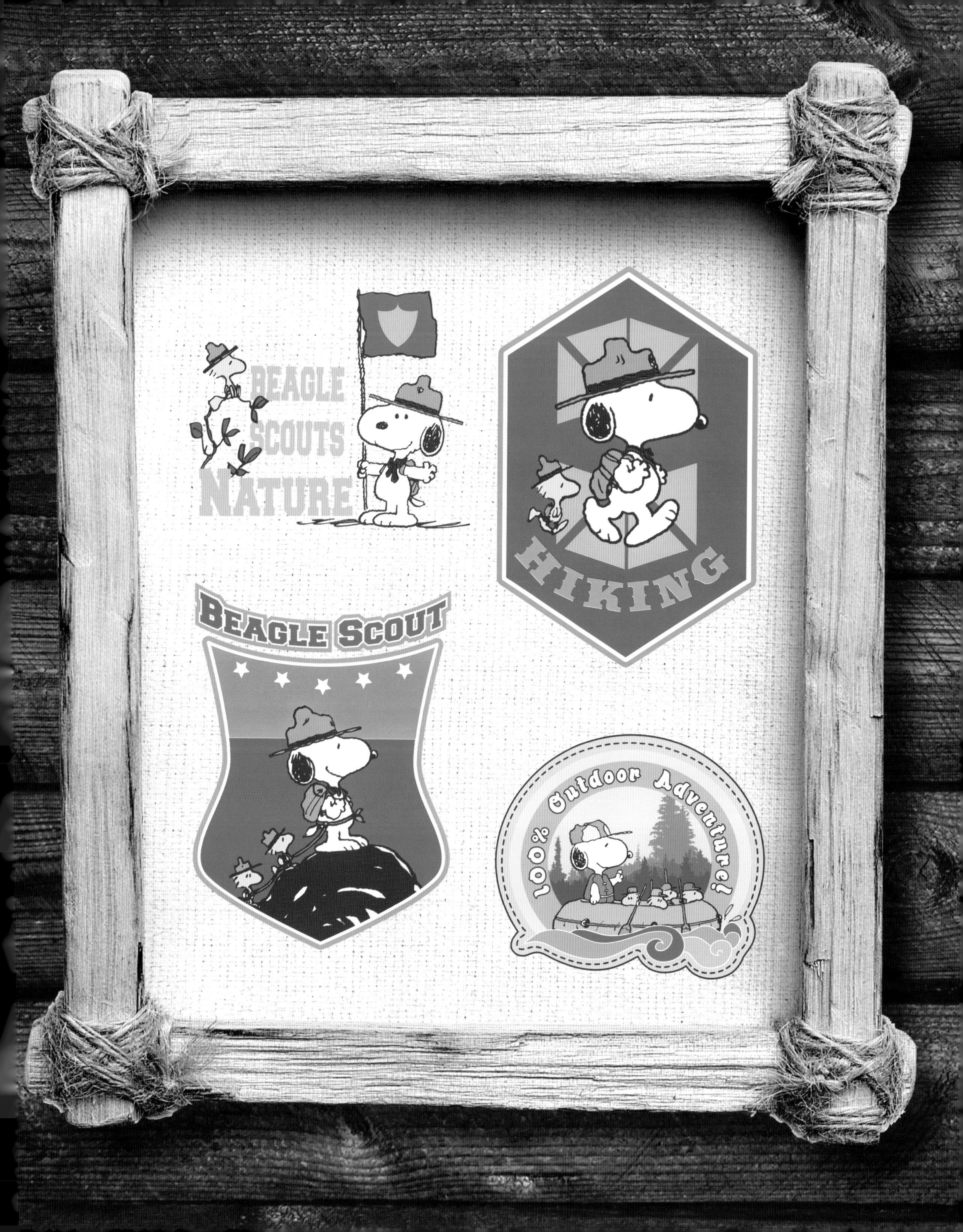
BEAGLE
SCOUTS
NATURE
HIKING
BEAGLE SCOUT
100% Outdoor Adventure!

# WORLD WAR II (THE CAT NEXT DOOR)

FIRST MENTIONED 11/23/1958, FIRST NAMED 10/20/1976

Snoopy has never been a "cat person," and he has a particularly contentious relationship with World War II, aka "The Cat Next Door." This vicious feline is known for his short temper, his razor-sharp claws, and his utter lack of appreciation for Snoopy and Woodstock's cat jokes.

Although Snoopy prefers to keep as much distance as possible between himself and World War II—whose claws are known to have reduced Snoopy's doghouse to splinters—Snoopy won't hesitate to leap into action to help a friend. At great personal risk, Snoopy ventures into World War II's territory to rescue both Peppermint Patty and Woodstock—fortunately for the little yellow bird (and unfortunately for Snoopy), World War II's target is a tiny yellow glove that drifted into his backyard. World War II is not on Snoopy's Christmas card list.

RIGHT: Peanuts, *Issue #4, Boom! Studios cover, 2014 - CSCA* | OPPOSITE: *Design by Cameron + Co*

SCHULZ

HE'S NOT UP HERE..
I TOLD YOU HE WASN'T
WHO'S THAT OVER THERE? IT LOOKS LIKE A DOG IN A CAT SUIT...
THAT'S "WORLD WAR II," THE CAT WHO LIVES NEXT DOOR...DON'T TANGLE WITH HIM... HE'S MEAN!!
10-20
YOU CAN'T FOOL ME, CHUCK! THAT'S SNOOPY IN A CAT SUIT! I'M GONNA GET 'IM!!!
OH, GOOD GRIEF!
SCHULZ

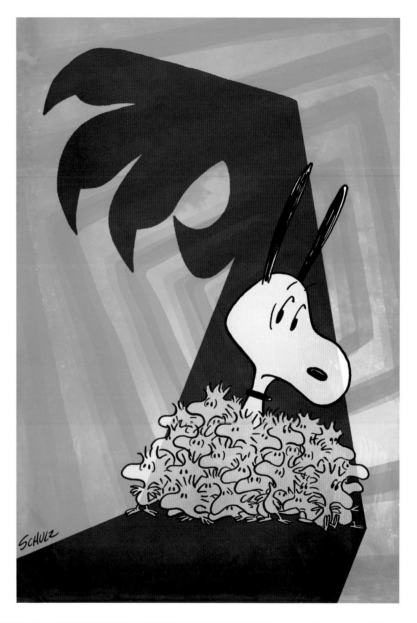

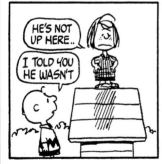

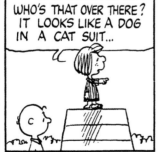

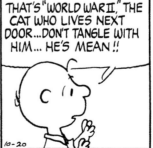

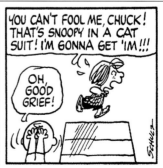

## WOODSTOCK'S GRANDFATHER

FIRST MENTIONED 01/04/1994, FIRST (AND ONLY) APPEARANCE 01/06/1994

Woodstock comes from a long line of unique birds. Snoopy gains new insight into his friend's roots when the pair discover a battered, empty birdcage and a journal kept by Woodstock's Grandfather, the cage's one-time occupant. The journal reveals his hatred of the cage and his intention to escape at the earliest possible opportunity.

Snoopy thoughtfully observes that Woodstock's Grandfather probably got out and that Woodstock should wave every time he sees a bird sitting on a telephone wire, since it might be his Grandpa.

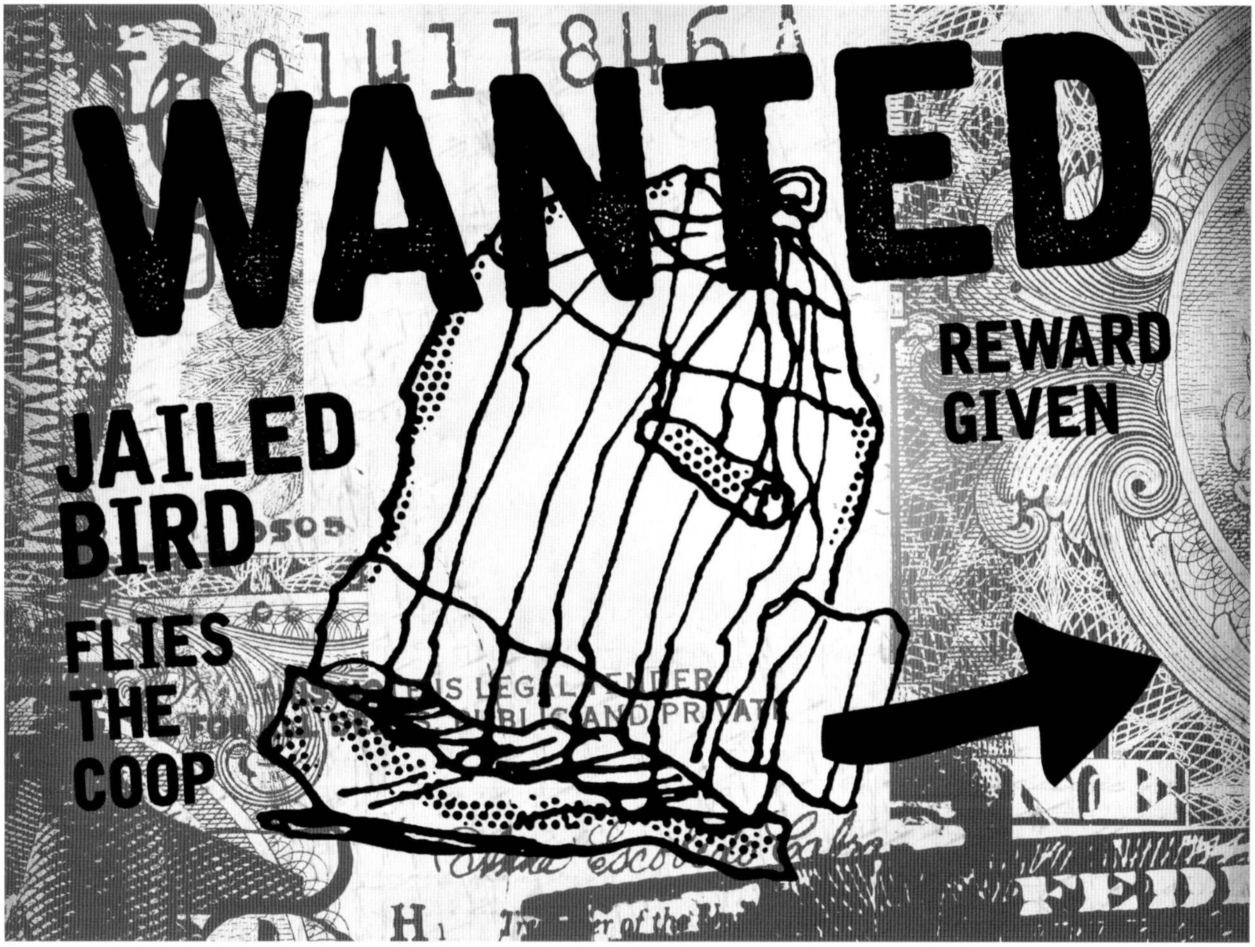
WANTED
JAILED BIRD
FLIES THE COOP
REWARD GIVEN

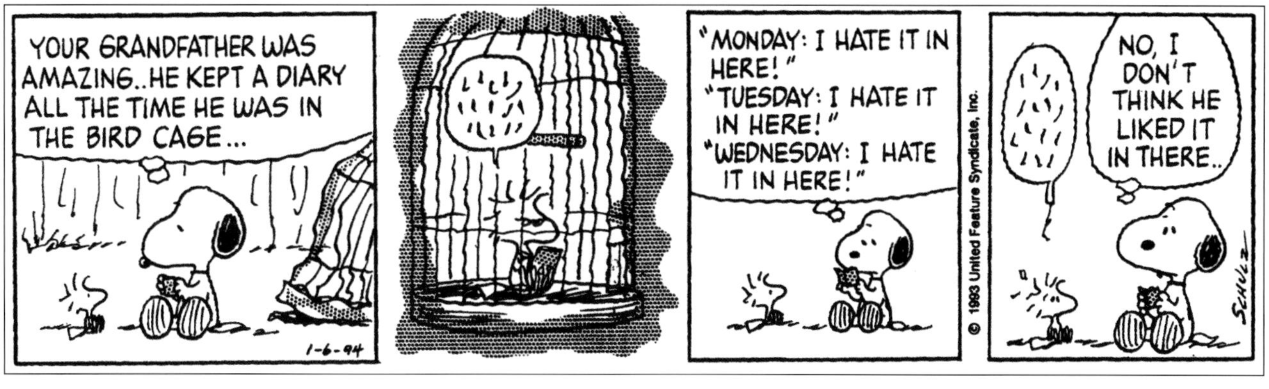
YOUR GRANDFATHER WAS AMAZING..HE KEPT A DIARY ALL THE TIME HE WAS IN THE BIRD CAGE...
1-6-94
"MONDAY: I HATE IT IN HERE!"
"TUESDAY: I HATE IT IN HERE!"
"WEDNESDAY: I HATE IT IN HERE!"
© 1993 United Feature Syndicate, Inc.
NO, I DON'T THINK HE LIKED IT IN THERE..
SCHULZ

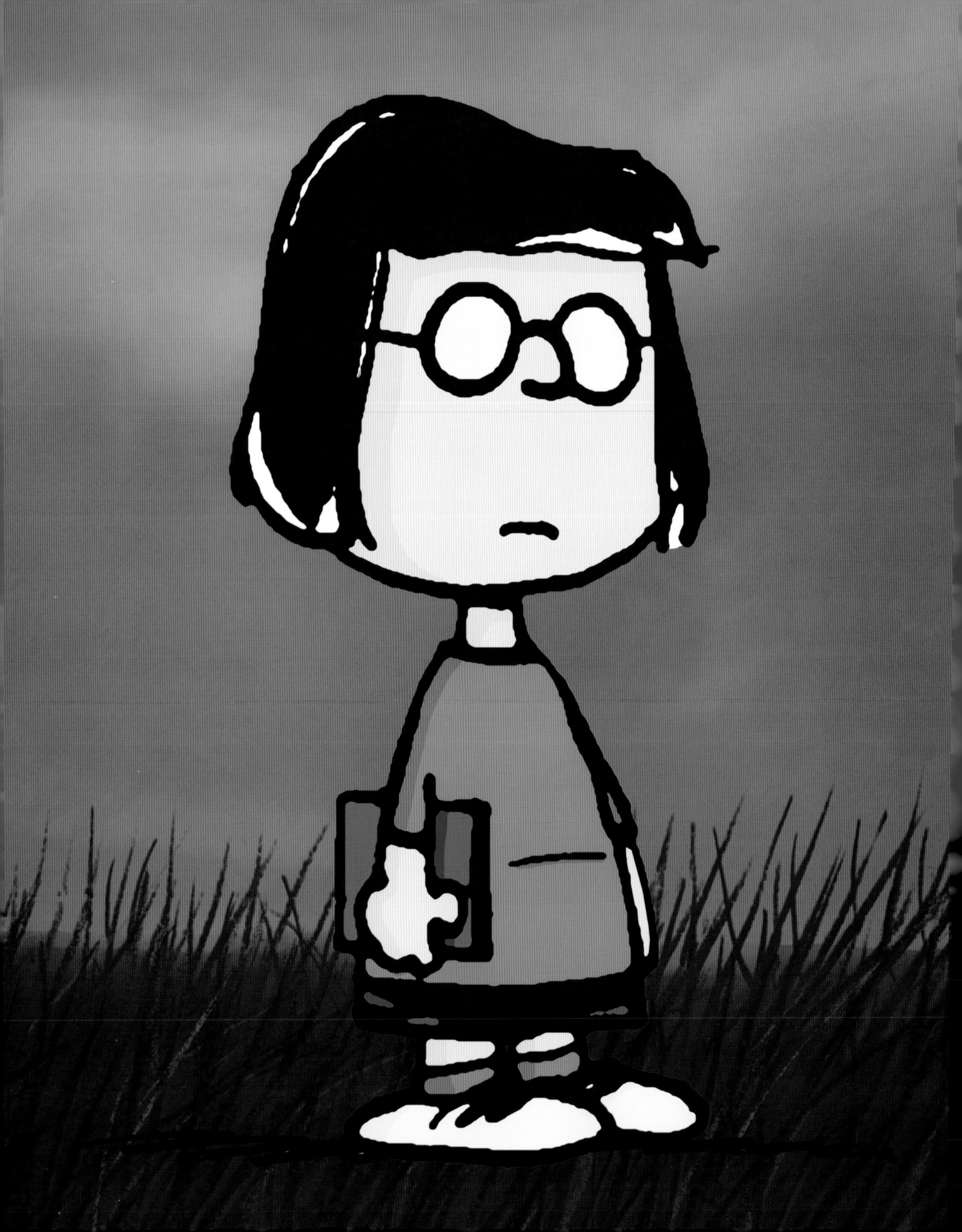

# Marcie

FIRST APPEARANCE
07/20/1971

Peppermint Patty and Marcie first meet at summer camp, when the pair are caught in a torrential downpour, and Marcie asks the experienced camper, "Sir, what time is lunch?" Peppermint Patty isn't quite sure what to make of Marcie, but the two become best friends—and Marcie still calls her "Sir!"

Unlike her classmate, Marcie is an excellent student and a patron of the arts, and has only a passing knowledge of sports, although she takes part when Peppermint Patty needs an extra player, to support equality for women more than out of enjoyment of the activity.

Marcie also differs from Peppermint Patty in her open admiration for Charlie Brown, whom she calls "Charles." She always treats Charlie Brown—and everyone else who earns it—with the utmost respect. Although she generally displays a quiet, reserved nature, she has been known to lose her temper on occasion and is one of the very rare people who won't back down from a confrontation with Peppermint Patty.

"Peppermint Patty, the tomboy, is forthright, doggedly loyal, with a devastating singleness of purpose, the part of us that goes through life with blinders on. This can be wonderful at times but also disastrous," noted Charles Schulz, when discussing their friendship. "Patty was never very smart. Then one day Marcie appeared. Marcie is devoted to her, calls her 'Sir' and doesn't mind following her around, which is deceptive. Marcie is one-up on Patty in every way. She sees the truth of things, where it invariably escapes Patty. I like Marcie."

WIN-LESS
BASEBALL CARDS
CLOMP!
MARCIE
"I HAVE THE BALL, SIR... WHAT DO YOU WANT ME TO DO WITH IT?"

PEANUTS
RAIN! GOOD GRIEF!
HOW CAN YOU HAVE FUN AT CAMP WITH DORKY WEATHER LIKE THIS? I WONDER HOW CHUCK IS DOING?
SIR, WHAT TIME IS LUNCH?
DON'T CALL ME "SIR"! WHAT KIND OF A DORKY KID ARE YOU?
DORKY?

PEANUTS
MARCIE, LOOK! I GOT AN "N"!
I GOT AN "N" ON MY ENGLISH TEST! THAT'S THE HIGHEST GRADE I'VE EVER GOTTEN!
THAT'S NOT AN "N," SIR... THAT'S A "Z"... YOU HAVE THE PAPER TURNED SIDEWAYS...
RATS! FOR ONE BRIEF EXCITING MOMENT I THOUGHT I HAD AN "N"!

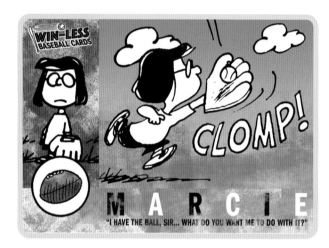

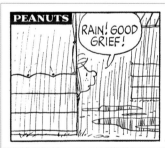

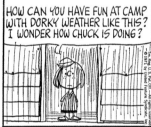

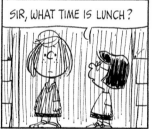

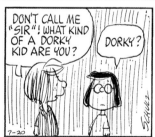

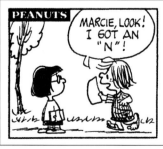

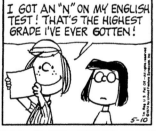

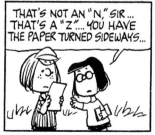

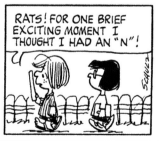

OPPOSITE: *Style Guide art – CSCA* | TOP RIGHT: *Design by Cameron + Co*

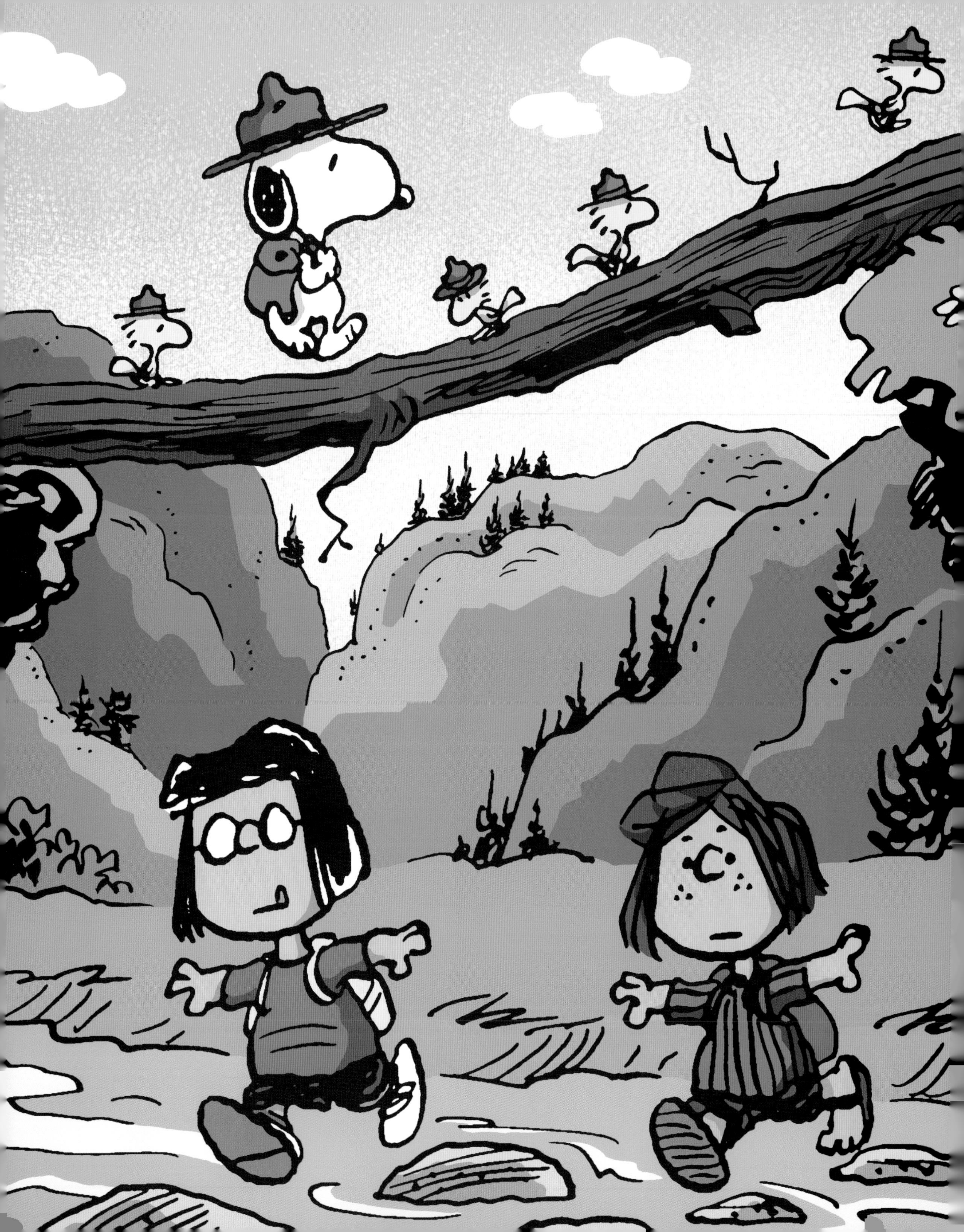

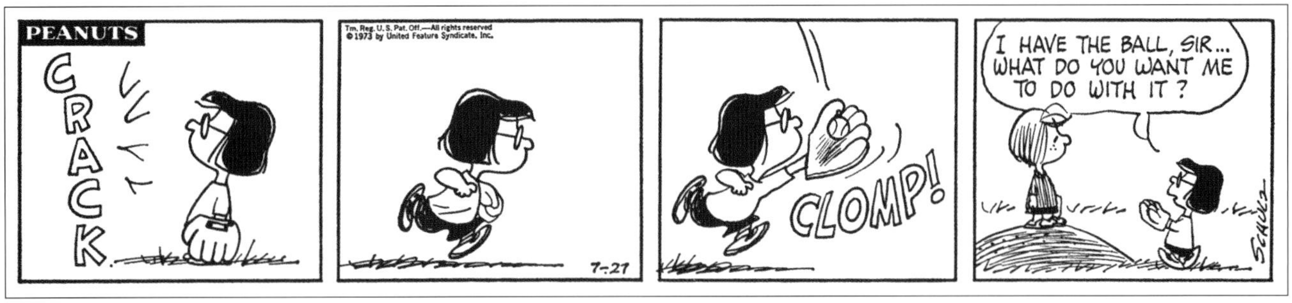
PEANUTS
Tm. Reg. U.S. Pat. Off.—All rights reserved
©1973 by United Feature Syndicate, Inc.
CRACK
7-27
CLOMP!
I HAVE THE BALL, SIR... WHAT DO YOU WANT ME TO DO WITH IT?
SCHULZ

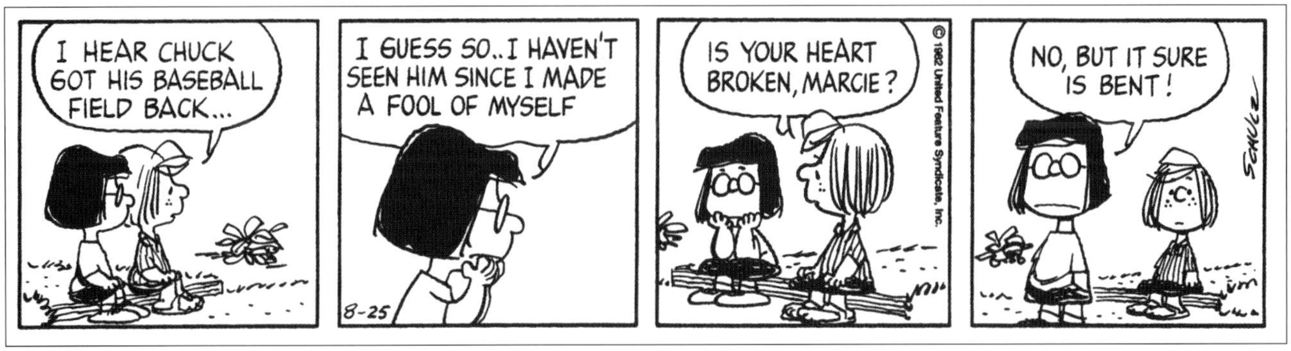
I HEAR CHUCK GOT HIS BASEBALL FIELD BACK...
I GUESS SO.. I HAVEN'T SEEN HIM SINCE I MADE A FOOL OF MYSELF
8-25
IS YOUR HEART BROKEN, MARCIE?
© 1982 United Feature Syndicate, Inc.
NO, BUT IT SURE IS BENT!
SCHULZ

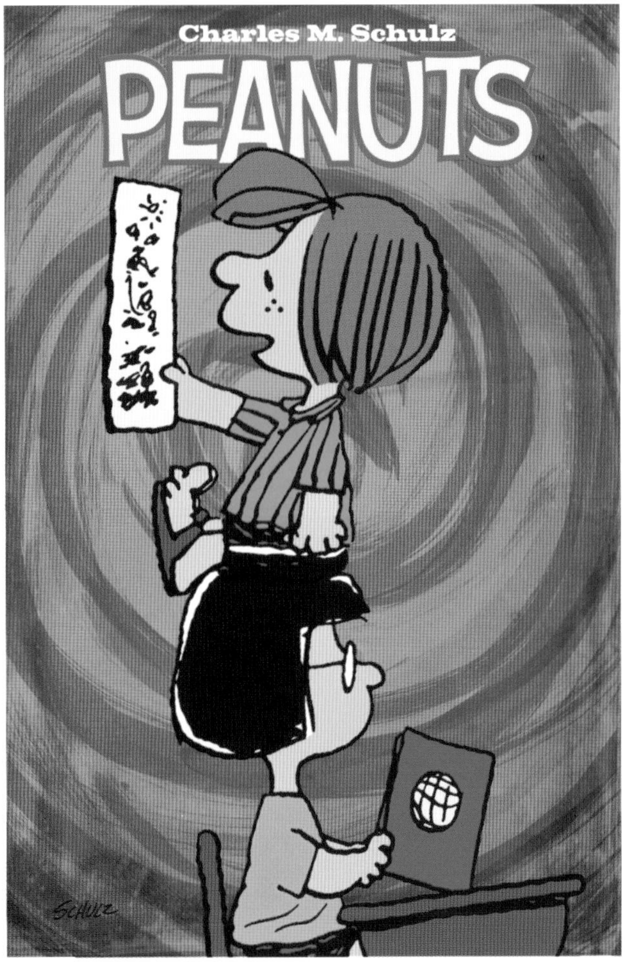
Charles M. Schulz
PEANUTS
SCHULZ

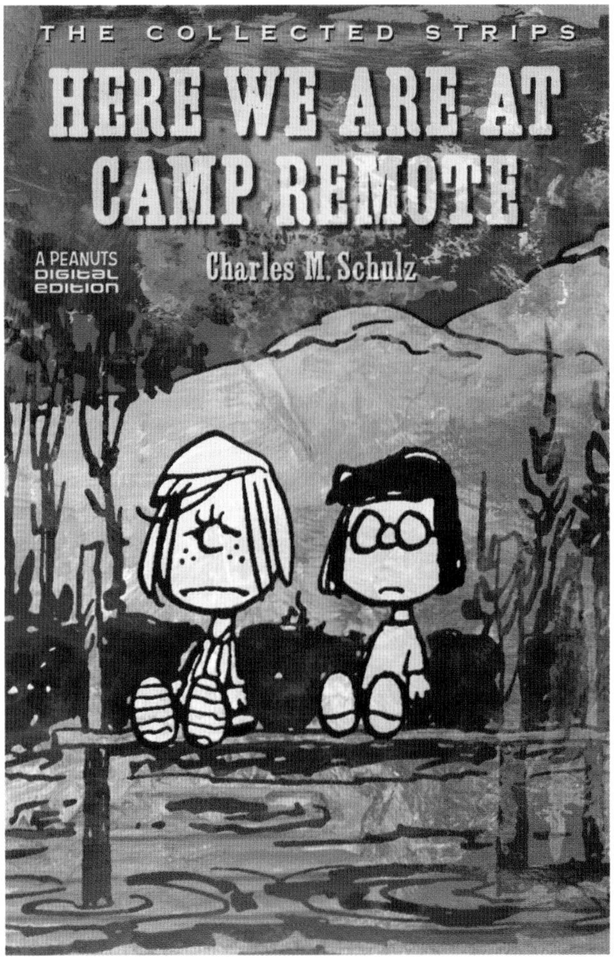
THE COLLECTED STRIPS
HERE WE ARE AT CAMP REMOTE
A PEANUTS DIGITAL EDITION
Charles M. Schulz

OPPOSITE: *Style Guide art – CSCA* | ABOVE LEFT: Peanuts, *Issue #12, Boom! Studios cover, 2014 – CSCA* | ABOVE RIGHT: Here We Are at Camp Remote, Peanuts *Digital Edition – CSCA*

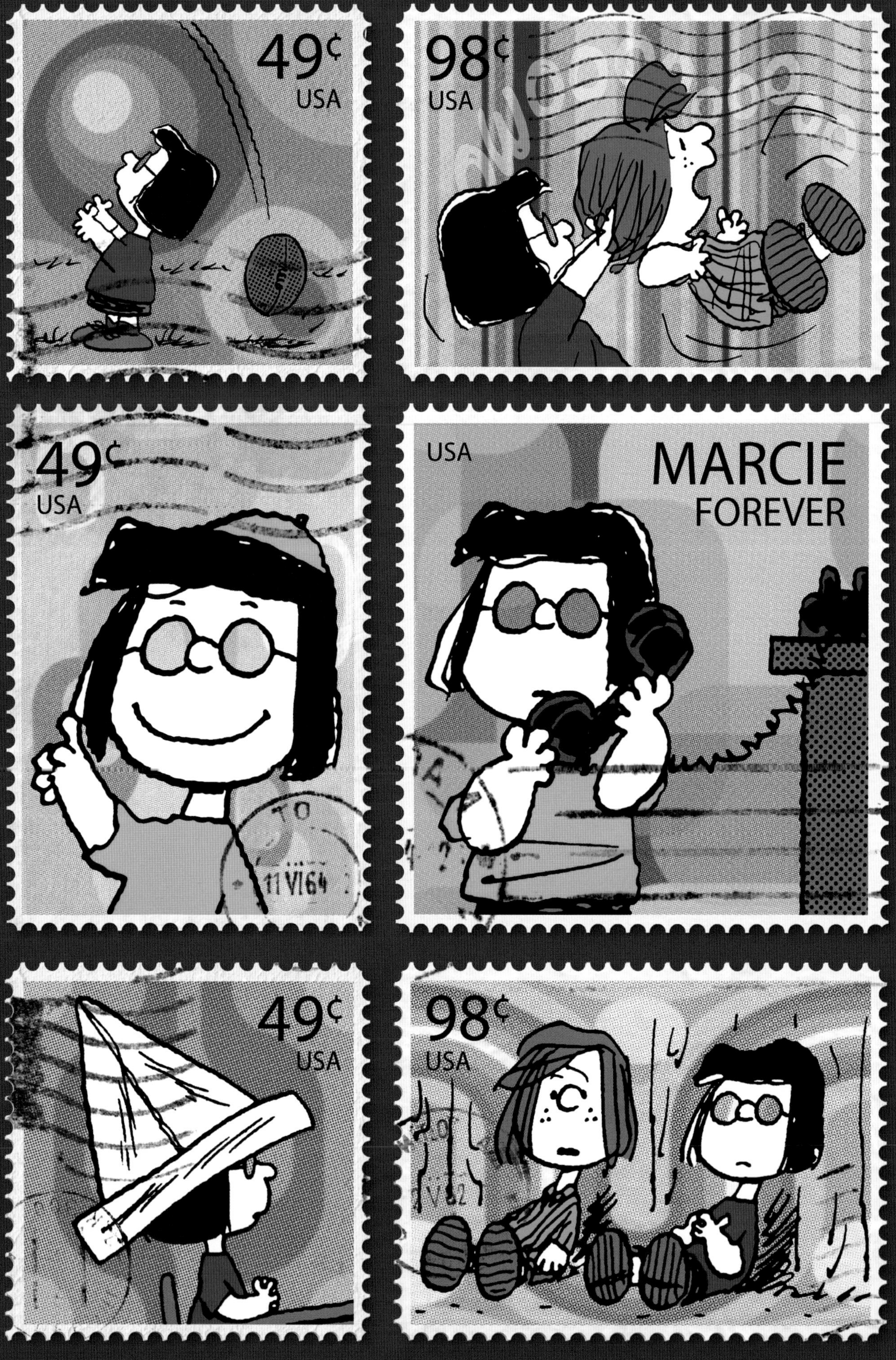
49¢
USA
98¢
USA
49¢
USA
11 VI64
USA
MARCIE
FOREVER
49¢
USA
98¢
USA

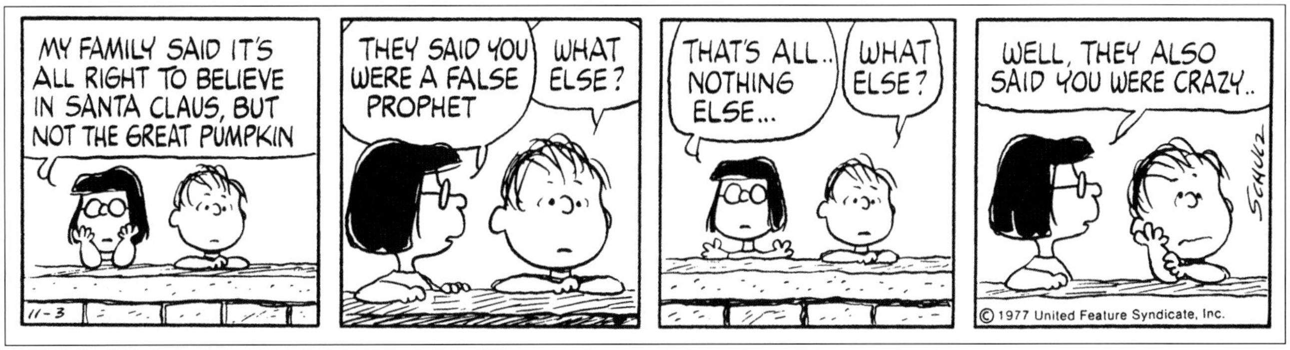
MY FAMILY SAID IT'S ALL RIGHT TO BELIEVE IN SANTA CLAUS, BUT NOT THE GREAT PUMPKIN
THEY SAID YOU WERE A FALSE PROPHET
WHAT ELSE?
THAT'S ALL.. NOTHING ELSE...
WHAT ELSE?
WELL, THEY ALSO SAID YOU WERE CRAZY..
SCHULZ
11-3
© 1977 United Feature Syndicate, Inc.

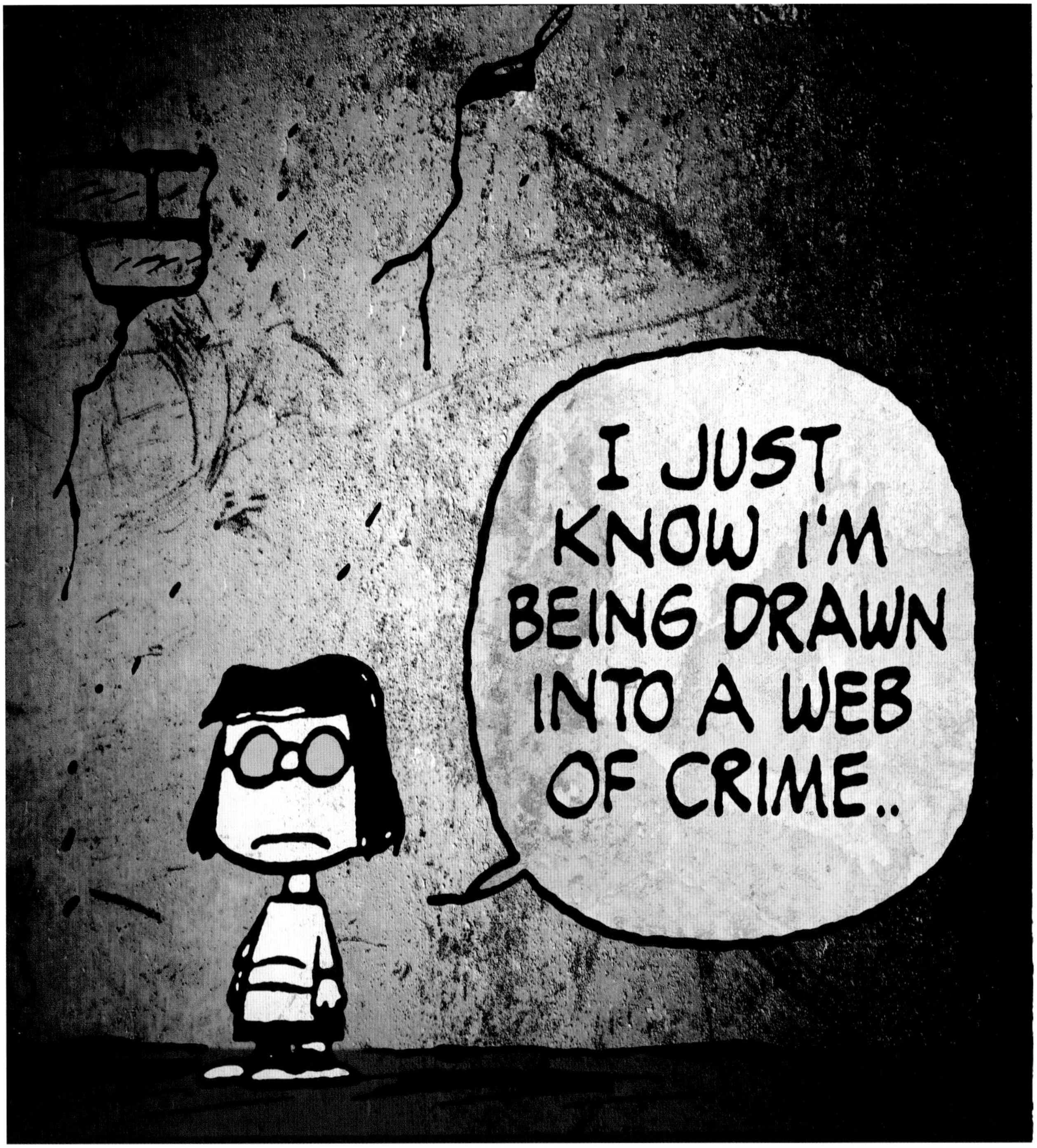
I JUST KNOW I'M BEING DRAWN INTO A WEB OF CRIME..

OPPOSITE AND ABOVE: *Design by Cameron + Co*

PEANUTS
YOU HAVEN'T HEARD WHAT THAT KID'S BEEN CALLING ME, HAVE YOU, SIR?
7-26
WELL, YOU JUST LISTEN... HE'S RIGHT BEHIND ME.. YOU JUST LISTEN...
PSST! HI, LAMBCAKE!
LAMBCAKE?
POW!
LAMBCAKE?
SCHULZ

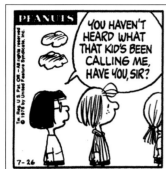

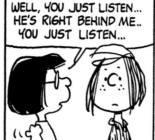

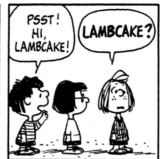

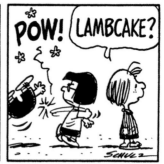

# FLOYD

FIRST APPEARANCE
07/26/1976

When you hear "Hey, Lambcake!" it can only mean one thing—Floyd is on the scene. Floyd makes his presence known when he first sees Marcie riding the bus to summer camp by calling her names and making a nuisance of himself. When he finally meets Marcie face-to-face, he

> **"Hey, Lambcake!"**
> **—Floyd**

confesses that he has developed a crush on her, but she is decidedly unimpressed—and his fondness for the nickname "Lambcake" never wins her over.

Although he promises to write to Marcie after summer's end, she fails to provide him with her last name and address as his bus speeds away from camp, and no one calls her "Lambcake" anymore.

POW!
LAMBCAKE?
SCHULZ
"I think she's beautiful... I think I'm in love with her..."
I DON'T KNOW YOUR LAST NAME! I DON'T KNOW YOUR ADDRESS!
POW!

RIGHT AND OPPOSITE: *Design by Cameron + Co*

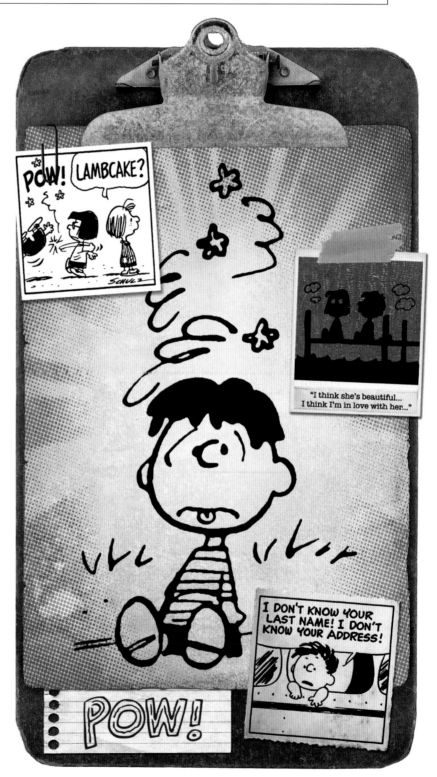

HI! I'M PEPPERMINT PATTY.. I GUESS WE'RE PLAYING IN THE SAME THREESOME...
DON'T GET TOO CLOSE! YOU MIGHT STEP ON MY GOLF SHOES OR SMUDGE MY WHITE TURTLENECK...
6-22
© 1981 United Feature Syndicate, Inc.
NEVER STRIKE ANOTHER PLAYER ON THE FIRST TEE, SIR...
SCHULZ

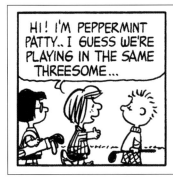

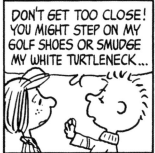

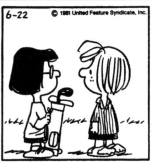

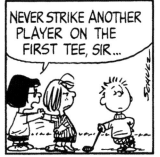

# JOE RICHKID

FIRST APPEARANCE
06/22/1981

The aptly named Joe Richkid is a talented golfer who first meets Peppermint Patty and Marcie when they're all assigned to the same group in a children's golf tournament. Peppermint Patty is leery of Richkid's fastidious ways, while Marcie is so irritated with Richkid's caddy that she shoves him into the lake—which Peppermint Patty is quick to point out is a two-stroke penalty.

Joe Richkid disappears after a single storyline, but Snoopy continues to hit the links on a regular basis, probably because of Charles Schulz's fondness for the sport. As he recalled, "I took up golf when I was 15 and became a real fanatic. I had seen Bobby Jones in a series of shorts he had made years ago, and I had always admired good golfers. But I had no one to show me the game. A friend of mine and I took an old borrowed set of clubs with wooden shafts and went up to a public course in St. Paul one morning at 5:30 and played our first game of golf. I remember I shot 156 and I thought the next time we go out, I'll do better. The next time I shot 165, but four months later I broke 80—I had my first 79. The next year I made the high-school golf team. From then on that was all I thought about—drawing cartoons and playing golf. I had this dream that some day I'd become a great cartoonist and win the National Open."

GOLFING
AT PEBBLE BEACH
THE RICHKID INVITATIONAL

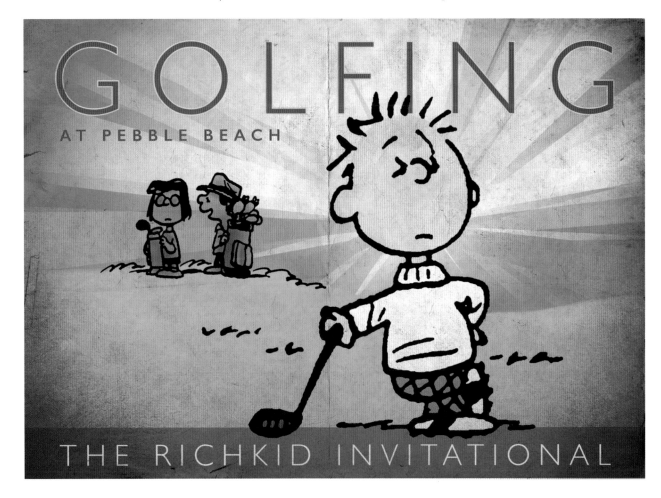

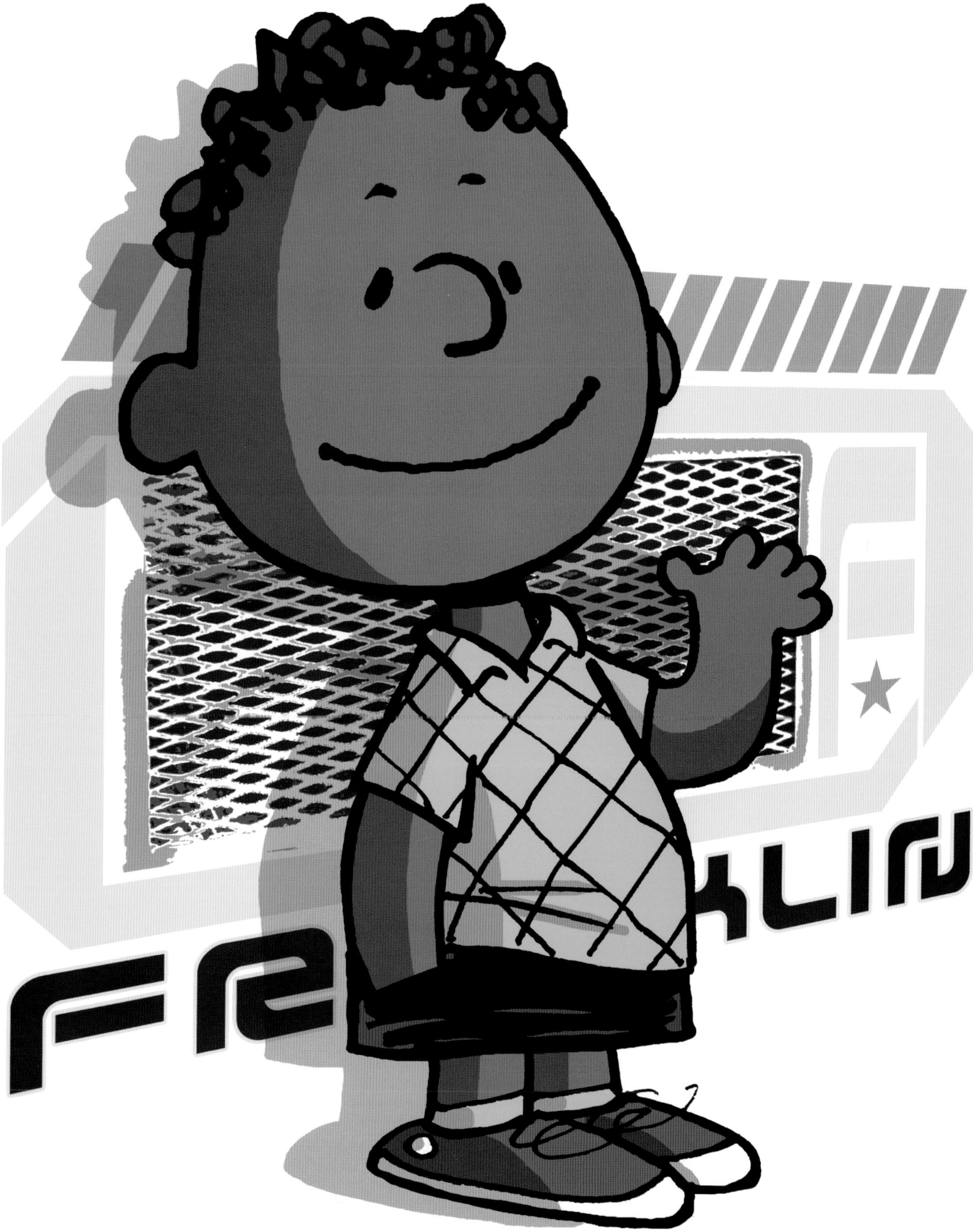
FR
KLIN

# FRANKLIN

FIRST APPEARANCE
07/31/1968

Calm, cool, and collected, Franklin is one of Charlie Brown's best friends and confidants. The two meet at the beach one summer when Franklin returns an errant beach ball that Sally tossed into the waves. That afternoon, they talk about their families and baseball as they build a giant sandcastle, and they are pals ever since.

Franklin lives in Peppermint Patty's neighborhood and plays center field for her baseball team. Even though he finds Charlie Brown's friends a little strange—on his first trip to his neighborhood, he was greeted by Lucy's

> **"In contrast with the other characters, Franklin has the fewest anxieties and obsessions."** — Charles Schulz

Psychiatric Booth and Snoopy in his guise as the World War I Flying Ace, and received testimonials about the Great Pumpkin and Beethoven—he takes it all in stride with his usual charm and tact.

Franklin is an "A" student and a deep thinker who enjoys spending time with Charlie Brown and Linus discussing philosophical issues or conversations that he has with his grandfather. "Franklin is thoughtful and can quote the Old Testament as effectively as Linus," Charles Schulz noted. "In contrast with the other characters, Franklin has the fewest anxieties and obsessions."

Despite his level-headed nature, Franklin is occasionally overwhelmed by his responsibilities and his many extracurricular activities, which are strongly encouraged by his parents. As he once notes when he declines Peppermint Patty's invitation to shoot marbles after school, "I have a guitar lesson at three-thirty . . . right after that I have Little League, and then swim club, and then dinner and then a '4H' meeting . . . I lead a very active Tuesday!"

Franklin's first appearance in *Peanuts* caused minor controversy, when a small number of readers expressed anger over his introduction. "The only editor who ever complained was when Franklin [a black character] came in in the 1960s," recalled Schulz. "The strip showed Franklin in school with Charlie Brown [the editor objected to an integrated school]. But I just ignored him."

PEANUTS
IS THIS YOUR BEACH BALL?
HEY! YEAH! THANK YOU VERY MUCH!
I WAS SWIMMING OUT THERE, AND IT CAME FLOATING BY..
MY SILLY SISTER THREW IT INTO THE WATER
I SEE YOU'RE MAKING A SAND CASTLE..
IT LOOKS KIND OF CROOKED
I GUESS MAYBE IT IS.. WHERE I COME FROM, I'M NOT FAMOUS FOR DOING THINGS RIGHT...
7-31
SCHULZ

HAVE YOU EVER NOTICED HOW CERTAIN HOMES HAVE DISTINCT COOKING ODORS?
YOU MEAN LIKE GARLIC OR SPAGHETTI ?
7-7
I KNOW ONE KID'S HOUSE THAT ALWAYS SMELLS LIKE THEY'VE BEEN COOKING CABBAGE
OURS SMELLS LIKE TV DINNERS!
SCHULZ
© 1980 United Feature Syndicate, Inc.


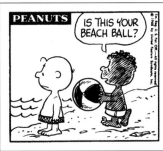

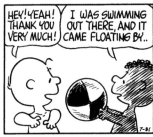

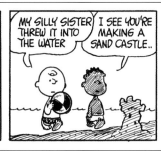

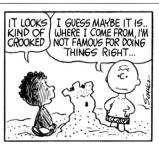

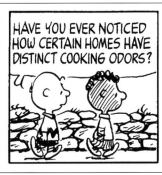

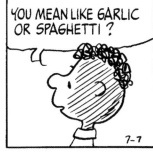

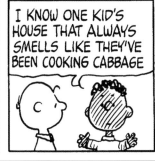

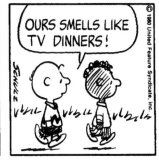

OPPOSITE: *Style Guide art – CSCA*

"I'm going home, Charlie Brown..
This neighborhood has me shook."

—Franklin

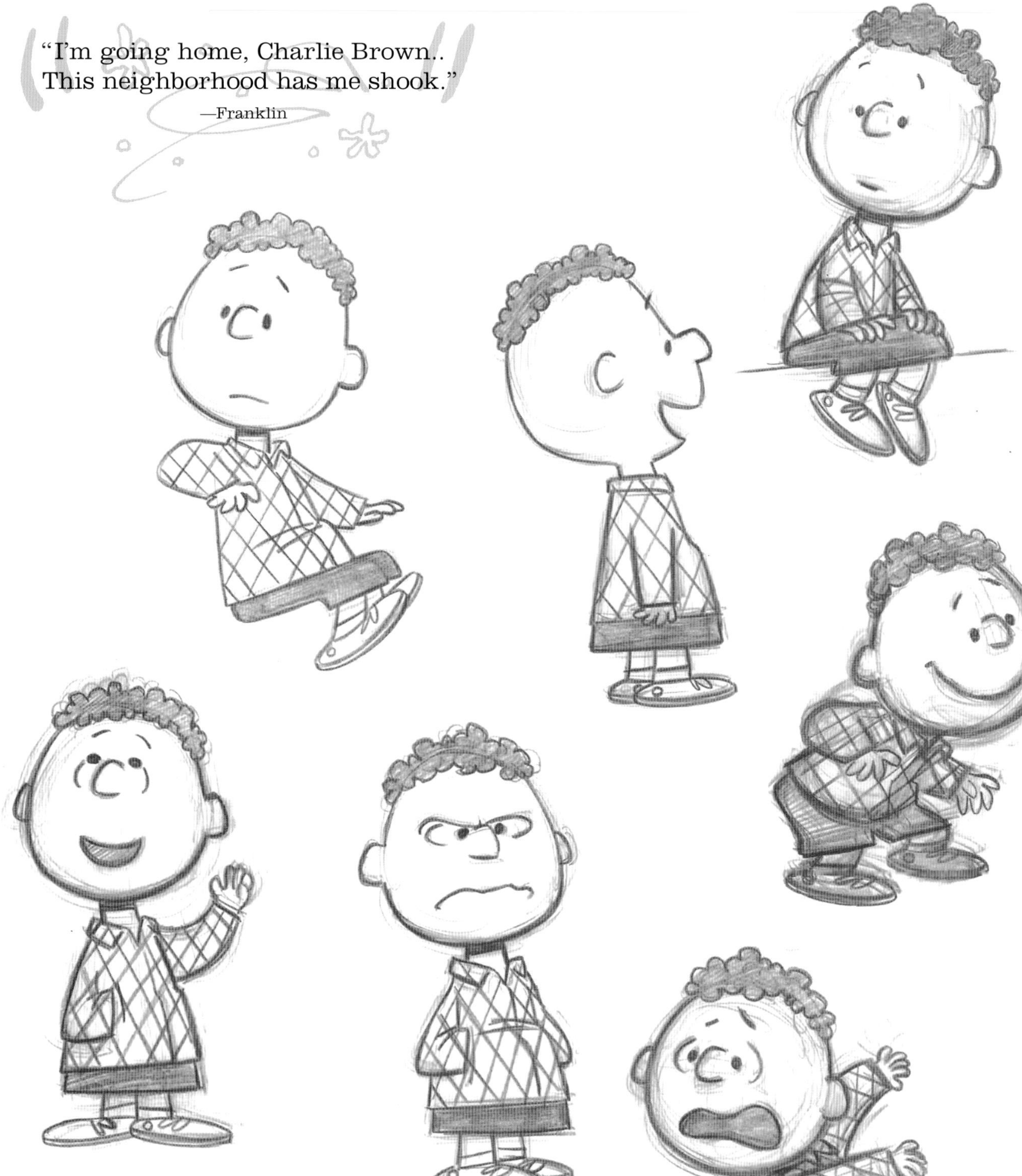

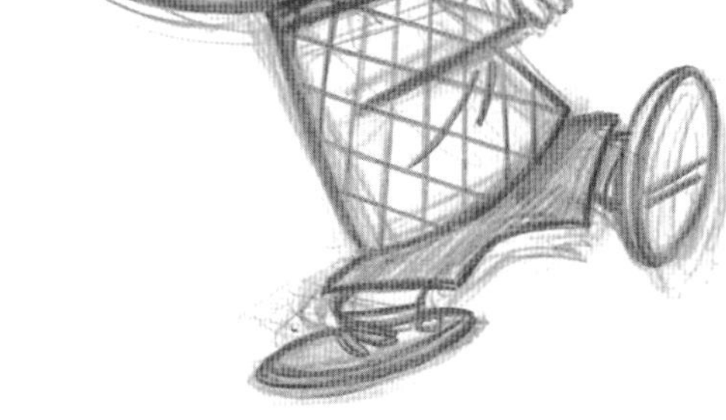

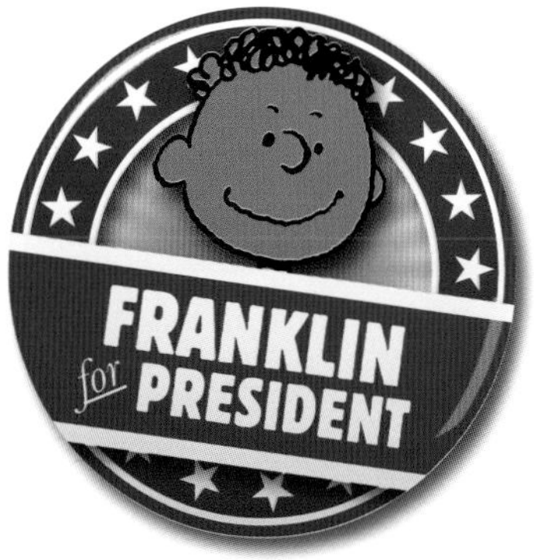
FRANKLIN
for PRESIDENT

LEFT: *Style Guide art – PW* | ABOVE AND OPPOSITE: *Franklin model sheet – CSCA* | OPPOSITE, BOTTOM RIGHT: *Style Guide art – CSCA*

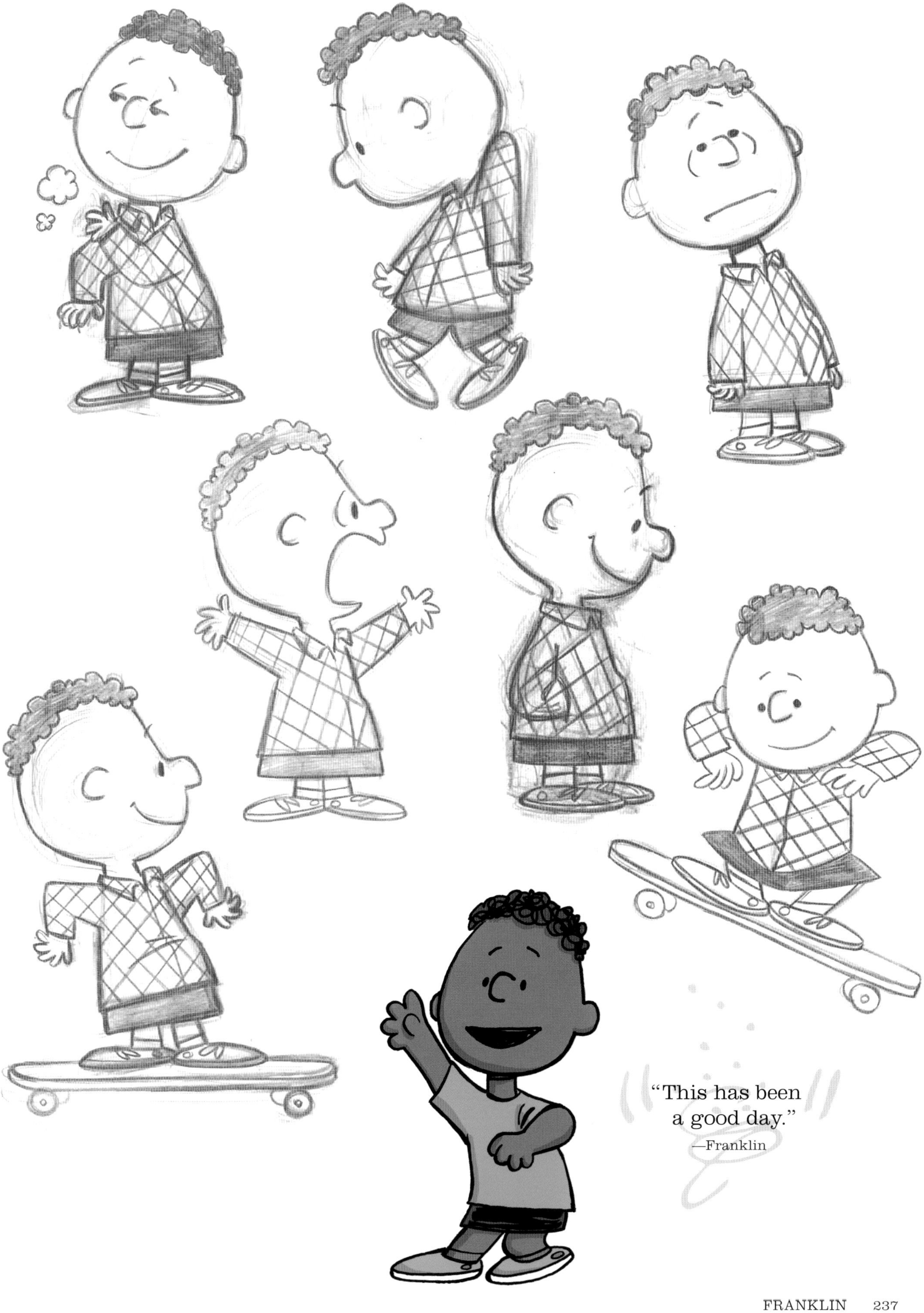

"This has been
a good day."
—Franklin

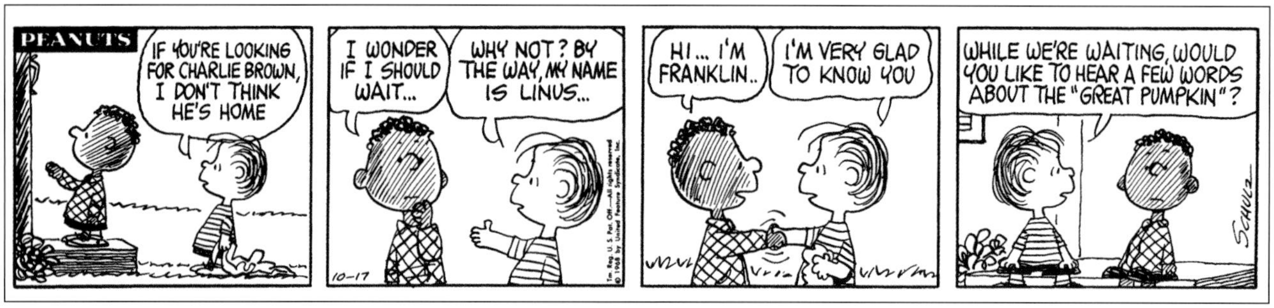
PEANUTS
IF YOU'RE LOOKING FOR CHARLIE BROWN, I DON'T THINK HE'S HOME
I WONDER IF I SHOULD WAIT...
WHY NOT? BY THE WAY, MY NAME IS LINUS...
10-17
HI... I'M FRANKLIN..
I'M VERY GLAD TO KNOW YOU
WHILE WE'RE WAITING, WOULD YOU LIKE TO HEAR A FEW WORDS ABOUT THE "GREAT PUMPKIN"?
SCHULZ

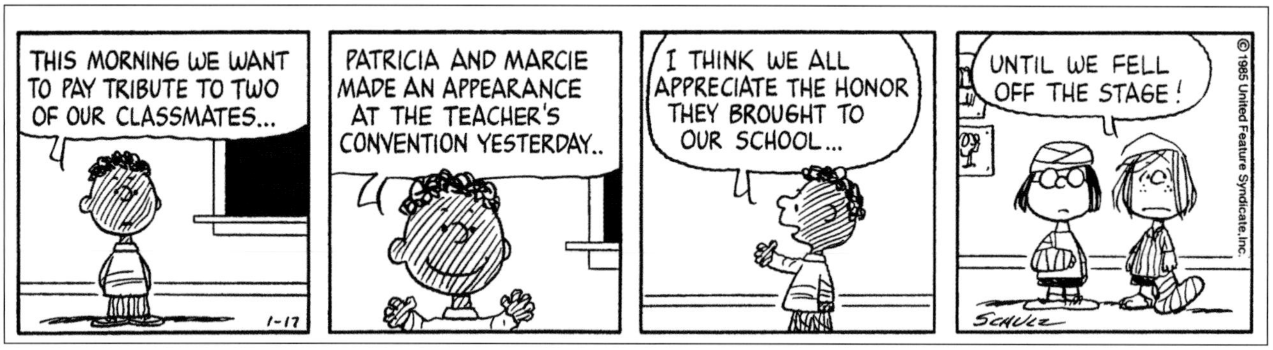
THIS MORNING WE WANT TO PAY TRIBUTE TO TWO OF OUR CLASSMATES...
1-17
PATRICIA AND MARCIE MADE AN APPEARANCE AT THE TEACHER'S CONVENTION YESTERDAY..
I THINK WE ALL APPRECIATE THE HONOR THEY BROUGHT TO OUR SCHOOL...
UNTIL WE FELL OFF THE STAGE!
© 1985 United Feature Syndicate, Inc.
SCHULZ

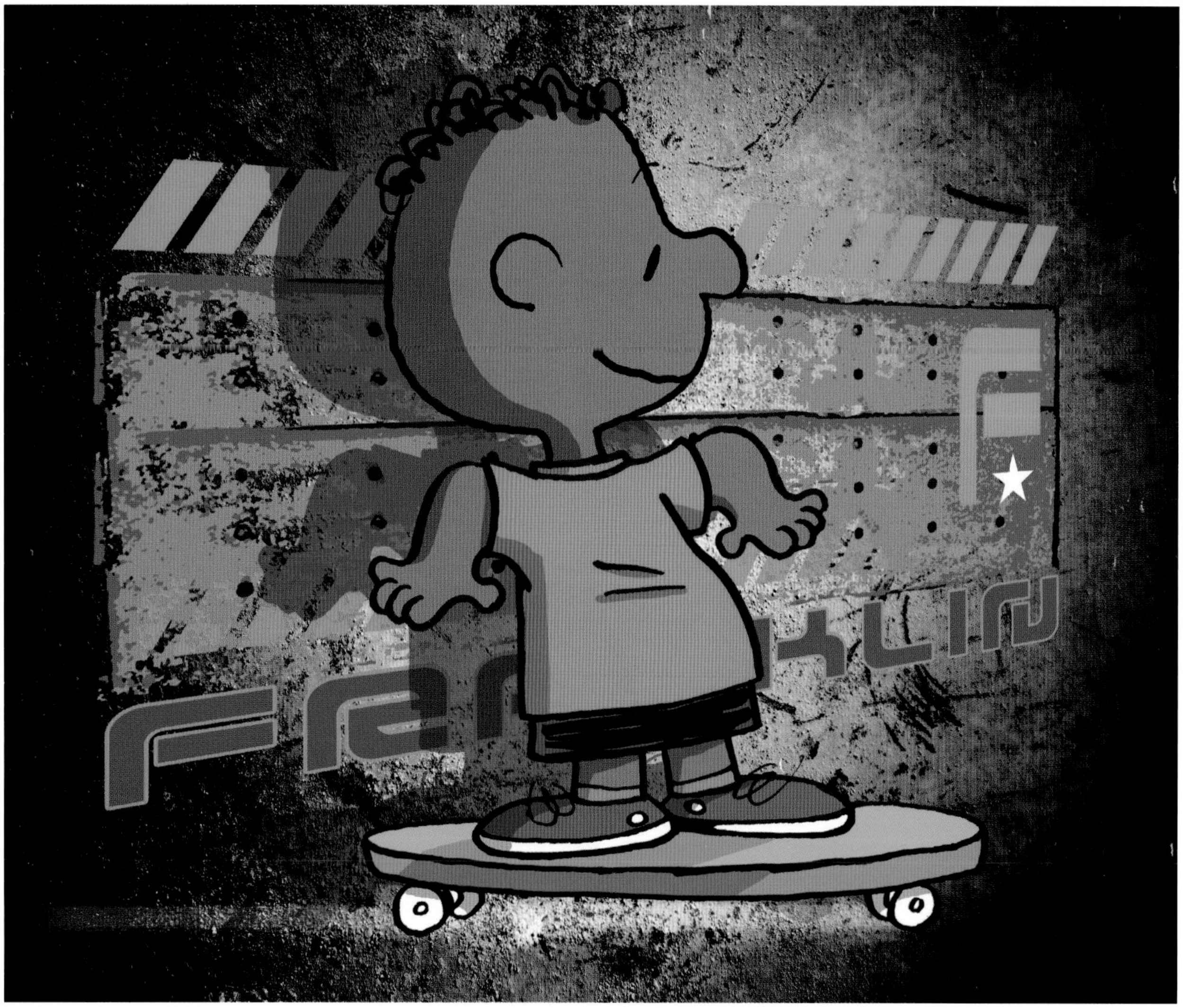

ABOVE: *Style Guide art – CSCA* | OPPOSITE: *Spot art from strip – Charles M. Schulz*

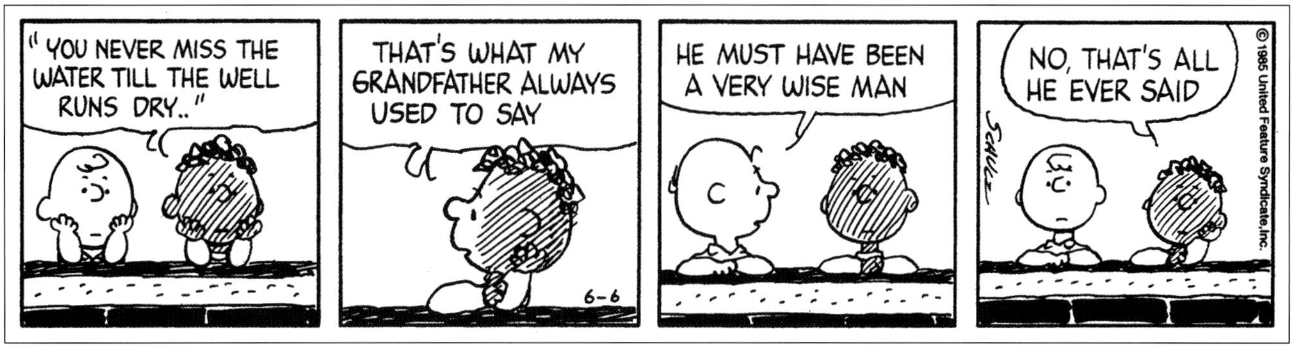
"YOU NEVER MISS THE WATER TILL THE WELL RUNS DRY.."
THAT'S WHAT MY GRANDFATHER ALWAYS USED TO SAY
HE MUST HAVE BEEN A VERY WISE MAN
NO, THAT'S ALL HE EVER SAID
6-6
© 1985 United Feature Syndicate, Inc.

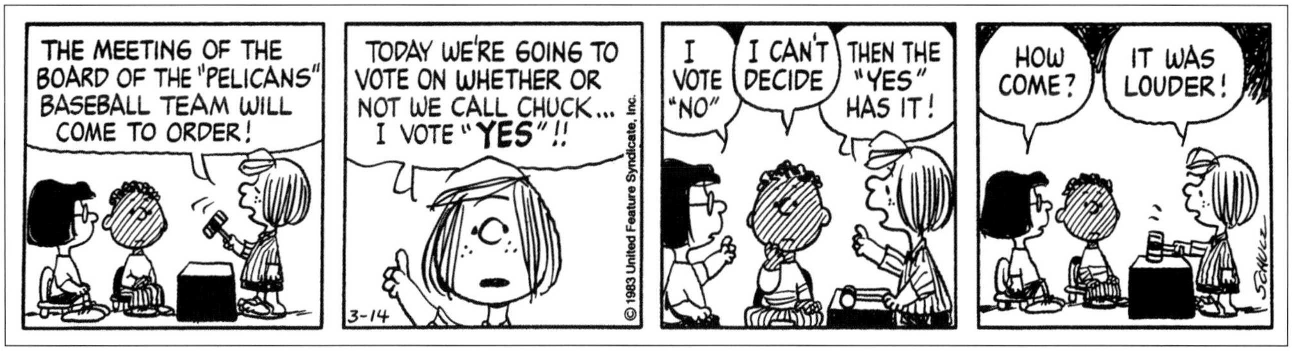
THE MEETING OF THE BOARD OF THE "PELICANS" BASEBALL TEAM WILL COME TO ORDER!
TODAY WE'RE GOING TO VOTE ON WHETHER OR NOT WE CALL CHUCK... I VOTE "YES"!!
3-14
© 1983 United Feature Syndicate, Inc.
I VOTE "NO"
I CAN'T DECIDE
THEN THE "YES" HAS IT!
HOW COME?
IT WAS LOUDER!

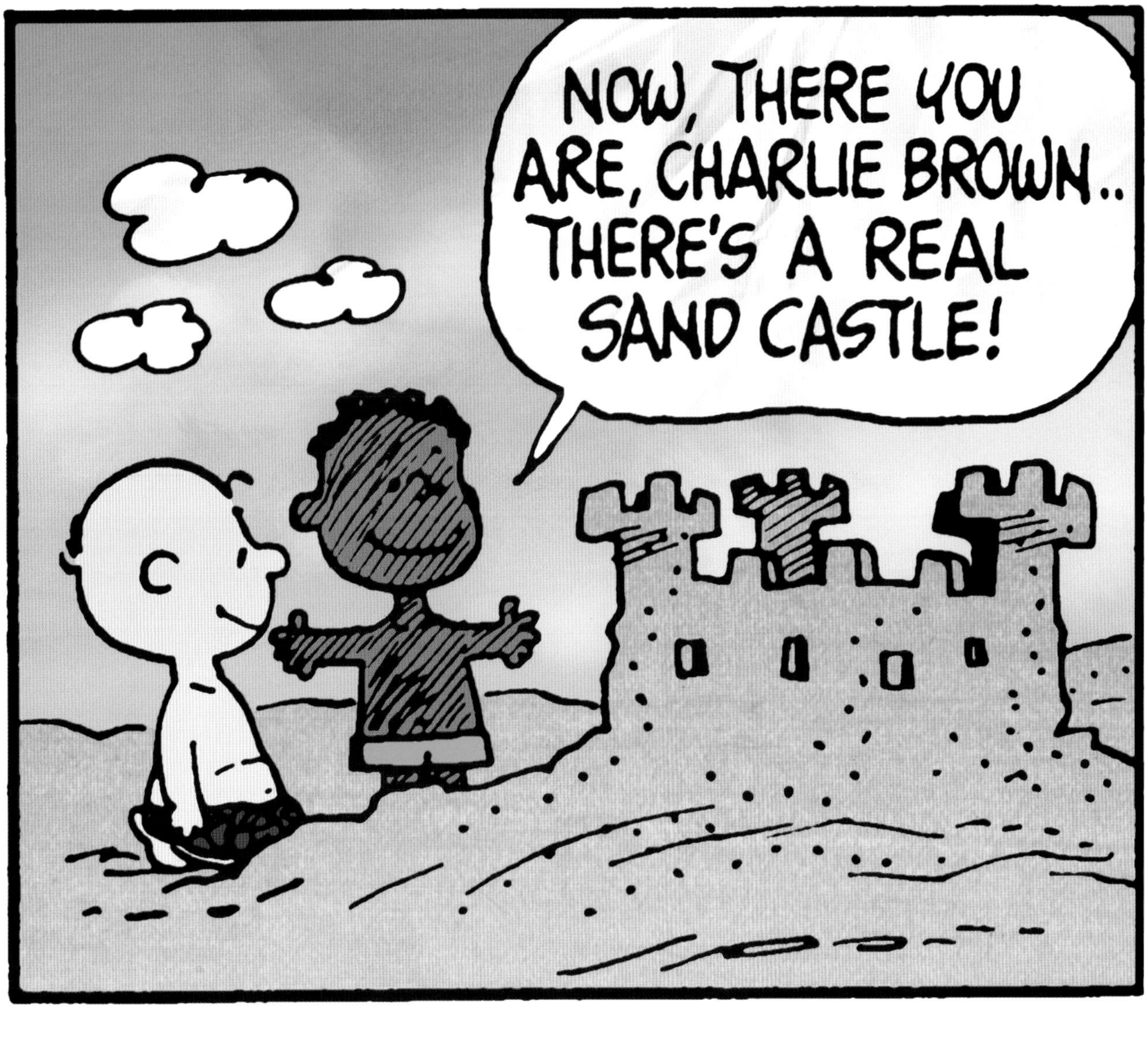
NOW, THERE YOU ARE, CHARLIE BROWN.. THERE'S A REAL SAND CASTLE!

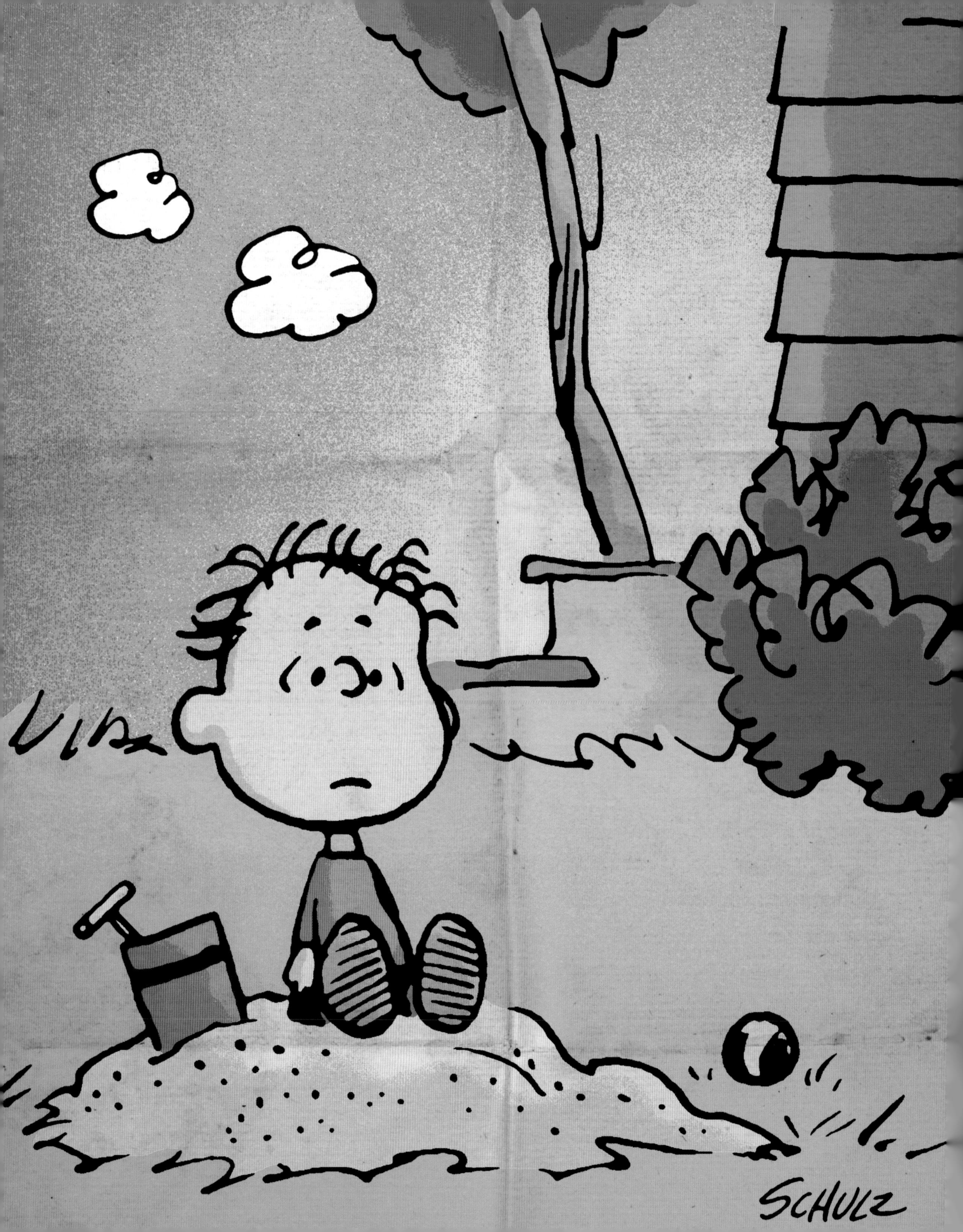
SCHULZ

# RERUN VAN PELT

FIRST MENTIONED 05/23/1972 FIRST APPEARANCE 03/26/1973

Lucy and Linus's younger brother, Rerun, earns his nickname when Lucy complains that she had a baby brother once, and that she sees no reason to go through that experience again, since it was like watching a rerun of a television program. Upon hearing this, Linus declares, "That's it! We'll call him 'Rerun'!" Despite her complaints, Lucy embraces her role of big sister and becomes very protective of Rerun.

When Rerun is not tagging along with his siblings, he's often seen racing across town on the back of his mother's bicycle as she dodges parked cars, sprinklers, and semitrucks on the way to the grocery store. Rerun does his best to enjoy the ride and encourage his mother, although he occasionally lapses into quoting Alfred, Lord Tennyson's poem The Charge of the Light Brigade, about a brave regiment of soldiers stoically accepting their fate.

When Rerun is safely on the ground, he can be found visiting Charlie Brown's house, hoping to play with Snoopy. The pair often play cards together (badly), but Snoopy generally rejects Rerun's offers to romp around the yard and chase sticks. Rerun's desire for a dog of his own is so great that he tries to adopt three of Snoopy's brothers, Spike, Andy, and Olaf, but his parents won't let him keep Andy and Olaf, and upon meeting Spike, Rerun isn't quite sure that he is actually a dog.

Although he often protests when it's time for him to go to kindergarten each morning, Rerun enjoys the challenges that he faces at school. He especially likes his art lessons, although he tends to ignore his teacher's instructions so that he can focus on his true passion, writing and drawing "underground comics."

Charles Schulz used Rerun sparingly throughout the 1980s, claiming that he'd exhausted all of his story options with him. "Rerun is still around," he reassured fans in 1984. "He rides on the back of his mom's bicycle now and then, and we're going to use him on some of the Saturday morning television shows but I just . . . run out of ideas on certain subjects, and lately I haven't been able to think of anything where he is on the back of his mom's bicycle. But he's still around." Schulz aged the character steadily over the next decade, and by the mid-1990s, Rerun's exploits took center stage in *Peanuts*, and he finally came into his own as a major character.

PEANUTS
WHAT I DON'T UNDERSTAND IS WHY YOUR MOTHER WOULD ALLOW LUCY TO THROW YOU OUT OF THE HOUSE...
MOM ISN'T HOME...SHE WENT TO THE HOSPITAL YESTERDAY
!
IS SHE ALL RIGHT?
I DON'T KNOW.. NOBODY EVER TELLS ME ANYTHING...
A NEW BABY BROTHER?!! BUT I JUST GOT RID OF THE OLD ONE!!!
SCHULZ
5-23

RIDING ON THE BACK OF YOUR MOTHER'S BICYCLE IN THE WINTER CAN BE AN EXPERIENCE
WE CAN'T SEE WHERE WE'RE GOING, AND WE SLIDE ALL OVER...
BUT WE FINALLY ARRIVE AT THE SUPERMARKET WHERE SHE BUMPS INTO AN OLD FRIEND...
12-9
COMPLETELY FORGETTING ABOUT YOU KNOW WHO!
SCHULZ
© 1980 United Feature Syndicate, Inc.

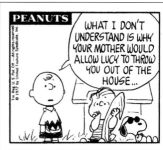

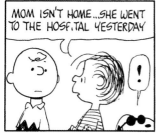

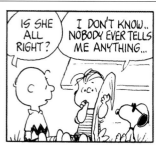

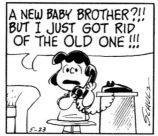

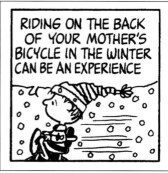

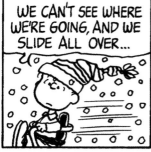

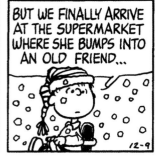

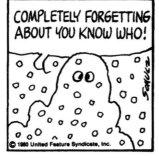

OPPOSITE: Peanuts, *Issue #21, Boom! Studios cover, 2014 – CSCA*

## THE ARTIST

Rerun has always had an uncomfortable relationship with education. He spends many mornings hiding under his bed to avoid going to school. That begins to change when he discovers art class and embraces his calling as an underground comic book artist. His disregard for authority and following instructions may frustrate his teacher, but who is he to fight his destiny?

Even if he's not quite sure what "underground comics" are.

"I think my future is in crayons." —Rerun

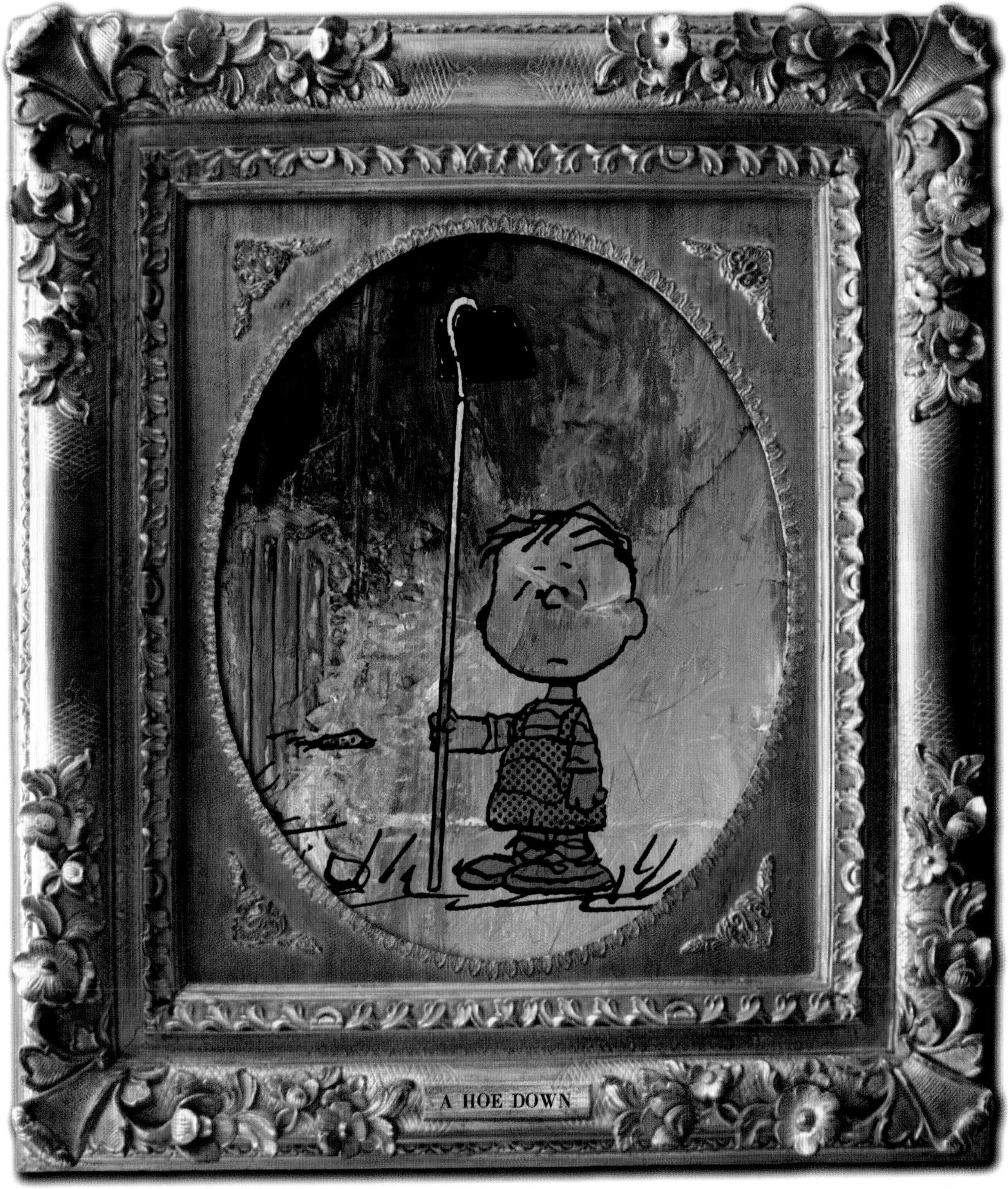
A HOE DOWN

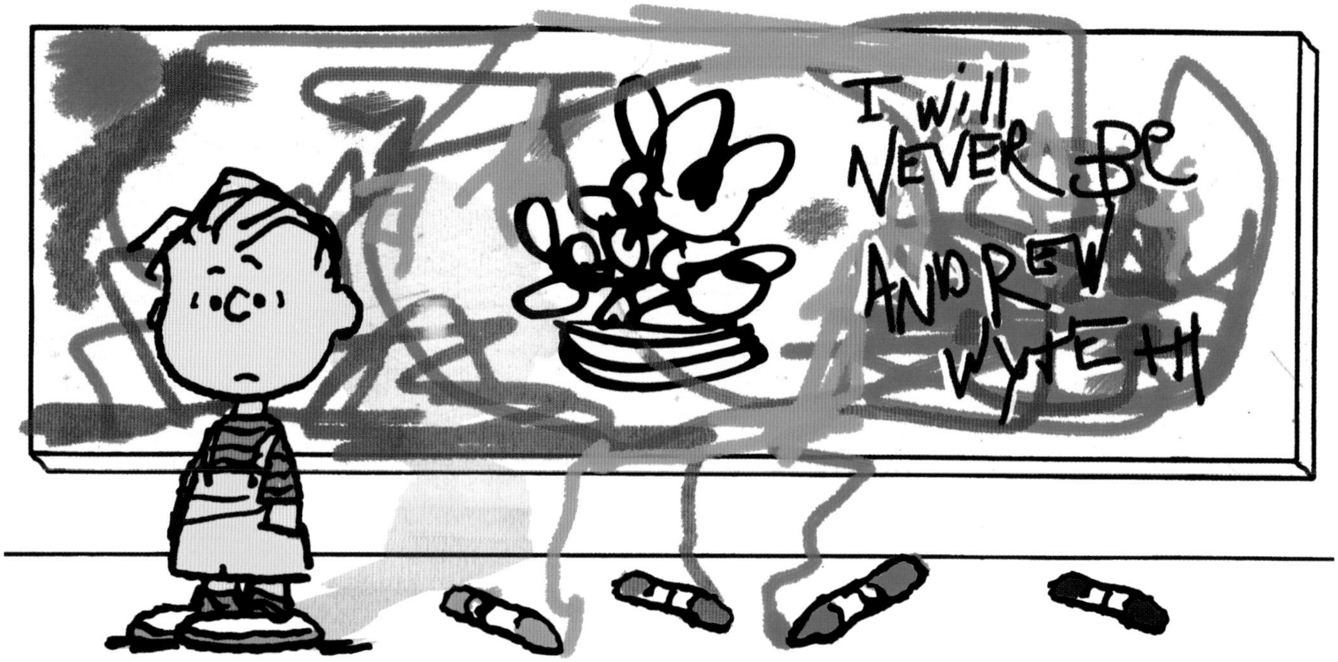
I will NEVER Be
ANDREW WYTEH

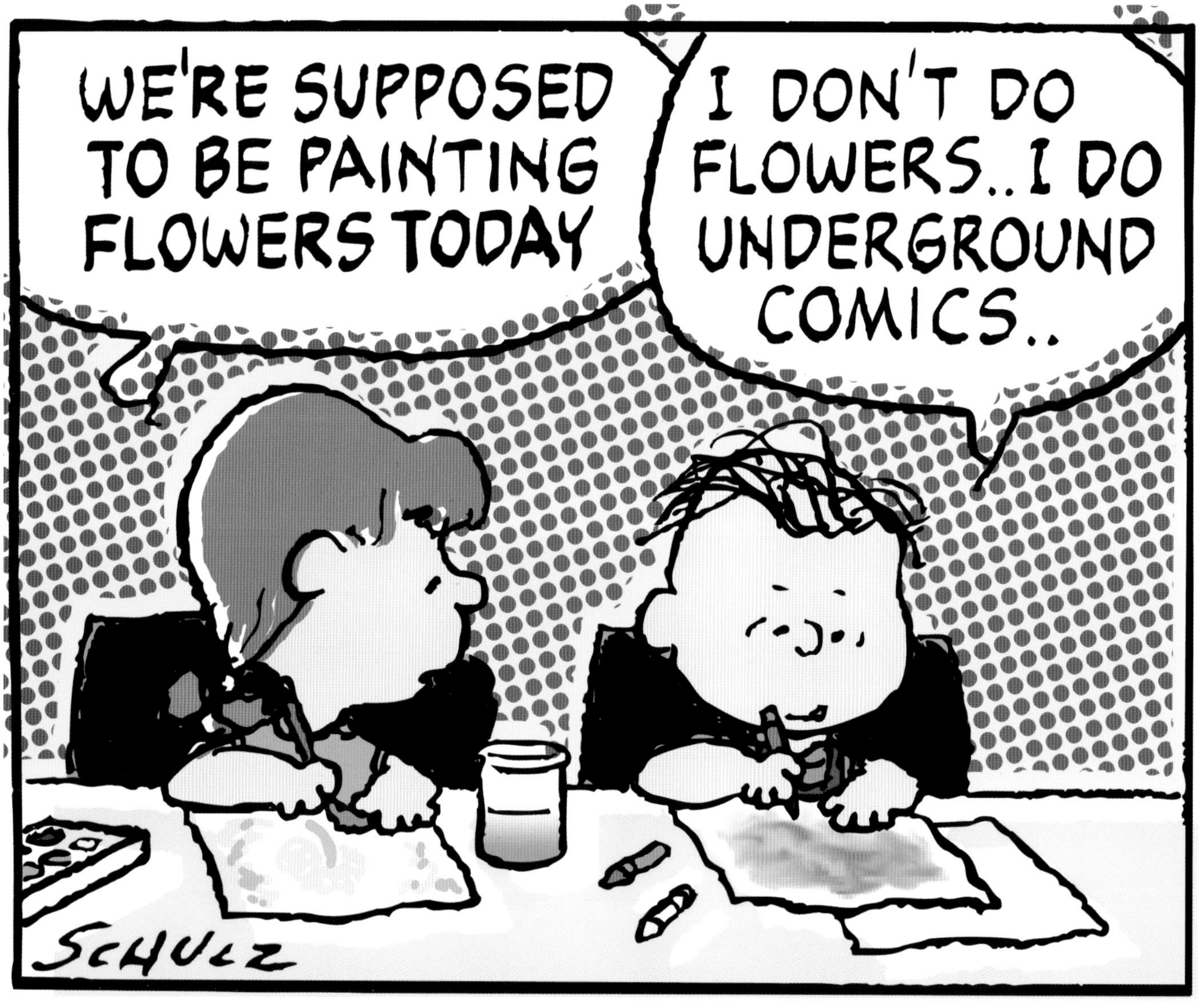
WE'RE SUPPOSED TO BE PAINTING FLOWERS TODAY
I DON'T DO FLOWERS..I DO UNDERGROUND COMICS..
SCHULZ

OPPOSITE: *Design by Cameron + Co* | TOP: *Design by Cameron + Co* | ABOVE: *Style Guide art – CSCA* | OVERLEAF, LEFT TO RIGHT: *Design by Cameron + Co*

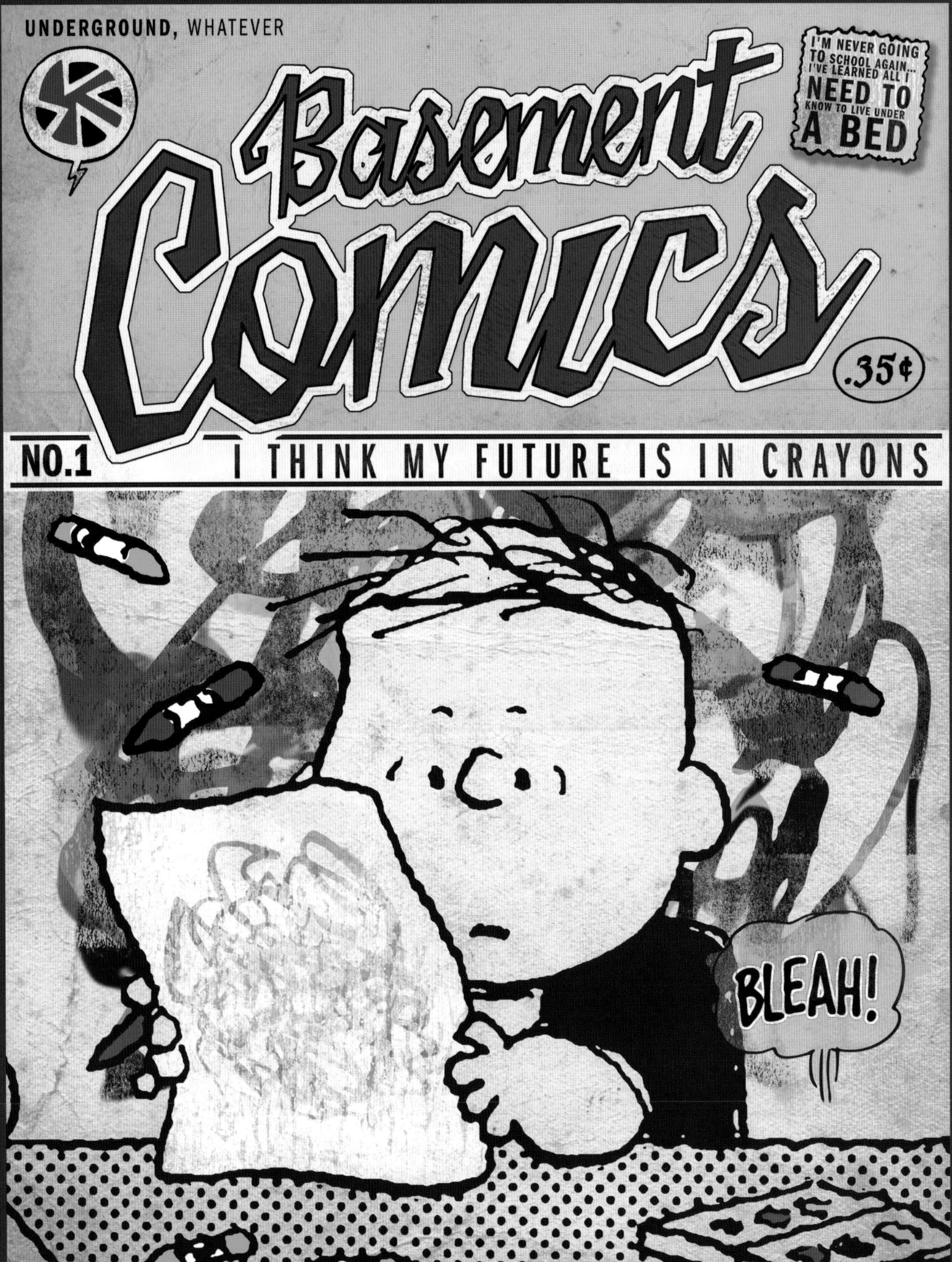
UNDERGROUND, WHATEVER
Basement Comics
I'M NEVER GOING TO SCHOOL AGAIN... I'VE LEARNED ALL I NEED TO KNOW TO LIVE UNDER A BED
.35¢
NO.1
I THINK MY FUTURE IS IN CRAYONS
BLEAH!

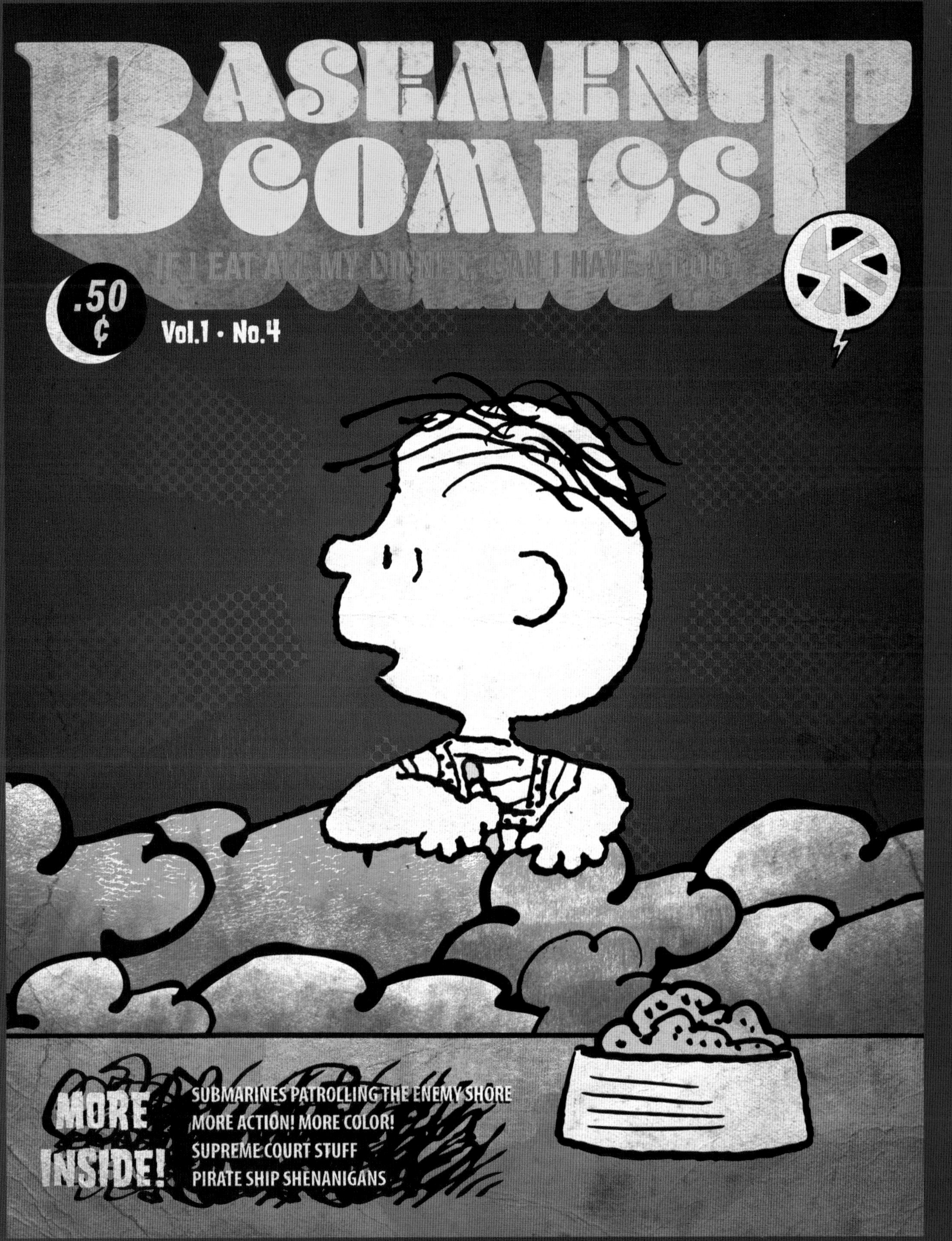
BASEMENT COMICS
IF I EAT ALL MY DINNER, CAN I HAVE A DOG
.50 ¢
Vol.1 • No.4
MORE INSIDE!
SUBMARINES PATROLLING THE ENEMY SHORE
MORE ACTION! MORE COLOR!
SUPREME COURT STUFF
PIRATE SHIP SHENANIGANS

# Joe Agate

FIRST APPEARANCE 04/07/1995

The best [marbles] player this side of the Mississippi," Joe Agate is also one of the most unscrupulous, challenging, young, and inexperienced marbles players to play for "keeps" so that he can build up his own massive marble collection. When he takes advantage of Rerun, the experienced sharpshooter, Charlie Brown knows what he has to do.

On his way to meet Joe Agate, Charlie Brown encounters Joe's latest victim and realizes that he has to teach the bully a lesson. Rerun and Lucy watch in awe as Charlie "Cool Thumb" Brown steps in and wins back all Rerun's marbles, along with Joe Agate's own collection, embarrassing Agate and driving him out of town in the process.

His triumph over Joe Agate is a rare decisive victory for Charlie Brown, who almost always winds up on the losing end of any competition.

"A lot of adults forget how difficult it is to be a child," Charles Schulz noted, recalling memories of his own childhood. "I've always despised bullies. They never let us play totally at peace. They made the playgrounds dangerous."

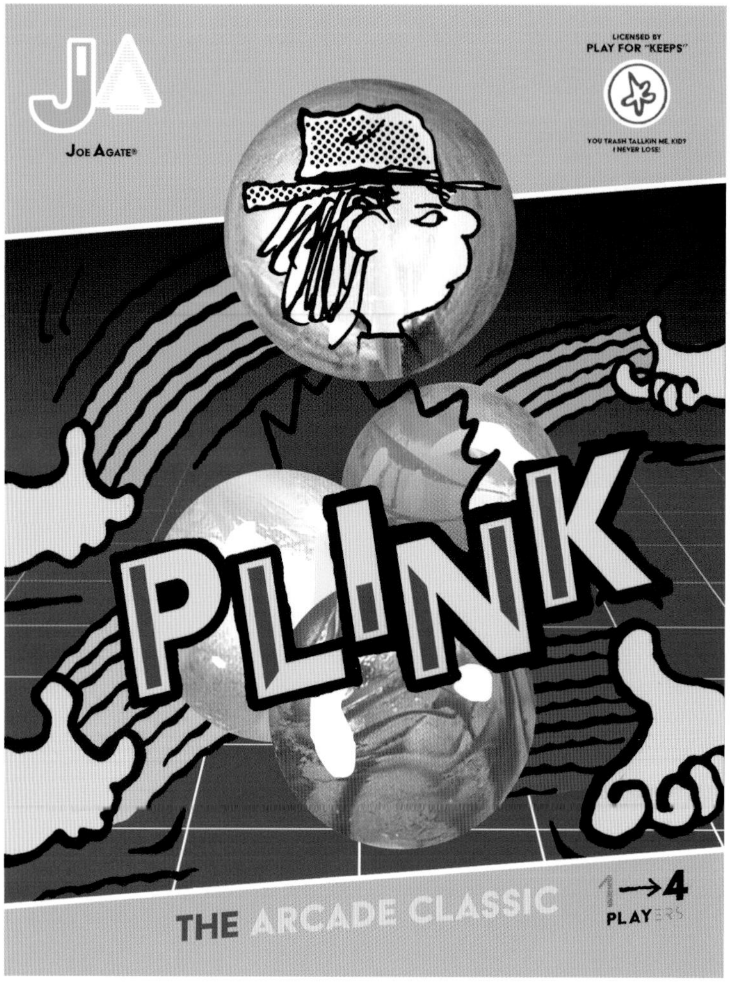
JA
Joe Agate®
LICENSED BY
PLAY FOR "KEEPS"
PLINK
THE ARCADE CLASSIC
1→4
PLAYERS

ABOVE: *Design by Cameron + Co*

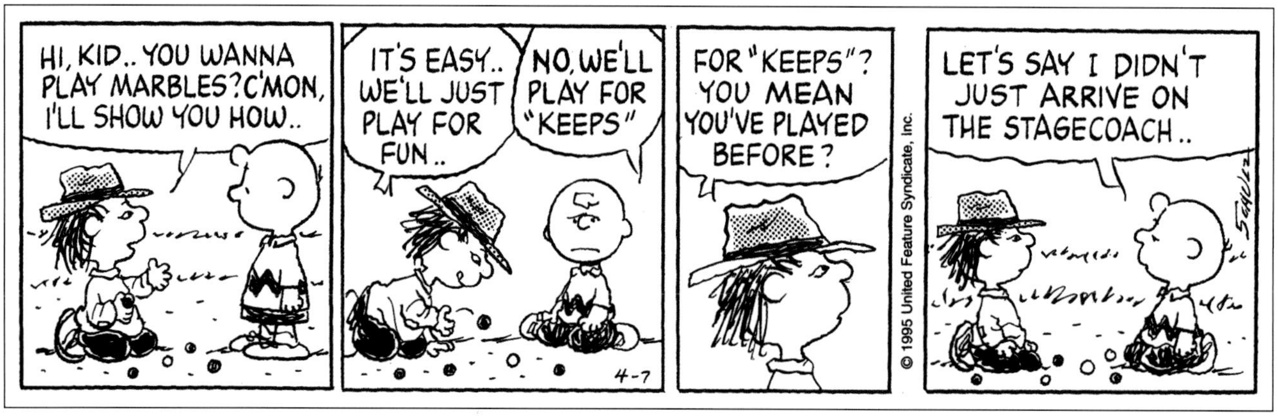
HI, KID.. YOU WANNA PLAY MARBLES? C'MON, I'LL SHOW YOU HOW..
IT'S EASY.. WE'LL JUST PLAY FOR FUN..
NO, WE'LL PLAY FOR "KEEPS"
4-7
FOR "KEEPS"? YOU MEAN YOU'VE PLAYED BEFORE?
© 1995 United Feature Syndicate, Inc.
LET'S SAY I DIDN'T JUST ARRIVE ON THE STAGECOACH..
SCHULZ

# SUPPORTING CAST

What's in a name? Some of the kids in the neighborhood made a big impression on their friends, even if those friends never bothered to learn their names. Despite their anonymity, they've proven themselves to be unforgettable additions to *Peanuts*.

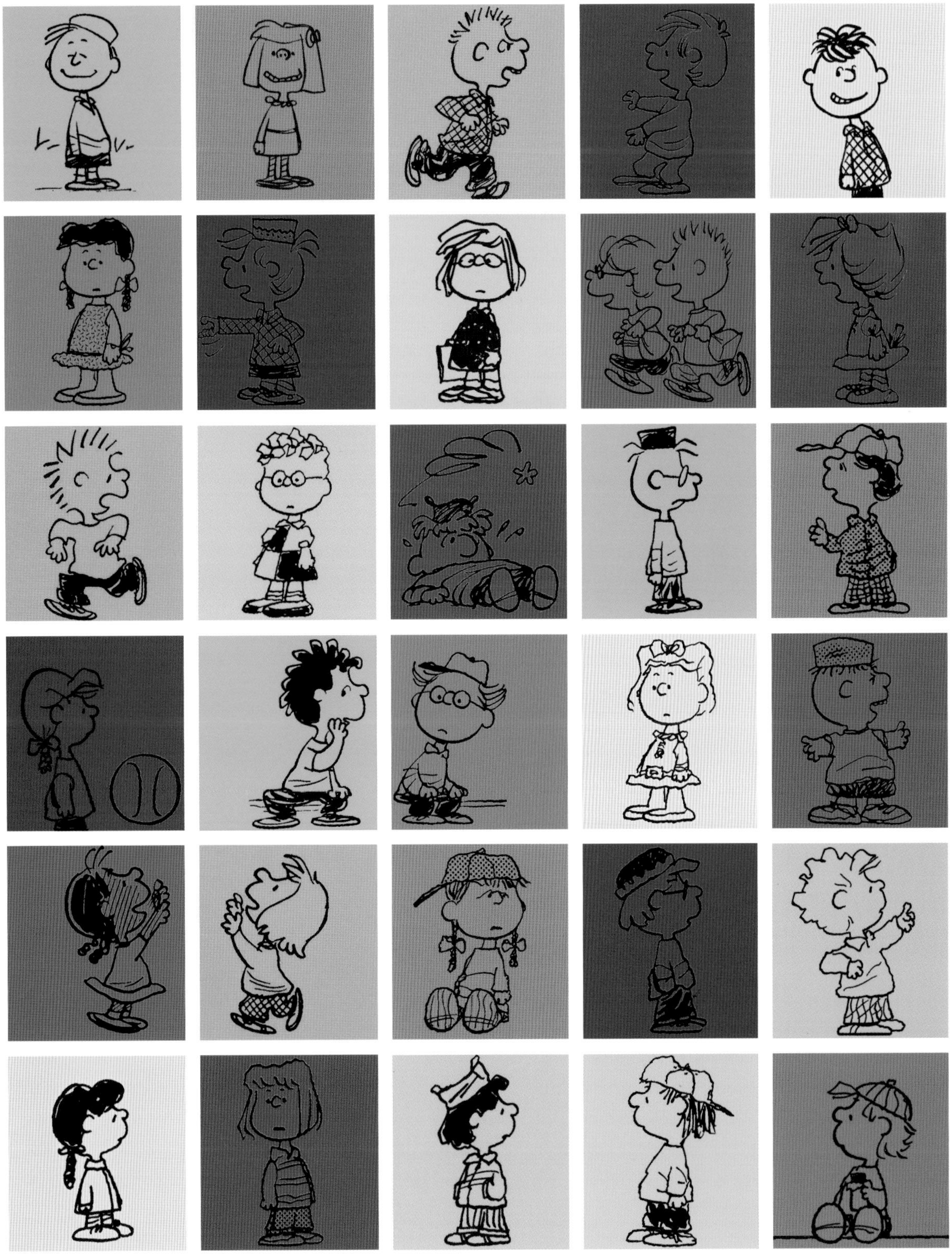

ABOVE: *Design by Cameron + Co*

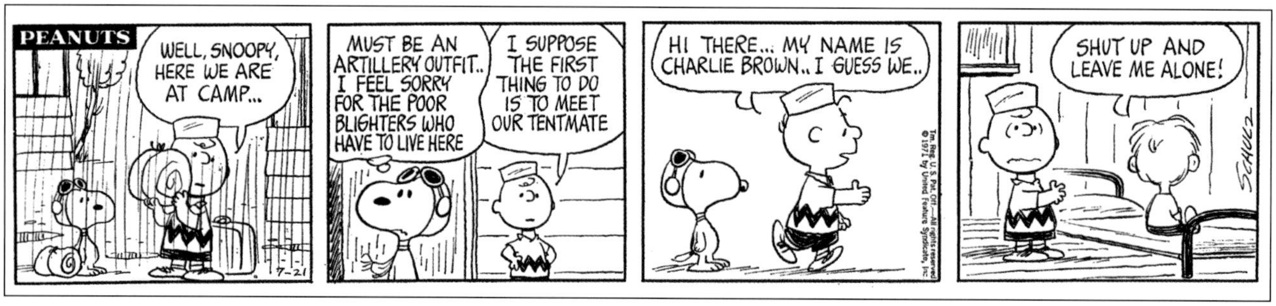
PEANUTS
WELL, SNOOPY, HERE WE ARE AT CAMP...
MUST BE AN ARTILLERY OUTFIT.. I FEEL SORRY FOR THE POOR BLIGHTERS WHO HAVE TO LIVE HERE
I SUPPOSE THE FIRST THING TO DO IS TO MEET OUR TENTMATE
HI THERE... MY NAME IS CHARLIE BROWN.. I GUESS WE..
SHUT UP AND LEAVE ME ALONE!
SCHULZ

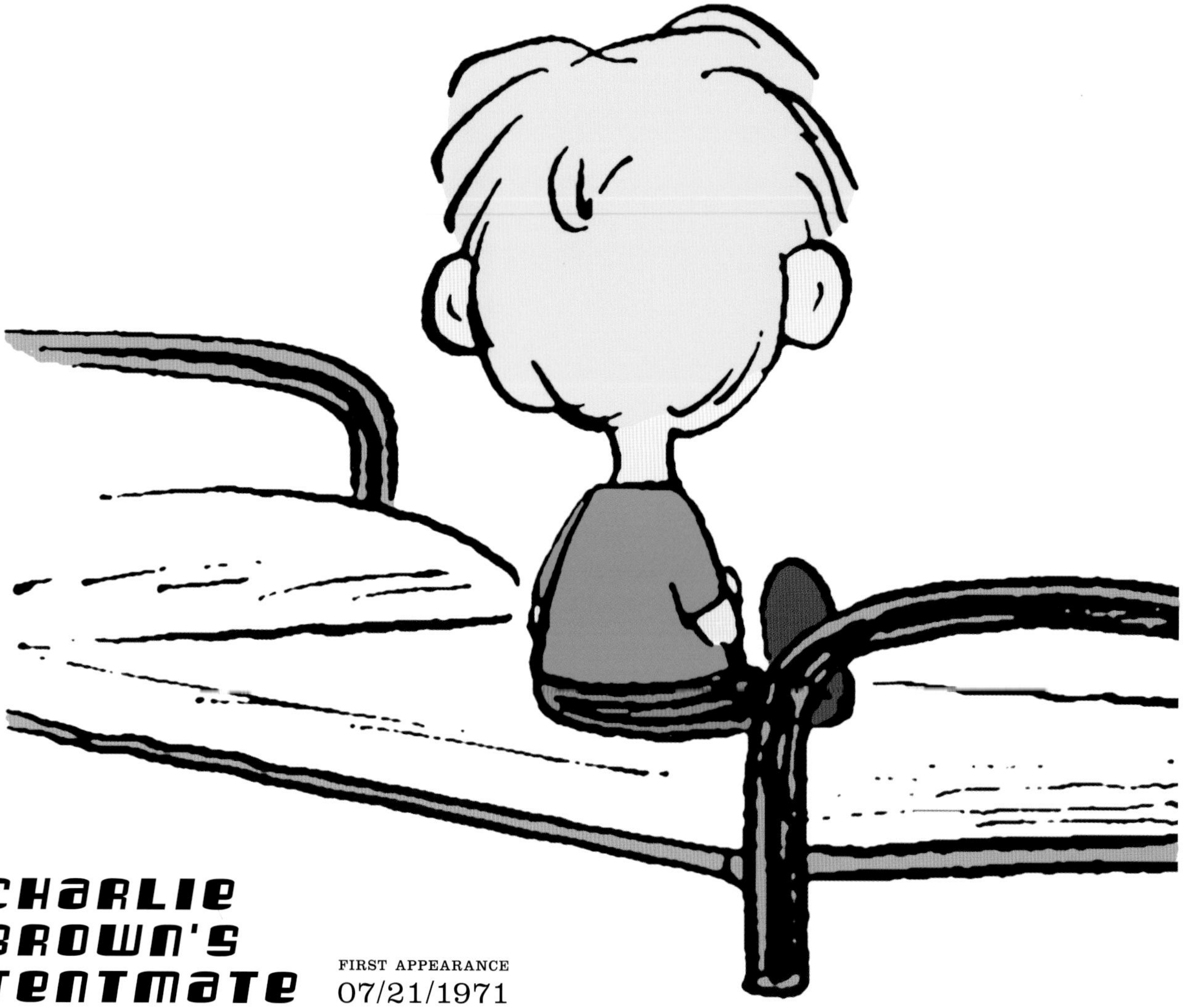

# CHARLIE BROWN'S TENTMATE

FIRST APPEARANCE
07/21/1971

Charlie Brown knows from experience that summer camp can be a very lonely place, so he always does his best to reach out to campers in need. One summer, he's greeted by a new tentmate who seems content to sit on his bunk facing the wall and ignore everyone around him. Charlie Brown does his best to engage him, but every greeting and invitation is met with the same response: "Shut up and leave me alone!" Dinner, astronomy class, and even a surprise visit from Peppermint Patty and Marcie aren't enough to get him to expand his vocabulary or turn his head.

A few weeks later, back at home, Charlie Brown writes a letter to his tentmate, hoping that they might be able to strike up a correspondence over their shared experience. Charlie Brown is surprised when his tentmate takes the time to respond, but not surprisingly, he only has one thing to say in his letter: "Shut up and leave me alone!"

WHO WAS ON THE PHONE?
© 1989 United Feature Syndicate, Inc.
A GIRL WHO SAID SHE WAS AN OLD FRIEND OF YOURS CALLING FROM OUT OF THE BLUE...
7-20
I DIDN'T KNOW WHERE THAT WAS SO I HUNG UP..
SCHULZ

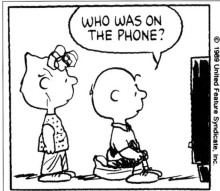

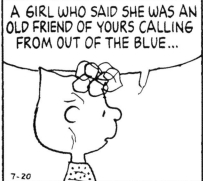

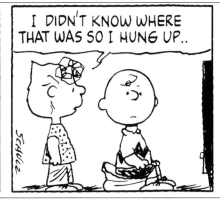

# Charlie Brown's Long-Lost Friend

FIRST MENTIONED 07/20/1989
FIRST APPEARANCE 07/28/1989

Charlie Brown receives a call from a long-lost friend, but he can't recall anything about her. When Charlie Brown and Snoopy go to meet her in person at the local mall, a little girl with a ponytail rushes up and embraces Snoopy—and is convinced that he is Charlie Brown! The unnamed girl treats Snoopy to five marshmallow sundaes as she reminisces about spending time with him at summer camp.

Charlie Brown doesn't remember her at all, unlike the other mysterious girls from Snoopy's past. And she doesn't recognize Charlie Brown, who has never seen her before in his life. None of her camp stories manage to clear up the mystery, but Snoopy is content as long as he's being treated to dessert. When they finally part ways, the ponytailed girl is elated, Charlie Brown is confused, and Snoopy is queasy—five marshmallow sundaes in one sitting are a lot for a beagle.

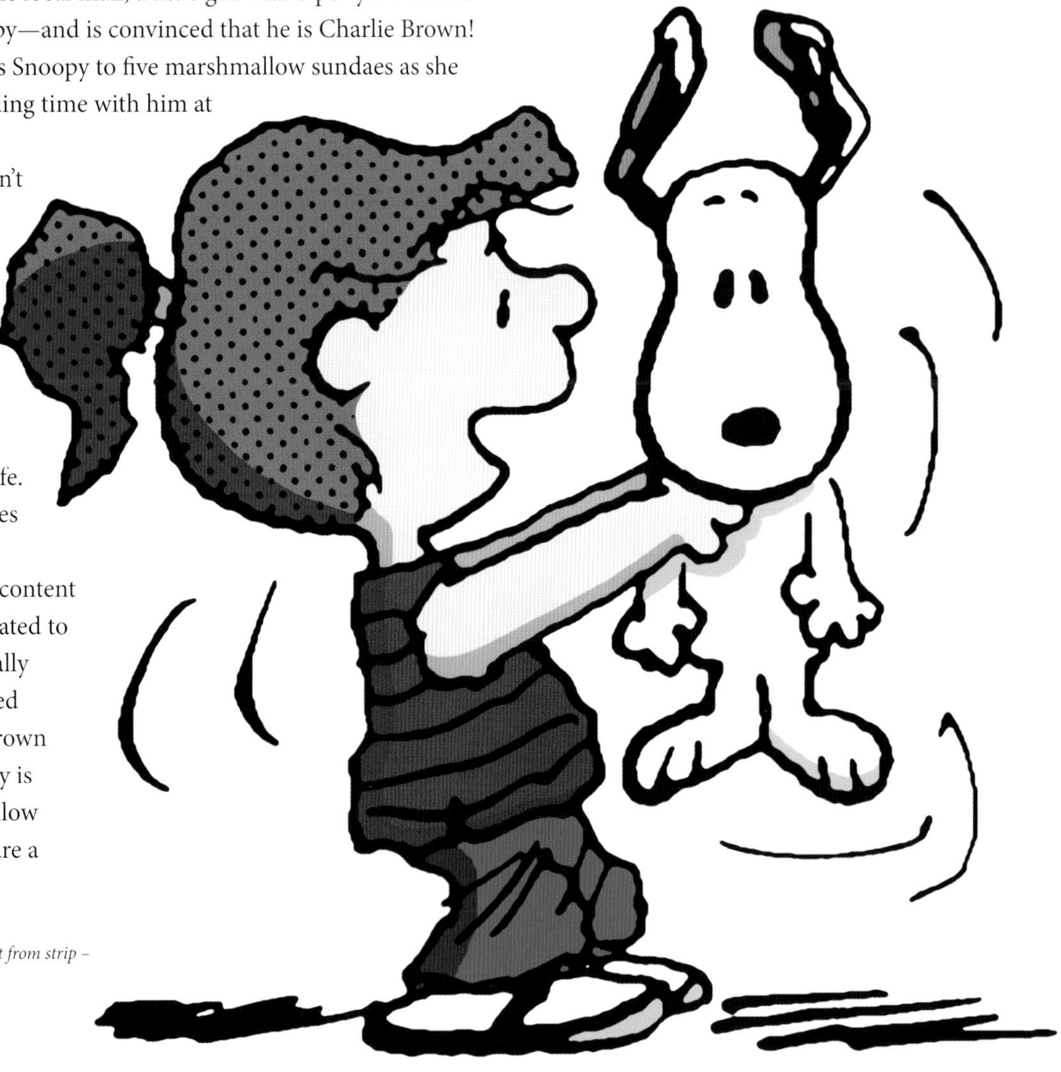

OPPOSITE AND RIGHT: *Spot art from strip – Charles M. Schulz*

# RERUN'S CLASSMATE

FIRST APPEARANCE 09/11/1996

**R**erun is in a class by himself—but a little girl with pigtails does her best to keep up with him in kindergarten. Unlike her easily distracted classmate, she always listens to her teacher, follows instructions, and shows a real commitment to her education. The little girl excels in art class and enjoys painting flowers and taking field trips to the museum.

The pigtailed girl doesn't seem to understand Rerun's very particular sense of humor, which is often a source of great confusion for the two of them. Despite these distractions, she stays on task, and once in a great while she even manages to get Rerun to pay attention to their teacher, which is an impressive task all its own.

"I knew that little kids live a life that is different from the adults," observed Charles Schulz, when discussing the younger *Peanuts* characters. "I always had this feeling that little kids are trapped on playgrounds or in other places and in order to get away you have to learn how to work your way around. It's tough to be a little kid."

RIGHT: *Spot art from strip – Charles M. Schulz* | OPPOSITE: Modern Painters *magazine cover, published by CTB (UK) Limited, 2005 – CMSM*

YES, MA'AM..MY NAME IS "RERUN"...I DON'T KNOW..THAT'S WHAT THEY ALL CALL ME..

YES, I KNOW I SHOULD HAVE BEEN HERE LAST WEEK.. WELL, I'M HERE NOW..

I HOPE WE DON'T HAVE TO READ "WAR AND PEACE" THE FIRST DAY..

© 1996 United Feature Syndicate, Inc.

www.unitedmedia.com

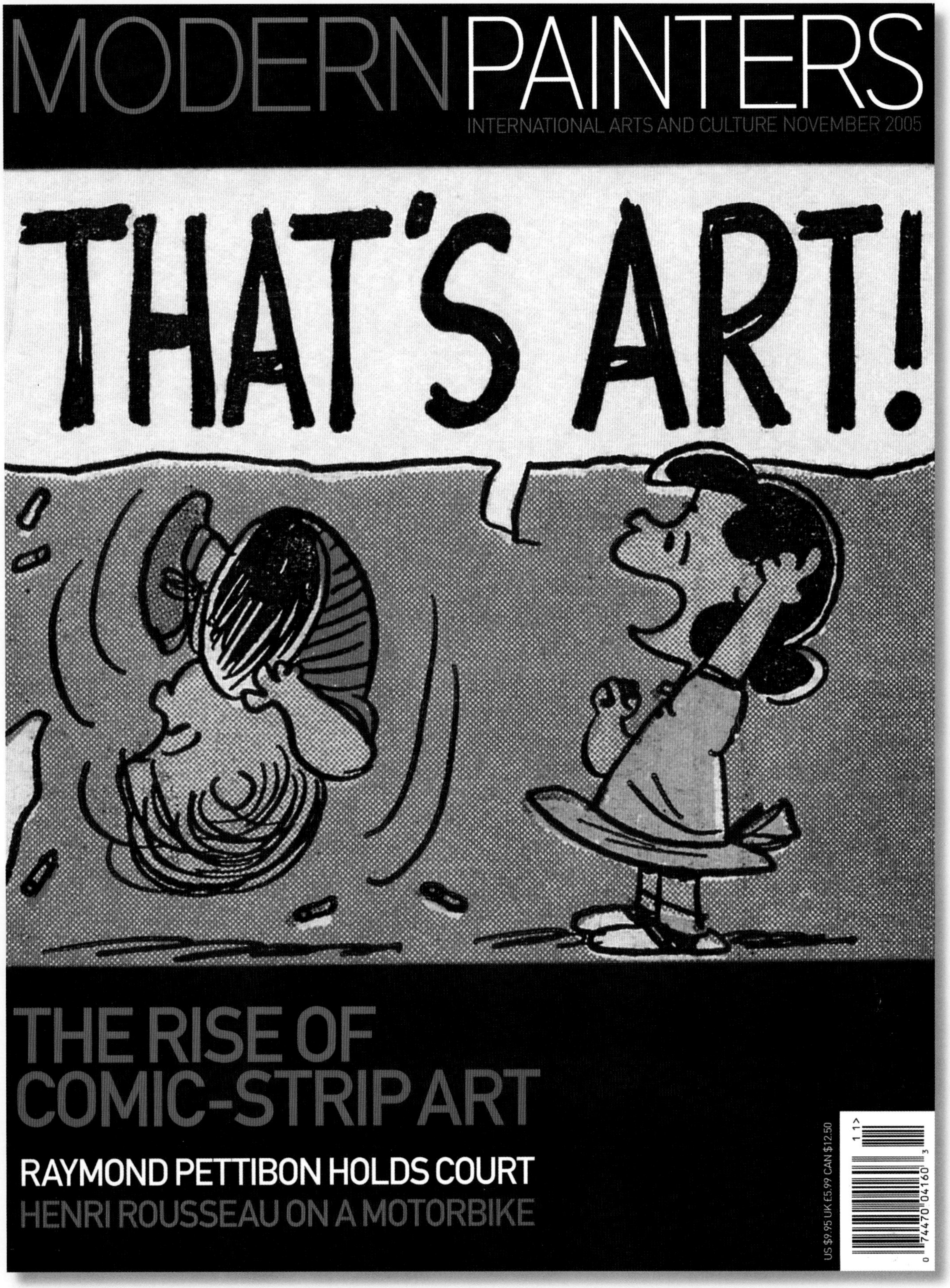
MODERN PAINTERS
INTERNATIONAL ARTS AND CULTURE NOVEMBER 2005
THAT'S ART!
THE RISE OF
COMIC-STRIP ART
RAYMOND PETTIBON HOLDS COURT
HENRI ROUSSEAU ON A MOTORBIKE
US $9.95 UK £5.99 CAN $12.50

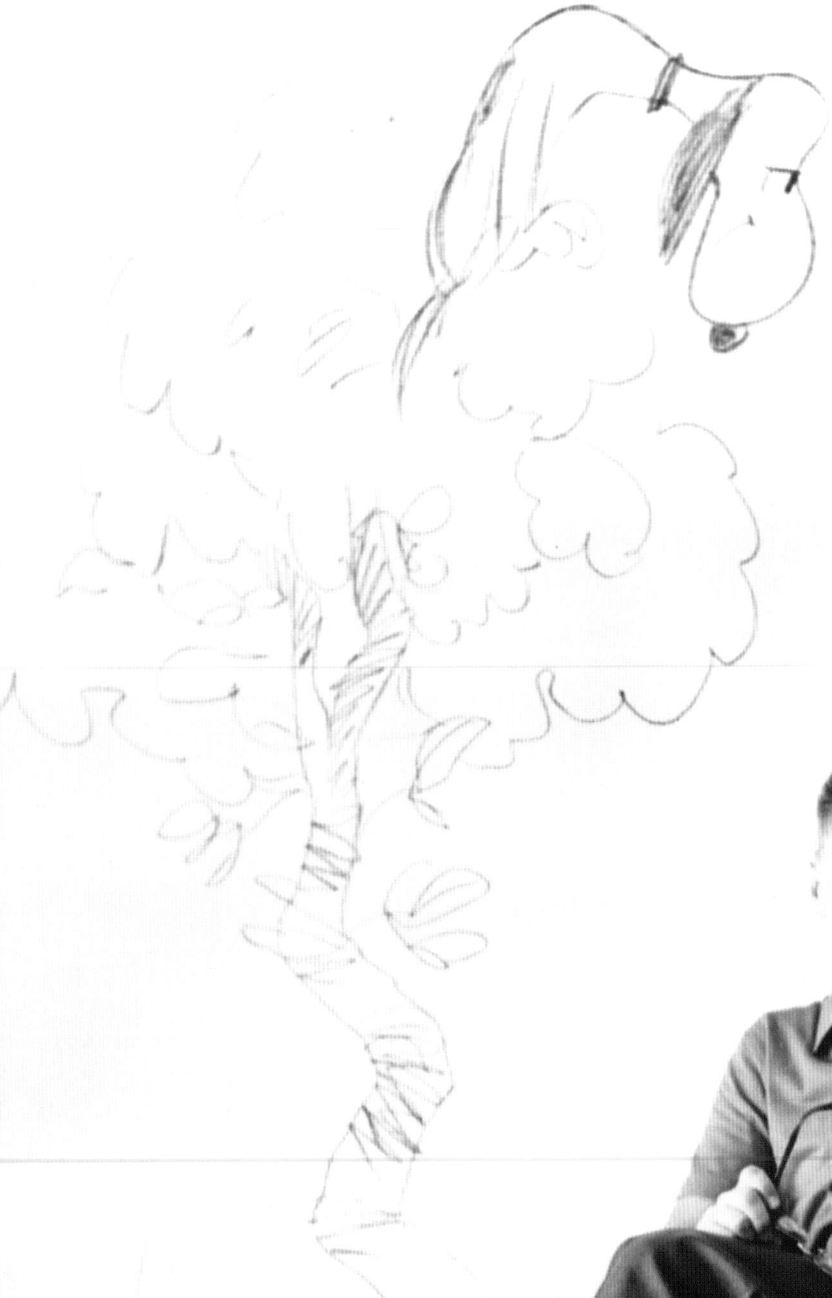

# CHARLES M. SCHULZ

Charles M. Schulz once described himself as "born to draw comic strips." Born in Minneapolis, at just two days old, an uncle nicknamed him "Sparky" after the horse Spark Plug from the *Barney Google* comic strip, and throughout his youth, he and his father shared a Sunday morning ritual reading the funnies. After serving in the Army during World War II, Schulz's first big break came in 1947 when he sold a cartoon feature called "Li'l Folks" to the St. Paul Pioneer Press. In 1950, Schulz met with United Feature Syndicate, and on October 2 of that year, PEANUTS, named by the syndicate, debuted in seven papers. Charles Schulz died in Santa Rosa, California, in February 2000–just hours before his last original strip was appear in Sunday papers.

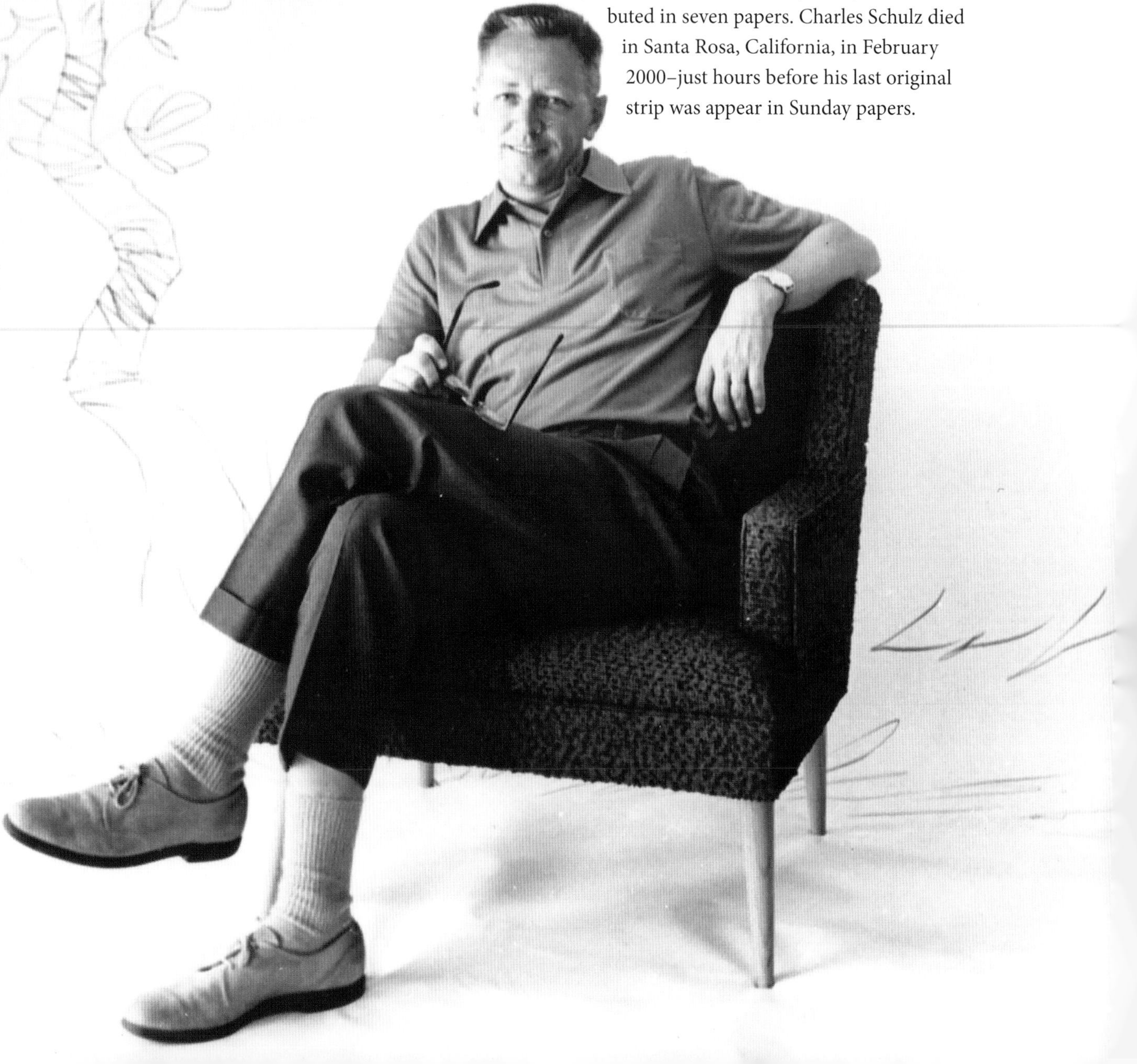

# ACKNOWLEDGMENTS

As always, thanks to Shaenon and Robin.

Thanks to Mom and Dad for introducing me to *Peanuts* in our local newspaper, and for making sure that my sister, brothers, and I always had at least a few of the *Peanuts* paperbacks on our bookshelf at home.

Thanks to the wonderful Charles Schulz for creating my favorite comic strip. I wouldn't be the person I am today without *Peanuts*, and I'm honored that I had this opportunity to pay tribute to the man and his work.

Tremendous thanks to Jeannie Schulz for her ongoing efforts to celebrate the legacy of *Peanuts*, her tireless support of the Charles M. Schulz Museum and Research Library as well as San Francisco's Cartoon Art Museum, and her endless enthusiasm for the comics medium.

Special thanks to the board and staff at the Cartoon Art Museum, especially Executive Director Summerlea Kashar, Program Coordinator Nina Taylor Kester, and the museum's founder, Malcolm Whyte.

Big thanks to Alexis Fajardo, senior editor at Charles M. Schulz Creative Associates for recommending me for this project and for going above and beyond the call of duty while this book came together. Iain Morris, Dustin Jones, and Jan Hughes of Cameron + Company guided this book every step of the way, and I couldn't have asked for a better team.

— *Andrew Farago*

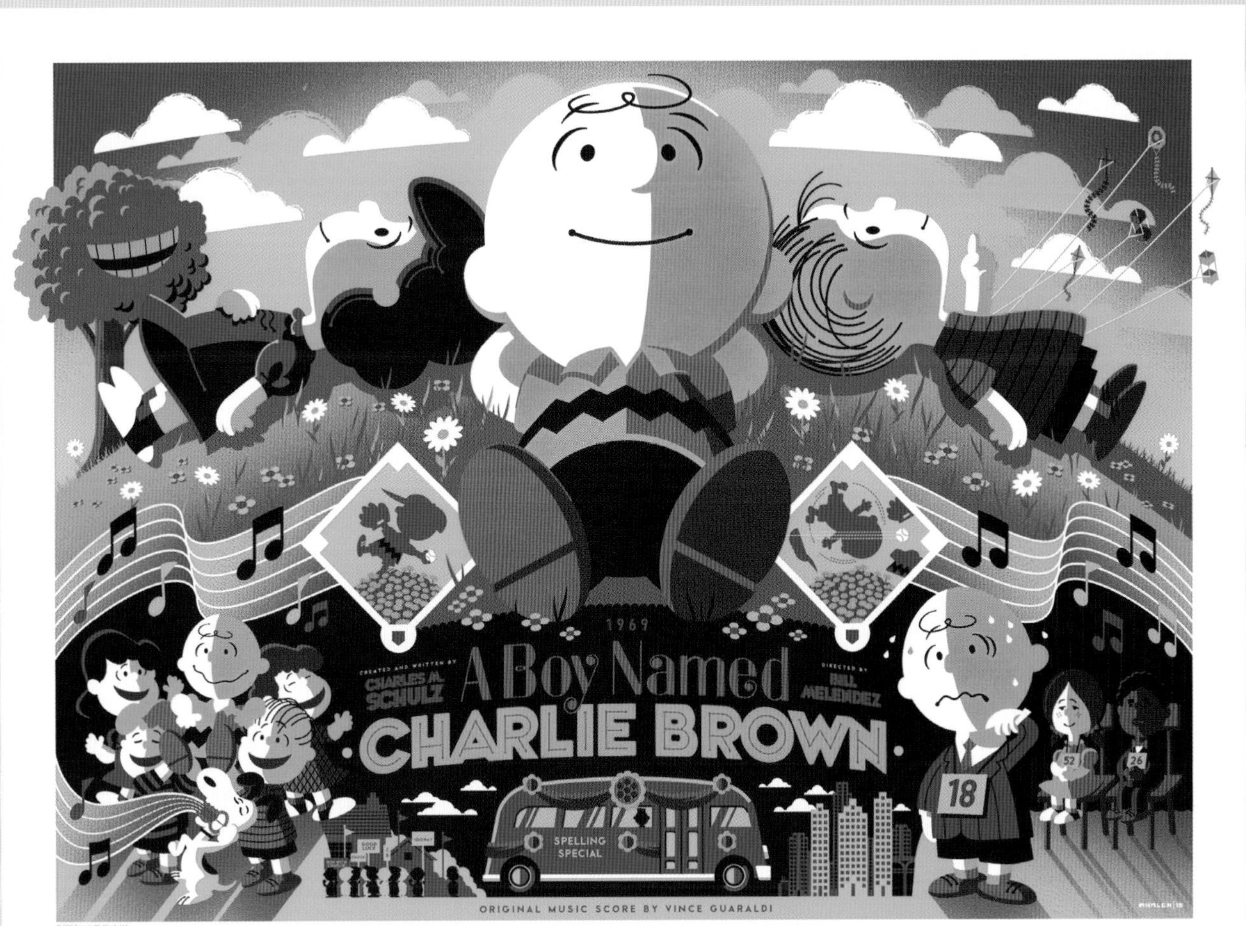
1969
CREATED AND WRITTEN BY
CHARLES M. SCHULZ
A Boy Named
DIRECTED BY
BILL MELENDEZ
CHARLIE BROWN
SPELLING SPECIAL
18
ORIGINAL MUSIC SCORE BY VINCE GUARALDI

OPPOSITE: *Courtesy of the Hallmark Archives, Hallmark Cards, Inc., Kansas City, Missouri* | ABOVE: A Boy Named Charlie Brown; *Artist: Tom Whalen; Limited Edition Print; Courtesy: Dark Hall Mansion* | FOLLOWING PAGE: It's the Easter Beagle, Charlie Brown!; *Artist: Tom Whalen; Limited Edition Print; Courtesy: Dark Hall Mansion*

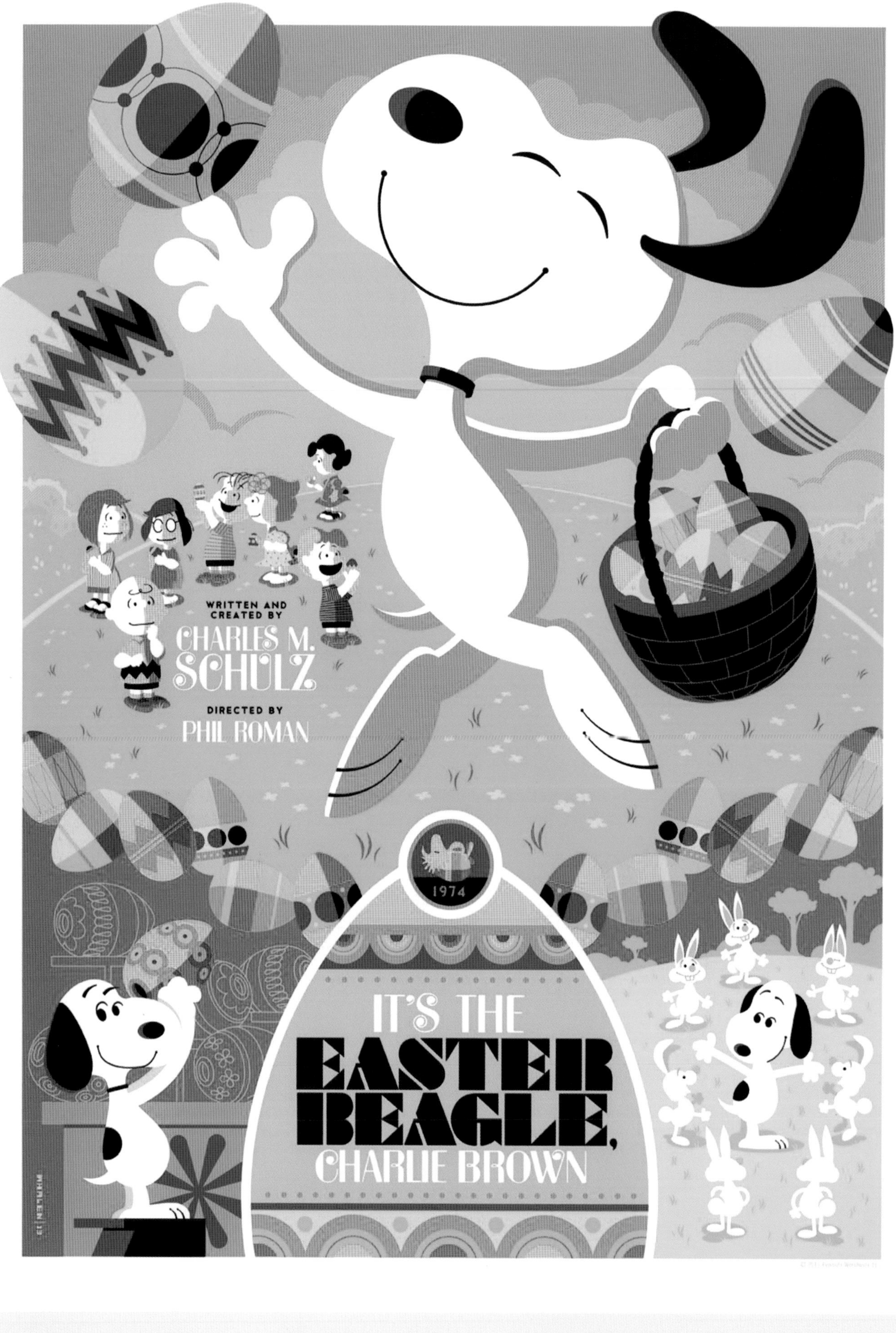
WRITTEN AND CREATED BY
CHARLES M. SCHULZ
DIRECTED BY
PHIL ROMAN
1974
IT'S THE
EASTER
BEAGLE,
CHARLIE BROWN

# CREDITS

**CHARLES M. SCHULZ** *is the artist for all strips, panels, and excerpts appearing in this book, unless otherwise cited.*

**COURTESY OF THE CHARLES M. SCHULZ MUSEUM AND RESEARCH CENTER (CMSM):** *pp 12; 14; 35 (top right); 37 (bottom right); 40–41; 64; 81 (3); 83 (top left); 91 (3, 4, 6); 96 (center); 117: (bottom left); 154 (2); 155 (5); 156: (1); 158; 178 (top); 179: (center); 180; 184; 187 (bottom left, right); 194; 221; 251; 252*

**CHARLES M. SCHULZ CREATIVE ASSOCIATES (CSCA):** *Cover: design Vicki Scott | PLC: color and design by Iain Morris | Endpapers: pencils by Vicki Scott | pp 1: pencils by Vicki Scott | 2: original artwork by Charles M. Schulz | 4–5: pencils by Vicki Scott, inks by Paige Braddock, color by Art Roche | 6: pencils by Bob Scott | 7: designed by Justin Thompson | 10–11: pencils by Vicki Scott, inks Paige Braddock, color by Art Roche | 15: (top row) design by Iain Morris; (bottom left) color by Alexis E. Fajardo; (bottom right) design by Katherine Efird | 16, 18: pencils and inks by Vicki Scott, color by Nina Kester, inks by Paige Braddock | 28–29, pencils by Bob Scott | 29: (center) pencils Vicki Scott, inks Paige Braddock, color Nina Kester | 30: (far left) color by Alexis E. Fajardo; (top right) design by Iain Morris | 31: design by Iain Morris | 33: pencils by Vicki Scott, inks by Paige Braddock, color and design by Iain Morris | 36: (left, right) design by Iain Morris | 37: (top, bottom left) design by Iain Morris, (center) design by Justin Thompson | 38: (left and right) design by Iain Morris | 39: (all) design by Iain Morris | 42: (1, 11) design by Iain Morris | 44: (top) pencils by Andy Beall; (center) pencils by Vicki Scott, inks by Paige Braddock, color by Nina Kester | 45: pencils by Bob Scott | 47: (center) pencils by Bob Scott; (bottom right) color by Alexis E. Fajardo | 48–49: design by Iain Morris | 50: design by Iain Morris | 51: design by Iain Morris | 52 (top) pencils by Bob Scott | 53 (bottom left) art by Bob Scott; (bottom right) design by Iain Morris | 56–57: design Iain Morris | 61: design by Iain Morris | 63: (bottom left) design by Iain Morris | 66: pencils by Scott Jeralds, inks by Justin Thompson, color by Nina Kester | 68–69: (1) art by Bob Scott; (2) pencils by Vicki Scott, inks by Paige Braddock, color by Art Roche | 71: design by Iain Morris | 78: (center) pencils by Vicki Scott, inks by Paige Braddock, color by Nina Kester | 78–79: pencils by Bob Scott | 80–81: (1, 2, 4, 5, 6) design by Iain Morris | 82: design by Iain Morris | 84–85: pencils by Bob Scott ; 84 (top) design by Iain Morris, (bottom left) pencils by Vicki Scott, inks by Paige Braddock, color by Nina Kester | 86–87: design by Iain Morris | 88: (2) design by Justin Thompson, (3) design by Iain Morris, (4) color and design by Donna Almendrala | 89: design by Iain Morris | 90: (1) design by Donna Almendrala, (2, 5) design by Iain Morris | 92: color and design by Iain Morris | 93: pencils by Vicki Scott, inks Paige Braddock, color Nina Kester | 94: (2) pencils by Bob Scott, (3) color by Iain Morris, (4) color by Alexis E. Fajardo | 95: (top row) design by Iain Morris | 97: (5) design by Iain Morris | 98: design by Iain Morris | 99: color by Donna Almendrala | 100–101: (1, 2, 4) design Iain Morris | 102: designs and color by Nomi Kane | 104–105: pencils by Bob Scott | 106: pencils by Bob Scott | 112–113: (1) design by Iain Morris; (3) design by Iain Morris; (6) art by Nick Lobianco; (8) pencils by Vicki Scott, inks by Paige Braddock | 115: color and design by Donna Almendrala | 116: (top) pencils by Bob Scott, (bottom) pencils by Andy Beall | 117: (bottom right) design by Iain Morris | 118: design by Iain Morris | 119: design by Iain Morris | 120: design by Iain Morris | 122–123: (2) pencils by Bob Scott | 123: (3) pencils by Vicki Scott, inks by Paige Braddock, color by Nina Kester; (4) design by Alexis E. Fajardo | 124: design by Iain Morris | 126: (top left) pencils by Vicki Scott, inks by Paige Braddock, color by Iain Morris; (bottom left) art by Nomi Kane; (bottom right) design by Alexis E. Fajardo | 127: (bottom left and right) design by Iain Morris | 132: (2) art from A Charlie Brown Christmas Storybook, art by Justin Thompson; (3) pencils Vicki Scott, Inks Paige Braddock, Color Art Roche | (6, 7) art by Bob Scott | 135: (6) art from A Charlie Brown Christmas Storybook, art by Justin Thompson | 138: (top left) pencils by Bob Scott; (top right) pencils Vicki Scott, inks by Paige Braddock, color Nina Kester; (center) pencils Vicki Scott, inks Paige Braddock, design Iain Morris | 139: design by Iain Morris | page 141 (top right) pencils by  Vicki Scott, inks by Paige Braddock, colors by Donna Almendrala | 143: design by Iain Morris | 144: (top left, center) design by Iain Morris | 146: (top) design by Iain Morris | 147: design by Iain Morris | 148: design by Iain Morris | 149: design by Iain Morris | 155: (7) design by Iain Morris | 156–157: (2) color by Justin Thompson; (3) color by Alexis E. Fajardo; (6) color by Justin Thompson; (8) pencils by Vicki Scott, inks Paige Braddock, design by Iain Morris; (9) pencils Vicki Scott, inks Paige Braddock | 164–165: pencils by Bob Scott | 166: (3) design by Iain Morris; (4) pencils by Bob Scott; (6) color by Alexis E. Fajardo | 167: pencils by Bob Scott, inks & color by Justin Thompson, design by Iain Morris | 168: design by Iain Morris | 172: (2, 5) design by Iain Morris | 174: (3) color by Justin Thompson; (5) art by Katharine Efird | 177: design by Iain Morris | 178: pencils by Vicki Scott, inks by Paige Braddock, color by Art Roche | 179: (bottom) design by Iain Morris | 181: color by Donna Almendrala | 183: design by Iain Morris | 185: (4) color by Justin Thompson | 189–191: design by Iain Morris | 193: design by Iain Morris | 196: design by Iain Morris | 198–199: design by Iain Morris | 201: design by Iain Morris | 204: (bottom) design by Iain Morris | 205: design by Iain Morris | 206: design by Iain Morris | 207: pencils by Vicki Scott, Inks by Paige Braddock, color design Iain Morris | 209: pencils by Vicki Scott, inks by Paige Braddock, color by Donna Almendrala | 212: pencils by Vicki Scott, inks by Paige Braddock, color and design by Iain Morris | 214: pencils by Bob Scott | 215: design by Iain Morris | 216: (left) design by Iain Morris; (right) color by Alexis E. Fajardo | 218: (top) design by Iain Morris; (bottom) design by Justin Thompson | 219: (top row, right) design by Iain Morris; (6, 8) design by Justin Thompson | 220: (left column) design by Iain Morris | 222: design by Iain Morris | 224: art by Bob Scott, design by Iain Morris | 226: design by Iain Morris | 228: color and design by Donna Almendrala | 229: design by Iain Morris | 234: pencils by Vicki Scott, inks by Paige Braddock, design Iain Morris | 236–237: pencils by Bob Scott | 237: (bottom) pencils by Vicki Scott, inks by Paige Braddock, colors Nina Kester | 238: pencils by Vicki Scott, inks by Paige Braddock, design Iain Morris | 240: color and design by Donna Almendrala | 242: design by Iain Morris | 243: (bottom) design by Justin Thompson | 256: (2, 3, 4) design by Iain Morris*

**PEANUTS WORLDWIDE (PW):** *pp 20–21: design by Chris Bracco | 28 (top left) design by Chris Bracco | 42 (2, 3, 4, 5, 6, 7, 9, 10) design Jessica Dasher | 60: design by Chris Bracco | 63 (bottom right) design by Ridge Rooms | 68–69: (4, 5) design by Chris Bracco; (7) design by Jessica Dasher; (8) design by Daniel Paz; (9) design by Ridge Rooms | 88: (1) design by Chris Bracco | 94 (1) design by Chris Bracco | 96: (1, 6) design by Jessica Dasher; (2, 4,) design by Ridge Rooms | 100: (4) design by Chris Bracco | 112–113: (2, 4, 5, 9) design by Chris Bracco | 122: (1) design by Chris Bracco | 123: (1) design by Chris Bracco; (4) design by Jessica Dasher | 125: design by Chris Bracco | 126: (top right) design by Ridge Rooms | 127: (top left) design by Chris Bracco; (top right) design by Daniel Paz | 134–135: (1, 4) design by Iain Morris; (2, 5) design by Chris Bracco; (3) design by Justin Thompson; (6) A Charlie Brown Christmas Story book, art by Justin Thompson | 146: (bottom) design by Jessica Dasher | 154–155: (1) art by Nick Lobianco; (3, 4, 6, 8) design by Chris Bracco; | 156–157: (4, 5) design by Chris Bracco; (7) design by Daniel Paz | 164: (top center) design by Chris Bracco | 166: (1, 2, 5) design by Chris Bracco | 172: (3) design by Daniel Paz | 173: (all) design by Chris Bracco | 182: design by Jessica Dasher | 183: (top right) design by Chris Bracco | 185: (2) art by Charles M. Schulz and Nick Lobianco; (3) design by Chris Bracco | 186: (top left) design by Daniel Paz; (top right) design by Ridge Rooms | 197: design by Chris Bracco | 213: design by Chris Bracco | 214: design by Daniel Paz | 217: design by Daniel Paz | 219: (3) design by Chris Bracco | 220: (top right) design by Chris Bracco; (bottom right) design by Daniel Paz | 223: (bottom right) design by Chris Bracco; (top row and bottom left) design by Daniel Paz | 236: (bottom left) design by Chris Bracco | 256: (1) design by Chris Bracco*

**CAMERON + CO:** *Iain Morris:* COLOR: *3, 35 (top left), 52, 58, 149, 152, 195, 201, 204 (top), 206, 210, 222, 239;* DESIGN: *66, 68–69 (6), 74, 75, 107, 108, 109, 110, 124, 129, 130, 131, 132, 134, 142, 145, 153, 159, 160, 161, 166, 173 (5), 174 (1), 200, 203, 211, 225, 230, 231, 232, 233 | Rob Dolgaard:* DESIGN: *9, 34, 59, 67, 72, 73, 150, 151, 202, 227, 243 (top), 244, 245, 246 | Melinda Maniscalco:* COLOR: *65, 156 (9), 175 (6), 185, 192, 208 | Amy Wheless:* COLOR: *30 (bottom right), 34 (top), 35 (top left), 46, 52, 54, 55, 70, 76, 77, 105, 110, 114, 128, 136, 140, 144 (top right), 202, 247, 249, 250;* DESIGN: *170–171*

weldon**owen**
Weldon Owen is a division of Bonnier Publishing USA
1045 Sansome Street, Suite 100, San Francisco, CA 94111
www.weldonowen.com



Library of Congress Cataloging in Publication data is available.
ISBN: 978-1-68188-292-5

First Published in 2017 • 10 9 8 7 6 5 4 3 2 1 • 2017 2018 2019 2020
Printed in China

**President & Publisher** Roger Shaw
**SVP, Sales & Marketing** Amy Kaneko
**Associate Publisher** Mariah Bear
**Acquisitions Editor** Kevin Toyama
**Creative Director** Kelly Booth
**Art Director** Allister Fein
**Senior Production Designer** Rachel Lopez Metzger
**Associate Production Director** Michelle Duggan
**Imaging Manager** Don Hill

**Produced in conjunction with Cameron + Company**
**Publisher** Chris Gruener
**Creative Director** Iain Morris
**Designer** Melinda Maniscalco
**Managing Editor** Jan Hughes
**Editor** Dustin Jones
**Copy Editor** Judith Dunham

Cameron + Company would first and foremost like to thank Charles M. Schulz for bringing *Peanuts* to the world. We would also like to thank Peanuts Worldwide LLC, Charles M. Schulz Creative Associates, and Charles M. Schulz Museum and Research Center for keeping his legacy alive and for their help in making this book possible—special thanks to Senior Editor Alexis E. Fajardo and Archivist Cesar Gallegos for their tireless efforts on our behalf. A resounding thank-you to Roger Shaw, Mariah Bear, and Kevin Toyama of Weldon Owen, for believing in this project and making this book possible. We are deeply indebted to Iain Morris for spearheading this project and creating much of the art that graces these pages, as well as with his inspired design; to Andrew Farago for his riveting text; to Melinda Maniscalo, Rob Dolgaard, Suzi Hutsell and Amy Wheless for their design and production contributions; to Jan Hughes and Dustin Jones for their editorial guidance; to Judith Dunham for her copyediting prowess.

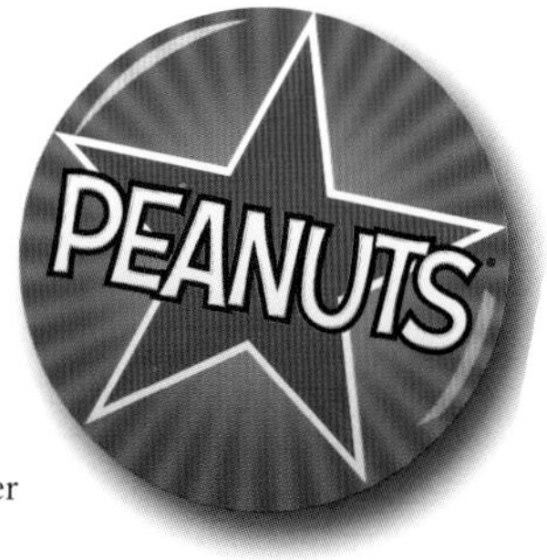
PEANUTS

1

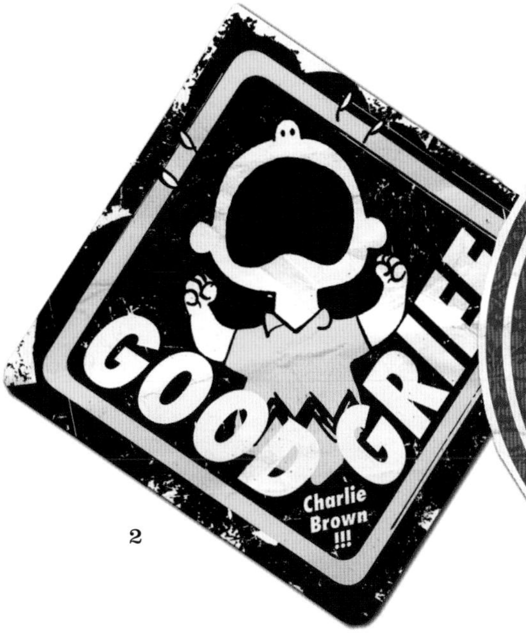
GOOD GRIEF
Charlie Brown !!!

2

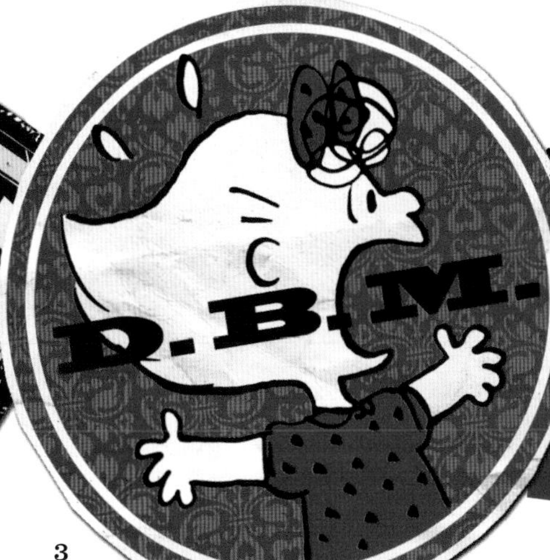
D.B.M.

3

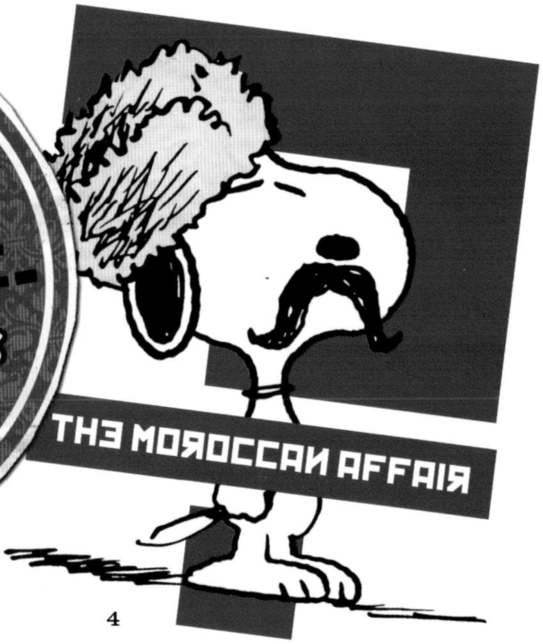
THE MOROCCAN AFFAIR

4

FRONT COVER: *Style Guide art, 2012 – CSCA*
ENDPAPERS: *Style Guide art, 2012 – CSCA*
PLC (FRONT, SPINE AND BACK): *Style Guide art, 2012 – CSCA*
THIS PAGE: *1: Style Guide art – PW, 2, 3, and 4: Style Guide art – CSCA*

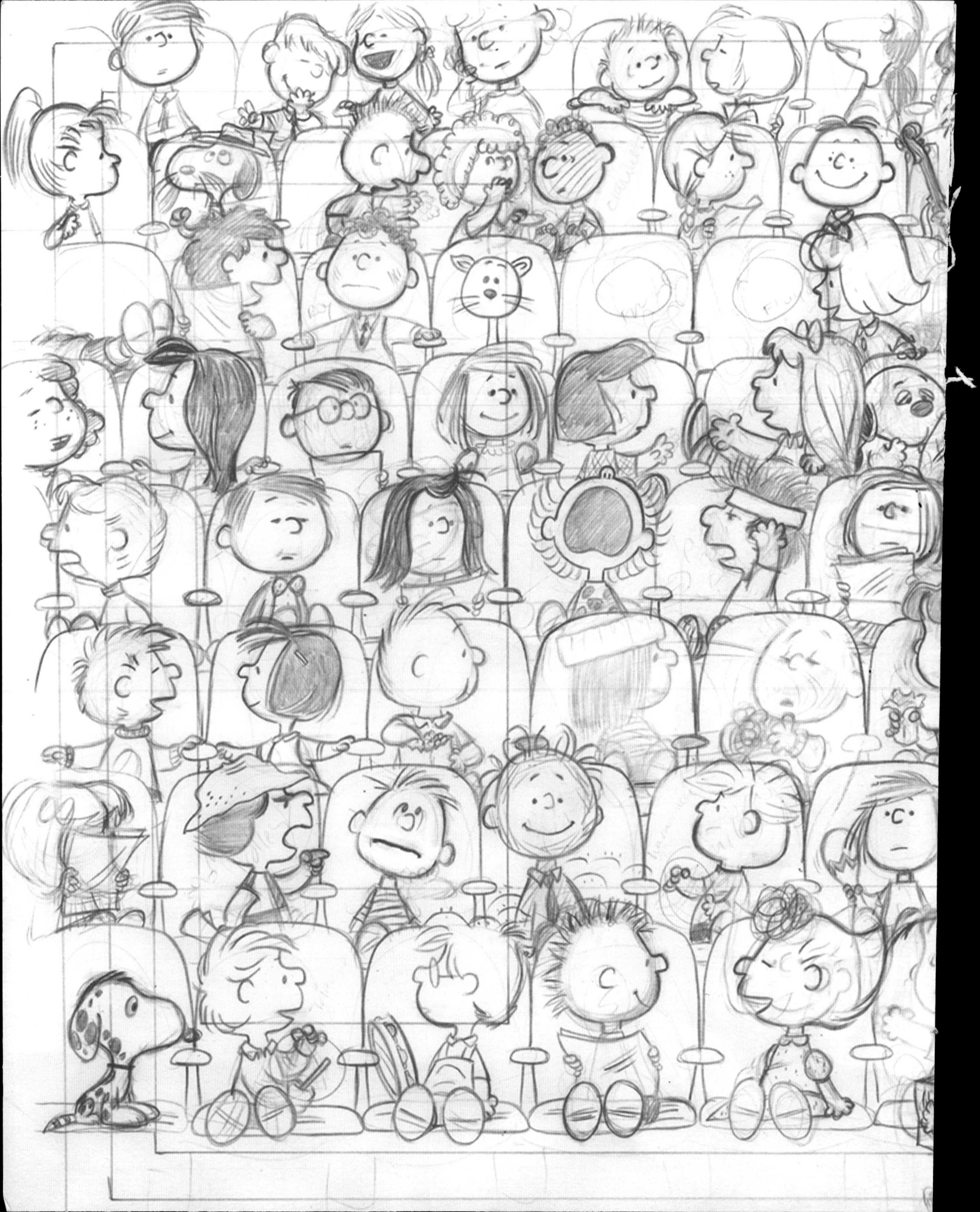